FOUNDATIONS OF PUBLIC INTERNATIONAL LAW

General editors: MALCOLM EVANS AND PHOEBE OKOWA

THE MAKING OF
INTERNATIONAL LAW

The Making of International Law

ALAN BOYLE

and

CHRISTINE CHINKIN

OXFORD

UNIVERSITY PRESS

OXFORD
UNIVERSITY PRESS

Great Clarendon Street, Oxford OX2 6DP

Oxford University Press is a department of the University of Oxford.
It furthers the University's objective of excellence in research, scholarship,
and education by publishing worldwide in

Oxford New York

Auckland Cape Town Dar es Salaam Hong Kong Karachi
Kuala Lumpur Madrid Melbourne Mexico City Nairobi
New Delhi Shanghai Taipei Toronto
With offices in
Argentina Austria Brazil Chile Czech Republic France Greece
Guatemala Hungary Italy Japan South Korea Poland Portugal
Singapore Switzerland Thailand Turkey Ukraine Vietnam

Oxford is a registered trade mark of Oxford University Press
in the UK and in certain other countries

Published in the United States
by Oxford University Press Inc., New York

ISBN 978-0-19-921379-5

Series Editors' Preface

The importance of understanding how international law comes into being is too obvious to dwell upon. However, this subject is usually approached in a rather formalistic fashion, focusing on the 'sources' of international law as traditionally understood with various 'non-traditional' modes of norm generation added as something of an afterthought. Alan Boyle and Christine Chinkin approach the generation of international law from a wholly different perspective, focusing on the actors, systems, and processes by whom and through which international law is generated rather than upon the forms into which that law is categorised. This approach unites norm creation with the interpretation, application, and development of international law, resulting in a more subtle, but far richer, vision of the making of international law. As such, this volume exemplifies the ambition of the *Foundations of Public International Law* series, which seeks to offer insightful expositions of key elements of international law which will inform and stimulate debate. There is no doubt that this agenda-setting work will do both.

Malcolm D. Evans
Phoebe N. Okowa
October 2006

Preface

This is a study of the principal multilateral processes and law-making tools through which contemporary international law is made. It does not seek to give an account of the traditional—and untraditional—sources and theories of international law, but rather to identify the processes, participants and instruments employed in the making of international law. It accordingly examines some of the mechanisms and procedures whereby new rules of law are created or existing rules are amended or abrogated. It concentrates on the UN, other international organisations, diplomatic conferences, codification bodies, NGOs and courts. Some of these bodies take decisions by majority vote, but more often consensus law-making has become the norm. We examine the implications of this development in an enlarged international community where law-making is no longer the exclusive preserve of states.

Every society perceives the need to differentiate between its legal norms and other norms of social, economic and political behaviour. But unlike domestic legal systems where this distinction is typically determined by constitutional provisions, the decentralised nature of the international legal system makes this a complex and contested issue. Moreover, contemporary international law is often the product of a subtle and evolving interplay of law-making instruments, both binding and non-binding, and of customary law and general principles. Only in this broader context can the significance of so-called 'soft law' and multilateral treaties be fully appreciated.

An important question posed by any examination of international law-making structures is the extent to which we can or should make judgments about their legitimacy and coherence, and if so in what terms. Put simply, a law-making process perceived to be illegitimate or incoherent is more likely to be an ineffective process. From this perspective, the assumption of law-making power by the UN Security Council offers unique advantages of speed and universality, but it also poses a particular challenge to the development of a more open and participatory process observable in other international law-making bodies. The range and diversity of these bodies provide another challenge to the coherence and systemic character of international law. While the specialised agencies, commissions and programmes of the United Nations illustrate the value of specialisation and expertise, they also contribute to the fragmentation of international law-making as a whole, through what Koskenniemi calls 'functional differentiation'. The risk is that there may then be competition between different subsystems of law and the values promoted by different international law-making institutions. Courts provide the ultimate affirmation for law-making undertaken by international organisations, treaty conferences and the International Law Commission. They can bring some measure of coherence to this fragmented institutional setting, insofar as they have to adjudicate on the inter-relationship of different norms, but they can do so only sporadically and are dependent on the establishment of jurisdiction. Moreover, the proliferation of international judicial tribunals creates its own problems. Most of these tribunals exercise specialised and limited jurisdiction outside any hierarchical structure and they do not necessarily have power to apply international law as a whole.

Understanding the character of contemporary international law-making is thus a complex and subtle undertaking. We do not pretend to have covered all of its aspects comprehensively. Our interest in the topic and some of our thinking reflect our own special interests, as well as the LLM teaching we both undertake in the subjects covered by this book. Our material has been chosen to illustrate the main themes, not to provide an encyclopedic treatment. A great many people in international organisations, NGOs, the International Law Commission and the United Kingdom Foreign and Commonwealth Office have been especially helpful and encouraging to us during our research for this book; their willingness to talk about international law-making and the experience of their own organisations provided us with a wealth of material, not all of which we have been able to use. Nevertheless, we cannot claim to offer the reader more than a selective snapshot of contemporary law-making processes. Their diversity and dynamics provide ample scope for further study and different points of view, but for anyone who reads this book from beginning to end the importance of understanding multilateral law-making in today's world is plain to see. We hope that something of our enjoyment in thinking about the topic has survived the writing.

Alan Boyle and Christine Chinkin
Edinburgh
July 2006

Acknowledgements

A great many people have helped make this book possible. The Leverhulme Trust provided funding for the research, including several visits to the UN in New York and Geneva, the FAO in Rome, and the WTO. We are immensely grateful to them and to our referees, Vaughan Lowe, David Freestone and Colin Warbrick, for their indispensable support. Iain McLeod, Alice Lacourt and Susan Macrory of the British missions in New York and Geneva went out of their way to facilitate access to meetings and people, and were the source of a lot of useful information and ideas in the early stages of our work. Louise de La Fayette of the UN Office of Legal Affairs and Bill Edeson and his colleagues at FAO were equally invaluable in the later stages. Tony Aust, Elizabeth Wilmshurst and John Grainger, all serving or former FCO lawyers, responded patiently and effectively to our questions about law-making processes and saved us from various misconceptions. Vaclav Mikulka arranged access to several sessions of the International Law Commission in Geneva, where Ian Brownlie, P. S. Rao, John Dugard, Alain Pellet, Bob Rosenstock and Bill Mansfield were especially supportive and hospitable, although they may not necessarily share the views we express about the Commission. Ralph Zacklin of the UN Secretariat, Gabrielle Marceau of the WTO, Edward Kwakwa and Tom Takahashi of WIPO, Francis Maupain of ILO, Gian Luca Burci of WHO, Mojtaba Kazazi of the UNCC, Louise Doswald-Beck of the International Commission of Jurists, Jelena Pejic of the ICRC, Melinda Ching of Amnesty International, Frieder Roessler of the Advisory Centre for WTO Law, Martin Stanford of UNIDROIT, and Professor Sir Nigel Rodley of Essex University all gave us much to think about and helped focus our initial ideas. We have not shared our analysis or our conclusions with any of them, so they bear no responsibility for the outcome of our research. Several academic colleagues have given us the benefit of their specialist knowledge, and we are particularly indebted to Sir Roy Goode, Campbell MacLachlan, Lorand Bartels, Joost Pauwelyn, Jutta Brunnée and Matthew Happold for their help. If we are still at sea on several issues the fault is not theirs. Our tireless research assistants, Sam McIntosh, Mark Gillespie, Felicity Stewart, Neil Craik, Neville Sorab and Emma Harling-Phillips have assembled material, drafted tables and remained cheerful and invaluable in innumerable ways. We are immensely grateful to all of them. Special thanks from Alan Boyle are owed to Drew and Simona Stirling for arranging the loan of an apartment in Geneva during his visits there, and to Bill Edeson and his wife for their hospitality at home on the shores of Lake Bracciano while visiting FAO. There can be few more delightful ways to appreciate the law relating to food and agriculture. Last but not least, John Louth of OUP has been supportive and above all patient in waiting for a manuscript that took rather longer to deliver than even he might have expected.

Contents

Abbreviations

AALCC	Asian–African Legal Consultative Committee
AC	Appeal Chamber
AfCHR	African Court of Human and Peoples' Rights
AI	Amnesty International
AJIL	American Journal of International Law
Am UJILP	American University Journal of International Law and Policy
ASIL	American Society of International Law
Australian YBIL	Australian Yearbook of International Law
BHRC	Butterworths Human Rights Cases
BIT	Bilateral Investment Treaty
BJIL	Brooklyn Journal of International Law
BYBIL	British Yearbook of International Law
CACT	Central American Court of Justice
Cardozo LR	Cardozo Law Review
CBD	Convention on Biological Diversity
CEDAW	Convention on the Elimination of All Forms of Discrimination against Women
CERD	Committee on the Elimination of Racial Discrimination
CESCR	Committee on Economic, Social and Cultural Rights
CHR	Commission on Human Rights
CITES	Convention on International Trade in Endangered Species of Wild Fauna and Flora
CMI	Comité Maritime International
Col HRLR	Columbia Human Rights Law Review
Col JIELP	Colorado Journal of International Environmental Law and Policy
Col JTL	Columbia Journal of Transnational Law
CONGO	Conference of Non-Governmental Organisations
COP	Conference of the Parties
COPUOS	Committee on Peaceful Uses of Outer Space
CSW	Commission on the Status of Women
CTR	Claims Tribunal Reports
CW	Committee of the Whole
CYBIL	Canadian Yearbook of International Law
DRC	Democratic Republic of the Congo
DSB	Dispute Settlement Body
DSU	Dispute Settlement Understanding
EC	European Community
ECHR	European Court of Human Rights
ECJ	European Court of Justice

ECOSOC	Economic and Social Council
ECOWAS	Economic Community of West African States
EEZ	Exclusive Economic Zone
EHRLR	European Human Rights Law Review
EHRR	European Human Rights Reports
EJIL	European Journal of International Law
Env Pol & Law	Environmental Policy and Law
EU	European Union
EWCA	England and Wales, Court of Appeal
FAO	Food and Agriculture Organisation
FCTC	Framework Convention on Tobacco Control
GAOR	General Assembly Official Records
GATS	General Agreement on Trade in Services
GATT	General Agreement on Tariffs and Trade
GC	Grand Chamber
Georgia JICL	Georgia Journal of International and Comparative Law
GMO	Genetically modified organisms
GYBIL	German Yearbook of International Law
Harv HRYB	Harvard Human Rights Yearbook
Harv ILJ	Harvard International Law Journal
Hastings ICLR	Hastings International and Comparative Law Review
HNS	Hazardous and noxious substances
HRLJ	Human Rights Law Journal
HRLR	Human Rights Law Review
HRQ	Human Rights Quarterly
IACHR	Inter-American Court of Human Rights
IAEA	International Atomic Energy Agency
IATA	International Air Transport Association
ICAO	International Civil Aviation Organisation
ICBL	International Campaign to Ban Landmines
ICC	International Criminal Court
ICCPR	International Covenant on Civil and Political Rights
ICESCR	International Covenant on Economic, Social and Cultural Rights
ICISS	International Commission on Intervention and State Sovereignty
ICJ	International Court of Justice
ICLQ	International and Comparative Law Quarterly
ICRC	International Committee of the Red Cross
ICSID	International Centre for the Settlement of Investment Disputes
ICSU	International Council of Scientific Unions
ICTR	International Criminal Tribunal for Rwanda
ICTY	International Criminal Tribunal for the Former Yugoslavia
IFRS	International Financial Reporting Standards
IGO	Intergovernmental Organisation
IJMCL	International Journal of Marine and Coastal Law

ILA	International Law Association
ILC	International Law Commission
ILM	International Legal Materials
ILO	International Labour Organisation
ILR	International Law Reports
IMO	International Maritime Organisation
INB	Intergovernmental Negotiating Body
Indian JIL	Indian Journal of International Law
Institut	*Institut de Droit International*
Int Org	International Organization
IPU	Inter-Parliamentary Union
ISO	International Standards Organisation
ITLOS	International Tribunal for the Law of the Sea
IUCN	International Union for the Conservation of Nature
IUU	Illegal, unreported and unregulated (fishing)
JEL	Journal of Environmental Law
JMLC	Journal of Maritime Law and Commerce
JWT	Journal of World Trade
LJIL	Leiden Journal of International Law
MAI	Multilateral Agreement on Investment
MARPOL	1973/78 Convention for the Prevention of Marine Pollution from Ships
Max Planck UNYB	Max Planck Yearbook of United Nations Law
MDGs	Millennium Development Goals
MEA	Multilateral Environmental Agreement
MEPC	Marine Environment Protection Committee
Mich JIL	Michigan Journal of International Law
MLR	Modern Law Review
MNF	Multinational Force
MOP	Meeting of the Parties
MSC	Maritime Safety Committee
NAFTA	North American Free Trade Area
NAIL	New Approaches to International Law
NATO	North Atlantic Treaty Organisation
NGO	Non-Governmental Organisation
NIEO	New International Economic Order
Nig SCt	Nigerian Supreme Court
NILR	Netherlands International Law Review
Nordic JIL	Nordic Journal of International Law
Northwestern UnivLR	Northwestern University Law Review
NRJ	Natural Resources Journal
NYBIL	Netherlands Yearbook of International Law

NYU	
Environmental LJ	New York University Environmental Law Journal
NYU JILP	New York University Journal of International Law and Politics
OAS	Organization of American States
OAU	Organization of African Unity
ODIL	Ocean Development and International Law
OECD	Organisation for Economic Cooperation and Development
OHCHR	Office of the High Commissioner for Human Rights
OPCW	Organisation for the Prevention of Chemical Weapons
OSPAR	
Convention	Convention for the Protection of the Marine Environment of the North-East Atlantic
Oxford JLS	Oxford Journal of Legal Studies
PCA	Permanent Court of Arbitration
PCIJ	Permanent Court of International Justice
Prepcom	Preparatory Committee or Commission
P5	The Five Permanent Members of the Security Council
RIIA	Royal Institute of International Affairs
S Ct	Supreme Court
SAARC	South Asian Association for Regional Cooperation
SARS	Severe Acute Respiratory Syndrome
SC	Security Council
SCCR	Scottish Criminal Cases Reports
S-G	Secretary-General of the United Nations
S-G SR	Secretary-General's Special Representative
SLO	Senior Legal Officer
SOLAS	1974 Convention on the Safety of Life at Sea
SPS	Sanitary and Phytosanitary Measures Agreement
Stan JIL	Stanford Journal of International Law
Swiss YBIL	Swiss Yearbook of International Law
TBT	Technical Barriers to Trade Agreement
TC	Trial Chamber
Texas ILJ	Texas International Law Journal
TNC	Transnational Corporation
TRIMS	Agreement on Trade-Related Investment Measures
TRIPS	Agreement on Trade-Related Aspects of Intellectual Property Rights
TWAIL	Third World Approaches to International Law
UDHR	Universal Declaration of Human Rights
UKHL	United Kingdom, House of Lords
UN	United Nations
UNAT	United Nations Administrative Tribunal
UNCED	United Nations Conference on Environment and Development

UNCITRAL	United Nations Commission on International Trade Law
UNCLOS I	First United Nations Conference on the Law of the Sea
UNCLOS III	Third United Nations Conference on the Law of the Sea
1982 UNCLOS	United Nations Convention on the Law of the Sea
UNCTAD	United Nations Conference on Trade and Development
UNDP	United Nations Development Programme
UNEP	United Nations Environmental Programme
UNESCO	United Nations Educational, Scientific and Cultural Organisation
UNGA	United Nations General Assembly
UNHCR	United Nations High Commissioner for Refugees
UNHRC	United Nations Human Rights Committee
UNIDROIT	International Institute for the Unification of Private Law
UNITAR	United Nations Institute of Training and Research
University of Richmond LR	University of Richmond Law Review
UNSC	United Nations Security Council
USSR	Union of Soviet Socialist Republics
UNTS	United Nations Treaty Series
Vand JTL	Vanderbilt Journal of Transnational Law
VCLT	Vienna Convention on the Law of Treaties
VJIL	Virginia Journal of International Law
V-P	Vice President
WEDO	Women's Environment and Development Organisation
WHO	World Health Organisation
WIPO	World Intellectual Property Organisation
Wis ILJ	Wisconsin International Law Journal
WLR	Weekly Law Reports
WMO	World Meteorological Organisation
WTO	World Trade Organisation
Yale LJ	Yale Law Journal
YBIEL	Yearbook of International Environmental Law
YBILC	Yearbook of the International Law Commission

List of Cases

A and others v. Secretary of State for the Home Department (HL) [2005] 3 WLR 1249; (2006) 45 ILM 503

Admission of a State to the United Nations Advisory Opinion (Article 4 of the Charter) (1948) ICJ Reports 57

Advisory Opinion on 'Other Treaties' Subject to the Consultative Jurisdiction of the Court IACHR OC-1/82, (1982) (1983) 22 ILM 51

Advisory Opinion on the Effect of Reservations IACHR OC-2/82, (1982) (1983) 22 ILM 37

Aegean Sea Continental Shelf Case (Greece v. Turkey) (1978) ICJ Reports 3

Al-Adsani v. United Kingdom (2002) 34 EHRR 11

Ambatielos (Greece v. United Kingdom) Preliminary Objections (1952) ICJ Reports 28

Amoco International Finance Corp. v. Iran (1987) 15 Iran-US CTR 189

Anglo-French Continental Shelf Arbitration (1978) 54 ILR 6

Anglo-Iranian Oil Co. Case (United Kingdom v. Iran) (1952) ICJ Reports 93

Armed Activities on the Territory of the Congo (New Application: 2002) (Democratic Republic of the Congo v. Rwanda) (2006) ICJ Reports

Armed Activities on the Territory of the Congo (Democratic Republic of the Congo v. Uganda) (2006) 45 ILM 271

Arrest Warrant Case (Democratic Republic of the Congo v. Belgium) (2002) ICJ Reports 3; (2002) 41 ILM 536

Asian Agricultural Products Ltd v. Republic of Sri Lanka ICSID, Case No. ARB/87/3 (1991) 30 ILM 577

Asylum Case (Colombia/Peru) (1950) ICJ Reports 266

Attorney-General of Israel v. Eichmann (1968) 36 ILR 277

Austro-German Customs Union Advisory Opinion PCIJ Series A/B No. 41 (1931)

Avena and other Mexican Nationals (Mexico v. USA) (2004) 43 ILM 581

Bankovic v. Belgium and others (2002) 11 BHRC (2001) 435; (2002) 41 ILM 517

Barcelona Traction Light and Power Company Limited (Belgium v. Spain) (1970) ICJ Reports 3

Belilos v. Switzerland (1988) ECHR Series A No. 132; (1988) 10 EHRR 466

Certain Expenses Advisory Opinion (1962) ICJ Reports 151

Certain German Interests in Polish Upper Silesia, (Germany v. Poland) PCIJ, Series A, No. 7 (1926)

Certain Phosphate Lands in Nauru (Nauru v. Australia) Preliminary Objections (1992) ICJ Reports 240

Commission of the European Communities v. Ireland, Case-459/03, 30 May 2006, WL 2294914

Competence of the General Assembly Regarding Admission to the United Nations Advisory Opinion (1950) ICJ Reports 4

Corfu Channel Case (UK v. Albania) (1949) ICJ Reports 4

EC Measures Affecting Asbestos, Appellate Body, WT/DS135/AB/R (2001) 40 ILM 1193

EC Measures Concerning Meat and Meat Products (Beef Hormones Case), Appellate Body, WT/DS26/AB/R (1997)

EC—Trade Preferences Case, Appellate Body, WT/DS246/AB/R (2004)

East Timor Case (Portugal v. Australia) (1995); ICJ Reports 90

El Salvador v. Nicaragua (CACT) (1917) 11 AJIL 674

List of Treaties and Other Instruments

Convention for the Conservation of Antarctic
  Marine Living Resources

1981

UNGA Res 36/39, 18 November

1982

United Nations Convention on the Law of
  the Sea

1984

Convention against Torture and Other Cruel,
  Inhuman or Degrading Treatment or
  Punishment
UNGA Res 39/229, 18 December

1985

Vienna Convention for the Protection of the
  Ozone Layer

1986

Vienna Convention on the Law of Treaties
  between States and International
  Organisations
  or between International Organisations
European Convention on the Recognition
  of the Legal Personality of International
  Non-Governmental Organisations
Convention on Registration of Ships

1987

SAARC Regional Convention on Suppression
  of Terrorism
Montreal Protocol to the Ozone Convention
European Convention for the Prevention of
  Torture

1988

Convention for the Suppression of Unlawful
  Acts against the Safety of Maritime
  Navigation
Protocol for the Suppression of Unlawful Acts
  against the Safety of Fixed Platforms Located
  on the Continental Shelf
UN Convention against Illicit Traffic in
  Narcotic Drugs
Convention for the Regulation of Antarctic
  Mineral Resource Activities
Resolution on Protection of Global Climate for
  Present and Future Generations of Mankind,
  UNGA Res 43/53, 6 December

1989

Timor Gap Treaty
Convention on the Rights of the Child
ILO Convention No. 169 concerning
  Indigenous and Tribal Peoples in
  Independent Countries
Basel Convention on the Control of
  Transboundary Movements of Hazardous
  Wastes and their Disposal
UNGA Res 44/39, 4 December
UNGA Res 44/225, 22 December

1990

Convention on the Protection of the Rights
  of All Migrant Workers and Members of
  their Families
UNGA Res 45/41, 28 November

1991

Protocol to the Antarctic Treaty on
  Environmental Protection
UNGA Res 46/215, 20 December
UNGA Res 46/54, 9 December
SC Res 687, 3 April
SC Res 688, 5 April

1992

Framework Convention on Climate
  Change
Convention on Biological Diversity
Convention on Civil Liability for Oil Pollution
  Damage
Convention on the Establishment of an
  International Fund for Compensation
  for Oil Pollution Damage
Rio Declaration on Environment and
  Development
UNGA Res 47/33, 25 November
UNGA Res 47/147, 18 December
UNGA Res 47/190, 22 December
UNGA Res 47/191, 22 December
SC Res 748, 31 March
SC Res 780, 6 October
SC Res 788, 19 November

1993

Convention for the Conservation of Southern
  Bluefin Tuna
UN World Conference on Human Rights,
  Vienna Declaration and Programme of
  Action, UN Doc A/CONF 157/23, 25 June

1

International Law-Making

1. Introduction

This book is about the constitutive processes[1] of contemporary international law—how international law is made. It does not give an account of the traditional sources or theories of international law,[2] but identifies the processes, participants and instruments employed in the making of international law. It examines the 'mechanisms and procedures whereby new rules of law are created or old rules are amended or abrogated'.[3] It does not do this through a structured methodology[4] but offers an account of how international law-making responds to the demands of international relations at the beginning of the 21st century.

In 2004, in its Report on United Nations (UN) Reform,[5] the High Level Panel on Threats, Challenges and Change called for the development of international regimes and norms, and of new legal mechanisms where existing ones were deemed inadequate for responding to the threats to collective security that it had identified. In this introductory chapter we commence our discussion by examining the international law-making processes that have been engaged in response to one particular such threat: the incidence and gravity of terrorist atrocities. We do this to illustrate the range of law-making mechanisms and institutions that has evolved, to suggest some of their strengths and weaknesses, and to introduce some of the recurrent themes of the book.

Following the overview of international law-making in the context of terrorism, this introductory chapter considers the impact of different theories of international law on law-making, for in some respects identification of law-making processes depends upon how one defines international law. It then considers some particular issues of law-making in the contemporary globalised world. Finally it

---

[1] H. Lasswell and M. McDougal, *Jurisprudence for a Free Society: Studies in Law, Science and Policy* (New Haven, 1992), especially 1131–54.
[2] There are numerous works on the sources of international law; see I. Brownlie, *Principles of Public International Law* (6th edn, Oxford, 2003) 3–29 and sources cited there.
[3] A. Cassese and J. Weiler, *Change and Stability in International Law-Making* (Berlin, 1988) 38.
[4] M. Bos, *A Methodology of International Law* (North Holland, 1984).
[5] *A More Secure World: Our Shared Responsibility*, Report of the High Level Panel on Threats, Challenges and Change, UN Doc A/59/565, 2 December 2004.

addresses briefly the question of reform in law-making. The following chapters discuss the 'who', 'how' and 'what' of international law-making. Chapter 2 considers some of the participants in international law-making processes. While states retain their primary position within the international legal order, other actors contribute in a variety of ways to the development of the rules and principles of international law. These include intergovernmental organisations (IGOs) and other non-state actors whose actions in cooperating with, confronting and contesting state actions all play a part in the evolution of international law. The latter are discussed in Chapter 2 and institutional law-making processes in Chapter 3. Law-making processes take place in many arenas including institutions, diplomatic meetings, conferences of states parties and judicial fora. The political processes are discussed in Chapter 3. We also examine the distinctive process of codification. The contemporary relevance of codification, especially the work of the International Law Commission (ILC), is analysed in Chapter 4. These multilateral processes result in a variety of law-making instruments,[6] including treaties and binding resolutions, as well as non-binding declarations, resolutions, and other forms of soft law. These different law-making instruments and their interrelationship within an increasingly complex legal system are examined in Chapter 5. In Chapter 6 we appraise judicial law-making. A marked change in the international legal system since 1920 has been the proliferation of international courts and tribunals. While the International Court of Justice (ICJ) remains the only international tribunal of general jurisdiction, other judicial and quasi-judicial bodies have jurisdiction over issues ranging from human rights to world trade, international criminal law and the law of the sea. Regional judicial bodies have also multiplied, notably in the areas of human rights and economic integration. Although the Statute of the ICJ, Article 38 (1) recognises judicial decisions only as a subsidiary source of international law, the impact of decisions of these international courts and tribunals on the development of international law cannot be ignored.

The book does not claim to provide a comprehensive account of the myriad ways in which contemporary international law is made. We use illustrative examples and case studies that inevitably draw upon our own specialised areas of interest to provide a flavour of the diversity of international law-making processes, the system's capacity for innovation, and its responsiveness to need. In particular it does not attempt to explain in detail the formation of customary international law. This topic has been well examined elsewhere.[7] That does not mean that customary international law is ignored, but rather that we consider it through its interlocking with other law-making processes, the contributions to its evolution

---

[6] R. Baxter, 'International Law in "Her Infinite Variety" ', 29 *ICLQ* (1980) 549.
[7] The customary international law-making process is especially well set out in the International Law Association, *Report of the 69th Conference*, Committee on the Formation of Customary International Law (London, 2000).

made by different participants, and the arenas in which claims about its existence and content are made. Nor do we consider, except incidentally, law-making through regional institutions. Where most developed, as in the European institutions, UN, this has taken on a *sui generis* character that is beyond the scope of this book.

2. International Law-Making: The Response to Global Terrorism

Terrorism is not a new threat to the international order but 'it is a threat that has grown more urgent in the last five years'[8] for reasons that are only too familiar in the aftermath of 11 September 2001. In the words of the UN Secretary-General in 2005:

> Transnational networks of terrorist groups have global reach and make common cause to pose a universal threat . . . Even one such attack and the chain of events it might set off could change our world forever.[9]

One response has been the adoption of international rules for the suppression and eradication of terrorism and terrorist activities and making accountable the perpetrators of such acts. A brief survey of international law-making in this context introduces many of the issues we discuss in this book: the range and diverse mandates of law-making institutions, the processes they engage in, participants within them, and the instruments adopted.

International law has long been engaged in addressing terrorism. After World War I delegates from states, IGOs and private international organisations considered terrorism at the International Conference for the Unification of Penal Law and amended some extradition treaties to exclude certain political offences from the category of non-extraditable offences.[10] The League of Nations sought to repress terrorist activity. After the 1934 assassination of King Alexander of Yugoslavia and the Foreign Minister of France a committee of experts was established by the League to work on the subject with a view to drawing up a convention. This resulted in the 1937 Convention for the Prevention and Punishment of Terrorism that failed however to come into force.

In the post-UN Charter era international law-making with respect to terrorism has been pursued along two lines through various institutions and in response to successive violent acts. First is the application of existing international law regulating the use of force to the commission of terrorist atrocities by non-state actors and demands for adaptation of those rules.[11] Second is the adoption of an international

---

[8] *In Larger Freedom: Towards Development, Security and Human Rights for All*, UN Doc A/59/2005, 21 March 2005, para 87.   [9] Ibid.
[10] T. Franck and B. Lockwood, 'Preliminary Thoughts Towards an International Convention on Terrorism', 68 *AJIL* (1974) 69.
[11] H. Duffy, *The 'War on Terror' and the Framework of International Law* (Cambridge, 2005).

regime that strengthens states' legal competencies to use criminal sanctions against terrorists and to prevent terrorist acts. Although issues relating to the use of force dominate the political and public space, this discussion focuses on the high level of international law-making generated by the second approach.

The adoption of an integrated and comprehensive international regime against terrorism has been thwarted by disagreement over a definition of what constitutes terrorist activity. Instead there have been multiple approaches to the issue. First has been the serial adoption of multilateral treaties that have identified and defined acts of violence against aviation,[12] at sea,[13] against identified protected persons,[14] through bombings,[15] and involving nuclear facilities.[16] These treaties have typically been adopted in response to specific incidents or crises[17] including aircraft hijacking, airport sabotage, seizure of ships such as the *Achille Lauro* and hostage taking. They have involved preparatory work within specialist bodies supplying technical assistance, for example the International Civil Aviation Organisation (ICAO) and the International Maritime Organisation (IMO), preparing draft texts, consideration of texts at diplomatic conferences of states' representatives, and treaty adoption for ratification through the UN General Assembly (GA). As we see in Chapter 4, the GA 6th (Legal) Committee has played a key role in the negotiation and adoption of some of the anti-terrorism conventions (for example the Convention on the Safety of UN and Associated Personnel, 1994) and is central to attempts to negotiate a comprehensive convention.[18] These treaties largely follow a consistent pattern: definition of the specific offence, its criminalisation under national law, the assertion of wide-based national jurisdiction, integration with extradition regimes and states' obligation to prosecute or extradite alleged offenders present on their territory. This piecemeal approach to law-making against terrorist activity continues. In 2005 the IMO convened a diplomatic conference that adopted new protocols to the 1988 Convention on the Safety of Maritime Navigation and its Protocol on the Safety of Fixed Platforms. The 2005 Protocols extend the range of prohibited offences, including new non-proliferation and counter-terrorism offences, and make

---

[12] 1963 Tokyo Convention on Offences and Certain Other Acts Committed on Board Aircraft; 1970 Hague Convention for the Suppression of Unlawful Seizure of Aircraft; 1971 Montreal Convention for the Suppression of Unlawful Acts against the Safety of Civil Aviation, with Protocol, 1988.

[13] 1982 United Nations Convention on the Law of the Sea, Articles 101–7 relating to piracy on the high seas; 1988 Convention for the Suppression of Unlawful Acts against the Safety of Maritime Navigation, Rome; 1988 Protocol for the Suppression of Unlawful Acts against the Safety of Fixed Platforms Located on the Continental Shelf.

[14] 1973 Convention on the Prevention and Punishment of Crimes against Internationally Protected Persons, including Diplomatic Agents; 1979 Convention against the Taking of Hostages.

[15] 1997 Convention for the Suppression of Terrorist Bombings.

[16] 1980 Convention on the Physical Protection of Nuclear Material; 2005 International Convention for the Suppression of Acts of Nuclear Terrorism.

[17] M. Reisman and A. Willard (eds), *International Incidents: The Law that Counts in World Politics* (Princeton, 1988); H. Charlesworth, 'International law: A Discipline of Crisis', 65 *MLR* (2002) 377.

[18] On the UNGA 6th Committee see Chapters 3 and 4.

available procedures to facilitate boarding a suspected vessel at sea. The negotiation of further protocols to existing treaties is a convenient way of developing further legal obligations within an already accepted framework.

The GA has taken a twin-track approach[19] in the fight against terrorism. In addition to its multilateral treaty activity it has more broadly condemned terrorism and specific terrorist attacks through a number of resolutions. However disagreement over what constitutes terrorist activity has meant that many of these were strongly contested and generated acrimonious debates, especially in the context of national liberation movements.[20] In 1972, on the recommendation of its 6th Committee, the GA established an *ad hoc* Committee on International Terrorism which sought unsuccessfully to resolve the definitional question. It operated through consensus which 'reflects the need for unanimity if an agreement is to be of any real use in solving the problem of terrorism and the extreme difficulty of getting any significant agreement at all'.[21] In 1994 '[d]eeply concerned by the increase, in many regions of the world, of acts of terrorism based on intolerance or extremism' the GA adopted by consensus a Declaration on Measures to Eliminate International Terrorism.[22] Although formally a legally non-binding instrument,[23] Sloan has argued that a declaration carries greater legal force than other resolutions. He finds a presumption that a declaration constitutes law where an intent to declare law is evinced and it has been adopted unanimously, or at least nearly unanimously, or by genuine consensus.[24]

Still unable to agree a definition of terrorism as such, the GA took a strong line in the Declaration by asserting that:

Criminal acts intended or calculated to provoke a state of terror in the general public, a group of persons or particular persons for political purposes are in any circumstance unjustifiable, whatever the considerations of a political, philosophical, ideological, racial, ethnic, religious or any other nature that may be invoked to justify them.

This language 'shut the door' to arguments that some violent acts could be justified by their objectives and opened the way for negotiating further resolutions and the broader-based Convention for the Suppression of the Financing of Terrorism.[25] The Declaration also recognised the involvement of states in terrorist activities. It specified states' obligations, urged states to become parties to the multilateral treaties (which are listed in the Declaration) and spelled out the continued goal of ensuring 'a comprehensive legal framework covering all aspects of the matter'. It also required action by the UN and the Secretary-General.

---

[19] M. Shaw, *International Law* (5th edn, Cambridge, 2003) 1049.
[20] However the 11 September 2001 attacks were strongly and immediately condemned by the UNGA; UNGA Res 56/1, 18 September 2001.
[21] Franck and Lockwood, 68 *AJIL* (1974) 69, 72. See discussion of consensus in Chapter 3.
[22] UNGA Res 49/60, 9 December 1994.
[23] See Chapter 5 for discussion of soft law.
[24] B. Sloan, 'General Assembly Resolutions Revisited (Forty Years After)', 58 *BYBIL* (1987) 39, 93.
[25] A. Aust, 'Counter-Terrorism—A New Approach', 5 *Max Planck UNYB* (2001) 1, 7.

The Declaration is based on the UN Charter and other principles of relevant international law. Its language picked up on earlier GA resolutions on other topics, for example the Declaration on Friendly Relations between States[26] and the Definition of Aggression.[27] Its reiteration that states 'must refrain from organizing, instigating, assisting or participating in terrorist acts in territories of other States, or from acquiescing in or encouraging activities within their territories directed towards the commission of such acts' comes from the principle prohibiting the use of force in the Declaration on Friendly Relations. The GA has linked terrorist activities and the *jus ad bellum* and thus brought the legal regime for the eradication of terrorism into other mainstream issues of international law, including the prohibition of the use of force.

Other UN bodies have done the same thing. The ILC[28] has considered terrorism in the context of international humanitarian law. Its Draft Code of Crimes against the Peace and Security of Mankind, Article 20 (f) (iv)[29] includes acts of terrorism (still not defined) as violations of international humanitarian law in non-international armed conflict. This provision is taken from Protocol II to the Geneva Conventions, Article 4 (2) (d)[30] and, according to the ILC Commentary, should be taken as having the same meaning as in the Protocol. The same provision had been included in the Statute of the International Criminal Tribunal for Rwanda (ICTR), Article 4 (d).[31] The ILC Draft Statute for an International Criminal Court (ICC) did not include offences under Protocol II in its concept of 'crimes pursuant to treaties' over which the proposed Court would have jurisdiction.[32] The ILC's Draft Statute did include the various defined crimes within the multilateral anti-terrorist conventions discussed above. However neither terrorism nor these specified treaty crimes were included within the jurisdiction of the Statute of the ICC adopted at Rome.[33] There is therefore no standing, permanent, international body with criminal jurisdiction over individuals accused of terrorist acts, although such acts may in extreme cases fall within the rubric of crimes against humanity. Moreover, *ad hoc* solutions are always available: for example, a special criminal process was designed for the prosecution and trial of alleged terrorists and the punishment of a convicted terrorist.[34]

---

[26] UNGA Res 2625 (XXV), 24 October 1970.

[27] UNGA Res 3314 (XXIX), 14 December 1974.

[28] The deliberative approach to international law-making taken by the ILC is discussed in Chapter 4.

[29] Adopted by the ILC at its 48th session; 1996 2 YBILC vol 2, para 47 ff.

[30] Protocol additional to the Geneva Conventions of 12 August 1949, and Relating to the Protection of Victims of Non-international Armed Conflicts, 8 June 1977, (Protocol II).

[31] SC Res 955, 8 November 1994.

[32] ILC Draft Statute, Article 20 (e). The text of the Draft Statute is at 33 ILM (1994) 253.

[33] 1998 Rome Statute of the International Criminal Court provides for jurisdiction over the crime of aggression (Article 5 (d)); genocide (Article 6); crimes against humanity (Article 7); and war crimes (Article 8).

[34] In the *Lockerbie* case a special criminal process was designed for the prosecution and trial of alleged terrorists and the punishment of a convicted terrorist—a Scottish tribunal, applying Scottish

In addition to formulating law in response to specific atrocities, the GA has adopted treaties directed at more general concerns in the fight against terrorism. In contrast to the earlier treaties, in the Convention for the Suppression of the Financing of Terrorism, 2000 it was not sufficient to define an exact form of terrorist act: instead what states sought to do was to identify prohibited acts of financing and to draft provisions that are precise in their regulation of particular situations. Work on the Convention was largely carried out by government legal experts and drafts were considered at meetings of the European Union (EU) and G8. After being tabled at the UN the Convention was considered in an *ad hoc* Committee and then in a working group of the GA 6th Committee. The 6th Committee recommended its adoption by the GA for ratification by states.[35]

The Preamble to the 1994 GA Declaration on Measures to Eliminate International Terrorism noted that suppression of terrorist acts is an essential element in the maintenance of international peace and security. It is not surprising that the Security Council (SC) has also addressed terrorism under its UN Charter, Chapter VII powers. Its initial response was to impose economic sanctions upon named states that refused to extradite alleged terrorists, harboured terrorists, or instigated or otherwise assisted the commission of terrorist acts within another state. Thus sanctions were imposed against Libya after the Lockerbie air disaster[36] and against the Taliban[37] after the 1998 attacks against US embassies in Kenya and Tanzania. Sanctions were subsequently also imposed on individuals—Usama Bin Laden and his associates.[38] These resolutions constituted Chapter VII enforcement action rather than legislative acts. However by over-riding the provisions of the Montreal Convention in the case of Libya, the SC created a hierarchy in international legal obligation between treaties and Chapter VII resolutions.[39]

Following the 11 September 2001 terrorist attacks in New York and Washington the SC has become more a explicitly law-making body.[40] Resolution 1373, 28 September 2001 adopts a holistic and comprehensive approach to terrorism applicable to all states (albeit the offence remains undefined) and is in marked contrast to the piecemeal response of the earlier treaties.[41] As we note in Chapter 5, many of the provisions of the Terrorist Financing Convention became binding upon all states through the Chapter VII resolution.[42] The SC has sought to ensure compliance with resolution 1373 through creation of a new institution, the Counter-Terrorism Committee, and has bestowed upon it far-reaching supervisory

---

law but situated in The Hague: see *Her Majesty's Advocate v. Abdelbaset Ali Mohmed al Megrahi and Al Amin Khalifa Fhimah* SCCR (2000) 177, case no. 1475/99, date of judgment 31/01/2001.

[35] Aust, 5 *Max Planck UNYB* (2001) 1. [36] SC Res 748, 31 March 1992.
[37] SC Res 1267, 15 October 1999. [38] SC Res 1333, 19 December 2000.
[39] *Questions of Interpretation and Application of the 1971 Montreal Convention Arising from the Aerial Incident at Lockerbie* Provisional Measures (1992) ICJ Reports, 114, paras 39–41. See Chapter 5.
[40] See Chapter 3. [41] Discussed in Chapters 3 and 4.
[42] UN Charter, Article 25: 'Members of the United Nations agree to accept and carry out the decisions of the Security Council'.

powers. The SC has continued this legislative trend through its adoption under Chapter VII of SC resolution 1540, 28 April 2004 on non-proliferation of weapons of mass destruction. This resolution links terrorism with non-proliferation of weapons regimes and seeks to prevent terrorist groups from obtaining such weapons. SC resolutions like 1373 and 1540 impose obligations upon states more quickly than the slower process of treaty-making, demonstrate the necessary institutional response to a particular crisis and are applicable to all states, not just to those that choose to become parties.

The multiple instruments and institutional mandates devoted to the eradication and suppression of terrorism have not resolved the dilemma of its definition; nor is there any 'joined-up' international law approach to combating terrorism. The ongoing urgent need for a comprehensive terrorism convention is part of the agenda for UN reform and in 2005 the Secretary-General again urged the GA to conclude such a convention, as well as a convention on the suppression of acts of nuclear terrorism.[43] Neither was a new proposal. As has been seen, the desirability of a terrorist convention has been expressed since at least 1937 and in its Summit Outcome Document the GA repeated the need to make every effort for its achievement.[44] It also uncompromisingly strengthened its 1994 denunciation of terrorism by condemning it 'in all its forms and manifestations, committed by whomever, wherever and for whatever purposes'.[45]

In 1996 the GA had established another *ad hoc* committee *inter alia* to work on a convention on the suppression of acts of nuclear terrorism.[46] In 1997 in response to a report by the Secretary-General, Russia proposed a draft convention to fill gaps in the 1980 Convention on the Physical Protection of Nuclear Material. The draft convention was considered by the GA 6th Committee and the *ad hoc* Committee but negotiations stalled, once again over the question of definition and also on that of the use of nuclear weapons by military forces.[47] The 6th Committee established a Working Group in 2002 to consider both these questions. While the comprehensive treaty remains elusive the GA adopted the Convention on the Suppression of Acts of Nuclear Terrorism on 13 April 2005— the first counter-terrorism convention so adopted since 11 September 2001. This Convention and SC Resolution 1540 on non-proliferation of weapons of mass destruction illustrate another change in law-making against terrorism: neither is in response to a specific act but rather they seek to lessen the possibility of such an eventuality.

This brief outline of the international legal responses to terrorism illustrates many facets of contemporary international law-making that are discussed throughout the book. It shows how international law evolves both rapidly in response to specific events and more slowly through policy deliberation. It also

---

[43] *In Larger Freedom*, paras 91, 92.
[44] 2005 World Summit Outcome, UNGA Res 60/1, 24 October 2005, para 83.
[45] Ibid, para 81.   [46] UNGA Res 51/210, 16 January 1997.
[47] Aust, 5 *Max Planck UNYB* (2001) 1.

illustrates the diversity of law-making approaches that international law now offers and that the choice of process depends upon context, political preference and purpose. In addition assessment has to be made as to whether a particular process is law-making, or whether the outcomes of specific deliberations are moral or political recommendations rather than legally binding norms.

Multilateral law-making is an intense process of negotiation. Even where there is widespread agreement as to the need for a legal framework certain issues may be hotly contested and compromise will be essential. In the case of terrorism the compromise of adopting sectoral multilateral treaties (in place of the elusive comprehensive treaty) remains in place after many years. The specificity of this approach has been accentuated by the adoption of further protocols as the need has arisen. The eclecticism of the international system is revealed as multiple institutions have been engaged, including the GA (through the plenary body, the 6th Committee, *ad hoc* committees and working groups), the SC (through its plenary body, Sanctions Committees and the Counter-Terrorism Committee), the Secretary-General, UN specialised agencies and the ILC. In the *Lockerbie* case the ICJ upheld the use of UN Charter Chapter VII powers in the context of terrorism. The choice of arena influences process and the form of outcome. Different institutions variously take centre-stage: the GA in 1994 through its adoption of the non-binding declaration of basic principles; the SC immediately after 11 September 2001 when an urgent and authoritative binding response was required; the GA again in 2005 with the adoption of the Convention on the Suppression of Acts of Nuclear Terrorism and further commitment to a comprehensive convention. Regional institutions have replicated these efforts resulting in further multilateral treaties, some of which are open to states outside the region.[48] Regional bodies have worked on initial drafts of global conventions as in the case of the EU with the Suppression of Financing Convention, 2000. Participants in the various law-making processes include specialist, technical and legal experts, international bureaucrats, and states' political representatives. Different processes have been engaged: detailed preparatory work and drafting, diplomatic conferences, adoption of treaties and resolutions, preparation, dissemination and discussion of expert reports, and development of compliance mechanisms.

Tackling global terrorism has also required cooperation between specialist networks of government and non-governmental agencies, for example banking communities, police, immigration and intelligence services. Behind the formal processes of international law-making such bodies also evolve law through their

---

[48] eg 1999 Convention of the Organization of the Islamic Conference on Combating International Terrorism; 1977 European Convention on the Suppression of Terrorism; 1971 OAS Convention to Prevent and Punish the Acts of Terrorism Taking the Form of Crimes against Persons and Related Extortion that are of International Significance; 1999 OAU Convention on the Prevention and Combating of Terrorism; 1987 SAARC Regional Convention on Suppression of Terrorism, Kathmandu; 1999 Treaty on Cooperation among the States Members of the Commonwealth of Independent States in Combating Terrorism; 1998 Arab Convention for the Suppression of Terrorism.

practices, exchanges, technical expertise and shared expediency.[49] Linkages between areas of international law (for example prohibition of the use of force in international relations, international criminal law, extradition, mutual assistance in criminal affairs, suppression of drug trafficking, non-proliferation of weapons) facilitate linguistic consistency and allow concepts and approaches developed in one legal context to be applied in another. Familiar language is more likely to be understood and thus less likely to be disputed. The outcomes of such processes combine hard and soft, global and regional law.

Alongside the multilateral negotiated law-making processes have been non-negotiated responses to international terrorism, primarily by the US acting alone or in conjunction with other states in a 'coalition of the willing'. The 'war on terror' has included targeted extra-territorial killings of individuals, long-term detention of 'enemy combatants', extraordinary rendition (the deportation of persons to places where they may be subject to torture) and forcible regime change in Afghanistan and Iraq. Depending on the responses of other actors, such unilateral acts may contribute to the mosaic of state practice foundational of customary international law but, as we argue in Chapter 3, they are more likely to do so only in the context of further multilateral law-making.

3.   Theories of International Law

In our discussion of law-making in the context of terrorism we have made no attempt to define international law. Nevertheless this cannot be ignored for individual answers to the question how international law is made may depend upon what one understands as comprising international law. In turn this determines the sources utilised and processes identified as 'law-making'. Theoretical approaches to international law and how it comes into being have burgeoned and '[i]dentifying international law-making today is not as easy as it used to be'.[50] President of the ICJ, Judge Higgins, has explained that 'international law has to be identified by reference to what the actors (most often states), often without benefit of pronouncement by the International Court of Justice, believe normative in their relations with each other'.[51] Traditional theories have been adapted and new theories evolved in response to the changing conditions of the international order. A brief survey of international legal theories[52] reveals diverse emphases and approaches. No survey can catch the current vitality in international legal theory and the many nuances that exist between scholars, even those supposedly following the same

---

[49] See Chapter 2.
[50] O. Schachter, 'Recent Trends in International Law-Making', 12 *Australian YBIL* (1989) 1.
[51] R. Higgins, *Problems and Process: International Law and How We Use It* (Oxford, 1993) 18.
[52] 'Symposium: Method in International Law', 93 *AJIL* (1999) 291–423 provides an overview of contemporary theories and methods of international law.

approach. In addition the work of many international lawyers does not fit within a single theoretical framework but draws from among them, or shifts in emphasis over time. In the following section we indicate how particular theoretical approaches to international law identify the processes of making law.

The origins of contemporary international law are rooted in natural law thinking categorised by Van Hoof under the umbrella of 'legal idealism'.[53] While many versions of natural law have been influential, especially (but by no means exclusively) in Western thought over many centuries, its 'constant factor has been the appeal to something superior to positive law, whether this superior factor was seen as a directive [rooted in religious doctrine, or secular appeal to reason] or as a guide to positive law'.[54] This 'superior law' offered universal principles for the determination of relations between states but natural law cannot offer any blueprint for its derivation, verification or guidance for detailed regulation. Nevertheless there are examples of recourse to 'moral law' in international law-making with evident affiliation with natural law reasoning, for instance in response to wartime atrocities[55] and humanitarian concerns such as discrimination. Law-making in accordance with the dictates of humanity has been provided for within treaties, most notably the celebrated Martens Clause.[56] The Treaty of Versailles, 1919, Article 227 provided for the trial of the German Kaiser for 'a supreme offence against international morality'. The inclusion of *jus cogens* within the Vienna Convention on the Law of Treaties was seen by some states as an expression of natural law, legal conscience or morality.[57] The GA has asserted moral law. For example the GA Resolution on the Crime of Genocide stated genocide to be 'contrary to moral law' and a 'crime under international law'[58] two years before the adoption of the Genocide Convention in 1948. The Preamble to the Rome Statute of the ICC refers to 'atrocities that deeply shock the conscience of humanity'. International judges upon occasion refer to guiding values such as justice, equity and considerations of humanity both to fill gaps in the law and to temper harsh application of legal principles.[59] In the *Legality of Nuclear Weapons* Judge

---

[53] Van Hoof categorises schools of international law under three headings: legal idealism, analytical, and sociological approaches to law: G. Van Hoof, *Rethinking the Sources of International Law* (Deventer and London, 1983) 30–44.   [54] Ibid 32.

[55] The prosecutor at the International Military Tribunal for the Far East, Keenan, considered that 'civilisation and humanity' demanded the trial. In his lengthy dissent Justice Pal rejected the argument that aggressive war was illegal at the time. He also challenged the 'politicization' of the Tribunal; E. Kopelman, 'Ideology and International Law: The Dissent of the Indian Justice at the Tokyo War Crimes Trial', 23 *NYU JILP* (1990–1) 373, 375, 397.

[56] Preamble to the Convention with respect to the Laws and Customs of War on Land, (Hague II), 29 July 1899: 'Until a more complete code of the laws of war is issued, the High Contracting Parties think it right to declare that in cases not included in the Regulations adopted by them, populations and belligerents remain under the protection and empire of the principles of international law, as they result from the usages established between civilized nations, from the laws of humanity, and the requirements of the public conscience.'

[57] eg Mexico, Italy, Ecuador, Monaco, Lebanon, Nigeria, Uruguay, Ceylon, Ivory Coast; UN Conference on the Law of Treaties, Official Records, First Session, 1969 at 294, 297, 298, 303, 311, 319, 320, 324.   [58] UNGA Res 96 (1), 11 December 1946, The Crime of Genocide.

[59] See Chapter 6.

Weeramantry considered that 'public conscience dictates the non-use of nuclear weapons'.[60] However the Secretary-General in his Report prior to the setting up of the International Criminal Tribunal for the Former Yugoslavia (ICTY) for the prosecution of war crimes and crimes against humanity committed at the break-up of the Former Yugoslavia did not draw upon moral or natural law but emphasised existing international customary and conventional law as essential for the prosecution of international crimes.[61] He thus affirmed a classic positivist approach for this innovative Tribunal.[62]

The legal positivist,[63] seeking rules deriving from state consent will tend to adhere to recognisable sources of authority, treaties and custom, and will give weight to those other sources identified in the Statute of the ICJ, Article 38 (1). The positivist is less willing to accept the normative effect of non-legal instruments such as GA resolutions or the final documents of global summit meetings, seeing any concept of so-called soft law[64] as seeking 'unprecedented expansion of the concept of law into areas of normative regulation which have never been considered as belonging to the law proper'.[65] While 'enlightened'[66] positivism retains the centrality of formal sources as the core of international legal discourse, it is more flexible, recognises change in patterns of state behaviour and wider methods of determining state consent and evidence of that consent. Further '[s]o-called soft law is an important device for the attribution of meaning to rules and for the perception of legal change'.[67] Perhaps strangely in that the classic exposition of sources of international law excludes any law-making role for non-state actors, among the strongest adherents to positivist law are civil society groups who seek the conclusion of treaties between states in as strong language as possible and to have input into those processes.[68] Civil society activists often have a faith in and commitment to the promise of international law whose law-making processes they seek to access.

The adherent to the New Haven (Yale) policy science approach to international law focuses not on rules but explicitly on the processes by which legal decisions and policies are made.[69] The method of analysis involves first identification of the

[60] *Legality of the Threat or Use of Nuclear Weapons* (1996) ICJ Reports 226, 487, diss op Judge Weeramantry.

[61] Report or the S-G Pursuant to Paragraph 2 of the Security Council Resolution 808 (1993), para 34.

[62] A major criticism of both Nuremberg and the International Military Tribunal for the Far East was that it applied *ex post facto* law; I. Bantekas and S. Nash, *International Criminal Law* (2nd edn, London, 2003) 333–5. The S-G's approach echoes the assertion of the ICJ that it could 'take account of moral principles only in so far as these are given a sufficient expression in legal form'. *SW Africa Case* (1966) ICJ Reports 6, para 49.

[63] ' "Positivism" is a label for a whole array of differing approaches to international legal theory.' B. Simma and A. Paulus, 'The Responsibility of Individuals for Human Rights Abuses in Internal Conflicts: A Positivist View', 93 *AJIL* (1999) 302, 303.   [64] See Chapter 5.

[65] G. Danilenko, *Law-Making in the International Community* (Dordrecht, 1993) 20.

[66] B. Simma and A. Paulus, ' "The International Community": Facing the Challenge of Globalization', 9 *EJIL* (1998) 266, 307.   [67] Ibid 308.

[68] See Chapter 2.

[69] For a concise account of the New Haven approach see M. Reisman, 'The View from the New Haven School of International Law', *ASIL Proceedings* (1992) 118. For emphasis on the communicative

observer's standpoint to allow disengagement and objectivity, second consciousness of the conceptual categories used by the observer to analyse particular situations, and third an understanding of the processes used to influence particular outcomes. The constitutive process therefore requires identification of trends in decision-making with reliance on past decisions in the light of their contexts (conditioning factors) and the desired outcome, thereby incorporating policy objectives and values. Unlike the positivist view, under the New Haven approach the decision-making process that generates international law is not limited to states or the actions of state officials. Instead it looks to:

the aggregate actual decision process, comprised, as it is, of governments, inter-governmental organizations, non-governmental organizations and, in no small measure, the media. All the actors, who assess, retrospectively or prospectively, the lawfulness of international actions and whose consequent reactions shape the flow of events, now constitute, in sum, the international legal decision process.[70]

For the New Haven school the over-riding and determinative value is the promotion of human dignity. While this is presented as an objective standard and the process as scientific, in reality in a world of deeply held diverse ideologies, religious beliefs and cultural practices, such values are inevitably subjective. Too often, by adopting this approach the Yale School has been found to favour law that is in accordance with US policy-making.[71]

Other scholars have urged that greater attention be given to the institutions established by states. Wilfred Jenks argued that international law discharges its community functions through 'a complex of international and regional institutions . . . calling for uniform regulation on an international basis'.[72] Other theorists also focus on process, including institutional process. Prescribed procedures and processes restrain policy-based decisions (one of the criticisms directed at the New Haven school) and when institutions act according to those procedures their decisions develop new legal standards. These institutions 'clarify ambiguities in the law, fill gaps, and thus make law beyond the consent of states'.[73] Institutional practice changes state behaviour and thus contributes to emergent customary international law.[74] Seeking to understand the ways in which global institutions act as regulators as well as standard setters and the shift to extra-state institutional

---

function see M. Reisman, 'International Lawmaking: A Process of Communication', *Proceedings of the 75th Anniversary Convocation of the American Society of International Law* (1981) 101.

[70] M. Reisman, 'Unilateral Action and the Transformation of the World Constitutive Process: The Special Problem of Humanitarian Intervention', 11 *EJIL* (2000) 3, 13.

[71] J. Hathaway, 'America, Defender of Democratic Legitimacy?', 11 *EJIL* (2000) 121.

[72] W. Jenks, *The Common Law of Mankind* (New York, 1958).

[73] M. E. O'Connell, 'New International Legal Process', 93 *AJIL* (1999) 334, 349.

[74] For a discussion of the operational processes of the World Bank see B. Kingsbury, 'Operational Processes of International Institutions as Part of the Law-Making Process: The World Bank and Indigenous Peoples', in G. Goodwin-Gill and S. Talmon (eds), *The Reality of International Law* (Oxford, 1999) 323.

forms of power and authority in global governance, Benedict Kingsbury and associates have enunciated the concept of a Global Administrative Law.[75] Harold Koh argues that international law derives from the transnational legal process which he describes as a 'complex process of institutional *interaction* whereby global norms are not just debated and *interpreted*, but ultimately *internalized* by domestic legal systems'.[76]

Critical legal scholars have used the form of legal argument to expose the indeterminacy of and contradictions in international (and national) legal rules and processes and thereby to challenge the view that law is rational, neutral, objective and principled. They emphasise that law is premised on substantive political or other values. David Kennedy for example has shown how positivists who adhere to treaties as the 'quintessential' form of hard law through their basis in state consent must fall back on the 'soft' principle of *pacta sunt servanda*[77] as their justification for holding states bound in some situations where they have not consented.[78] The self-designated task of the critical legal scholar is to reveal the concealed biases and hierarchies of international law and hence to expand its discourse. Accordingly the decision-maker should not rely solely on either rules or process but must use 'sociological enquiries into causal relationships and political enquiry into acceptable forms of containing power'.[79] Critical scholars in what has become known as the 'New Approaches to International Law' (NAIL) have exposed a range of different biases that are obscured and marginalised by accounts of law-making that ignore the interests of disempowered groups. Studies include the gendered nature of international law,[80] Third World Approaches to International Law (TWAIL) that show the failure to take account of third world analyses and resistance movements,[81] and historical accounts that have demonstrated the 'dark' side of international law in upholding the interests of the colonial powers, for example by masking their violent acquisition and exploitation of overseas territories through the civilising doctrines of legality.[82] Critical analysis has also charged that international law-making is in fact 'part of the problem' and that lawyers mistake law-making for problem-solving and substitute process for substantive solutions.[83]

---

[75] B. Kingsbury, N. Krisch, R. Stewart and J. Wiener (eds), 'The Emergence of Global Administrative Law', 68 *Law and Contemporary Problems* (2005).

[76] H. Koh, 'Why Do Nations Obey International Law?', 106 *Yale LJ* (1996–7) 2599, 2602. (Italics in original; footnotes omitted). The purpose of internalisation of norms is of course their application by national bodies.   [77] 1969 Vienna Convention on the Law of Treaties (VCLT), Article 26.

[78] D. Kennedy, 'The Sources of International Law', 2 *Am UJILP* (1987) 1, 25.

[79] M. Koskenniemi, *From Apology to Utopia: The Structure of International Legal Argument* (Helsinki, 1989) 485.

[80] H. Charlesworth and C. Chinkin, *The Boundaries of International Law: A Feminist Analysis* (Manchester, 2000).

[81] B. Rajagopal, *International Law from Below: Development, Social Movements and Third World Resistance* (Cambridge, 2003).

[82] M. Koskenniemi, *The Gentle Civilizer of Nations: The Rise and Fall of International Law 1870–1960* (Cambridge, 2001); A. Anghie, *Imperialism, Sovereignty and the Making of International Law* (Cambridge, 2004).

[83] D. Kennedy, 'The International Human Rights Movement: Part of the Problem?', 15 *Harvard Human Rights Journal* (2002) 101.

The critiques just addressed might be perceived as coming from the 'left' of the political spectrum. Other challenges to the place of international law in the contemporary world come from its other end. Commitment to an international rule of law has long been challenged by the realists who dispute the applicability of law to the powerful when it restrains their choices.[84] Another challenge to the position of law in international affairs has gained prominence in the post-cold war era, especially from within the US. Writers such as Goldsmith and Posner have argued that international law empirically results from state interests: 'international law emerges from states acting rationally to maximise their interests, given their perceptions of the interests of other states and the distribution of state power.'[85] On this reasoning law is no more than a factor to be taken into account in decision-making and the concept of *opinio juris* is rendered meaningless. Treaty-making is also reduced in importance for the text has little bearing on state behaviour.

In 1959 Wolfgang Friedmann argued for a 'cooperative international law'[86] based upon mutual interest in achieving common benefits, especially through common institutional participation. This vision of positive international collaboration was necessitated by the broadening vertical and horizontal scope of international law and a response to the then prevailing cold war concept of co-existence. There is an instrumentality—a need to address global problems through negotiated law-making rather than through confrontation and division—that is most readily addressed in areas of technical regulation devoid of significant ideological or moral content. Another evolutionary trend that has gained force since the 1960s is that of a hierarchy of international norms that was given conventional weight through the controversial inclusion of the concept of peremptory norms—*jus cogens*—in the Vienna Convention on the Law of Treaties.[87] Similar manifestations of a value-based hierarchy have generated the argument that the international legal system is moving from a system of bilateral law-making and state voluntarism to one of multilateral law-making and community values.[88] These manifestations include the negotiation of multilateral law-making treaties on such issues as human rights and environmental law incorporating obligations owed *erga omnes*;[89] the ILC's concept of a 'State other than an injured State';[90] and the invocation of the will of the 'international community' that is inherent in all these developments.[91]

---

[84] H. Morgenthau, *Politics Among Nations: The Struggle for Power and Peace* (5th edn, New York, 1978).

[85] J. Goldsmith and E. Posner, *The Limits of International Law* (Oxford, 2005) 3.

[86] W. Friedmann, *Law in a Changing Society* (London, 1959) 460. This argument is expanded in W. Friedmann, *The Changing Structure of International Law* (New York, 1964; 2nd edn, 1966).

[87] 1969 VCLT, Articles 53, 64, 66 (a) and 71.

[88] C. Chinkin, *Third Parties in International Law* (Oxford, 1993) 349–56; B. Simma, 'From Bilateralism to Community Interest in International Law', 250 *Recueil des Cours* (1994) 217.

[89] *Barcelona Traction Light and Power Company Ltd* (1970) ICJ Reports 3, para 33.

[90] ILC Articles on the Responsibility of States for Internationally Wrongful Acts, Article 48.

[91] Ibid, Articles 33, 42 (b). H. Mosler, 'The International Society as a Legal Community', 140 *Recueil des Cours* (1974) 17; B. Simma and A. Paulus, ' "The International Community": Facing the Challenge of Globalization', 9 *EJIL* (1998) 266.

The abandoned Article 19 of the ILC's Draft Articles on State Responsibility on international crimes of state[92] encompassed some of these same ideas. These concepts involve a dilution of state consent in law-making, assume harmony of purpose within the international community, a shared value system and a willingness to wade in on behalf of others, even against one's own self-interest. As Judge Bedjaoui expressed it:

> The resolutely positivist, voluntarist approach of international law still current at the beginning of the [20th] century . . . has been replaced by an objective conception of international law, a law more readily seeking to reflect a collective juridical conscience and respond to the social necessities of States organized as a community.[93]

In a manner reminiscent of natural law, there have been attempts in international law-making to give some content to abstract notions of community values that have been espoused across a number of differing theoretical perspectives on law. For example international courts have determined norms to constitute *jus cogens*,[94] 'intransgressible principles',[95] or obligations owed *erga omnes*.[96] There has been at least some shift from impunity to accountability for gross violations of human rights through the development of international criminal courts and assertions of universal jurisdiction by national courts. Theorists have urged that the process of establishing customary international law should take account of moral standards, for example by discounting contrary state practice where there are moral dictates for pronouncing the existence of such a rule.[97] Explicitly Teson has drawn upon Kantian thought to argue that 'only a theory of international morality firmly grounded on human rights can avoid the pitfalls of realism. By extension, human rights (and not the rights of states) provide the ethical foundation of international law.'[98] This approach is taken up by the International Commission on Intervention and State Sovereignty that considered a 'Responsibility to

---

[92] Draft Articles on State Responsibility provisionally adopted by the ILC on First Reading (1996) in J. Crawford, *The International law Commission's Articles on State Responsibility* (Cambridge, 2002) 348.

[93] *Legality of the Threat or Use of Nuclear Weapons* (1996) ICJ Reports 226, Declaration, President Bedjaoui, 268, para 13.

[94] eg *Prosecutor v. Furundzija* (IT-95–17/1) (judgment 10 December 1998), paras 153–4 (prohibition of torture as *jus cogens*); Inter-American Court of Human Rights, *Juridical Condition and Rights of the Undocumented Migrants* (Adv Op 17 September 2003) (non-discrimination on the basis of race and sex as *jus cogens*); *Armed Activities on the Territory of the Congo* (2006) ICJ Reports, para 64 (prohibition of genocide as *jus cogens*).

[95] *Threat or Use of Nuclear Weapons* (1996) ICJ Reports, para 79; *Legal Consequences of the Construction of a Wall in the Occupied Palestinian Territory* (2004) ICJ Reports, para 157.

[96] *East Timor Case* (1995) ICJ Reports 90, para 29 (judgment of 30 June) (the right to self-determination); *Armed Activities on the Territory of the Congo*, para 64 (prohibition of genocide).

[97] F. Kirgis, 'Custom on a Sliding Scale', 81 *AJIL* (1987) 146; for discussion see A. Roberts, 'Traditional and Modern Approaches to Customary International Law: A Reconciliation', 95 *AJIL* (2001) 757, 766. Charney urged acceptance of a 'universal international law' developed through multilateral fora and binding upon all states without exception because of the need to provide speedy and comprehensive solutions to problems of a fundamental nature; J. Charney, 'Universal International Law', 87 *AJIL* (1993) 529. See Chapter 5.

[98] F. Teson, 'Realism and Kantianism in International Law', 86 *ASIL Proceedings* (1992) 113, 118.

Protect' to be founded upon 'a duty to protect communities from mass killing, women from systematic rape and children from starvation'.[99]

However the concept of international community is an artificial construct and both its constitution and the content of the values derived therefrom are contested. Although states remain the dominant international actors, it is not apparent that the *omnes*—or international community—must be identified exclusively with states rather than expressed through a wider range of voices. John Tasioulas for example has recognised the place of non-state actors in identifying fundamental norms and obligations owed *erga omnes*.[100] Even if the understanding of the international community were extended in this way, international law-making remains unrepresentative as participants are largely drawn from elite groups within and across societies. The input of those who remain stranded at the peripheries— women, indigenous persons, displaced persons—remains minimal.[101]

Nor is there necessarily agreement on the content of community values. There is no authoritative list of *jus cogens* norms and the ILC deliberately refrained from providing examples because this might 'lead to misunderstanding as to the position concerning other cases'.[102] Nor did it specify any law-making process for norms of *jus cogens* leaving the 'danger that in the absence of clearly defined procedures . . . their emergence and subsequent identification may become a matter of conflicting assertions reflecting political preferences of different groups of states'.[103] Critics have challenged the biases inherent in accepted contenders for *jus cogens* and in those not accepted as such. For example the supposedly objective and neutral assessment of core values is exposed as being founded upon male visions of the 'good life'[104] or as espousing an ideology 'shaped in a "peculiarly Western concept of law" which disregards the "partial, multilayered and fragmented nature of international society"'.[105] A 'doctrine of international community' has been put forward as a political objective for international law reform by UK Prime Minister Tony Blair, who sees it as essential in an interdependent, globalised world.[106] In language reminiscent of Friedmann, Blair seeks an echo of the notion of community that he finds in domestic politics and which fosters partnership and cooperation. This vision ignores the fragmentation of both domestic and international

---

[99] Report of the International Commission on Intervention and State Sovereignty, *The Responsibility to Protect* (Ottawa, 2001) 17. See further Chapter 2.

[100] J. Tasioulas, 'In Defence of Relative Normativity: Communitarian Values and the *Nicaragua* Case', 16 *Oxford JLS* (1996) 85.   [101] See Chapter 2.

[102] 1966 YBILC, vol II, 248.

[103] G. Danilenko, 'International *Jus Cogens*: Issues of Law-Making', 2 *EJIL* (1991) 42, 43.

[104] H. Charlesworth and C. Chinkin, 'The Gender of *Jus Cogens*', 15 *HRQ* (1993) 63.

[105] J. Weiler and A. Paulus, 'The Structure of Change in International Law or Is There a Hierarchy of Norms in International Law?', 8 *EJIL* (1997) 545, 552 citing A. Carty, 'Critical International Law: Recent Trends in the Theory of International Law', 2 *EJIL* (1991) 66, 68.

[106] T. Blair, 'Doctrine of the International Community', speech to the Economic Club of Chicago, Hilton Hotel, Chicago, USA, 22 April 1999, available at <http://www.globalpolicy.org/globaliz/politics/blair.htm>.

politics. The delivery of the speech in the US and Blair's appeal that the 'EU and US should prepare to make real step-change in working more closely together' suggest that fulfilment would reinforce the 'project of organising the administration of the international society by the Rule of Law in the image of the liberal West'.[107]

Further, there are other, opposing indications that signal that so-called community values or ideals are either not part of the contemporary law-making process, or at best play only a minor role. One such indication is that states rarely make claims of violations of fundamental norms. For example, outside the regional systems no state has availed itself of the right of inter-state complaint for violations of the human rights treaties. States do not always accept the restraints of peremptory norms. In the *East Timor* case Australia did not accept that the *erga omnes* nature of the right of self-determination prevented it from entering into a treaty for the allocation of maritime resources with a state that was clearly violating that right.[108] Nor has the ICJ developed procedural rules commensurate with the substantive obligations it has enunciated.[109] By reasserting the principle of jurisdictional consent and not hearing the merits of Portugal's claim in light of Indonesia's absence, the ICJ left the East Timorese peoples' right to self-determination (that it had asserted to be *erga omnes*) without practical consequences. In the *Arrest Warrant* case the ICJ upheld the immunity of the foreign minister of the Democratic Republic of the Congo before Belgian courts even when he was facing charges of crimes against humanity.[110] The United Nations Convention on the Jurisdictional Immunities of States and their Property, 2004 makes no exception to immunity for violations of *jus cogens* norms.[111] The 'trumping' argument—that a norm of *jus cogens* is hierarchically superior to the requirements of immunity—has not been widely accepted.[112] Despite human rights reports setting out the adverse impact of neo-liberal economic ideology and globalisation on the human rights of the poor, of women and of other vulnerable peoples, there has been little real attempt to address these issues within the framework of international law. International law has played an insignificant role in the Millennium Development Goals (MDGs),[113]

---

[107] M. Koskenniemi, ' "The Lady Doth Protest Too Much": Kosovo and the Turn to Ethics in International Law', 65 *MLR* (2002) 159, 160.

[108] Portugal claimed that by entering into the Timor Gap Treaty, 1989 with Indonesia, Australia had violated the right of the people of East Timor to self-determination.

[109] In the *Armed Activities on the Territory of the Congo* (3 February 2006) the ICJ reiterated that the fact that a dispute concerned obligations *erga omnes* and compliance with a *jus cogens* norm has no bearing on consent to the jurisdiction of the ICJ; para 64. However in *Armed Activities on the Territory of the Congo* (*Democratic Republic of the Congo v. Uganda*) Judge Simma considered Uganda to have standing to bring a claim of violations of obligations owed *erga omnes; (*2005) ICJ Reports, para 37 sep op Judge Simma.   [110] *Arrest Warrant of 11 April 2000* (2000) ICJ Reports 3.

[111] *Jones v. Ministry of the Interior* [2006] 2 WLR 1424, para 26 per Lord Bingham.

[112] K. Parlett, 'Immunity in Civil Proceedings for Torture: The Emerging Exception', 2006 (1) *EHRLR* 49, 51.

[113] P. Alston, 'Ships Passing in the Night: The Current State of the Human Rights and Development Debate seen through the Lens of the Millennium Development Goals', 27 *HRQ* (2005) 755.

the blueprint agreed to by all the world's states and leading development institutions for achieving social justice. In these various ways, claims that contemporary international law gives effect to some commonly held values and that international law-making should take account of this appear somewhat thin.

This account has assumed that attempts to make contemporary international law-making conform with ethical values and to introduce a hierarchy of norms are desirable. But this stance is not unchallenged. Some writers have strongly reasserted the need for law-making to be based upon state consent and have deplored attempts to develop norms of *jus cogens* as fostering uncertainty and relative normativity.[114] In turn such arguments have been decried 'as a slightly hysterical effort to stop the world from changing'.[115] But no theory of international law offers a comprehensive or scientific guide to international law-making. In all cases the outcome is dictated by the subjective evaluations and value preferences of those making the determination whether they are government policy-makers, members of the international bureaucracy, international judges, academics or civil society activists. Even from the standpoint of positivism relativity is unavoidable in international law.[116]

4. International Law-Making in a Globalised World

The complexity of contemporary international relations and the changing international environment has been noted by many commentators over the years and has generated arguments in favour of expansion of law-making processes, as well as of the forms and substance of international regulation.[117] Indeed the inadequacy of international law in changing conditions is a perennial concern, as are claims for a dynamic international legal system incorporating processes for amending and making laws that are commensurate to the demands upon it. Whatever view is preferred about the ethical basis of international law, it is clear that this law is fundamental to a globalised world: the movements of people, goods and capital across state borders demand international standards and processes. So too do the movements of deadly viruses, arms and drugs. The discussion of law-making in the context of terrorism illustrates the need for global solutions to such threats to international peace and security. Other challenges are raised by the despoliation of the environment, climate change, gross human rights violations, the need to control the spread of disease, and to regulate scientific and technological advances such as human cloning or genetically modified products.

---

[114] P. Weil, 'Towards Relative Normativity in International Law?', 77 *AJIL* (1983) 413.
[115] A. Cassese and J. Weiler, *Change and Stability*, 137 (per Richard Falk).
[116] U. Fastenrath, 'Relative Normativity in International Law', 4 *EJIL* (1993) 305, 306.
[117] eg G. Palmer, 'New Ways to Make International Environmental Law', 86 *AJIL* (1992) 259.

The requirements of contemporary international law-making have involved diverse participants. In some instances demand for international regulation has come from civil society that perceives its interests as in conflict with those of states, especially in contexts such as human rights, disarmament and the environment. Non-state actors purport to speak on behalf of diverse interests. Epistemic communities comprising those with scientific, technical or other expertise come together in treaty-making alongside government representatives and members of international bureaucracies.[118] Scientific and technological advance does not necessarily lead to uncontested law-making. Divergent interests over such issues as technology transfer and access to data and different views as to the reliability of, and the appropriate economic response to, scientific evidence lead to clashes between law-makers. These may prevent or delay successful negotiation of a new instrument, or full participation in an adopted instrument,[119] or become subject to judicial interpretation as to the legal requirements of an adopted regime.[120]

An often discounted participant in international law-making is the media, whose role in making instantly generated images available worldwide may hasten legal change. In 1991 the intense media focus on the plight of the Kurds in the aftermath of the Gulf War (in contrast to the attacks on them in the 1980s) put pressure on states that had been in the alliance against Iraq to come to their assistance. SC Resolution 688, 5 April 1991 insisted that Iraq allow access to humanitarian organisations and appealed to member states to contribute to humanitarian relief efforts. In Operation Provide Comfort the UK, France and US established safe havens in northern Iraq. This was an important step towards an emergent principle of humanitarian intervention, at least with SC authorisation, although it is impossible to tell whether it would have occurred without such media attention. While the 'CNN factor' in the making of international law should not be discounted, it must be remembered that media attention is selective and often short-lived. The media are not and should not be a 'reliable long-term substitute for an institutionalized international decision process'.[121]

Globalisation continues to collapse spatial and temporal boundaries. It is a truism that this is not a new phenomenon. In the 1950s Philip Jessup used the expression 'Transnational Law' to encompass the regulation of actions or events transcending national boundaries.[122] By the last years of the 20th century the expansion of the power and areas of operation of multinational corporations

---

[118] eg P. Haas, 'Do Regimes Matter? Epistemic Communities and Mediterranean Pollution Control', 43 *Int Org* (1989) 377; see further Chapter 2.

[119] eg by April 2006 163 states and regional economic integration organisations were parties to the 1997 Kyoto Protocol to the UN Framework Convention on Climate Change, excluding the US, which claims, *inter alia* that reducing carbon dioxide emissions would seriously harm its economy.

[120] eg European resistance to biotech foods led to a case brought against the EU by the US, claiming breach of WTO rules for blocking the import of genetically modified food. In early 2006 the press announced that the US claim had been upheld by a WTO Panel, although at time of writing the Panel Report had not been issued; *Washington Post*, 8 February 2006, D01.

[121] Reisman, 11 *EJIL* (2000) 3, 18.   [122] P. Jessup, *Transnational Law* (New Haven, 1956).

(globalisation from above)[123] and the proliferation of civil society movements (globalisation from below) had highlighted the need for legal regulation to mediate the often violent confrontation between these two forces. The challenges of globalisation have exposed some of the inadequacies of both national and international law mechanisms.[124] National legal systems face obstacles in exercising effective jurisdiction over entities that operate across state borders while international law based upon the regulation of state behaviour is ill-equipped to respond to corporate behaviour, or that of other non-state actors. As Michael Reisman has stated:

For better or worse, participants in a civilization of science and technology are locked in a relentless process of research and a frenzied, competitive drive to apply the results wherever they promise enhanced productivity and profit. Each innovation stimulates further innovations and the juggernaut of development roars on. As for the law that would regulate it all, thanks to its characteristic deliberative and measured methods, it often lags behind the innovations, leaving intervals of legal gap in which authority becomes uncertain.[125]

The contemporary relevance of customary international law in the face of such realities has sparked much debate.[126] The processes of its creation and determination have undoubted deficiencies. Despite assertions of 'instant'[127] customary law, this mode of informal and unwritten law-making is inherently conservative and backward-looking because of its reliance upon existing state practice. Uncertainties about the existence and content of rules of customary law allow opportunistic claims lacking any content in state practice or *opinio juris*.[128] Customary international law allows states to reject treaty regulation while claiming the benefits of those parts of an unratified treaty they perceive as desirable. In contrast, multilateral treaty-making 'involves a deliberate and rational effort to meet perceived needs by general rules applicable to all'.[129] Broad participation enhances the democratic nature of the process,[130] but is often slow and cumbersome and subject to political hijacking. Complex treaties comprise interwoven provisions that frequently cannot be viewed in isolation. This makes attempting to renegotiate an existing treaty a risky affair as opening up a text may lead to dissent where it had

---

[123] R. Falk, 'The Nuclear Weapons Advisory Opinion and the New Jurisprudence of Global Civil Society', 7 *Transnational Law and Contemporary Problems* (1997) 333.

[124] The inadequacy of international law in the face of globalisation is aptly captured by P. Alston, 'The Myopia of the Handmaidens: International Lawyers and Globalization', 8 *EJIL* (1997) 435.

[125] M. Reisman, 'Assessing Claims to Revise the Laws of War', 97 *AJIL* (2003) 82.

[126] eg P. Kelly, 'The Twilight of Customary International Law', 40 *VJIL* (2000) 449; J. Kammerhofer, 'Uncertainty in the Formal Sources of International Law: Customary International Law and Some of its Problems', 15 *EJIL* (2004) 523.

[127] B. Cheng, 'United Nations Resolutions on Outer Space: "Instant" International Customary Law?', 5 *Indian JIL* (1965) 23. See Chapter 5.

[128] P. Alston, 'Making Space for New Human Rights: The Case of the Right to Development', 1 *Harv HRYB* (1988) 3.

[129] O. Schachter, 'Entangled Treaty and Custom', in Y. Dinstein (ed), *International Law at a Time of Perplexity* (Dordrecht, 1989) 717, 720.

[130] At the UN Conference of Plenipotentiaries for the establishment of an International Criminal Court, 15 June–17 July 1998 there were 120 votes in favour, seven negative votes and 20 abstentions.

been thought there was consensus—or at least a willingness to live with the treaty provisions—and the attempt may generate more contested provisions. For example any change in SC membership would require UN Charter amendment in accordance with Article 108. The need for SC reform has been widely asserted: by the High Level Panel on Threats, Challenges and Change;[131] the Secretary-General, who considered that 'no reform of the United Nations would be complete without reform of the Security Council'; [132] and the GA, which in its Millennium Declaration resolved to intensify efforts 'to achieve a comprehensive reform of the Security Council'.[133] Models for reform encompassing the size of the SC and the powers of any additional members have been put forward. However SC membership is inextricably tied to highly charged issues of international peace and security and the political structures of the contemporary international order. At the 2005 Outcome Summit, there was insufficient political will to affirm any proposals for UN Charter amendment with respect to SC membership (or indeed any other issue), only a general expression of support for early reform.[134]

Some more flexible law-making processes have been engaged,[135] for example decision-making by consensus,[136] institutional procedures[137] and the use of Framework Conventions and subsequent Protocols to create new substantive obligations,[138] to bring additional matters within the scope of the original treaty,[139] and to create new procedures.[140] Multilateral treaties incorporate provisions for amending or updating without the need for recourse to a further diplomatic conference or other formal process. Recourse is also had to interpretative devices[141] and institutional practice.[142] Multiple institutions are engaged simultaneously and sequentially in law-making, as seen in the context of terrorism discussed above. Nevertheless frustration with slow, or what is perceived as an inappropriate, institutional response

---

[131] Report of the High Level Panel on Threats, Challenges and Change, para 250.
[132] *In Larger Freedom*, para 169.   [133] UNGA Res 55/2, 8 September 2000, para 30.
[134] UNGA Res 60/1, 2005 World Summit Outcome, para 153.
[135] In the context of customary international law see Chapter 6.
[136] See Chapter 3.   [137] See Chapter 3.
[138] eg Optional Protocol to the Convention on the Rights of the Child on the Involvement of Children in Armed Conflicts, GA Res 54/263, Annex I; Optional Protocol to the Convention on the Rights of the Child on the Sale of Children, Child Prostitution and Child Pornography, GA Res 54/263, Annex II, 16 March 2001.
[139] eg 1973 Convention on International Trade in Endangered Species of Wild Flora and Fauna and appendices; 2001 UNIDROIT Convention on International Interests in Mobile Equipment and Protocols.
[140] eg Optional Protocol to the Convention on the Elimination of All Forms of Discrimination against Women, UNGA Res 54/4, annex, 15 October 1999; Optional Protocol to the Convention against Torture and other Cruel, Inhuman or Degrading Treatment or Punishment, UNGA Res 57/199, 18 December 2002.
[141] eg the General Comments or Recommendations adopted by the UN human rights treaty bodies discussed in Chapter 3.
[142] eg the practice of the SC, whereby an abstention by a permanent member does not constitute a veto. On law-making by international institutions see J. Alvarez, *International Organizations as Law-Makers* (Oxford, 2005).

encourages unilateral action, as was the case with the NATO military action against Serbia in March 1999. Unilateral action and the ensuing responses, including legal claims,[143] political[144] and academic[145] analysis allows for assessment of the state of the law. But unless unilateral state action is endorsed by SC resolution or becomes accepted as a first step in the adoption of a uniform state practice for the evolution of a new rule of customary international law, it remains illegal and has the potential to undermine the role of international law.

Contemporary international law offers a fragmented landscape.[146] The ILC identified three forms of fragmentation: the emergence of deviating interpretations of general international law; emergence of institutionalised exceptions to general international law; the clash of particular laws.[147] Fragmentation is also seen in the variety of law-making processes and the separate legal regimes that exist alongside and within the international legal order. Regional groupings of states form their own horizontal systems that operate within, or may exclude, the general system. For example the EU has observer status within the UN,[148] is a participant in multilateral law-making and enters into treaties in its own name. However the separate legal order of the European Community (EC) may displace general international law. In the *Mox Plant* arbitration between Ireland and the UK instituted under the UN Convention on the Law of the Sea, Annex VII, the UK successfully claimed that the Annex VII arbitral Tribunal had no jurisdiction because matters before it were under the exclusive jurisdiction of the European Court of Justice, such matters extending to the interpretation and application of the Convention. The arbitral Tribunal had suspended its proceedings pending those of the ECJ.[149]

Fragmentation is also seen in the enormous variety of law-making processes. Contextualised legal regimes[150] now abound, generated by the need for specialist or technical regulation in a globalised world. These include legal regimes for human rights, the environment, economic regulation, trade, resources and disarmament. A specialised regime is understood as a self-contained, self-referential system of law

[143] *Legality of Use of Force (Serbia v. Belgium)* (1999) 1CJ Reports (Order of 2 June); 2004 ICJ Reports (judgment of 15 December). Separate cases were commenced by Serbia against the NATO countries.

[144] House of Commons, Foreign Affairs Committee, Fourth Report, Kosovo, vol I, Report and Proceedings of the Committee (London, 2000).

[145] I. Brownlie, C. Chinkin, C. Greenwood and V. Lowe, 'Kosovo: House of Commons, Foreign Affairs Committee, 4th Report, June 2000, Memoranda', 49 *ICLQ* (2000) 878–943.

[146] The ILC has undertaken the topic 'Fragmentation of International Law: Difficulties arising from the Diversification and Expansion of International Law', GAOR A/55/10, 2000, para 729; GAOR A/57/10, 202, paras 492–4. It has determined to concentrate upon substantive aspects of fragmentation in light of the VCLT; ILC, Report of the 57th Session, GAOR A/60/10 (2005), para 447. See Chapter 4.   [147] ILC, Report of the 56th Session, 283–303, GAOR A/59/10 (2004).

[148] See Chapter 2.

[149] *Mox Plant Arbitration*, Order No. 3, Suspension of Proceedings on Jurisdiction and Merits and Request for further Provisional Measures, 24 June 2003; *Commission of the European Communities v. Ireland*, Case C-459/03, 30 May 2006. See Chapter 6.

[150] The ICJ raised the concept of a specialised regime in the *Case Concerning United States Diplomatic and Consular Staff in Tehran* (1980) ICJ Reports 3, paras 85–6.

(*lex specialis*) that is governed by a set of principles and rules which either excludes general international law or modifies it to accommodate the needs of the particular regime. The purpose of a self-contained regime is to regulate behaviour within the particular sector and to that end it can be developed to give effect to its relevant needs, priorities and agendas. Special regimes co-exist and their provisions may overlap or conflict. The ICJ has elucidated that the relevant *lex specialis* should be used to interpret or define the terms of another applicable regime. In the *Nuclear Weapons* advisory opinion the Court considered the application of human rights law (the right to life) in determining the legality of nuclear weapons. It asserted that:

> In principle, the right not arbitrarily to be deprived of one's life applies also in hostilities. The test of what is an arbitrary deprivation of life, however, then falls to be determined by the applicable *lex specialis*, namely, the law applicable in armed conflict which is designed to regulate the conduct of hostilities.[151]

This statement does not however resolve the question as to which regime provides the primary applicable law, or the extent to which one legal regime is applicable within a different legal regime, for example whether the WTO panels and Appellate Body are required to take account of human rights or environmental law. We return to this question in Chapter 5.

The relevant question for our purposes is whether we can speak of a generalised system of international law-making or whether certain methodologies and processes apply exclusively to specific issue areas. Evidently there are specialised institutions that have developed their own procedures and there is a growing number of courts and tribunals of limited jurisdiction.[152] Certainly contemporary international law is made and operates through special regimes within a framework of generally applicable principles. As evidenced by the *Mox Plant* arbitration, there is the potential for jurisdictional and substantive conflict which may increase with time. Nevertheless we consider that the conclusions of Charney's study of multiple tribunals remain valid: 'Although differences exist, these tribunals are clearly engaged in the same dialectic. The fundamentals of general international law remain the same regardless of which tribunal is deciding the issue.'[153]

5. Legitimacy

5.1 Process Legitimacy

A recurring theme throughout the book is that of legitimacy—the normative belief that a rule or institution ought to be obeyed. The expansion of international law-making processes, and consequentially the corpus of international law, reflects a

---

[151] *Legality of the Threat or Use of Nuclear Weapons* (1996) ICJ Reports 226, paras 23–5.
[152] See Chapter 6.
[153] J. Charney, 'Is International Law Threatened by Multiple International Tribunals?', 271 *Recueil des Cours* (1998) 101, 347.

belief in the international rule of law and that an international system subject to law benefits all international actors, the strong as well as the weak. The concept of legitimacy is used to enhance the moral persuasiveness of international law by importing other values such as those of justice or equity, and conversely the centrality of international law is undermined by assertions of its illegitimacy, either of the system as a whole or, more frequently, of particular rules. Franck has explained that one facet of the latter—rule legitimacy—is that a rule derives 'from a perception on the part of those to whom it is addressed that it has come into being in accordance with right process'.[154] Hurd has similarly noted that an 'actor's perception [of legitimacy] may come from the substance of the rule or from the procedure or source by which it was constituted'.[155] Franck further argues that legitimacy is a significant factor in the 'compliance pull',[156] that a law-making process perceived to be illegitimate is likely to be disregarded and undermined. We accordingly use legitimacy as one criterion for assessing the different law-making processes discussed throughout the book.

Process is an essential element of law-making. It provides limits to arbitrary power. As Koskenniemi has asserted: 'formalism constitutes a horizon of universality, embedded in a *culture* of restraint, a *commitment* to listening to others' claims and seeking to take them into account'.[157] In a decentralised system no process can claim priority and different processes may be engaged simultaneously or in competition with each other. There are no easy pointers to the most appropriate way of approaching law-making in a specific instance, or as to which process will more likely be regarded as legitimate and by whom. Although for some critics of international law legitimacy is little more than a tool with which to reassert the sovereignty of states in an increasingly globalised world, for most governments the consensual basis of general international law through international agreements and decisions taken thereunder legitimises consequential restraints on sovereignty. In that sense legitimacy both derives from state consent, and is an essential pre-condition if governments are to be persuaded to give their consent to regulatory regimes. Accordingly where law is made through a long-established process that gives effect to state consent there is less likelihood of its being deemed illegitimate, while the legitimacy of new or adapted law-making processes may be challenged, especially where in one way or another they by-pass expressly given state consent.

Apparent distancing from well-established rules of international law can also lead to claims of illegitimacy. For example the assertion of jurisdiction based on the nationality of an alleged perpetrator even if that person's state is not a party to the Rome Statute is one challenge to the legitimacy of the ICC. The Sierra Leone

---

[154] T. Franck, 'Legitimacy in the International System', 82 *AJIL* (1988) 705, 706; id, *The Power of Legitimacy Among Nations* (New York, 1990).

[155] I. Hurd, 'Legitimacy and Authority in International Politics', 53 *Int Org* (1999) 379, 381.

[156] On compliance see A. Chayes and A. Chayes, *The New Sovereignty: Compliance with International Regulatory Agreements* (Cambridge, Mass, 1998); D. Shelton (ed), *Commitment and Compliance: The Role of Non-binding Norms in the International Legal System* (Oxford, 2000); B. Kingsbury, 'The Concept of Compliance as a Function of Competing Conceptions of International Law', 19 *Mich JIL* (1998) 345.

[157] Koskenniemi, 65 *MLR* (2002) 159, 174.

Special Tribunal was established by treaty between the UN and the Sierra Leone government. International pressure from some governments and human rights organisations urged the arrest and return for trial of former Liberian President Charles Taylor from Nigeria. The Nigerian response was that it would only accede to a request from a democratically elected Liberian government. Implicit in this response is that such a request would be deemed legitimate, unlike one from a Tribunal established by a treaty to which Nigeria is not a party.

The direct impact of international law upon individuals and organisations means that it is not just states that are concerned about the legitimacy of international law-making. Again there are differing views. For example the assertion of individual criminal responsibility for the commission of international crimes has led to assertions by accused persons that the establishment of international war crimes tribunals by the SC is illegal because that body lacks the requisite competence[158] and that proceedings before these bodies are illegitimate.[159] On the other hand human rights NGOs herald the legitimacy incurred through individual criminal responsibility pronounced by international tribunals.

Charges of illegitimacy may also be made because of procedural irregularity, changed procedural rules that had not been widely accepted, the application of what are seen as double standards, or participation by actors deemed unacceptable. We discuss in Chapter 2 US claims that the Landmines Convention was negotiated through the wrong institutional fora and that the Chair of the Rome Conference gave inadequate time for consideration of the final text of the ICC Statute before its adoption. In the *Reservations* case the difficulty of applying the compatibility rule espoused by the majority was a further concern for the dissenting judges. Although they did not express it in terms of legitimacy, their opinion that a new rule 'should be easy to apply and calculated to produce final and consistent results'[160] covers similar ground. The legitimacy of an unworkable rule is not easy to uphold.

As is also discussed in Chapter 2 non-state actors seek to influence international law-making in a variety of ways. Their participation may be perceived either as unacceptable and as depriving a process of legitimacy or as redressing the democratic deficit of international processes.[161] In the *Nuclear Weapons Advisory Opinion* Judge Oda complained that:

Some NGOs seem to have tried to compensate for the vainness of their efforts by attempting to get the principal judicial organ of the United Nations to determine the absolute illegality of nuclear weapons, in a bid to persuade the member States of the United Nations to press for their immediate and complete prohibition in the political forum.

---

[158] The Appellate Chamber of the ICTY asserted the legality of its establishment in *Prosecutor v. Tadic*, IT-94-1, Decision on the Defence Motion for Interlocutory Appeal on Jurisdiction, 2 October 1995, para 40.

[159] A challenge that the ICTY failed to comply with the fair trial requirements of the European Convention on Human Rights, Article 6 (including impartiality and independence) failed in *Naletilic v. Croatia* (Application No. 51891/99), 121 *ILR* (2002) 209.

[160] *Reservations to the Convention on the Prevention and Punishment of the Crime of Genocide* (1951) ICJ Reports 15, 44, diss op Judges Guerrero, Sir Arnold McNair, Read, Hsu Mo.

[161] See Chapter 2.

Judge Oda continued that this pressure meant 'that the Request [for an advisory opinion] did not reflect a meaningful consensus of the member States of the United Nations or even of its Non-Aligned Members' and that the Request was therefore not legitimate. But to other judges this broad expression of popular concern enhanced the importance and legitimacy of the Request. Judge Weeramantry noted that 'A multitude of organizations, . . . have also sent communications to the Court . . . and nearly two million signatures have been actually received by the Court from various organizations and individuals from around 25 countries'. These submissions 'evidence a groundswell of global public opinion which is not without legal relevance'.[162] These differences of opinion demonstrate both the subjectivity of any evaluation of legitimacy and the ready blending of assessments of both legality and legitimacy.

Franck has suggested four indicators of legitimacy: determinacy, symbolic validation, coherence and adherence to a normative hierarchy.[163] Current standards of good governance as promoted by the World Bank may offer other objective criteria as guidance to process legitimacy, for example the requirements of procedural transparency, democratic decision-making,[164] reasoned decisions and review mechanisms. The legitimacy of an international law-making process may be found in domestic systems. For example Slaughter has argued that the legitimacy of international law-making through government networks[165] is based upon the checks and balances that surround democratic governmental structures.[166] But one of the concerns about government networks is precisely that they have no formal constitutional status and thus lack domestic safeguards. It is evident that criteria of legitimacy are not easy to apply in particular cases and there may be debate about the conclusion in particular instances.

We have two final comments on this point. First, illegitimacy must be distinguished from illegality. If a body fails to observe its procedural rules it will have acted illegally and any outcome may lack legal force.[167] Second we reject the concept of legitimacy as a substitute for legality where the designated and accepted procedures have not been followed, or where substantive laws have been breached. Some commentators have concluded that unauthorised uses of force may be illegal but legitimate, for example because they are supported by humanitarian objectives.[168] Similarly in the context of the war on terror there is debate about whether torture may be legitimate, such as in the so-called 'ticking bomb' scenario. In the

---

[162] *Threat or Use of Nuclear Weapons* 1996 ICJ Reports 226, 438, diss op Judge Weeramantry.

[163] Franck, 82 *AJIL* (1988) 705, 712.

[164] See Chapter 2 for discussion of whether non-state actor participation in international law-making democratises the process. [165] See Chapter 2.

[166] A.-M. Slaughter, *A New World Order* (Princeton, 2004).

[167] The effects of illegality in international law are contested. E. Lauterpacht, 'The Legal Effect of Illegal Organisations', in *Cambridge Essays in International Law: Essays in Honour of Lord McNair* (London, 1965) 88.

[168] eg military action by NATO with respect to Kosovo, 1999. See generally E. Milano, *Unlawful Territorial Situations in International Law: Reconciling Effectiveness, Legality and Legitimacy* (Leiden, 2006).

absence of changed law such action must remain illegal although legitimacy is an important measure for assessing evolving international law-making processes.

5.2   System Legitimacy

Behind many of the discussions about contemporary international law-making and legitimacy lie the role and actions of the world's sole superpower, the US. The US has had an equivocal stance with respect to international law-making. On the one hand it has been a key player in shaping the contemporary legal order, including playing a central role in the creation of the UN, the International Financial Institutions, human rights instruments and other multilateral regimes. There has always been a US judge on the World Court and a US member on the ILC. On the other hand it has failed to become a party to core multilateral instruments, or has delayed for a long period before doing so. At the outset of the 21st century there are concerns that by resorting to unilateralism and rejecting the multilateralism of contemporary international law-making the US is weakening the legitimacy of the international system as a whole. Claims of American exceptionalism, its unique constitutional order and of its global responsibilities are raised to justify this stance. These are considered below and some of the law-making dilemmas created by its stance are discussed in the relevant places throughout the book.

As a starting point, 'theorizing international legitimacy var[ies] across countries, regions and political traditions'.[169] This is relevant to the reality that the most powerful states have long played a particular role in the making of international law.[170] The actions of the most powerful states in the international legal system have traditionally carried greater weight in the formation of customary international law. As remarked by De Visscher, 'Every international custom is the work of power'.[171] Schachter also noted that it is 'a historical fact, [that] the great body of customary international law was made by remarkably few States'.[172] International law rules such as those relating to acquisition of territory, diplomatic protection of aliens, or compensation for alienation of foreign investment were formulated by a small number of powerful states to uphold their interests. Unequal status was discounted in international law. Capitulatory regimes were imposed upon weaker states by European powers; economic coercion was excluded from the body of the Vienna Convention of the Law of Treaties and located in an Annex, and there is no generalised doctrine of unequal treaties

---

[169] B. Kingsbury, 'The International Legal Order', in P. Cane and M. Tushnet, *The Oxford Handbook of Legal Studies* (Oxford, 2003) 272, 284.

[170] G. Simpson, *Great Powers and Outlaw States: Unequal Sovereigns in the International Legal Order* (Cambridge, 2004).

[171] C. De Visscher, *Theory and Reality in Public International Law* (2nd edn, P. Corbett trans, Princeton, 1968) 154.

[172] O. Schachter, 'New Custom: Power, *Opinio Juris* and Contrary Practice', in J. Makarczyk, *Theory of International Law at the Threshold of the 21st Century: Essays in Honour of Krzysztof Skubiszewski* (The Hague, 1996) 531, 536.

within that Convention. Actions of the powerful were legitimated by the concept of the civilising mission. Resistance was discounted since the doctrine of protest and lack of acquiescence was not applied to relieve the burden of the rules for those who had been made subject to them.[173] The non-democratic nature of the customary international law process undermines its legitimacy and it is rendered illegitimate to those who have been adversely subjugated by it. Indeed the 'rational, ruthlessly [legally] ordered world of sovereign states had no place for those portrayed as unruly, disordered, subversive, primitive, or irrational'.[174] To such outsiders— those who are marginalised 'from full citizenship in Western democracies . . . such as women, indigenous peoples, the mentally ill or refugees', international law may hold little legitimacy.

There has been some change in both customary international law and treaty-making processes. The contrary practice of a large number of states may outweigh that of a smaller number of more powerful states,[175] destabilise an accepted rule of customary international law and in time replace it. For example challenges to a three mile territorial sea and claims to broader preferential fishing zones, or more generally economic zones, were made by states such as Iceland and the maritime states of South America and were at first rejected by more powerful states. In time such states accepted the emergence of new customary law and have made their own claims.

Nevertheless the practice of the most dominant states tends to retain a particular force in claims of emerging customary law and the ICJ has affirmed that the practice of states 'whose interests are specially affected' is an 'indispensable requirement' to the process.[176] But this leaves open the identity of a 'specially affected' state. There remains an assumption that it is the most dominant state.[177] As Danilenko explained:

. . . the notion of 'specially affected states' may be used as a respectable disguise for 'important' or 'powerful' states which are always supposed to be 'specially affected' by all or almost all political-legal developments within the international community.[178]

For example, it has been claimed that the military intervention in Kosovo in 1999 by NATO member states without explicit SC authorisation provides evidence of an emergent (or existing) rule of customary international law of humanitarian intervention. But must a 'specially affected state' be the one that provides military

---

[173] Rajagopal, *International Law from Below*.

[174] A. Orford, 'The Politics of Collective Security', 17 *Mich JIL* (1996) 373, 400.

[175] For the view that the US is less influential in the making of customary international law than 'is often assumed' see S. Toope, 'Powerful but Unpersuasive? The Role of the United States in the Evolution of Customary International Law', in M. Byers and G. Nolte, *United States Hegemony and the Foundations of International Law* (Cambridge, 2003) 287.

[176] *North Sea Continental Shelf Cases* (1969) ICJ Reports 3, para 74.

[177] M. Byers, *Custom, Power and the Power of Rules: International Relations and Customary International Law* (Cambridge, 1999) chapter 3.

[178] G. Danilenko, *Law-Making in the International Community* (Dordrecht, 1993) 96.

support rather than the state targeted for intervention? In a globalised world many states can claim to be especially affected in different ways by the actions of other states, making the concept of a 'specially affected' state unhelpful. Judge Weeramantry questioned any assumption that nuclear weapon states are those most specially affected by nuclear weapons for although they:

> possess the weapons, . . . it would be unrealistic to omit a consideration of those who would be affected once nuclear weapons are used. They would also be among the States most concerned, for their territories and populations would be exposed to the risk of harm from nuclear weapons no less than those of the nuclear powers, if ever nuclear weapons were used.[179]

In the context of humanitarian intervention, a new rule of customary international law would uphold human rights values but also legitimate intrusion into states that would likely be one way: from the North to the South. But this assessment too is simplistic: in assessing relevant state practice a global view must be taken. In this instance there is further support for a customary principle allowing for humanitarian intervention in practice from Africa[180] where ECOWAS states have intervened without SC authorisation, for example in Liberia, and subsequently had their actions endorsed.[181]

In treaty-making, leading states are inevitably highly influential within multi-lateral processes. They are able to provide substantial briefing, draw upon and finance a pool of skilled negotiators, and secure communications allow regular contact with further expertise at home. In the words of a British diplomat: 'diplomacy is skewed in their [powerful and affluent countries'] favour'.[182] Nevertheless US experience at the multilateral law-making processes leading to the adoption of the Rome Statute of the ICC, the Landmines Convention, the Convention on Climate Change and the Kyoto Protocol shows that a dissentient state—even the most powerful—cannot assume it will be able to dictate the outcome against the wishes of the majority. In Chapter 2 we discuss how so-called 'like-minded' states and non-state actors acted in conjunction in these instances to promote legal change through treaty-making. This alliance strengthened the negotiating power of weaker states and provided a bulwark against US demands. It is these changes that most likely lie at the heart of US disquiet with what it perceives as the constraints of international law.

But the case must not be over-stated. Despite such negotiation success multilateral treaty-making may still be dictated by the agendas of the powerful, especially where practical application is not considered feasible in their absence. An example

---

[179] *Threat or Use of Nuclear Weapons* (1996) ICJ Reports 226, 535, diss op Judge Weeramantry.

[180] The analysis is facilitated in Africa by the Constitution of the African Union that asserts the right of the Union 'to intervene in a Member State pursuant to a decision of the Assembly in respect of grave circumstances, namely war crimes, genocide and crimes against humanity'. Constitutive Act of the African Union, Togo, 11 July 2000, Article 4 (h).

[181] SC Res 788, 19 November 1992 (commending the actions of ECOWAS in Liberia).

[182] C. Ross, 'We must hear the unheard for a more stable world', *Financial Times*, 5 April 2006.

is the renegotiation of Part XI of the UN Convention on the Law of the Sea when it became apparent that the regime for the regulation of the deep seabed would otherwise be supported only by the less economically powerful states.[183] There has been no multilateral renegotiation of the ICC but the US has achieved some part of its objectives (non-submission of US nationals to the Court) through a series of bilateral negotiations[184] with states persuaded or threatened to accept its position and through recourse to the over-riding UN Charter Chapter VII powers of the SC.[185]

Further, whatever the reaction to the political stance of the US some of its actions in thwarting multilateral law-making are unexceptional in legal terms. Its withdrawal from the ICJ's compulsory jurisdiction under Article 36 (2) of its Statute and from the Anti-Ballistic Missile Treaty, and its repudiation of the ICC Statute and Kyoto Protocol to the Convention on Climate Change, 1997[186] have been critically received by some commentators. A state is, however, legally able to withdraw from a treaty or process in accordance with its terms,[187] or with those of the Vienna Convention on the Law of Treaties.[188] Similarly it is unarguable that a state is free to choose not to become a party to a treaty and the US can legitimately so decide with respect to such influential and widely adopted contemporary treaties as the UN Convention on the Law of the Sea,[189] the Comprehensive Test Ban Treaty, 1996, the Landmines Convention,[190] the Convention on the Elimination of All Forms of Discrimination against Women, 1979[191] and the Convention on the Rights of the Child, 1989[192] where it considers they do not support its interests. The principle of accession to treaties keeps the door open for the US to become a party to any such treaty even where it is not a signatory. Nevertheless the UN Secretary-General has noted that universal participation in multilateral conventions strengthens the rule of law and (without naming any state) has urged ratification of treaties relating to civilian protection.[193] But another factor of some concern is that in all these instances the US participated in the negotiations. This highlights that there can be no assumption that all actors enter an international law-making process with the same intentions. States (and other participants) may seek an effective regulatory regime, but individual states

---

[183] Discussed in Chapter 3.   [184] So-called Article 98 agreements, discussed in Chapter 2.
[185] See Chapter 2.
[186] The US signed the Kyoto Protocol, 12 November 1998 and withdrew on 29 March 2001. It signed the ICC Statute, 31 December 2000 and withdrew on 6 May 2002.
[187] It is arguably the case that the US withdrawal from the Treaty between the United States of America and the Union of Soviet Socialist Republics on the Limitation of Anti-Ballistic Missile Systems, Moscow, 1972 is in accordance with Article XV.
[188] The US action in 'unsigning' the Rome Statute of the ICC is in accordance with the VCLT, 1969, Article 18 which provides: 'A State is obliged to refrain from acts which would defeat the object and purpose of a treaty when: (a) it has signed the treaty . . . , until it shall have made its intention clear not to become a party to the treaty'. The US is not a party to the VCLT.
[189] As of April 2006 there are 149 states parties.
[190] As of April 2006 there are 151 states parties.
[191] As of May 2006 there are 184 states parties.
[192] The US is one of only two states not to have become a party to the Children's Convention. The other is Somalia.   [193] *In Larger Freedom*, para 136.

may participate in a treaty-making process in order to achieve certain goals, whether or not it intends to become a party to the treaty. Indeed its objective may be to secure the best possible regime for itself as a non-party to the treaty. The willingness of other negotiating states to concede points in the hope of persuading that state to join the regime may result in a weakened compromise text that is unsatisfactory to many. When this is followed by measures to undermine its operation as has been the case with the ICC,[194] the charge that the US is undermining international law-making has greater force.

A crucial issue in law-making is who chooses the arena and process. US practice demonstrates the fluid nature of such choices and how they shift according to institutional composition, predicted voting patterns and the assessment of national advantage. In the early years of the UN, Western powers dominated the GA. The formally recommendatory character of GA resolutions was ignored as that body 'affirmed' the legal nature of the principles of law contained in the Nuremberg Charter, a treaty adopted by four states.[195] Similarly it 'declared' genocide to be an international crime,[196] two years before the adoption of the Genocide Convention. In 1950 when the SC was unable to exercise its primary responsibility for the maintenance of international peace and security the US promoted the powers of the GA through the Uniting for Peace resolution.[197] The changed composition of the GA in the wake of decolonisation and the shift to universal membership following the two *Admissions* cases[198] meant that it could no longer assume concurrence with its position from the majority of members. The newly independent states (the so-called Group of 77) used their numerical majority in the GA to pursue their own economic and political agendas through the adoption of resolutions.[199] Arguments for the normative status of such resolutions were also put forward.[200] These were strongly resisted by Western states who formed a bloc of abstentions or negative votes in such key instruments as those for the New International Economic Order (NIEO), the Right to Development and resolutions with respect to the common heritage of mankind. Western states reasserted the generally non-binding nature of GA resolutions, their political character[201] and that the majority could not use this arena to impose their will upon a minority. The use of the GA for pursuit of their goals has meant the institutionalisation

---

[194] See Chapter 2.
[195] UNGA Res 95 (1), 11 December 1946, Affirmation of the Principles of International Law Recognized by the Charter of the Nuremberg Tribunal.
[196] UNGA Res 96 (1), 11 December 1946, The Crime of Genocide.
[197] UNGA Res 377 (V), 3 November 1950.
[198] *Conditions of Admission of a State to Membership in the United Nations (Article 4 of the Charter)* (1948) ICJ Reports 57; *Competence of the General Assembly for the Admission of a State to the United Nations* (1950) ICJ Reports 4.
[199] Third World states did not ignore other arenas; for example a number of such states from Africa, Asia and the Caribbean attended the Vienna Conference on the Law of Treaties in 1969 and the UNCLOS commencing in 1973.
[200] eg G. Abi-Saab, 'Cours Général de Droit International Public', 207 *Recueil des Cours* (1987) 33, 160–1.
[201] In *Texaco Overseas Petroleum Co. v. Libya* the (French) arbitrator rejected the binding nature of resolutions establishing the NIEO because of their ideological strategy of development, lack of support from industrialised states, and lack of reference to international law; 53 *ILR* (1977) 389, paras 87–90.

and dilution of Third World radicalisation including in law-making.[202] For the US there has been a move back to the SC where it holds a veto.[203] In many instances in the post-cold war world the US has been able to secure its objectives through SC resolution, perhaps most visibly in the immediate aftermath of 11 September 2001. In resolutions 1368, 12 September 2001 and 1373, 28 September 2001 the SC unequivocally condemned the terrorist attacks, recognised the inherent right of self-defence, implicitly acknowledging its applicability to armed attacks by non-state actors, and decided upon a slew of measures against terrorist activity. However where the requisite SC resolution has not been forthcoming, the US has undertaken unauthorised action in conjunction with other willing states, as for example in the action against Serbia on behalf of the Kosovars in 1999 and the invasion of Iraq in 2003.

There are a number of points relevant to law-making. First, institutional development has lessened to some degree the ability of great powers to make international law in their own interest. This has particular relevance to the position of the United States in the post-cold war era. As Friedmann commented in 1959:

> . . . in the former, less organised, international society, a new State had to make its place in the family of nations slowly, by a gradual process of recognition, diplomatic relations and effective role in international affairs, today new States . . . obtain international status and an equal vote, almost immediately after their creation through their admission to the United Nations.[204]

As we have seen in this chapter, the G77 sought legal change through the GA once they acquired full international status through membership. In Chapter 3 we also show how in WTO negotiations the US no longer controls the agenda or dictates the outcome.

Second, the US position with respect to customary international law is somewhat equivocal. Its actions have been instrumental in developing customary international law in the past: the Truman Declaration on the continental shelf and its outer space activities come to mind.[205] In the context of the law of the sea the US has not become a party to the 1982 Convention on the Law of the Sea although in 1994 Part XI was renegotiated in part to meet its concerns.[206] However it has claimed some of the Convention's benefits through assertion of their customary international law status. In other contexts the US has not explicitly claimed reliance on existing custom, nor to be creating custom when expounding apparently new practice. For example, in the War on Terror one of its most controversial claims has been that of pre-emptive self-defence as enunciated in its National Security Strategy, 2002. However the doctrine put forward as a policy statement, 'was not taken seriously as a legal proposition, since it was not remotely advanced as a new reciprocal right, one tenable by any nation'[207] and was not claimed as the

---

[202] Rajagopal, *International Law from Below*, 73–94.   [203] UN Charter, Article 27 (3).
[204] Friedmann, *Law in a Changing Society*.   [205] See Chapter 4.   [206] See Chapter 3.
[207] T. Franck, 'The Power of Legitimacy and the Legitimacy of Power: International Law in an Age of Power Disequilibrium', 100 *AJIL* (2006) 88, 98.

basis for its 1993 military action in Iraq. Without any such supporting practice verbal claims lack weight[208] and the widespread resistance also weakens any arguments for pre-emptive self-defence attaining the status of customary international law.

Third, the US has *not* consistently rejected multilateral law-making and it normally supports initiatives where they accord with its interests. Its broad agenda, notably a commitment to neo-liberal economic policies, has been dominant in *inter alia* the WTO, the Organisation for Economic Cooperation and Development (OECD), the International Financial Institutions and the legal frameworks for post-conflict reconstruction in such places as Bosnia, Kosovo, Afghanistan and Iraq. Indeed 'many . . . areas of international law are generally characterised by a marked imbalance in favour of western influence, heightened by the relative paucity of expert scholars, practitioners, regulators, and leading corporations based outside the OECD'.[209] In pursuing its agenda through international law it has strengthened the requisite institutions. For example there has been much discussion of the harm to the authority of the SC caused by the unauthorised military action against Iraq in 2003. Rather less notice has been taken of the strengthening of the SC, for example in the establishment of the Counter-Terrorism Committee, with its far-reaching mandate and intrusion into national legal systems.

The US has also on some occasions used its diplomatic muscle effectively in securing adoption of law-making resolutions under Chapter VII that uphold its interests. The veto enables the US (or any other P5—the five permanent members of the Security Council—member) to prevent any substantive resolution it considers to be against its interests, while it can benefit from SC authority for actions where it can engender agreement. Of course, even the US cannot guarantee that it will always get its own way, even in the SC.

Fourth, although its counter-terrorist activities have seen assertions of the non-applicability of international law (for example the Geneva Conventions with respect to prisoners in Guantánamo Bay), the US has pursued law-making through other arenas such as the Convention on the Suppression of Acts of Nuclear Terrorism 2005, discussed above. Finally there is a genuine concern that certain principles of international law have become outmoded and require amendment and reform. This has been recognised by the High Level Panel on Threats, Challenges and Change, the Secretary-General and the 2005 GA Summit Outcome Document. All explicitly accept the need for some changes in the law in areas of concern to the US: intervention in cases of widespread, gross violations of human rights and further powers in the war against terror. But these documents stress the need for multilateral law-making through deliberation and negotiation,

---

[208] There has been much debate about the weight to be accorded to a state's words as opposed to its actual practice; eg A. D'Amato, *The Concept of Custom in International Law* (Ithaca, NY, 1971) and K. Wolfke, *Custom in Present International Law* (2nd rev edn, Dordrecht, 1993); M. Akehurst, 'Custom as a Source of International Law', 47 *BYBIL* (1974–5) 1.

[209] Kingsbury, in Cane and Tushnet, *The Oxford Handbook of Legal Studies*, 275.

not unilateral action. Nevertheless the fact that the US asked for a recorded vote and registered a negative vote[210] in relation to the GA resolution adopting the mandate of the newly established Human Rights Council[211] does nothing to abate concerns about the US unwillingness to accept legal change where it is unable to assert its will. This tension constitutes the contemporary backdrop to international law-making.

6.   Reform of International Law-Making

The international legal system has moved far beyond the categorisation of the sources of international law in the Statute of the ICJ. Flexibility has been engendered as long-standing law-making processes have adapted to changed conditions and new processes have evolved. Some have been contentious and the nature of the adopted instruments disputed, for example the legal effect of GA resolutions. Adaptations include such techniques as opting into (or out of) treaty amendments that allow for technical changes, or extension to the scope of existing treaties without the need for formal processes such as diplomatic conferences. As we discuss in Chapter 5, new multilateral processes may become accepted as law-making. Initially non-binding outcomes may become binding through their acceptance as customary international law; any other way of bestowing legally binding status on any instrument other than a treaty would be a revolutionary change in the structure of the system, based as it is on the consent of states.[212] It is striking that while the High Level Panel on Threats, Challenges and Change urged law-making initiatives, it did not offer any new modalities of law-making. Its suggestions were for treaty-making through the GA and for institutional reform. The most significant change to date, establishment of the Human Rights Council as a subsidiary body of the GA, in place of the Commission on Human Rights, has been achieved through GA Resolution.[213]

A further question is: who determines an instrument to be law-making? It is no longer the case (if indeed it ever was) that such decisions are made by Heads of Governments or Ministers of Foreign Affairs. The ICJ has noted the increasing frequency with which other officials speak for their states on issues of foreign affairs, for example holders of technical ministerial portfolios within the area of their competence.[214] Such people may well have to determine whether they accept

---

[210] The voting was 170 in favour; four against; three abstentions.

[211] UNGA Res 60/251, 3 April 2006.

[212] O. Garibaldi, 'The Legal Status of General Assembly Resolutions: Some Conceptual Observations', 73 *ASIL Proceedings* (1979) 324, 325.

[213] UNGA Res 60/251, 3 April 2006. UN Charter, Article 22 authorises the UNGA to establish such subsidiary bodies as are necessary for performance of its functions. The UNGA also decided to establish a Peacebuilding Commission as an intergovernmental advisory body, UNGA Res 60/1, 24 October 2005, para 97.

[214] *Armed Activities on the Territory of the Congo* (*DRC v. Rwanda*) (2006) ICJ Reports, para 47.

certain instruments as law-making and their responses thereto. National judges increasingly find themselves having to decide what constitutes international law. The growing impact of international law upon individuals means that such claims are likely to increase. When acted upon, national judicial decisions contribute to the development of international law that is applied throughout diverse arenas.[215]

There have been constant proposals for changes to international law-making processes. Some have envisaged 'elaborate constitutional blueprints for global reform'[216] including such measures as staggered voting blocks in the GA, change in the composition of, and veto power in, the SC and hence to law-making with respect to collective security. However, proposed reforms of the existing institutional structure have been described as 'at best a very partial or incomplete form of democracy in international life' in that they remain rooted in a state-centred model of international affairs.[217] Other proposals have looked to giving greater prominence to the law-making role of non-state actors. This is not new. Writing about the sources of law in 1925 Sir Hersch Lauterpacht considered that:

> The definition of the sources of rules of international law as historical events to which their establishment can be traced, is, I think, correct; but there is no reason to restrict these historical events to those only which are evidenced by acts of statesmen or written documents; the legal conviction and the sense of right of masses of men [*sic*] is a historical fact of no less force.[218]

One such proposal is that activities of NGOs should be accepted as constitutive of practice for determining rules of customary international law, reflecting the contemporary dynamics of the formation of international law.[219] Participation by NGOs and other non-state actors in international law-making is discussed in Chapter 2 but we note here that such a proposal entails considerable theoretical and logistic difficulties. For example: which of the thousands of NGOs in existence would have this status? Which of their myriad and diverse activities could constitute 'practice'? Whose actions would constitute those of an NGO? Would this equate the international legal personality of NGOs with that of states, or of IGOs? And as we discuss in the following chapter, NGO agendas are not necessarily produced with greater democracy or transparency than the agendas of states or IGOs.

---

[215] See Chapter 2.   [216] Friedmann, *Law in a Changing Society*, 478.
[217] D. Held, *Democracy and the Global Order: From the Modern State to Cosmopolitan Governance* (Cambridge, 1995) 270.
[218] H. Lauterpacht, 'Westlake and Present Day International Law', 15 *Economica* (1925) 307, 318. See Chapter 2.
[219] I. Gunning, 'Modernizing Customary International Law: The Challenge of Human Rights', 31 *VJIL* (1991) 211. For a critique of these proposals see K. Knop, 'Re/statements: Feminism and State Sovereignty in International Law', 3 *Transnational Law and Contemporary Problems* (1993) 293, 311–15.

Other proposals are rooted in the assumption that the legitimacy of international law-making would be enhanced by according a greater role to civil society through institutional processes. In the words of Anderson and Rieff:

... international NGOs have gradually taken a leading role in providing what is declared to be the legitimate, and politically legitimising, input of the world's peoples across a myriad of issues and causes.... International NGOs come together to advocate for the peoples of the world, those who would otherwise have no voice, given that the actors they seek to influence, which include both economic actors and the world's superpower, are globally unregulated.[220]

In response to what was considered to be the undemocratic character of the SC and the need to revitalise the GA, the 1995 Commission on Global Governance proposed an International Assembly of People and a Forum of Civil Society with direct access to the UN system.[221] In 2000 the UN Secretary-General proposed an NGO Millennium Forum held in conjunction with the Millennium Assembly.[222] Richard Falk and Andrew Strauss have argued for a standing Global Peoples Assembly, organised and represented by civil society. Their vision is for a 'globally democratic institutional structure that would enable the peoples of the world to have a meaningful and effective voice'.[223] Falk and Strauss consider that the transformative potential of such a supra-national law-making body would derive from the freeing of delegates from parochial nationalist or state interests,[224] enabling delegates to identify common purposes and solutions across other lines. In particular a standing global forum would allow the development of coherent policy and offer an alternative to the *ad hoc* nature of civil society access to, and participation in, institutional law-making described in Chapter 2. Clearly any such proposal raises major problems of logistics, organisation, representation and legitimacy.[225] It would require 'many and substantial changes to the way in which the world is governed'.[226] However there is no obvious reason why, given the requisite political will, the powers and status of a global parliamentary body could not be allowed to evolve over time, as has been the case with the European Parliament.[227]

---

[220] K. Anderson and D. Rieff, ' "Global Civil Society": A Sceptical View', in H. Anheier, M. Glasius and M. Kaldor (eds), *Global Civil Society 2004/5* (London, 2005) 26, 28.

[221] *Our Global Neighbourhood: Report of the Commission on Global Governance* (Oxford, 1995) 259.

[222] UN Doc A/52/850, 31 March 1998.

[223] R. Falk and A. Strauss, 'On the Creation of a Global Peoples Assembly: Legitimacy and the Power of Popular Sovereignty', 36 *Stan JIL* (2000) 191, 195 n. 16 (citing the Perugia Assembly of the United Nations of Peoples).

[224] Cf the vision of Alfred Lord Tennyson in *Locksley Hall* (1842):

> Till the war-drum throbb'd no longer, and the battle-flags were furl'd
> In the Parliament of man, the Federation of the world.
> There the common sense of most shall hold a fretful realm in awe,
> And the kindly earth shall slumber, lapt in universal law.

[225] See also the discussion of Peoples' Tribunals in Chapter 2.

[226] R. Buchanan, 'Perpetual Peace or Perpetual Process: Global Civil Society and Cosmopolitan Legality at the World Trade Organisation', 16 *LJIL* (2003) 673, 695.   [227] See Chapter 3.

We have some final questions. First how *should* international law be made? Since the early 1990s this question has had great practical application, for instance in the context of international criminal law. As the following chapters explain, many institutions and processes have been engaged in making international criminal law procedures and substance. International criminal procedures have been created in diverse ways: the ICTY and ICTR were established by SC resolution following a fact-finding commission and a feasibility study by the Secretary-General; the ICC through state treaty negotiation with broad NGO participation; and the Sierra Leone Special Tribunal through treaty negotiation between the UN and the Sierra Leone government pursuant to SC resolution 1315, 14 August 2000. The judges drafted the Rules of Procedure and Evidence of the ICTY and ICTR; states parties negotiated them for the ICC; the Statute for the Sierra Leone Special Tribunal provided that the Rules of Procedure of the ICTR apply, although the judges could amend them if needed, guided by Sierra Leone criminal procedure. Unlike the other international criminal courts, this body has both international judges and judges appointed by the local government and has jurisdiction over crimes under Sierra Leone law as well as international law. As with the discussion of law-making responses to global terrorism, these different procedures demonstrate the flexibility of contemporary law-making and responsiveness to political and legal situations on the ground. Similarly substantive international criminal law has been crafted by the ILC; the SC; the GA through espousal of general principles; states through sustained treaty negotiation and subsequently meetings of the ICC Assembly of States Parties; and by international and national judicial decision-making. But from where should each of these bodies derive the starting points for development of substantive law? From earlier international law treaties and jurisprudence, albeit often inadequate and providing only a skeletal framework? From domestic legal systems? From jurisprudence on analogous areas such as that of the regional human rights bodies? From the works of criminologists, political and social scientists? From the advocacy of civil society? Does the crafting of new legal principles from all these sources lack coherence? Or does it provide a broad legitimacy to a complex enterprise?

Second, the second half of the 20th century was characterised by a vast amount of new international law generated through diverse multilateral processes. Rules and principles of international law now formally constrain, empower, and structure state behaviour (and in some instances that of non-state actors) across numerous areas of political, social and economic life. But law-making is not the end of the story, only its beginning; questions of implementation, compliance, effectiveness and enforcement are self-evidently important. Moreover, having laws is not the same as having effective law, even when fully complied with. Full compliance with the Climate Change Convention will not save humanity from global warming, to take only one example. In the midst of widespread international legal regulation there also remain 'law-free zones'[228] or 'legal black holes'[229]—areas where states claim that there is no applicable international law against which their behaviour can be assessed. The refusal of some states to apply the Refugee Convention, 1951 to persons on the high seas before they can land and claim non-refoulement is a good example.[230] The collapsing of territorial boundaries through the internet has created other challenges—as yet unresolved—for international legal regulation.[231] We suggest that what is now needed is not still more international law-making but greater efforts at ensuring the integration, coherence, effectiveness and universal reach of existing international law.

Third, international law is a regulatory tool for pursuing such goals as orderly and equitable distribution of global assets, sustainable development and global social justice. It is also an instrument of control. Who determines the international law-making agenda and the allocation of resources to law-making are therefore crucial. As we discuss in Chapters 2 and 3, while states continue to dominate these issues, other actors are also influential. But it is also evident that the use of international law to promote a social justice agenda is limited: as noted earlier, the blueprint agreed to by all the world's countries and leading development institutions—the MDGs—is not the outcome of any law-making process and is not in binding legal form. Their language of identified and time-specific targets is that of political, not legal, commitment. International lawyers barely engage with them. Their implementation rests *inter alia* with economists and development agencies but not with lawyers, international or national. What is the impact of the acceptance of the MDGs on international law-making? Is the fact that legal processes were not engaged indicative of an unwillingness to incur legal responsibility for lack of performance, cynicism about the role or 'value-added' of international law, or recognition that agreement would have been unlikely to legally binding norms? Was there even a hope that their undermining of internationally accepted standards of human rights would pass unnoticed?

We do not have answers to these and other questions, but we do hope that the book will stimulate debate and show why it is important that international law-making must be evaluated alongside other political, social and economic institutional processes.

---

[228] The expression was used by Sharryn J. Aiken, Queens University, Ontario in a presentation, 'Immigration and Refugee Law', University of Toronto, 3 June 2006.

[229] J. Steyn, 'Guantánamo Bay: The Legal Black Hole', 53 *ICLQ* (2004) 1.

[230] See R. Barnes, 'Refugee Law at Sea', 53 *ICLQ* (2004) 47.

[231] F. Mayer, 'Europe and the Internet: The Old World and the New Medium', 11 *EJIL* (2000) 149.

Further Reading

A. Anghie, *Imperialism, Sovereignty and the Making of International Law* (Cambridge, 2004).

M. Byers and G. Nolte, *United States Hegemony and the Foundations of International Law* (Cambridge, 2003).

G. Danilenko, *Law-Making in the International Community* (Dordrecht, 1983).

T. Franck, *The Power of Legitimacy Among Nations* (New York, 1990).

International Law Association, *Report of the 69th Conference*, Committee on the Formation of Customary International Law (London, 2000).

M. Koskenniemi, *The Gentle Civilizer of Nations: The Rise and Fall of International Law 1870–1960* (Cambridge, 2001).

D. Shelton (ed), *Commitment and Compliance: The Role of Non-binding Norms in the International Legal System* (Oxford, 2000).

'Symposium: Method in International Law', 93 *AJIL* (1999) 291.

2

Participants in International Law-Making

1. Introduction

The traditional statement of the sources of international law, the Statute of the International Court of Justice (ICJ), Article 38 (1) assumes states to be the primary actors in international law-making and gives no indication of the ways in which non-state entities impact upon this function. Although states enter into binding agreements with non-state entities, treaties are defined as legal agreements between states,[1] or between states and international organisations or international organisations *inter se;*[2] state practice and *opinio juris* are the constitutive elements of customary international law; general principles of law are gleaned from the domestic legal systems of states. In the traditional schema of sources the contribution of non-state actors is recognised only with respect to the subsidiary sources: the writings of publicists. As President of the ICJ, Judge Higgins, has put it: 'States are, at this moment of history, still at the heart of the international legal system.'[3] But focus solely on state actions gives a misleading picture of international law-making. Account must also be taken of the role and influence in multilateral law-making of the state-based intergovernmental organisations (IGOs) that are discussed in the following chapter. The present chapter considers the place in international law-making of other non-state actors, in particular those that are variously termed civil society, transnational advocacy networks,[4] social movements,[5] and in an institutionalised form, non-governmental organisations (NGOs). In general terms, such non-state actors have sought access to international governmental institutions and law-making processes to advance their own agendas. Their role must be considered in order to understand some of the political influences behind international law-making and some of the ways in which alliance with civil society enhances the profile of some apparently weaker states within international law-making arenas and diffuses centralised state power.

---

[1] 1969 Vienna Convention on the Law of Treaties (VCLT), Article 2 (1) (a).
[2] 1986 Vienna Convention on the Law of Treaties between States and International Organisations or between International Organisations, Article 2 (1) (a) (i) and (ii).
[3] R. Higgins, *Problems and Process: International Law and How We Use It* (Oxford, 1993) 39.
[4] M. Keck and K. Sikkink, *Activists beyond Borders: Advocacy Networks in International Politics* (Ithaca, NY, 1998) 9.   [5] R. Cohen and S. Rai, *Global Social Movements* (London, 2000).

Past examples of non-state actors that have left their mark on the international legal system include mediaeval political structures, religious institutions, commercial enterprises such as the East India Company and other chartered bodies engaged in the colonial enterprise in its so-called informal era.[6] Significant social movements have campaigned since at least the 18th century around such issues as the abolition of the trade and institutions of slavery, women's suffrage, international peace and international workers' rights. Some at least of their efforts resulted in significant changes in international law and practice. The International Committee of the Red Cross (ICRC) was founded in 1863 and its pre-eminent position in the formation and implementation of international humanitarian law is well known.

At the end of the 19th century the belief of non-governmental movements in international law as a powerful force for beneficial change was evidenced in the popular and church support for a permanent institution for international arbitration at the 1899 and 1907 Hague Peace Conferences.[7] At the Hague Conferences non-governmental groups submitted petitions to the delegates and organised a salon as an informal meeting place between government delegates and groups and individuals.[8] As another example of activity by non-state actors at this time, Charnowitz notes that the Convention Creating the International Institute of Agriculture, 1905, Article 9 provided for consultation with 'international or other agricultural congresses or congresses of sciences applied to agriculture . . . '.[9] Civil society groups sought legal status even prior to the League of Nations[10] and many groups became actively involved with the League,[11] seeking cooperation and demanding international law reform with respect to issues such as the nationality of married women[12] and human trafficking. The Constitution of the International Labour Organisation provided for the participation of employers' and workers' organisations at its meetings, including with voting rights.[13]

---

[6] M. Koskenniemi, *The Gentle Civilizer of Nations: The Rise and Fall of International Law 1870–1960* (Cambridge, 2001) chapter 2; A. Anghie, *Imperialism, Sovereignty and the Making of International Law* (Cambridge, 2004) esp. 67–8.

[7] M. Janis, 'Protestants, Progress and Peace: Enthusiasm for an International Court in Early Nineteenth Century America', in M. Janis (ed), *The Influence of Religion on the Development of International Law* (Dordrecht, 1991) 223.

[8] H. Anheier, M. Glasius and M. Kaldor (eds), *Global Civil Society 2001* (Oxford, 2001) 5.

[9] S. Charnovitz, 'Non-Governmental Organisations and International Law', 100 *AJIL* (2006) 348, 357.

[10] Charnovitz describes attempts within the ILA and *Institut de Droit International* to promote a convention granting international legal personality to NGOs; ibid 356.

[11] S. Charnovitz, 'Two Centuries of Participation: NGOs and International Governance', 18 *Mich JIL* (1997) 183; L. Cromwell White and M. Ragonatti Zocca, *International Non-governmental Organisations Their Purposes, Methods and Accomplishments* (New Brunswick, NJ, 1951); J. Connors, 'NGOs and the Human Rights of Women at the United Nations', in P. Willetts (ed), '*The Conscience of the World': The Influence of Non-governmental Organisations in the UN System* (Washington, 1996) 147.

[12] K. Knop and C. Chinkin, 'Remembering Chrystal Macmillan: Women's Equality and Nationality in International Law', 22 *Mich JIL* (2001) 523.

[13] 1919 Constitution of the International Labour Organisation, Articles 3 and 4.

Similarly, the determination of primarily American NGOs at San Francisco resulted in the adoption of human rights articles within the UN Charter,[14] paving the way for the growth of international human rights law.

Civil society's impact on international affairs was given further impetus by the populist movements that grew up in Eastern Europe after the Helsinki Final Act, 1975 which sculpted the political space to challenge the communist regimes. Peoples' movements have brought down governments in countries as diverse as Iran, Nicaragua, the Philippines, South Africa and Ukraine. The end of the cold war, the removal of oppressive regimes in states in Central and South America, Asia and Africa and demands for some form of accountability for the human rights violations of such regimes all contributed to what has been claimed as an emergent international legal entitlement to democratic rule.[15] It has been argued that bringing civil society movements into the state-centric system of international law has itself been part of this democratisation trend.

Scholars from different theoretical perspectives have acknowledged the broad range of participants in the contemporary processes of international law-making. For example, among modern positivists Bruno Simma and Andreas Paulus recognise that '[o]ther actors than states are assuming growing importance: intergovernmental organizations, as well as nongovernmental organizations, global economic players and the global media'.[16] From the New Haven school, Michael Reisman asserts the importance of actors who lack formal law-making competence but who nevertheless influence decisions, including IGOs, NGOs, pressure groups, interest groups, gangs and individuals.[17] Harold Koh describes the transnational legal process as involving a range of public and private actors, including nation states, international organisations, multinational enterprises, non-governmental organisations and private individuals that interact in a 'variety of public and private, domestic and international fora to make, interpret, internalize, and enforce rules of transnational law'.[18]

It is apparent that transnational non-governmental bodies have never and still do not form a homogeneous grouping. Non-state actors today encompass *inter alia* sub-state entities and entities denied statehood, national and international

---

[14] Charter of the United Nations, Articles 1 (3), 55 and 56. J. Humphrey, *Human Rights and the United Nations: A Great Adventure* (Dobbs Ferry, 1984); W. Korey, *NGOs and the Universal Declaration of Human Rights: A Curious Grapevine* (New York, 1998) 29–39; on the particular contribution of the organised Christian churches see Paul Lauren, *The Evolution of International Human Rights: Visions Seen* (2nd edn, Philadelphia, 2003); J. Nurser, 'The "Ecumenical Movement", Churches, "Global Order" and Human Rights', 25 *HRQ* (2003) 841.

[15] T. Franck, 'The Emerging Right to Democratic Governance', 86 *AJIL* (1992) 46.

[16] B. Simma and A. Paulus, 'The Responsibility of Individuals for Human Rights Abuses in Internal Conflicts: A Positivist View', 93 *AJIL* (1999) 302, 306.

[17] M. Reisman, 'The View from the New Haven School of International Law', 86 *ASIL Proceedings* (1992), 118, 122.

[18] H. Koh, 'Why Do Nations Obey International Law?', 106 *Yale LJ* (1996–7) 2599, 2626.

issue-based NGOs, individuals, 'kitchen-tablers',[19] the corporate and business sector, shareholders, churches and religious groupings, trade unions and employees, academics, think tanks, consumer groups, para-military forces, professional associations, including those of judges, lawyers, parliamentarians and law enforcement agencies, expert communities, sport associations and criminal and terrorist organisations.

The range and diversity of non-state actors make it impossible to do more than generalise about their law-making activities. Nevertheless there is little doubt that various non-state actors contribute in different ways to the emergence of international norms.[20] The exponential growth in their numbers throughout the twentieth century means that this influence is likely to become greater.[21] So too do the information technology and electronic communications that have made global networking immeasurably easier to create and to maintain.[22] Debates are conducted in the public arena of the web as individuals and organisations across many countries exchange information instantaneously and mobilise an inestimable audience while controlling costs. People who cannot attend meetings can participate and present their views. The collapse of obstacles of time and space brought about by the information revolution has played a significant if unmeasured role in enhancing input by non-state actors into international law-making.[23] It must also be remembered that the advantages of technology are also used by those seeking to destroy the international legal order such as terrorist organisations.

What is more problematic is to determine empirically the precise role of such bodies in international law-making: do they act as little more than a catalyst to traditional forms of state law-making or can they be accurately described as free-standing participants in international law-making? Are their activities primarily lobbying and campaigning or can they be appropriately termed law-making?[24] Do they represent a paradigm shift away from a state-centric model of international

---

[19] J. Mertus, 'Considering Non-state Actors in the New Millennium: Toward Expanded Participation in Norm Generation and Norm Application', 32 *NYU JILP* (2000) 537.

[20] For an overview of NGO law-making activity across a number of areas of international law see A. Zimmermann and R. Hoffmann, *Unity and Diversity in International Law* (Berlin, 2005).

[21] The UN Secretary-General reported that the number of international NGOs 'grew forty-fold over the course of the twentieth century to more than 37,000 in 2000'. Report of the S-G, *Strengthening of the United Nations; An Agenda for Further Change*, UN Doc A 57/387, 9 September 2002, para 134; over 2,000 NGOs have consultative status with ECOSOC, ibid, para 138.

[22] In 1907 Baldwin noted how 'steam and electricity' have played their part in facilitating 'unofficial congresses' of those working on common international problems; S. Baldwin, 'The International Congresses and Conferences of the Last Century as Forces Working toward the Solidarity of the World', 1 *AJIL* (1907) 565, 574.

[23] J. Gamble and C. Ku, 'International Law—New Actors and New Technologies: Center Stage for NGOs?', 31 *Law and Policy in International Business* (2000) 221.

[24] The transnational activities of non-state actors go well beyond law-making. We do not consider other activities such as delivery of humanitarian services, verification and information gathering, and political activism, except to the extent that they contribute to the emergence of legal norms.

law-making? Further questions follow relating to the desirability, legitimacy and accountability of such bodies: does their participation in law-making processes constitute a desirable democratisation of international legal processes, or a new form of legal imperialism?[25]

We consider these questions in this chapter. We examine first the distinctive position of some different entities with respect to participation in law-making processes and then in more detail one form of non-state actor, international NGOs. In Chapter 4 we discuss the work of non-governmental associations formed in the late 19th century explicitly for the purpose of promoting international law through codification-like processes, notably the International Law Association and the *Institut de Droit International*.[26] These professional associations are somewhat different from both 'social justice' NGOs that seek to make international law advance their agendas within special issue areas, such as human rights, the environment and disarmament, and from business oriented non-state entities. We discuss the definition of an NGO, their different roles and their access to IGOs, in particular whether NGOs have a right to participate in IGO processes and whether such participation enhances the legitimacy of international law-making. We then look at NGO participation in various state law-making processes: treaty-making (including case studies), law-making through institutional resolutions and global summits, and advocacy within national, regional and international tribunals. Where state processes are inadequate or do not exist, NGOs have developed their own. We discuss one such example, that is Peoples' Tribunals. We conclude with an overview of the relationship between NGOs and IGOs and an assessment of the contribution of the former to international law-making.

We single out NGOs for greater attention because they alone among civil society actors are given international legal status by the UN Charter. Article 71 provides that the Economic and Social Council (ECOSOC) 'may make arrangements for consultation with non-governmental organizations which are concerned with matters within its competence'. NGOs have used this consultative status to demand access to the law-making activities of international institutions. Indeed a symbiotic relationship has developed between NGOs and IGOs: IGOs acquire some additional legitimacy from the participation of NGOs in their processes while NGOs can point to this participation as evidence of their status and the importance of their activities—a matter of considerable interest to donors. This mutually reinforcing relationship is recognised by the fact that ongoing proposals for UN reform include strengthening NGO participation.

---

[25] K. Anderson, 'The Ottawa Convention Banning Landmines, the Role of International Non-Governmental Organizations and the Idea of International Civil Society', 11 *EJIL* (2000) 91.

[26] 'Non-governmental organizations of jurists have had an important influence upon governmental organizations devoted primarily to the codification of international law.' Q. Wright, 'Activities of the Institute of International Law', *ASIL Proceedings* (1960) 195.

2.   Non-state Actors and Law-Making

2.1   Non-state Entities

In this section we look at some state-like entities that for political reasons are denied full participation in UN and other multilateral law-making activities. They may be afforded limited access and procedural rights through observer status. Observer status is not provided for within the UN Charter. It is accorded to 'Non-Member States, entities and organizations'[27] by GA resolution on a case by case basis after consideration by the GA 6th (Legal) Committee. The privileges observer status bestows are dependent upon the terms of the particular resolution, practice and interpretation by the UN Secretariat. In the exceptional case of the Holy See, these privileges are barely distinguishable from those of states and it participates as such in multilateral diplomatic conferences and meetings.[28] The Holy See governs the Vatican City and is regarded as the 'juridical personification' of the Roman Catholic Church. It maintains a permanent observer mission to the UN and is a full member of UN specialised agencies and European IGOs. It has exercised considerable influence in the negotiation of treaties and soft law instruments. For example it led a group of Catholic states at the 1994 Cairo Conference on Population and Development and the 1995 Beijing World Conference on Women. At both these conferences the Vatican combined forces with a number of Islamic states to resist international recognition of women's sexual and reproductive rights and freedoms.[29] At the 1998 Diplomatic Conference in Rome it influenced drafting of the provisions on 'forced pregnancy' and the meaning of gender within the ICC Statute.[30] In these actions it was opposed by many women's NGOs, who questioned why a particular religious community should enjoy privileged status within international fora.

Entities with observer status before the GA form an eclectic group. They include Guam, the Organisation of the Islamic Conference, Palestine, the Sovereign Military Order of Malta, the Inter-Parliamentary Union (IPU) and a number of IGOs. Exceptionally the International Committee of the Red Cross, an NGO, was accorded observer status in 1990. The IPU is of particular significance as it links national legislators with the GA and secures parliamentary input into the latter's work.[31] In its application for observer status it stated that it could

---

[27] UN Doc A/INF/60/4, 30 November 2005 lists those entities with standing invitations to observer status.

[28] H. Cardinale, *The Holy See and the International Order* (Toronto, 1976); H. Charlesworth and C. Chinkin, *The Boundaries of International Law: A Feminist Analysis* (Manchester, 2000) 134–5.

[29] H. Charlesworth, 'Women as Sherpas: Are Global Summits Useful for Women?', 22 *Feminist Studies* (1996) 537, 542–3.

[30] Rome Statute of the International Criminal Court, 17 July 1998, UN Doc A/CONF 183/9, Articles 7 (2) (f) and 7 (3).

[31] Cooperation between the United Nations and the Inter-Parliamentary Union, Report of the Secretary-General, UN Doc A/56/449, 8 October 2001.

'channel to the United Nations the views of the people, in all their diversity, as expressed in parliamentary debates and discussions at the IPU'.[32] The importance of this relationship is echoed in the GA's call for 'strengthened cooperation between itself and national and regional Parliaments in particular through the IPU'.[33]

Political controversy denies certain entities statehood or even observer status and other techniques have to be found to allow them any form of participation in international law-making. For example, the uncompromising stance of the People's Republic of China to even implied recognition of the Republic of China (Taiwan) as a state denies Taiwan access to UN bodies. The disadvantages of Taiwan's exclusion—a sizeable entity that constitutes the world's fourteenth largest economy—from the ambit of international regulatory regimes has led to seeking ways of facilitating its participation. Participation in most modern treaties is limited to states and regional organisations for economic integration such as the EU, but some treaties unusually allow for less restricted participation and access for non-state entities. Serdy has described how advantage has been taken of such treaty provisions in the case of Taiwan.[34] For example the WTO Agreement, Article XII provides that 'Any state or customs territory having full autonomy in the conduct of its trade policies is eligible to accede to the WTO on terms agreed . . . '. Taiwan negotiated membership in January 2002 under the name of the 'Separate Customs Territory of Taiwan, Penghu, Kimmen and Matsu' or 'Chinese Taipei'.

Taiwan's significant deep sea fishing fleet has also made it important to bring it within fishing conservation regimes. Progress has been made by granting Taiwan observer status at technical and scientific meetings, followed in some cases by full membership. Articles 305–6 of the 1982 UN Convention on the Law of the Sea allow for self-governing associated states and territories to become parties and the UN Fish Stocks Agreement, 1995 provides for 'fishing entities' (such as Taiwan) to become members of regional fisheries commissions. On that basis, as 'Chinese Taipei', it participated in negotiation of the 2000 Convention on the Conservation and Management of Highly Migratory Fish Stocks in the Western and Central Pacific, and is a member of the commission established by the treaty. Taiwan similarly attended the trilateral scientific meetings of the Commission for the Conservation of Southern Bluefin Tuna. This was made possible by Article 14 of the 1993 Convention for the Conservation of Southern Bluefin Tuna which allowed states parties to invite 'any State or entity' to such meetings. A Resolution adopted by the Commission in 2001 to establish an 'Extended Commission' was

---

[32] IPU, *Cooperation with the United Nations System*, Report adopted by the IPU Council at its 170th session, Marrakech, 23 March 2002, available at <http://www.ipu.org/cnl-e/170-un1.htm>.

[33] 2005 World Summit Outcome, UNGA Res 60/1, 24 October 2005, para 171.

[34] A. Serdy, 'Bringing Taiwan into the International Fisheries Fold: The Legal Personality of a Fishing Entity', 75 *BYBIL* (2005) 185.

negotiated with Taiwan's participation and led to its becoming a member as the 'Fishing Entity of Taiwan'. Taiwan is also a 'Cooperating Fishing Entity' in the International Commission for the Conservation of Atlantic Tuna.

2.2   Indigenous Peoples

A particular category of non-state actors has had some considerable success in institutional development but less in successful law-making in the sense of adoption by states of the international legal standards they have worked towards. Indigenous peoples across many states hold a unique position in the world and have sought to have their status and rights given effect under international law. There has long been engagement between international institutions and indigenous peoples. The ILO began working on issues pertinent to indigenous peoples as early as 1921, especially in connection with what they termed the 'native workers' of Latin America. In the UN era the ILO adopted Convention No. 107 on Indigenous and Tribal Populations in 1957. This Convention identified members of indigenous peoples as requiring special protection of their human rights but this was within a framework of assimilation that does not 'envisage a place . . . for robust, politically significant cultural and associational patterns of indigenous groups'.[35] The Convention was revised in 1989 by ILO Convention No. 169. In the meantime there had been a significant change. Indigenous peoples had ceased to be solely 'objects' of international law but had become active participants 'in an extensive multilateral dialogue that has engaged states, non-governmental organisations, and independent experts, a dialogue facilitated by human rights organs of international institutions'.[36] There was some participation by representatives of indigenous peoples in negotiating the 1989 Convention. The assimilationist perspective had largely given way to one that recognises the importance of maintaining and developing the identities, languages and religions of indigenous peoples within their own states of residence. Nevertheless, for some people there remained concerns about the 1989 Convention, including the qualified use of the word 'peoples'[37] and the definition of 'indigenous'.

Another instrument negotiated through the wide participation of indigenous representatives was still needed. The mechanism through which this has been sought was the Commission on Human Rights (CHR) Sub-Commission on Prevention of Discrimination and Protection of Minorities.[38] In 1971 ECOSOC authorised the Sub-Commission to work on the subject and in 1982 the Sub-Commission established a Working Group on Indigenous Populations to work on

---

[35] J. Anaya, *Indigenous Peoples in International Law* (Oxford, 1996) 44.   [36] Ibid 45.

[37] ILO Convention No. 169, Article 1 (3) states that 'use of the term "peoples" in this Convention shall not be construed as having any implications as regards the rights which may attach to the term under international law'. This is intended not to imply any right of self-determination.

[38] In 1999 its name was changed to the Sub-Commission on the Promotion and Protection of Human Rights; ECOSOC decision 99/256, 27 July 1999.

a draft instrument. The Working Group began work in 1985, thus pre-dating ILO Convention No. 169. Indeed the latter became an 'effective extension'[39] of the Working Group, although with less active participation by indigenous persons than in the Working Group. The latter pioneered innovative working methods within the UN, most importantly according speaking rights to indigenous representatives without requiring them to have affiliation to any NGO with ECOSOC consultative status. Alongside states, such representatives were able to comment on proposals and to make their own suggestions. In 1994 the Sub-Commission adopted the Working Group's Draft Declaration on the Rights of Indigenous Peoples. It was hoped that the Draft Declaration would be discussed and adopted in turn by the CHR, ECOSOC and finally the GA. However the process was long stalled in the CHR. In 1995 the CHR established an open-ended inter-sessional working group to elaborate a draft declaration on the rights of indigenous peoples, considering the Sub-Commission's draft.[40] Unlike the Sub-Commission (and its Working Group) this body comprised state representatives, although it followed the practice of the Sub-Commission Working Group by authorising as observers participation by organisations of indigenous people not in consultative status with ECOSOC. Controversial issues included the right to self-determination and land rights. At the first session of the Human Rights Council in 2006, nearly 25 years after the establishment of the Sub-Commission Working Group and after eleven sessions of the Working Group, the non-binding declaration was adopted,[41] although of course this is still a long way from the adoption of a binding convention.[42] Change in 2006 rested upon the apparent willingness of some states to offer support to the Declaration, illustrating that the political will of states remains crucial to the law-making activities of non-state actors—a recurrent theme throughout this chapter. Other factors were the support for the declaration in the World Summit Outcome Document and perhaps too the desire for the newly established Human Rights Council to be seen to take a significant law-making step at its first meeting.[43]

Institutionally there was faster progress. In 1993 the Vienna World Conference on Human Rights recommended consideration of the establishment of a permanent forum for indigenous people within the framework of an international decade of the world's indigenous people.[44] Workshops were held to explore the feasibility of this recommendation and a CHR *ad hoc* Working Group established. Indigenous representatives participated throughout these processes. The recommendation of the *ad hoc* Working Group to the CHR was accepted by ECOSOC, which adopted by

---

[39] Anaya, *Indigenous Peoples*, 52.   [40] CHR Res 1995/32, 3 March 1995.

[41] UN Doc A/HRC/1/L3, 23 June 2006. The Human Rights Council recommends to the UNGA that it adopt the Declaration as a resolution.

[42] Although ILO Convention 169 remains in force for states parties and contains legal obligations.

[43] The Human Rights Council also adopted the text of the International Convention for the Protection of All Persons from Enforced Disappearances, UN Doc A/HRC/1/L2, 23 June 2006.

[44] UN Doc A/CONF 157/24, Part II, 12 July 1993, para 32.

consensus a resolution establishing the Permanent Forum on Indigenous Issues.[45] The Forum is a subsidiary organ of ECOSOC with advisory status on issues within its mandate. Eight members are nominated by governments and elected by ECOSOC, and eight members are nominated by the ECOSOC president 'on the basis of broad consultations with indigenous organizations'. All members serve in their personal capacity 'as independent experts on indigenous issues'. This composition makes the Forum a unique global body[46] in which indigenous representatives access a UN body on an equal footing with states' representatives. Further, ECOSOC has provided that 'organizations of indigenous people may equally participate as observers in accordance with the procedures which have been applied in the Working Group on Indigenous Populations of the Sub-Commission on the Promotion and Protection of Human Rights'. It appears that through the processes evolved for the drafting and adoption of the draft Declaration by the Sub-Commission and the creation of the Permanent Forum there is now a principle, backed by supporting state practice, that rights of indigenous peoples cannot be determined without their participation and consent. Nevertheless the long delay in the adoption of the draft Declaration demonstrates that where states deem their interests to be threatened, even extensive participation by non-state actors does not lead to timely international law-making.

2.3   Transnational Networks

It has been convincingly argued that international law-making through negotiation of treaties or other instruments rests upon a unitary model of the state that speaks through the mouth of the head of government (or other relevant ministry).[47] Anne-Marie Slaughter has criticised this model for discounting the way government networks disaggregate the state and carry out law-making functions. People working in sub-state sectors such as courts, administrative agencies, legislatures and parliamentarians share professional and technical expertise with those in similar positions in other states.[48] Through their working relationships they develop networks across state borders in a horizontal system of what Slaughter terms 'transnational regulatory cooperation'. Such networks may work in conjunction with, or be initiated by, those in expert positions in IGOs, for example financial networks including World Bank and International Monetary Fund personnel.[49]

---

[45] ECOSOC Res 2000/22, 28 July 2000.

[46] The European Roma and Travellers Forum was established as an NGO registered in Strasbourg in September 2004 with special links to the Council of Europe.

[47] Those bodies accorded full powers under the 1969 VCLT, Article 7.

[48] A.-M. Slaughter, 'Governing the Global Economy through Government Networks', in M. Byers (ed), *The Role of Law in International Politics* (Oxford, 2000) 177. See generally A.-M. Slaughter, *A New World Order* (Princeton, 2004).

[49] A.-M. Slaughter, 'Sovereignty and Power in a Networked World Order', 40 *Stan JIL* (2004) 283, 299.

Experts from civil society groups also assist within public sector transnational networking. Membership of networks is flexible without the formal criteria for participation that are required for non-state actor access to IGOs. Networks facilitate devising solutions to common problems that are formulated through rules and principles in soft law forms such as codes of conduct, guidelines and best practices. Guiding rules and principles may also be more formally agreed through Memoranda of Understanding. They are implemented by the network participants within their own states. These flexible and informal agreements on common approaches and regulatory mechanisms create the expectation of compliance, in effect international standard setting. Slaughter gives as examples the Basle Committee on Banking Supervision, the International Organisation of Securities Commissioners and the International Association of Insurance Supervisors.[50] The soft character of their agreements[51] avoids the formality of treaty negotiation and the need for incorporation into national law. Transnational networks are facilitated by electronic communications that avoid the expense and time of meetings, or in the case of government networks, the formality of diplomatic meetings. These networks emphasise technical expertise, practice and functional efficiency, although at the expense of openness and transparency.

Similar forms of transnational networking take place through expert groups within the private sector, for example professional associations and similar epistemic communities.[52] Such networking has had a long history. Writing in 1907 Baldwin listed some 600 meetings of what he termed 'leading congresses, associations and societies of an unofficial description'.[53] He noted that international regulation of matters of public moment often resulted from private congress inspired by commercial, scientific, philosophic or altruistic motives.[54] A contemporary example is what has been called the 'globalization of accounting standards'.[55] Standard setting for accounting has traditionally been carried out by national authorities but this has shifted to the International Accounting Standards Board, a London-based organisation whose parent body is a US private corporation and which is largely financed by the 'big four' accountancy firms. Since 2005 the International Financial Reporting Standards (IFRS) prepared by this body have been adopted by all publicly listed companies in the EU and by some 70 other states. The IFRS have, in effect, become international accounting standards and provide an example of international regulation of technical matters by an epistemic professional community. 'What stands out . . . is the strong role of the [accounting profession] and of a very narrow group of private actors [the Big Four] in the process of formal rule setting.'[56]

---

[50] Slaughter, 'Governing the Global Economy', 177, 181–6.
[51] See Chapter 5 for discussion of soft law instruments.   [52] See Chapter 3.
[53] Baldwin, 1 *AJIL* (1907) 565, 572.   [54] Ibid 576, citing the Geneva Conventions of 1864.
[55] A. Nolke, 'Introduction to the Special Issue: The Globalization of Accounting Standards', 7 (3) *Business and Politics* (2005) 1.   [56] Ibid 4.

The various ways in which non-state entities are brought into the law-making processes and the activities of sub-state and professional networks illustrate different forms of participation and their diverse outcomes. Innovative solutions are possible to allow participation where the political will (or economic reality) requires measures to redress the anomaly of an entity's exclusion from UN institutional law-making (as in the case of Taiwan), or of a long marginalised group (as in the case of indigenous peoples). Expert networks are a pragmatic (albeit bureaucratic) response in the public or private sector to complex specialist demands which can best be met through transnational cooperation. Treaty-making may be too cumbersome a process to address effectively these demands.

3.   NGOs and the UN

3.1   What is an NGO?

This section considers the distinctive role played by NGOs in the institutional processes of international law-making. In accordance with the UN Charter, Article 71, ECOSOC has accorded consultative status to NGOs whose mandates are 'in conformity with the spirit, purposes and principles of the Charter'.[57] Different categories of NGO status (general, special and 'roster') determine the level of participation.[58] ECOSOC is thus the 'gatekeeper' between NGOs and the UN. Some specialised agencies also provide for some form of consultative or other status for non-governmental entities. For example UNESCO's Constitution allows the Organisation to 'make suitable arrangements for consultation and cooperation with non-governmental international organizations concerned with matters within its competence, and may invite them to undertake specific tasks'.

In 1996 ECOSOC reconsidered its criteria for according consultative status[59] and determined that an NGO (international, regional, sub-regional or national) must have *inter alia* established headquarters, a democratically adopted constitution, representative structure, appropriate mechanisms for ensuring accountability to its members and transparent decision-making processes. Any financial support from a government must be declared to the ECOSOC Committee on NGOs.[60]

Despite the elaboration of criteria for consultative status, neither the Charter nor ECOSOC have spelled out what constitutes an NGO. NGOs are primarily defined through what they are not: they are not established by a government or by intergovernmental agreement and their resources should come primarily from

---

[57]   ECOSOC Res 1296 (XLIV), 23 May 1968.

[58]   C. Chinkin, 'The Role of Non-Governmental Organisations in Standard Setting, Monitoring and Implementation of Human Rights', in J. Norton, M. Andenas and M. Footer (eds), *The Changing World of International Law in the Twenty First Century: A Tribute to the Late Kenneth R. Simmonds* (The Hague, 1998) 45, 48–50.

[59]   Consultative Relationship between the United Nations and Non-Governmental Organizations, ECOSOC Res 1996/31, 25 July 1996.

[60]   The ECOSOC Committee on NGOs is a standing committee comprising 19 member states.

voluntary contributions. They may operate solely or primarily in a single state (national NGOs) or across a number of states (international NGOs). Such general criteria provide a broad umbrella for a range of institutional arrangements[61] whose interests, strategies, target audiences and objectives do not necessarily coincide. Although the term NGO is often used to distinguish organisations with humanitarian or social justice 'public' objectives from commercial interests, NGO status is the route through which non-governmental industry and corporate entities are brought within the UN framework. These include associations representing commercial interests (for example the International Chamber of Commerce, the International Chamber of Shipping, and the International Air Transport Association) and transnational corporations (TNCs). Some international instruments now draw a distinction between NGOs and the private[62] or business[63] sector, although the same entitlements may be extended to both categories. The objectives of private sector bodies may be at odds with environmental, human rights and other public interest NGOs. The objective of the former category is typically to ensure that governments are informed of, and take into account, their specialist knowledge and profit-oriented business interests.[64] They seek to ensure that governmental delegates who lack industry-specific expertise are informed of the potential impact of particular measures on their industries.

The relationship between all types of non-state entity and the UN has been (and remains) an evolving one. The granting of consultative status was the first formal step into the UN for NGOs, which was the starting point for their much greater influence today. The language of consultative status or 'honoured guests'[65] has since shifted to that of 'loose creative coalitions'[66] and 'partnership' at the conceptual, operational and economic levels. In the words of UN Secretary-General Kofi Annan:

I think it is clear that there is a new diplomacy, where NGOs, peoples from across nations, international organizations, the Red Cross and governments come together to pursue an objective. When we do . . . this partnership . . . is a powerful partnership for the future.[67]

---

[61] The 1986 European Convention on the Recognition of the Legal Personality of International Non-Governmental Organisations, Article 1 provides that to qualify for recognition as an NGO an entity must have a non-profit aim of international utility, be established under internal law, pursue activities in at least two states and maintain a statutory office on the territory of a party.

[62] eg UNGA Res 53/182, 2 February 1999 invites the Secretary-General to make arrangements for the participation of civil society in the 3rd UN Conference on Least Developed Countries including 'non-governmental organizations and the private sector', cited S. Tully, 'Corporations and International Law-Making' (University of London, PhD thesis, 2004) 282.

[63] The Secretary-General has referred to the invitation by the SC to 'NGO representatives and the business sector' to participate in debates; Report of the Secretary-General in Response to the Report of the Panel of Eminent Persons on United Nations–Civil Society Relations, UN Doc A/59/354, para 13.

[64] B. Boczar, 'Avenues for Direct Participation of Transnational Corporations in International Environmental Negotiations', 3 *NYU Environmental LJ* (1994–5) 1.

[65] E. Reddy, UN Special Committee against Apartheid cited in Korey, *NGOs and the Universal Declaration of Human Rights*, 95.

[66] *We the Peoples of the United Nations in the 21st Century*, Millennium Report of the Secretary-General (2000) 70.

[67] NGO Forum on Global Issues, 30 April 1999, cited W. Pace and J. Schense, 'The Role of Non-Governmental Organisations', in A. Cassese, P. Gaeta and J. Jones, *The Rome Statute of the International Criminal Court: A Commentary* (Oxford, 2002), vol I, 105.

Partnership entails a mutually beneficial and equal relationship. Many IGOs and UN organs have established units, working groups or other focal points for liaison with NGOs and issued guidelines for their mutual relations. The concept of partnership has also been used to induce regulation of non-state actors, even if only voluntary self-regulation, as for example in the setting up of the Global Compact between companies, UN agencies, labour and environment movements in 2000.[68]

As part of his strategy for strengthening the UN, in 2004 the Secretary-General appointed a Panel of Eminent Persons to consider UN–Civil Society Relations. The Panel considered that the UN should become 'more outward looking' and to this end recommended increased NGO participation, including streamlining accreditation to the UNGA and its committees.[69] Implementation would enhance the opportunities for NGOs to influence international law-making. The UNGA in its 2005 consideration of UN reform stressed the importance of continued engagement between governments, IGOs, the private sector and other civil society bodies but made no reference to the suggestions of the earlier Panel.[70] Nor did it make any specific proposals of its own.

3.2   An NGO Right to Participation?

An important consequence of ECOSOC consultative status is that there is now widespread provision for national and international NGOs qualified in relevant fields to be accorded observer status at meetings of treaty parties, in law-making diplomatic conferences, global summits and other meetings held under UN auspices. Upon occasion, a government may select NGO representatives as members of its own delegation.[71] Otherwise a range of modalities exist for NGO participation at particular meetings.[72] This may depend upon their accreditation, which is carried out by a designated preparatory committee or commission (prepcom). Accreditation also determines the privileges of participation, for example which meetings NGO representatives may attend, which documents they may receive, and whether, when and for how long they are entitled to speak. The criteria are often inconsistent and uncertain.[73]

---

[68] The Global Compact was suggested in a speech by UN Secretary-General Kofi Annan in a speech to the World Economic Forum, 31 January 1999 and launched on 26 July 2000.

[69] Panel of Eminent Persons on United Nations–Civil Society Relations, UN Doc A/58/817, 2004, paras 123–8; this was endorsed in *A More Secure World: Our Shared Responsibility*, Report of the Secretary-General's High Level Panel on Threats, Challenges and Change, UN Doc A/59/565, 2 December 2004, para 243.

[70] 2005 World Summit Outcome, UNGA Res 60/1, 24 October 2005, para 172.

[71] At the UN Conference on Environment and Development, 1992, Rio de Janeiro, 14 government delegations included NGO representatives; P.-T. Stoll, 'Questionnaire International Environmental Law', in Zimmermann and Hoffmann, *Unity and Diversity in International Law*, 138.

[72] Report of the Secretary-General in Response to the Report of the Panel of Eminent Persons on United Nations–Civil Society Relations, UN Doc A/59/354, para 7.

[73] See Office of the President of the GA of the United Nations, *Reference Document on the Participation of Civil Society in UN Conferences and Special Sessions of the General Assembly during*

While there is no general right to observer status, and some treaties continue to exclude NGOs, many agreements now presume admission unless at least one third of member states object.[74] In some instances NGO observers have been admitted to meetings of treaty parties even without any specific treaty provision.[75] Unusually, a global convention, the 1995 UN Fish Stocks Agreement, Article 12, provides that relevant NGOs have a right to take part in the meetings of regional fisheries bodies.

Which NGOs are qualified to participate will usually be determined by the rules of procedure of the organisation or treaty in question. For example the Convention on the Rights of the Child, Article 45 allows the committee of experts[76] to invite 'other competent bodies' to provide expert advice on the Convention's implementation. Other instruments refer explicitly to NGOs with consultative status. The Rules of Procedure for Meetings of States Parties to the 1982 UN Convention on the Law of the Sea allow NGOs recognised by ECOSOC whose activities are 'relevant to the law of the sea' and other invited NGOs to attend as observers.[77] Such NGOs may attend public meetings and make oral and written statements. The criteria of relevance or expertise are relied on in the Convention on International Trade in Endangered Species of Wild Fauna and Flora (CITES), Article XI (7) so that a body 'technically qualified in protection, conservation or management of wild fauna and flora' may inform the Secretariat that it wishes to be represented at a conference of the parties and shall be admitted unless at least one-third of the Parties object. Such representation bestows no voting rights. FAO's Rules of Procedure, rule XVII (3) allow an observer of an NGO with consultative status to attend Conference plenary meetings, commission and technical committee meetings, to speak before such bodies but not to vote. The Rules of Procedure for the Rome Conference of the International Criminal Court, rule 63 allowed 'invited' NGOs to attend plenary meetings and unless decided otherwise by the Conference for specific meetings, formal meetings of the Committee of the Whole and to receive official documents. Some NGO representatives were able to make oral statements at the beginning and end of the Conference. Only states could vote. Under the 1997 Ottawa Landmines Convention, 'relevant' NGOs may be invited to Meetings of States Parties, Review Conferences and Amendment Conferences, in each case as observers in accordance with the Rules of Procedure. The Rules of Procedure for the First Review Conference,[78] held at Nairobi in 2004, stated that certain specified non-state entities (including the ICRC, the International

---

the 1990s (2001), available at http://www.globalpolicy.org/ngos/role/policymk/conf/2001/0518 refdoc.htm#equal>.

[74] 1973 CITES Convention, Article 11 (7) and 1985 Vienna Convention for the Protection of the Ozone Layer, Article 6 (5) are the two principal provisions and are repeated in many later treaties.

[75] eg to meetings of states parties to the 1946 Convention for the Regulation of Whaling and the 1972/1996 London Dumping Convention.   [76] See Chapter 3.

[77] SPLOS/2/Rev 4, 24 January 2005, Rule 18.

[78] Rule 1 (3), UN Doc APLC/CONF/2004/3/Rev 1, 15 November 2004.

Federation of Red Cross and Red Crescent Societies and the International Campaign to Ban Landmines (ICBL))[79] and other bodies 'that have received an invitation from the Coordinating Committee' could attend as observers. Rule 24 prevented observers from participating in decision-making, making any procedural motion, raising a point of order or appealing against any ruling of the President. The 1998 Aarhus Convention entitles a 'qualified' NGO to participate as an observer at a meeting of the Parties, unless at least one third of the Parties present objects.[80] This last formulation (also found in CITES) provides a procedural mechanism for resolving any disputed claim to participate. It also shifts the determination away from a conference bureaucracy to the states parties.

It will have been noted that in all these examples observer status gives no right to vote. Thus while access to NGOs has been quite widely accorded, allowing the acquisition of knowledge about the progress of international negotiations and the opportunity to influence state delegates,[81] states have been unwilling to permit such non-state actors to take a crucial part in law-making decisions.

NGO access was initially less readily accepted in the WTO.[82] The WTO Agreement, Article V (2) provides that the 'General Council may make appropriate arrangements for consultation and cooperation with non-governmental organizations concerned with matters related to those of the WTO'. In 1996 the General Council adopted Guidelines for Arrangements on Relations with Non-Governmental Organizations.[83] However the motivation was not to allow participation in decision-making but rather to facilitate the role of NGOs in increasing 'the awareness of the public in respect of WTO activities' and improving transparency. Although NGOs were recognised as a 'rich resource' it was explicitly spelled out that 'the special character of the WTO' as an 'intergovernmental treaty of rights and obligations among its Members and a forum for negotiations' led to 'a broadly held view that it would not be possible for NGOs to be directly involved in the work of the WTO or its meetings'. However, NGOs may be accredited to attend Ministerial Conferences and plenary sessions, and increasing numbers have done so.[84] The majority of these are trade and industry associations although others represent a broad range of interests, including human rights, development, environmental protection, protection of animals, and aid agencies. While the vast majority are based in Europe and North America, many of these

---

[79] A coalition NGO which we discuss below.

[80] 1998 Convention on Access to Information, Public Participation in Decision-Making and Access to Justice in Environmental Matters, Article 10 (5).

[81] Participation also legitimates attempts to influence state delegates; R. Falk and A. Strauss, 'On the Creation of a Global Peoples Assembly: Legitimacy and the Power of Popular Sovereignty', 36 *Stan JIL* (2000) 191, 198. [82] See Chapter 3.

[83] WTO Doc WT/L/162, 23 July 1996.

[84] R. Buchanan, 'Perpetual Peace or Perpetual Process: Global Civil Society and Cosmopolitan Legality at the World Trade Organisation', 16 *LJIL* (2003) 673, 678–84 tracks 'transnational advocacy' at the WTO.

exist to promote the interests of developing states. The NGO focus has been primarily on process, that is transparency, accountability, access and inclusivity as hallmarks of procedural legitimacy.[85]

The more frequent presence of NGOs (and their larger numbers) at multilateral law-making processes raises the question of whether there is an NGO right to participation. Where there is a specific treaty entitlement the answer is determined by the treaty terms, although there may remain ambiguity and uncertainty as to who may make the final determination. Where NGOs were active participants in the treaty negotiations they are likely to have sought provision for their own inclusion in subsequent processes, as was the case with UN Charter, Article 71. Without such treaty provision there is undoubtedly a growing practice towards, and expectation of, NGO participation. The UN Secretary-General has commented that 'a major United Nations gathering without the involvement of civil society in all its various forms is scarcely imaginable'.[86] However it seems premature to assert that there is a right to access and participation.[87] The very existence of accreditation procedures by a designated body indicates a discretion as to whether access is granted and the fact that some applications for accreditation to global diplomatic conferences have been refused reinforces this conclusion. For example Tibetan (and other) NGOs were denied accreditation for the 1995 Beijing Women's Conference and for the 1996 Istanbul Habitat Conference on Housing and Sustainable Communities. Such refusals may be politically motivated and cause considerable disquiet.[88]

In practice another concern is that of logistics. Attendance by NGO representatives requires greater meeting space, wider production and distribution of materials and, where they are permitted to speak in formal sessions, longer time. This all adds to the expense and burdens of meetings. There are also concerns about the size and composition of NGO delegations. These practical considerations impinge upon the more theoretical issues discussed in the following section.

3.3   Democratisation of International Law-Making?

The Panel of Eminent Persons on UN–Civil Society Relations, the UN Secretary-General and the UNGA at its 2005 Summit all supported increased access for NGOs to the UN and its agencies and their greater participation in international law-making. As UN S-G, Kofi Annan has stated, '[The UN] must be open not

---

[85]   Ibid 680.

[86]   Report of the S-G, *Strengthening of the United Nations; An Agenda for Further Change*, UN Doc A 57/387, 9 September 2002, para 12.

[87]   Tully, 'Corporations and International Law-Making', 278.

[88]   eg in 1994 the consultative status of the International Gay and Lesbian Association was withdrawn; D. Otto, 'Non-Governmental Organisations in the United Nations System: The Emerging Role of International Civil Society', 18 *HRQ* (1996) 107.

only to States but also to civil society, which at both the national and international levels plays an increasingly important role in world affairs'.[89]

Despite this level of agreement it must be asked what extensive NGO participation in international law-making processes achieves and whether it is appropriate. The first concern is addressed in Section 4 below. With respect to the second, it has been suggested that NGO participation constitutes a 'sea-change' in international law-making[90] by democratising and thus legitimising the essentially non-democratic processes of international law.[91] It strips away the myth of the monolithic state and allows disagreement with the official state view to be voiced at the international level. The expression of a cosmopolitan,[92] popular will through the NGO voice—the 'conscience of the world'—is itself seen by some as a basis of legitimacy.[93] More instrumentally the Secretary-General has stated that '[m]ore effective engagement with NGOs also increases the likelihood that United Nations decisions will be better understood and supported by a broad and diverse public'.[94] As international law impacts more often and directly upon individuals it becomes more important that it is seen as legitimate to a broader based community.

Nevertheless caution is required against assuming the democratisation of international law-making through NGO participation.[95] Judge Higgins presents well the alternative views: 'To some, these radical phenomena represent the democratisation of international law. To others it is both a degradation of the technical work of international lawyers in the face of pressure groups and a side-stepping of existing international law requirements and procedures.'[96]

Some of the areas of concern are the following. NGOs are often non-democratic, self-appointed, may consist of only a handful of people and determine their own agendas with an evangelical or elitist zeal. There is no guarantee that the views expressed by even high-profile NGOs are representative, either generally, or with respect to their claimed constituencies. Their internal decision-making processes may not be transparent and are often concealed within a deluge of information. NGOs do not have to address the full range of options that must be considered by state elites but can limit themselves to their own, often limited or even single issue,

---

[89] *In Larger Freedom: Towards development, security and human rights for all*, UN Doc A/59/2005, 21 March 2005, para 153.   [90] Anderson, 11 *EJIL* (2000) 91.

[91] J. Crawford, 'Democracy and International Law', 64 *BYBIL* (1993) 113.

[92] D. Held, *Democracy and the Global Order: From the Modern State to Cosmopolitan Governance* (Cambridge, 1995).

[93] C. Reus-Smit (ed), *The Politics of International Law* (Cambridge, 2004) 35.

[94] Report of the S-G in Response to the Report of the Panel of Eminent Persons on United Nations–Civil Society Relations, UN Doc A/59/354, para 4.

[95] For a broader discussion of global civil society and democracy see K. Anderson and D. Rieff, ' "Global Civil Society": A Sceptical View', in H. Anheier, M. Glasius and M. Kaldor (eds) *Global Civil Society 2004/5* (London, 2005) 26, 33–5.

[96] R. Higgins, 'The Reformation of International Law', in R. Rawlings (ed), *Law, Society and Economy: Centenary Essays for the London School of Economics and Political Science 1895–1995* (Oxford, 1997) 208, 215.

concerns. The need for many NGOs to account to donors for their expenditures gives rise to questions about the latter's influence on setting priorities.

Another source of unease is whether the NGOs that are most prominent in an international forum do in fact speak for a broader constituency. NGO coalitions are one way of enhancing their representative character, as well as creating a single, and therefore more forceful, NGO voice.[97] But coalition building does not necessarily answer the concern. The fact of a coalition may conceal deep divisions between its members.[98] Some NGOs may feel they are being asked to make unwelcome compromises, or that bigger, better funded NGOs wield excessive influence. Dissenting voices might be silenced in order to maintain the appearance of unity, or those who have not joined the coalition may become invisible. On the other hand opposing alliances may form. Diversity of NGO views fosters fuller debate but may be seen as detrimental by majority NGOs that apprehend the dilution of their voice and consequential weakening of their influence. Divisions may cause hostility, accusations of unfair tactics and seeking different allies among states. Contestation between NGO alliances can impact upon the final text. For example at Rome, Cairo and Beijing, women's interests were contested between the Vatican and other religious-based pro-life groups on the one side and the Women's Caucus on the other. Although the Women's Caucus was successful in securing the inclusion of gender crimes within the ICC Statute, the influence of the former ensured restrictive definitions of gender and of forced pregnancy as a crime against humanity, and the rejection of persecution on the basis of sexuality as a crime against humanity.[99]

Individual NGOs must determine whether their objectives are more likely to be achieved through joint action with other NGOs or by remaining outside any coalition. Some NGOs prefer to remain outside the established processes of international law creating a dichotomy between 'insider' and 'outsider' NGOs. States may be more likely to consult or otherwise work with the 'insiders' and claim popular legitimacy for their actions by having done so. This carries the risk of marginalising the 'outsiders' and silencing voices that are unwilling to compromise within the state-dominated international fora. Outsider groups (for example women's groups, indigenous persons) seeking to move from the margins of meetings devoted to their concerns to the mainstream of international law may have to compromise with 'mainstream' NGOs whose agendas and priorities do not accord

[97] Coalition building has been part of NGO strategy with respect to NGO/UN relationships almost since the outset. The Conference of Non-Governmental Organizations in Consultative Relationship with the United Nations (CONGO) was founded in 1948 as an 'umbrella' coalition of NGOs, to ensure that NGO voices are heard throughout the international arena.

[98] The Report of the Open-Ended Working Group on the Review of Arrangements for Consultations with Non-Governmental Organisations, UN Doc A/49/215 (1994), para 63 expressed concern that seeking consensus through NGO coalitions risked losing the range and diversity of opinions.

[99] C. Steains, 'Gender Issues', in R. Lee (ed), *The International Criminal Court: The Making of the Rome Statute—Issues, Negotiations, Results* (The Hague, 1999) 357, 368.

with their own. All these considerations undermine a claim of democratisation through NGO participation.

In light of the imbalance between international NGOs from the northern industrialised countries and those from the developing countries,[100] another effect of enhancing the role of international civil society in international law-making might be to replicate state power structures by furthering the bias in favour of the agendas of the North. The global disparity in computer access may also disadvantage membership participation in NGOs from the South. The 'paradigmatic shift' in international society towards geo-governance may in fact amount to little more than another means of validating essentially Northern liberal interests in a post-colonial, post-cold war world. Indeed it may promote still further a Western/ Northern domination through the culture of law as an instrument of NGO activism. The Secretary-General has made some attempt to address this concern through the establishment of a trust fund to support NGO representatives from developing countries to attend meetings.[101]

A misleading perception is to regard all intervention in international law-making by non-state actors as moving in the same direction. The law-making activities of social interest NGOs—the apparent moral authority and benign face of 'globalisation from below'—may conflict with each other and with the normative activities of other non-state actors, for example those of the corporate/financial forces of 'globalisation from above'.[102] The 'processes of economic globalisation are transferring unprecedented power to . . . transnational business and financial interests'.[103] The business sector's greater access to all forms of resources allows them to attract state attention[104] and to occupy greater political and participatory space. It forms the most prominent non-state participation at meetings of states parties where business interests are at stake. Thus Krut has noted the proliferation of TNCs within the UN and described how their disproportionate financial power enables them to lobby more effectively in law-making processes than other non-state actors.[105] Similarly business associations have had greatest access to the WTO. Sixty-five per cent of the non-state organisations accredited to the Singapore Ministerial Conference represented business interests.[106] TNCs typically seek

---

[100] Report of the S-G, *Strengthening of the United Nations; An Agenda for Further Change*, UN Doc A 57/387, 9 September 2002, para 139.

[101] Report of the S-G in Response to the Report of the Panel of Eminent Persons on United Nations–Civil Society Relations, UN Doc A/59/354, para 22.

[102] R. Falk, 'The Nuclear Weapons Advisory Opinion and the New Jurisprudence of Global Civil Society', 7 *Transnational Law and Contemporary Problems* (1997) 333.

[103] Anderson and Rieff, ' "Global Civil Society" ', 26, 27.

[104] P. Spiro, 'New Global Potentates: Nongovernmental Organizations and the "Unregulated" Marketplace', 18 *Cardozo LR* (1996) 957 at 966.

[105] WEDO, 'Transnational Corporations in the United Nations' cited in R. Krut, *Globalization and Civil Society: NGO Influence in International Decision-Making* (Geneva, 1997) 1, 23.

[106] J. A. Scholte, R. O'Brien and M. Williams, *The WTO and Civil Society*, Centre for the Study of Globalisation and Regionalisation, University of Warwick, Working Paper No. 14 (1998) 17.

minimal legal regulation and to remain outside the framework of international legal accountability by preserving the differentiation between public and private activity. Much social-based NGO activity is directed precisely towards ensuring government regulation and control over other non-state actors and making such bodies accountable, as in the movement to make TNCs accept responsibility for human rights and environmental abuses. Accordingly NGOs are likely to seek law-making in hard form while business organisations favour soft, self-regulatory guidelines or codes of conduct. Alternatively, different solutions might be sought by diverse non-state interests: in the area of climate change environmental NGOs lobby for stronger controls on fossil fuel use, while industry sectors may be focused on achieving greater flexibility in ways of meeting pollution targets.

Such conflicting objectives may mean that the state or IGO becomes less of an initiator or law-maker and more of a mediator between conflicting forces. Arenas of confrontation within and between non-state bodies for the upper hand in the articulation of norms may be highly visible as in civil society demonstrations against the WTO in Seattle, 1999 and in the locations for summit meetings of the G8. The internet provides both an organising tool and a site for mobilising sufficient antagonism to particular proposals to make them politically unacceptable as was the case with the proposed Multilateral Agreement on Investment (MAI) described below.

Work with social justice NGOs, including seeking changes in international law, is becoming an alternative career route for public advocacy-minded international lawyers: a job in Amnesty International (AI) may be sought as providing an effective basis for challenging corporate and state interests in international law-making. The direct influence of international law-making in the former may be hard to determine but is nevertheless seen as being progressive and on the side of the 'good'. However it must be remembered that governments comprise recognised state representatives and arguments that states are non-representative are weakened by the growing number of states where elections are held. Anderson argues that the non-democratic nature of the NGO-driven process for the adoption of the Landmines Convention, which we discuss below, justifies the democratically elected US government refusing to become a party and indeed that NGO pressure is a new form of illegitimate imperialism.[107] Another perspective is that in an environment where the US is putting its power against multilateral law-making, NGOs provide a counter-balance and support for those governments willing to resist US pressure.

NGO commitment to seeking access to international institutional arenas and change through international law strengthens both the institutions and body of international law. Since states retain their central position in international law-making it also paradoxically reinforces state power. It is not chance that the strongest civil society movements emanate from the most powerful states: by taking account

---

[107] Anderson, 11 *EJIL* (2000) 91, 95.

of civil society activity, a more complete assessment of power within the state may be achieved but it does not mean that the role of the state is displaced.

4.　NGOs and Treaty-Making

This section examines NGO strategies for participation in treaty-making. As stated above, a central focus throughout the discussion of NGO participation is to determine whether they are autonomous participants in international law-making or whether it is more accurate to see them as additional players within the state-centred processes described in the following chapters. There can be little doubt that the NGO presence changes the dynamics of such processes but their actual impact on the topics that are selected for international law-making and the substance of any agreed outcome remains less clear.

4.1　Treaty Negotiation

NGO influence on international treaty negotiation is not new. One of the earliest examples is the work of the ICRC. In *A Memory of Solferino* Henri Dunant questioned whether military authorities could draw up 'some international principle, sanctioned by a convention and inviolate in character, which, once agreed upon and ratified, might constitute the basis for societies for the relief of the wounded in the different European countries?'[108] Gustave Moynier, a Geneva lawyer, responded by presenting the question to the Geneva Public Welfare Society, a charity of which he was the chair. The society established a five-person committee which first met on 17 February 1863 and soon became known as the ICRC. On 25 August 1863, the ICRC decided under its own responsibility to convene an international conference in Geneva to which it invited all European governments and numerous leading personalities. Fourteen government delegates, six delegates from various organisations and seven private individuals participated in the conference which commenced in October 1863. The conference took as its starting point a draft convention prepared by the ICRC and adopted ten resolutions. The ICRC then prepared for a diplomatic conference to adopt the ten resolutions in treaty form. The initiative passed to the Swiss government, which agreed to organise the diplomatic conference and invited all European governments, the USA, Brazil and Mexico to participate. Delegates from 16 states participated in the 1864 diplomatic conference and working from the ICRC's draft text, adopted the Geneva Convention for the Amelioration of the Condition of the Wounded in Armies in the Field. 'Modern international humanitarian law was born.'[109] This account

---

[108]　Henri Dunant, *A Memory of Solferino* (Geneva, 1986) 63.
[109]　Website of the ICRC, <www.icrc.org/>.

illustrates what has become a familiar pattern: NGO initiative in identifying an area for potential legal reform, intensive work for its introduction onto the international agenda, and states assuming control at the crucial law-making stage.

The ICRC continues its law-making function in areas within its (expanded) concerns. For example, it was instrumental in the drafting and adoption of the Convention on Conventional Weapons,[110] especially Protocol IV on Blinding Laser Weapons,[111] and was an active participant in the negotiation of the Landmines Convention and the Rome Statute of the ICC, both discussed below. The ICRC has also contributed to customary international law through its two-volume compendium of the current (2005) customary international rules of international humanitarian law. This is based on a study of all available sources carried out by national and international research teams, legal and governmental experts and the ICRC.[112]

International NGOs working in such areas as human rights, the environment, disarmament and those focusing on the interests of particular groups such as women, children, indigenous persons and refugees have been especially active in seeking to make international law responsive to their demands.[113] Indeed the level of commitment they place on achieving change in international law is perhaps surprising, especially in those areas where enforcement is regarded as especially weak such as human rights. Nevertheless to this end NGOs have proceeded at a number of levels and through diverse strategies.

Following the example of the ICRC, one strategy is to seek the inclusion of their political and social agendas within the accepted fabric of international law, that is by the adoption of a treaty or soft law instrument. To this end NGOs have typically engaged in a range of activities. Their campaigns 'often conducted in concert with the United Nations, have helped to raise—and alter—the consciousness of the international community and to change the behaviour of states on many critical global issues'.[114] Many tasks are preparatory to the issue appearing on the agenda of any IGO and are targeted at this objective.[115] The issue must first be defined and brought to public attention. One of the most dramatic (and ultimately successful) examples of inducing new international law was the role of

---

[110] The Diplomatic Conference on Reaffirmation and Development of International Humanitarian Law applicable in Armed Conflicts, Geneva 1974–7, Resolution 22 led to the Diplomatic Conference for the drafting of the Convention on Prohibitions or Restrictions on the Use of Certain Conventional Weapons which may be deemed to be Excessively Injurious or to have Indiscriminate Effects, Geneva 1980. The ICRC acted as observer and expert at this conference; ICRC, *Annual Report, 1980* (1981) 69.

[111] Protocol IV on Blinding Laser Weapons, October 1995.

[112] J.-M. Henckaerts and L. Doswald-Beck, *Customary International Humanitarian Law Vol. I: Rules; Vol. II: Practice* (Cambridge, 2005). See also Chapter 4.

[113] R. Geiss, 'Non-State Actors: Their Role and Impact on the Fragmentation of International Law', in Zimmermann and Hoffmann, *Unity and Diversity in International Law*, 303, 326.

[114] *'We the Peoples': The Role of the United Nations in the 21st Century*, Millennium Report of the Secretary-General of the United Nations (New York, 2000), para 323.   [115] See Chapter 3.

Raphael Lemkin in the adoption of the Genocide Convention. He formulated the concept of genocide, brought documentary evidence of Nazi atrocities against the Jews to the US in the early 1940s, conducted seminars on the concept, lobbied ambassadors at the UN to adopt a resolution and urged the adoption of a treaty.[116] Lemkin's work also shows that a sufficiently committed and tireless individual can generate change in international law. Other preparatory tasks include intensive and detailed background research, dissemination of that research, fact-finding and reporting, legal analysis on the subject matter, drafting policy papers, texts or reports in the hope of assisting international institutions or governments in determining an appropriate approach to issues of international law, securing support for international action from governments and experts in the field,[117] and raising public awareness of, and mobilising support for, the campaign. For example the detailed preparatory works by the AI International Secretariat on a permanent international criminal court set out the issues and options in a way that was accessible to other NGOs and members of the public. These became widely referred to sources of information, often in preference to the more legalistic International Law Commission (ILC) draft text discussed in Chapter 4.

Preparatory work continues after an issue comes onto an international agenda and may have to continue for many years. The ICRC secured its first convention in a remarkably short period of time but NGOs may expect a long period of work before the convening of an international conference, or the adoption of a text. The GA adopted the Genocide Convention in 1948, 15 years after Lemkin's first call for a treaty. The draft protocol to the Torture Convention took ten years to negotiate and the Rome Statute of the ICC was adopted nearly 50 years after the GA first proposed the subject to the ILC. NGO involvement may commence at a low level, perhaps in some particular national organisation, and then become an important aspect of the work of major international NGOs. Background work typically takes on a higher profile once the issue has reached the international agenda and the law-making process advances. NGOs may undertake such tasks as scrutinising and commenting on government or international secretariat drafts and attending government meetings, regional or international preparatory committees (prepcoms) and finally participating in an international diplomatic conference, as described in Chapter 3.

At multilateral law-making meetings (diplomatic conferences and meetings, or conferences of states parties) NGOs are frequently a highly organised and professional presence. They typically engage in intensive lobbying of government delegates and seek regular briefings and meetings. They work on draft texts, changing wording in response to the debates and negotiations, or strengthening their earlier

---

[116] Keck and Sikkink, *Activists beyond Borders*, 87–8.

[117] eg the International Council of Scientific Unions played a major role in bringing scientific opinion around to the reality of climate change and the need for international regulation; R. Falk and A. Strauss, 'On the Creation of a Global Peoples Assembly: Legitimacy and the Power of Popular Sovereignty', 36 *Stan JIL* (2000) 197.

language, and bring such texts to the attention of government delegates in the hope that they will incorporate them into the treaty. They seek to make themselves indispensable to the process by supplying information and expertise; accordingly keeping themselves well-informed is vital.

Non-governmental industry and corporate entities seek access to diplomatic conferences, conferences of the parties and institutional meetings to further their business interests. In Chapter 3 we discuss the participation of representatives of industrialised states' mining industries and other technical experts at UNCLOS III. Depending upon the subject matter, they may be the most numerous participants in international negotiations. Industry-based NGOs may bring into the international processes technological or scientific advances about which government negotiators may be unaware and hence facilitate agreement on less expensive and more efficient solutions to problems. As noted, these actions may also expose divergent interests between different commercial sectors and between commercial and non-commercial interests that government officials have to weigh.

Recourse to the media may publicise NGO concerns and put pressure upon states, for example by exposing intransigence in states' positions. NGO production of a daily newspaper has become a regular feature.[118] A paper typically details positions, progress (or lack of progress) in negotiations, exchanges and views. Since NGOs do not all speak with a single voice, there may be negotiations between different bodies in an attempt to secure a common position and thus to strengthen their bargaining power *vis-à-vis* state representatives. As discussed above, coalitions may also make it easier for states to accommodate the smaller number of actors when NGOs come together to speak collectively on an issue.[119] Networking, alliance and coalition building between NGOs have been important features of many a successful NGO treaty campaign.[120] Industry-based NGOs also form coalitions to speak with a concerted voice, for example the participation of NGOs representing the automobile and oil industries at meetings of the parties to the Convention on Climate Change and the Kyoto Protocol and whose activities form a significant counterweight to environmentalist NGOs.

Coalition building can also generate innovative substantive arguments by borrowing from one issue area to make progress in another. For example the ICBL brought together NGOs with very different mandates and expertise, including

---

[118] An independent activist produced a daily newspaper at the Hague Peace Conferences, 1899 and 1907; Anheier et al (eds), *Global Civil Society 2004/5*, 5.

[119] Report of the S-G, *Strengthening of the United Nations; An Agenda for Further Change*, UN Doc A 57/387, 9 September 2002, para 140; Report of the S-G in Response to the Report of the Panel of Eminent Persons on United Nations–Civil Society Relations, UN Doc A/59/354, para 8 supports the recommendation that NGOs form groups and networks to participate in UN activities.

[120] On the NGO coalition in the drafting of the 1989 UN Convention on the Rights of the Child and its Protocols of 2000 see C. Cohen, 'The Role of Nongovernmental Organizations in the Drafting of the Convention on the Rights of the Child', 12 *HRQ* (1990) 137; C. Breen, 'The Role of NGOs in the Formulation of and Compliance with the Optional Protocol to the Convention on the Rights of the Child on Involvement of Children in Armed Conflict', 25 *HRQ* (2003) 453.

human rights, humanitarian assistance, medical assistance, public health and disarmament. Mechanisms drawn from human rights (state reporting), disarmament (verification) and humanitarian law (fact finding) were all introduced into the 1997 UN Convention on the Prohibition of the Use, Stockpiling, Production and Transfer of Anti-Personnel Mines and on their Destruction (Landmines Convention).

State delegations may be willing to accept NGO proposals into treaties for a number of reasons. They may be convinced that there is a sizeable political constituency behind the demands. They may accept the expertise or field experience of a particular organisation (or individuals within an organisation) and recognise that this exceeds their own. Recognition of the value of NGO expertise and specialist knowledge extends into participation at subsequent conferences or meetings of states parties, as described in Chapter 3. The terms of the treaty may need to be fleshed out, made more precise and capable of application. NGO expertise may be important in collecting examples of national best practice from which international standards can be formulated. In other cases NGOs may provide scientific or technical expertise. The Comité Maritime International (CMI), an association of maritime lawyers, has a longstanding role in the regulatory work of the International Maritime Organisation.[121] The International Council of Scientific Unions (ICSU) has cooperated with WMO and UNESCO in scientific studies relating to climate change and other environmental issues.[122] The value of most of these bodies is that they represent 'a diversity of knowledge and expertise',[123] and provide an independent source of publicly accessible data. Scientists or lawyers cannot be expected to take policy decisions that are ultimately the responsibility of politicians; rather their role as experts is 'to refine problem definition and to identify and expand the range of response options', setting out uncertainties, assumptions and the probable consequences of action or inaction.[124]

Every treaty-making process is distinctive, involving different participants, institutional and other arenas, agendas, timetables and outcomes. Inevitably historical accounts of the process vary according to the particular perspective and it is often difficult to determine the impact of NGO participation. Evidence of NGO influence on the pre-history of an international instrument is found in diverse sources, such as the minutes of NGO meetings and personal accounts, but the official history (the *travaux préparatoires* of a treaty) may obscure the extent or nature of NGO activity, much of which takes place outside the formal sessions. Nevertheless there are a number of international instruments where the NGO contribution has been widely recognised. The next section briefly outlines four examples that illustrate some of the more general points made above and draws some conclusions.

---

[121] See Chapter 3.
[122] D. Tolbert, in R. Churchill and D. Freestone (eds), *International Law and Global Climate Change: International Legal Issues and Implications* (London, 1991) 95; L. Kimball, *Treaty Implementation: Scientific and Technical Advice Enters a New Stage* (Washington, 1996) 188–9.
[123] Kimball, *Treaty Implementation*, 7.   [124] Ibid.

4.2   Treaty-Making: Case Studies

4.2.1   The Torture Convention

The first example is the role played by Amnesty International (AI) in the development of international norms prohibiting torture, culminating in adoption of the 1984 Torture Convention and the 2002 Optional Protocol.[125] The Torture Convention has been described as 'one of the most successful initiatives ever undertaken by an NGO' [126] and is a landmark in the contemporary history of NGO law-making. When AI commenced in 1972 what it anticipated to be a year-long Campaign for the Abolition of Torture, the right to be free from torture was already well entrenched in human rights law through the Universal Declaration of Human Rights, Article 5, the International Covenant on Civil and Political Rights, Article 7, the European Convention on Human Rights, Article 3 and the American Convention on Human Rights, Article 5 (2). The campaign's objective was not to create new law, or to amend existing law, but to expose the reality of non-observance of the law. The campaign was backed by detailed research and publication on the widespread use of torture. It generated a massive petition and an international conference on the abolition of torture. UNGA delegates took up the issue and called for concrete proposals. This resulted in the adoption of UNGA Resolution 3059 (XXVIII)[127] which condemned torture and placed the issue squarely on its own agenda. Buoyed by this success AI continued its campaign beyond the initial year, notably though an urgent action campaign. The UNGA remained seised of the issue and in 1974 called for specific action against torture through the 5th UN Congress on the Prevention of Crime and the Treatment of Offenders.[128] AI prepared fully for this Congress and sponsored two seminars on torture at it. Korey notes the importance of another seminar in The Hague involving the Dutch section of AI which brought in and mobilised a further sector in support—the police. The Netherlands became a leading state in the UN drafting process. A declaration against torture was adopted by the Crime Congress, which was followed by further personal lobbying at the UN to ensure its adoption by the UNGA in 1975.[129] The UNGA adopted the Declaration without referring the text to the CHR. In this instance other bodies—AI and the Crime Congress—displaced the more usual route for human rights law-making,[130] showing AI's success in mobilising the GA. AI continued its work through employing the same techniques—urgent action campaigns, publicity, petitions, focused country campaigns (in particular against Uruguay) and 'bombardment'[131] of the UN with

---

[125]   UNGA Res 57/199, 18 December 2002.

[126]   Korey, *NGOs and the Universal Declaration of Human Rights*, 171. This account is largely taken from Korey, chapter 7, 'Amnesty International and the "Prisoners of Conscience"'.

[127]   5 November 1973.   [128]   UNGA Res 3218 (XXIX), 6 November 1974.

[129]   Declaration on the Protection of all Persons from being subjected to Torture and Other Cruel, Inhuman or Degrading Treatment or Punishment, GA Res 3452 (XXX), 9 December 1975.

[130]   P. Alston, 'The Commission on Human Rights', in P. Alston (ed), *The United Nations and Human Rights* (Oxford, 1992) 126, 135.

[131]   Korey, *NGOs and the Universal Declaration of Human Rights*, 177.

reports and accounts of torture. In 1984 the UNGA adopted the Torture Convention.

This process followed a well-trodden law-making path—GA adoption of a non-binding declaration followed by a legally binding treaty. Although law-making was not the primary focus of this NGO campaign, the Torture Convention did in fact evolve new law, procedures and institutions, for example the definition of torture (Article 1), the obligation of non-refoulement (Article 3), the requirement to extradite or prosecute those suspected of torture (Articles 6 and 7) and the rejection as evidence of any statement established to have been made as a result of torture (Article 15). There can be little doubt that the adoption of the Convention has facilitated acceptance of the prohibition of torture as customary international law and indeed a peremptory norm of international law, imposing upon states obligations owed *erga omnes*, and of its various provisions as law-making.[132]

Subsequent NGO attention focused on the need to develop an international regime of inspection of prisons and other centres of detention as a means of preventing torture. NGOs, including AI, the International Commission of Jurists and the Association for the Prevention of Torture, pushed for this goal despite the initial lack of any government support and they gradually built up a further coalition around the issue. Lobbying became a two-way process as NGOs lobbied governments to support the inspection regime and like-minded governments lobbied NGOs to back a compromise text. In Chapter 3 we discuss how this NGO/governmental coalition successfully piloted the 2002 Protocol to the Torture Convention through the CHR, ECOSOC and the GA in the face of strenuous opposition.

4.2.2   *The Landmines Convention*

The second example is the negotiation of the Landmines Convention. This differed from the campaign to suppress torture in that there was no existing international prohibition of landmines. The campaign was initiated by NGOs,[133] notably the ICRC, at a time when governments were entirely negative about either the desirability of a convention or its feasibility.[134] It gained impetus from the formation in the early 1990s of a global NGO coalition, the ICBL. The coalition membership eventually reached some 1,200 NGOs across 60 states. NGOs organised local and regional meetings and conferences to build support for a treaty. Despite initial government scepticism, some states came on board and took steps within their domestic law to limit the use and export of landmines. State inertia—or preference for the *status quo*—can jeopardise a law-making initiative, so the offer by

---

[132]   eg *A and others v. Secretary of State for the Home Department* [2005] 3 WLR 1249.

[133]   Anderson, 11 *EJIL* (2000) 91.

[134]   For an account of the adoption of the Landmines Convention from diverse perspectives see M. Cameron, R. Lawson and B. Tomlin (eds), *To Walk Without Fear: The Global Movement to Ban Landmines* (Canada, 1998).

Canada to put its weight and financial resources behind the project was significant. An important planning meeting was held in Ottawa in 1996 at which Canada committed to hold a treaty-signing meeting a year later. This put pressure on those involved to maintain the momentum in order to have a treaty to sign. After the 1996 Ottawa meeting a draft text was produced by Austria and another text was offered by the ICBL. Although amendments were made through various expert and diplomatic meetings, the short time span limited negotiations and opportunities for weakening the text. The GA added its weight to a speedy process through urging states 'to pursue vigorously an effective, legally binding international agreement to ban the use, stockpiling, production and transfer of anti-personnel landmines with a view to completing the negotiation as soon as possible'.[135]

The ICBL made careful and extensive preparations for the 1997 diplomatic conference in Oslo. These included logistics (locating its own office and meeting rooms directly opposite the negotiation room, thereby ensuring regular informal contact with government delegates), generating publicity, producing brief but pointed (and memorable) slogans, preparing for briefings and press conferences, and looking ahead to strategies for the post-Oslo phase. The ICBL had observer status at Oslo under the Conference Rules of Procedure allowing representatives to be present at all sessions, including smaller working group sessions, and to make oral interventions. Coalition representatives were not able to make formal drafting proposals but could (and did) informally circulate their preferred texts.

The role of NGOs in the achievement of the Landmines Convention is spelled out in its preamble:

Stressing the role of public conscience in furthering the principles of humanity as evidenced by the call for a total ban of anti-personnel mines and recognizing the efforts to that end undertaken by the International Red Cross and Red Crescent Movement, the International Campaign to Ban Landmines and numerous other non-governmental organizations around the world . . .

The 'fast-track' negotiation of the treaty can be contrasted with the slow negotiation process of, for example, the 1982 UNCLOS.[136] It can be attributed to a number of factors. First was the strength and simplicity of the humanitarian message backed by data about the numbers and devastating effects of landmines.[137] Second was formation of the powerful and broad-based NGO coalition and the mobilisation of public opinion. Third was the determination to move away from the traditional diplomatic negotiating process associated with disarmament

---

[135] UNGA Res 51/45, 10 December 1996, S (1).   [136] See Chapter 3.

[137] In UNGA Res 51/45, 10 January 1997, it was estimated that there are more than 110 million landmines in more than 60 countries; that an estimated 2 million new landmines are laid each year; and that landmines kill or maim hundreds of mostly innocent and defenceless civilians, especially children, every week, obstruct economic development and reconstruction, inhibit the repatriation of refugees and the return of internally displaced persons, and have other severe consequences for years after emplacement.

treaties, including that engaged in 1996 for the Review Conference of the Convention Prohibiting the Use of Certain Weapons.[138] The Review Conference adopted an amended Protocol II restricting the use of landmines, booby traps and other devices. The adoption of further restrictions on landmine use disappointed those states that considered regulation to be insufficient and were convinced of the necessity of outright prohibition. They became convinced that this objective could not be achieved through the disarmament process and that a new approach was required. This became the Ottawa process. Fourth was the commitment of a small number of like-minded states that came together around this objective before the Oslo conference and their expectation that others would join the process. A coalition of like-minded states echoes NGO coalition-building and, as with NGOs, a state may join such a grouping for any of a number of reasons: that it considers the risks of financial or political fallout to be low; that it is a means of responding to domestic NGO pressure and allows for partnership with civil society groups; that it is a means of resisting US domination in the post-cold war era. Many commentators have seen the negotiation of the Landmines Convention as a genuine partnership between like-minded states, IGOs and NGOs which demonstrated that 'coalitions of NGOs and governments could work together to change international law more quickly and radically than traditional diplomacy'.[139] Fifth was the commitment of Canadian Minister of Foreign Affairs Lloyd Axworthy to the concept of human security of which the Landmines Campaign was one aspect.[140] Sixth was the skilled chairing of the diplomatic conference by South African Ambassador Selebi, including his expressed determination at the outset that the text be finalised within a specified short time frame.

Hard to gauge in terms of law-making is the involvement of high profile celebrity figures. The death of Princess Diana (who had publicly supported a legal ban on landmines) just a couple of weeks before the Oslo Conference in September 1997 heightened media attention on the conference and public awareness of its occurrence. In the words of Jody Williams, this 'increased attention might have made it that much more difficult for governments to seriously consider any changes that would affect the integrity of the mine ban treaty'.[141] While celebrity international law-making is not extolled, publicity can make it hard to ignore well-orchestrated NGO campaigns.

The separateness of the 'Ottawa process' from the UN disarmament processes[142] was deliberate and was represented by the procedural decision to adopt the text by a

---

[138] 1980 Convention on Prohibitions or Restrictions on the Use of Certain Conventional Weapons which May be Deemed to be Excessively Injurious or to Have Indiscriminate Effects.

[139] M. Bleicher, 'The Ottawa Process: Nine Day Wonder or a New Model for Disarmament Negotiations?', 2 *Open Forum* (2000) 69, 73.

[140] L. Axworthy, *Human Security: Safety for People in a Changing World* (Ottawa, 1999).

[141] J. Williams, 'Stopping the Coward's War', at <http://www.peacejam.org/pages/laureates_jody/laureates_jody_Unit1_Ch5_Pt2>.

[142] The Geneva Conference on Disarmament was described by the GA as the 'single multilateral disarmament forum'; Bleicher, 2 *Open Forum* (2000) 69.

two thirds majority if consensus could not be achieved,[143] although in the event no vote was taken. The traditional disarmament negotiating process was perceived as too slow[144] and the quest for unanimity as likely to dilute the text.[145] The Ottawa process also provided a symbolic link with international humanitarian law, underscoring the humanitarian objectives of the treaty rather than the more strategic and militaristic thinking of non-proliferation/disarmament regulation. Indeed the process has been perceived as a return to the style of humanitarian treaty negotiation that had prevailed before UN institutionalisation of multilateral processes: it operated outside the UN disarmament process; it was called for by a single state (the 1899 Hague Conference was called by Tsar Nicholas II and the 1907 Hague Conference was convened by the US and Russia); voting was by two thirds majority; and it was conducted within a short time frame.[146]

4.2.3   The Rome Statute of the International Criminal Court (ICC)

The third case study is the Rome Statute of the ICC. The idea of an international criminal court has been on the international agenda since the 19th century. In 1937 the League of Nations adopted the Convention for the Creation of an International Criminal Court but it failed to receive the requisite ratifications to enter into force. The UN almost immediately took up the idea. The Genocide Convention, 1948, Article 6 refers to 'such international penal tribunal as may have jurisdiction'. The ILC Special Rapporteur presented his first report on the subject in 1950. Cold war rivalries prevented the project from progressing until it was reactivated in the early 1990s when the end of the cold war offered a window of opportunity for its realisation. Non-state actors had been instrumental in keeping the concept alive, for example through ILA committee reports,[147] and public international law scholars, most notably Cherif Bassiouni.[148] It was revitalised in 1989 by the call by some Caribbean states for an international court with jurisdiction over major drug traffickers. Other factors in the early 1990s that stimulated interest were the lack of any international tribunal for the trial of war crimes after the 1991 Gulf War and the creation by SC resolution of the *ad hoc* international war crimes tribunals for Former Yugoslavia (ICTY) and Rwanda (ICTR). The Secretary-General's report prior to the setting up of the ICTY referred to the

---

[143]   Rules of Procedure, APL/CRP2, 1 September 1997, rule 35: 'decisions of the Conference on all matters of substance shall be taken by a two-thirds majority of the representatives present and voting'.

[144]   S. Maslen, *Commentaries on Arms Control Treaties, Volume I, The Convention on the Prohibition of the Use, Stockpiling, Production and Transfer of Anti-Personnel Mines and on their Destruction* (Oxford, 2004) 27.   [145]   Bleicher, 2000 (2) *Open Forum* 69, 72.

[146]   Ibid 74.

[147]   An ILA Committee had concluded in 1926 that a permanent international criminal court was 'highly expedient and practicable'; cited in M. Glasius, 'Expertise in the Cause of Justice: Global Civil Society Influence on the Statute for an International Criminal Court', in M. Glasius, M. Kaldor and H. Anheier (eds), *Global Civil Society 2002* (London, 2003) 137, 139.

[148]   J. Crawford, 'The ILC's Draft Statute for an International Criminal Tribunal', 88 *AJIL* (1994) 140, 141 n. 4.

comments he had received from NGOs on the desirability and feasibility of an *ad hoc* international criminal tribunal in Former Yugoslavia.[149] The *ad hoc* tribunals showed the potential of international trials, but also raised concerns about selective application of the law. Thus, unlike in the case of the Landmines Convention, NGO campaigns with respect to an ICC took place in conjunction with the activities of many other actors.

The initial work of the ILC, the GA, the *ad hoc* Committee and prepcoms is described in Chapter 4. Of relevance here is that when the GA established an *ad hoc* Committee in 1994 in place of convening a diplomatic conference, NGOs committed to accountability for perpetrators through an international criminal process feared this would stall progress, perhaps indefinitely.[150] In response, in February 1995, some 30 NGOs formed a global coalition to work for the establishment of a permanent international criminal court. The convenor of the Coalition[151] has identified three central tenets that were critical to its coordinated work: that unless NGOs pooled their political strengths, expertise and resources an ICC might never happen; that the complexity and technicality of the subject matter would require different NGOs to work on different aspects of the law and procedures; and that states and NGOs would have to be integrally involved throughout the entire process.

As the process moved through the *ad hoc* Committee and preparatory committee meetings, a group of supportive states came to work together in what—as in the case of the Landmines Convention—was known as the 'like-minded' group committed to establishing a strong, effective and independent permanent international criminal court. The NGO Coalition organised itself with a secretariat and officials, developed various working methods that evolved over the different stages (and years) of the process and became politically and diplomatically more sophisticated. Throughout the six prepcoms Coalition activities included NGO-government consultations and expert dialogue; activity to raise awareness of, and garner civil society support for, the ICC; documentation and dissemination of relevant information; meetings with state delegations from both those opposing the Court and from members of the like-minded group; holding meetings for information-giving and lobbying in different regions of the world; and making full use of the internet and electronic communications to pass information and maintain constant contact.

The Coalition membership expanded from its 30 original members to over 800 by 1998. NGO participation at the diplomatic conference in Rome was through observer status for invited NGOs and over 200 were accredited to participate.[152]

---

[149] Report of the S-G pursuant to paragraph 2 of Security Council Resolution 808 (1993), UN Doc S/25704, 3 May 1993, para 14.

[150] For a detailed account of the role of NGOs throughout the drafting of the Rome Statute see Pace and Schense, 'The Role of Non-Governmental Organisations', 105.

[151] William Pace of the World Federalist Movement, which served as the Secretariat of the Coalition.   [152] UN Doc A/CONF 183/INF/3, 5 June 1998.

This meant that the number of NGOs represented was larger than the number of participating states (160) and larger than any single state delegation. In addition some NGO members became state delegates at the prepcoms and at Rome. Despite these large numbers the Coalition largely maintained, and even increased, solidarity between its members, including those from the South. The Coalition Secretariat maintained neutrality as between NGOs and 'worked to identify and expand areas of commonality among its members and encouraged them to develop joint positions and strategies where possible'.[153] For efficient working it created 12 separate teams that each carried out liaison, reporting and documentary functions. NGO activities went beyond the formal activities listed in the Conference Rules of Procedure, rule 63. They included encouraging wide state participation in the process, assisting smaller countries in their preparations, producing expert analyses of various issues within the areas of expertise of particular NGOs, and disseminating information and draft texts. Specialist caucuses formed, for example the Women's Caucus,[154] to ensure focused in-depth attention with respect to issues of special concern and to counter-balance organised opposition as occurred through the alliance between the Vatican and certain Islamic states. The Women's Caucus drew attention to the lack of any provisions on crimes against women in the ILC draft Statute, provided background papers on the importance of the issue and provided texts to remedy the omission.[155] The NGO No Peace Without Justice provided a technical assistance programme to state delegations.[156] Other important steps were the development of good relationships with the UN Secretariat and the prepcom bureau and of common guiding principles with the like-minded states. NGOs also acted as global publicists of the Conference achievements.[157] After the adoption of the Rome Statute the Coalition committed itself to ensuring its entry into force, which occurred on 1 July 2002. NGOs continue to participate in the Assembly of States Parties.[158] The Coalition promotes education and awareness of the ICC; facilitates the effective participation of civil society and NGOs as observers at the Assembly of States Parties, including especially representatives from the South; expands and strengthens the global network of organisations working on the ICC; promotes universal acceptance and ratification of the Rome Statute; and promotes and facilitates technical cooperation to ensure the adoption of strong domestic implementing legislation. Specialist groups also continue their work, for example the

---

[153] Pace and Schense, 'The Role of Non-Governmental Organisations', 125.

[154] Other thematic groups included caucuses on victims, children, peace and a faith-based caucus; Glasius, 'Expertise in the Cause of Justice', 143, 147.

[155] Steains, 'Gender Issues', 360.   [156] Glasius, 'Expertise in the Cause of Justice', 151.

[157] Ibid 128.

[158] Rules of Procedure of the Assembly of States Parties, ICC-ASP/1/3, Rule 93 allows for observer status for NGOs invited to Rome, registered to the Preparatory Commission for the ICC or with ECOSOC consultative status whose activities are relevant to the Court's activities and other NGOs invited by the Assembly.

Women's Caucus disbanded to be replaced by the Women's Initiatives for Gender Justice in The Hague. This group monitors developments at the ICC, acts as a gender watch, lobbies the Court on gender issues and offers training on issues of gender justice to ICC staff.

It cannot be claimed that NGOs legislated the Rome Statute but NGO influence on the process and outcome was considerable. First, many observers and commentators have concluded that without NGO participation the ICC could not have come into existence. The process is seen 'virtually everywhere . . . as the triumph of international civil society in favor of the judicialization of that last fortress of sovereignty, criminal law'.[159] It was 'international lawmaking of historic proportions'.[160] Second, some causes that NGOs especially promoted that had not been in the ILC draft Statute were included in the text adopted in Rome, for example an independent prosecutor with the power to initiate investigation subject to the permission of a pre-trial Chamber.[161] Third, special interest NGOs were instrumental in securing attention to their concerns. For example, the Rome Statute provides for jurisdiction over crimes against women (Articles 7 (1) (g) (h), 8 (b) (xxii), 8 (e) (vi)); a 'fair representation' of women and men on the Court (Article 36 (8) (a) (iii)) and a definition of gender (Article 7 (3)). While these were not all that was sought by the Women's Caucus, there seems little doubt that without its participation throughout the entire process such provisions would not have been secured.[162] Unlike at Rome, NGOs have no formal access to the ILC[163] and it is noticeable that the ILC draft Statute contained no reference to gender-specific matters.

4.2.4   *The UNIDROIT Convention on Mobile Equipment*

The final example is the UNIDROIT Convention on Mobile Equipment (the 'base' Convention).[164] The Convention's objective is the 'efficient financing of mobile equipment'.[165] The Convention and its Protocol on Matters Specific to Aircraft Equipment provide an interesting contrast to the previous case studies in that they concern highly technical areas of private law and lack the popular appeal of torture and landmine prohibition, combating impunity for perpetrators of atrocities, and upholding human rights. Non-state actor input into their drafting and adoption was thus specialist and industry oriented. In addition the base

---

[159] J. Alvarez, 'The New Dispute Settlers: (Half) Truths and Consequences', 38 *Texas ILJ* (2003) 405, 407.

[160] *The Times of India*, Editorial, 1 August 1998, cited Pace and Schense, 'The Role of Non-Governmental Organisations', 106.   [161] Glasius, 'Expertise in the Cause of Justice', 154.

[162] Steains, 'Gender Issues', 357, 360.

[163] Informally it is likely that members are subject to their influence, for example through academia.

[164] Convention on International Interests in Mobile Equipment, Cape Town, 2001; Iwan Davies, 'The New *Lex Mercatoria*: International Interests in Mobile Equipment', 52 *ICLQ* (2003) 151.

[165] R. Goode, *Convention on International Interests in Mobile Equipment and Protocol Thereto on Matters Specific to Aircraft Equipment Official Commentary* (Rome, 2002) 5. This account draws heavily on this work.

Convention and the Aircraft Protocol were developed in close collaboration with two international organisations: UNIDROIT[166] and the International Civil Aviation Organisation (ICAO).

In response to a proposal from the Government of Canada, UNIDROIT set up a Restricted Exploratory Working Group to examine the need for, and feasibility of, uniform rules on security interests in cross-border transactions.[167] This was followed by a Study Group, a sub-committee of which prepared the first draft text. Three aspects of this treaty-making process are especially worthy of note. First, the work was from the outset strongly influenced by the expertise and commitment of the Chairman of the Study Group, Professor Roy Goode. Second, there was early interest in the proposal from the aviation industry leading to the development of an Aircraft Protocol alongside the Convention. Input into this Protocol (and thus the Convention) was directed through an Aviation Working Group comprising aerospace manufacturers and financial institutions. This group was set up by the expert consultant to the UNIDROIT Study Group, Jeffrey Wool, and collaborated with the International Air Transport Association (IATA). The Aviation Working Group, IATA and representatives from the ICAO worked together on the Aircraft Protocol. Third, the drafting of the Aircraft Protocol alongside the base Convention meant that that industry had greater input than other industries into the structure and substance of the base Convention. This raised the important question of how the legal framework could be adapted to other categories of mobile equipment. A unique and innovative relationship was devised whereby the base Convention on its own has no practical effect. The Convention takes effect with respect to each particular protocol (including future protocols such as for railway stock and space assets), which will modify and supplement the Convention to make it relevant in the context of financing the specific class of equipment to which the particular protocol relates. This ground-breaking solution facilitates the inclusion of new sectors within an umbrella of general principles, provides flexibility and demonstrates the benefits of bringing a problem-solving, international commercial law approach to treaty-making.

The texts went through a lengthy process and were scrutinised by a range of bodies. A Steering and Revisions Committee established by the UNIDROIT Governing Council worked on the draft texts before their transmission to governments; Joint Sessions of a UNIDROIT Committee of Governmental Experts and the Legal Sub-Committee of the ICAO Legal Committee continued the process; three specialist working groups on public international law, insolvency and registration also contributed. These various groups comprised sectoral, government, academic and institutional experts. The UK Department of Trade and Industry issued a Consultation Document. The texts were also considered by the ICAO Legal Committee and approved by the UNIDROIT Governing Council before their adoption by consensus at a diplomatic conference in Cape Town 2001. The

---

[166] See Chapter 3.   [167] Goode, *Convention on International Interests*, 3.

preparation of a detailed Commentary[168] providing an overview and article by article analysis of the Convention and Aircraft Protocol by Professor Goode is a final important step in the process. This drafting process shows well how a range of different experts can work under the auspices of specialist IGOs to develop law in a particularly complex and technical area.

4.2.5   The MAI

NGOs have also prevented treaty-making. A notorious example is that of the MAI that was being negotiated within the Organisation for Economic Cooperation and Development (OECD) in the mid-1990s. Concern was expressed about the proposed treaty when it was leaked in 1997.[169] A coalition of NGOs and consumer groups reacted strongly to what they saw as secret negotiations over a treaty to protect the rights of foreign investors and restrict the ability of governments to legislate in the public interest, for example with respect to the environment and labour rights. The MAI became the focus of anti-globalisation and anti-multinational corporate activity. A global campaign was waged against it, primarily through the internet. Different reasons have been put forward for the success of NGOs in their confrontation with the business community and the OECD negotiators. First, the OECD discounted likely NGO opinion and omitted to put an appropriate 'NGO strategy' in place. It laid itself open to allegations of lack of transparency and pursuing 'a conspiracy against democracy and civil society'.[170] Second, was the influence of committed individuals who took it upon themselves to provide information, offer analysis and forceful explanations. Third, was the crucial role of the internet in coordinating global activities. Unlike other campaigns there was no formal NGO secretariat but instead the formation of ever-growing networks through e-mail distribution lists between known activists and others. NGOs directed their campaigns at citizens (raising awareness, education on the issues and framing arguments) and at governments (through similar strategies). NGO activity has been described as follows:

Hundreds of advocacy groups, attempting to galvanize opposition to the MAI, used terms and examples that brought their message home to the public. Their sites on the World Wide Web were colorful and easy to use, offering primers on the MAI that anyone could understand.[171]

By the time the OECD negotiators accepted the need for consultation with NGOs the atmosphere had become too confrontational for cooperation.

---

[168] A treaty commentary assists states in identifying required domestic legislation and facilitates uniform interpretation. It thus also contributes to acceptance of a treaty as customary international law, for example J. Pictet (ed.), *The Geneva Conventions of 12 August 1949: Commentary* (Geneva, 1952–60).

[169] K. Tieleman, 'The Failure of the Multilateral Agreement on Investment (MAI) and the Absence of a Global Public Policy Network', UN Vision Project on Global Public Policy Networks, available at <http://www.globalpublicpolicy.net/>.   [170] Ibid.

[171] Gamble and Ku, 31 *Law and Policy in International Business* (2000), 221, 256.

Eventually the negotiations were abandoned in December 1998, although there have been suggestions of its resurrection through the WTO, or elsewhere. The failure of the MAI is seen as a success for concerted NGO action against the power of organised business. 'This experience represents one of the fastest, most resounding defeats for a treaty—a defeat attributable to the efforts of NGOs.'[172] However, frustrating the adoption of a multilateral treaty was to some extent a pyrrhic victory; the network of hundreds of bilateral investment treaties (BITs) through which international investment is now regulated have achieved some law-making effect that might not be so different from what was anticipated for the MAI.[173]

5. NGOs and Institutional Law-Making

5.1 The General Assembly

Non-governmental bodies have not confined their input to international law-making to treaty-making processes. They have also sought to influence institutional processes, including those of the UN. NGOs are increasingly becoming involved in the deliberations of the GA and its committees 'informally through round-table meetings and panel discussions, and formally, through invitations to the special sessions and conferences convened under its auspices, and more recently, through the biennial high-level dialogue'.[174] Although GA resolutions are not formally binding, the adoption of a resolution may be an early step towards the eventual conclusion of a treaty, may represent state *opinio juris*, generate practice, or have effect as soft law.[175] Accordingly in many instances NGOs lobby for a GA resolution on a particular topic and seek to participate in its drafting and adoption in the same ways as in treaty-making. Special interest NGOs seeking to develop international law in accordance with their own agendas may make a strategic determination that a formally non-binding General Assembly resolution is more achievable—at least in the short term—than a treaty and campaign accordingly. Success in this objective may be a step towards the eventual negotiation of a treaty.[176]

The expertise of non-governmental bodies may be utilised to assist in developing international law through UN processes. For example in 1999 and 2000 UN

---

[172] Ibid 255.

[173] A growing body of jurisprudence is developing through arbitrations, eg under the International Centre for the Settlement of Investment Disputes and North American Free Trade Area Dispute Settlement Procedures. However the language of BITs varies and arbitral awards turn on the particular language of the instrument in question.

[174] Report of the S-G in Response to the Report of the Panel of Eminent Persons on United Nations–Civil Society Relations, UN Doc A/59/354, para 9.   [175] See Chapter 5.

[176] eg the Torture Convention was preceded by UNGA resolutions against torture, as discussed above.

Secretary-General, Kofi Annan, appealed to member states to seek a consensus around the legality of humanitarian intervention. In response the Canadian government set up the International Commission on Intervention and State Sovereignty (ICISS) to draft proposals. Although it received some funding and other assistance from the Canadian government, the ICISS was not a Canadian state body. Its members (from 11 countries) were drawn from NGOs, academia, IGOs and current or former politicians. It is perhaps best described as a *sui generis* non-state expert body. In its Report the Commission deliberately moved away from the language of intervention and introduced the concept of the Responsibility to Protect.[177] The language was picked up and used by the Secretary-General in his Report, *In Larger Freedom*.[178] It is spelled out as a commitment by the GA in its Outcome Document, 2005.[179] While the parameters of any change in law must depend upon further elaboration and relevant state practice, the seed of possible legal change can be seen in the reasoning and language of the ICISS as taken up by the GA.

5.2   The Security Council

In contrast to other UN bodies and global conferences, the SC has remained largely aloof from NGO demands for access. Its key role within the global collective security system has ensured its state-centred focus. Accordingly, longstanding practice restricted speaking at SC meetings and consultations to official delegations, government officials of Council members and UN officials. Nevertheless there has been some consideration of the potential benefits of having a wider discursive base. This has to some extent been achieved by the adoption of the so-called Arria formula that was devised in 1993. The Arria formula allows an SC member to invite other members to an informal meeting chaired by the inviting member. The meeting is held outside the SC Chamber and is usually convened to enable SC members to be briefed by experts on some matter of concern to the Council. Such meetings are scheduled so as not to clash with the SC's formal business and are typically well-attended by Council members. There has been more frequent recourse to the process.[180] Use of the Arria formula allows NGOs to give the SC information on particular issues or in specific crises. SC Resolution 1325 on Women and Peace and Security[181] is

---

[177] Report of the International Commission on Intervention and State Sovereignty, *The Responsibility to Protect* (Ottawa, 2001).   [178] *In Larger Freedom*, para 132.
[179] UNGA Res 60/1, 24 October 2005, paras 138–9. In particular the responsibility to protect is envisaged as extending beyond the requirements of the Genocide Convention to other large-scale loss of life.
[180] Report of the S-G in Response to the Report of the Panel of Eminent Persons on United Nations–Civil Society Relations, UN Doc A/59/354, para 13.
[181] SC Res 1325, 31 October 2000.

an example of a resolution adopted through NGO influence and by means of this process.

In 1999 International Alert (a London-based NGO) commenced discussions about women in conflict with what it identified as appropriate SC members. At the annual session of the UN Commission on the Status of Women in March 2000 an NGO caucus on Women, Conflict and Peacebuilding was formed. This was followed by the establishment in August 2000 of an NGO Working Group on Women and International Peace and Security, comprising International Alert, AI, the Women's International League for Peace and Freedom, the Women's Commission on Refugee Women and Children, and the 1999 Hague Appeal for Peace. The Working Group performed many tasks: it identified key organisations and individuals with expertise in women and peace building; shared concerns 'in ensuring that women's peace and security are recognized by the international community';[182] entered into bilateral discussions; and presented information, data, recommendations and a draft resolution to SC members. Throughout September 2000 the Working Group sought to build consensus through meetings with policy-makers worldwide and liaison with key UN bodies such as the Department of Peacekeeping Operations and the Division for the Advancement of Women. NGOs cannot place matters on the SC agenda, so the support of a member state in this regard is essential. The government of Namibia agreed to place the item on the SC agenda under its presidency.

On 23 October the SC held an Arria formula meeting where representatives of women's NGOs met SC members. The joint NGO Working Group statement was presented and the next day the SC held an official Open Debate where the views of other UN member states were expressed. Namibia presented a draft resolution which was circulated among SC members for amendments and comments. On 31 October this campaign resulted in the unanimous adoption of Resolution 1325. Although this is an example of how NGOs can induce the adoption of a SC resolution, it is not a UN Charter Chapter VII resolution and is not worded in mandatory language. Its legislative effect is thus limited and it has not generated uniform and consistent practice with respect to the inclusion of women in peace processes and post-conflict reconstruction.

The Panel of Eminent Persons on United Nations–Civil Society Relations noted that informal consultations between the SC and NGOs are oriented towards Northern-based—and especially US—human rights and humanitarian NGOs. It recommended improving the planning and effectiveness of Arria formula meetings, including covering travelling costs to bring representatives 'from the field'.[183]

---

[182] International Alert, 'Women Building Peace from the Village Council to the Negotiating Table', No. 4, October-December 2000, 3.

[183] Panel of Eminent Persons on United Nations–Civil Society Relations, UN Doc A/58/817, 2004, paras 95–100.

5.3   Global Summit Meetings

Global summit meetings organised under the auspices of the UN constitute another arena for highly visible NGO activity. High profile global meetings have sought to enhance international cooperation through soft law instruments, as described in Chapter 5, on a range of social, economic and development issues, for example the Rio Conference on the Environment, 1992, the Vienna Conference on Human Rights, 1993, the Cairo Conference on Population and Development, 1994, the Copenhagen Conference on Social Development, 1995 and the Beijing Fourth World Conference on Women, 1995, as well as the five- and ten-year follow-up meetings to these Conferences. The Millennium Summit was in some ways a culmination of these meetings.

States are the formal participants at UN global conferences and are accordingly the key players in agreeing the declarations and agendas for action typically adopted. However global summit meetings also create a space that NGOs have been able to exploit within both the parallel NGO fora and through their presence at the official conferences. NGOs have followed similar strategies to those described for treaty-making processes and have imbued the negotiation of volu-minous but formally non-binding texts with considerable significance.[184] A num-ber of the final documents have explicitly provided for future consultative and advisory roles for NGOs,[185] thus ensuring their continued participation.

Global conferences have been an important way of seeking consensus around change in expectations of international behaviour. The complex and interlocking agendas of these conferences have made a holistic treaty an unrealistic prospect. For example at Beijing there were 12 critical areas of concern: poverty; education and training; access to health care and related services; violence against women; women in armed conflict; inequality in economic structures and policies; power sharing and decision-making; insufficient mechanisms to promote women's advancement; human rights of women; women and the media; natural resources and the environ-ment; and the girl child. Each area required analysis of the current position, identi-fication of obstacles, formulation of positions and the devising of strategies targeted at governments, IGOs and NGOs. Controversies abounded. What was needed was not formalistic legal language but practical and feasible programmes of action and allocation of tasks. In the words of the UN Secretary-General:

The United Nations conferences of the 1990s were sometimes marked by discord, but they have played a central role in forging normative consensus and spelling out practical solu-tions on the great issues of the day. Nowhere else has it been possible for the international

---

[184] C. Tomuschat, 'The Concluding Documents of World Conferences', in J. Makarczyk (ed), *Theory of International Law at the Threshold of the 21st Century: Essays in Honour of Krzysztof Skubiszewski* (The Hague, 1996) 563.
[185] eg Vienna Declaration and Programme of Action, I para 38; Beijing Platform for Action, UN Doc A/CONF 177/20, 15 September 1995, para 344.

community as a whole to sketch out responses to the dawning challenge of globalization on which all, or almost all, could agree.[186]

As one commentator has concluded: 'Low legal profile was the price to be paid for the tremendous reach of these documents.'[187] A further price for agreement was the lack of high cost commitments such as allocation of resources, the setting of performance targets and compliance dates. Although these were to some extent addressed in the Millennium Summit with the adoption of the Millennium Development Goals, these too were not in legally binding treaty form.[188]

6.   NGO Monitoring and Norm Generation

The adoption of a treaty or soft law instrument may be celebrated by NGOs as a significant victory. However, NGO activity does not stop at standard setting but continues through encouraging states to become parties[189] and subsequently insisting on state accountability for failure to comply with its obligations. NGOs remind states of their commitments and through 'naming and shaming' for non-compliance seek to promote the internalisation of international law norms so that they become part of the internal map of state decision-making.[190] This in turn builds up consistent state practice, thereby strengthening such norms and ensuring the durability of the earlier formal law-making process.

NGOs participate in treaty monitoring and verification processes. One example is the mobilisation of national NGOs around the state reporting requirements under the UN human rights treaties that are discussed in Chapter 3. Although only the Children's Convention provides formally for NGO participation in the state reporting process,[191] this has become an increasingly important site for intervention across all the human rights treaty bodies. Since sessions are held in public, NGO representatives can attend and meet with members of the relevant committee. Committees also receive information from NGOs, including through so-called 'shadow' reports. International NGOs alert local contacts to the state reporting schedules, offer training in reporting to local bodies and supply information to the respective committees. The treaty bodies have responded favourably by providing greater opportunity for NGO participation at their meetings. The annual meeting of chairpersons of the

---

[186] '*We the Peoples*', Millennium Report of the S-G of the United Nations, para 322.
[187] Tomuschat, 'The Concluding Documents of World Conferences', 565.
[188] See Chapter 1.
[189] eg in Japan, 17 NGOs launched an appeal on the 25th anniversary of the Universal Declaration of Human Rights to persuade the government to ratify human rights treaties. They continued this action in 1974, 1976 and 1977. Other national and international NGOs lobbied the government, attempting to embarrass it in comparison with the ratification record of other countries; A. Gurowitz, 'International Law, Politics and Migrant Rights', in C. Reus-Smit (ed), *The Politics of International Law* (Cambridge, 2004) 131, 139.
[190] H. Koh, 'Why Do Nations Obey International Law?', 106 *Yale LJ* (1996–7) 2599.
[191] Convention on the Rights of the Child, Article 45.

treaty bodies also holds informal consultations with NGOs. Proposals for reform of the treaty bodies have taken account of NGO participation.[192]

NGO verification is not limited to human rights treaties. Monitoring compliance with environmental standards goes back to at least 1984 when the GA expressed its appreciation of NGO cooperation in compiling a list of products banned because of their harmful effects on health or the environment and urged their continued activity in this regard, in effect monitoring adherence to international standards.[193] NGOs and IGOs may work in conjunction with each other in such tasks. In 1988 the World Conservation Monitoring Centre was founded jointly by the World Wildlife Fund, IUCN and the United Nations Environmental Program (UNEP). Since 2000 it has become integral to UNEP. Its function is to assess and monitor information on conservation and biodiversity for the secretariats of the major treaties. The ICBL has established a network to monitor states' obligation to report annually under the Landmines Convention, Article 7. This global reporting network—a civil society verification system—provides coordinated and systematic monitoring of compliance with the Convention and disseminates information through annual reports, fact sheets and independently produced country reports.

NGOs have drawn little distinction between legally binding and non-binding instruments. They have accordingly pursued follow-up strategies to the latter, for example seeking compliance with the final instruments of global summit meetings not just in states but within and across other local and global communities. In some instances NGOs have a mandate for such action. For example the recommended strategies for action adopted at the Beijing World Conference on Women were directed at NGOs as well as at states and IGOs. NGOs uphold the proposition that 'if a government makes a formal statement, it must be held to comply with its own words'.[194] Subsequent activity has centred upon what has been called the 'translation'[195] of conference statements into concrete projects for change in social practice at the local level in anticipation of, and in conjunction with, similar local actions elsewhere. Such 'interpretative communities' may give meaning to and incorporate international instruments into their own local regimes through a mix of their own narratives,[196] experiences, values, visions and dreams. Legal academics or practitioners (publicists in the old sense) may offer plausible (or implausible) interpretations of the instruments that they advocate should be adopted in states' policy and practice, in a sense acting as intermediaries between activists and states.

---

[192] eg Report of a Meeting on Reform of the Human Rights Treaty Body System (Malbun, Liechtenstein, 4–7 May 2003), UN Doc A/58/123, 8 July 2003, para 3; Concept Paper on the High Commissioner's Proposal for a Unified Standing Treaty Body, UN Doc HRI/MC/2006/2, 22 March 2006, para 29.

[193] UNGA Res 39/229, 18 December 1984; R. Geiss, 'Non-State Actors: Their Role and Impact on the Fragmentation of International Law', in Zimmermann and Hoffmann, *Unity and Diversity in International Law*, 303, 310.

[194] Tomuschat, 'The Concluding Documents of World Conferences', 568.

[195] S. Ratner, 'Does International Law Matter in Preventing Ethnic Conflict?', 32 *NYU JILP* (2000) 591, 623.   [196] Mertus, 32 *NYU JILP* (2000), 537, 540.

The global processes have been re-engaged through the five- and ten-year anniversary meetings. For example, in preparation for Beijing +5, the UN Commission on the Status of Women devised a questionnaire requiring states to indicate the progress made in fulfilling their commitments under the Beijing Platform for Action. This engendered further action from states such as domestic legislation on violence against women or changes in policing in conformity with the Platform. As we discuss more fully in Chapter 5, such interactive processes are potentially law-making insofar as they generate state practice as a basis for customary international law, help establish general principles of law, or constitute evidence for the interpretation and application of existing norms and principles. Vaughan Lowe has described a diffuse process of international law-making through the fleshing out of crucial policy concepts that are based neither in state practice nor treaty provisions, but which emerge through exposition, exchanges, policy reports, scientific and social investigations.[197] Lowe sees the generation of such 'interstitial norms' as the 'dominant mode of change in international law within the next two or three decades'.[198] The post-conference interactions between non-governmental 'interpretive communities', IGOs and state agencies are precisely a way of generating such exchanges and evolving interstitial norms.

These various complex interactions collapse the binary perception of states as international law-makers and other actors merely as claimants under those laws. Non-state entities are recognised as constituting both subjects and objects of international law. They illustrate Teubner's understanding of global law as norms produced in 'self-organized processes of structural coupling of law with ongoing globalised processes of a highly specialized and technical nature'.[199]

7. Advocacy

7.1 Litigation Strategies

Another NGO strategy is seeking to ensure the application of international law through litigation. In Chapter 6 we discuss how judicial pronouncements from authoritative tribunals can crystalise customary international law and thus promote the development of international law in accordance with the Statute of the ICJ, Article 38 (1) (d). This strategy is deliberately (and sometimes aggressively) pursued through advocacy[200] in contentious cases before national, regional and international judicial bodies.

NGOs seek out test cases to bring before appropriate tribunals. Individuals appearing before international and regional courts or tribunals (in particular the

---

[197] A. V. Lowe, 'The Politics of Law-Making: Are the Method and Character of Norm Creation Changing?', in Michael Byers (ed), *The Role of Law in International Politics* (Oxford, 2000) 207, 212.
[198] Ibid 219.   [199] G. Teubner (ed), *Global Law without a State* (Aldershot, 1997) 8.
[200] The Beijing Platform for Action, para 228 recognised the catalytic role played by NGOs, women's groups and feminist activists in the promotion of women's human rights, including by networking and advocacy.

regional human rights bodies) may be assisted by NGOs, or NGOs may appear in their own right.[201] Other non-state actors are given standing before international bodies, for example NAFTA Chapter 11, ICSID, Article 36 and the Statute of the International Tribunal for the Law of the Sea, Article 20. By initiating claims within the terms of these various treaties, non-state actors are able to ensure that international legal arguments have been presented in their terms and states forced to respond, rather than the other way round.

NGOs have also participated as third parties before international judicial bodies, for example through the submission of *amicus curiae* briefs or interventions. The proliferation of international courts described in Chapter 6 means that there are more judicial fora open to NGO participation. The ICJ has remained largely closed to NGOs,[202] but other courts have allowed NGOs to raise issues or arguments not presented by the parties,[203] for example the European[204] and American Human Rights Courts. [205] The indeterminate and imprecise language of human rights treaties has allowed innovative arguments that have led to far-reaching reconceptualisation of substantive provisions. For example *Velasquez Rodriguez v. Honduras*[206] is widely considered a landmark decision with respect to the recognition of disappearances as a human rights violation, state responsibility for omission, and for the assertion of a state's positive duty to exercise due diligence to respect and ensure the right to life. A cluster of NGOs—AI, the Association of the Bar of the City of New York, the Lawyers Committee for Human Rights and the Minnesota Lawyers International Human Rights Committee—all made submissions to the American Court of Human Rights. The extended understanding of state responsibility expounded by the American Court has been picked up and incorporated in other contexts as discussed in Chapter 6. This has been a reiterative and mutually reinforcing process between NGOs, adjudicative bodies,

---

[201] The Protocol to the African Charter on Human and Peoples' Rights on the Establishment of an African Court of Human and Peoples' Rights, 1998, Article 5 (3) allows NGOs with observer status before the Commission to institute cases before it.

[202] On the ICJ and NGOs see C. Chinkin, *Third Parties in International Law* (Oxford, 1993) 226–37. There have been some inroads into the ICJ's advisory jurisdiction. ICJ Practice Direction XII, 2004, states that NGO submissions in an advisory opinion do not form part of the case file. They are however 'publications readily available' and may be used by states and IGOs in their statements. Statements and documents submitted by NGOs are placed in a designated location and states and IGOs making statements under the Statute of the ICJ, Article 66 will be so informed.

[203] On the importance of *amicus curiae* briefs before international courts and tribunals see C. Chinkin and R. Mackenzie, 'Intergovernmental Organizations as "Friends of the Court"', in L. Boisson de Chazournes, C. Romano and R. Mackenzie (eds), *International Organizations and International Dispute Settlement: Trends and Prospects* (Ardsley, 2002) 135, 136–9.

[204] 1950 European Convention for the Protection of Human Rights and Fundamental Freedoms, as amended by Protocol 11, Article 36 (2). Sometimes the European Court refers extensively to an NGO intervention, eg *MC v. Bulgaria* (Application no. 39272/98), judgment of 4 December 2003 cited sections of a brief submitted by Interights.

[205] There is no provision in the American Convention on Human Rights permitting this but the Court has received NGO submissions from the outset; Chinkin, *Third Parties*, 242–4.

[206] *Velsaquez Rodriguez v. Honduras* (1988) IACHR OAS/SerL/V/III.19, doc 13.

UN human rights treaty bodies, the GA and expert working groups. It has clarified the legal standard of state obligation and evolved new processes of accountability. In the particular context of the movement against violence against women, the first special rapporteur on violence against women has called it:

Perhaps the greatest success story of international mobilization around a specific human rights issue, leading to the articulation of international norms and standards and the formulation of international programmes and policies.[207]

NGOs act as non-party advocates before other courts.[208] The *ad hoc* international criminal courts have had a particular law-making role in that they have had to mould a workable international criminal law primarily from the minimalist provisions in their Statutes and dated precedents from the World War II war crimes trials. When faced with novel issues of substance and procedure, they have on occasion sought assistance from NGOs and academics. For example in *Blaskic* the ICTY had to determine whether it could issue a *subpoena* to Croatia and Croatian officials. Judge Kirk McDonald made an order inviting requests for leave to submit *amicus* briefs on the power of the Tribunal to issue a *subpoena* to a sovereign state, to a high government official of a state and remedies for non-compliance with such a *subpoena*.[209] A range of individuals and NGO representatives responded and submitted *amicus* briefs on these issues.[210]

National courts are also relevant to international law-making.[211] NGOs such as AI have collected and collated evidence of human rights violations against the possibility of its use in legal proceedings.[212] NGOs commence or intervene in litigation involving issues of international law. Inevitably the regularity and success of this strategy depends upon whether national law allows for such processes and whether there is a culture of NGO legal activism. NGOs have been most active in

---

[207] R. Coomaraswamy, 'The Varied Contours of Violence against Women in South Asia', paper presented to Fifth South Asia Regional Ministerial Conference, Celebrating Beijing +10, Pakistan, May 2005, 2.

[208] On the controversy with respect to NGO submissions to the WTO Panels and Appellate Body that have not been requested, see Chinkin and Mackenzie, 'International Organizations' 135, 149–53.

[209] *Prosecutor v. Tihomir Blaskic*, (IT-95–14) Order Submitting the Matter to Trial Chamber II and Inviting *amicus curiae*, 14 March 1997.

[210] Judge Lal Chand Vohrah, 'Pre-trial Procedures and Practices', in G. K. McDonald and O. Swaak-Goldman (eds), *Substantive and Procedural Aspects of International Criminal Law*, vol 1 (The Hague, 2000) 481, 526.

[211] Former President of the ICJ Jennings notes the importance of reporting of decisions of municipal courts that contain questions of international law; R. Jennings, 'The Judiciary, International and National and the Development of International Law', 45 *ICLQ* (1996) 1.

[212] This became public knowledge when a Spanish magistrate requested an arrest warrant against Former President of Chile Senator Pinochet during the latter's visit to London in October 1998. In the subsequent litigation AI, the Medical Foundation for the Care of Victims of Torture, the Redress Trust and the Association of the Relatives of the Disappeared Detainees intervened. AI was exceptionally given leave to make oral submissions and Human Rights Watch made a written submission; *R v. Bow Street Metropolitan Stipendiary Magistrate, ex parte Pinochet Ugarte (No. 3)* [1999] 2 WLR 827.

this respect in the US. The Alien Torts Claims Act, 1789 has been used in numerous cases to bring the human rights violations of a range of actors, including military generals and corporations, before the courts. Summary proceedings in the absence of the defendant allow victims to present their claims, place their accounts on the record and secure a ruling from the bench. Bodies such as the Center for Constitutional Rights, Washington DC and the Center for Justice and Accountability, San Francisco (an anti-impunity organisation established by AI in 1998), assisted by human rights law clinics such as those at the Yale Law School and the City University of New York, have researched and presented arguments in a number of such cases. This litigation for transnational civil responsibility has been criticised as being so intertwined with the US judicial system that it appears a 'unilateralist imposition of US interests'.[213] Nevertheless it has allowed judicial statements as to the customary international law status of such crimes as the prohibition of torture[214] and rape as a war crime or an act of genocide[215] and in developing a non-coercive form of intervention in response to human rights abuses. This judicial activity has contributed to the international pressure for accountability for human rights abuses that has seen the establishment of the international criminal tribunals and growing state practice relating to the exercise of universal jurisdiction. However the activity of US courts in this regard may be lessened after the Supreme Court narrowed the scope of Alien Torts Claims litigation in *Sosa v. Alvarez-Machain.*[216]

In the particular context of individual criminal responsibility for international crimes NGOs have used international argument across a number of fronts: preparing for and intervening in national and international litigation; campaigning for the detention of alleged perpetrators and subsequently for the exercise of universal jurisdiction within national courts; campaigning first for the *ad hoc* international criminal tribunals and for an ICC; and adding to the subsequent commentary. It is perhaps significant that a decision upholding the immunity of a government official against allegations of crimes against humanity was made by the ICJ[217] where NGOs have been unable to secure participatory rights.

However use of national courts may be a somewhat high risk strategy: there is no guarantee that a national court will be receptive to NGO arguments of international law, or that the decision will support the hoped-for view. The assessment must be made that raising the profile of the particular issue is worthwhile even in the face of a disappointing decision. It must also be remembered that the decisions of national courts do not, of themselves, constitute customary international law and that national judges may (rightly) be cautious in pronouncing rules of international law. In *Jones v. Ministry of the Interior* the Redress Trust, AI, Interights and Justice

---

[213] B. Kingsbury, 'The International Legal Order', in P. Cane and M. Tushnet, *The Oxford Handbook of Legal Studies* (Oxford, 2003) 272, 278.

[214] *Filartiga v. Peña-Irala* 630 F 2d 876 (US CA, 2nd Circ).

[215] *Kadic v. Karadžić* 70 F 3d 232 (2nd Circ).

[216] 124 S Ct 2739, 29 June 2004. See B. Roth, 98 *AJIL* (2004) 798 for analysis of the case.

[217] *Case Concerning the Arrest Warrant* (*Democratic Republic of the Congo v. Belgium*) 2002 ICJ Reports 3 (Judgment of 14 February).

intervened in the House of Lords arguing for an exception to state immunity in cases of civil claims against torture. In rejecting such a rule of international law Lord Hoffmann stated:

. . . the ordering of competing principles according to the importance of the values which they embody is a basic technique of adjudication. But the same approach cannot be adopted in international law, which is based upon the common consent of nations. It is not for a national court to 'develop' international law by unilaterally adopting a version of that law which, however desirable, forward-looking and reflective of values it may be, is simply not accepted by other states.[218]

Whatever the outcome, national judicial decisions must not be given excessive weight as evidence of customary international law. Nevertheless a positive decision contributes to state practice[219] and thus to evolving or crystalising a rule of customary international law. Former ICJ President Judge Jennings has noted the view that domestic courts may contribute to the transformation of law-making treaties into customary international law through their application in non-party states.[220] National judicial decisions are subsidiary sources of international law under ICJ Statute, Article 38 (1) (d) and should be considered alongside other jurisprudence, as discussed in Chapter 6.

7.2 NGO Innovations

Where international procedures have not existed NGOs have sought their introduction. For example women's NGOs were to the forefront of an effective advocacy campaign for the adoption of an individual complaints mechanism for the Convention on the Elimination of All Forms of Discrimination against Women, 1979 and NGOs were active in seeking the establishment of an African Court of Human Rights. The former campaign was conducted through the Vienna[221] and Beijing[222] global summit meetings to gain support for the proposal. Practical steps were taken through the preparation of a draft text by NGO representatives and academics for presentation to the appropriate bodies—the Commission on the Status of Women and the Committee on the Elimination of Discrimination against Women.[223] It reached fruition through the adoption by the GA of the Optional Protocol to CEDAW which provides for both individual complaints and an inquiry

---

[218] *Jones v. Ministry of the Interior* [2006] UKHL 26; [2006] 2 WLR 1424, para 63 per Lord Hoffmann.

[219] In the *Arrest Warrant Case* the ICJ stated that it had 'carefully examined State practice, including national legislation and those few decisions of national higher courts, such as the House of Lords or the French Court of Cassation'. *Arrest Warrant Case*, para 58.

[220] R. Jennings, 'The Judiciary, International and National and the Development of International Law', 45 *ICLQ* (1996) 1, 2 citing K. Zemanek, in *Festschrift für Rudolf Bernhardt* (1995), 289, 294.

[221] 1993 Vienna Declaration and Programme of Action, II, para 40.

[222] Beijing, Platform for Action, para 230 (l).

[223] A. Byrnes and J. Connors, 'Enforcing the Human Rights of Women: A Complaints Procedure for the Women's Convention?', 21 *Brooklyn JIL* (1996) 679, 692.

procedure.[224] Two NGOs, Equality Now and Casa Amiga, initiated the first inquiry procedure under the Optional Protocol by submitting 'reliable information indicating grave or systematic violations' by Mexico with respect to the large number of murdered and disappeared women in the Ciudad Juarez area of Mexico. The inquiry and report[225] allowed the Committee to set out more fully its understanding of violence against women as a human rights violation than was possible in its General Recommendation on the subject.[226] Establishing and using a complaints mechanism is a law-making strategy through both providing a forum for authoritative articulation of the legal principles and fostering consistent state practice.

Where NGOs are denied access to an international institution they have sought ways around the limitation. For example, NGOs have circumvented their lack of access to the contentious jurisdiction of the ICJ by turning to its advisory jurisdiction as in the requests by the World Health Organisation[227] and the GA[228] with respect to the legality of nuclear weapons. These requests were motivated by the World Court Project, an NGO initiative.[229] The Court exercised its discretion to respond to the GA request, despite the argument that it should not do so, because NGO involvement had rendered the questions political and that the unorthodox origin of the request had tainted the process.[230] Indeed NGOs may indirectly participate in the contentious jurisdiction of the Court. In the 1995 *Nuclear Tests Cases* some South Pacific states had assistance from environmental NGOs in preparing their request to intervene under the Statute of the ICJ, Article 62 and declaration of intervention under Article 63. Although the contentious case was dismissed, these examples show that NGOs can access state-controlled arenas through the instrumentality of states. They can contribute to judicial proceedings, directly through 'invoking court procedures or appearing before courts, or indirect[ly], in making information or arguments available in cooperation with states'.[231]

8.   Autonomous NGO Activity

Where NGOs are unable to access international law-making bodies, or have found such bodies inadequate, they have sought to affirm and enforce international law through their own initiatives. Two relevant strategies are the drafting

---

[224]   UNGA Res 54/4, 6 October 1999.

[225]   Report on Mexico produced by the Committee on the Elimination of Discrimination against Women under Article 8 of the Optional Protocol to the Convention and the reply by Mexico, UN Doc CEDAW/ C/2005/OP8/Mexico, 27 January 2005.

[226]   Committee on the Elimination of All Forms of Discrimination Against Women, General Recommendation No. 19, 29 January 1992, UN Doc HRI/GEN/1/Rev. 1, (1994) 84.

[227]   *Legality of the Use by a State of Nuclear Weapons in Armed Conflict* (1996) ICJ Reports 66.

[228]   *Legality of the Threat or Use of Nuclear Weapons* (1996) ICJ Reports 226.

[229]   R. Falk, 'The Nuclear Weapons Advisory Opinion and the New Jurisprudence of Global Civil Society', 7 *Transnational Law and Contemporary Problems* (1997) 333, 340–2.

[230]   See Chapter 1.

[231]   L. Boisson de Chazournes and P. Sands (eds), *International Law, the International Court of Justice and Nuclear Weapons* (Cambridge, 1999) 10.

and publication of texts (often in conjunction with academics) in a variety of forms—codes of conduct and guidelines, interpretative treaty commentaries, principles—in the hope that they will be adopted by other international actors, cited and accepted as contributing to the corpus of international law. Examples include the International Law Association, Helsinki Rules on the Use of Waters of International Rivers, 1966; the Limburg Principles on the Implementation of the International Covenant on Economic, Social and Cultural Rights, 1987;[232] the Maastricht Guidelines on Violations of Economic, Social and Cultural Rights, 1997;[233] the Montreal Principles on Women's Economic, Social and Cultural Rights, 2000; [234] the Princeton Principles on Universal Jurisdiction.[235] NGOs rely upon the weight and authority of their organisation and of those responsible for the texts in a variation on the 'teachings of the most highly qualified publicists' as a subsidiary source of international law.

A second strategy is the establishment of Peoples' Tribunals of which there have been a number since the Bertrand Russell Tribunals that considered the legality of US actions in Vietnam.[236] The essence of a Peoples' Tribunal is that a panel of eminent 'adjudicators' determines the international legal validity of some state action that is unlikely to be adjudicated upon by the formal mechanisms of international law. Evidence and arguments are presented at a public hearing and the panel members issue a determination based upon what they have heard. An example was the International Women's War Crimes Tribunal that sat in Tokyo, December 2000 to determine individual criminal responsibility and state responsibility for the crimes committed against the so-called 'Comfort Women'. The Tribunal was set up by Asian NGOs from Japan, South Korea and the Philippines. The 'judges' prepared an opinion on international law with respect to sexual slavery as a crime against humanity. Another is the World Tribunal on Iraq which between 2003 and 2005 held over 20 sessions in different parts of the world to hear oral testimony and to evaluate the actions of the US and UK in Iraq against legal and moral criteria. The Tribunal culminated in a final session in Istanbul in June 2005 to summarise the findings of the preceding sessions on the legal, political, social and ethical wrongs committed against the people of Iraq in the 2003 military action and subsequent occupation, through analysis of specific crimes and violations.

Peoples' Tribunals reject the claim that the application and determination of international law rest solely in states. They seek legitimacy through a number of

---

[232] UN Doc E/CN4/1987/17, Annex.

[233] The initiative for both the Limburg and Maastricht Principles was taken by NGOs and academic institutions—the International Commission of Jurists, the Urban Morgan Institute on Human Rights and the Centre for Human Rights of the Faculty of Law of Maastricht University.

[234] 26 *HRQ* (2004) 760.

[235] Princeton Project on Universal Jurisdiction, *Princeton Principles on Universal Jurisdiction* (Princeton University, 2001).

[236] E. Haslam, 'Non-Governmental War Crimes Tribunals: A Forgotten Arena of International Criminal Justice', in C. Harding and C. Lim, *Renegotiating Westphalia: Essays and Commentary on the European and Conceptual Foundations of Modern International Law* (The Hague, 1999) 153.

devices including their global reach; reliance upon official UN reports and documents; symbolic legitimacy through following ritualistic and formal courtroom procedures, associating the Tribunal with the indicia of state judicial legitimacy; the reputation and quality of work of the lawyers and the involvement of eminent public figures; and the issuing of fully reasoned and referenced legal opinions. However it must be accepted that any law-making function of such a tribunal rests upon its credibility acquired through the strength of the arguments and the academic worth of the work which is put out into the public domain to be responded to by states as they see fit.

9.   The Relationship between IGOs and NGOs

There is a symbiotic and fluid—even 'romantic'[237]—relationship between IGOs and NGOs that has evolved over the years. IGOs are created by states, generally with state membership, and take on their own independent existence and reality. The shortfall between the demands placed on IGOs by states and the resources committed for their performance provides space for well-resourced and expert non-state actors to fill. Inadequate IGO budgets and resources have meant that many have looked to NGOs for assistance. Epistemic communities have built up around an IGO comprising specialist staff from the NGO community. The head of the then UN Centre for Human Rights commented that 'We [the UN Centre for Human Rights] have less money and fewer resources than Amnesty International, and we are the arm of the U.N. for human rights. . . . This is clearly ridiculous.'[238] In examining what she calls the 'powershift' towards NGOs, Jessica Matthews has stated that '[t]oday NGOs deliver more official development assistance than the entire U.N. system (excluding the World Bank and the International Monetary Fund)'.[239]

As well as working to accomplish the mandates of IGOs, NGOs and business enterprises access intergovernmental arenas (especially UN bodies) and intervene in their processes in pursuit of their own agendas, including in international law-making. Their presence has enhanced the UN's role as a 'global convenor of diverse constituencies relevant to an issue'.[240] Working relationships have been established between NGOs and their functional equivalents in IGOs. This process should not be seen as uncontested or inevitable. For example there were heated battles in the Committee for NGOs, ECOSOC and the Commission on Human Rights in the first decades of the UN that have only eased as the UN human rights system has developed and cold war rivalries abated.

---

[237] Anderson, 11 *EJIL* (2000) 91, 104.
[238] J. Matthews, 'Powershift', 76 *Foreign Affairs* (1997) 50, 53, citing Ibrahima Fall, head of the then UN Centre for Human Rights.   [239] Ibid.
[240] Report of the S-G in Response to the Report of the Panel of Eminent Persons on United Nations–Civil Society Relations, UN Doc A/59/354, para 4.

The relationship is, however, rarely explained and the contribution of external actors in law-making initiatives of international institutions remains unspecified. In the examples of the Torture Convention, the UNIDROIT Mobile Equipment Convention and the ICC discussed above international institutions provided institutional and logistic support and to some degree shaped the process. In contrast, the Ottawa Landmine process largely by-passed IGOs. The lack of clear distinction between state and NGO action in the context of IGOs is another factor that makes it difficult to assess the extent to which NGOs play an autonomous role in international law-making.

NGO input into international law-making can derive legitimacy from its association with an IGO, for example by having a report documented under the UN system or having it referenced within an official document. It is interesting to consider the various human rights monitoring and enforcement mechanisms in this light. The UN human rights treaty bodies blend governmental and non-governmental elements. They have been established by states through treaties which define their jurisdiction. Treaty body members are elected by governments for their individual expertise, sometimes acquired through NGO activity. They serve as individuals, not government delegates. NGOs have interacted readily with the treaty bodies. In addition to the human rights treaty bodies there is a range of UN Charter human rights mechanisms, largely created by resolution of the CHR, often after NGO intervention (for example, special rapporteurs, working groups, experts, fact-finding missions)[241] that add to the body of human rights understandings through a seamless blend of law, soft law, reports, recommendations and aspirations. They build upon the undoubted law of the human rights treaties through processes of articulation, case analysis, interpretation, claim and counter-claim, cross-fertilisation, building upon each other's work and drawing upon academic or other writings, including NGO studies.

We now have a proliferation of institutional and non-institutional actors working within the international legal arena. The number is magnified if regional bodies are also taken into account. The body of reports, expert opinions, guidelines and studies produced by these actors is immense. Those advocating a particular rule of law, for example in litigation or in lobbying, can invariably find support for their viewpoint, as can those taking the opposite side. Judges and other decision-makers can draw on a wealth of international instruments made through a variety of processes. While assigning formal legal authority to the respective instruments may be problematic, the citation of an instrument in a judgment from a prestigious court undoubtedly enhances its status.[242]

---

[241] In 2006 the status of the special procedures after the abolition of the Commission on Human Rights had not been clarified.

[242] eg the House of Lords (UK) in *R v. Immigration Officer at Prague Airport ex parte European Roma Rights Centre and Others* [2004] UKHL 55, [2005] 2 WLR 1 referred to a range of formally non-binding documents deriving from IGOs and NGOs, including: UNHCR, *Handbook on Procedures and Criteria for Determining Refugee Status*, 1992; Declaration on Territorial Asylum,

IGOs and NGOs each derive legitimacy from each other. Bodies operating within the IGO framework, for example the CHR special procedures, increasingly draw their personnel from the NGO sector rather than from among the former diplomats, civil servants or UN bureaucrats who were originally favoured, often from among the very people who argued for the creation of the position. Indeed in some instances the establishment of particular posts or institutions or enhanced NGO access has been in response to allegations of IGO institutional illegitimacy. For example the establishment of the World Bank Inspection Panel came after NGO criticisms of the Bank's lack of transparency in applying its own procedures.[243] Similarly, in the OECD 'it was out of a moment of crisis and contestation (around the Multilateral Agreement on Investment) that efforts at greater transparency and inclusion emerged'.[244] Once accorded status or access, NGOs derive legitimacy from their IGO-granted mandate. Where their function involves reporting, their reports are adopted by the same IGO and may be recorded as official UN documents. The NGO allegiance gives an aura of independence and credibility while UN affiliation gives reports weight and authority. This becomes a self-referential system: the human rights thematic machinery has been largely inspired by NGOs and then 'NGOs are the main source of information for the thematic machinery, whose reports are themselves influential in the determination of situations appropriate for special scrutiny'.[245] To paraphrase Teubner: '[h]ere the vicious circle of [NGO self-validation] is transformed into the virtuous circle of two [institutional] processes.'[246] Practice is evolved through conferences and other institutional arenas and validated through the same institutional imprimatur. On the one hand the richness and diversity of contemporary expressions of international law deriving from these various bodies should not be ignored; on the other hand their very volume may undermine their overall usefulness.

1967; American Law Institute, *Restatement of the Foreign Relations Law of the United States (Third)*; Bangkok Principles, Asian-African Legal Consultative Committee, 1966; resolutions of the Committee of Ministers of the Council of Europe; reports from the UNHCR Executive Committee; reports of the International law Association; UN Human Rights Committee, General Comment No. 31, 29 March 2004; study for the European Council on Refugees and Exiles, 1999; reports by the Inter-American Commission for Human Rights and UN Committee on the Elimination of Racial Discrimination; numerous academic articles (including one by a former refugee officer for AI) and books.

[243] C. Chinkin, 'International Environmental Law in Evolution', in T. Jewell and J. Steele (eds), *Law in Environmental Decision-Making* (Oxford, 1998) 229, 238–40.

[244] B. Kingsbury, N. Krisch and R. Stewart, 'The Emergence of Global Administrative Law', 68 (3 and 4) *Law and Contemporary Problems* (2005) 15, 60.

[245] World Conference on Human Rights Preparatory Committee, UN Doc A/CONF. 157/PC/60/Add6, 1 April 1993, 16 cited Korey, *NGOs and the Universal Declaration of Human Rights*, 259.

[246] G. Teubner, 'Legal Pluralism in the World Society', in Teubner, *Global Law without a State*, 3, 17.

10. Conclusions

This chapter has considered a number of the strategies adopted by different non-state actors to influence international law-making. Increased NGO partici-pation undoubtedly brings diverse interests and objectives into international law-making processes. Whether this is viewed as beneficial depends upon the par-ticular perspective. NGO activity opposing government initiatives (for example the campaign against the MAI) may be applauded as offering resistance or con-demned as frustrating desired law-making objectives, or as diverting attention away from the original focus. Sometimes states go to considerable lengths to keep NGOs out of negotiations in order to protect the process from what they see as harmful and counter-productive influences as was the case with the WHO Framework Convention on Tobacco Control.[247] This may be an extreme example but it helps explain some of the WTO's reluctance to deal with NGOs. Some of the large number of industry NGOs with observer status at the WTO are prob-ably more interested in protecting their members from the effects of free trade than in encouraging the WTO to promote further liberalisation.[248] It may also explain why the Security Council has allowed only very limited access to NGOs through the so-called Arria formula. Effective and timely decision-making relating to international peace and security could not readily accommodate the widespread opposing views that are typically held in any such situation.

There remain outstanding a number of important empirical and theoretical questions. The most relevant is whether non-state actors (and in particular social and business sector NGOs in light of their ECOSOC consultative status) play an independent law-making role or whether they merely exert influence on govern-ments. While there is undoubtedly an ever-growing number of international NGOs, many of which are exceedingly active in promoting international law-making, and there has certainly been a greater NGO presence at institutional meetings, expert groups, diplomatic conferences, prepcoms, meetings of states parties and other crucial meetings, the actual influence they have had on the development of international law is empirically uncertain. NGOs do have a cata-lytic effect. They bring issues onto the international agenda, make recommenda-tions in their own name at international meetings, and wording emanating from NGOs has found its way into texts. However their participation is determined by the treaty or particular Rules of Procedure and invariably their accreditation excludes voting. Their precise influence on a final text can be difficult to gauge after what might have been a long and complex negotiation process. Where there

---

[247] See Chapter 3.
[248] eg the shipping industry, which successfully secured exclusion from the principal commit-ments under the General Agreement on Trade in Services: see 1994 GATS, Annex and Ministerial Decision on Negotiations on Maritime Transport Services.

has been an initial NGO draft text this can be compared with the final document and scrutiny of the *travaux préparatoires* may reveal the pattern of debate and textual changes but not the informal corridor negotiations and deals. These may be numerous. For example the ICC negotiations were mostly conducted through informal meetings from the preparatory stages through to the Rome Conference.[249] The *travaux* may be incomplete: 'there is now a lack of verbatim, or even summary, records of treaty negotiations'.[250] The numerous informal and differing accounts and oral histories of any negotiation process in which individuals and groups assign credit for crucial wording make impossible generalisation about NGO impact on the outcome.

Nevertheless there are examples where it is safe to say that a treaty (or other instrument) would not have been adopted, or would not have been adopted in the particular form or at that time, without NGO action. This is surely true of the four conventions discussed in the case studies on treaty-making. All have entered into force. Three have generated widespread acceptance.[251] The Torture Convention has contributed to the development of customary international law; the definitions of crimes in the Rome Statute and Elements of Crimes 'correspond in a general sense to the state of customary international law'[252] and may be said to have crystallised such understanding. Other provisions are likely to be similarly accepted and claims may be successfully made in the future about the customary international law status of the Landmines Convention.[253] There are other treaties that we might have chosen to illustrate NGO influence on law-making. This leads one to ask what factors are likely to make NGO campaigns for change in international law successful.

NGOs have been most influential in law-making in special issue areas, notably human rights, environmental matters and international humanitarian law (the last through the unique position of the ICRC). These are areas of international regulation that impact directly upon individuals, which may explain the high level of NGO involvement compared with, for example, the law of the sea and the WTO. Geiss concludes that environmental law has displayed the highest area of NGO involvement and human rights the most progressive.[254] As is apparent from the examples where NGOs pushed for an international treaty where there was no government interest, it is not crucial at the initial stages to have the support of a major government, although not engaging the active opposition of important military, political or economic interests might be.[255] A simple message that can be put

---

[249] Foreword, Lee, *The International Criminal Court*, vii.

[250] A. Aust, 'Limping Treaties: Lessons from Multilateral Treaty-Making', 50 *NILR* (2003) 243. Eg there are no formal records for the Oslo Landmines Conference.

[251] The Torture Convention and the Landmines Convention each have over 140 states parties; the Rome Statute has 100 states parties.

[252] W. Schabas, *An Introduction to the International Criminal Court* (Cambridge, 2001), 23.

[253] R. Price, 'Emerging Customary Norms and Anti-Personnel Landmines', in Reus-Smit, *The Politics of International Law*, 106, 107.   [254] Geiss, 'Non-State Actors', 303, 326.

[255] Anderson, 11 *EJIL* (2000) 91, 106.

forward in straightforward language, as was the case with the AI anti-torture campaign and the campaign to ban landmines, may readily gain popular support. Although the details of the Rome Statute are complex, the message of the ICC is simple: the need for effective measures against impunity for the commission of grave crimes against humanity and genocide. Other factors assisting NGO effectiveness include the availability of financial and other resources; careful research and campaign preparation; commitment and input from individual experts, including competent legal advisers; broad-based NGO membership and members willing to lobby governments, including their own; effective coalition building; an efficient and well-coordinated NGO secretariat that can provide resources and a central focus point; the involvement of, and interplay with, the UN and its agencies. The internet has become an inestimable asset although international campaigns were also successful before its creation.[256] Another factor is timing, for example the coincidence of the AI anti-torture campaign with the seizing of power by a number of brutal regimes such as those in Chile, Uruguay and Argentina gave impetus to the need to strengthen international responses to torture.

A practical point is that NGO effectiveness may be constrained by the very nature of their organisation and action. NGOs may be victims of their own success. The number of NGOs wishing to participate in international law-making events means the imposition of restrictions because of lack of time and space. Member states have become wary of NGO demands[257] and states inevitably give greater time and attention to those NGOs with which they feel most comfortable. The large numbers make this an acceptable position for states to adopt but it also allows states to represent that they have consulted widely and risks NGO co-option.

Nevertheless, despite the multiple NGO activities described in this chapter and their often forceful presence, states retain a tight grip on the formal law-making processes, even in those areas where NGOs have had greatest impact. States control the agenda and access to the international arenas relevant for hard and soft law-making, in particular through accreditation to consultative status with ECOSOC and to meetings. Other devices such as imposing high admission fees,[258] limiting space, ticket allocations and speaking time all reduce the effectiveness of NGO attendance at particular meetings. NGOs may be excluded from crucial stages of negotiations[259] and states have the final word in the adoption of the text. The participation of NGOs throughout all the preparatory stages of the negotiation of the Rome Statute did not prevent the Conference Chair preparing

---

[256] The account of the campaign to eradicate footbinding in China, 1874–1911, is illuminating for its consideration of factors leading to success; Keck and Sikkink, *Activists beyond Borders*, 60–6.

[257] Report of the S-G, *Strengthening of the United Nations; An Agenda for Further Change*, UN Doc A 57/387, 9 September 2002, para 139.

[258] eg NGOs attending as observers at meetings of the Northwest Atlantic Fisheries Organisation have to pay a fee to cover the additional costs involved; D. Konig, 'Questionnaire International Law of the Sea', in Zimmermann and Hoffmann, *Unity and Diversity in International Law*, 29.

[259] M. Posner and C. Whittome, 'The Status of Human Rights NGOs', 25 *Col HRLR* (1994) 269, 283.

the final text as a package that he thought would be an acceptable compromise for states, with some NGOs disappointed with some aspects of the outcome.[260] States retain the final word through adoption, accession and ratification procedures and the power in some cases to make reservations. Soft measures of enforcement may also minimise changes sought by NGOs.

The approach of the Conference Chair to the final negotiation stages at Rome highlights different views about the legitimacy of international law-making processes, especially where non-state actors play a significant role. This was regarded as illegitimate by the US whose delegates complained that they had not had the appropriate time to study the text. The text was adopted with some negative votes cast, including that of the US. Nor has the US become a party. Similarly some of the most powerful states have not become parties to the Landmines Convention.[261] While US courts accepted the prohibition of torture as contrary to customary international law in 1980,[262] it did not ratify the Torture Convention until 1994. The alliance between NGOs and like-minded states to make international law in the face of US opposition raises the issue of law-making by the majority against the minority, albeit most powerful, state. Unlike earlier attempts at majority law-making, such as the New International Economic Order (discussed in Chapter 3), these instruments are in legally binding treaty form. Despite the principle that treaties do not bind third parties (discussed in Chapter 5), the US has felt the need to take measures to ensure that its forces are not brought within the ICC's jurisdiction. These include turning to the SC. Accordingly in 2002 the US threatened to veto renewal of the UN mission in Bosnia-Herzegovina. In response the SC adopted resolution 1422, 12 July 2002 using its Chapter VII powers to request the ICC not to commence or proceed with any prosecution of personnel from a non-party state serving on a UN established or authorised mission for a 12-month period, unless the SC otherwise decides.[263] SC resolution 1497, 1 August 2003 establishing the multinational force (MNF) in Liberia goes further by deciding that MNF personnel from a non-party state are subject to the exclusive jurisdiction of the sending state unless expressly waived by that state. Although some states assert its compatibility with Article 16 of the Rome Statute,[264] this device allows the US to use its powers within the SC to challenge the integrity of an internationally binding treaty. Nevertheless, the US cannot simply ignore the establishment of an international institution by the majority of the world's states and strong public opinion. It seemingly recognised this when in 2005 it did not veto SC resolution 1593, which referred the Darfur

---

[260] Pace and Schense, 'The Role of Non-Governmental Organisations', 139.

[261] eg China and Russia.   [262] *Filartiga v. Pena-Irala* 630 F 2d 876 (US CA, 2nd Circ).

[263] This was followed by SC Res 1487, 12 June 2003, but no similar resolution has since been adopted.

[264] For a summary of the different arguments about the compatibility of these resolutions with ICC Statute, Article 16 see ILA Committee on the International Criminal Court, First Report, *Report of the 71st Conference*, Berlin (London, 2004) 295.

situation to the ICC prosecutor. However, the resolution contained a similarly worded jurisdictional exclusion to SC resolution 1497. The nature of the Landmines Convention or the Rome Statute makes it harder for the US to pick and choose sections of those conventions as customary international law, while disregarding other parts as it has done with the UN Law of the Sea Convention. The latter has no core proposition but comprises a package of rights and duties unlike the undertakings never to use anti-personnel mines or to allow submission of its nationals to the jurisdiction of the ICC.

As we argued in Chapter 1, the future of institutional regimes established against the will of the US remains uncertain. Nevertheless, there is little doubt that by working together, less powerful states and international NGOs have changed international law-making. Focus on the continued exclusion of NGOs from formal aspects of international law-making misses the political and social reality of their increased participation and the impact of that participation on state and IGO behaviour—whether this is deemed favourable or otherwise. It would be myopic to insist on the classical view of states as the sole makers of international law;[265] rather we must recognise the multi-layered, multi-partite nature of the international law-making enterprise.

[265] C. Harding and C. Lim, 'The Significance of Westphalia: An Archaeology of the International Legal Order', in C. Harding and C. Lim, *Renegotiating Westphalia* (The Hague, 1999) 1.

Further Reading

H. Anheier, M. Glasius and M. Kaldor (eds) *Global Civil Society* (Yearbooks, from 2001 onwards).

S. Charnovitz, 'Non-Governmental Organizations and International Law', 100 *AJIL* (2006) 348.

M. Keck and K. Sikkink, *Activists beyond Borders: Advocacy Networks in International Politics* (Ithaca, NY, 1998).

W. Korey, *NGOs and the Universal Declaration of Human Rights: A Curious Grapevine* (New York, 1998).

A.-M. Slaughter, *A New World Order* (Princeton, 2004).

G. Teubner (ed), *Global Law without a State* (Aldershot, 1997).

A. Zimmermann and R. Hoffmann, *Unity and Diversity in International Law* (Berlin, 2005).

3

Multilateral Law-Making: Diplomatic Processes

1. Introduction

In this chapter we consider the main multilateral diplomatic processes through which most modern international law-making takes place. These include not only intergovernmental organisations such as the United Nations, but also commissions, conferences or meetings of the parties to multilateral treaties (COPs/MOPs), and *ad hoc* negotiating conferences, of which the 3rd UN Conference on the Law of the Sea (UNCLOS III) and the 1998 Rome Conference to adopt the Statute of the International Criminal Court are the leading examples in modern times. In the century and a half following the Congress of Vienna *ad hoc* conferences of this kind became the main mechanism for negotiating and adopting multilateral treaties and declarations. They remain an important feature of contemporary international diplomacy, although the UN and other international bodies have to some extent taken over their role.

The processes considered in this chapter have certain common features. They are all primarily political in character; they mainly operate through 'quasi-parliamentary procedures',[1] usually affording a significant degree of deliberation and transparency, and in most cases their voting membership is dominated by and generally open only to states or quasi-state entities.[2] This does not preclude the involvement of legal and technical experts, whether on an *ad hoc* basis, or through permanent bodies such as the International Law Commission (ILC) or the UN specialised agencies, and we explore several examples later in this chapter and Chapter 4. Nor does it mean that other entities do not participate in other ways. On the contrary, as we observed in Chapter 2, one of the most striking features of modern international law-making is the interaction of states, intergovernmental organisations (IGOs), and non-governmental organisations (NGOs) in what have been variously

---

[1] O. Schachter, in C. Joyner (ed), *The UN and International Law* (Cambridge, 1997) 24. The significant exception is the UN Security Council.
[2] The significant exception is the International Labour Organisation, created in 1919, with a tripartite membership of governments, trade unions and employers.

described as 'epistemic communities' or 'transnational networks' of officials, experts and interest groups whose quasi-autonomous character allows them to constitute a broader international community than the states that nominally make the decisions.[3] Through such bureaucratic networks states and other actors seek to accomplish in cooperation what formerly was undertaken on a narrower basis.[4] Understanding the role of such groups contributes to an awareness of the multiple influences on the politics of international law-making, and also helps explain why some states sometimes appear to have more or less influence on outcomes than their relative size or importance might suggest. Participation goes directly to a central question: who makes international law? Is it only a community of national governments, or a transnational epistemic community of experts and diplomats, or a broader community including NGOs or other representatives of civil society and operating beyond or across national borders? We addressed this question mainly in Chapter 2, but the numerous examples noted in this chapter show how significant the broadening of participation considered there has become.

2. Legitimacy and Multilateral Law-Making

Simply put, a law-making process perceived as illegitimate by states and other relevant actors is more likely to be an ineffective process, which either fails to make law at all or which undermines the likelihood of compliance with adopted rules or standards. An important question posed by any examination of international law-making structures therefore is the extent to which we can make judgments about their legitimacy and in what terms. In this context legitimacy becomes a critical issue once international institutions acquire power to take decisions binding on states without their specific consent, and more especially so when those decisions amount in effect to legislating for all states.[5] Nevertheless, the consent of states is increasingly attenuated by the scale and scope of law-making by multilateral institutions, and by some of the methods they employ. As Franck observes: 'It is only by reference to a community's evolving standards of what constitutes right process that it is possible to assert meaningfully that a law . . . is legitimate'.[6] Brunnée and Toope argue that periodic meetings of the parties to multilateral treaties—and by extension the argument must also apply to IGOs and law-making conferences

---

[3] P. M. Haas, 'Do Regimes Matter? Epistemic Communities and Mediterranean Pollution Control', 43 *Int Org* (1989) 377; P. Szasz, in Joyner, *The UN and International Law*, 34–5; A.-M. Slaughter, 'The Real New World Order', 76 *Foreign Affairs* (1997) 183.

[4] A. Chayes and A. Chayes, *The New Sovereignty: Compliance with International Regulatory Agreements* (Cambridge, Mass, 1998).

[5] The arguments reviewed in D. Bodansky, 'The Legitimacy of International Governance', 93 *AJIL* (1999) 596 have general relevance.

[6] T. Franck, *Fairness in International Law and Institutions* (Oxford, 1995) 26.

such as UNCLOS III—constitute 'ongoing, interactional processes', and that 'It is this broader process and not the formal act of consent that infuses the legal norms generated within [a multilateral agreement] with the ability to influence state conduct'.[7] From that perspective legitimacy is essentially a sociological question about the process of law-making—the way law is created—rather than the outcome of the process. Moreover, if general law-making is the product of interactive processes, then the question who participates in these processes assumes added importance. Finally, Brunnée and Toope's argument points additionally to the conclusion that norms do not necessarily have to be adopted in binding form to influence or contribute to law-making. We return to this important issue in our discussion of soft law in Chapter 5.

Most of the law-making processes we consider in the following sections are also deliberative to some degree, although rarely to the same extent as is evident within the ILC. Deliberation is an essential lubricant of any law-making process because it facilitates discussion, negotiation, compromise, persuasion, influence and participation. It is what allows participants a voice, whether or not they also have a vote. Just as importantly, contemporary international law-making has also become generally more transparent than in earlier times. This is partly a consequence of wider participation, but it also reflects a significant change in the way governments and international organisations view their role as international law-makers. In that sense the system as whole has come a good deal closer to Woodrow Wilson's classic prescription of 'open covenants openly arrived at',[8] although there remain significant exceptions, most notably the Security Council. Our study suggests that international law-making in general is more open and transparent than some aspects of European Union law-making.[9] Moreover, in the authors' experience it is often easier to understand the inner workings of a multilateral treaty negotiation than to find out who or what has influenced national legislation or how it has evolved.

Although international law-making often proceeds within the constitutional structures of international organisations, international law itself lacks an identifiable constitutional structure.[10] The law-making system is eclectic, unsystematic, overlapping, and often poorly coordinated. The UN is a central element, but by no means the only one, nor even the principal one in certain contexts, such as

---

[7] J. Brunnée, 'COPing with Consent: Law-Making under Multilateral Environmental Agreements', 15 *LJIL* (2002) 1, 6. For a fuller account see also J. Brunnée and S. Toope, 'International Law and Constructivism: Elements of an Interactional Theory of International Law', 39 *Col JTL* (2000) 19.

[8] Not all treaty negotiations are transparent however: compare A. Aust, 'Limping Treaties: Lessons from Multilateral Treaty-Making', 50 *NILR* (2003) 243, 245.

[9] Compare C. Harlow, *Accountability in the European Union* (Oxford, 2002), notably at 37–47.

[10] But there have been many sophisticated attempts to envisage one: see most recently E. De Wet, 'The International Constitutional Order', 55 *ICLQ* (2006) 51; D. M. Johnston, in R. St. J. Macdonald and D. M. Johnston (eds), *Towards World Constitutionalism* (Leiden, 2005) 3; B. Fassbender, 'The United Nations Charter as Constitution of the International Community', 36 *Col JTL* (1998) 529–619.

international economic law. Moreover, the UN is not a coherent whole but comprises multiple organs, specialised agencies, working groups and programmes which operate through various procedures and mechanisms. Constitutionalism, however defined, is not the most obvious perspective from which to address legitimacy in this fragmentary setting, and we have not focused on it as a major element of our analysis.[11] This is not to suggest that we should overlook academic debate about the constitutionalisation of particular institutions, most notably the WTO, and we return to the question in that context. Nevertheless, it is worth emphasising that our focus is on the international law-making process in general, and on how specific institutions function as part of that process. We do not view any of these bodies, including WTO, as having become part of some separate constitutional order. On the other hand the existence of multiple institutions promoting international law-making within their own specialised areas poses an obvious challenge for the coherence and integrity of international law, and we consider this crucial question both here and in subsequent chapters.

A further perspective on legitimacy is offered by the notion of democratisation. In Chapter 2 we considered whether multilateral law-making processes have been democratised by NGO participation. But what is meant by democracy in this context is an open question. Some writers point to the democratic deficit inherent in transferring effective law-making responsibility from elected national parliaments to unelected intergovernmental fora. There are various responses to this criticism. If escaping democratic accountability at home by pursuing international law-making abroad merits accusations of illegitimacy, one obvious answer would be to improve domestic parliamentary oversight of governments when they act internationally.[12] Others argue that in a globalised world it is no longer enough to address democracy at the national level alone. 'If politics has become global, then so too must democracy.'[13] Here again a more cosmopolitan notion of participation in international law-making provides a possible solution, exemplified by the election of parliamentary organs in international institutions such as the Council of Europe, the Nordic Council or the Organisation for Security and Co-operation in Europe.[14] The International Labour Organisation's tripartite structure of governments, trade unions and employers represents another version of this approach, although despite

---

[11] For a powerful but sceptical assessment of the concept see D. Cass, *The Constitutionalization of the World Trade Organization: Legitimacy, Democracy, and Community in the International Trading System* (Oxford, 2005), and more positively N. Walker, 'The EU and the WTO: Constitutionalism in a New Key', in G. de Búrca and J. Scott (eds), *The EU and the WTO: Legal and Constitutional Issues* (Oxford, 2001) 31.

[12] See eg on the EU, Harlow, *Accountability in the European Union*, 45 and 79–92, and on WTO, chapters by G. Shaffer, D. Skaggs, M. Hilf and E. Mann, in E. -U. Petersmann (ed), *Reforming the World Trade System* (Oxford, 2005) 381–428.

[13] S. Marks, 'Democracy and International Governance', in J. -M. Coicaud and V. Heiskanen (eds), *The Legitimacy of International Organisations* (Tokyo, 2001) 52.

[14] H. Schermers and N. Blokker, *International Institutional Law* (The Hague, 1995) 383–4; E. Stein, 'International Integration and Democracy', 95 *AJIL* (2001) 489.

its relative antiquity in the pantheon of international organisations, it remains unique in this respect. Structures of this kind, or others which exceptionally employ weighted voting, such as the International Monetary Fund and World Bank, to some extent respond to the critique that giving all states equal voting power is fundamentally unfair and illegitimate in the eyes of the larger, wealthier or more populous states.[15] But it might also be said that the equal participation of all sovereign states in the process of law-making can be viewed as inherently democratic, particularly when the negotiating power of individual states, however small, is strengthened by consensus negotiating procedures. In that context both the weak and the strong have to be accommodated, and resort to actual voting is minimised. In this chapter we observe how far such procedures have proved useful in securing widespread consent and thereby helping to generate genuinely global law. From this perspective, how decisions are taken within the process of law-making, and by whom, may be among the more important elements of legitimacy, a point we consider towards the conclusion of the chapter.

It is tempting to suggest that the present international law-making 'system'—in reality more bric-a-brac than system—should evolve into something closer to the European Union, the only functioning model of a multilateral legislative system currently available. On that model the UN General Assembly might become the Parliament, the Security Council would be the equivalent of the Council of Ministers, and the Secretariat would perform the functions of the European Commission. Analogies of this kind are potentially misleading, and the context is clearly very different. Nevertheless, the institutions of European law-making have themselves evolved, most notably in the present sharing of legislative functions by the Parliament and the Council of Ministers, a power originally exercised by the Council alone. The institutions of international law-making also evolve; currently the most important development is the emergence of the Security Council as a significant legislator. How to legitimise and democratise the involvement of such a body is perhaps the most interesting challenge posed in this chapter. One obvious answer might be to accept that the Security Council should be empowered to legislate, but only with the involvement and approval of the General Assembly.[16] Another answer looks to a more democratic composition of the Security Council, a reform mooted by the Secretary-General but not accepted by the General Assembly's 2005 Summit. Both would require a significant reform of the UN Charter, or at least a change in the practice of the two principal organs and the acquiescence of member states to that change, but if carried out would constitute a genuine legislative body. Whether the world needs such an institution is another

---

[15] T. Franck, *Fairness in International law and Institutions* (Oxford, 1995); Bodansky, 93 *AJIL* (1999) 596, 612–17.

[16] On possible ways of involving the UNGA in UNSC decisions see D. Caron, 'The Legitimacy of the Security Council', 87 *AJIL* (1993) 552, 575–6, and M. Happold, 'SC Resolution 1373 and the Constitution of the UN', 13 *LJIL* (2003) 593.

question, but the point should remind us that the UN's centrality in the present system for international law-making has come about despite, not because of, the institutional architecture created in 1945.

3.   Agenda-Setting

3.1   Law-Making, Power and International Relations[17]

The Anglo-American invasion of Iraq, the surrounding debates in the US Congress and the UK parliament, and the subsequent decisions on the jurisdiction of US and UK courts over the treatment of prisoners,[18] clearly show that international law is not merely an academic discipline. It has real-world importance, of serious concern to governments and electorates. Nor is international law-making principally undertaken by lawyers. It is a political activity, which requires above all political initiative, energy and skill to set the process in motion and sustain it thereafter. Regardless of where proposals originate, marshalling the support of coalitions of like-minded states is normally essential. These do not necessarily have to be powerful states. The success of the Group of 77 developing states in UNCLOS III or the Association of Small Island States in the negotiation of the Framework Convention on Climate Change demonstrates that power and influence are not synonymous in the real world of multilateral diplomacy.[19] On the contrary, the UN system has empowered weaker states in a way that would not have been possible previously.[20] As we noted in Chapter 1, during the 1960s and 1970s developing states began using their growing dominance of the UN General Assembly with some success to promote a law-making agenda that focused *inter alia* on decolonisation, sovereignty over natural resources, the adoption of a new international economic order, and the refashioning of the law of the sea.

In the post-cold war era developing states have somewhat fragmented as a group and no longer seek to use their majority in the General Assembly to refashion international law in quite the same way. Initiative and influence in the UN have to some extent passed back to the Security Council, even in the sphere of international law-making. Moreover in certain contexts, notably the WTO, developing states have so far had insufficient leverage over the major trading economies to be able to promote their own agenda effectively. Although the Doha Development Round of trade negotiations initiated in 2001 ostensibly reflected

---

[17] See generally M. Byers, *Custom, Power, and the Power of Rules: International Relations and Customary International Law* (Cambridge, 1999); M. Byers and G. Nolte (eds), *United States Hegemony and the Foundations of International Law* (Cambridge, 2003).

[18] *Rasul v. Bush* 321 F. 3d 1134 (2004); *Hamdan v. Rumsfeld, Secretary of Defense*, US S Ct, 29 June 2006; *A, X & Ors v. Secretary of State for the Home Department* [2005] 2 AC 68.

[19] See J. Evensen, 'Working Methods and Procedures in the 3rd UNCLOS', 199 *Recueil des Cours* (1986-IV) 425, 455; I. Mintzer and J. Leonard, *Negotiating Climate Change* (Cambridge, 1994).

[20] M. J. Peterson, *The General Assembly in World Politics* (Boston, 1986) 51.

the concerns of developing countries, after five years of unsuccessful negotiations it had become apparent that progress depended entirely on the willingness of Europe, Japan and the United States to make the necessary concessions to developing countries.[21] Like the climate change negotiations, however, the WTO example also shows that 'developing countries' are no longer a cohesive group. The trading interests and objectives of newly industrialised China, India or Brazil, for example, are different from those of the least-developed agricultural producers in Africa and the Caribbean, and not easy to reconcile.

The perception that the US can and should operate more effectively outside many of the constraints of international law poses the greatest contemporary challenge to the post-1945 system of multilateral law-making exercised principally through the United Nations. Whether there are imperial alternatives to multilateralism is a question for consideration elsewhere.[22] Nevertheless it would be naïve to assume that in a multipolar world an international law-making agenda can simply be dictated by supposedly powerful states; even the US has signally failed to control the development of international law on climate change, human rights or international criminal law, among many other examples. Nor, as we saw in Chapter 2, could it secure acceptance of the proposed Multilateral Agreement on Investment (MAI) against sustained NGO lobbying and opposition from other states. Effective multilateral diplomacy remains a necessary condition for exercising political leadership at an international level. Similarly, effective political leadership by individuals within international organisations may make the difference between a successful law-making initiative and failure.[23] The political dynamics will also be heavily influenced by the decision-making procedures employed. Securing global consensus in favour of some new initiative is very different from achieving a simple majority of votes, and in a world of nearly 200 states it requires considerable diplomatic skill and the right personal attributes.

3.2   Setting the International Law-Making Agenda

How then do new topics for international law-making reach the agenda of intergovernmental organisations or become the subject of diplomatic conferences? There is no simple answer. Some topics emerge in response to unilateral claims made by a single state or a small group of states. Thus the 1945 Truman Proclamation in which the US claimed exclusive jurisdiction over the continental shelf initiated a process of law-making in the ILC, the 1958 UN Conference on the Law of the Sea (UNCLOS I), the ICJ, and the 1973–82 UN Conference on

---

[21] See Petersmann, *Reforming the World Trading System*.

[22] But see M. Koskenniemi, 'International Legislation Today: Limits and Possibilities', 23 *Wis ILJ* (2002) 61.

[23] eg the impact of Dr H. S. Amerasinghe as President of UNCLOS III, Dr Maurice Strong at UNCED, Dr Mostafa Tolba as head of UNEP or Dr Gro Harlem Brundtland at WHO.

the Law of the Sea (UNCLOS III). Icelandic and Canadian claims to high seas fisheries jurisdiction also resulted in multilateral negotiations that led to changes in international law.[24] But unilateral action is inherently risky and unpredictable in its effects. Success depends entirely on the response of other states; significant opposition may lead at best to new law opposable only to other like-minded states,[25] or at worst to litigation and failure.[26] If a new practice does emerge it may do so in terms very different from the initial intention. This fate befell the other 1945 Truman Proclamation in which the United States claimed limited powers over high seas fisheries and to which some Latin American states responded with 200-mile territorial sea claims.[27] This is not the best way to promote universal law-making.

Proposals for law-making more often originate in the principal political organs of the UN, usually the UN General Assembly or the Economic and Social Council, or in UN subsidiary bodies such as the UN Environment Programme (UNEP) or the Commissions on Human Rights, Women, or Sustainable Development, or in a specialised agency. One example to which we return later is the reform of the law of the sea. UNCLOS III had its genesis in a Maltese proposal in the General Assembly to designate deep seabed resources as the common heritage of mankind. The UNGA first established an *ad hoc* Committee on Peaceful Uses of the Seabed and Ocean Floor Beyond the Limits of National Jurisdiction to consider this proposal.[28] Then, when it became apparent that there was pressure for more comprehensive reform, especially from developing states, the Seabed Committee's mandate was broadened and UNCLOS III was convened by the General Assembly.[29] Legal regulation of the oceans touches upon many diverse and emergent interests, however, and has continued to generate proposals for further development from various bodies, including the 1992 UN Conference on Environment and Development ('the Rio Conference'),[30] the Commission on Sustainable Development,[31] the UN General Assembly,[32] and the Informal Consultative Process on Law of the Sea.[33] Law-making on ocean affairs and on other topics within their mandates may also be initiated by the political organs of specialised agencies, such as the security-related revisions to the 1988 Convention

---

[24] See A. E. Boyle, 'EU Unilateralism and the Law of the Sea', 21 *IJMCL* (2006) 15.

[25] As in the *Fisheries Jurisdiction Cases*, 1974 ICJ Reports 3 and 175.

[26] As in the *Swordfish Case* (*Chile/EC*) ITLOS No. 7, Order No. 2000/3 (2000), and EC-Chile: *Measures Affecting the Transit and Importation of Swordfish* WT/DS193 (2000).

[27] See generally A. Hollick, *US Foreign Policy and the Law of the Sea* (Princeton, 1981).

[28] See UNGA Res 2467 (XXIII), 21 December 1968.

[29] See UNGA Res 2750 (XXV), 17 December 1970; 2881 (XXVI), 21 December 1971; 3067 (XXVIII), 16 November 1973. On UNCLOS III, see below.

[30] UN, *Agenda 21* in *Report of UNCED* (1992), vol I, chapter 17.

[31] CSD, *Report of 7th Session*, Decision 7/1.

[32] See in particular the annual UNGA resolutions on fisheries.

[33] eg on IUU fishing, on which see FAO below. The 1994 Agreement on Implementation of Part XI of UNCLOS was negotiated in an informal process convened by the S-G of the UN.

on the Suppression of Unlawful Activities Against the Safety of Maritime Navigation adopted by IMO in 2005, and the Convention on Underwater Cultural Heritage adopted by UNESCO in 2001. Here we can clearly see the diversity of contemporary international law-making fora.

As we saw in Chapter 2, states are sometimes persuaded to initiate law reform by individuals, NGOs or expert bodies such as the Comité Maritime International.[34] It is well-known that the 1973 Convention on International Trade in Endangered Species was proposed, and initially drafted, by the International Union for the Conservation of Nature (IUCN).[35] The UN Convention against Torture was negotiated on the initiative of Amnesty International,[36] while negotiation of the 2002 Protocol to the same convention was promoted by a coalition of NGOs and like-minded states. The idea of instituting a scheme of preventive visits based on the practice of the ICRC originated in a draft proposed in 1977 by the Swiss Committee Against Torture and was subsequently taken up by the International Commission of Jurists.[37] Successfully bringing a topic onto the international agenda does not guarantee speedy conclusion, however. Although by 1987 the European Convention for the Prevention of Torture made provision for such prison visits, it took a quarter of a century to negotiate the international Torture Protocol in the face of strong opposition from the United States, supported by Cuba, China and Iran.

The agenda of an international law-making conference will itself be the subject of negotiation and compromise. The 1992 Rio Conference illustrates how what eventually emerges for adoption at such a gathering may differ significantly from what was envisaged by those who initiated the process. The genesis of the Rio Conference can be traced to the report of the 1987 World Commission on Environment and Development (Brundtland Report). This was not an intergovernmental body, but a group of eminent politicians, scientists and lawyers convened by the UNGA, acting on a proposal from UNEP, and nominated by the UN Secretary-General.[38] Following further proposals from governments and the UNEP, the UN General Assembly decided to convene a Conference and it established a Preparatory Commission (Prepcom) in which most of the negotiations took place.[39] Political objections from developing countries ensured that intergovernmental negotiating committees established by the General Assembly, rather

---

[34] On the CMI see the section on IMO below.

[35] In 1995 IUCN unsuccessfully proposed a codification of international environmental law in the form of a draft Covenant on Environment and Development.

[36] On the adoption of the Torture Convention and other examples of NGO initiation of law-making treaties, see Chapter 2.

[37] See M. D. Evans and C. Haenni-Dale, 'Preventing Torture: The Development of the Optional Protocol to the UNCAT', 4 *HRLR* (2004) 19.

[38] UNGA Res 161/38, 19 December 1983.

[39] UNGA Res 44/228, 22 December 1989. See P. Sand, 'UNCED and the Development of International Environmental Law', 3 *YBIEL* (1992) 3; D. Freestone, 'The Road from Rio: International Environmental Law After the Earth Summit' (1994) 6 *JEL* 193; Symposium: UNCED, in 4 *ColJIELP* (1993) 1.

than UNEP, the World Meteorological Organisation (WMO) or the Food and Agriculture Organisation (FAO), were given responsibility for drafting conventions on climate change and biological diversity.[40] Developing states also worked hard to coordinate their negotiating position, although in the intergovernmental negotiating committee on climate change they could not agree on a common position and separated into different groups.[41]

It was initially hoped by some of the sponsoring states and NGOs that the Rio Conference would produce an 'Earth Charter' setting out comprehensive principles for environmental protection and sustainable development and consider proposals for conventions on forestry and land-based sources of marine pollution, together with agreements on biodiversity and climate change. In practice, significant differences between the proposals of developed and developing states resulted in a much less ambitious outcome.[42] A declaration on environment and development, a detailed programme of action, known as Agenda 21, and framework conventions on climate change and biological diversity were adopted by consensus. A non-binding 'statement of principles' on forests papered over fundamental differences on this highly charged issue, and Agenda 21 set in motion further law-making conferences on straddling and highly migratory fish stocks and desertification.[43]

Since international law-making agendas serve political purposes, it is unsurprising that they are sometimes driven by immediate political needs and dramatic events. When the Security Council legislated on international terrorism post-9/11, or created criminal tribunals to deal with genocide, or when IMO adopted measures on oil tanker disasters post-*Torrey Canyon*, or IAEA on nuclear accidents post-Chernobyl, we can see how attitudes and agendas may suddenly change, and law reform then becomes an urgent priority. In some cases the need to be seen to be doing something will result in an essentially symbolic response; in others it may bring about long-needed and real legal change. Law-making of this kind is very different from the attempt to give systematic coherence to international law which has characterised much of the work of the ILC.[44] Crisis-driven law-making is sporadic, selective and often requires a process that will deliver results quickly, rather than prolonged deliberation or systematic coherence.[45] From this perspective it is easy to understand why the Security Council has emerged as one of the more significant elements in contemporary international law-making, and why the General Assembly of the UN has comparatively declined in influence, and the ILC even more so.

[40] See D. Bodansky, 'The UN Framework Convention on Climate Change', *Yale JIL* (1993) 451, 471–92.
[41] See Beijing Ministerial Declaration on Environment and Development, UN Doc A/CONF 151/PC/85 (1991); South Centre, *Environment and Development: Towards a Common Strategy of the South in the UNCED Negotiations and Beyond* (Geneva, 1991); Bodansky, *Yale JIL* (1993) 451.
[42] See *Report of the UNCED*, UN Doc A/CONF 151/26/Rev 1, vols I–III (1992).
[43] See the 1994 Convention to Combat Desertification and the 1995 Agreement on Straddling and Highly Migratory Fish Stocks.   [44] See Chapter 4.
[45] H. Charlesworth, 'International Law: A Discipline of Crisis', 65 *MLR* (2002) 377, 386–92.

International law-making is generally not dictated by disasters, however. It is mainly policy-driven, and reflects ongoing concerns of the international community or of groups of states and NGOs. Thus the Stockholm, Rio and Johannesburg Conferences on the Human Environment and Sustainable Development show how international policy and law on these topics have emerged progressively from a process of periodic review in which new agendas are set, existing goals confirmed or modified, or old policies and institutions reformed in line with emerging priorities. Even when they do not themselves create new law, policy declarations adopted by the UN or by inter-state conferences may influence the development of international law insofar as policies endorsed by the international community create expectations and pressure for implementation and change. The UN General Assembly's Millennium Declaration is an example.[46] Intended to complement Agenda 21 and other international instruments, it sets goals and targets for combating poverty, hunger, disease, illiteracy, environmental degradation and discrimination against women. It commits member states *inter alia* to take action against international crime and terrorism, to try to eliminate weapons of mass destruction, to promote economic development and so on. Some of these objectives will lead to law reform initiatives in various organisations, and the policies endorsed by the Declaration may also influence the interpretation and application of existing treaties and international law. Moreover, subsequent reviews by the UN in 2005 and no doubt also in future years may have continuing effects on the law-making agenda, notably in the WTO, the newly established Human Rights Council and the UN General Assembly.

4.   Law-Making by the United Nations

As Oscar Schachter pointedly observed, 'Neither the United Nations nor any of its specialised agencies was conceived as a legislative body'.[47] This is true insofar as the authority of international organisations to adopt binding rules remains limited. Nevertheless, in the modern world, the United Nations has in practice assumed the role of principal promoter of international law-making.

It is potentially well-suited for this purpose, for several reasons. First, in the eyes of many member states it has legitimacy. As an intergovernmental organisation with universal membership, all states have in theory an equal voice and an equal vote in the General Assembly. Their right to participate in its law-making activity is assured. However, as we shall see below, the same cannot be said of the Security

---

[46] UNGA Res 55/2, 8 September 2000.
[47] In C. Joyner (ed), *The United Nations and International Law* (Cambridge, 1997), 3. See generally Szasz, ibid, 27–64; R. Higgins, *The Development of International Law through the Political Organs of the United Nations* (Oxford, 1963); J. Alvarez, *International Organizations as Law-Makers* (Oxford, 2005).

Council, nor of other elected bodies with limited membership such as the Human Rights Council established in 2006.[48] Second, the UN is a political organisation. Deliberation, negotiation and compromise are its working currency and the principal rationale of its existence. If greater inclusivity and consensus are thereby facilitated, then global law-making is more likely to be successful. Third, it has universal competence. The powers it possesses under the UN Charter embrace, potentially, all areas of political, economic and social affairs.[49] Some important areas of UN law-making, such as human rights, are explicitly envisaged in the Charter. Others, such as suppression of international crime, or the promotion of sustainable development and environmental protection, have emerged through subsequent interpretation to meet the evolving needs of international society. The Charter has proved a very flexible instrument for accommodating such needs.

The UN is also the centrepiece of an eclectic system of international organisations, specialised agencies, programmes, commissions, councils and other bodies with responsibility for law-making in specific areas such as human rights, the environment or criminal justice. We consider the work of several of these bodies in later sections of this chapter.

4.1   Law-Making by the UN Security Council

The conventional view is that the Security Council 'is not, properly speaking, an organ that creates law', but merely one that interprets and applies existing law.[50] A less conventional view is that in the absence of due process, transparency or judicial review, 'the redefinition of a political process as a law-applying process presents more problems than it solves'.[51] Nevertheless, following the end of the cold war, the Security Council has largely been freed from the use of the veto power that had previously inhibited it. Since then, and notwithstanding that its powers under Chapter VII of the UN Charter are limited to the maintenance of international peace and security, it has interpreted these terms very broadly and acted in a number of innovative ways that demonstrate a capacity and willingness to lay down rules and principles of general application, binding on all states, and taking precedence over other legal rights and obligations.[52] In effect it has asserted and

---

[48]   Membership consists of 47 states elected by the UNGA taking into account candidates' contribution to 'the promotion and protection of human rights': UNGA Res 60/251, 3 April 2006.

[49]   UN Charter, Article 1.

[50]   M. P. de Brichambaut, in M. Byers (ed), *The Role of Law in International Politics* (Oxford, 2000) 275.

[51]   M. Koskenniemi, 'Solidarity Measures: State Responsibility as a New International Order', 72 *BYBIL* (2001) 337, 356.

[52]   The scope of the Council's authority to act is dealt with in Chapter 5. See generally F. Kirgis, 'The Security Council's First Fifty Years', 89 *AJIL* (1995) 506, 520; Caron, 87 *AJIL* (1993) 552; V. Gowlland-Debbas, in Byers, *The Role of Law in International Politics*, 277. But for a more cautious view compare T. Sato in Coicaud and Heiskanen, *The Legitimacy of International Organisations*, 335, who emphasises the particularity of most UNSC resolutions.

extended its authority where the inadequacies of law-making by treaty might undermine the pursuit of its objectives.

4.1.1   Legally Binding Determinations

First, Security Council decisions may have legal effects. In the *Namibia Advisory Opinion* the ICJ held that 'a binding determination made by a competent organ of the United Nations to the effect that a situation is illegal cannot remain without consequence'.[53] The Court affirmed the power of the UNSC to declare illegal South Africa's occupation of Namibia, require it to withdraw from the territory, and impose on other states a duty to recognise the illegality. Another notable example is the 1991 Gulf War ceasefire resolution.[54] Iraq disputed provisions of that resolution on the grounds that, *inter alia*, the Security Council had no authority to impose a boundary, a position that was not without support from other UN member states.[55] The same resolution declared that Iraq 'is liable under international law for any direct loss, damage, including environmental damage and the depletion of natural resources, or injury to foreign governments, nationals and corporations, as a result of Iraq's unlawful invasion and occupation of Kuwait'. It established a Compensation Commission to determine claims brought pursuant to the resolution.[56] Subsequently the Council determined that Iraq was in 'material breach' of its disarmament obligations under the ceasefire resolution, although neither UN inspectors nor US-led occupation forces could find any evidence of weapons of mass destruction or illegal weapons programmes. These examples show how the Security Council may make legally binding determinations on questions of law of a kind that are more typically made by courts, but without the normal safeguards of due process inherent in judicial procedures.

Another example shows how the Council has also used its power to override both customary law and applicable treaties. UN peacekeeping personnel are potentially subject to the criminal jurisdiction of the sending state, the host state, the International Criminal Court, and any other state exercising universal jurisdiction over international crimes. Because the US is not a party to the Statute of the Court and objects to the possibility of the ICC having jurisdiction over its forces when engaged on UN peacekeeping missions, SC resolution 1497 (2003) provides that personnel drawn from non-parties to the ICC Statute on UN duty in Liberia are subject to the exclusive jurisdiction of the sending state. This effectively exempts US personnel in Liberia not only from the jurisdiction of the ICC, but also from Liberian territorial jurisdiction in customary law, or indeed that of any other state exercising universal jurisdiction. They may thus be tried only by

---

[53] (1971) ICJ Reports 16. See also *Legal Consequences of the Construction of a Wall in Occupied Palestinian Territory* (2004) ICJ Reports; (2004) 43 ILM 1009.   [54] SC 687 (1991).

[55] C. Gray, 'Iraq, the Security Council and the Use of Force', 65 *BYBIL* (1994) 135, 146–50; M. Mendelson and S. Hulton, 'The Iraq-Kuwait Boundary', 64 *BYBIL* (1993) 135; Kirgis 89 *AJIL* (1995) 506, 531–2.

[56] A. Gattini, 'The UNCC: Old Rules, New Procedures on War Reparations', 13 *EJIL* (2002) 161.

the US. This is a very particular case,[57] but it shows clearly the power the Council has assumed to rewrite or dispense with existing law, a controversial argument we consider further in Chapter 5. Insofar as the Council's reading of the Charter is correct and is accepted by states, the potential for law-making is readily apparent.

4.1.2   Interpretation and Application of the UN Charter

Second, like the General Assembly, the Security Council may in effect extend or develop the law through its interpretation and application of the UN Charter.[58] An important recent example is the body of law relating to the use of military force in response to humanitarian catastrophes. Under the UN Charter the use of force in international relations is permitted only under Article 51 (self-defence in response to an armed attack) or Chapter VII (Security Council collective action in response to a threat to or breach of the peace or act of aggression). Since 1991 when the SC insisted that Iraq allow 'immediate access by international humanitarian organizations' to those in need in Iraq (notably the Kurds),[59] the Security Council has authorised the use of 'all necessary means' to provide humanitarian assistance in, *inter alia*, Somalia, Bosnia-Herzegovina, Rwanda,[60] and to restore the elected government in Haiti.[61] Through such resolutions the Security Council has established the principle that a humanitarian crisis may constitute a situation that triggers Chapter VII action, although the parameters remain imprecise. For example in the case of East Timor, Indonesian consent to intervention was deemed necessary, but not in relation to Somalia, where there was no functioning government. This practice has helped promote the argument that states may, without UNSC authorisation, use military force for humanitarian objectives under customary international law.[62] The legal position remains controversial,[63] but what is indisputable is the potential for extrapolation from Security Council practice on the basis of which claims for the evolution of customary international law may be made. Such claims need not be limited to humanitarian intervention but could be made in any context in which the SC has acted expansively.

4.1.3   Establishment of UN Courts

Third, the Security Council has established international courts. In response to widespread allegations of war crimes and crimes against humanity in Bosnia-Herzegovina, the Security Council established the International Criminal

---

[57] See N. Jain, 'A Separate Law for Peacekeepers: The Clash between the SC and the ICC', 16 *EJIL* (2005) 239. See also SC Res 1593 (2005) authorising the first SC referral to the ICC (Darfur), but excluding jurisdiction over personnel from ICC non-parties.

[58] See Kirgis, 89 *AJIL* (1995) 506, 511–18. On the General Assembly's power to interpret the Charter, see the *Certain Expenses* case (1962) ICJ Reports 151.   [59] SC Res 688, 5 April 1991.

[60] S. Murphy, *Humanitarian Intervention: The United Nations in an Evolving World Order* (Philadelphia, 1996).   [61] SC 940, 31 July 1994.

[62] C. Greenwood, 'International Law and the NATO Intervention in Kosovo', 49 *ICLQ* (2000) 926.

[63] See I. Brownlie and C. Apperley, 'Kosovo Crisis Inquiry: Memorandum on the International Law Aspects', 49 *ICLQ* (2000) 878; C. Chinkin, 'The Legality of NATO's Action in Yugoslavia', ibid 910; V. Lowe, 'International Legal Issues Arising in the Kosovo Crisis', ibid 934.

Tribunal for Former Yugoslavia (ICTY) in 1993. This tribunal became the first international tribunal exercising criminal jurisdiction since the Nuremberg and the Tokyo trials at the end of World War II. The ICTY was followed in 1994 by the International Criminal Tribunal for Rwanda (ICTR) and since then the Security Council has been instrumental in setting up a special court for Sierra Leone. The authority of the Security Council to create subsidiary organs and to bestow criminal jurisdiction on them as a means of addressing threats to international peace and security was affirmed by the appellate chamber of the ICTY in the *Tadic* case.[64] This decision recognised that, in accordance with international human rights law, any such tribunal had to comply with fundamental guarantees of a fair trial by an independent and impartial court. It also accepted that in accordance with the principle of *nullum crimen sine lege*, a tribunal could only apply existing international humanitarian law. Thus the UNSC 'would not be creating or purporting to "legislate" that law'.[65] Nevertheless, as we will see in Chapter 6, the decisions and orders of these tribunals constitute an innovative and increasingly well-developed body of jurisprudence on contemporary international criminal law and procedure.[66]

In the process of establishing the ICTY, the Security Council engaged the services of a range of actors: the Secretary-General,[67] a fact-finding Commission of Experts,[68] and the Special Rapporteur of the Commission on Human Rights. The UNGA also condemned acts of ethnic cleansing in Former Yugoslavia, but it went further than the SC by locating primary responsibility for these acts in the 'Serbian leadership in territories under their control in Bosnia and Herzegovina, the Yugoslav Army and the political leadership of the Republic of Serbia'.[69] The UNGA also asserted individual criminal liability for crimes against humanity and grave breaches of the Geneva Conventions. Thus the SC's unique response to conflict and atrocities was bolstered by the unequivocal support of the UNGA,[70] which was at the same time requesting the ILC to draft a Statute for an International Criminal Court. While the UNGA cannot determine the legality of the SC's exercise of its Chapter VII powers, repeated approval and endorsement 'by the "representative" organ of the United Nations' further legitimates SC action.[71] The most obvious process for establishing such a tribunal would have

---

[64] *Prosecutor v. Tadic* Decision on the Defence Motion for Interlocutory Appeal on Jurisdiction, 2 October 1995 (1996) 35 *ILM* 32, paras 11–43.

[65] *Report of the Secretary General*, UN Doc S/25704 (1993), para 29. See also ICC Statute, Article 22.

[66] See W. von Heinegg, in A. Zimmerman (ed), *International Criminal Law and the Current Development of Public International Law* (Berlin, 2003) 27; R. Kolb, 'The Jurisprudence of the Yugoslav and Rwandan Criminal Tribunals on their Jurisdiction and on International Crimes', 71 *BYBIL* (2000) 259, and Chapter 6. [67] SC Res 808, 22 February 1993.

[68] SC Res 780, 6 October 1992.

[69] UNGA Res 47/147, 18 December 1992 (adopted without a vote).

[70] See also UNGA Res 48/88, 20 December 1993; 48/143, 20 December 1993; 49/10, 8 November 1994 and 49/205, 23 December 1994.

[71] *Prosecutor v. Tadic*, para 44.

been by treaty. This would have allowed states the opportunity to undertake 'detailed examination and elaboration of the issues' and to express their sovereign will in determining whether to become parties.[72] But treaty-making is slow and further time is required before ratification and entry into force. There can be no guarantee that those states whose participation is most needed if the treaty is to be effective will in fact ratify.[73] The Secretary-General also considered that treaty negotiations involving the UNGA could not be reconciled with the urgency expressed by the SC.[74] In contrast, the process of establishment by SC resolution was completed within the year and was binding upon all relevant states under Article 25 of the UN Charter.

4.1.4 *Legislative Competence and UN Reform*

Lastly, the Council has shown that it is willing to legislate more generally on matters relating to peace and security. Two striking and unprecedented examples are SC resolutions 1373 (2001) and 1540 (2005), both Chapter VII resolutions passed in the aftermath of the 11 September 2001 attacks in New York and Washington and later atrocities. In resolution 1373 the Security Council decided that states must take a range of anti-terrorist activities, including prevention and suppression of the financing of terrorism; refraining from any form of support for persons involved in terrorism; providing early warning to states by exchange of information; denying safe havens to those who finance, plan, support or commit terrorist acts; and affording the greatest measure of assistance in criminal investigations. Such obligations would previously have been adopted by treaty, leaving states free to participate or not. The resolution calls upon (although it does not require) states to become parties to the 1999 Convention for the Suppression of the Financing of Terrorism,[75] the provisions of which are in significant respects similar to those found in resolution 1373. States are required to report to a Counter-Terrorism Committee explaining how they have implemented the resolution. The Committee may take further measures where it deems the response to be inadequate. Yet the resolution provides no definition of international terrorism, which had long been debated within the United Nations and other international arenas. In effect this Security Council committee makes authoritative determinations on what constitutes international terrorism and adequate steps to counter it. All UN member states must comply with these decisions. In resolution 1540 (2004) the Council has again legislated in general terms to ensure that non-state actors are prevented from obtaining nuclear, chemical or biological weapons. Implementation is also monitored by the UNSC. Resolution 1540 adds to rather than changes existing treaty law. Its terms expressly disavow any conflict with the

---

[72] Report of the S-G Pursuant to para 2 of SC Res 808 (1993), para 19.
[73] Ibid, para 20.   [74] Ibid, para 21.
[75] The Convention did not enter into force until 10 April 2002. See P. Szasz, 'The Security Council Starts Legislating', 96 *AJIL* (2002) 901, at 903.

rights or obligations of states parties to the Nuclear Non-proliferation Treaty, the Chemical Weapons Convention and the Biological and Toxic Weapons Convention, and it leaves unchanged the responsibilities of the IAEA and the Organisation for the Prohibition of Chemical Weapons.

The exercise of what might be termed legislative or quasi-legislative power by the Security Council is not unproblematic. Its main advantages, as resolutions 1373 and 1540 show, are that where there is political support within the SC it can produce quick, universal and immediately binding obligations in a manner that no treaty negotiation or General Assembly resolution could replicate.[76] At the same time its most obvious drawbacks are that the UNSC is not a fully representative body and that pushed too far such legislative actions may lack legitimacy and acceptability among the wider community of states.[77] The Council consists of only 15 states, five of which are permanent members,[78] the remainder elected on a rotating basis. Non-members whose interests are specially affected may be invited to participate in the Council's discussions, without a vote,[79] and procedures also exist to enable NGOs to have some input into its deliberations.[80] It negotiates its decisions in private, however, but acts on behalf of and can place legally binding obligations on all UN member states, and arguably also on non-members.[81] The power which this gives the Council, and particularly its five permanent members, undermines both the principle of sovereign equality of states and the conception that individual states are not bound by *new* law to which they have not consented. The last point is all the more important when it is appreciated that the Council has acted on the basis that it may over-ride existing law by which states had previously believed themselves bound or empowered to act.[82] As we note in Chapter 5, the possibility of challenging the legality of the Council's actions is limited and the scope of judicial review uncertain. At the same time, any permanent member may veto a resolution which affects its own interests or those of its friends and allies. There can thus be little assurance that the Council will act consistently or at all. This conception of international law-making is especially unappealing to developing states represented on the Security Council only by a few non-permanent members.[83] Moreover, it can also be criticised for the essentially *ad hoc* and unsystematic approach to law-making which results from Council action on specific issues.[84]

---

[76] The General Assembly adopted resolutions on terrorism in 1994 and 1996: see UNGA Res 49/60, 9 December 1994 and 51/210, 17 December 1996 respectively. See Chapter 1.

[77] See Caron, 87 *AJIL* (1993) 552 and Szasz, 96 *AJIL* (2002) 901.

[78] UN Charter, Article 27.

[79] UN Charter, Article 31. Some 25% of UN members did participate in the discussions on resolution 1540.   [80] See Chapter 2.

[81] Articles 2 (6) and 25.   [82] See Chapter 5.

[83] See South Centre, *For a Strong and Democratic United Nations* (London, 1997) 127–49. See also the letter on weapons of mass destruction from the Permanent Representative of India to the United Nations to the President of the Security Council, 27 April 2004.

[84] A. Bianchi, 'Ad-hocism and the Rule of Law', 13 *EJIL* (2002) 263–72.

Whether viewed in terms of accountability, participation, procedural fairness or transparency of decision-making, the Security Council is a seriously deficient vehicle for the exercise of legislative competence. Dominated by the permanent members, or sometimes by only one or two of them, unrepresentative and undemocratic, its quasi-legislative powers can only be justified by reference to the paramount urgency and importance of its responsibility for the maintenance of international peace and security. From this perspective, while the process may seem unfair and illegitimate, the Council has shown that on some occasions it can be effective at taking decisions, and this is an important standard by which to judge it.[85] At the same time, as we noted earlier, the increasing prominence of the UNSC in the dynamics of international law-making marks an important shift of power and influence away from the General Assembly. For many states that see the General Assembly as the paramount 'law-making' institution of the UN this is not a welcome development, nor is it necessarily one foreseen or intended by the drafters of the Charter.[86] The Council's powers are not unlimited, and in Chapter 5 we consider how far, if at all, it may have authority to act in a legislative capacity.

Moreover, the *de facto* broadening of the Council's competence within the Charter system has strengthened demands from some states for procedural and institutional reform. In 2004, as part of a broader review of the objectives and structure of the UN, a High Level Panel appointed by the S-G recommended that the UNSC should be made more democratic and accountable, and that more countries, especially from the developing world, should be involved in its decisions.[87] The Panel's report also makes far-reaching recommendations about the conditional nature of sovereignty within the Charter system and the collective responsibility of states for promoting the objectives of the UN. Although the report says nothing about the implications for international law-making of what Slaughter calls a 'tectonic shift' in the role of the UN, an organisation more committed to the exercise of collective responsibility could scarcely avoid enhancing its own law-making role.[88] In that context reform of the Council would be essential. As the Secretary-General noted in a speech marking the UN's 60th anniversary: 'do not underestimate the slow erosion of the UN's authority and legitimacy that stems from the perception that it has a very narrow powerbase, with just five countries calling the shots.'[89] However, the Summit meeting held in 2005 made no progress on reform of the Council.

---

[85] See Sato, in Coicaud and Heiskanen, *The Legitimacy of International Organisations*, 327–9.

[86] South Centre, *For a Strong and Democratic United Nations*, 138 ff; M. Happold, 'SC Resolution 1373 and the Constitution of the UN', 16 *LJIL* (2003) 593, 607.

[87] Report of the High Level Panel on Threats, Challenges and Change, UN Doc A/59/565 (2004). See also Y. Z. Blum, 'Proposals for UN Security Council Reform', 99 *AJIL* (2005) 632.

[88] A.-M. Slaughter, Security, 'Solidarity and Sovereignty: The Grand Themes of UN Reform', 99 *AJIL* (2005) 619.   [89] Kofi Annan, London, 31 January 2006.

4.2   The UN General Assembly in International Law-Making

The UN General Assembly is a forum for discussion, negotiation and coordination.[90] It also has responsibility for 'encouraging the progressive development of international law and its codification'.[91] With minor exceptions it has no power to take decisions binding on states. In this respect it is very different from the Security Council. Nevertheless, although not a legislative body in any sense, its ability to adopt resolutions on any subject, convene law-making conferences, adopt treaties and initiate codification projects has given it a central role in the development of international law.[92] Law-making conferences on, *inter alia*, the Human Environment (Stockholm, 1972), the Law of the Sea (1973–82), Environment and Development (Rio, 1992), Fish Stocks (New York, 1993–5) and the International Criminal Court (Rome, 1998) have been convened and their results endorsed by the General Assembly. Moreover, as we will see in Chapter 5, UNGA resolutions on such diverse matters as human rights, the legal status of the deep seabed and outer space, decolonisation, friendly relations between states, and global climate change have influenced the evolution of treaties, general principles and customary law on these and many other topics.

In other cases multilateral treaties are negotiated within various committees of the General Assembly. These include the 1st Committee (Disarmament), the 3rd Committee (Social and Humanitarian Affairs), and the 6th Committee (Legal Committee), the Committee on Peaceful Uses of Outer Space (COPUOS), and various *ad hoc* or special committees. Subsidiary bodies of the UNGA also play a prominent role in law-making and the negotiation of multilateral treaties, in particular the Human Rights Commission, the Commission on the Status of Women, the UN Environment Programme and others which we examine below. The work of some of these bodies involves the negotiation of new law, such as the development of international human rights law or international environmental law, while in other cases more modest codification or progressive development of existing law is the objective. The ILC is the principal UNGA subsidiary body responsible for codification and progressive development, but other UN bodies also undertake such work. We examine codification and progressive development in Chapter 4, but as we suggest there, it is neither possible nor particularly useful to draw a sharp distinction between the law-making which is the focus of this chapter and codification which is the focus of the next: the two often overlap, and the distinction is one of degree. Moreover, in many cases the process of negotiation involves participation by a range of different bodies: for example the UNGA may take the initiative by remitting an issue for codification by the ILC, whose

---

[90]   UN Charter, Articles 10–11. See generally Peterson, *The General Assembly in World Politics*.
[91]   UN Charter, Article 13. See Chapter 4.
[92]   See generally Joyner, *The United Nations and International Law*, and A. Roberts and B. Kingsbury (eds.), *United Nations, Divided World* (2nd edn, Oxford, 1993), chapter 10.

proposals will then be considered by the 6th Committee, then they will possibly be taken further by an *ad hoc* committee, remitted back to the ILC, refined in the 6th Committee and finally be adopted by the UNGA. Human rights treaty negotiations may involve the UNGA, the 3rd Committee, the Economic and Social Council, the Human Rights Council and an intergovernmental conference. The range of possibilities is very great, and they do not end there.

Even when it does not itself promote the negotiation of new treaties or other instruments, the General Assembly's power to coordinate the legal and policy agendas of specialised agencies and other UN bodies gives it a continuing role at the heart of the law-making process. With so many different bodies potentially involved in international law-making, the task of allocating responsibilities and coordinating policy is an increasingly important feature of the General Assembly's role. Where, for example, should responsibility for developing international law relating to forests be located? FAO's mandate covers forestry, while promoting trade in timber is the main objective of the International Tropical Timber Organisation. The World Heritage Convention adopted by UNESCO protects some forest areas, while forests generally are also covered by the Convention on Biological Diversity. Sustainable use of natural resources falls within the mandate of UNEP, while afforestation and deforestation are potentially significant issues for parties to the Kyoto Protocol and the Convention on Climate Change. Where such cross-cutting areas of policy are involved, no single forum is self-evidently the right one to undertake the development of new law.[93]

Moreover, the choice of forum may affect not only the perspective from which the issues are approached but also the constituencies most likely to become involved and whose interests are most strongly favoured by the governmental representatives concerned. To give responsibility for a convention on forests to FAO, for example, would tend to favour the perspectives of agriculture and forestry ministries and the relevant industries. To give it to UNEP would be more likely to favour environmental ministries and organisations. In either case, the influence of developing countries may not be as strong as it is in the General Assembly, and forests are a matter of strong interest to a number of important developing states. In such circumstances there is a tendency for the UNGA to take upon itself responsibility for coordinating action.[94] Alternatively, as we shall see below, one agency may lead while other interested agencies cooperate and coordinate their policies. This gives each of them a say, but ensures—or may ensure—that the UN as a whole pursues a single coherent policy.[95]

A specialised agency with undisputed competence may not, however, be the best forum to take the relevant measures. Specialised agencies, both national and

---

[93] The UN first established an Intergovernmental Panel on Forests, then an Intergovernmental Forum on Forests to coordinate policy and recommend a programme of action to the Commission on Sustainable Development.

[94] See eg UNGA Res 59/25, 17 December 2004 which gives directions on fisheries policy to FAO, IMO and UNEP.

[95] See discussion of the WHO Framework Convention on Tobacco Control, below, Section 4.

international, tend to be strongly influenced by special interests and particular ministries. For instance, IMO, dominated by shipping states, has been notably reluctant to strengthen international law relating to flag of convenience vessels.[96] FAO, in which fishing states have a powerful voice, may be slow to react to unsustainable practices such as drift-netting or flag of convenience trawling. In all of these cases it may become necessary for the General Assembly with its universal membership and broader view to take action, as it did when adopting a ban on driftnet fishing,[97] or establishing an inter-agency task force on flags of convenience in response to lobbying by Greenpeace, IUCN and the International Transport Workers' Federation.[98]

Coordination of the policies of so many different international organisations necessarily falls to the UN, usually the General Assembly, the Secretary-General, or a subsidiary body such as UNEP or the Commissions on Human Rights or Sustainable Development. Thus, when the General Assembly endorsed the 1992 Rio Declaration on Environment and Development, referring to its 'fundamental principles for the achievement of sustainable development', it also called on the Commission on Sustainable Development and the UN Secretary-General to promote incorporation of the principles of the declaration in the implementation of Agenda 21 and in UN programmes and processes, and urged governments to promote their widespread dissemination.[99] The Rio Agenda has gradually affected the application and the development of law and policy by most of the relevant international organisations, including FAO, IMO, The World Bank and the WTO, as well as by treaty bodies such as the International Tropical Timber Organisation and the European Energy Charter.[100] International law-making by all of these organisations on issues such as the precautionary approach, sustainable use of natural resources and environmental impact assessment reflects the changes brought about through the mechanism of UN soft law since 1992.

The point is not that the General Assembly has usurped the powers of other bodies, merely that it can perform a necessary role in bringing some measure of consistency to the policies and law-making activities of an otherwise diverse range of organisations. However, there is also good reason for some scepticism concerning the UN's success at coordinating either its own programmes or those of the rest of the UN 'family'. As the Director General of IUCN pointed out: 'Despite all the emphasis on co-ordination . . . the programmes of UN agencies, and other organisations, including my own, are still conceived too independently, operated too

---

[96] See below, Section 4.
[97] UNGA Res 44/225, 22 December 1989; 45/197, 21 December 1990; 46/215, 21 December 1991; 59/25, 17 December 2004.
[98] Consisting of the UN, FAO, IMO, UNEP, UNCTAD, ILO and OECD. See UN Doc A/59/63 (2004), *Report of the Consultative Group on Flag State Implementation*.
[99] UNGA Res 47/190 and 191, 22 December 1992 and 48/190, 21 December 1993.
[100] See P. W. Birnie and A. E. Boyle, *International Law and the Environment* (2nd edn, Oxford, 2002), chapter 2.

separately and involve too many overlaps and inefficiencies . . . '.[101] This can result in multiple agencies reinventing the wheel each time they adopt measures on similar topics. Further, the UNGA has no power to coordinate the policies of non-UN bodies such as the WTO. We consider below whether this could result in potential conflicts of interest between WTO and other international organisations.

4.3   ECOSOC Commissions and Programmes

In the UN Charter the Economic and Social Council (ECOSOC) is the principal UN organ responsible for the promotion of international cooperation on economic and social matters and the protection of human rights.[102] It is also the body to which UN specialised agencies, commissions and programmes report, and with which NGOs may have consultative status.[103] ECOSOC does not have any formal law-making competence as such. Its principal powers are to initiate studies and reports on economic, social, health and related matters; to make recommendations on these matters to the General Assembly and to specialised agencies, whose activities it also coordinates; to prepare draft conventions for submission to the General Assembly, and to convene international conferences.[104] This is potentially a huge area of responsibility for a body with limited membership (54 states). In practice some of its functions, for example with respect to coordination, have been assumed by the General Assembly. Others are exercised by functional programmes, such as the UN Environmental Programme (UNEP) and the UN Development Programme (UNDP), or by a number of Commissions, including the former Commission on Human Rights (CHR), the Commission on the Status of Women (CSW), the Commission on Crime Prevention and Criminal Justice, and the Commission on Sustainable Development.

Some of these ECOSOC subsidiary bodies have taken a leading role in preparing conventions and promoting international law-making in various ways. UNEP, for example, has been the most active UN body in the development of international environmental law. In this context it has pioneered the use of soft law and framework agreements, as well as promoting treaty implementation and coordinating some of the growing number of treaty secretariats and meetings of parties.[105] It has also to some extent sought to codify the law on natural resources, sustainable development, environmental impact assessment and so on. Another

---

[101] M. Holdgate, 19 *Env Pol & Law* (1989) 86, 92. See also P. Szasz, in E. Brown Weiss, *Environmental Change and International Law* (Tokyo, 1992) 340–84.
[102] UN Charter, Articles 55, 62.   [103] UN Charter, Articles 64, 71.
[104] UN Charter, Articles 62–6.
[105] UNCED Agenda 21, Chapter 38, para H (1) (h); UNGA Res S/19–2, 19 September 1997; UNGA Res 53/242, 28 July 1999; 1997 Nairobi Declaration on the Role and Mandate of UNEP, adopted by UNEP Governing Council decision 19/1 (1997). See generally Birnie and Boyle, *International Law and the Environment*, chapter 2.

example is the Commission on Crime Prevention and Criminal Justice, which has responsibilities covering many of the areas of organised crime that threaten international security, such as money laundering, corruption, trafficking. A significant achievement for this body was the negotiation of the Convention on Transnational Organised Crime, adopted in 2000, including two protocols on Migrant Smuggling and Human Trafficking.[106] The latter introduced for the first time a now widely accepted definition of 'human trafficking' and set out states' obligations with respect to cooperation in prosecuting traffickers and assisting trafficked persons.[107]

One of ECOSOC's most prominent responsibilities for international law-making has been the elaboration of international human rights law through subsidiary commissions. In 1946, pursuant to Article 68 of the UN Charter, it established the Commission on Human Rights (CHR) and the Commission on the Status of Women (CSW).[108]

4.3.1 The Commission on Human Rights

From the outset it was anticipated that the CHR would draft an international bill of rights and in the first two decades it concentrated on setting human rights standards though the non-binding Universal Declaration of Human Rights (UDHR) and binding treaties, principally the 1966 International Covenants on Civil and Political Rights (ICCPR), and on Economic, Social and Cultural Rights (ICESCR).

The articulation of human rights principles in the UDHR was an important first step in fleshing out the general human rights provisions of the UN Charter. Much has been written about the various influences within the Commission throughout the drafting of the UDHR. Different weight has been given to the impact of individual members—their intellectual and personal priorities, their willingness to compromise and their level of involvement—to the role of the UN Human Rights Division, in particular its first Director John Humphrey, and of various civil society bodies.[109] Thereafter the task of transforming the Declaration into treaty form proved to be long and arduous. The 17-year negotiation process for the 1966 Covenants has been described as follows:

The Commission then worked on the draft covenants at every annual session from 1949 to 1954, during which time it circulated early drafts to governments and intergovernmental organizations for comment. In 1950, during the UN Fifth Session, all member states were

---

[106] Protocol against the Smuggling of Migrants by Land, Sea and Air; Protocol to Prevent, Suppress and Punish Trafficking in Persons, especially Women and Children, both supplementing the 2000 UN Convention against Transnational Organized Crime, UNGA Res 55/25, 8 January 2001.
  [107] See eg 2005 Council of Europe Convention on Action against Trafficking in Human Beings, Article 4; OHCHR, Recommended Principles and Guidelines on Human Rights and Human Trafficking, UN Doc E/2002/68/Add 1 (2002). See also T. Obokata, 'Trafficking Human Beings as a Crime Against Humanity', 54 *ICLQ* (2005) 445, who argues that trafficking is now a crime against humanity in general international law.   [108] ECOSOC Resolution 11 (II), 21 June 1946.
  [109] See eg M. A. Glendon, *A World Made New: Eleanor Roosevelt and the Universal Declaration of Human Rights* (New York, 2001).

given opportunity to comment on the several substantive issues pertaining to the draft covenants. This was arguably the moment when diplomats exercised greatest influence on the shape and content of the two human rights covenants.

The UNGA's Third Committee (Social, Humanitarian and Cultural Affairs) discussed the initial draft for several weeks and sent it back to the Commission with instructions for changes. When the Human Rights Commission finalized its draft of the covenants in 1954, they were referred to . . . ECOSOC, which in turn passed them on to the UNGA for formal review and debate in the UNGA's Third Committee. That fall the Third Committee began an article-by-article scrutiny of the draft covenants, a process that would ultimately span twelve years.[110]

The work of the CHR in these early years has been likened by Alston to that of the International Law Commission,[111] in that it was primarily a drafting body for the General Assembly with the many difficult political impasses being mainly resolved within the Assembly. Indeed Alston observes that the CHR played a minimal role in the drafting of other human rights instruments and that the Assembly at times deliberately by-passed it, preferring to undertake the drafting process itself. It had little or no input into such instruments as the Genocide Convention, the Women's Convention, the Declaration against Torture and the Convention on the Human Rights of Migrant Workers and their Families. On the other hand the CHR was responsible for significant work on the Torture Convention and the Convention on the Rights of the Child. It provided technical drafting assistance and through its sub-commission and various specialist working groups carried out considerable preparatory work, research and drafts on a wide range of human rights topics.[112]

The CHR was an intergovernmental body, rather than a body of independent members.[113] States were elected periodically, and no state was guaranteed membership. This structure was not necessarily inappropriate for a body with responsibility for the negotiation and development of human rights law acceptable to governments but the Commission came under considerable criticism for its growing politicisation. In the words of UN Secretary-General, Kofi Annan:

> . . . the Commission's capacity to perform its tasks has been increasingly undermined by its declining credibility and professionalism. In particular, States have sought membership of the Commission not to strengthen human rights but to protect themselves against criticism or to criticize others. As a result, a credibility deficit has developed, which casts a shadow on the reputation of the United Nations system as a whole.[114]

As part of the 2005 UN reforms the CHR was replaced by the Human Rights Council.[115] The Human Rights Council may make recommendations to the GA

---

[110] S. Waltz, 'Universal Human Rights: The Contribution of Muslim States', 26 *HRQ* (2004) 799, 806.

[111] P. Alston, 'The Commission on Human Rights', in P. Alston (ed), *The United Nations and Human Rights* (Oxford, 1992) 126, 129–30. [112] For further details see ibid 131–8.

[113] Contrast the sub-commission whose members are independent experts.

[114] Report of the S-G, *In Larger Freedom: Towards Development, Security and Human Rights for All*, UN Doc A/59/2005 (2005), para 182. [115] UNGA Res 60/251, 3 April 2006.

'for the further development of international law in the field of human rights'. Like the CHR, it has a limited membership of states elected periodically by the GA. It is hoped that by specifying human rights credentials for membership, including 'voluntary pledges and commitments made thereto' the credibility and legitimacy of the new institution will be ensured. In its first meeting the Human Rights Council adopted two standard-setting instruments—the International Convention for the Protection of All Persons from Enforced Disappearances[116] and the Declaration on the Rights of Indigenous Peoples.[117]

4.3.2   The Commission on the Status of Women

Other ECOSOC Commissions have also been responsible for drafting human rights instruments within their areas of expertise. The mandate of the Commission on the Status of Women includes preparing recommendations and reports on 'promoting women's rights in political, economic, civil, social and educational fields'. To this end standard setting comes within its functions. The CSW has particularly sought to influence the standard setting work of the CHR, ensuring the inclusion of sex equality provisions within the UDHR and the Covenants, and has undertaken its own drafting of instruments.[118] A commentator has noted that 'Its legislative activities mirror its historical development, from an exclusive concern with legal equality in specific areas, to a concern with integration and participation and efforts to achieve global synthesis'.[119]

Thus the particular importance of the CSW as a law-making body is that it has sought to ensure the integration of women's rights throughout the human rights system, including international criminal law. This movement can be illustrated by three law-making initiatives. First, from its origin to the early 1960s CSW identified specific issues where women suffered disadvantage and sought to rectify the position through what have been called 'corrective treaties'. These include the 1952 Convention on the Political Rights of Women, the 1957 Convention on the Nationality of Married Women and the 1962 Convention on Consent to Marriage, Minimum Age for Marriage and Registration of Marriages. In each case there was disagreement between members of the CSW and ECOSOC, with drafts being sent back for reworking.

After this initial phase the CSW turned to its major achievements, first a Declaration on the Elimination of Discrimination against Women,[120] and then the 1979 Convention on the Elimination of All Forms of Discrimination against Women (CEDAW), both global instruments addressing inequality. The latter was the most significant outcome of the UN Decade for Women (1975–85) and was

---

[116] UN Doc A/HRC/1/L.2, 23 June 2006.
[117] UN Doc A/HRC/1/L.3, 23 June 2006. See Chapter 2. On the Human Rights Council see P. Alston, 'Reconceiving the UN Human Rights Regime: Challenges Confronting the New Human Rights Council', 7 *Melbourne Journal of International Law* (2006) 185.
[118] L. Reanda, 'The Commission on the Status of Women', in Alston, *The United Nations and Human Rights*, 265, 279.   [119] Ibid 281.
[120] UNGA Res 2263 (XXII), 7 November 1967.

adopted in time for the mid-term Conference at Copenhagen in 1980. Modelled on the earlier Declaration and Convention on the Elimination of Racial Discrimination, the text was prepared by working groups within the CSW during 1976. Between 1977 and 1979 it was subject to extensive deliberations by a working group of the UNGA 3rd Committee. Concerns were expressed in the UNGA that the speed with which the working group completed the draft convention cut short discussion over last-minute amendments and at the way in which the 3rd Committee took decisions on a legal instrument.[121] Nevertheless, the CEDAW was adopted by the UNGA, quickly becoming the 'crowning achievement of the Commission in the field of standard setting'.[122] It is the second most widely ratified human rights treaty and has greatly contributed to the evolution of the international norm of non-discrimination on the basis of sex.

Since completing its work on CEDAW, the CSW's role has turned primarily to promoting the themes of global summit meetings, notably the Third and Fourth World Conferences on Women at Nairobi (1985) and Beijing (1995): Equality, Peace and Development. Although these conferences did not produce any legally binding texts, the final documents do contain a blend of normative propositions, recommendations and strategies for women's equality and empowerment. As we saw in Chapter 2, a particular feature of both the CHR and CSW has been the participation of NGOs in a range of law-making functions including researching, drafting, lobbying and mobilising opinion. The enormous presence of women's NGOs at Nairobi and Beijing (as well as the Vienna Conference on Human Rights) was part of a global campaign for women's advancement that has sought to work through and alongside international governmental bodies. The focus has been on implementation of legal standards rather than adoption of new ones, although it has promoted with some success instruments relating to the acceptance of violence against women as a human rights concern and the adoption of an Optional Protocol to the Women's Convention.

4.4 Specialisation in UN Law-Making: Some Conclusions

The point about the Commissions on Human Rights or the Status of Women, like the UN Environmental Programme, or the UN Development Programme, is that although not specialised agencies separate from the UN, these bodies are institutions with a commitment to promote the relevant objectives of the UN Charter through law-making where appropriate or necessary. They have built up an expertise in their special fields of law, while at the same time operating through finely tuned political processes. In taking law-making initiatives they can draw upon experience derived from compliance monitoring and reporting procedures. NGOs and other international organisations can participate in and influence their agendas

---

[121] eg Mr Edis (UK), GA 107th Plenary Meeting, UN Doc A/34/PV 107, 1992 (1979).
[122] Reanda, in Alston, *The UN and Human Rights*, 286.

and their work. In many of these respects they are very similar to UN specialised agencies. They are quite unlike the International Law Commission, which we consider in Chapter 4. These differences help explain why the ILC has not been more involved in these specialised fields of international law-making. As Koskenniemi points out, 'Human rights, humanitarian law and refugee protection (like trade law, environmental law and so on) come with a political direction and a set of preferences and it was far from clear that the [International Law Commission] would share those preferences—in fact it was likely not to share them'.[123]

All of these bodies are in other words variants of the 'epistemic communities' we discussed in Chapter 2. They illustrate the value of specialisation and expertise, but they also contribute to the fragmentation of international law-making as a whole, through what Koskenniemi calls 'functional differentiation'. The need for coordination can up to a point be supplied by the UNGA, but to see the problem of specialisation solely in these terms 'underestimates the degree to which it manifests a deliberate challenge and attempt by one instrumental idea to impose itself on others'.[124] The risk is that there may then be competition between different subsystems of law and the values promoted by different international law-making institutions. If this manifests itself within the UN itself—in essence a competition between the different bureaucratic mandates of the CHR, UNEP, the ILC and so on—then it should be no surprise that it arises just as strongly in the law-making activities of specialised agencies and other international organisations outside the UN.

5.   Other International Organisations

The network of UN specialised agencies and other global and regional organisations is too diverse to permit a comprehensive study of their contribution to international law-making, and that is not the purpose of this chapter. It is possible here only to give some sense of their role in the law-making process, and their strengths and limitations. Some, such as the World Trade Organisation (WTO) and its predecessor, the General Agreement on Tariffs and Trade (GATT), have an ongoing responsibility for negotiation, interpretation and enforcement of law within their specialised field. In that sense law-making is one of their most significant responsibilities. Others, such as the North Atlantic Salmon Conservation Organisation, only very occasionally and incidentally undertake any law-making. We have deliberately said very little about several agencies with a long record of law-making, notably the International Civil Aviation Organisation (ICAO), the International Atomic Energy Agency (IAEA) and the International Labour Organisation (ILO), because they have been fully examined by others and further treatment here would provide few additional insights to the present chapter.[125]

---

[123] Koskenniemi, 23 *Wis ILJ* (2002) 64.   [124] Ibid 81.
[125] On IAEA see Birnie and Boyle, *International Law and the Environment*, chapter 9. On the ILO see Section 7.2 below. For an overview see J. Alvarez, *International Organizations as Law-Makers* (Oxford, 2005).

Some common features of all such bodies affect their ability to participate in or to promote international law-making. First, in contrast to the UN, the competence of every other IGO is limited. While their powers may be broadly construed, and can be implied from functional necessity or practice, they are nevertheless specific to the purposes of each organisation, and therefore vary widely.[126] Second, no IGO is in any sense independent of their member states; all are controlled by and answerable to the governments who constitute their decision-making bodies. They can undertake law-making only if member states so decide, although in some cases those with the power to decide constitute only a proportion of the total membership elected for this purpose to a governing council or executive body, which is not necessarily reflective of the views of all states parties.[127] Third, within the UN system specialised agencies are the principal repositories and disseminators of technical expertise, and it is this attribute which arguably constitutes their most significant contribution to the law-making process. Moreover, NGOs and national experts often influence the decisions of specialised agencies and other bodies, sometimes to a greater extent than is possible in the UN itself.

The range of law-making activities undertaken and instruments produced by these bodies is very varied. Their most important role is best understood as international standard setting. The adoption of soft law codes and guidelines on nuclear installations by the IAEA, the Codex Alimentarius of the WHO and FAO, the radiological protection standards established by the International Commission on Radiation Protection, the annexes to IMO treaties on ship safety and pollution, or the establishment of domain-name standards by the World Intellectual Property Organisation typify this aspect of their work.[128] Essentially technical in character, these instruments seek to establish internationally agreed minimum standards for the regulation of internationally important industries. Their precise legal status will depend on the organisation involved, the basis on which the standards are adopted and the form of the instrument. We explore this question further in Chapter 5.

Specialised agencies also negotiate and adopt multilateral treaties. In many cases, these treaties provide the legal framework for international regulatory regimes which provide the basis for standard setting, monitoring processes and compliance mechanisms. The regulation of maritime, aviation and nuclear safety, security and liability by IMO, ICAO and IAEA respectively is among the most important examples of this genre. All three organisations are responsible for adopting new treaties and treaty amendments, revising or adding annexes, and setting additional soft law standards on related matters. In effect they each constitute a standing diplomatic forum, whose ongoing oversight enables law-making to evolve relatively quickly in response to new problems, priorities or opportunities. Less convincingly, they also enable

---

[126] See *Reparations for Injuries Case* (1949) ICJ Reports 174; *Certain Expenses Case* (1962) ICJ Reports 151; *Nuclear Weapons Advisory Opinion* (1996) ICJ Reports 66 (WHO).

[127] eg the Council of IMO, on which see below.

[128] See F. Kirgis, in Joyner, *The UN and International Law*, 82–8.

member states to exercise some degree of oversight over implementation and compliance by member states.

Lastly, as we shall see below, major UN agreements such as the 1982 UNCLOS and the Convention on Biological Diversity, or policy statements such as the Millennium Development Goals or Agenda 21 of the Rio Conference often require further implementation by specialised agencies. In the following sections we consider law-making by some of these agencies and other international organisations in more detail.

5.1   The Food and Agriculture Organisation

Within its specialised sphere of fisheries and agriculture, FAO has promoted international law-making in various ways.[129] Article XIV of its Constitution empowers the Organisation to 'approve' conventions and agreements negotiated, drafted and submitted by a technical commission or conference composed of member states. While the majority of Article XIV treaties mainly establish regional fisheries commissions rather than adding to the corpus of international law, a few have laid down rules of more general significance, most notably the 1993 Agreement to Promote Compliance with International Conservation and Management Measures by Fishing Vessels on the High Seas (Compliance Agreement) and the 2001 International Treaty on Plant Genetic Resources for Food and Agriculture. FAO technical consultations have provided expert and influential advice in the negotiation of several UN treaties, including the 1958 Convention on Fishing and Conservation of the Living Resources of the High Seas, the 1982 UNCLOS and the 1995 Agreement on Straddling and Highly Migratory Fish Stocks. The Organisation collaborated with UNEP in securing the negotiation and adoption of the 1998 Convention on the Prior Informed Consent Procedure for Certain Hazardous Chemicals and Pesticides in International Trade. Finally, when the adoption of binding agreements is not possible, FAO has made some use of non-binding agreements, including the 1983 International Undertaking on Plant Genetic Resources, now superseded by the 2001 treaty considered below.

FAO has also been the principal body responsible for developing international fisheries law and promoting implementation of the fisheries provisions of the 1982 UNCLOS, the 1995 UN Fish Stocks Agreement and Agenda 21 of the 1992 UN Conference on Environment and Development. It has employed a mixture of hard and soft law for this purpose, including the 1993 Agreement to Promote Compliance with Conservation Measures on the High Seas, [130] the 1995 Code of Conduct on Responsible Fishing,[131] the 2001 Reykjavik Declaration on

---

[129] See J. P. Dobbert, in O. Schachter and C. Joyner (eds), *United Nations Legal Order* (ASIL, 1995), 902.

[130] G. Moore, in E. Hey (ed), *Developments in International Fisheries Law* (The Hague, 1999) 91–2.

[131] See W. Edeson, 'The Code of Conduct for Responsible Fisheries: An Introduction', 11 *IJMCL* (1996) 97.

Sustainable Fisheries and various voluntary undertakings.[132] As required by Article XIV of the FAO Constitution, all of these fisheries instruments were considered initially by a 'technical consultation' of industry and government experts; they were then negotiated by consensus in the Committee on Fisheries before adoption by the FAO Council. Here we can see how, within the framework of a UN law-making treaty—the 1982 UNCLOS—a specialised agency can further develop the law within its own special field in response to emerging needs and priorities. At the same time, we can also see that a variety of law-making instruments allows added flexibility and increases the likelihood of reaching agreement.[133]

FAO played only a limited role in the negotiation of the Convention on Biological Diversity (CBD), but it has subsequently been involved in implementation of the Convention and related elements of Agenda 21. To this end, the International Treaty on Plant Genetic Resources for Food and Agriculture adopted in 2001 replaces the earlier non-binding 1983 Undertaking and creates a multilateral scheme for access to certain agricultural crops, an issue not specifically dealt with in the CBD.[134] Negotiations were initiated by the FAO Council and conducted mainly in the Commission on Genetic Resources for Food and Agriculture, in which a large number of states participated, together with observers from WIPO, the CBD Secretariat, the International Union for the Protection of New Varieties of Plants, and a variety of NGOs and agricultural research institutes. However, the negotiations straddled issues of concern to several other international bodies, including UNEP, WTO, UNCTAD, WIPO and the Conference of the Parties to the CBD and could have been allocated accordingly.[135] Three factors helped ensure the choice of FAO. First, that is where the issue had previously been dealt with, mainly at the insistence of developing countries, which did not have the same influence or level of participation in WTO. Second, the CBD recognised that further negotiations on agricultural biodiversity would be required, and should take place within FAO.[136] FAO's promotion of a new treaty whose objectives included 'harmony with the Convention on Biological Diversity'[137] was not inherently problematic. At Brazil's insistence it

---

[132] eg the International Plans of Action on Longline Fisheries, Conservation and Management of Sharks, Management of Fishing Capacity, adopted by FAO in 1999, and the International Plan of Action on Illegal, Unreported and Unregulated Fishing, adopted in 2001. Some states expressed significant reservations when adopting the 2001 Plan of Action: see FAO, *Report of the Committee on Fisheries*, 24th Session (2001). See Chapter 5, Section 2.4. [133] See Chapter 5.

[134] See Dobbert, in Schachter and Joyner, *United Nations Legal Order*, 930–8; K. Raustiala and D. G. Victor, 'The Regime Complex for Plant Genetic Resources', 58 *Int Org* (2004) 277.

[135] See M. Petit et al, *Why Governments Can't Make Policy: The Case of Plant Genetic Resources* (Lima, 2001) 6; B. Chambers, 'Emerging International Rules on the Commercialisation of Genetic Resources', 6 *J World Intellectual Property* (2003) 311.

[136] Petit et al, *Why Governments Can't Make Policy*, 10, and Resolution 3, Nairobi Final Act, 1992 CBD. The parties to the CBD subsequently adopted the Bonn Guidelines on Access to Genetic Resources, but like the CBD itself these are broader than the 2001 Treaty. Moreover they are nonbinding. See Chambers, 6 *J World Intellectual Property* (2003) 311.

[137] Article 1. A draft clause dealing with other agreements was deleted by the FAO Legal Committee. See FAO, *Report of 72nd Cttee on Constitutional and Legal Matters* CL121/5 (2001).

became a 'treaty', rather than a 'convention', a meaningless gesture supposed to minimise confusion with the CBD. Third, the United States and other developed countries had already largely secured their objectives in intellectual property negotiations at the WTO, and to that extent whatever happened in FAO would matter less.[138]

The negotiation of this treaty illustrates several points of more general importance for international law-making. First, international law-making is necessary in such cases in order to coordinate potentially disparate national policies, even if in the end consensus eludes the delegates, in this case largely because US attitudes to intellectual property issues could not be accommodated. But as this example shows, the result may be a treaty which coordinates the policies of only some states, and which in this case will not be supported by the US. Second, it shows that the complexity of modern law-making is not simply a product of the need to secure agreement among a large number of states and other actors. Coordination with the work of other bodies, with UN policy and with other treaties is often necessary and equally important. This is a point we return to below and in Chapter 5. The need for law-making on plant genetic resources within FAO was largely driven by developments in law and policy elsewhere within the UN system and not by FAO. Nevertheless, locating the negotiations within FAO ensured both an influential role for FAO specialist technical expertise and the conduct of subsequent negotiations by representatives with a food and agriculture perspective rather than a trade or intellectual property viewpoint.[139] Whether this is the right 'epistemic community' for such a task need not concern us here, but choices of this kind do have important consequences for the outcome of negotiations. Lastly, it is apparent that FAO has not succeeded in shaping the whole of international law on plant genetic resources: important elements have been determined in the WTO and the CBD.

5.2   The World Health Organisation

Unlike FAO or IMO, the WHO has until recently had relatively little involvement in international law-making. This is not because it lacks the necessary powers. Unusually for an international organisation, WHO may adopt 'regulations' which will be binding on all member states except those who register an objection, but this power is rarely used, and in practice non-binding recommendations have become the main regulatory instrument.[140] Even serious global health risks, such as the threat of severe acute respiratory syndrome (SARS), have been dealt with

---

[138] See TRIPS Agreement, Article 27 (3) (b); Raustiala and Victor, 58 *Int Org* (2004) 277.

[139] Petit et al, *Why Governments Can't Make Policy*, 58.

[140] 1948 WHO Constitution, Articles 21–3. See S. Fidler, 'The Future of the WHO: What Role for International Law?', 32 *Vand JTL* (1998) 1079; G. L. Burci and C.-H. Vignes, *WHO* (The Hague, 2004), 124–55.

through non-binding guidelines rather than regulations.[141] The reason for this is simple. As a respected expert body, WHO's recommendations will normally be followed—or even exceeded—by national health administrations. In this respect WHO standards have a significance very similar to the soft-law standards set by IAEA for the nuclear industry: they represent the consensus of expert opinion. For this purpose they do not necessarily need binding force. On the other hand, if severe medical threats of this sort did require mandatory powers over all states, then at present only the Security Council has such competence. In resolution 1308 (2000) the Council recognised that the HIV/AIDS pandemic has the potential to risk international stability and security but it has not yet taken any legislative action under Chapter VII in response to global health concerns.

The WHO constitution also provides for the adoption of conventions and agreements with respect to health, but the Framework Convention on Tobacco Control, adopted unanimously in 2003, remains the sole treaty concluded under these powers.[142] Nevertheless, this is an interesting and informative example of modern international law-making. The objective of the Convention is to provide 'a framework for integrated tobacco control measures to be implemented by the Parties'. As a framework convention, modelled on earlier environmental agreements, it is intended to be further developed by the addition of more detailed optional protocols negotiated and adopted by the Conference of the Parties.[143] The decision to negotiate a treaty rather than more soft law was important because it ensured that whatever was agreed would, once in force for most states, over-ride any inconsistent commitments of a more general kind undertaken by states.[144] For that reason the policies and law-making agenda of other international organisations would also have to take the Tobacco Convention into account, for example within the WTO or the World Bank.

WHO policy on tobacco control was substantially based on a strategy approved by the 9th World Conference on Tobacco and Health in 1994. In initiating the negotiation of a convention, WHO was responding to resolutions adopted by its own member states and by ECOSOC.[145] A new Director-General, Dr Gro Harlem Brundtland, gave the negotiations added priority and serious political leadership. Two important political problems had to be addressed, and doing so contributed greatly to the eventual success of the negotiations. First, WHO sought to ensure that tobacco industry lobbying could not undermine the negotiations. A Committee of Experts' report highlighted the extent to which the industry had influenced

---

[141] WHO guidelines for the global surveillance of SARS, WHO/CDS/CSR/ARO/2004.1.

[142] Under Articles 2 (k) and 19 of the WHO Constitution a two thirds majority of the Assembly is required for adoption of a convention. A Convention comes into force for members when it is accepted in accordance with national constitutional requirements.

[143] Article 23(4). On framework conventions see Chapter 5. The Convention entered into force in 2005 and at that point no protocols had been adopted.   [144] See Chapter 5.

[145] Notably WHA.49.17 (1996) and WHA.52.18 (1999). See also ECOSOC 1999/56.

international policy on tobacco control by diverting attention towards other issues. Their report showed, in the view of Dr Brundtland, 'that the tobacco companies planned and implemented global strategies to discredit and impede WHO's efforts to carry out its mission'.[146] To counter these strategies WHO introduced new procedures to ensure transparency and prevent conflicts of interest among staff and others involved in the negotiations. It also held hearings to give the public health community, tobacco farmers and the tobacco industry the opportunity to make their case in public.

Second, it was essential to ensure that WHO's efforts would not be hampered by other elements of the UN system. An inter-agency task force was established to ensure that 'one United Nations' voice is heard throughout the FCTC process'.[147] Strenuous efforts were made to ensure cooperation, in particular from the World Bank, the UNDP, FAO and the WTO. Some countries had a substantial tobacco-growing industry; controls on tobacco would affect trade, economic development and farmers. It was important to establish that UN policy on tobacco control was not simply an issue for WHO to promote, but required the support of other agencies with different mandates and potentially different priorities. That over 50 states pledged their support for the negotiations in the 1999 session of the WHO Assembly would not of itself have been enough to ensure success without these other political strategies.

The negotiations themselves were handled in two stages. First, a Working Group was established. This body was responsible for producing the elements of a draft text and identifying possible topics for protocols.[148] Open to all WHO member states and observers, participation by developing states was facilitated through payments from a trust fund. Legal and health experts were also consulted. The draft then went to the WHO Assembly, providing states with a further opportunity for comment.[149] Once approved by WHO, the draft elements then formed the basis for the second stage of negotiations, conducted by an Intergovernmental Negotiating Body (INB) composed of all member states and observers. NGOs could participate in meetings and make statements if they met WHO's criteria, or if specifically admitted by the INB.[150] The INB determined what should go in the draft convention, and what would be deferred for later protocols, and it convened a series of working groups to advance the negotiations and develop compromise solutions.[151] Prior to the second session, regional preparatory meetings were held in Africa, the Caribbean and Southeast Asia to help familiarise governments with the issues. NGOs also produced commentaries. Ultimately, as in

---

[146] WHO, *Response of the D-G to the Report of the Committee of Experts*, WHO/DG/SP (2000).
[147] UN, Interagency Task Force on Tobacco Control, *Report of 1st Session* (1999) 1. See also the 2nd, 3rd and 4th Reports produced in 2000–1.
[148] See WHO, *1st Report of the WG on the FCTC*, A/FCTC/WG1/7 (1999).
[149] See WHO, *Comments of the 53rd World Health Assembly*, A/FCTC/INB1/2 Add1 (2000).
[150] See WHO, *Participation of NGOs*, A/FCTC/INB3/DIV/6 (2001).
[151] UN, Interagency Task Force, *Report of 3rd Session* (2000) 8–9.

many other major negotiations, it was the responsibility of the Chair of the INB, a Brazilian diplomat, to produce a consensus draft based on the working group texts and submissions from governments and observers.[152] Intersessional meetings and informal negotiating groups helped the Chair reach agreement on a final text at the fifth session of the INB. Finally, the Convention was adopted by the WHO Assembly in 2003 and opened for signature.

This is a typical example of the negotiating process for multilateral treaties. Much more could be said about the inevitable bargaining and last-minute horse-trading that characterise any negotiation of this kind, and about which states held particular views, but these matters belong to diplomatic history. For our purposes, what matters is to observe the role of WHO in this process. WHO neither drafted the Convention nor dictated its content. That was a matter for states to determine, even at the earliest stage. It is of course possible for an international organisation, or an NGO, to provide a negotiating text, but this will inevitably be redrafted in the process of negotiation by states. WHO's role in this case was twofold. First, it provided the necessary leadership and organisation to make the negotiations possible. In that respect, the impact of a dynamic and politically shrewd Director-General should not be underestimated. Second, it provided or facilitated access to the necessary technical expertise, whether on health, law or other policy issues. It is this combination of political and technical expertise which gives specialised agencies their most distinctive contribution to international law-making.

5.3   The International Maritime Organisation

IMO is the principal body responsible for the international regulation of shipping. Its role as 'the competent organisation' in this respect is referred to implicitly in several articles of the 1982 UN Convention on the Law of the Sea.[153] It is empowered to promote 'the general adoption of the highest practicable standards in matters concerning the maritime safety, efficiency of navigation and prevention and control of marine pollution from ships'.[154] Responsibility for regulatory developments is divided between a Maritime Safety Committee (MSC), a Marine Environment Protection Committee (MEPC) established following a recommendation of the 1972 Stockholm Conference,[155] and a Legal Committee.[156] The IMO Council, whose 32 members are drawn on an equitable geographical basis

---

[152] See WHO, *Letter from the Chair of the INB*, A/FCTC/INB5/DIV/5 (2002).

[153] Notably Articles 211, 217, 218. See IMO, *Implications of the Entry into Force of the UNCLOS for the IMO*, LEG/MISC/2 (1997).

[154] Article 1, 1948 Convention Establishing the International Maritime Consultative Organisation (changed to IMO in 1982).

[155] IMO Res A297 (VIII) (1973). See L. de La Fayette, 'The MEPC: The Conjunction of the Law of the Sea and International Environmental Law', 16 *IJMCL* (2001) 155.

[156] See N. Gaskell, 'Decision Making and the Legal Committee of the IMO', 18 *IJMCL* (2003) 155.

from the largest maritime states and other states with a 'special interest in maritime transport and navigation', supervises the work of these bodies. As a result, the Council is dominated by shipping states,[157] but all member states are represented in the Assembly, the governing body of the Organisation, and in the various committees referred to above. Coastal states and those with limited maritime interests can thus participate fully in the Organisation's main rule-making bodies; however, it does not follow that they will necessarily be influential.[158]

IMO has negotiated almost 40 conventions, as well as adopting non-binding codes, recommendations and guidelines on related matters. The most important regulatory treaties are the 1973/78 Convention for the Prevention of Marine Pollution from Ships (MARPOL) and the 1974 Convention on the Safety of Life at Sea (SOLAS). These agreements establish internationally recognised standards for the construction and operation of ships and the prevention of pollution at sea. The principal regulations are found not in the text of the conventions themselves but in the annexes, participation in which is not necessarily obligatory,[159] and which are easily and regularly supplemented or amended by decision of the MEPC or MSC.[160] Apart from their character as treaty law, many of the relevant provisions of these annexes have become 'generally accepted international rules and standards' for the purposes of Articles 211 and 217–20 of the 1982 UNCLOS. As such they will in many cases define the obligations of flag states and the powers of coastal states not only under UNCLOS but also, potentially, under customary international law. They may thus become Law for states not party to the treaties themselves. To that extent, the parties to MARPOL and SOLAS are not merely implementing UNCLOS but in a very real sense making law for all states. We return to this important point in Chapter 5.

Another important role for IMO law-making is the development of treaty regimes whose principal purpose is to harmonise and progressively develop national law on liability for marine pollution. Starting with the adoption of the 1969 Convention on Civil Liability for Oil Pollution Damage and the 1971 Convention on the Establishment of an International Fund for Compensation for Oil Pollution Damage, IMO has gradually extended the scope of maritime liability. The original treaties on oil pollution were replaced by revised agreements negotiated in 1992, and these have since been joined by conventions on liability for hazardous and noxious substances and bunker fuel oil. These agreements simplify recovery of compensation for pollution damage and they are an important precedent for other forms of hazardous activity. Nevertheless, the most recent tanker accidents have strained the financial limits that are an inherent part of the

---

[157] See R. M'Gonigle and M. W. Zacher, *Pollution, Politics and International Law* (London, 1979).

[158] Gaskell, 18 *IJMCL* (2003) 171 points out that US interventions in the Legal Committee are 'more notable for their quality than for their influence'.

[159] For example states parties to the 1973/78 MARPOL Convention are automatically bound by Annexes I and II, but may opt out of Annexes III–V.

[160] But only the states parties have a vote: see MARPOL Convention, Article 16.

regime, and some states have begun to question whether they are too favourable to the interests of the shipping and oil industries. This criticism points to one of the main problems with bodies like IMO.

IMO exhibits many of the strengths and weaknesses of international regulatory agencies. In its favour it enables the law-making process to draw upon appropriate technical expertise and it is rather more than a forum within which interested states negotiate and revise global standards. Industry associations, mainly representing shipping companies, seafarers and insurers, participate actively and they are often influential, as are some environmental NGOs.[161] Bodies typically involved include the International Chamber of Shipping, the International Confederation of Trade Unions, P&I Clubs, Friends of the Earth International and IUCN. Moreover, IMO conventions on private law aspects of maritime law—civil arrest, limitation of liability and salvage—are usually proposed and initially drafted by the Comité Maritime International, an association of lawyers with a longstanding role in the development of maritime law. In all these respects IMO's relationship with the shipping and insurance industries is a positive one, quite unlike WHO's experience with the tobacco industry.

Among its weaknesses, IMO inevitably finds it difficult to act against the opposition of flag of convenience states, many of which coordinate their positions in advance and are influential members of the IMO Council. Repeated disasters with single hull oil tankers eventually resulted in the adoption of IMO regulations accelerating the phasing out of these ships, but only after unilateral action was taken first by the United States and then by the European Union.[162] Another weakness has been IMO's failure to give enough attention to non-implementation and non-compliance with existing conventions and standards. In 1992 a new Sub-Committee on Flag State Implementation was asked 'to identify measures necessary to ensure effective and consistent global implementation of IMO instruments, paying particular attention to the special difficulties faced by developing countries'. The main outcome has been the adoption of some useful recommendations and guidelines clarifying the responsibilities of flag states,[163] but there is still no mechanism for investigating and dealing with non-performing parties, and IMO's Flag State Implementation Committee does not provide one. The problem highlights IMO's limited powers as a supervisory body.[164]

Substandard shipping is not simply the product of non-compliance with MARPOL and SOLAS, but it is clear that while IMO has been an active regulatory body, with a good record in securing wide acceptance for safety and environmental standards, and in updating them, it has not been wholly convincing in its handling

---

[161] Gaskell, 18 *IJMCL* (2003) 172–4; de La Fayette, 16 *IJMCL* (2001) 213–16.

[162] See 1973/78 MARPOL Convention, Annex I, regulations 13F and 13G, as amended in 2003.

[163] de La Fayette, 16 *IJMCL* (2001) 215–26.

[164] de La Fayette, ibid 223; A. Roach, in M. Nordquist and J. Moore (eds) *Current Maritime Issues and the IMO* (The Hague, 1999) 151.

of the modern shipping industry.[165] Domination by flag of convenience states is a significant factor in its inability to deliver stronger measures and better compliance mechanisms. Like some other regulatory agencies IMO is thus open to the criticism that it too often serves the interests of the industry it is meant to regulate.[166] It is significant that pressure for action on flags of convenience has come from the UNGA rather than from IMO. Lastly, the whole process of negotiating and renegotiating maritime conventions can be very slow. The 1989 Salvage Convention took 11 years to negotiate, the 1996 HNS Liability Convention almost 20, and ten years later it was still not in force. In this respect IMO compares unfavourably with the work of the CMI in the years prior to IMO's involvement in maritime law-making.[167] IMO can act quickly, as its response to disasters such as the sinking of the *Torrey Canyon* or the *Erika* shows.[168] Nevertheless, it is unsurprising if some states sometimes opt for unilateral measures rather than waiting for the IMO.

5.4   The World Trade Organisation

5.4.1   The Institution

The WTO came into existence as an international organisation only in 1994, but its origins date from the adoption of the General Agreement on Tariffs and Trade in 1947 (GATT). The GATT established the core rules and principles of international trade law, but it also provided for further meetings of the contracting parties 'for the purpose of giving effect to those provisions of this Agreement which involve joint action and, generally, with a view to facilitating the operation and furthering the objectives of this Agreement'.[169] Subsequently, provision was also made for additional negotiations on tariffs.[170] On this basis, successive conferences of the parties negotiated and adopted additional trade measures and agreements since 1947. The most significant of these negotiations, the so-called 'Uruguay Round', concluded in 1994 with the adoption by consensus of a package of important agreements, understandings and decisions that *inter alia* regulated trade in agricultural produce, trade in textiles, services (GATS), intellectual property rights (TRIPS), investment (TRIMS), technical barriers to trade (TBT Agreement), sanitary and phytosanitary measures (SPS Agreement), and established both the WTO and a quasi-judicial dispute settlement system.[171] The

---

[165] See M. Hayashi, 'Toward Elimination of Sub-standard Shipping: The Report of the International Commission on Shipping', 16 *IJMCL* (2001) 501; Birnie and Boyle, *International Law and the Environment*, chapter 7; de La Fayette, 16 *IJMCL* (2001) 215–20.

[166] Another example of the same problem is IAEA, on which see Birnie and Boyle, *International Law and the Environment*, chapter 9.   [167] Gaskell, 18 *IJMCL* (2003) 212–14.

[168] See de La Fayette, 16 *IJMCL* (2001) 195–6.   [169] 1947 GATT, Article 25 (1).

[170] GATT, Article 28 *bis*.

[171] For the full package of agreements, understandings and decisions adopted by the conference see WTO, *The Legal Texts: The Results of the Uruguay Round of Multilateral Trade Negotiations* (Cambridge, 1999). See generally A. Lowenfeld, *International Economic Law* (Oxford, 2002), chapter 5.

GATT itself was re-adopted, incorporating amendments and interpretations agreed since 1947.

The WTO is an intergovernmental organisation. Like other such organisations, it has an influential secretariat, but it is in no sense an autonomous regulatory or law-making body. As Howse observes, the organisation is 'simply the collective voice of the members themselves, and not an independent decision-making institution'.[172] Article 5 of the WTO Agreement requires it to cooperate effectively with related IGOs; it also allows for consultation and cooperation with NGOs concerned with WTO-related matters. As we saw in Chapter 2, unlike most international organisations, WTO does not have a history of openness towards NGOs, and its members tend to take the view that it is not possible for NGOs to become directly involved in the work of WTO bodies. There are some good reasons for this caution, including the opposition of member states, but also arguments in favour of some form of participation.[173] In practice, increasingly large numbers of NGOs, including many trade and industry associations, have been allowed to participate in WTO Ministerial Conferences.

The WTO undertakes law-making in two senses. First, like IMO and various other international organisations, it is in effect a regulatory agency. All WTO members must sign up to all the main agreements adopted in 1994. While many of these agreements are detailed and comprehensive, some, such as TRIMS, are little more than an outline or framework requiring further negotiations, while the whole package of WTO law assumes the need for continued evolution. In this respect the WTO is the forum for agenda-setting and policy review, as well as the negotiation, adoption, amendment and authoritative interpretation of WTO agreements.[174] For these purposes all members are represented on the General Council and the Ministerial Conference, the two main political organs of the organisation. The 1947 GATT allowed decisions to be taken by majority vote,[175] but the parties have normally operated on the basis that consensus is desirable (defined for this purpose to mean the absence of objections by any member present when a decision is taken) and that practice is retained expressly in the WTO Agreement.[176] Voting is thus allowed only if the objections of a member government cannot otherwise be overcome. Although in these circumstances individual countries may not be able to exercise a veto over negotiations, the opposition of a major trading state, such as the US, China or Japan, or a major bloc of states, such as the EU or the Cairns Group of agricultural producers, will effectively render an agreement pointless even if there is a large majority in favour. While the US and the EU often set the agenda for earlier rounds of trade negotiations, the increased

---

[172] R. Howse, in Coicaud and Heiskanen (eds), *The Legitimacy of International Organisations*, 359. However these comments do not apply to the Dispute Settlement Body.

[173] See Chapter 2, and G. Marceau and P. Pedersen, 'Is the WTO Open and Transparent?' (1999) 33 *JWT* 5; D. Esty, 'NGOs and the WTO', 1 *JIEL* (1998) 123.

[174] 1994 WTO Agreement, Articles 3, 9–10.   [175] Article 25 (4).

[176] Article 9 (1).

influence of developing states and various *ad hoc* groups now has to be accommodated and it is less easy for developed states to dominate the organisation in this way.

The dynamics of trade negotiations thus tend towards a 'package deal' outcome (known as a 'single undertaking' in WTO), with various parties making mutually interdependent agreements in order to achieve a compromise acceptable to all.[177] In negotiations of this kind no one state or group of states can usefully push agreements through without making appropriate concessions to others; only when there are enough benefits for all groups is consensus likely. For example, during the Uruguay round, developing countries eventually accepted the TRIPS Agreement but only in return for concessions on agriculture and textiles. It took eight years of negotiations, a threatened US walkout and a lot of patient diplomacy by the Director-General of the secretariat to conclude the Uruguay Round.[178] As they become more familiar with WTO and better organised, developing states have been less susceptible to the diplomatic coercion employed by the US during earlier negotiating rounds; for this reason the Doha Round remained deadlocked in 2006 after several ministerial conferences had failed to produce a package deal on services, agriculture and development.

Second, and very unusually for an international organisation, the WTO itself has exclusive compulsory jurisdiction over disputes arising under the relevant agreements (covered agreements).[179] The role of the Dispute Settlement Body (DSB) is to secure a 'satisfactory settlement' in accordance with the covered agreements, interpreted 'in accordance with the customary rules of interpretation of public international law'.[180] This function is performed by expert panels, whose decisions are subject to appeal to an Appellate Body consisting of lawyers of recognised authority and independence. The Appellate Body's decisions can in theory be overturned by consensus of the members of DSB; to that extent they are unlike judicial decisions, but in practice it would be pointless to challenge them in this way unless even the successful party opposed adoption. In reality, they have without exception become final and binding.

The Appellate Body's decisions are significant for several reasons. Most obviously, they provide a consistent and authoritative jurisprudence on the interpretation and application of the covered agreements in accordance with the relevant provisions of the Vienna Convention on the Law of Treaties, whose provisions are treated for the purpose of the DSU as a codification of international law.[181] Critics have argued that the Appellate Body has taken a more expansive view of its role

---

[177] Lowenfeld, *International Economic Law*, 61–7. On the significance of consensus/package deal negotiations see discussion of the UNCLOS III conference in Section 5 below.

[178] See Howse, in Coicaud and Heiskanen, *The Legitimacy of International Organisations*, 360–1.

[179] 1994 Dispute Settlement Understanding.

[180] 1994 DSU, Articles 3 (2)–(4). See Chapter 5.

[181] 1994 DSU, Article 3 (2). See *Standards for Reformulated Gasoline*, Appellate Body WT/DS2/AB/R (1996), in 35 ILM (1996) 603; *Taxes on Alcoholic Beverages*, Appellate Body WT/DS8/AB/R (1996).

than the pre-WTO panels,[182] but this ignores its judicial character as well as the other changes mandated by the Dispute Settlement Understanding (DSU), and it overstates the nature of the jurisprudence that has emerged.[183] In contrast, the old panel system essentially delivered conciliation awards designed to secure an outcome politically acceptable to all the contracting parties.[184] Often characterised by inconsistency and an absence of legal reasoning, pre-WTO awards were easily blocked because they became binding only when confirmed by consensus of the parties. Equally unlike the old panels, the Appellate Body has sought to integrate WTO law within international law as a whole. Its decisions have shown that the covered agreements can when necessary be interpreted and applied consistently with general international law and other treaties, as required by Article 3 of the DSU.[185] As we argue in Chapters 5 and 6, the importance of this integration function cannot be overestimated. Without it, a coherent system of international law could not even be envisaged. From this perspective the DSU gives WTO law an essential bridge into the values and principles of general international law, although how far it does so and with what effect remain controversial.[186]

Nevertheless, the Appellate Body performs a law-making function only in the limited sense that it has to decide arguable and unsettled questions of law; that is the task the members of WTO have given it. If the outcome is an unacceptable precedent for future cases, a three-fourths majority of the General Council or the Ministerial Council remains free in accordance with Article 9 (2) of the WTO Agreement to change the law by agreeing on a different interpretation of a covered agreement. By virtue of Article 31 (3) (a) of the Vienna Convention on Treaties, such an agreement will necessarily prevail over an earlier judicial decision. In that sense, as in general international law, WTO members continue to make the law, not the Appellate Body.

5.4.2 The WTO and the Regulation of Trade-Related Matters

What can the WTO legitimately regulate? The Agreement Establishing the WTO envisages that it will provide a 'common institutional framework for the conduct of trade relations among its Members . . .'.[187] At the same time it is not the only international body with responsibilities related to international trade and its jurisdiction in this respect is not exclusive. The UN Conference on Trade and Development is

---

[182] See eg R. H. Steinberg, 'Judicial Law-Making at the WTO', 98 *AJIL* (2005) 247.
[183] See L. Bartels, 'The Separation of Powers in the WTO: How to Avoid Judicial Activism', 53 *ICLQ* (2004) 861.
[184] See generally Lowenfeld, *International Economic Law*, chapter 7.
[185] See especially *Import Prohibition of Certain Shrimp and Shrimp Products (Shrimp-Turtle case)*, Appellate Body WT/DS58/AB/R (1998). Contrast two decisions under the old system: *Restrictions on Imports of Tuna*, GATT (1991) 30 ILM 1598 (*Tuna/Dolphin I Case*) and *Restrictions on Imports of Tuna*, GATT (1994) 33 ILM 839 (*Tuna/Dolphin II Case*).
[186] See generally J. Pauwelyn, 'The Role of Public International Law in the WTO: How Far Can We Go?', 95 *AJIL* (2001) 535 and contrast J. Trachtman, 'The Domain of WTO Dispute Resolution', 40 *Harv ILJ* (1999) 333.   [187] 1994 WTO Agreement, Article 2 (1).

also a forum in which policy on trade matters is formulated, with specific focus on developing countries. During the 1970s UNCTAD was active in promoting a new international economic order,[188] and several conventions on shipping and commodities were adopted under its auspices.[189] Neither initiative has had lasting success or succeeded in changing international law.[190] UNCTAD was more successful in securing special treatment for developing countries in the GATT, but it has not in practice sought to compete with WTO in the regulation of international trade, and the Doha Round of trade and development negotiations falls firmly within the WTO's authority. The OECD has also been a forum for at least one set of trade-related negotiations—the otherwise abortive Multilateral Agreement on Investment.

A small number of non-WTO multilateral treaties regulate harmful forms of international trade. These include the 1988 UN Convention against Illicit Traffic in Narcotic Drugs, the Conventions on International Trade in Endangered Species and Transboundary Movements of Hazardous Wastes negotiated by UNEP in 1973 and 1989 respectively, and a protocol on trade in genetically modified organisms adopted by the parties to the Convention on Biological Diversity.[191] Provided they are non-discriminatory and not a 'disguised restriction on international trade',[192] there is no obligation for states to choose WTO as the forum in which to conduct negotiations on such matters. At the same time, since trade regulation is the central purpose of all of these agreements, there is no reason in principle why the WTO should not address similar concerns. Moreover, since the WTO is not a UN specialised agency, its law-making activities cannot easily be coordinated or dictated by the UN General Assembly. Member governments are largely free therefore to decide for themselves what the scope of WTO law-making should be.

A more difficult question is whether the WTO can also regulate issues that do not themselves involve trade but which have a direct impact on conditions of trade. Obvious examples would include the protection of intellectual property rights, the protection of labour standards, or the establishment of health and safety standards for goods or agricultural produce traded internationally. In all these examples other international bodies with primary responsibility for international regulation already exist, including WIPO, ILO, FAO, WHO and the International Standards Organisation. There are no hard and fast jurisdictional boundaries between these organisations and WTO, and it is possible to advance policy arguments of various kinds for and against the WTO taking on a more

---

[188] See in particular the Declaration on the Establishment of a New International Economic Order, UNGA Res 3201 (S–VI), 1 May 1974 and the Charter of Economic Rights and Duties of States, UNGA Res 3281 (XXIX), 12 December 1974.

[189] eg the 1986 Convention on Registration of Ships; 1965 Convention on Transit Trade of Land-Locked States.

[190] But see B. Rajagopal, *International Law from Below Development: Social Movements and Third World Resistance* (Cambridge, 2003), chapter 4.   [191] 2000 Protocol on Biosafety.

[192] See especially 1992 Rio Declaration on Environment and Development, Principle 12.

expansive role in regard to the regulation of these matters and many others.[193] It might well make sense, for example, to link negotiations on trade issues with setting standards for reducing CO_2 emissions and promoting energy efficiency, since it is far from obvious why a country that subsidises pollution by failing to take action on climate change should reap the benefits of free trade. We should not assume therefore that such trade-related issues could not be dealt with by WTO.

Ultimately it is for the contracting parties to decide on the forum in which they wish to negotiate, and if, for example, they choose to conclude the TRIPS Agreement in a WTO context rather than at WIPO they are free to do so. In this particular instance developing countries would have preferred WIPO, but eventually yielded to pressure from the US and EU in return for concessions on other issues.[194] This is no different from the similar choices made when preferring to negotiate a plant genetic resources agreement at FAO rather than the CBD, or a tobacco convention at WHO rather than FAO or WTO. In all these cases states have treated the question as essentially a pragmatic one: which forum is more appropriate and why? The answer in many instances is best understood in political rather than jurisdictional or constitutional terms.

WTO has also made use of standards set by other international bodies where appropriate. It has not so far sought to substitute its own, although here too there is no constitutional impediment. Thus the SPS Agreement relies *inter alia* on standards set by the Codex Alimentarius Commission, the International Plant Protection Convention and so on. When taking exceptional national measures under Article 20 of the GATT to protect the health of humans, plants and animals, members are entitled to invoke WHO and other internationally agreed standards as evidence that their actions are necessary and justifiable.[195] The TRIPS Agreement seeks to establish a 'mutually supportive' relationship with WIPO and it expressly requires members to comply with the various articles of the relevant WIPO conventions.[196] The principal safeguard against the WTO over-extending itself by seeking to regulate such matters is the need for consensus among the membership.

On the other hand, WTO has stopped short of requiring members to comply with ILO labour conventions, or with UN human rights conventions, or with multilateral environmental agreements. Trade measures have in the past been used by states to promote compliance with international standards on such matters, and present WTO law does not necessarily prohibit all such action in appropriate cases.[197] But we can see from this example that WTO does not have the same kind

---

[193] See J. Alvarez and others, 'Symposium: The Boundaries of WTO', 96 *AJIL* (2002) 1–158.

[194] See Lowenfeld, *International Economic Law*, 98–101.

[195] See *EC Measures Concerning Meat and Meat Products (Beef Hormones)*, Appellate Body WT/DS26/AB/R (1997).

[196] In particular the 1967 Paris Convention for the Protection of Industrial Property and the 1971 Berne Convention for the Protection of Literary and Artistic Works.

[197] See eg *EC—Trade Preferences case*, Appellate Body WT/DS246/AB/R (2004), and the *Shrimp-Turtle case* and Principle 12 of the 1992 Rio Declaration referred to earlier.

of 'mutually supportive' relationship with other law-making organisations that it has with WIPO.

5.4.3   WTO: Legitimacy, Constitutionalisation and Law-Making

The present WTO represents a major evolution in the law-making machinery for international trade. Compared to the arrangements in place before 1994, its membership is more inclusive, although still not universal, its negotiations are more open and transparent, even if there is room for further improvement, and the dominance of the US and EU has been replaced by the need for a broader consensus involving developing states. Moreover the agreements it adopts now have a genuinely legal character, and trade relations among the parties are largely governed by rules rather than by non-transparent compromises and understandings brokered *ad hoc* by a secretariat wielding what one author has described as a 'technocratic, epistemic, "*eminence grise*"' kind of power.[198] Dispute settlement is also no longer determined by the secretariat but proceeds within a recognisably judicial and rules-based structure. As an international regulatory body WTO can now be compared to UN specialised agencies such as IMO or ICAO.

Given all these changes, it could hardly be denied that the WTO has greater legitimacy as a law-making institution than the old GATT structure, even if it could be improved in several ways. At the same time, the potential scope of its law-making, and its actual or perceived impact on economic and social life worldwide is far greater than any other international regulatory body. Its policies are not universally appreciated. Scholars have advanced very different views about the legitimacy and role of the WTO, and their debate is of wider relevance. Some take the view adopted in this chapter that the WTO is simply another intergovernmental regulatory body operating within a pragmatically determined but nevertheless limited ambit. They generally favour additional measures to enhance openness, NGO participation and a more mutually supportive relationship with other international organisations and with international law in general, but otherwise they tend to see an improved WTO as the best solution to the regulation of trade relations.[199] A rather different approach would elevate WTO law to the status of a new constitutional order, conferring on individuals trade rights directly enforceable in national courts, expanding its ambit into additional areas of economic and social life, using WTO to promote compliance with international human rights law, and democratising the institutions by involving civil society in the law-making process.[200] This vision of WTO as an institution of global governance has obvious resemblances to the European Union. Its law-making activities would,

---

[198] Howse, in Coicaud and Heiskanen (eds), *The Legitimacy of International Organisations*, 358.

[199] See especially Howse, ibid; A. Guzman, 'Global Governance and the WTO', 45 *Harv ILJ* (2004) 303–51; J. Pauwelyn, 'The Sutherland Report', 8 *JIEL* (2005) 329–46.

[200] See especially E.-U. Petersmann (ed), *Reforming the World Trading System* (Oxford, 2005); id, 'European and International Constitutional Law: Time for Promoting "Cosmopolitan Democracy" in the WTO', in de Búrca and Scott (eds), *The EU and the WTO: Legal and Constitutional Issues*, 81.

like the EU's, become ever more expansive and the sovereignty of individual states would be markedly diminished, but it would no longer be making international law. Instead we would have a new and distinct legal order. Deborah Cass has argued powerfully, however, that free trade is not the right starting point for a new global legal order and that WTO must remain situated within the broader structure of international law-making so that other values and concerns can be adequately and more democratically addressed by the international community.[201]

It is not necessary here to pursue this specifically WTO debate. Its shows, however, that the more ambitious the law-making aspirations of an international institution, and the more extensive the transfer of powers away from member states, the more important become the indicators of legitimacy: openness, transparency, participation and democratisation. As we saw when considering the Security Council, contemporary international law-making processes are generally inadequate to meet such challenges without radical structural reform. It is also evident, however, that process alone will not guarantee legitimacy if the substance is unacceptable. In the present Balkanised system of international law-making, the specific focus of one organisation may prove harmful or inadequate if it results in the legal system disregarding other concerns, values or perspectives. The point sharply made by Cass is that there is more to life than free trade, and we need a legal system that reflects this. Thus, while the boundaries between different organisations cannot be laid down in a systematic way, the need for a supportive relationship is obvious. In Chapter 5 we take further the question whether international law itself has a coherent approach to the inter-relationship of different bodies of law, including WTO law.

6. International Conferences

The negotiation of treaties in multilateral conferences dates back at least to the Treaty of Westphalia in 1648 and the Congress of Vienna in 1814–15, but was relatively rare until the 20th century. The first truly law-making conferences were those convened at The Hague in 1899 and 1907. With 45 states represented, the latter was the largest treaty negotiation then held.[202] A reassessment on the 100th anniversary concludes that 'The mixture of lofty rhetoric, prophetic international legal vision, and narrow political interest of the Hague Conferences became a characteristic, even an unexpected feature, of collective international law-making efforts in this century'.[203] In practice, the more important global treaties and declarations

---

[201] Cass, *The Constitutionalization of the WTO*.
[202] On the early history of international conferences see N. Hill, *The Public International Conference* (Stanford, Calif, 1929).
[203] G. Aldrich and C. Chinkin, 'The Hague Peace Conferences: A Century of Achievement and Unfinished Work', 94 *AJIL* (2000) 90.

continue to be negotiated and adopted using *ad hoc* conference procedures, although in many cases the preliminary negotiations are now conducted at the UN or in some other international organisation.[204] Major examples include the 1969 Vienna Convention on the Law of Treaties, the 1982 UNCLOS, the 1994 Agreement Establishing the WTO, the 1998 International Criminal Court Statute, and the various instruments, binding and non-binding, adopted at the 1992 Rio Conference on Environment and Development. Other non-binding instruments have also been adopted at global conferences of this kind, including declarations on human rights, population and development, and women.[205]

The process has evolved significantly since its 19th and early 20th century antecedents. Decisions at The Hague Peace Conferences had to be adopted unanimously, but they were not open to IGOs, NGOs or observers, and their proceedings were held in private.[206] Today, UN-convened global conferences are in principle open to all states, and for some time have not necessarily excluded non-members of the UN. For example, Switzerland participated in UNCLOS III although not a UN member at the time. Other participants include IGOs and other bodies with observer status, as discussed in Chapter 2. Participation by NGOs is nowadays also the norm.[207] UN conferences are very much more open to scrutiny than in 1899 and unanimity is no longer required. However certain features have remained constant, including the practice of concluding some instruments in legally binding form while other statements are in the form of *voeux* or declarations.

Multilateral conferences remain strange law-making phenomena: they have 'no regular sessions, no permanent venue and no constitutional infrastructure'.[208] Nevertheless, prominent among the modern examples of conference diplomacy, two negotiating models can broadly be distinguished: the one codified by the Vienna Convention on the Law of Treaties in 1969 (and followed by the interstate negotiating conference which adopted that convention), and the other based on the procedures followed by UNCLOS III from 1973 to its conclusion in 1982.

6.1   The Vienna Convention Model

Early international conferences favoured unanimity or near unanimity as the voting requirement for adoption of multilateral treaties or individual treaty provisions. As the international community of states expanded, later practice tended towards majority voting, and it was this practice which the International Law

---

[204] See generally, J. Kaufmann, *Conference Diplomacy* (3rd edn, Basingstoke, 1996).

[205] UN World Conference on Human Rights, Vienna Declaration and Programme of Action, UN Doc A/CONF 157/23, 25 June 1993; International Conference on Population and Development, Cairo, 1994, UN Doc A/CONF 171/13/Rev 1; 4th UN World Conference on Women, Beijing Declaration and Platform for Action, 1995, UN Doc A/CONF 177/20. See Chapter 2.

[206] Aldrich and Chinkin, 94 *AJIL* (2000) 97–8.   [207] See Chapter 2.

[208] C. W. Pinto, 'Modern Conference Techniques: Insights from Social Psychology and Anthropology', in R St J. Macdonald and D. M. Johnston (eds), *The Structure and Process of*

Commission preferred.[209] Article 9 (2) of the Vienna Convention on the Law of Treaties thus provides that ' . . . adoption of the text of a treaty at an international conference takes place by the vote of two-thirds of the States present and voting, unless by the same majority they shall decide to apply a different rule'. The Commission rejected the option of a simple majority in order to protect the interests of large but unwilling minorities. Sohn notes that in addition to a two-thirds majority of those present and voting, 'there is great merit in adding to it the requirement of at least majority, and preferably two-thirds majority, of the states participating in the Conference'.[210] UNCLOS III rules of procedure for all votes accordingly required both a two-thirds majority of states *voting* and a simple majority of states *participating*. One proposed amendment failed solely on that basis. Nevertheless, the principle advantage of majority voting is that it makes treaty adoption easier but does not preclude a dissenting state from subsequently ratifying. Minority interests are further protected by the right to make reservations to particular provisions, provided they are not incompatible with the object and purpose of the treaty, or prohibited by the treaty itself.[211]

Many ILC treaties have been adopted on this basis, including the 1958 Geneva Conventions on the law of the sea and the Vienna Convention on Treaties itself. However, the problems posed by majority voting are obvious. There is no necessity to negotiate a text capable of accommodating all participants, and the result may be that a significant minority of states vote against specific provisions, or the whole text, and they may then refuse to ratify the adopted convention. While reservations may to some degree alleviate opposition,[212] they will not save a treaty that in the view of dissenting states is fundamentally flawed. As an exercise in global law-making such a procedure is quite likely to fail. It will neither ensure enough support for a treaty to function effectively, nor provide a potential basis for state practice and new customary law. The 1958 Geneva Convention on Fishing and Conservation of the Living Resources of the High Seas provides a good example. Adopted by the necessary majority, but against the opposition of major coastal fishing states, it limped into force without their participation and signally failed to establish the stable relationship between distant water and coastal fishing states that was needed. Further disputes ensued,[213] and the whole issue

---

International Law: Essays in Legal Philosophy, Doctrine and Theory (Dordrecht, 1986) 305, 308. See also J. Gamble and C. Ku, 'International Law—New Actors and New Technologies: Center Stage for NGOs?', 31 *Law and Policy in International Business* (2000) 221, 247.

[209] Commentary to draft Article 8, in A. D. Watts, *The ILC 1949–1998* (Oxford, 1999), vol II, 634. See C. W. Jenks, 'Some Constitutional Problems of International Organisations' (1945) 22 *BYBIL* 34; L. Sohn, 'Voting Procedures in United Nations Conferences for the Codification of International Law', 69 *AJIL* (1975) 310; R. Sabel, *Procedure at International Conferences* (Cambridge, 1997) 281–6.　　　　　　　　　　　　　　　　　　　　　　[210] 69 *AJIL* (1975) 353.

[211] 1969 VCLT, Articles 19–23. See also *Reservations to the Genocide Convention Advisory Opinion* (1951) ICJ Reports 15.

[212] For example the 1958 Convention on the Continental Shelf became widely ratified and generally indicative of customary law despite reservations to Article 6: see *North Sea Continental Shelf Case* (1969) ICJ Reports 3.　　　　　　[213] See the *Fisheries Jurisdiction Cases* (1974) ICJ Reports 3 and 175.

ultimately had to be reconsidered by UNCLOS III. It is true that majority voting may enable a stronger text to be adopted, since it will sideline the recalcitrant few, but as the fisheries example shows, this may be a hollow victory. The compulsory dispute settlement provisions of the above-mentioned 1958 Convention are admirable but have remained unused because the states that objected to these and other provisions are not bound.

The Vienna Convention model is residual, so it is open to states to opt for a different approach. There are still situations where majority voting is favoured—it remains the norm for UN human rights treaties and ILC codification conventions for example—but in other fields such as the environment and law of the sea it has increasingly been abandoned in favour of a model based on the procedure used at UNCLOS III.

6.2   Third UN Conference on the Law of the Sea (UNCLOS III)

UNCLOS III remains something of a milestone in international law-making for several reasons. Above all, it succeeded where its predecessors had failed. Whatever the position may have been when it was adopted, the 1982 Convention on the Law of the Sea has become accepted, in most respects, as a statement of contemporary international law on nearly all matters related to the oceans. Most of its provisions, including those that were new or emerging law in 1982, are not only treaty law for the large number of states parties, but customary law for all or nearly all states.[214] Even the United States, which originally voted against adoption of the text in 1982, and had not yet become a party in 2006, by then took the view that the Convention's principal provisions were or had become customary law. Given the differences among states that prevailed before negotiations began, and which still had to be reconciled after the negotiations concluded, this is a remarkable achievement. To a significant degree, success can be attributed to the innovative and largely unprecedented negotiating methods and procedures employed at UNCLOS III, and to certain consequential features of the Convention itself. Those elements have in turn become a model for subsequent law-making conferences.[215] It is for this reason that they merit attention here.

Unlike the first two UN Conferences on the Law of the Sea held in 1958 and 1960, the ILC was not asked to produce preliminary draft articles for UNCLOS III.[216] The negotiation of what became the 1982 Convention was therefore not an exercise in codification by legal experts; rather it was understood from the outset that a political process 'emanating directly from the General Assembly' and

---

[214]   See Chapter 5.
[215]   See A. W. Koers, 'The Third UNCLOS', in W. P. Heere (ed), *International Law and its Sources: Liber Amicorum Maarten Bos* (Deventer, 1989) 23, 35.
[216]   For the fullest account of the UNCLOS III process and how radically it differed from previous UN conferences see T. Koh and S. Jayakumar, in M. Nordquist (ed), *UN Convention on the Law of the Sea: A Commentary*, vol. I (Dordrecht, 1985) 29 ff.

involving governmental representatives would be necessary in order to secure the appropriate compromises and produce a consensus treaty that could be universally supported.[217] Involving the ILC would take too long and above all would not guarantee a text that reflected the vital and very diverse interests of the large number of states concerned. Preparatory work was therefore undertaken initially by an *ad hoc* committee of states which, however, proved unable to agree on a draft. Thereafter, a treaty text slowly evolved within the Conference itself. Proposals were made by individual states or more often by groups of states. These included various regional groups, the Group of 77 representing developing states, and other overlapping interest groups of coastal states, maritime states, landlocked and geographically disadvantaged states, archipelagic states and so on. There was also a considerable NGO presence, both in state delegations and as observers. Among other activities such bodies (including those representing mining industries from industrialised countries) provided states with technical and expert help. Gamble and Ku argue that 'the duration of the conference, the complexity of the issues, including the need for technical expertise, created a rare opportunity for NGO influence because states needed information often available only from NGOs'.[218]

Consolidated negotiating drafts eventually emerged from committees with influential chairs, coordinated by the Conference President, actively seeking consensus and providing 'the crucial source of momentum the negotiations had lacked up to 1975'.[219] They were assisted by a series of informal meetings and negotiating groups, which in the words of one insider 'became a general characteristic of the working methods of the Conference'.[220] Legal experts participated in their personal capacities, and lawyers had particular influence in the negotiations on the dispute settlement provisions of the Convention. Perhaps the least useful elements of the whole process were the plenary meetings of the Conference.[221] Although the negotiations took ten years to complete, the final outcome was a comprehensive treaty consisting of 320 articles and eight annexes that made extensive changes to existing law, while creating new law on previously unregulated matters such as deep seabed mining, the marine environment and marine scientific research.

How was such a difficult task made possible? Two closely related features of the process stand out and differentiate it from the Vienna Convention model used

---

[217] J. Evensen, 'Working Methods and Procedures in the 3rd UNCLOS', 199 *Recueil des Cours* (1986-IV) 425, 435–8, 450–3.

[218] Gamble and Ku, 31 *Law and Policy in International Business* (2000) 221.

[219] B. Buzan, 'Negotiating by Consensus: Developments in Technique at the UN Conference on the Law of the Sea', 75 *AJIL* (1981) 324, 334–5. He identifies the process of active consensus as the key procedural innovation that saved UNCLOS III.

[220] Evensen, 199 *Recueil des Cours* (1986-IV) 425, 465; B. Buzan, 'United We Stand: Informal Negotiating Groups at UNCLOS III', 4 *Marine Policy* (1980) 183.

[221] Nordquist, *UNCLOS Commentary*, vol I, 95.

before. First, the negotiations proceeded on the basis that 'the Conference should make every effort to reach agreement on substantive matters by way of consensus, and there should be no voting on such matters until all efforts at consensus have been exhausted'.[222] The reason for avoiding votes if at all possible was simple. As Evensen points out, 'it would be an exercise in futility to work on the assumption that one or more major groups of the Conference should be occasionally or consistently outvoted . . . '.[223] The reason for retaining the option of voting was equally simple—to ensure that the negotiations did not become deadlocked.[224] This compromise formula worked successfully, and the only votes taken throughout the Conference came at the end, on whether to amend the final text, and whether to adopt the Convention.[225] Throughout the negotiations up to that point consensus had prevailed, and with the exception of Part XI on the deep seabed, had helped produce a text that almost all participants could live with. This was an outcome very different from UNCLOS I at Geneva in 1958.

Second, consensus was only possible because of the many compromises reached on different elements of the emerging draft. The General Assembly had stressed that 'the problems of ocean space are closely inter-related and need to be considered as a whole . . . '.[226] This gave rise to the so-called 'package deal' approach aptly summarised by Evensen: 'The essence of the procedural system adopted for the Conference was that compromises arrived at in one part had to be weighed against compromises arrived at in other parts as a "quid pro quo".'[227] To take one well-known example—maritime states agreed to the extension of the territorial sea to 12 nautical miles and the creation of an exclusive economic zone of 200 miles provided their rights of maritime navigation were strengthened and safeguarded. As the negotiations proceeded it thus became increasingly difficult to amend certain draft articles without unpicking other elements of the package deal. Consensus was sometimes reached simply on that basis, with delegations reluctantly withdrawing potentially divisive proposals rather than pressing for a vote. By the time the final Conference session convened in 1982, further changes could in practice be made only if the Conference President was satisfied that they had substantial support and that no state objected. Three amendments proposed by Turkey and Spain were voted on in the final session: all were rejected.

---

[222] UNGA Res 2750 (XXV), 17 December 1970; UNGA 3067 (XXVII), 16 November 1973. The Conference Rules of Procedure in fact provided for adoption of articles by two-thirds majority vote, but a 'Gentleman's Agreement' incorporated consensus decision-making into the working procedure of the conference. See Sohn 69 *AJIL* (1975) 310; Buzan, 75 *AJIL* (1981) 324; P. Allott, 'Power Sharing in the Law of the Sea', 77 *AJIL* (1983) 1; A. W. Koers in Heere (ed), *International Law and its Sources* 23.   [223] Evensen, 199 *Recueil des Cours* (1986-IV) 483; Buzan, 75 *AJIL* (1981) 326.

[224] Evensen, in R. B. Krueger and S. Riesenfeld (eds), *The Developing Order of the Oceans* (Honolulu, 1984) 23, 28.

[225] The final vote was demanded by the United States. The Convention was adopted by 130 to 4, with 17 abstentions.   [226] UNGA 3067 (XXVII), 16 November 1973.

[227] Evensen, 199 *Recueil des Cours* (1986-IV) 485. See also H. Caminos and M. Molitor, 'Progressive Development of International Law and the Package Deal', 79 *AJIL* (1985) 871; Koers, in Heere (ed), *International Law and its Sources*, 23.

At the final conference session, however, the consensus negotiating process collapsed. US President Reagan (who had been elected in the last stages of the negotiations) sought major changes to the deep seabed regime in Part XI of the Convention and he made it clear that the Convention would be unacceptable to the US unless Part XI was renegotiated. Other industrialised states also had reservations about Part XI. But Part XI was a major part of the package deal: it reflected the ambitions of developing states for a new international economic order and for protection of land-based mineral producers. These states were understandably reluctant to forego the benefits of the package deal as negotiated. In their view they had already made significant concessions in order to secure consensus on Part XI and they rejected last-minute attempts to make the extensive changes sought by the United States. The Convention was adopted overwhelmingly, with only four votes against, including the US. But many of the industrialised states abstained on the final vote and it soon became clear that, without further change, the Convention would enter into force mainly on the strength of participation by developing states.

Eventually, the need to facilitate universal participation in the Convention regime, the reality that the economic advantages of the seabed-mining regime had not been and were not likely to be realised, and the global shift towards a market-oriented economy, combined to create the environment for renegotiation prior to entry into force. Achieving this outcome required another innovative approach to international law-making. The UN Secretary-General took the initiative by convening informal consultations. Through 15 meetings between 1990 and 1994 the issues of concern were identified and solutions were sought on some very detailed points. Various possible approaches were canvassed. Imminent entry into force of the Convention created a strong sense of urgency and the General Assembly then invited all states to participate in the consultations. A draft resolution and a draft Agreement relating to the Implementation of Part XI of the 1982 UNCLOS were agreed by consensus, including the US and other Western states. The Resolution was adopted by the General Assembly and the Agreement was opened for signature on 28 July 1994.[228]

The use of an 'Implementation Agreement' was deliberately intended to avoid formal amendment of the Convention, a process in which only the parties could have participated, and which in any case could not have taken place ahead of entry into force. Nevertheless, the Agreement disapplies certain provisions of Part XI and revises others. It also prevails over inconsistent provisions of the Convention. This looks very like amendment in practice. To encourage participation in the Agreement there are complex and innovative arrangements for states to become bound. Not all states that were parties to UNCLOS in 1994 have in fact done so, but as they continue to participate in the meetings of the International Seabed

---

[228] See D. Anderson, 'Further Efforts to Ensure Universal Participation in the UNCLOS', 43 *ICLQ* (1994) 886; J. Charney, 'Entry into Force of the 1982 UNCLOS', 35 *VJIL* (1995) 381.

Authority without protest it must be assumed that these states have acquiesced in the changes made to the Convention. By 2005 there were 149 states parties, including nearly all the industrialised states which had abstained in 1982, and the amended Convention has now been in operation without protest since 1994. Many of its provisions are generally regarded as customary law by almost all states and by the UN. This is a very significant success in law-making terms.

The UNCLOS III procedure is in some respects a reversion to the older ways of negotiating treaties.[229] In practice most of the text was adopted by unanimity and there was little or no preparatory work by legal experts before the Conference convened; the participants themselves undertook the essential work. But the advantage of the package deal approach is clear. It sustained the necessary compromises through ten years of negotiations and enabled the parties to conclude a comprehensive treaty text, even if it did fall at the final hurdle. The Convention was thus negotiated as an integral interlocking whole and reflected a complex balance of interests. Moreover, its package deal character is protected in various ways, including compulsory settlement of disputes.[230] It can be ratified only in full, without reservations, or not at all.[231] Unlike the 1958 Geneva Conventions, states cannot pick and chose the provisions they are willing to accept, unless like the US they treat them as customary law.[232] Article 311 further limits the possibility of derogating from the package deal via *inter se* agreements,[233] while amendments must be adopted by consensus, although voting is permitted once all efforts at consensus are exhausted.[234] However, every negotiation has its own dynamics, and the process is only part of the story. The most that can be concluded is that the UNCLOS III procedures worked eventually and that subsequent experience has shown their continuing value in other contexts.[235] We consider the broader significance of this and other consensus law-making procedures in Section 7 below.

6.3   The Rome Conference

In contrast to UNCLOS III the Rome Conference on the establishment of an International Criminal Court was a speedier process. It was held from 15 June to 17 July 1998 and even including the work of *ad hoc* and preparatory committees

---

[229] Sohn, 69 *AJIL* (1975) 310, 352.   [230] See Articles 279–99.

[231] See Article 309. But states can make 'declarations and statements' in accordance with Article 310. See L. D. M. Nelson, 'Declarations, Statements and Disguised Reservations with Respect to the Convention on the Law of the Sea', 50 *ICLQ* (2001) 767.

[232] However not all parties would necessarily accept that a non-party is entitled to benefit in this selective way from every new element of the Convention.   [233] See Chapter 5.

[234] Articles 312–13.

[235] See especially R. Benedick, *Ozone Diplomacy* (London, 1998); Mintzer and Leonard, *Negotiating Climate Change*; S. Oberthür and H. Ott (eds), *The Kyoto Protocol* (Berlin, 1999), and FAO, *Structure and Process of the 1993–5 UN Conference on Straddling Fish Stocks* (Rome, 1995). Buzan, writing in 75 *AJIL* (1981) 347, was much more cautious about the possible importance of UNCLOS as a model for later negotiations.

(prepcoms) the process lasted only from 1994 to 1998.[236] However, as we will see in Chapter 4, the International Law Commission had already undertaken significant preparatory work on a draft statute, starting in 1991. Thus the intergovernmental negotiating process did not start with a blank sheet of paper. This chapter considers aspects of the Conference process, but for the important work of NGOs reference should also be made to Chapter 2.

The prepcom divided the issues requiring consideration into sections and allocated them to working groups which reported to the plenary meeting. From this process a draft statute emerged that was significantly different from the text prepared by the ILC. Delegates at Rome were faced with some 1,400 square brackets—the device used to indicate disagreement on the text—and numerous alternative texts for disputed provisions. The working process to move from this highly divisive text to a statute that could be adopted by the Conference was thus all-important. The work was again divided between 13 working groups responsible to the Committee of the Whole (CW). The overall process has been well described by the Chair of the Bureau of the CW and another member of the Canadian delegation:

The plenary dealt with the organization of work, the delivery of policy statements . . . and the formal adoption of the Statute at the end of the conference. The CW was responsible for the development of the statute and the Drafting Committee was responsible for ensuring proper and consistent drafting throughout the statute in all languages. . . . issues once debated in the CW were referred to working groups or coordinators. The latter then reported the results of their work to the CW, and texts accepted by the CW were referred to the Drafting Committee. Texts refined by the committee had again to be approved by the CW. The final report was sent from the CW to the plenary, with a complete text on the final day of the conference.[237]

This account does not reflect the many sticking points, diverse interests and frenzied informal and formal exchanges and consultations that took place throughout the conference, including meetings between various political and regional state groupings such as the non-aligned movement, the Arab Group, the Latin-American Group and the Caribbean Group.[238] Other alliances formed around particular issues, some of which were especially forceful, for example between the Holy See and some Catholic and Arab states with respect to the crime of forced pregnancy.[239]

Most important in the acceptance of the Statute by the Conference was the proactive role taken by the bureau of the CW, the body with the responsibility for

---

[236] For a full account see R. Lee (ed), *The International Criminal Court: The Making of the Rome Statute: Issues, Negotiations, Results* (The Hague, 1999).

[237] P. Kirsch and J. Holmes, 'The Rome Conference on an International Criminal Court: The Negotiating Process', 93 *AJIL* (1999) 2, 3 n. 5.

[238] M. Arsanjani, 'The Rome Statute of the International Criminal Court', 93 *AJIL* (1999) 22, 23.

[239] C. Steains, 'Gender Issues', in Lee, *The International Criminal Court*, 357, 366–9.

managing the conference. The bureau required coordinators to take the initiative in drafting texts and to refer only unbracketed texts to the CW. Towards the end of the Conference, when success had begun to seem out of reach, it prepared bureau discussion papers that contained proposals and narrowed options so as to move the negotiations forward. Through the CW chairs also held bilateral talks with particular delegations to try to reach compromise. Finally, when there was still no agreement on a number of important points and growing concern that if this conference failed the prospects of agreeing an international criminal court would recede, the bureau pulled together a package deal that it presented to the conference in the early hours of the final day. The plenary had to accept or reject this package. The text included a provision that no reservations were allowed. As at UNCLOS III, attempts at the final session to propose further amendments (including from the US) were rejected and the Statute was put to the vote. It was adopted by 120 votes in favour, seven against (including the US) and 21 abstentions. This process has been criticised. For example David Scheffer, Head of the US delegation, has remarked on the lack of time to consider 'extraordinary' changes that delegates were 'confronted' with on the last day and the rejection of any further proposals for amendment.[240]

Consensus package-deal negotiations come in several forms, and the negotiating techniques employed at the Rome Conference differ in detail from those used in the more leisurely atmosphere of UNCLOS III. Nevertheless there remain fundamental similarities. First, the process was designed to secure the widest possible consensus, and in both cases that was largely though not completely achieved. The active role of the chairman at UNCLOS III and of the Bureau at the ICC Conference was in both cases essential to securing agreement on the draft text. It is obvious that a consensus process will not necessarily keep all states happy or completely eliminate opposition, and later in this chapter we will have to consider the nature of consensus as revealed by these and other international negotiations. At the same time it is not obvious that the Vienna Convention model of negotiation based on majority voting would have delivered a better outcome; it remains the case that more states are likely to be dissatisfied when adoption by voting is the norm.

Second, the involvement of the International Law Commission in preparing an initial draft for the ICC negotiations indicates an important role for the Commission when legal expertise is central to the subject matter of a diplomatic conference. This is not quite so different from UNCLOS III as it might seem, since the negotiators there also had the benefit of the preparatory work undertaken by the ILC for the 1958 UNCLOS I Conference and incorporated in the Geneva Conventions. Both sets of negotiations also show, however, that diplomats operating through a political process will inevitably refashion the work of

---

[240] David J. Scheffer, 'Testimony Before the Senate Foreign Relations Committee', Washington, 23 July 1998.

legal experts into a compromise text that is more likely to secure agreement. In its own work there is no point the ILC trying to second-guess the compromises that may emerge from such negotiations, nor should its failure to do so be a cause for criticism or concern. The final ICC Statute is not the work of the ILC, but it is unlikely that a statute would have emerged at all without the ILC's initial preparatory work.[241]

7. Law-Making by Treaty Bodies

Law-making treaties need to evolve. Human rights treaties are especially perceived as 'living instruments' that must take account of developing social conditions and perceptions of rights.[242] Framework regulatory agreements, such as the 1992 Convention on Climate Change or the 2003 Convention on Tobacco Control, also need to be filled out with more detailed provisions and kept up-to-date. A common way to facilitate further development and implementation of a treaty is to establish institutions for this purpose. These may be existing intergovernmental organisations, such as IMO or IAEA, or they may be autonomous treaty bodies.[243] Alternatively, independent expert bodies may be established, an approach confined mainly to human rights treaties.

7.1 Intergovernmental Treaty Bodies

Whether they are autonomous bodies or part of an international organisation, the essential elements of intergovernmental treaty institutions are threefold. First, and most importantly, the parties must meet regularly. Conferences or meetings of the parties (COPs/MOPs) may be provided for in the treaty itself, or may be convened by the UN or one of its specialised agencies, or by a commission established to manage the treaty. It is this ongoing role which institutionalises these gatherings and distinguishes them from the *ad hoc* conferences considered in the previous sections.[244] Second, it will usually be the responsibility of the parties to keep the relevant treaty under review and take whatever measures they are empowered to adopt to further its object and purpose. They must therefore have power to adopt the necessary amendments, protocols, regulations, decisions or recommendations which add to and develop the legal regime created by the treaty. COPs are usually the forum in which these measures are negotiated and adopted, and it is in this sense that they are law-making bodies.[245] Third, they will usually be assisted

---

[241] See Chapter 4.   [242] See Chapter 5.
[243] See R. Churchill and G. Ulfstein, 'Autonomous Institutional Arrangements in Multilateral Environmental Agreements', 94 *AJIL* (2000) 623; J. Brunnée, 'COPing with Consent: Law-Making Under MEAs', 15 *LJIL* (2002) 1.   [244] Churchill and Ulfstein, 94 *AJIL* (2000) 623.
[245] Brunnée, 15 *LJIL* (2002) 1.

by expert bodies providing scientific, technical and legal advice where appropriate. These bodies may be the source of recommendations for further regulation, or they may be concerned with treaty implementation, or they may have other functions. Finally, some treaty bodies also have a responsibility for supervising compliance with the treaty regime, but this is not a necessary feature of a law-making agreement and it falls beyond the scope of this chapter.

Law-making or regulation by these intergovernmental institutions gives treaties a dynamic character and enables the parties to respond to new problems or priorities. The Antarctic Treaty System is a particularly good example of this feature. Through periodic review meetings, the parties have negotiated treaties or protocols to regulate the conservation of seals, marine living resources, mineral exploitation and the environment.[246] Both the 1985 Ozone Convention and the 1992 Convention on Climate Change have similarly evolved following regular meetings of the parties, with additional protocols, amendments, adjustments and decisions.[247] The Framework Convention on Tobacco Control considered earlier is also drafted in these terms.

The form in which such standards or regulations are adopted varies widely.[248] In some cases new treaties may be required. As we have seen, the Antarctic Treaty System has extended its regulatory scope mainly in this way. Other treaties provide for the negotiation of protocols or annexes to lay down detailed standards. The 1973/78 MARPOL Convention, the 1979 Convention on Long-Range Transboundary Air Pollution, the 1985 Ozone Convention and the 1992 Climate Change Convention have all relied principally on this method. Treaties of this kind are sometimes described as 'framework treaties', a concept we consider more fully in Chapter 5. The 1982 UNCLOS incorporates 'generally accepted' treaty regulations on dumping and pollution from ships which can be changed and updated by IMO without the need to amend UNCLOS itself.[249] The 1982 Convention has also been amended and added to by a number of 'implementing agreements'.[250] Some treaties contain technical annexes in which specific standards are set and which can be amended by the parties more easily than amending the treaty.[251] The phasing out of dumping at sea and commercial whaling brought

---

[246] See eg 1972 Convention for the Conservation of Antarctic Seals; 1980 Convention for the Conservation of Antarctic Marine Living Resources; 1988 Convention for the Regulation of Antarctic Mineral Resource Activities; 1991 Protocol to the Antarctic Treaty on Environmental Protection; and generally F. Francioni and T. Scovazzi (eds), *International Law for Antarctica* (2nd edn, The Hague, 1996); O. Stokke and D. Vidas (eds), *Governing the Antarctic: The Effectiveness and Legitimacy of the Antarctic Treaty System* (Cambridge, 1996).

[247] See Birnie and Boyle, *International Law and the Environment*, chapter 10 and Brunnée, 15 *LJIL* (2002) 1.   [248] See Kirgis, in Joyner (ed), *The UN and International Law*, 65–94.

[249] Articles 210–11. The regulations in question are mainly located in the annexes to the 1973/78 MARPOL Convention and the 1996 London Dumping Convention. ICAO has similar power to set standards for aviation.

[250] 1994 Agreement on the Implementation of Part XI of UNCLOS; 1995 Agreement on Straddling and Highly Migratory Fish Stocks.   [251] See following para.

about by amending the annexes to the 1972 London Dumping Convention and the 1946 Whaling Convention has amounted in practice to a very substantial revision of the treaties themselves.[252] Many treaties also provide for more informal methods of 'soft law' rule-making, such as recommendations, resolutions, codes of practice, guidelines or agreed interpretations of the treaty. The legal effect of these instruments is considered further in Chapter 5.

Whether formally binding or not, all of these various methods of rule-making have in common that no obligation may be imposed on any state without its consent.[253] Differences exist in the manner in which consent is achieved, but requirements of consensus, three-quarters or two-thirds majority voting, are the typical conditions for adoption of new regulatory measures in whatever form. Moreover, new treaties, protocols or amendments thereto will normally require positive ratification by a sufficient number of states to enter into force. This often-slow 'opt-in' process can be a serious impediment, and states which fail to ratify, whether through inertia or otherwise, will not be bound. An alternative approach relies on tacit consent or non-objection to bring implementing agreements or amendments into force within a set time limit.[254] This 'opt-out' method reverses the normal procedure and is widely used *inter alia* for annexes to environmental treaties, since it enables schedules of protected species, prohibited substances or conservation regulations to be changed speedily as circumstances require.[255] Although states still remain free to opt out of these measures if they object within the prescribed time limit, the onus is on them to do so.

The 1987 Montreal Protocol shows that a more radical approach to the problem of regulatory opt-outs is possible. Combined majorities of industrialised and developing states are empowered to amend standards set by the protocol for production and consumption of controlled ozone-depleting substances.[256] Once adopted, these adjustments are automatically binding on all parties to the protocol. No objections are permitted. Withdrawal from the protocol is then the only option left for any state which finds such an amendment unacceptable. In practice isolated opposition to majority decisions is pointless and all such adjustments have been adopted by consensus. The Montreal Protocol precedent remains unique among multilateral regulatory treaties, an indication of the particular

---

[252] Revised Annexes I and II of the 1972 London Dumping Convention adopted in 1993 by the 16th Consultative Meeting of the Parties; revised Schedule to the 1946 Whaling Convention adopted in 1982, para 10 (e). See Churchill and Ulfstein, 94 *AJIL* (2000) 638–41.

[253] A point very fully developed by Brunnée, 15 *LJIL* (2002) 1.

[254] ICAO, IMO and WHO all use tacit consent procedures. See Kirgis, in Joyner (ed), *The UN and International Law*, 70–6. One unusual example is the 1994 Agreement on Implementation of Part XI of UNCLOS. See Article 4.

[255] See eg 1973/78 MARPOL, Article 16 (2) (g) (ii) (but compare sub-para (i)); 1985 Ozone Convention, Article 10 (2); 1973 CITES Convention, Article 30; 1989 Basel Convention on the Control of Transboundary Movements of Hazardous Wastes, Article 18.

[256] Article 2 (9), as amended 1990.

determination of states to tackle ozone depletion, but amendments to the constitutions of international organisations usually also become binding for all parties once the specified majority have ratified.[257]

In contrast, the more usual freedom to opt out of regulations adopted by majority vote has seriously limited the ability of a number of COPs to function effectively as regulatory bodies. Fisheries commissions in particular have had difficulty setting appropriate catch quotas. The so-called Turbot war in 1994 between Canada and Spain resulted from the abuse by the European Community of its power to object to quotas set under the 1978 Northwest Atlantic Fisheries Convention.[258] In an attempt to overcome this problem the 1995 UN Fish Stocks Agreement now requires parties to regional fisheries agreements to 'agree on decision-making procedures which facilitate the adoption of conservation and management measures in a timely and effective manner'.[259] Any failure to do so in respect of fishing for straddling or highly migratory fish stocks on the high seas could be dealt with under the compulsory dispute settlement provisions of the Agreement. The International Whaling Commission has also had difficulty in persuading Japan and Norway not to opt out of moratoria on commercial whaling approved by large majorities of non-whaling states. Nevertheless, due to the relative ease of amending regulations, the Whaling Convention 'has proved a most useful and flexible instrument for reflecting changes in attitude and practice'.[260] So too has the CITES Convention, enabling the parties to list and de-list protected species easily and regularly.[261]

The success of the parties to the London Dumping Convention and the Basel Convention in progressively adopting stricter standards leading to the elimination of hazardous waste exports for dumping at sea or disposal in developing countries shows how in the right conditions substantial changes can come about by agreement within the terms of an existing treaty.[262] Comparable developments within IMO, ICAO and IAEA demonstrate the same point. We can see clearly that without some such process regulatory treaties would quickly ossify and become devalued.

7.2   Human Rights Treaty Bodies

The evolution of human rights treaties is in part the responsibility of the parties, through the adoption of protocols that add new substantive provisions or procedures (as in the case of the Optional Protocol to the Torture Convention, discussed

---

[257] See eg UN Charter, Article 108; 1982 UNCLOS, Articles 159 and 314.

[258] See P. Davies, 'EC-Canada Fisheries Dispute', 44 *ICLQ* (1995) 927.

[259] Article 10 (j).

[260] P. Birnie, 'International Legal Issues in the Management and Protection of the Whale: A Review of Four Decades of Experience', 29 *NRJ* (1989) at 913; id, 'Are 20th Century Marine Conservation Agreements Adaptable to 21st Century Goals and Principles?', 12 *IJMCL* (1997) 488.

[261] P. Sand, 'Whither CITES? The Evolution of a Treaty Regime on the Borderland of Trade and Environment', 8 *EJIL* (1997) 29.

[262] See Birnie and Boyle, *International Law and the Environment*, chapter 8.

above). In these cases negotiation and adoption will take place through the relevant intergovernmental institutions, whether the UN Commission on Human Rights or elsewhere. To that extent there is some similarity with the treaties discussed in the previous section. But human rights treaties also make use of independent, expert bodies to receive reports on and monitor treaty compliance, and in some cases to make recommendations and give opinions on the interpretation of a treaty as a 'living instrument'. The UN human rights institutions provide a good example of how these independent specialist bodies can interact with states in evolving law-making.

Members of the Human Rights Committee, established by the ICCPR, are not state delegates but are elected for their individual expertise. Similar committees have been established under the other human rights treaties.[263] Through a range of activities, including the adoption of General Comments and Recommendations, asking questions of states' representatives at periodic reporting sessions, adopting Concluding Comments to the reporting procedure, and issuing opinions in response to individual complaints, these human rights treaty bodies have articulated their understanding of the requirements of their respective treaties. Their statements may either be viewed as interpretative of the treaty provisions, or as going beyond the treaty and as such developing the law.

For example, there is no specific provision on violence against women in the Convention on the Elimination of All Forms of Discrimination against Women, an obvious omission. In 1992 the Committee on the Elimination of Discrimination against Women adopted General Recommendation No. 19 on Violence against Women. It rooted this Recommendation firmly in the Convention by emphasising that violence against women is a form of discrimination that prevents women's enjoyment of their Convention rights on a basis of equality with men. The General Recommendation shows how specific articles of CEDAW are violated by violence against women. While the Recommendation contains innovative provisions (for example the definition of gender-based violence), it is drafted so as to derive its legal authority from the Convention itself. States parties are accordingly expected to report on the measures taken to comply with the Recommendation and are questioned upon them by the Committee. On this basis it is now clear that violence against women may violate human rights treaty obligations.

In contrast, the Human Rights Committee went beyond the terms of the ICCPR and general international law in its General Comment 24 on reservations. While framing the Comment in terms of the need to maintain the integrity of the

---

[263] ICCPR, Article 28 (Human Rights Committee); ICESCR (Committee on Economic, Social and Cultural Rights established by ECOSOC Resolution in 1987); Race Convention, Article 8 (Committee on the Elimination of Race Discrimination); Women's Convention, Article 17 (Committee on the Elimination of Discrimination against Women); Torture Convention, Article 17 (Torture Committee); Children's Convention, Article 43 (Committee on the Rights of the Child); Convention on the Protection of the Rights of All Migrant Workers and Members of Their Families, Article 72.

objects and purposes of the Covenant, the Committee's assumption that it should determine the compatibility of a reservation with the Covenant was seen by some states (notably the US, UK and France) as usurping their powers under the Vienna Convention on the Law of Treaties. We will see in Chapter 4 how the General Comment contributed to the controversy over reservations and whether human rights treaties should be treated differently from other treaties because of their non-reciprocal, standard-setting character.

The various instruments and opinions issued by the human rights committees are often cited, and may well be viewed as forms of soft law.[264] When supplemented by the reports and recommendations of special rapporteurs, working groups and independent experts, a body of persuasive jurisprudence is developed. For example, for evaluating whether states respect, protect and fulfil the right in question the Committee on Economic, Social and Cultural Rights has adopted this layered typology that breaks down a state's obligations under the Covenant.[265] The Committee has further elaborated each of these obligations, both in general terms and in the context of particular rights. Other experts and NGOs have also reiterated and added to an understanding of the typology,[266] which has entered case law through an opinion of the African Commission on Human Rights.[267]

While none of these comments, reports or recommendations is formally binding, their consistent repetition creates a consensus that a lawyer would be foolish to ignore. This process of soft law formation is further strengthened where the various human rights committees adopt a consistent approach. An example is the development of a normative practice of gender mainstreaming, endorsed by global summit meetings such as the Vienna World Conference on Human Rights, the Fourth World Conference on Women and the Durban Conference on Racism and Xenophobia. The objective of gender mainstreaming was endorsed by ECOSOC Resolution and the Secretary-General. The human rights treaty bodies sought to turn these statements into practice, for example through General Comments such as Human Rights Committee General Recommendation No. 28 on Equality of Rights between Men and Women[268] and the CERD General Comment No. 25 on race and gender mainstreaming,[269] and by questioning

---

[264] This is not to say they are accepted by all states as such. See for eg the Joint Statement by the Australian Minister for Foreign Affairs, the Attorney-General, and the Minister for Immigration and Multicultural Affairs, on Improving the Effectiveness of United Nations Committees, 29 August 2000.

[265] See eg CESCR, General Comment No. 12, UN Doc E/C/1999/5 (1999) on the right to adequate food, para 15; 1997 Maastricht Guidelines on Violations of Economic, Social and Cultural Rights, para 6.

[266] eg Maastricht Guidelines, para 6; 2002 Montreal Principles on Women's Economic, Social and Cultural Rights, 26 *HRQ* (2004) 760.

[267] African Commission on Human and Peoples' Rights, *Re Communication 155/96, ACHPR/COMM/A044/1*, 27th May 2002 (Federal Republic of Nigeria).

[268] UN Doc CCPR/C/21/Rev1/Add10 (2000), reprinted in *Compilation of General Comments and General Recommendations Adopted by Human Rights Treaty Bodies*, UN Doc HRI/GEN/1/Rev6 at 179 (2003).   [269] A/55/18, Annex V, 20 March 2000.

states on the steps they have taken towards mainstreaming and including its desirability in their Concluding Comments.

The practice of these various committees represents one of the rare instances in which bodies whose members are formally independent of governments (but which are not courts) play a significant role in international law-making. The human rights context largely explains this unusual development, since it has no parallels in any of the regulatory treaties considered in the previous section. Only the International Labour Organisation, responsible for international standard setting in the field of labour law, has any similarity. In some ways the ILO is entirely unique in the history of international organisations: its tripartite membership of governments, employers and trade unions has no analogy elsewhere; it has a systematic and coordinated procedure for the adoption of Conventions, of which there are over 200;[270] and highly developed systems for monitoring compliance.[271] ILO is one of the most prolific of all treaty negotiating bodies, but its unique structure makes it difficult to derive wider lessons about its significance for the institutional process of international law-making in general.[272]

8.   Consensus Law-Making: An Assessment

8.1   The Nature of Consensus

As we have seen, treaty conferences, commissions and COPs are increasingly required to take decisions by consensus. Many IGOs also in practice take some of their decisions by consensus, including the UNGA, IMO, WHO and WTO, even if they are not required to do so.[273] What do we mean by consensus in such cases? Unlike a unanimous decision, consensus is arrived at without a vote. It does not follow that all participants are necessarily in favour of such a decision: for example, Article 161 of UNCLOS defines 'consensus' simply as 'the absence of any formal objection'.[274] There may be various explanations for the absence of

---

[270] Under the ILO Constitution, Article 19 (5) (b) members undertake to bring a Convention before the appropriate authorities for the enactment of legislation within a year from the Conference closing session. Under Article 19 (6) recommendations also have to be brought 'before the authority or authorities within whose competence the matter lies for the enactment of legislation or other action'.

[271] V. Leary, 'Lessons from the Experience of the International Labour Organisation', in Alston (ed), *The United Nations and Human Rights*, 580, 581.

[272] On the ILO's particular approach to law-making see F. Maupain, 'The ILO's Standard Setting Action: International Legislation or Treaty Law?', in V. Gowlland-Debbas (ed), *Multilateral Treaty-Making* (The Hague, 2000) 129.

[273] On the evolution of consensus decision-making in the UN see Peterson, *The General Assembly in World Politics*, 81–90; H. Schermers and N. Blokker, *International Institutional Law* (The Hague, 1995), 506–15.

[274] So does the WTO Agreement. See generally R. Sabel, *Procedure at International Conferences* (Cambridge, 1997), chapter 16.

such objections, and one of the more subtle advantages of a consensus procedure is that some states might indeed have voted against if offered the option. Indeed they sometimes indicate their reservations, or even their opposition, in subsequent statements. One formula used by certain delegates in the UN runs as follows: 'My government does not agree with the proposal but it will not obstruct the consensus'. But this is not so different from unanimity in some cases. A decision is unanimous even if some states abstain, and abstention may similarly conceal unexpressed opposition.[275]

Consensus in UNCLOS III and in other law-making conferences is also generally arrived at in circumstances where a vote is possible, and 'The vote is then a threat, an inducement to achieve consensus'.[276] This kind of consensus can be a very double-edged sword. A state that is reluctant to disturb the consensus may nevertheless have little incentive to ratify a treaty or implement a decision arrived at in this way. The 1995 UN Fish Stocks Agreement was negotiated as a package deal between coastal and distant water fishing states, and adopted by consensus in which all the important fishing states participated,[277] but a number of these have subsequently expressed opposition to the Agreement or have failed to become parties. Despite following closely the UNCLOS III model, it thus risks sharing the same fate as the 1958 Fisheries Convention. Of course, as the UNCLOS III conference shows, consensus on one item in a negotiation to which a state might otherwise be opposed may be the product of consensus on another of which it very much approves. As Buzan points out: 'It is hard to overstress the importance of the integral link between consensus procedures and a package deal outcome . . . '[278] Where there is no such package deal, the potential law-making impact of a consensus text may be much less predictable. On the other hand, even if consensus cannot always be interpreted as approval, it is still different from the outright opposition expressed by a negative vote. Again, the subtle point is that states with less of an interest in the outcome may be willing to go along with a decision reached by consensus, whereas voting requires them to take a position for or against, or to abstain. Before establishing that there is no opposition, however, it is also important to ensure that there is positive support. Securing consensus thus places greater demands on chairs to evaluate the sense of a meeting and to take an active role in promoting consensus through informal negotiations or soundings.

[275] Kaufmann, *Conference Diplomacy*, at 27–32. But *contra* A. Cassese, *International Law in a Divided World* (Oxford, 1990) 196, who regards unanimity as 'full agreement'.

[276] D. Vignes, 'Will the Third Conference on the Law of the Sea Work According to the Consensus Rule?', 69 *AJIL* (1975) 119. Compare consensus decision-making where no vote is allowed: in effect this requires unanimity and will allow any state to block a decision.

[277] See FAO, *Structure and Process of the 1993–5 UN Conference on Straddling Fish Stocks* (Rome, 1995); J. de Yturriaga, *The International Regime of Fisheries* (Leiden, 1997) 187–201.

[278] Buzan, 75 *AJIL* (1981) 339.

8.2 When is Consensus Law-Making Appropriate?

A consensus procedure has benefits and drawbacks.[279] As we saw above, the UNCLOS III precedent shows that it can work in favour of a complex, comprehensive and inclusive agreement that will stand the test of time and generate widely acceptable new law for parties and non-parties alike. The success of the procedure, still uncertain in 1982, can also be gauged *inter alia* from its use in negotiating the 1992 Climate Change and Biological Diversity Conventions, the 1994 Uruguay Round agreements establishing the WTO, and many other subsequent agreements. At the same time, as the stalemate in WTO negotiations in 2006 illustrates, consensus requires compromises that may be unobtainable, or may result in a text that is weaker or more ambiguous than might be thought desirable by some states or NGOs. Moreover, certain topics may be inherently unsuited to a consensus negotiating process. Human rights and humanitarian treaties fall into this category mainly because they do not readily lend themselves to the package deal approach we observed in UNCLOS III and WTO negotiations. Thus the negotiating practices of the ICRC and the former UNCHR remain firmly based on the majority voting plus reservations model favoured by the ILC. While some countries will use reservations to emasculate the human rights treaties to which they become party,[280] other participants will have the satisfaction of adopting a text that can nevertheless represent an aspirational ideal even if not accepted by everyone. Rather obviously, such an approach would not advance the 'politics of interdependence' that characterises regulation of world trade, the oceans, or the global environment.[281] Put simply, while consensus negotiations aim to produce a set menu for everyone, human rights negotiators prefer to offer an à la carte selection from a gourmet menu. And as we all know, those who dine à la carte often eat very different meals.

8.3 The Significance of Consensus Procedures

The significance of consensus negotiating procedures can be evaluated in several ways. First, they inevitably generate a greater need to engage in diplomacy, to listen, to bargain than would be the case when decisions can be taken by majority vote. The negotiation of the 1982 UNCLOS and the Climate Change Convention both show how a consensus process tends to democratise decision-making by diminishing disparities in power among states.[282] This works in two

---

[279] See generally K. Zamenek, in Macdonald and Johnston (eds), *The Structure and Process of International Law* (Dordrecht, 1986) 49–52; Buzan, 75 *AJIL* (1981) 324; Sabel, *Procedure at International Conferences*, chapter 16.

[280] See eg the US reservations to the 1966 ICCPR or the Saudi reservations to CEDAW.

[281] Buzan, 75 *AJIL* (1981) 329.   [282] Ibid 326–8.

ways. The point has already been made that the G77 developing states had a strong influence on the UNCLOS III negotiations. But, in strictly numerical terms, the G77 (in reality a much larger group) could easily have commanded a two-thirds majority on many issues. Had they wanted to do so they could have driven through a treaty that suited their interests alone. Of course, the United States, Europe and Japan would never have supported or ratified such a text. The consensus procedure made such an outcome unlikely, but it did not empower developing states alone; rather, it empowered all states. No participating state could be ignored, every state had to compromise. Thus the United States, Europe and Japan had to be accommodated throughout the negotiations. At the same time, none of these powerful states or groups of states could dictate what should be in the treaty without risking ultimate disagreement on a text. They too had to compromise, since the possibility of voting when efforts at consensus have failed ensures that no one state or group of states can block final agreement unreasonably. Much the same can be said of the climate change negotiations concluded by consensus in 2005 despite prolonged US hostility and a theatrical but pointless walkout. Even for so-called hyper powers, consensus procedures will ensure that minority interests are respected only if opposition is not pressed too far.[283]

Second, as the 1982 UNCLOS clearly demonstrates, the adoption of a consensus package-deal treaty can have a powerful law-making effect, even before the treaty enters into force. Although the outcome very much depends on the circumstances in which consensus is achieved and the nature of what has been agreed, securing widespread support for such a text not only legitimises and promotes consistent state practice, but makes it less likely that other states will object to immediate implementation. New customary law may come into being very quickly by this method. In this broader sense a consensus process becomes not merely a more effective way of negotiating universally acceptable treaties, decisions or soft law instruments but, in effect, a specific form of law-making process. We pursue this very important point in Chapter 5.

9. Conclusions

This chapter has outlined the variety of international processes which now exist for the negotiation and adoption of treaties, decisions, and soft law instruments of various kinds, but it has not so far addressed the sense in which we can speak of any of them as 'law-making'. With the debatable exception of the UN Security Council, we have not argued that any of the processes reviewed here constitutes a body formally endowed with the power to legislate—and in that sense a legislature. Rather, as Charney has explained, 'the products of multilateral forums substantially

---

[283] Koers, in Heere (ed), *International Law and its Sources*, 23, 36.

advance and formalize the international law-making process'.[284] This is a subtle but important distinction.

At the most basic level it might be suggested that all these processes are mainly mechanisms for generating treaties or other instruments with a treaty foundation, and as such they at most bind only the parties to those treaties. In some cases this is correct and only in that very limited sense could we identify these processes as law-making. But there would be little point writing this book if that was all that could be said. More importantly, we have seen that some of the institutions considered above have power by virtue of their constituent treaties to prescribe generally applicable rules, albeit in very limited circumstances. The most notable of these is the UNSC, acting under the authority of the UN Charter, but we have also seen how majority decisions taken by some treaty COPs are in a small number of cases binding on all parties. Certain rules and standards established by international regulatory agencies such as IMO and IAEA have been given binding force for all states once they become 'generally accepted' within the terms of applicable other conventions. These are exceptional cases, but in their own fields they are significant.

We can only begin to talk seriously about international law-making processes, however, if we identify some other sense in which the instruments they adopt become 'law' beyond the specific context of participation in a treaty or the affirmation of a soft law instrument. For that purpose we have to consider the circumstances in which those instruments may be translated into customary international law or general principles of law, or become binding on all states in some other way. As we will see in Chapter 5, the processes considered in this chapter do generate generally applicable international law in some or all of these senses. Treaties, decisions and soft law instruments may either generate *opinio juris* and state practice and thereby constitute the material elements of customary law, or afford evidence of generally accepted principles of law. This is the most important sense in which we can point to *law-making* processes. The use of consensus-negotiating techniques significantly advances the formation of new law in this way. Moreover, if law is the product of such interactional processes, a formalist approach focused only on binding norms cannot explain the reality of the contemporary international law. A broader, more nuanced, conception is required. From that perspective even non-binding soft law may become an element of 'law-making'. Finally, there remains the more radical but controversial argument that consensus itself generates law. We explore all these issues further in Chapter 5.

As we saw earlier, no law-making process is likely to prosper unless generally perceived as legitimate by the community it serves; in that sense the process of law-making is as important as the law itself. The Security Council's evolution into a law-making body is problematic because of its unrepresentative membership

---

[284] J. Charney, 'Universal International Law', 87 *AJIL* (1993) 529, 547.

and great power domination and because it was never intended to act in this way. It presents a lopsided and deceptive model for any study of modern international law-making, posing serious problems of legitimacy. For all these reasons expansive use of its power is more likely to be resisted by some states regardless of the binding character of its decisions.

Legitimacy is less of a problem for more genuinely universal bodies whose law-making has a consensual and 'interactional' basis or where it provides technical solutions to global problems. When examining various diplomatic conferences and international organisations, we noted the considerable efforts that have been made to enhance the universality and inclusivity of modern international law-making, and thus to address issues of process legitimacy. Moreover the ability of individual states to withhold consent from most forms of law-making tends to insulate them against the criticisms that apply to Chapter VII resolutions. A state which questions the process by which international law emerges has no obligation to participate, or to join in any consensus, or to accept what is emerging as law. From this perspective, in an essentially voluntaristic system, an illegitimate process may not result in law-making at all.

Further Reading

P. Alston (ed), *The United Nations and Human Rights* (Oxford, 1992).

J. Alvarez, *International Organizations as Law-Makers* (Oxford, 2005).

D. Bodansky, 'The Legitimacy of International Governance', 93 *AJIL* (1999) 596.

B. Buzan, 'Negotiating by Consensus: Developments in Technique at the UN Conference on the Law of the Sea', 75 *AJIL* (1981) 324.

J. Charney, 'Universal International Law', 87 *AJIL* (1993) 529.

R. Churchill and G. Ulfstein, 'Autonomous Institutional Arrangements in Multilateral Environmental Agreements', 94 *AJIL* (2000) 623.

J.-M. Coicaud and V. Heiskanen (eds), *The Legitimacy of International Organisations* (Tokyo, 2001).

V. Gowlland-Debbas (ed), *Multilateral Treaty-Making* (The Hague, 2000).

R. Higgins, *The Development of International Law through the Political Organs of the United Nations* (Oxford, 1963).

C. Joyner (ed), *The UN and International Law* (Cambridge, 1997).

P. Kirsch and J. Holmes, 'The Rome Conference on an International Criminal Court: The Negotiating Process', 93 *AJIL* (1999) 2.

A.-M. Slaughter, 'Security, Solidarity and Sovereignty: The Grand Themes of UN Reform', 99 *AJIL* (2005) 619.

4

Codification and Progressive Development of International Law

1. Introduction

In this chapter we turn to a distinctive element of the international law-making process: codification and progressive development. The unwritten character of customary international law rarely makes its identification easy. The evidence of state practice and *opinio juris* may be scattered, difficult to access, incomplete or contradictory. The claims of states and other relevant actors often differ, as do their views on what constitutes custom. Nor are general principles of law always easy to identify or to define with precision. Judicial decisions and advisory opinions provide an authoritative but far from comprehensive picture of the law on those matters which happen to come before courts. Moreover, judicial pronouncements may conflict, they can become obsolete or outdated, and it may be unwise to attribute too much weight to some of them. Writers of scholarly texts can partly overcome these obstacles but, as with judges and officials, their views and conclusions inevitably reflect differences of background, legal training and experience. In these circumstances, as in any system of unwritten law, codification directed by a more representative body or commission of experts offers a means of restating, clarifying and revising the law authoritatively and systematically. Not until the creation of the United Nations was an International Law Commission established with this objective in mind, meeting for the first time in 1949. We discuss the ILC at length in this chapter, as well as a number of other bodies which also contribute to the codification and progressive development of international law.

The concept of codification is not new, however. The Institutes of Justinian codified Roman law in the late imperial era; the Code Napoleon, drafted by a commission of learned experts, initiated the modern era of European civil law codification, while the Indian Criminal Code of 1860 remains an early landmark of codification in common law jurisdictions. Bentham, Bluntschli and Lorimer were among the earliest advocates of the codification of international law. Their writings helped to inspire the creation of the International Law Association (ILA) and the Institut de

Droit International (*Institut*), both founded in 1873. Koskenniemi describes how the founders of these associations embodied their concept of the 'legal conscience of the civilized world'[1] while Cryer observes how they 'took the place of an absent international legislature'.[2] These two bodies represent the origins of the international legal profession, and they remain the principal private associations of legal experts dedicated to the codification of international law. Their work continues to provide material on which governments, international organisations and NGOs can draw when engaged in international law-making. The membership of the ILA, the *Institut* and national or regional associations of international lawyers together form what Schachter has called the 'invisible college of international lawyers'.[3]

The *Institut* has always been a small body of professors and judges. It produces detailed studies of contemporary international legal issues, in effect an informal codification of particular topics.[4] Founded as the Association for the Reform and Codification of the Law of Nations, the ILA has a broader membership, consisting mainly of academic and practising international lawyers within universities, IGOs, NGOs, government and private practice, and students. Its constitutional objectives are the 'study, elucidation and advancement of international law, public and private, the study of comparative law, the making of proposals for the solution of conflicts of law and for the unification of law, and the furthering of international understanding and goodwill'. Working through a range of specialist committees, each comprising jurists from the 50 ILA national branches, reports and recommendations on a wide range of topics are considered and adopted at biennial conferences. This method of working ensures diverse perspectives on the issues under discussion, but developing countries are poorly represented in both organisations.

In practice both the ILA and the *Institut* have in most cases taken a fairly conservative view of codification, rather more so than the ILC, for example. Koskenniemi concludes that the actual impact of these professional associations has been limited, despite the authority of their members within the discipline. Nevertheless, although long since overshadowed by the International Law Commission and the broader law-making activities of the UN, both institutions have survived. ILA Committees continue to produce some influential reports and recommendations. They have made important contributions to some areas of law that have not been addressed by the International Law Commission, notably in the Final Report of the Committee on Formation of Customary General International Law.[5] Members of the committee brought a range of scholarly and

---

[1] M. Koskenniemi, *The Gentle Civilizer of Nations: The Rise and Fall of International Law 1870–1960* (Cambridge, 2001) 41.

[2] R. Cryer, 'Déjà vu in International Law', 65 *MLR* (2002) 931, 932.

[3] O. Schachter, 'The Invisble College of International Lawyers', 72 *Northwestern UnivLR* (1977) 217.

[4] See Q. Wright, 'The Activities of the Institute of International Law', *ASIL Proceedings* (1960) 195, and reports published in the Institute's *Yearbooks*.

[5] ILA, *Report of the 69th Conference*, held in London, 2000.

practical perspectives to bear on the problem, and drew upon the earlier reports of the *Institut*. Over many years ILA committees have also supplemented the work of the International Law Commission. Thus for over 50 years the ILA worked on various aspects of international water law and in 1966 adopted the Helsinki Rules on the Use of Waters of International Rivers, which 'played a key role in formulating the rule of equitable and reasonable utilization as the basic rule of international law for the transboundary use and development of waters'. The preamble to the 1997 UN Watercourses Convention also refers to the 'valuable contribution' of NGOs in the 'codification and progressive development' of international law in this field. The Helsinki Rules have periodically been supplemented and updated to take account of changes in international law, including developments affecting the sustainable use of water and the protection of watercourse ecosystems. Substantially revised Berlin Rules on Water Resources were adopted in 2004.

Unlike the ILA or the *Institut*, the Hague Conference on Private International Law was established as an intergovernmental organisation in 1893 for the purpose of 'progressive unification' of the rules of private international law. It is still the principal forum for this purpose and remains very active in concluding treaties, many of which are widely ratified. Another international organisation, the Pan-American Union (now the Organisation of American States), was the earliest regional body to promote the codification of international law. However, it was not until the Hague Peace Conferences of 1899 and 1907 that the first opportunity arose for inter-state diplomatic conferences to codify certain principles of public international law. The Hague Peace Conferences have rightly been described as the first quasi-legislative assembly for the international community, although only the 1907 Conference was attended by a significant number of non-European states.[6]

The birth of the League of Nations ushered in a new era in the codification of international law. Starting in 1924, the League Assembly adopted a series of resolutions which recognised the need for 'progressive codification' in order to 'define, improve and develop' international law.[7] It referred to 'The spirit of codification, which should not confine itself to the mere registration of existing rules, but should aim at adapting them as far as possible to contemporary conditions of life'.[8] At much the same time, another intergovernmental organisation known as UNIDROIT was established with the objective of modernising, harmonising and coordinating national commercial law.[9] Already we can see in the mandate of both institutions an understanding that codification could not be limited to restating existing law.

---

[6] R. Dhokalia, *The Codification of Public International Law* (Manchester, 1970) 87–109 (hereafter '*Codification*'). The literature on the Hague Peace Conferences is extensive, but for a recent reassessment of their significance see the Symposium edited by G. Aldrich and C. Chinkin in 94 *AJIL* (2000) 1–98.
[7] Resolutions adopted by the Assembly of the League, 22 September 1924; 27 September 1927 and 25 September 1931.   [8] 1927 Resolution para 6 (d).
[9] See Section 6.2 below.

In 1930 the League of Nations Conference for the Codification of International Law met in Geneva for the purpose of considering codification conventions on a number of topics.[10] However, there was no agreement on the extent to which codification should involve explicit law-making or address the most politically sensitive matters. Some delegations thought that the whole of international law should be codified systematically while others favoured a more piecemeal approach. These disagreements and the lack of preparatory work by experts independent of governments contributed to the inability of the Conference to adopt any of the proposed conventions or to make recommendations to the League, but much of value was learned from the experience and subsequently influenced the organisation and work of the International Law Commission.[11] Dhokalia considered that the 1930 Codification Conference 'taught the lesson that the legislative element in the attempt to codify any part of international law was not merely subordinate or incidental but far outweighed the codifying element'.[12] A more nuanced conclusion, however, is that much depends on the subject and the aspirations of those involved. While some subjects are more amenable to codification and reformulation after thorough deliberation and preparation by legal experts, others require an essentially political negotiating process from their inception.[13] Not surprisingly, no single process fits all forms of international-lawmaking. This lesson is very much reflected in the subsequent history of codification and progressive development in the UN.

2.   Codification and Progressive Development by the UN

Unlike the Covenant of the League of Nations, Article 13 of the UN Charter expressly gives the General Assembly of the UN the power to initiate studies and make recommendations for the purpose of 'encouraging the progressive development of international law and its codification'.[14] Less radical than some of the proposed alternatives, which would have given the General Assembly the power to legislate, this provision originated in a Chinese proposal adopted and revised by the UK, US, and USSR at San Francisco.[15] Although Watts argues that law reform is not contemplated by Article 13 or by the concepts of codification and progressive

---

[10] See S. Rosenne (ed), *League of Nations Conference for the Codification of International Law* (New York, 1975), vol 1. The topics were nationality, territorial waters and responsibility for injury to aliens.   [11] Ibid xlv–xlvi.

[12] Dhokalia, *Codification*, 130. See also UN, *Survey of International Law in Relation to the Work of the International Law Commission* (1949) UN Doc A/CN4/Rev1, para 9 (hereafter '*UN Survey*') reproduced in M. Anderson, A. E. Boyle, A. V. Lowe and C. Wickremasinghe (eds), *The International Law Commission and the Future of International Law* (London, 1998) 63–149.

[13] R. Y. Jennings and A. D. Watts, *Oppenheim's International Law* (London, 1996) 111.

[14] UN Charter, Article 13 (1) (a).

[15] C.-A. Fleischauer, in B. Simma (ed), *The Charter of the UN: A Commentary* (2nd edn, Oxford, 2002) 300.

development, Fleischauer describes the provision as 'the starting point for the vast efforts deployed by the UN in this field'.[16] In practice nothing turns on the interpretation of Article 13 and it covers a wide spectrum of law-making activity, some of which does amount to law reform. Equally, some of the law-making we considered in the previous chapter includes significant elements of codification, including the 1982 UN Convention on the Law of the Sea. It would be foolish therefore to pretend that it is possible to draw a sharp line between law-making covered by this chapter and by the previous one: at best they reflect different parts of the same spectrum.

Institutionally, however, there are important differences. The task envisaged by Article 13 is principally carried out by the International Law Commission (ILC), whose work we consider later in this chapter, or in more specialised fields by the Commission on International Trade Law (UNCITRAL), the Committee on Peaceful Uses of Outer Space (COPUOS) and the UN Environment Programme (UNEP).[17] Nevertheless, the General Assembly also retains the option of undertaking codification and progressive development through diplomatic means, mainly *ad hoc* committees reporting to the 6th Committee. *Ad hoc* committees have become a regular feature of UN law-making and are established when a specific issue needs to be addressed outside the 6th Committee's normal agenda.[18] Codification projects requiring legal expertise but not considered appropriate for prolonged study by the ILC have been handled in this way. Terrorism (considered below) is the most important recent example. A politically controversial Declaration on Human Cloning was also adopted in the General Assembly following negotiations in an *ad hoc* committee and in the 6th Committee.[19] All members of the UN or the specialised agencies may participate in these negotiations and make or comment on proposals, but apart from the International Committee of the Red Cross,[20] there is almost no evidence of NGO participation, except in negotiations on the ICC Statute, considered below. Lawyers from the UN Secretariat's Codification Division service all of these activities, as well as the ILC, undertaking research, providing information on national and international law and the practices of states and international organisations. Legal advisers from member states may also participate in the negotiations.[21] Although political perspectives plainly motivate and dominate this process, legal expertise plays a significant role.

[16] Compare A. D. Watts, *The ILC 1949–98* (Oxford, 1999), vol I, 7–10 (who accepts however that the line between revision and progressive development is not sharp), and Fleischauer in Simma, *The Charter of the UN*, 299–301.

[17] Fleischauer, ibid, 305–11. On COPUOS see R. Steinhardt, in C. Joyner (ed), *The UN and International Law* (Cambridge, 1997) 338–41; on UNEP see P. Birnie and A. E. Boyle, *International Law and the Environment* (Oxford, 2002) 53–7.

[18] Fleischauer, in Simma, *The Charter of the UN*, 308–9.

[19] UNGA Res 59/280, 8 March 2005, adopted 84 to 34, with 37 abstentions.

[20] For example the ICRC was an observer in the *ad hoc* Committee on the Convention on the Safety of UN Personnel. The ICRC, unusually, also has observer status in the UNGA: see Chapter 2.

[21] M. Wood, 'The Role of Legal Advisers at Permanent Missions to the United Nations', in C. Wickremasinghe (ed), *The International Lawyer as Practitioner* (London, 2000) 71, 75–81.

2.1   The 6th Committee of the UNGA

While the 6th Committee does not itself codify or develop international law, we will see below that it approves the codification programme of the ILC, is consulted on its work, and decides whether to convene intergovernmental negotiating conferences for the purpose of revising and adopting draft conventions. This can have negative as well as positive consequences; failure to do anything further with an ILC draft will inevitably reflect adversely on the acceptability and status of the Commission's work on a topic. In a few cases the 6th Committee has become the forum within which ILC draft conventions are renegotiated and redrafted to make them more generally acceptable to states, usually in conjunction with an *ad hoc* committee. Its more political character, in contrast to the ILC, and the ability to produce compromise texts acceptable to governments, have helped to save at least three ILC draft conventions from probable oblivion. The most prominent example is the Statute of the International Criminal Court, which we consider in greater detail in Section 4 below. Another is the 1997 Convention on Non Navigational Uses of International Watercourses. Consistently with earlier UN policy declarations, including the 1992 Rio Declaration, the ILC draft was revised by the 6th Committee in order to accord greater weight to sustainable utilisation.[22] A more difficult task was presented by the 2005 Convention on State Immunity. The ILC draft had failed to bridge the gap between states supporting a narrow concept of immunity and those wishing to retain a broader version. Here again, prolonged negotiations in the 6th Committee and in an *ad hoc* committee eventually provided the necessary mixture of political and legal input to secure adoption of a revised text by consensus.[23] In contrast, the ILC's draft articles on state responsibility were simply noted by the 6th Committee without further comment or renegotiation. All of these examples suggest that the ILC cannot function in isolation from broader political input into the overall process of codification and progressive development. We return to this point below.

The 6th Committee also reviews the work of *ad hoc* committees and considers comments and proposals from governments on draft conventions or declarations they produce, in much the same way as it responds to ILC drafts. Two of the more significant examples of this genre are the *ad hoc* committees on terrorism and on the safety of UN personnel.

2.2   *Ad Hoc* Committee on Terrorism

The *ad hoc* Committee on Terrorism merits special mention here because of its longstanding work on codification and progressive development of the law on this subject. The earliest conventions on international terrorism were adopted not by

---

[22] UN, 6th Cttee, *Report of the Working Group*, GAOR A/51/869 (1997).
[23] See Section 4 below.

the UN but by ICAO and IMO.[24] They were aimed, naturally enough, at attacks on aircraft and ships, in response to particular incidents which occurred in the 1970s and 1980s. The IMO Convention was amended in 2005 to take account of post-9/11 concerns about the use of shipping for terrorist purposes. Apart from elaborating principles of jurisdiction over the relevant offences, these and other conventions also established the obligations of states to prosecute or extradite suspects, and to provide mutual legal assistance. The IMO and ICAO conventions were widely accepted, and many of the principles they established have been incorporated into other treaties[25] and have helped to shape general international law.

As we saw in Chapter 1, it was only in 1994 that the UN General Assembly began to develop more broadly focused measures, starting with a Declaration on Measures to Eliminate International Terrorism.[26] The Declaration and subsequent resolutions encouraged states to review the scope of existing international law, and provided the basis for establishing an *ad hoc* committee to prepare the 1997 Convention for the Suppression of Terrorist Bombings, the 1999 Convention for the Suppression of the Financing of Terrorism and the Convention for the Suppression of Acts of Nuclear Terrorism, adopted by the General Assembly in 2005. The first two were partially put into immediate effect by binding Security Council resolutions adopted following the attacks of September 2001.[27] Work begun by the *ad hoc* committee in 2000 on the drafting of a comprehensive convention on measures to eliminate international terrorism had not yet produced consensus on its scope or relationship to other treaties five years later, but by 2005 enough progress had been made with assistance from the Secretary-General and the High Level Panel on Threats, Challenges and Change for a possibly over-optimistic committee to predict 'imminent' success.[28]

It is not necessary here to go further into the substance of these treaties or the process of negotiation, which we have already considered in Chapter 1; the important point is that they show how codification and progressive development of international law is not confined to the International Law Commission. Although driven by increasingly urgent political imperatives, all three agreements build on existing law, including the obligation to prosecute or extradite suspects, the provision of mutual legal assistance, and extradition law. They also incorporate human rights guarantees and due process requirements not found in the older ICAO and

---

[24] See *inter alia* 1971 Montreal Convention for the Suppression of Unlawful Acts Against the Safety of Civil Aviation; 1988 Convention for the Suppression of Unlawful Acts Against the Safety of Maritime Navigation.

[25] Ten other treaties are referred to in the reports of the *ad hoc* Committee.

[26] UNGA Res 49/60, 9 December 1994, as supplemented by UNGA Res 51/210, 17 December 1996.

[27] See Chapter 3. The 1997 Convention entered into force on 23 May 2001 and the 1999 Convention on 10 April 2002.

[28] See UN, *Report of the ad hoc Committee*, GAOR A/60/37 (2005); UN, 6th Cttee, *Report of the WG on Measures to Eliminate International Terrorism*, GAOR A/C.6/60/l.6 (2005).

IMO treaties, but reflected in the subsequent development of international criminal law. They do not define terrorism, since no agreement on that term has proved possible, but they do set out the offences covered and deal with other matters in relative detail. Writing in terms applicable to all of these negotiations, the chairman reported that

> . . . the mandate of the *Ad Hoc* Committee is to draft a technical, legal, criminal law instrument that would facilitate police and judicial cooperation in matters of extradition and mutual assistance. Our mandate is not to draft a political definition of terrorism . . . the comprehensive convention on terrorism must preserve and build upon the *acquis* of the previous 12 conventions on terrorism. The elements common to the previous instruments are already incorporated in our draft.[29]

The need for legal expertise when negotiating such agreements is obvious; why then was the task not given to the ILC? As suggested earlier, one answer is that the topics were too urgent for consideration by the ILC. Governments already knew what they wanted, and apart from the inability to agree a definition of terrorism, the negotiating process was relatively straightforward and could be handled directly by diplomats and government lawyers. Moreover, although we argue below that legal expertise is the ILC's principal justification, it does not necessarily have the right legal expertise for this task, in the same way that it was not asked to draft a declaration on reproductive cloning. But fundamentally, like the negotiation of the 1982 UNCLOS considered in Chapter 3, agreements of this kind rest on the ability of the participants to reach a political compromise. For that reason consensus is essential and nothing is agreed until everything is agreed. Codification and progressive development of the law remain political tasks that will be effective only while they retain the support of states; when they become predominantly political it is less likely that the ILC will be asked to undertake the necessary work.

2.3 *Ad Hoc* Committee on the Safety of UN Personnel

In contrast to the terrorism conventions considered above, the 1994 Convention on the Safety of UN and Associated Personnel provides a less successful example of a treaty negotiated through an *ad hoc* committee and the 6th Committee. Following proposals by New Zealand and Ukraine aimed at reducing the growing number of attacks on UN personnel undertaking peacekeeping missions, and based on existing conventions on hijacking and other crimes, this convention was negotiated by consensus in only nine months—an unusual achievement—and entered into force in 1999.[30] There is little doubt that urgency was the principal reason for preferring an *ad hoc* committee to any other forum, but if so it has proved counter-productive. Although nearly 80 states had become parties at the time of writing, very few hosted a UN peacekeeping mission. Moreover, a report

---

[29] *Report of the WG*, ibid, paras 32–3.
[30] See E. Bloom, 'Protecting Peacekeepers', 89 *AJIL* (1995) 621.

from the UN Secretary-General in 2000 concluded that the Convention was inadequate in several important respects and recommended urgent revision.[31] Although attacks on UN staff continued to escalate, somewhat leisurely discussions lasted until 2005 when an optional protocol expanding the scope of the original treaty was rapidly agreed following strong political support from the 2005 World Summit.[32] The rather unsatisfactory history of the 1994 treaty may suggest that even the 6th Committee is not immune from a failure of political realism, or it could simply show that states in need of UN peacekeeping forces are unlikely to put negotiation and ratification of new treaties at the top of their priorities. Haste is not usually a virtue in any legislative process and with the benefit of hindsight it might have been better to approach this topic in some other way.

3. The International Law Commission

The principal body established in 1947 for the purpose of progressive development and codification of international law is the International Law Commission.[33] The ILC differs from older codification bodies in several respects. First, it is a permanent body of independent experts on international law, not an *ad hoc* conference of government representatives like the 1930 Hague Codification Conference, nor an intergovernmental organisation like the Hague Conference on Private International Law or UNIDROIT, nor a private association like the ILA. It remains the only such international body ever created, and it long pre-dates the national law commissions established in the United Kingdom and other common law countries from 1965 onwards.[34] Independent law commissions of this kind are entirely unknown in civil law countries. Second, it proceeds deliberatively rather than rapidly (though taking 46 years to conclude draft articles on state responsibility may seem excessive even from this perspective). Third, where the particular priorities of governments had tended to determine the work of the 1907 Hague and 1930 Geneva Conferences,[35] the ILC's agenda reflects a more independent and systematic approach to the codification of international law than had previously been possible. Finally, although the ILC has not been a forum for the development of wholly new bodies of law, by recognising the impossibility of undertaking codification without progressive development, it has given effect to some significant changes in international law.[36] This is most obviously true of the law of treaties and state responsibility, which we consider in Section 4 below.

---

[31] GAOR A/55/637 (2000).

[32] H. Llewellyn, 'The Optional Protocol to the 1994 Convention', 55 *ICLQ* (2006) 718–28.

[33] ILC Statute, Article 1.

[34] But the American Law Institute is older. Established in 1923 to promote 'clarification and simplification' of US law, this is a private, scholarly body, more like the ILA than a national law commission.

[35] See Section 1.

[36] See *Report of the ILC* (1996), chapter vii, paras 157–8; R. Ago, 'Nouvelles réflexions sur la codification du droit international', 92 *RGDIP* (1988) 532 f; I. Sinclair, *The International Law Commission*

Most of the Commission's work has resulted in draft conventions that remain subject to further negotiation, adoption, and ratification by states. To that extent it can be seen as a provider of expert preparatory input into the processes of international law-making by the UN reviewed in the previous chapter. On the other hand, as we will see below, the ILC has significant power of initiative in setting its own agenda, and it would be a mistake to portray it simply as a body which merely responds to or assists the UN. One measure of its success must be the adoption on its own initiative of conventions codifying a significant part of international law, although in some cases participation has been poor and not all have entered into force.[37] The Commission's work has also influenced state practice and the jurisprudence of the ICJ, and in that sense it has contributed to the development of general international law.[38] At its best, the ILC's real strength is the ability to take a systematic view of international law as a whole, to integrate new developments and different bodies of law, and to articulate in its commentaries reasoned and fully researched conclusions. As Crawford observes,

What the ILC can do is to consolidate developments in a particular area of law, making them part of the *droit acquis* . . . it is progressive when seen against a background of slow development of the international community and its institutional need for a coherent body of law.[39]

At the same time, our study of some examples of the work of the Commission summarised in Section 4 suggests that its ability to give coherence to international law can be over-stated. We should not expect too much from an innately conservative body with limited influence on many of the organisations that undertake much of modern international law-making. We argue below, however, that in selecting as topics the fragmentation of international law and reservations to treaties, the ILC has attempted to strengthen its focus on coherence within the system of international law as a whole, even if it has at the same time moved beyond its more traditional role of codifying particular areas of law. Given the eclecticism of modern international law-making processes reviewed in Chapter 3, the proliferation of international courts and tribunals which we consider in Chapter 6, and the resulting potential for fragmentation of international law, these developments seem to mark something of a necessary change of emphasis for the Commission.

3.1　The Commission as an Independent Expert Body

The International Law Commission currently consists of 34 unpaid, part-time members nominated by governments and elected by the General Assembly. The most significant features of the Commission are that its members sit as independent

---

(Cambridge, 1987) 46–7 and 120–7; H. W. Briggs, *The International Law Commission* (Cornell, 1965) 129–41; M. Koskenniemi, 'Solidarity Measures: State Responsibility as a New Legal Order', 72 *BYBIL* (2001) 337; B. Simma, in UN, *The ILC Fifty Years After: An Evaluation* (New York, 2000) 43.

[37] See Anderson et al, *The ILC and the Future of International Law* (London, 1998).
[38] See Section 5 below.
[39] Professor J. Crawford, then a member of the ILC, letter to the author, 7 October 1997.

experts with 'recognised competence in international law', not as delegates of their governments, and that its composition is intended to represent 'the main forms of civilisation and the principal legal systems of the world'.[40] In reality this has come to mean ensuring equitable geographical representation, although the permanent members of the UN Security Council have normally secured the election of their candidates to the Commission.[41] Those ILC members who work or who have worked for states as legal advisers, diplomats or judges bring an important element of practical experience to the Commission, even if they are not always able to participate fully in the Commission's work while still in government service.[42] A small number (four in 2002) also represent their governments at the UNGA 6th Committee when ILC matters are discussed. A minority of ILC members are professors of international law, but they frequently have experience of international litigation or government service. Discussion at public sessions of the Commission is often dominated by this group, which also provides many of the special rapporteurs responsible for preliminary research and drafting on each topic. Viewed as a whole, the composition of the Commission is generally a successful blend of different practical and theoretical legal skills and backgrounds.[43] Several ICJ judges previously served on the ILC, including Simma, Tomka and Sepulveda, elected to the Court in 2003 and 2005. However, only in 2002 were the first two women members elected to the Commission (from Portugal and China).

Rosenne refers approvingly to 'the continuous interaction, throughout the development of a codification draft, between professional expertise and governmental responsibility, between independent vision and the realities of international life'.[44] Nevertheless, while diversity of expertise, a measure of independence from direct government control, and a representative character continue to give the Commission its principal claim to speak as a global body on international law, none of these points should be exaggerated. The election of ILC members by the General Assembly has as much to do with politics as with professional expertise. Ensuring more equitable geographical representation has resulted in increased participation by developing countries and in that sense gives the Commission's work greater legitimacy, but the consequential addition of more serving diplomats or governmental lawyers does not necessarily broaden or deepen its expertise and adds nothing to its independence. The breadth and increasing specialisation of contemporary international law also means that real expertise on any individual topic may be thinly spread within the Commission. Moreover, Koskenniemi, a former member of the ILC, draws attention to the doubts shared by other UN specialised agencies and programmes about 'the very idea of international legislation being

---

[40] ILC Statute, Articles 2 (1) and 8.
[41] UNGA Res 36/39, 18 November 1981. See Sinclair, *The ILC*, 15.
[42] Sinclair, *The ILC*, 16–18.
[43] M. El Baradei, T. Franck and F. Trachtenberg, *The ILC: The Need for a New Direction* (UNITAR, 1981) 29, on which see T. Franck and M. El-Baradei, 'The Codification and Progressive Development of International Law: A UNITAR Study', 76 *AJIL* (1982) 630.
[44] Rosenne, *League of Nations Conference for the Codification of International Law*, at xxxv.

prepared by a body of international lawyers, somewhat like experts in a domestic justice department . . . '.[45] As he observes, from the perspective of these institutions 'international legislation through the traditional method by UN lawyers and diplomats was not a key to solving the world's problems but part of these problems itself'.[46]

3.2   Codification and Progressive Development by the ILC

To understand the ILC's strengths and limitations as a law-making body we need first to understand what constitutes codification and progressive development in the practice of the Commission. Article 15 of the Commission's Statute misleadingly suggests a clear dividing line between the two. According to this provision, codification is 'the more precise formulation and systematisation of rules of international law where there has already been extensive state practice, precedent and doctrine'. Progressive development on the other hand covers 'the preparation of draft conventions on subjects which have not yet been regulated by international law or in regard to which the law has not yet been sufficiently developed in the practice of states'. The Statute also envisages different procedures according to whether the exercise is one of codification or development.[47]

In reality the Commission quickly concluded that few topics divide neatly in this way. It has never sought to identify which of its draft conventions or articles fall into either category, nor has it interpreted codification as a limited exercise of restating existing law. The reasons for this are easy to identify. First, if the existing customary law is clear and satisfactory for most states there is little point expending energy on codifying it or turning it into a treaty binding only on the parties. Any exercise of useful codification will inevitably entail resolving uncertainties, filling in gaps, settling disagreements, and if necessary changing settled law that is out-dated, unsatisfactory or unacceptable to states.[48] As Lauterpacht cogently noted in the 1949 *UN Survey of International Law in Relation to the Work of the ILC* (hereafter '*UN Survey*'): 'Codification which constitutes a record of the past rather than a creative use of the existing materials—legal and others—for the purpose of regulating the life of the community is a brake upon progress.'[49] To that extent all codification contains significant elements of progressive development and law reform, and the real question is how far it is politic or prudent to go.[50]

Second, even in those topics where the element of progressive development of new law is necessarily larger, such as the legal regime of the continental shelf, shared

---

[45]   M. Koskenniemi, 'International Legislation Today: Limits and Possibilities', 23 *Wis ILJ* (2002) 60, 64.   [46]   Ibid 64.

[47]   ILC Statute, Articles 16–17 (progressive development) and Articles 18–22 (codification).

[48]   R. Y. Jennings, 'The Progressive Development of International Law and its Codification', 24 *BYBIL* (1947) 301.

[49]   GAOR A/CN4/Rev1 (1949), paras 3–14 (hereafter '*UN Survey*') reproduced in Anderson et al, *The ILC and the Future of International Law*, 69–79.   [50]   *UN Survey*, para 13.

groundwater, or unilateral acts, there are usually some indications of state practice and general principles, however fragmentary, on which to build. The Commission can also draw on analogies from existing law and practice in cognate areas, for example when expanding its work on the law of treaties to cover those concluded by international organisations. Rarely, if ever, is the Commission starting from a blank sheet. It has, however, left the development of wholly new areas of law to other institutions discussed in Chapter 3, and to that extent it has taken a limited view of the meaning of progressive development in Article 15 of the Statute. In effect, if codification by the ILC necessarily entails progressive development, it seems that progressive development by the ILC generally entails some element of codification. These points help explain the Commission's approach to the choice of topics on its agenda. They show why it is unlikely that the ILC would decide to draft a set of principles on, for example, reproductive cloning.

3.3 Choice of Topics

What determines the Commission's selection of topics? Article 18 of the Statute requires it to 'survey the whole field of international law with a view to selecting topics for codification . . . '. The 1949 *UN Survey* treated the selection of topics as a pragmatic question of 'fitting the work of the Commission at any particular time into the orbit of a comprehensive plan'—with the codification of the entirety of international law as the 'ultimate object' of the Commission's work. The survey's plan proved too ambitious, but it enabled the Commission to draw up a shorter list of 14 topics from which much of the subsequent agenda has emanated. It is true that it has not achieved the impossible task of codifying the whole of international law, a subject now more extensive than in 1949, but it has nevertheless been remarkably successful.[51] The choice of topics over 60 years has enabled the Commission to work on many matters of fundamental doctrinal significance, such as treaties, state responsibility, diplomatic relations, state immunity, law of the sea, international crimes and international organisations. The extent of its work is now such that there have more recently been doubts as to what is left of comparable significance for the future.[52] Moreover, one commentary concludes that in its more recent work 'the ILC has been more haphazard and less strategic in its orientation'.[53]

Some of the topics chosen by the Commission are far less fundamental or of limited scope, such as diplomatic bags, while some matters of fundamental significance are notably absent from the Commission's agenda, such as the use of force. This may reflect a realistic appreciation that some matters are too important and politically sensitive to leave to a body of lawyers: it is notable that when, following

---

[51] Koskenniemi, 23 *Wis ILJ* (2002) 60, 70.
[52] But for a possible agenda see Anderson et al, *The ILC and the Future of International Law*.
[53] Ibid 8.

the Anglo-American invasion of Iraq in 2003, the UN Secretary-General sought a review of the UN Charter provisions on the use of force, he did not refer the issue to the ILC for advice but instead set up an *ad hoc* body of eminent persons, mainly composed of former politicians, diplomats and soldiers.[54] Many of the newer branches of international law such as human rights, environmental protection and international trade are also under-represented in or absent from its programme of work, although the ILC's contribution to the development of international criminal law has been more significant. But as Koskenniemi points out, 'Any intervention in environmental, humanitarian or human rights law, or indeed an attempt to fix the law in *any* field that has to do with the distribution of spiritual or material values will seem eminently political. Why would a body of technical experts be entrusted with it?'[55] The picture that emerges is of a body whose choice of topics continues to be useful, but no longer central to international law-making within the UN system as a whole. This may well be the price of success in restating the fundamentals of international law, but it relegates the Commission to a role of diminishing value, or in Koskenniemi's dismissive phrase, 'increasingly useless'.[56]

3.4 Relations with Other Bodies

Although it was accepted in 1949 that the Commission is entitled to determine what topics it will pursue and in what form, the UN General Assembly may also refer matters to it and such requests have priority.[57] Since 1951 the latter have not been numerous; topics referred include the Nuremberg Principles (1947), crimes against peace and security (1947), the definition of aggression (1950), reservations to treaties (1950), the status of the diplomatic bag (1976), international criminal jurisdiction (1948 and 1991) and international liability (2002). Thus, while the General Assembly must be consulted on the choice of topics,[58] and its views will necessarily be important, it has in practice left the Commission considerable freedom to set its own agenda.

Other UN organs, specialised agencies and states may also refer matters to the ILC under Article 17 of the Statute. Only two such references have been made, both by ECOSOC in 1950.[59] One reason for the paucity of such references under Article 17 is that the Commission has been reluctant to give them priority or to become a drafting body for proposals it has not itself initiated; if it did this its

---

[54] See UN, *Report of the High Level Panel on Threats, Challenges and Change*, GAOR A/59/565 (2005).   [55] (2002) 23 *Wis ILJ* 60, 76.
[56] Ibid 74.   [57] ILC Statute, Articles 16 and 18. See Briggs, *The ILC*, 142–52, 161–78.
[58] ILC Statute, Article 18 (2). This article does not oblige the Commission to obtain the prior *consent* of the UNGA: see Briggs, 164–71.
[59] In 1950 ECOSOC Res 304 D (XI) and 319B III (XI) requested the ILC to draft conventions on the status of women and on statelessness. See Briggs, *The ILC*, 155–9. After receiving the special rapporteur's report the Commission took no further action on the former topic; the latter eventually resulted in adoption of the 1961 Convention on the Reduction of Statelessness.

freedom to set its own agenda would undoubtedly be compromised.[60] This does mean, however, that in practice only the UN General Assembly has any real say in the work of the Commission. Given the limited capacity of the part-time ILC it may be inevitable that it cannot easily respond to the needs of other bodies. Equally, other bodies may not wish to involve the ILC in their projects. Since 1950 ECOSOC has not sought ILC assistance but has resorted instead to the UN Human Rights Commission and the Commission on the Status of Women to further the development of international human rights law, as we saw in Chapter 3. It is notable that this is an area of international law-making from which the ILC has largely been absent. Nevertheless, the result is that when other international bodies or UN organs need the services of a body of legal experts for codification and development of relevant areas of international law they have appointed their own *ad hoc* or in house. The Commission could play a larger role here if it wanted to. It does not have to wait for an Article 17 request, but could actively propose cooperation on areas of mutual concern. Without greater openness to bodies other than the UNGA it seems unlikely that the ILC will be able to promote a more systematic and coherent approach across the fragmented and sometimes overlapping processes of international law-making we observed in Chapter 3.

However, the ILC has remained largely untouched by notions of broader participation now commonplace elsewhere in the UN system, and considered in Chapter 2. In particular it has not generally encouraged participation by NGOs in its work. The reasons for this reluctance have nothing to do with the Statute. The Commission has broadly drafted powers to consult other UN organs, any other official or non-official organisation, scientific institutions and individual experts should it wish to do so.[61] It has used these powers relatively infrequently. Only international organisations are routinely consulted on topics of direct interest, such as the law of treaties and accountability of international organisations. More unusually, UN and regional human rights treaty monitoring bodies and tribunals were consulted after (but not before) the Commission had formulated provisional conclusions on the subject of reservations to human rights treaties.[62] Observers are also exchanged with regional organisations involved in codification, such as the Council of Europe or the Asian-African Legal Consultative Committee, but these relations are usually more formal than productive.[63] The Commission has held meetings with the officers of relevant ILA and *Institut* committees, and there are also informal contacts. Technical advice is occasionally sought: specially commissioned reports from hydrographic experts influenced the maritime delimitation provisions of the Conventions on the Territorial Sea and Continental Shelf, while more recently experts from UNESCO and FAO have advised the Commission in its

---

[60] Briggs, *The ILC*, 153–60.   [61] ILC Statute, Articles 16 (e), 17 (2) (b), 25 and 26.
[62] A. Pellet, *5th Report on Reservations to Treaties*, GAOR A/CN4/508 (2000), para 9.
[63] Sinclair, *The ILC*, 136. Cooperation with the AALCC and the Committee of Legal Advisers of the Council of Europe on the question of reservations to treaties is noted in Pellet, *4th Report*, GAOR A/CN4/491 (1999), paras 27–30.

work on groundwater law. Nevertheless, there is little sense of a working relationship with any of these bodies, and their influence on the ILC is difficult to judge.

Nor is the growing involvement of NGOs in international law-making reflected in the ILC. Rather surprisingly and with the important exception of the ICC Statute which we consider below, NGOs have shown almost no interest in attempting to influence the ILC's work, although increasingly the Commission's draft conventions and other proposals have a potential impact, *inter alia*, on human rights law, environmental law and development law. The Commission's handbook observes that: 'Feeling in the Commission, however, has in general not been favourable to consultation with national official organisations and non-governmental organisations'.[64] One problem that confronts NGOs and anyone seeking to influence the Commission is that 'The Commission has not regarded the right of consultation given to it by Article 16(e) and by implication, by Article 21 of its Statute, as conferring on any individual the right to be heard by the Commission'.[65] But, as the Commission's dealings with the Chairs of the UN Human Rights and Torture Committees over reservations to treaties demonstrate, carefully argued responses to ILC proposals are taken seriously and are unlikely to be ignored even if they had come from an NGO.[66]

Of greatest importance, however, is the Commission's relationship with the General Assembly, because its work can only be successful if it is politically acceptable to member states. One study concludes: 'the fact that certain topics have not commanded a broad spectrum of support or consensus either within the Commission or in the international community at large, affords a more convincing explanation for their failure'.[67] Equally, where the ILC and states are in agreement, the ILC's work is much more likely to meet with general approval.[68] The Commission is required to seek and take account of the views of governments and of the General Assembly on its programme of work,[69] but the difficulties of securing information or representative feedback from states and international organisations are the most important weakness in the ILC's process. In many cases relatively few governments avail themselves of the opportunity to respond to the Commission's questionnaires or to submit written observations after the first and second readings of draft articles. For example, by 2000 only 32 out of 188 governments and 24 out of 65 international organisations had replied to the questionnaire on reservations to treaties sent out in 1995. The special rapporteur regarded this response as encouraging because it was higher than normal, but nonetheless disappointing.[70] Most respondent states were European, eight were Latin American

---

[64] UN, *The Work of the ILC* (5th edn, New York, 1996) 24.
[65] Briggs, *The ILC*, 148.
[66] See Pellet, *5th Report*, GAOR A/CN4/508 (2000), paras 11–15.
[67] Anderson et al, *The ILC and the Future of International Law*, 16.
[68] See the discussion of state responsibility in Section 4.1 below.
[69] ILC Statute, Articles 18 (2), 21 and 22.
[70] Pellet, *5th Report*, UN Doc A/CN4/508 (2000), para 4. Only three governments replied to the ILC questionnaire on unilateral acts.

and five Asian, but no African states replied. The European Community, which concludes more treaties than any other organisation, had also not responded. In the General Assembly, governments, and particularly their legal advisers, have an opportunity to provide comments when the Commission's annual reports and draft articles are considered by the 6th Committee. These meetings are not a real debate on the issues, but they do give ILC chairs and special rapporteurs a feel for how some states are responding, both to what is in a draft and also to what the ILC has chosen to leave out. However, while keeping in touch with the views of states is clearly an essential element of successful codification, the practice is not without serious shortcomings.

For example, during the 6th Committee's discussion of the ILC Report for 2002, one of the main items under consideration was the ILC's draft articles on diplomatic protection, an issue of relevance to all states. The responses of delegations varied. Some encouraged the Commission to adopt a more progressive approach to the topic (for example Mexico), while others took a more conservative approach (for example the US). Some statements were detailed and included substantial comments on the law and the proposals. Others simply listed articles or proposals which they approved or disapproved. Some identified key issues and concerns that should be addressed. Very few developing countries had any comments. Latin American contributions were limited to Guatemala and Mexico. Morocco was the only African country to speak, although the ILC special rapporteur presenting the report was a South African. The debate, such as it was, was dominated by European states, the US, Australia and New Zealand, together with China, Japan, India and Iran. All the P5 states participated.

For many smaller or developing states with limited resources in international law it is not easy to contribute usefully to such discussions. There are several reasons for this. Too many of these states are represented by diplomats rather than lawyers, but Western states, and especially the P5 states, usually send their legal advisers with prepared and detailed comments. Developing states can secure changes to ILC draft articles when these are submitted to a negotiating conference, a good example being the revision of the draft convention on the non-navigational uses of international watercourses in 1997, but by then it may be too late to make significant changes. During the 6th Committee's consideration of the draft articles on diplomatic protection in 2002, some 86 national delegations were represented, of which only 31 were developing states.[71] Can the consultation process really be regarded as either legitimate or representative when so many states or regions do not participate meaningfully, or at all? How can the 6th Committee exercise meaningful oversight of the Commission in such circumstances? And just as importantly, how can the ILC gauge the views of states from

[71] Liberia, Mozambique, Yemen, Venezuela, Tanzania, UAE, Bahrain, Barbados, PRK, Cuba, Gabon, Guatemala, Kuwait, Laos, Iran, India, Dominican Republic, Egypt, Burkina Faso, Brunei, Brazil, Zambia, Thailand, Singapore, Saudi Arabia, Uganda, Niger, Malaysia, Maldives, Kenya, Kiribati. Three Observers were present: the Holy See, the EU and the ICRC.

such a limited selection? Referring specifically to the lack of response from states on the Commission's draft articles on state immunity and international water-courses, it has been suggested that this 'lulls the Commission and other organs of the United Nations into a false sense of security'.[72] The process of codification and progressive development envisaged by the ILC Statute can only work if there is some level of useful dialogue between the representative political body—the 6th Committee—and the representative expert body—the ILC. As we will see in Section 4 below, the evidence suggests that this cannot always be relied upon.[73]

3.5   Working Procedures

The Commission's working practices provide ample opportunity for deliberation and reflection on topics under consideration.[74] In most cases, once the choice of topic is accepted by the General Assembly, a working group will first be appointed by the Commission to identify the scope of the topic and give some guidance to whoever is appointed as special rapporteur with responsibility for directing work on that issue. Normally, the special rapporteur will produce a series of annual reports outlining the topic, setting out the present law and any difficulties which need to be addressed, and making proposals. In some cases the topic is developed entirely by a small working group or study group without appointing a special rapporteur. The preparation of an initial draft of a statute for the International Criminal Court is the most significant example of this abbreviated process.[75] Whatever the method used to produce them, the reports which emerge will even-tually be debated by the Commission in public session. Once a sufficient measure of agreement is reached, draft articles and a commentary are referred to a smaller drafting committee for further detailed study and reworking in private. Progress will be reported to the UN General Assembly in the Commission's annual report. Any ensuing comments or criticisms can then be addressed in the following year's work. When draft articles and commentary are complete, the Commission will provisionally adopt them at first reading and invite states to comment. After fur-ther revision, if necessary, draft articles are adopted on second reading and sent to the General Assembly with a recommendation for further action. Possible out-comes include recommending that the articles be adopted as a treaty by a diplomatic conference (for example, the draft articles on treaties), or taken note of by the General Assembly pending a further decision (for example, state responsibility), or there may be no recommendation.

---

[72] L. Caflisch, in UN, *The ILC Fifty Years After: An Evaluation* (New York, 2000) 67.

[73] But contrast the much more positive assessment by Crawford in relation to state responsibility at n. 89 below.

[74] Sinclair, *The ILC*, 32–44. The Commission's working methods have changed since Sinclair's time on the ILC. See also B. Graefrath, 'The ILC Tomorrow: Improving its Organization and Methods of Work', 85 *AJIL* (1991) 595; S. McCaffrey, 'Is Codification in Decline?', 20 *Hastings ICLR* (1997) 639.   [75] See Section 4 below.

Since the Commission meets for no more than three months of the year, working simultaneously on five or more topics, progress will usually be relatively slow. Some topics have been the subject of very prolonged discussion. Consideration of the law of treaties began in 1949, went through several major revisions under a succession of rapporteurs, and resulted first in the 1969 Vienna Convention on the Law of Treaties, second, the 1978 Vienna Convention on Succession of States in Respect of Treaties, and finally the Vienna Convention on the Law of Treaties between States and International Organisations adopted in 1986. In 1994 the topic of reservations to treaties, already covered by provisions of the earlier conventions, returned to the ILC's agenda for reconsideration in view of subsequent developments, and was still under discussion in 2006. Draft articles on state responsibility were finally adopted in 2001, but the topic had first been considered in 1955. These articles underwent substantial change over that period, and finalising the text required extensive reconsideration and revision. The draft articles on non-navigational uses of international watercourses adopted in 1994 took only 20 years from start to finish. Each of these topics occupied no less than five special rapporteurs.

Some of this prolonged consideration is due to the complexity of certain topics or the difficulty in securing a consensus within the ILC; as we have seen the process is deliberative, states have to be consulted, and membership of the Commission changes from year to year. In other cases, such as Liability for Injurious Consequences, it took many years of largely wasted effort before a realistic conception of the subject emerged. In that instance the Commission eventually found it useful to appoint a small group of members to reconsider the outlines of the topic and make proposals for the future direction of the topic.[76] Not all ILC projects are so slow. Draft articles on diplomatic and consular relations took respectively five and seven years to complete, and the Commission's work on law of the sea in the 1950s was similarly expeditious. The draft Statute of the International Criminal Court was concluded in a mere three sessions, although it benefited from earlier ILC work on a draft code of crimes against peace and security, initiated in 1949 and completed in 1996. Overloading the Commission's agenda became a significant source of delay in the 1980s until it began to restrict the number of topics it was willing to tackle. In 2005, however, there were again no fewer than nine topics on its agenda. Nevertheless, it is not obvious that the UNGA 6th Committee or the other negotiating processes we considered in Chapter 3 have proved to be any faster.

3.6   Codification by Treaty or Soft Law?

Given the relative advantages of soft law over treaties, it is perhaps surprising that the multilateral treaty has been the International Law Commission's preferred instrument for the codification of international law. Articles 17 and 23 of the

---

[76] See Section 4 below.

Statute of the Commission refer expressly to the conclusion of conventions, but other possibilities are left open.[77] As we saw in Chapter 3, one important feature of the treaty as an instrument of codification is that states have significant input into the negotiations and they have sometimes made substantial changes to ILC drafts.[78] This renegotiation does not necessarily happen when the UN General Assembly simply adopts or takes note of a declaration of principles drafted by the Commission. A treaty basis may also be required when creating new international organisations or institutions, such as the International Criminal Court, or for dispute settlement provisions. Finally, for many states ratified treaties become part of their national law, and adoption of a text in this form thus becomes a convenient way of changing national law. The latter point explains why these states ultimately favoured adoption of a treaty on the law of state immunity, rather than a simple declaration.

Nevertheless, in some situations soft law instruments appear to be just as useful a means of codifying international law as treaties. The Commission's draft articles on the law of state responsibility are an example. Although views within the ILC and the 6th Committee on the eventual form of the articles were divided, both bodies recommended that the UNGA initially 'take note' of the draft articles, in the expectation that in this form they would 'exert an influence on the crystallization of the law of State responsibility through application by international courts and tribunals and State practice', deferring for later consideration a decision on whether to proceed with a codification treaty.[79] Why has this topic been treated differently from almost all its predecessors? It cannot be said that the state responsibility articles are unsuited to adoption in the form of a multilateral treaty; on the contrary they are drafted as if in treaty form. A UNGA resolution may in this case be more effective than a treaty for two reasons. First, a treaty runs the risk of securing only a relatively small number of parties. The Commission's work on the law of treaties is among its most successful and authoritative codifications, but it is difficult to suggest that this owes much to the Vienna Convention's treaty status, or to the relatively small number of states parties. Second, referring the draft articles to a diplomatic conference might re-open debates on a text which already rests on a delicate compromise between differing views.[80] Further negotiations might have a destabilising rather than a reinforcing effect. In this respect, the fate of the state responsibility articles may suggest a recognition that in some cases it can be better for states simply to endorse a consensus in the Commission and then argue about

[77] On the comparative advantages of different forms see J. Crawford, *The International Law Commission's Articles on State Responsibility* (Cambridge, 2002) 58–60.

[78] eg the 1969 Vienna Convention on the Law of Treaties and the 1997 International Convention on the Non-navigational Uses of International Watercourses.

[79] J. Crawford and S. Olleson, 'The Continuing Debate on a UN Convention on State Responsibility', 54 *ICLQ* (2005) 959, and see Section 4 below.

[80] Ibid 961, and M. Koskenniemi, 'Solidarity Measures: State Responsibility as a New International Order', 72 *BYBIL* (2001) 337, 341.

the status of the rules in their dealings with each other and in litigation. Thus in this case, the form of the articles is more significant for what it tells us about the process of international law-making than about the nature or legal status of the rules themselves. There can be few better illustrations of the flexibility of the process.

It is possible that the ILC will make greater use of soft law instruments in future. Articles on Prevention of Transboundary Harm adopted in 2001 were drafted in treaty form, and were similarly taken note of by the General Assembly, but without commitment to negotiation of a treaty, and proposed articles on shared natural resources may also be adopted in this form. Re-examination of the law and practice on reservations to treaties was not conceived as leading to any amendment of or addition to existing conventions, but may conclude with the adoption of guidelines.[81] Guidelines can be expressed differently from treaty articles, their purpose is more practical and they do not create binding commitments, although they may help interpret such commitments, or simply disseminate a better understanding of the legal system. Principles on the Allocation of Loss in the Case of Transboundary Harm Arising out of Hazardous Activities have also been drafted in this form, although as we argue below the Commission has in this case been excessively cautious. A study of the fragmentation of international law initiated in 2000 is another topic which does not fit the normal pattern and on which a report and guidelines are envisaged.[82] Such an outcome would itself tell us that the ILC has evolved. Not only does its agenda in the new millennium begin to look different from the original conception laid out by Lauterpacht in the 1949 UN Survey,[83] but its role would be seen to have subtly expanded in new directions. We consider some of these changes in the following sections.

4. Codification and Progressive Development in Practice

No sense of the significance and limitations of the ILC's contribution to the codification and progressive development of international law can be gleaned without reference to some of the more telling examples of its work.

4.1 State Responsibility

The law relating to state responsibility is a classic example of 'lawyer's law' ripe for codification by an expert body of international lawyers. There were remarkably few precedents for the ILC to draw upon. Work undertaken for the 1930 Hague Conference and the Harvard Research project had dealt with the subject only in relation to the treatment of aliens, but the 1949 *Survey of International Law in Relation to Codification* identified it as a distinct topic occupying a broader field. From the outset it featured on the ILC's list of potential topics, although not until

---

[81] See Section 4.   [82] *Report of the ILC*, GAOR A/60/10 (2005).   [83] Above, n. 49.

1955 did work begin, and it was only when Ago was appointed special rapporteur in 1963 that the eventual shape of the topic emerged. In this form, the ILC set out to codify only secondary rules relating to breach of international obligations rather than the primary rules of obligation themselves.[84] Nevertheless, it would take nearly 40 years to conclude work on the topic. Draft articles were finally adopted by the Commission in 2001 and, as we saw earlier, at the Commission's suggestion the 6th Committee recommended that the UNGA 'commend [the articles] to the attention of governments without prejudice to the question of their future adoption or other appropriate action'.[85] Unusually, therefore, although skilfully drafted in treaty language that is 'lean and polished',[86] they remain soft law, whose legal significance will derive only from whatever authority they possess as evidence of customary law. But as Koskenniemi has observed, 'A convention could hardly have attained more'.[87]

The prolonged consideration of the topic by the Commission may seem excessive, but it had a number of advantages. First, it allowed for genuine deliberation within the Commission and the 6th Committee. The draft articles received their first reading as a whole in 1996 and their second in 2001, but the general principles contained in part I of the draft had already received a first reading as far back as 1980.[88] Substantial changes to the 1996 draft were made in the final stages of the Commission's consideration of the articles. In this respect, Crawford, who served as the last special rapporteur on the topic, has drawn attention to the regularity and importance of the feedback from governments, particularly in the later stages. Comments from states resulted in the eventual deletion of Article 19 on international crimes of state, the abandonment of dispute settlement clauses, and the reduction of Article 54 from a substantive provision on collective countermeasures to a savings clause which left the matter open for future development. Other changes also resulted from consultations with states. In Crawford's view, the interplay with the 6th Committee contributed greatly to the 'benign reception' the final draft articles received there in 2001.[89]

Second, the very long gestation also allowed for significant debate within the wider community of international lawyers.[90] Few ILC topics can have been the subject of so much academic comment and scrutiny.[91] More importantly, by the time the final draft articles were adopted, they had already become widely cited by foreign

---

[84] ILC, *Report of Subcommittee on State Responsibility*, 2 *YBILC* (1963) 227. For a fuller account of the history of the topic, see J. Crawford, *The ILC's Articles on State Responsibility: Introduction, Text and Commentaries* (Cambridge, 2002) 1–60 and D. Bodansky and J. R. Crook, 'Symposium: The ILC's State Responsibility Articles', 96 *AJIL* (2002) 773, on which the following account is largely based.

[85] UNGA Res 56/83, 12 December 2001. The articles and commentary are reproduced in Crawford, *The ILC's Articles on State Responsibility*.

[86] Bodansky and Crook, 96 *AJIL* (2002) 787.   [87] Koskenniemi, 72 *BYBIL* (2001) 341.

[88] UN, *Report of the ILC*, GAOR A/35/10 (1980) 49–133.

[89] J. Crawford, 'The ILC's Articles on State Responsibility for Internationally Wrongful Acts: A Retrospect', 96 *AJIL* (2002) 874, 875.   [90] Bodansky and Crook, 96 *AJIL* (2002) 774.

[91] See eg I. Brownlie, *System of the Law of Nations: State Responsibility Part I* (Oxford, 1983); M. Spinedi and B. Simma (eds), *UN Codification of State Responsibility* (New York, 1987).

ministries, practising international lawyers, and international courts and tribunals, most notably by the ICJ in the *Gabčíckovo-Nagymaros* case.[92]

It has been suggested that some of the articles have 'a bootstrapping quality, helping to shape the law to match the draft',[93] but this tells us only that any attempt to set out a systematic account of the law built largely on international judicial decisions and awards by claims commissions cannot be a mere codification of existing rules. In significant respects it was far from clear what those rules were, still less what they should be. The prolonged debate on countermeasures, *erga omnes* obligations, the role of fault, and the definition of 'injured state' are only some of the elements where the Commission's work can be said to develop the law rather than merely codify it. Indeed some went so far as to characterise the Commission's work as an attempt to construct a 'system of multilateral public order' rather than codifying the law of state responsibility.[94] Others criticised it as mostly a backward-looking endeavour which failed to address the expanding scope of contemporary international law or the emergence of non-state entities as significant actors. Some saw the whole endeavour as flawed because it presumed that a unified body of law could cater for a multiplicity of special regimes. Crawford argues that the articles are neither as inflexible nor as conservative as some of these comments might suggest, and that the level of controversy is 'overstated'.[95] Nor is the process finished: 'The articles will have to prove themselves in practice, and that is a process which will require careful assessment. Indeed, the point of the ILC's recommendation, in the first place at least, was to allow such a process of testing and assessment to continue . . . on a case-by-case basis.'[96] Here we can see the Commission itself pointing to the very important impact which ICJ decisions and those of other international courts have on the status of ILC draft articles and conventions as customary law.[97]

It is not necessary here to enter further into an account of the ILC draft articles on state responsibility.[98] Whatever their merits may be, they show the value of an expert body which can give systematic shape to legal principles of quite fundamental importance to the character and scope of contemporary international law. In this case, unlike some others that we examine below, it cannot be said that the Commission failed to rise to the challenge, even if some might have preferred it to go further. It is not surprising that the draft articles on state responsibility have been referred to as one of the ILC's most significant accomplishments.[99]

---

[92] (1997) ICJ Reports 7.

[93] Bodansky and Crook, 96 *AJIL* (2002) 788, referring specifically to articles on necessity and countermeasures.

[94] *Report of the ILC*, GAOR A/55/10 (2000) 112, para 365. Others viewed this development as the topic's main merit: see B. Simma, in UN, *The ILC Fifty Years After*, 43.

[95] Crawford, 96 *AJIL* (2002) 889.   [96] Ibid.   [97] See Section 5 below.

[98] For a full debate see 'Symposium: The ILC's State Responsibility Articles', 96 *AJIL* (2002) 773–890 and 'Symposium: Assessing the Work of the International Law Commission on State Responsibility', 13 *EJIL* (2002) 1037–256.

[99] Crawford, *The ILC's Articles on State Responsibility*, 60; Simma, in UN, *The ILC Fifty Years After*, 43.

4.2   State Immunity

In 2004 the UN General Assembly adopted a Convention on the Jurisdictional Immunities of States and their Property.[100] This was not the first attempt to codify international law relating to state immunity. Draft articles were adopted by the *Institut de Droit International* in 1891 and in 1927 the Committee of Experts on Progressive Codification of International Law recommended to the League of Nations that the subject was ripe for codification, in response to which a convention of 28 articles was drafted by American lawyers as part of the Harvard research programme.[101] None of these projects came to anything, but in 1949 the subject reappeared on the list of topics provisionally selected by the ILC for codification. Not until 1978 did the Commission decide to proceed with the topic, and the draft articles it adopted in 1991 proved controversial and failed to reconcile the significant differences between states. It took a further 13 years of negotiations at the UN to produce a partially revised text that was finally adopted without a vote.

Whether the new convention will become accepted as a codification of international law on the subject cannot at this stage be certain. Its impact will depend significantly on how far it succeeds in encouraging states to harmonise existing national laws. It is unlikely to change the national law of non-parties and to that extent it will be important that as many states as possible become parties: mere acquiescence alone will not suffice. Moreover, the Convention is not a package deal and reservations are not prohibited. So long as they do not undermine the object and purpose of the Convention, it will be open to individual states to pick and choose those elements which they are willing to accept while reserving others. There is thus no guarantee that national laws will be harmonised even among the parties unless reservations are kept to a minimum. Even then, there remain uncertainties in a text which may be interpreted in significantly different ways.[102] Finally, the important question of immunities with respect to proceedings brought by victims of torture, crimes against humanity, or other breaches of human rights obligations remains unresolved, nor is immunity from criminal prosecution covered by the Convention. In all of these respects the customary international law will continue to evolve, if at all, on the basis of national law and judicial decisions, although the difficulty of resolving conflicting trends through adjudication is apparent in the case law, national and international, that has developed during the past decade.[103]

---

[100] UNGA Res 59/38, 16 December 2004. For a fuller analysis of the convention see comments by E. Denza, H. Fox, R. Gardiner, C. Hall, A. Dickinson and L. McGregor in 55 *ICLQ* (2006) 395–445, and papers by G. Hafner, D. Akande, C. Greenwood, L. Livada and A.V. Lowe given at a symposium held at the RIIA, Chatham House, London, in October 2005. The following section draws on all of these sources without further attribution, but our conclusions are very much our own.

[101] 26 *AJIL* Supp (1932) 451. For a fuller account of the early precedents see H. Fox, *The Law of State Immunity* (Oxford, 2002), chapter 4.

[102] For example the applicability of the Convention to military activities, on which see A. Dickinson, 'Status of Forces under the UN Convention on State Immunity', 55 *ICLQ* (2006) 427.

[103] See eg *Ex Parte Pinochet* [2000] 1 AC 147; *Jones v. Ministry of the Interior of Saudi Arabia* [2006] 2 WLR 1424.

Nevertheless, even if it is not comprehensive and may not fully harmonise national laws, the adoption of a global convention on state immunity is a significant achievement. It articulates for the first time a common international standard of limited immunity based largely on the practice of those jurisdictions, such as the United Kingdom, whose most recent legislation has sought to ensure that foreign states can be sued in respect of commercial contracts and other essentially non-sovereign transactions. There is now agreement on the exceptions to immunity, both from suit and from execution of judgments or actions in respect of state property, and on what constitutes the 'state' for this purpose. For a number of civil law countries it will provide a valuable means of modernising national law and the immunity provisions of their civil codes. For states such as China which had formerly adhered on ideological grounds to the doctrine of absolute immunity from suit, the Convention offers the opportunity to move to a common conception of immunity limited to the exercise of sovereign authority.[104]

The 2004 Convention thus addresses the main problems which had originally persuaded the ILC to start work on the topic and on which the majority of states had from the beginning sought agreement. Faced with widely differing national laws on the subject, and no clear consensus on what immunities international law either permitted or required, the working group which recommended the choice of topic in 1978 concluded that 'it was in the interest of states generally that the rules of international law governing state immunities should be made generally more ascertainable so as to give general guidance to states for the adoption and maintenance of a consistent attitude . . . '.[105] However, the ILC clearly underestimated the extent to which strong national interests would impede the special rapporteur's attempts to limit the immunity of states, and the ideological differences with regard to the personality, capacity and functions of the state. The result was a draft convention adopted by the Commission in 1991, which was unsatisfactory to many states in various ways.[106] It delegated the distinction between commercial and non-commercial transactions largely to national law. It also failed to reconcile broader and narrower conceptions of what constituted the state or how far states could be held liable for the commercial transactions of state enterprises, and it left states with extensive immunity from any form of execution of judgments. Moreover, the end of the cold war found former communist states with extensive state-owned enterprises uncertain how to proceed with a draft that could expose them to liabilities from which they might no longer be immune. The impact of privatisation and economic globalisation made harmonisation of the law on state immunity more important, but 1991 was not the right moment politically to proceed to do so. Not surprisingly, when the ILC sent its draft articles to the

---

[104] See comments by China in UNGA, *Report of the SG on Jurisdictional Immunities of States*, A/56/291(2001).   [105] *YBILC* (1978), vol I, 1524th meeting, 24 July 1978.

[106] See Caflisch, in UN, *The ILC Fifty Years After: An Evaluation* (UN, 2000) 56–61; UNGA, 6th Cttee, *Report of Chair of WG on Jurisdictional Immunities of States*, A/C6/54//L12 (1999), paras 13–45, and for a more detailed analysis, Fox, *The Law of State Immunity* 230–50.

6th Committee for consideration, they proved too politically controversial. Nor could the 6th Committee itself resolve differences of view among states on the most fundamental issues; consultations undertaken in 1993/4 failed to agree on solutions. Indeed participants could not even agree on whether the differences *could* be resolved.

The ILC cannot be blamed for failing to foresee the end of the cold war and the collapse of communism, or for the prolonged inability of the 6th Committee to reach agreement. As the Italian government observed, 'the ILC draft was the result of a study which had been carried out during a period in which the institutional and economic landscape were far different from now'.[107] Nevertheless, apart from its understandable inability to reconcile the irreconcilable, the Commission's difficulties with state immunity betray other failings of a more systemic kind. Hafner, who chaired the 6th Committee working group and the *ad hoc* committee which eventually negotiated the final text of the Convention, has pointed to the absence of any interaction or exchange between the ILC and the 6th Committee.[108] He confirms the point made earlier that lack of response from states left the ILC inadequately informed about what would be acceptable,[109] and concludes that the topic shows the lack of a proper relationship between states and the ILC. Politics alone do not explain all the problems with the ILC's work on state immunity; deficiencies of process also play a role.

Ultimately, the problems left unsolved in 1994 were finally dealt with ten years later, after further negotiations in a 6th Committee working group and an *ad hoc* committee.[110] These bodies took into account further comments from states, including China, Japan and Italy, and also had the benefit of proposals for revision from a working group of the ILC, which the 6th Committee had requested. Significant revisions to the ILC draft resulted, most notably in the definitions of 'State' and 'commercial transaction', in the article on contracts of employment, and in articles limiting the immunity of state property from pre- and post-judgment measures.[111] The *ad hoc* committee also agreed on a dispute settlement clause and an annex setting out interpretations of certain articles. In effect this committee became a negotiating conference of states. Comments made by China in 2001 in support of the revised ILC draft show the extent to which political change made legal change easier.[112] Thus, when finally adopted, the UNGA resolution was able to note 'the broad support for the conclusion of a convention on jurisdictional immunities of States and their property'.

---

[107] UNGA, *Report of the SG on Jurisdictional Immunities of States*, A/56/291/Add1 (2001), para 2.
[108] UN, *The ILC Fifty Years After*, 66. See also Caflisch ibid, 67.
[109] See Section 3 above.
[110] UNGA, 6th Cttee, *Report of Chair of the WG on Jurisdictional Immunities*, A/C6/54/L12 (1999) and A/C6/55/L12 (2000); UNGA, *Report of the ad hoc Cttee on Jurisdictional Immunities*, A/57/22 (2002); A/58/22 (2003); A/59/22 (2004).
[111] 2004 Convention, Articles 2, 11, 18–21.
[112] UNGA, *Report of the SG on Jurisdictional Immunities of States*, A/56/291(2001).

Probably the most important conclusion to draw from the codification of international law on state immunity is that timing is crucial. For over a century successive bodies had concluded that the time for codification was ripe; the experience of the ILC appears to show that for most of this period it was never ripe, and with hindsight it seems unsurprising that nothing was achieved for so long. If the ILC was wrong in its timing, it nevertheless produced a draft that offered a substantial basis for further negotiation and eventual agreement between states when the time did become very ripe only a few years later. Most of its original text remains in the new Convention unchanged or changed only to a limited extent. If the 1991 version was unsatisfactory in some respects, the Commission's work had succeeded in highlighting the central areas of disagreement.

Viewed as part of a larger process of international law-making and harmonisation of very disparate national laws, this is not an insignificant achievement. It is not realistic to expect treaties to emerge from the ILC fully formed, universally supported and wholly unblemished by ambiguities or inelegant compromises. As we emphasised earlier, the ILC is an expert body of international lawyers, not a drafting committee of states. Faced initially with strong ideological differences surrounding the topic, and then with serious changes in the political landscape, it is to be expected that only significant political involvement in the process could secure ultimate consensus. Of course, earlier input from governments would have helped the Commission determine what states really thought, but this presupposes that states had fully formed views on the topic that they could have shared with the Commission during its work rather than afterwards. This may be an optimistic view of governments, and it discounts the possibility that the ILC's work helps the views of states to evolve, even if the evolution may be in contrary directions. The notion that some element of dialogue exists between the Commission and states is not entirely fanciful, even if it is imperfect and sporadic. Certainly, without such a dialogue codification projects cannot be expected to prosper, as we saw earlier. Lastly, it is also worth noticing the absence of other participants in a dialogue which has important implications, *inter alia* for remedying breaches of human rights law and international criminal law. No doubt the involvement of human rights NGOs would have made agreement on the convention text even harder to achieve, but their influence will nevertheless be felt at national level and that may now make ratification harder for some states.[113]

4.3 The Law of Treaties

No other topic has occupied the ILC for longer; few ILC conventions have established such a universally accepted, comprehensive and enduring codification than the 1969 Vienna Convention on the Law of Treaties; none has been so widely

---

[113] See in particular C. Hall, 'UN Convention on State Immunity: The Need for a Human Rights Protocol', 55 *ICLQ* (2006) 411.

relied on by governments and courts. By any measure, this is one of the ILC's successes, despite a relatively poor record of ratification of or accession to the 1969 Convention and the even worse record of the 1986 Vienna Convention on the Law of Treaties between States and International Organisations.[114] Moreover, even for those states which are parties, the Vienna Conventions do not apply to all treaties. Neither Convention is retrospective, so prior treaties continue to be governed by customary law, as do treaty relations between parties to the Vienna regime and non-parties. Thus the real significance of the ILC's achievement lies not in the conventions themselves, but in the extent to which they have successfully become accepted by international and national courts, or by governments and foreign ministries, as restatements of customary law.

The 1969 Vienna Convention is not solely the work of the ILC. As a draft convention it was submitted to a UN diplomatic conference that undertook some significant revision and redrafting. The most notable addition is Article 66 providing for compulsory dispute settlement procedures in respect of Part V of the Convention, although ironically these procedures have never been used. Without this compromise text it was likely that the diplomatic conference would have failed.[115] Articles 11 (consent to be bound), 13 (exchange of instruments), 46 (2) (violation of internal law), 60 (5) (material breach of humanitarian treaties) and 74 (diplomatic and consular relations) were also proposed by states rather than by the ILC. The 1969 Convention and its 1986 counterpart, with their subtle *mélange* of codification and progressive development, have undoubtedly shaped the modern law of treaties,[116] but it is the interaction of the ILC, the diplomatic conferences, subsequent practice and judicial decisions which have brought this about.

While building on existing law, the 1969 Convention nevertheless made important clarifications, reformulations and additions, most notably in regard to interpretation, invalidity, reservations and *jus cogens*. Some provisions go beyond previous precedents, such as Article 18 on the obligation not to defeat the object and purpose of a treaty pending signature, or Article 20 on the effect of objections to reservations. The degree of progressive development contained in Part V of the Convention, dealing with invalidity, termination and suspension, was acceptable to many states only because Article 66 provides for compulsory settlement procedures in the event of a dispute.[117] Nevertheless, the ICJ has been willing to accept many of these articles as evidence of current customary law, and thus applicable to states not bound by the Convention. Article 62 on change of circumstances was applied by the ICJ in the *Icelandic Fisheries* cases,[118] although the Convention was

---

[114] 81 and 23 parties respectively in 2004. The latter convention is not in force.

[115] I. Sinclair, *The Vienna Convention on the Law of Treaties* (Manchester, 1982) 231–2.

[116] See Sinclair, *The Vienna Convention*; A. Aust, *Modern Treaty Law and Practice* (Cambridge, 2000) chapter 1; P. Daillier and A. Pellet, *Droit International Public* (7th edn, Paris, 2002) 119.

[117] Sinclair, *The Vienna Convention*, 226–36.

[118] *Fisheries Jurisdiction Case (UK v Iceland)* (Jurisdiction) (1973) ICJ Reports 3.

not then in force and had been adopted only four years previously. Similarly, Article 60 on breach of treaty was relied on in the *Namibia Advisory Opinion* [119] and in the *ICAO Council* case.[120] Most notable of all is the ICJ's reliance on various articles from Part V of the 1969 Convention in the *Gabčíkovo* case,[121] notwithstanding that the 1977 treaty at issue in that case pre-dated entry into force of the Vienna Convention. A few entirely new provisions, such as Article 53 (on *jus cogens*), were also controversial for some states. Notwithstanding these objections, however, the concept of *jus cogens* has acquired a significant pedigree in case law, although none of the judicial decisions deals with the specific issue of validity of a treaty that contravenes such a norm.[122]

Indeed, it can be said that on most questions both conventions have come to be widely, if not universally, accepted as authoritative statements of the customary law of treaties. On that basis the 1969 Convention's provisions on interpretation (Articles 31 and 32) have been applied in the case law of nearly all international tribunals and many national courts.[123] Commenting on the *Gabčíkovo* case, Aust concludes that it is not unreasonable to assume that the International Court will apply the same approach to virtually all of the provisions of the 1969 Convention, and as he points out there is no case in which the Court has found that the Convention does not reflect customary law.[124]

Only in one respect has the 1969 Vienna Convention failed to generate consensus on the applicable law, but the failure is illuminating. With one important modification,[125] the ILC's proposals on reservations to treaties were adopted as Articles 19–23 of the 1969 Convention, but they have never become fully established. When the permissibility of reservations was considered in the *Reservations to the Genocide Convention Advisory Opinion*,[126] the ICJ held only that states were free to make reservations to humanitarian conventions, provided that the reservation was compatible with the object and purpose of the convention, and subject to the right of other parties to object. This departure from the then prevailing practice which disallowed reservations except with the consent of other parties was justified in the interests of promoting wider participation in humanitarian treaties. The ILC adopted the Court's approach and with some amplification applied it to all treaties in its draft articles on reservations, which subsequently became Articles 19–23 of

---

[119] (1971) ICJ Reports 16.   [120] (1972) ICJ Reports 46.   [121] (1997) ICJ Reports 7.
[122] *Al-Adsani v. United Kingdom* (2002) 34 EHRR 11, 273, paras 52–67; *Prosecutor v. Furundzija* (1999) 38 ILM 317 (ICTY); *Nicaragua Case* (Merits) (1986) ICJ Reports 14, 92–8, paras 172–86; *Arrest Warrant Case* (2002) ICJ Reports 3, para 56.
[123] See eg *Golder v. UK* (1975) 1 EHRR 524; *Advisory Opinion on 'Other Treaties' Subject to the Consultative Jurisdiction of the Court*, IACHR OC-1/82, 24 September 1982; *Legal Consequences of the Construction of a Wall in Occupied Palestinian Territory* (2004) ICJ Reports, para 94; *R v. Immigration Officer at Prague Airport ex parte European Roma Rights Centre* [2005] 2 AC 1.
[124] Aust, *Modern Treaty Law and Practice*, 11.
[125] 1969 Vienna Convention, Article 20 (4) (b) provides that objection to a reservation does not preclude entry into force of a treaty as between the states concerned unless a contrary intention is expressed. This reverses the presumption against treaty relations in the ILC's proposed article.
[126] (1951) ICJ Reports 15. See Chapter 6.

the 1969 Vienna Convention. In the *Anglo-French Continental Shelf Arbitration* [127] the arbitrators generally followed the Vienna Convention provisions when determining the permissibility and effect of reservations in customary law.

However, in a number of later cases it became apparent that human rights tribunals and treaty-monitoring bodies were taking a different approach to these questions. [128] Instead of leaving it to states in accordance with Vienna Convention rules to object to or acquiesce in reservations, and to treaty relations *inter se*, tribunals and monitoring bodies were deciding questions relating to the permissibility and effect of reservations themselves. Reservations determined to be impermissible were in some cases disregarded and in others no objections to permissible reservations were allowed. Moreover, as several studies observed, neither the Vienna Convention nor state practice had fully clarified the consequences of making an impermissible reservation, regardless of the category of treaty concerned. [129]

Given such divergent views, and continuing uncertainty over other matters, such as the distinction between reservations and interpretative declarations, the ILC once more returned to the topic of reservations in 1993. It envisaged drafting a guide to practice for states and international organisations rather than a new or amended treaty. [130] The resulting guidelines are essentially an amplification of the Vienna regime, clarifying uncertainties or filling in gaps. In this form the Commission's draft has been the subject of very extensive consultation with states and international organisations. [131] Nevertheless, one reason why the topic has proceeded so slowly is that views remain divided and the special rapporteur has been reluctant to allow matters to come to a premature conclusion.

This is particularly true with respect to the problem of impermissible reservations to human rights treaties, which the special rapporteur did not begin to address until 2005. [132] In 1994 the UN Human Rights Committee had explicitly found that 'the provisions of the Vienna Convention on the role of State objections are inappropriate to address the problem of reservations to human rights treaties'. [133] Despite this, the ILC provisionally concluded in 1996 that the Vienna

---

[127] (1978) 54 ILR 6.

[128] See *Belilos v. Switzerland* (1988) ECHR Series A No. 132; *Louizidou v. Turkey (Prelim. Objs)* ECHR Series A, No. 310, paras 90–8; *Advisory Opinion on the Effect of Reservations*, IACHR (1983); 22 ILM 37; *Kennedy v. Trinidad and Tobago*, UNHRC Comm. No. 845/1999 CCPR/C/67/D/ 845/1999, 31 December 1999. For a full account of the practice of human rights bodies see Y. Tyagi, 'The Conflict of Law and Policy on Reservations to Human Rights Treaties', 71 *BYBIL* (2000) 181, especially 219–36; K. Korelia, 'New Challenges to the Regime of Reservations under the ICCPR', 13 *EJIL* (2002) 437–77; R. Goodman, 'Human Rights Treaties, Invalid Reservations and State Consent', 96 *AJIL* (2002) 531; S. Marks, 'Reservations Unhinged: The Belilos Case before the ECHR', 39 *ICLQ* (1990) 300.

[129] See C. Redgwell, 'Universality or Integrity? Some Reflections on Reservations to General Multilateral Treaties', 64 *BYBIL* (1993) 245; D. Bowett, 'Reservations to Non-restricted Multilateral Treaties', 48 *BYBIL* (1976–7) 67.   [130] *Report of the ILC* (1996), para 105.

[131] See eg Pellet, *5th Report on Reservations to Treaties*, GAOR A/CN4/508 (2000), paras 32 ff.

[132] Pellet, *10th Report on Reservations to Treaties*, GAOR A/CN4/558 and Add 1 (2005).

[133] General Comment 24 (1994), in *Compilation of General Comments and General Recommendations Adopted by Human Rights Treaty Bodies*, UN Doc HRI/GEN/1/Rev6 (2003), paras 17–18.

Convention was intended to afford a single legal regime for reservations, and that this regime remained suited to all types of multilateral treaty, including human rights treaties.[134] It could therefore see no need for 'normative diversification'. However, the ILC accepted that monitoring bodies were competent to decide on the permissibility of reservations, although not definitively unless so empowered. The UN 6th Committee was divided on this question.[135] Some states felt that it was for them alone to determine the permissibility of a reservation. Others disagreed, including the chairs of the UN human rights bodies, who reiterated that the role of universal and regional bodies in monitoring compliance with treaties necessarily entails a duty to assess the compatibility of a reservation with the object and purpose of the treaty.[136] They expressed their continued support for the approach taken by the UN Human Rights Committee, which noted that states have little interest in objecting to reservations to human rights treaties, and concluded: 'The normal consequence of an unacceptable reservation is not that the Covenant will not be in effect at all for a reserving party. Rather, such a reservation will generally be severable, in the sense that the Covenant will be operative for the reserving party without benefit of the reservation.'[137] The ILC was urged to adjust its conclusions accordingly, but in his 2005 report the special rapporteur concluded only that 'It is too early for the Commission to take a position on whether the nullity of the reservation invalidates the consent to be bound itself'.[138]

Faced with the clearly opposed views of UN treaty bodies and decisions of regional human rights courts, it is obvious that the Commission's guidelines cannot, as originally hoped, unify international practice or prevent the consolidation of a special regime for human rights treaties, unless the Commission adopts that regime for all treaty reservations. The Commission has not articulated a reasoned case in opposition to the views of human rights bodies, if there is one. But the problem here is not the role of the Commission, but rather a dilemma which confronts all those who make law—at what point are differentiated rules justified? The question whether to enhance the authority of human rights bodies to adjudicate on treaty commitments by governments is a question of policy. It cannot be answered simply by reiterating the need for coherence in the legal system or by expressing alarm at the perils of fragmentation when the dynamics of human rights law point in the direction of a necessarily different approach.[139] It remains to be seen whether the Commission can produce a draft of sufficient subtlety and finesse to accommodate such distinctive positions.

Apart from revealing the Commission's limitations as a body of generalist lawyers, this debate shows once again that the success of the ILC as a law-making

---

[134] *Report of the ILC* (1996), paras 116–35. See Tyagi, 71 *BYBIL* (2000) 181, 248–52.
[135] *Report of the ILC* (1997), chapter V, para 135.
[136] See Pellet, *5th Report*, paras 11–15; Tyagi, 71 *BYBIL* (2000) 181, 248–52.
[137] General Comment No. 24 (1994).   [138] Pellet, *10th Report*, para 200.
[139] The arguments are reviewed in Redgwell, 64 *BYBIL* (1993) 244; Tyagi, 71 *BYBIL* (2000) 181, and R. Baratta, 'Should Invalid Reservations to Human Rights Treaties be Disregarded?', 11 *EJIL* (2000) 413.

body is entirely dependent on the acceptability of its work to states, international organisations and international courts. This cannot be taken for granted. Unless there is seen to be a need to reorder divergent practice or judicial decisions, no proposal from the Commission is likely to prosper.[140]

4.4   International Criminal Law and the International Criminal Court

We have already outlined the negotiating process for the Rome Statute of the International Criminal Court in Chapter 3. The contribution made by the International Law Commission to the successful outcome of this process is significant, and it is one of the better examples of the Commission's role in international law-making by the UN. The concept of a permanent international criminal court has a long history. In 1872 Gustav Moynier, one of the founders of the International Committee of the Red Cross, proposed a permanent court to adjudicate some of the serious crimes committed in the Franco-Prussian war. James Lorimer, then Regius Professor of the Law of Nations at Edinburgh, was another early advocate for such a court.[141] Similarly in 1919 an *ad hoc* criminal tribunal to try the Kaiser and other German leaders for war crimes was envisaged, but never established.[142] Thus, when in 1945 the allies created the Nuremberg and Tokyo Tribunals to try German and Japanese leaders for crimes against international law, these became the first such international courts ever set up.[143]

With this experience in mind, the General Assembly's first request to the ILC in 1947 was to 'formulate the principles of international law recognized by the Charter and the Judgment [of the Nuremberg Tribunal]', and secondly to draw up a more comprehensive Code of Offences against the Peace and Security of Mankind.[144] As one commentary has noted, 'The Commission's formulation of the Nürnberg Principles has been very influential in the development . . . of an international criminal law for violation of which individuals as well as states may be held responsible.'[145] Although a draft Code of Offences was also adopted by the Commission in 1951 and revised in 1954, the response was less positive, and action by the UNGA was deferred pending agreement on a definition of aggression.[146] The cold war effectively put an end to further work on this project until it was resumed in 1981 at the request of the General Assembly. An expanded and

---

[140]   See the caution expressed in the 6th Cttee at GAOR A/CN4/529 (2003), paras 73–9.

[141]   J. Lorimer, *Institutes of the Law of Nations* (Edinburgh, 1884), vol II, 284–5.

[142]   1919 Treaty of Versailles, Article 227.

[143]   1945 London Agreement; 1945 Charter of the International Military Tribunal; 1946 Charter of the International Military Tribunal for the Far East.

[144]   UNGA Res 177 (II), 21 November 1947.

[145]   Watts, *The ILC*, III, 1658. See Principles of International Law Recognized in the Charter and Judgment of the Nürnberg Tribunal; UNGA Res 488 (V), 12 December 1950.

[146]   UNGA Res 897 (IX), 4 December 1954. See 1954 Draft Code of Offences, Articles 1–4, in Watts, *The ILC*, III, 1657–85.

revised Code of Offences eventually adopted by the Commission in 1996 included aggression, genocide, crimes against humanity, war crimes and crimes against UN personnel. It also covered general principles of individual criminal responsibility, universal jurisdiction, the obligation to try or extradite, guarantees of a fair trial, defences, non-retroactivity and the *ne bis in idem* rule.[147] Although the 1996 Code progressed no further, the ILC's work did form part of the preparatory material available to the Commission and to governments when the drafting process for the Rome Statute was initiated.

Creation of an international criminal court was also an early item on the ILC's agenda. On 9 December 1948 (the same day as it adopted the Genocide Convention) the General Assembly resolved that there was an 'increasing need for an international judicial organ for the trial of certain crimes under international law',[148] an option already anticipated by Article 6 of the 1948 Genocide Convention. Accordingly the ILC was invited to 'study the desirability and possibility' of establishing such a body. The Commission reported and in 1950, seeking concrete proposals, the Assembly set up an *ad hoc* committee of 17 states to work on preparing a draft text.[149] This committee prepared a report and draft statute but, as it had received little input from other states, in 1952 the UNGA referred the matter to another *ad hoc* committee for further consideration and study of specified issues.[150] A revised Statute was submitted to the General Assembly in 1954, but it was decided to take no further action.[151]

Not until 1989 was the ILC again asked by the UNGA to consider international criminal jurisdiction.[152] Having explored the topic of international criminal jurisdiction in the context of its renewed work on the Code of Offences, the Commission was able to respond with some urgency to the General Assembly's further request to elaborate a draft statute for an international criminal court 'as a matter of priority'.[153] Unusually, the ILC text was developed by a working group, rather than by a special rapporteur, and consideration by the Commission was kept to a minimum.[154] Several other factors helped the ILC react with uncharacteristic speed, including the work already done by the UN in drafting statutes for the two *ad hoc* tribunals established by the UNSC.

Extensive comments on the ILC draft were made by states in the 6th Committee and in writing and by 1994 the Commission had delivered a substantial draft statute to the General Assembly. Faced with opposition from France, the United

---

[147] 1996 Code of Offences against the Peace and Security of Mankind, Final Draft Articles 1–20, in Watts, *The ILC*, III, 1686–765.   [148] UNGA Res 260 B (III), 9 December 1948.

[149] UNGA Res 489 (V), 12 December 1950.

[150] UNGA Res 687 (VII), 5 December 1952.

[151] UNGA Res 898 (IV), 14 December 1954.

[152] UNGA Res 44/39, 4 December 1989; 45/41, 28 November 1990; 46/54, 9 December 1991. The initial request came from Trinidad and Tobago and included drug trafficking, which was later dropped from the proposal.

[153] UNGA Res 47/33, 25 November 1992; 48/31, 9 December 1993.

[154] For an account of the ILC process see J. Crawford, 'The ILC's Draft Statute for an International Criminal Court', 88 *AJIL* (1994) 140.

Kingdom and the United States to the immediate convening of a diplomatic conference, the UNGA instead established an *ad hoc* committee of interested states to consider the matter further. Thereafter it was possible to convene a preparatory committee of all interested states to finalise a 'widely acceptable consolidated text' for a diplomatic conference.[155] The prepcom based its text on the ILC draft and the work of the *ad hoc* committee. It also looked at the evolving experience of the *ad hoc* tribunals for Yugoslavia and Rwanda, and exchanged views with the members of the ICTY Office of the Prosecutor. Unlike the ILC, the prepcom was open to NGO participation which, over the continuing sessions, became more coordinated and effective through the submission of commentaries and recommendations.[156] Political alliances that formed through the prepcoms, in particular the formation of the 'like-minded group' committed to a strong and independent court, continued to the Rome Conference.[157] Developing states were slower to participate in the prepcom process but by the sixth session more had begun to contribute.

While the ILC had provided legal analysis of the issues, once the process moved from there it became highly politicised. Through disagreements between states, the formation of coalitions, and the determined input of NGOs, the draft statute moved ever further away from the ILC's starting point. Finally, at the Rome Conference, the decision of a forceful chair of the Committee of the Whole to present a 'package deal' to the Conference for acceptance or rejection resulted in a text that as finally adopted differed in many ways from the one submitted by the ILC.[158] In particular, the Rome Statute redefined and extended the categories of crimes against humanity and war crimes, broadened the applicable law to draw in general principles of law, and empowered the judges to define elements of crimes. Although the crime of aggression could not be prosecuted until redefined, the most important and controversial departure from the ILC scheme involved reducing the role of the UNSC in other respects. Instead of needing UNSC approval for prosecutions, which would require nine votes with no veto, the Council was now empowered only to prohibit them for a period of 12 months, which would likewise require nine votes and no veto. This reversal helps explain US opposition, since it no longer had an effective veto over the prosecution system; it must secure the support of the other P5 states plus another four votes.[159]

Crawford, chairman of the ILC Working Group on the ICC, has described the ILC draft as 'modest enough to gain initial support and not to scare potential and

---

[155] UNGA Res 50/46, 11 December 1995.   [156] See Chapter 2.

[157] C. Hall, 'The First Two Sessions of the UN Preparatory Committee on the Establishment of an ICC', 91 *AJIL* (1997) 177; id, 'The Third and Fourth Sessions of the UN Preparatory Committee on the Establishment of an ICC', 92 *AJIL* (1998) 124; id, 'The Fifth Session of the UN Preparatory Committee on the Establishment of an ICC', 92 *AJIL* (1998) 331; id, 'The Sixth Session of the UN Preparatory Committee on the Establishment of an ICC', 92 *AJIL* (1998) 548.

[158] P. Kirsch and J. Holmes, 'The Rome Conference on an ICC: The Negotiating Process' (1999) 93 *AJIL* 2. See Chapter 3 for a fuller account of the Rome Conference.

[159] See Chapters 1 and 2.

influential states . . . '.[160] The perceived need to balance the conflicting demands of political realism and legal principle thus led the Commission to give the UN Security Council a central role in authorising prosecutions and to confine itself to listing existing treaty crimes. In fact, for reasons already explained, a political constituency for a more ambitious system developed quite quickly. Here, as in most of the other examples examined in this chapter, we can once again see the innate conservatism of the ILC at work—a conservatism that is often belied by the actual response of more radically minded governments. It is a matter for conjecture whether this is the best way to secure effective progress in international law-making. On this occasion it may have been the right strategy, but other examples are less clear-cut, most notably in environmental matters.

4.5   International Environmental Law

International environmental law has proved to be one of the Commission's most troublesome topics. It is here that we can see the real limitations of law-making by independent experts in a new and fast-developing area of law. Lacking a political constituency, the Commission has been reluctant to engage too deeply in creative thinking.[161] At the same time its more cautious approach has also lacked the authority in this field that comes more naturally with work on longer established subjects such as the law of treaties or international watercourses. The ILC has thus played no part in creating what might be called the architecture of international environmental law: sustainable development, global environmental responsibility and environmental rights. It has confined itself to the more limited role of codifying and modestly developing those elements which have become established law during the 25-year period of its work on this topic—in practice the law relating to transboundary risk. Even then, its efforts have sometimes been deeply troubled and confused, and inevitably raise the question whether the Commission should have any role in the development of new areas of law.

In the view of many commentators much of the ILC's early work on environmental matters was based on a fundamentally confused view of international environmental law.[162] When it initiated work on the topic 'Liability for Injurious Consequences of Acts Not Prohibited by International Law' the Commission appeared to believe that no primary obligations of environmental protection existed. They seemed unable to grasp that international law might, as in the 1982 UNCLOS, impose obligations of regulation, diligent control and prevention of

---

[160] A. Cassese, P. Gaeta and J. Jones (eds), *The Rome Statute of the International Criminal Court: A Commentary* (Oxford, 2002) vol I, 23 ff.

[161] Koskenniemi, 23 *Wis ILJ* (2002) 60, 76.

[162] M. Akehurst, 'International Liability for Injurious Consequences Arising out of Acts Not Prohibited by International Law', 16 *NYBIL* (1985) 8; A. E. Boyle, 'State Responsibility and International Liability for Injurious Consequences of Acts Not Prohibited by International Law: A Necessary Distinction?', 39 *ICLQ* (1990) 1; M. Fitzmaurice, 'International Environmental Law as a Special Field', 25 *NYBIL* (1994) 181.

harmful emissions even in respect of lawful activities without either prohibiting the activity or excluding the possibility of state responsibility for breach of these obligations. Even in 1978 the Commission's view of the law seemed extraordinary. At a theoretical level it was not clear how the topic was distinguished from state responsibility. At a more practical level, it was questionable whether such a distinction provided a useful basis for codification and development of existing law and practice relating to environmental harm. Eventually, after much wasted effort, the Commission succeeded in codifying largely pre-existing law on transboundary risk management.[163] It also included some important environmental provisions in its draft convention on international watercourses.[164]

These were useful achievements, but they remained modest when compared to the development of international environmental law as a whole. That it is easier to identify what the ILC has not contributed to this evolution than what it has tells us much about the ILC in the contemporary law-making process. The larger canvasses of sustainable development, global environmental responsibility and environmental rights have not only emerged from other processes, they have done so with a rapidity it is doubtful the ILC could match. This is law-making far removed from codification and progressive development as conceived by the ILC. Legal architecture of this kind is indispensable to contemporary international society, but as we have seen in Chapter 3 it has mostly fallen to bodies other than the ILC to supply it.

Moreover, after 25 years the ILC had still not managed to produce a draft specifically dealing with liability for transboundary damage in international law. The problem of liability was one that states had consistently evaded, and on which the ICJ had not had the opportunity to adjudicate. In every context in which the issue arose for negotiation it was postponed for further development, as it was, again, in the 1992 Rio Declaration.[165] In an attempt to move beyond the limitations of the existing law on state responsibility, the ILC's 1996 draft articles on International Liability would have made states strictly liable for significant transboundary harm caused by an activity covered by the articles.[166] The obligation to compensate other states would not have covered unforeseeable risks, but would have included harm which the source state could not prevent by exercising due diligence. In this situation the harm would in effect be unavoidable and there would be no fault on the part of the state. These were relatively novel proposals, however, and they did not rest on any clear foundation in general international law. A decision was taken in 1997 to suspend further consideration of liability for damage and concentrate instead on other related but less controversial issues.

Nevertheless, liability is, *par excellence*, a lawyer's question, clearly within the competence of a body of legal experts. If the Commission could not develop the

---

[163] 2001 Articles on Prevention of Transboundary Harm from Hazardous Activities, *Report of the ILC* (2001) GAOR A/56/10, paras 366–436.

[164] 1997 UN Watercourses Convention, Articles 20–3.   [165] See Principle 13.

[166] Draft Article 5. For the full text of the 1996 draft see *Report of the Working Group on International Liability, Report of the ILC* (1996) GAOR A/51/10, Annex 1, at 235.

law on such topics, even if it was to a significant extent developing new law, then it would indeed have failed to live up to the aspirations of its founders. Here was a challenging, but far from impossible, task. Not surprisingly, in 2001, largely at the behest of developing states, the General Assembly requested the ILC to resume work on liability, 'bearing in mind the interrelationship between prevention and liability, and taking into account the developments in international law and comments by Governments'.[167] The Commission proceeded quickly and in 2004 a set of draft principles was adopted and sent to states for consultation.[168]

This draft was not a straightforward exercise in codification or progressive development, however. First, it was clear from the General Assembly's response that earlier proposals to make states liable would not be politically acceptable. The state's duty would not be to provide reparation but to ensure that polluters and others who cause damage do so. Second, attempts to harmonise national tort law even on a regional basis had proved notoriously difficult and the ILC had little expertise in this area of private law, as its members are mainly public international lawyers. Third, the issues of private international law which potentially arise in transnational legal actions were themselves complex and had not been addressed by the principal body responsible for such questions, the Hague Conference on Private International Law. Finally, while there were several possible models for sophisticated international liability regimes, most of them dealt with very specific matters such as oil pollution from ships or nuclear accidents.[169] Those exclusively European agreements which addressed liability issues on a wider basis had not attracted much support and were not in force.[170] Attempting to draft another such agreement on a global basis would be no more likely to appeal to many states. Thus despite a clear political mandate for its work and a wealth of precedents from which to choose, the Commission had in reality very limited room for creativity.

The draft liability principles adopted by the Commission in 2004 were far from radical, and in that respect they fully reflected its traditional conservatism and caution. The main elements of the proposed scheme were drawn from existing civil liability treaties, showing how the Commission can also make use of general

---

[167] UNGA Res 56/82, 18 January 2002.

[168] See 2004 *Report of the ILC*, GAOR A/59/10, paras 158–76. For preparatory work see 2002 *Report of the ILC*, GAOR A/57/10, paras 430–57; Special Rapporteur Rao's 1st Report (2003) A/CN4/531; 2003 *Report of the ILC*, GAOR A/58/10, paras 154–231; Special Rapporteur Rao's 2nd Report (2004) A/CN4/540.

[169] See especially 1960 Paris Convention on Third Party Liability in the Field of Nuclear Energy (in force 1968); 1963 Brussels Agreement Supplementary to the 1960 Convention on Third Party Liability (in force 1974); 1992 Convention on Civil Liability for Oil Pollution Damage (in force 1996); 1992 Convention on the Establishment of an International Fund for Compensation for Oil Pollution Damage (in force 1996); 1997 Protocol on Civil Liability for Nuclear Damage and Convention on Supplementary Compensation.

[170] 1993 Lugano Convention on Civil Liability for Damage Resulting from Activities Dangerous to the Environment; 2003 Protocol on Civil Liability and Compensation for Damage Caused by the Transboundary Effects of Industrial Accidents on Transboundary Waters. See generally J. Brunnée, 'Of Sense and Sensibility: Reflections on International Liability Regimes as Tools for Environmental Protection', 54 *ICLQ* (2004) 351.

principles of law as 'an indication of policy and principle'.[171] At the heart of its codification was an international standard for compensation—a requirement of promptness and adequacy which would affect not only the compensation itself but also the procedures and remedies through which it was to be obtained. This element would have represented its most significant contribution to the progressive development of the subject. However, due mainly to resistance within the Commission, the final text was pure soft law, employing the term 'should' rather than 'shall' throughout. States were thus given guidance on what a liability regime 'should' look like, but they had no obligation to make any form of redress available to injured claimants. Yet the Commission's own reports suggested that there were enough precedents on which to build something more than a soft law compensation principle. As we saw earlier, the Commission does not normally differentiate between the codification of existing international law and the progressive development of new law, and its endorsement has not infrequently proved sufficient to endow what might otherwise have been regarded as *lex ferenda* with enough added authority to elevate it into law.[172] Thus apart from illustrating how slow and constrained the process of law-making can become in the hands of the ILC, it is doubtful whether the draft adopted in 2006 gives effect to the wishes of the General Assembly or the Rio Conference. This looks more like a collective failure of nerve than a reasoned outcome.

5. The ILC and Customary International Law

We saw earlier that because the Commission has not drawn a sharp distinction between codification and progressive development, it has been possible for it to engage in a certain amount of creative law-making or law reform. This has also enabled the ICJ and other tribunals to rely on ILC conventions without overtly enquiring whether particular articles represent existing law, revision of existing law or a new development of the law. Moreover, the deliberative and sometimes slow pace of its work enables states to influence, appreciate and in some cases apply the law as articulated and shaped by the Commission. Use by foreign ministries of the Vienna Convention on the Law of Treaties and the draft articles on state responsibility are the most obvious examples, but by no means the only ones. The response of national legal advisers to the Commission's work thus assumes a potentially constitutive effect. Lastly, the reports of individual special rapporteurs may be especially influential and as 'teachings of the most highly qualified publicists' are themselves a subsidiary source of international law.[173] Thus, although the ILC does not 'make' international law it has become a significant part of the subtle

---

[171] See *South West Africa Advisory Opinion* (1950) ICJ Reports 128, sep op Lord McNair, 148.
[172] See Section 5 below.
[173] ICJ Statute, Article 38 (1) (d). Much will depend on the quality of the report and the rapporteur.

process by which general international law is identified, changes and comes into being. Because of its character and process the Commission has an authoritative quality. Its influence can be observed in the jurisprudence of the ICJ.

The best example is the *Gabčíkovo-Nagymaros* case,[174] decided by the ICJ in 1997. Here the Court showed remarkably little inclination to search for evidence of widespread, consistent and prolonged state practice as it did for example in its judgment in the *North Sea Continental Shelf* cases.[175] Instead, on questions of treaty law, the law relating to international watercourses, state responsibility and state succession, it relied more heavily than in any previous case on the work of the Commission as representing customary law. The Commission's work on state responsibility was then incomplete, its articles on watercourses had only just been adopted as a treaty, and its convention on state succession had not been widely ratified. If the Court's endorsement is testimony to the authority of the ILC's reports on these topics, it also suggests that the UN's attempts to economise by cutting back on time-consuming commentaries may place at risk its most valuable contribution to the law-making process.[176]

The case was concerned with construction of a system of dams across the Danube, and Hungary's attempt to terminate an agreement to build and operate them. In deciding whether Slovakia's diversion of the river into a new channel was internationally wrongful, the Court relied on Hungary's right as a riparian to an equitable and reasonable share of the natural resources of the river. It also noted that the effects of Slovakia's actions on the ecology of the 'riparian area' (not just the river) further added to the unlawfully disproportionate results between the parties. As authority for its conclusions the Court referred both to the case relating to the *Territorial Jurisdiction of the International Commission of the River Oder*[177] and to Article 5 of the newly concluded UN Convention on the Law of the Non-Navigational Uses of International Watercourses. This codification treaty had been drafted by the ILC, but it had no parties and even in 2006 it was still far from entry into force.

What is also interesting about the *Gabčíkovo-Nagymaros* judgment is the Court's application to a watercourse dispute of a large body of international environmental law, both as an aspect of equitable utilization and as independent norms. Applying international law in an integrated way is very much in line with the ILC's work and with the UN Watercourses Convention, which was revised by states in the final negotiating stages to include express reference to sustainable utilisation of watercourses. There are important lessons here. Equitable utilisation, a long-established general principle, and sustainable utilisation, a very new one, are not the same—a use may be equitable as between two parties without necessarily

---

[174] (1997) ICJ Reports 7. For a more general review of the Court's reliance on ILC material see Sinclair, *The ILC*, 127–35.   [175] (1969) ICJ Reports 3.
[176] See *Report of the International Law Commission to the UN General Assembly*, GAOR A/51/10 (1996), Chapter VII: 'Programme, Procedures and Working Methods of the Commission and its Documentation'.   [177] PCIJ Series A No. 23 (1929).

being sustainable. The Watercourses Convention recognises this implicit tension and the inevitable conclusion that, as in international fisheries law,[178] equitable utilisation of an international resource must be set in the broader context of sustainable development. If this is correct, it will stand as perhaps the most radical rewriting of the law relating to international watercourses since the *River Oder* case. Yet it is worth noting that this particular development is not the work of the ILC but of states exercising a more political judgment during the treaty negotiation, thereby bringing an unsatisfactory ILC draft into line with global policies adopted at the Rio Conference on Environment and Development in 1992.

When dealing with international environmental law, the Court made no reference to the ILC's more troubled and still unsatisfactory work on International Liability for Injurious Consequences Arising Out of Acts Not Prohibited by International Law,[179] but relied instead on cryptic references to new norms of international law concerned with the environment and 'set forth in a great number of instruments during the last two decades'.[180] One can only guess at which instruments the Court had in mind, but they presumably included at least the Stockholm and Rio Declarations as well as the large body of environmental treaty law. The fact that the Court seemed happy to treat a number of these new norms as law that the parties would have to take account of without further reference to state practice or authority poses some serious questions about the nature of customary law and the use of general principles by courts which we consider more fully in Chapter 6.

Here we can see very clearly the interplay of codification by the ILC, re-negotiation and revision of the text in a diplomatic forum, and application of that revised text by an international court, even though it was not in force or binding on the parties. Moreover, the fortuitous conjunction of litigation so soon after the UN's adoption of the Watercourses Convention resulted in a rapid endorsement of its efforts at redrafting the law in a more integrated and systematic way. There are few better examples of the process of international law-making. It also helped that although the UN Convention was not adopted by consensus, very few states opposed the text as a whole and only a handful voted against individual articles.[181] Even so, as McCaffrey observes, acceptance by most delegations of an obligation of prior notification 'provides further evidence that the international community as a whole emphatically rejects the notion that a state has unfettered discretion to do as

---

[178] See 1995 Agreement for the Implementation of the Provisions of the UN Convention on the Law of the Sea Relating to the Conservation and Management of Straddling Fish Stocks and Highly Migratory Fish Stocks (UN Fish Stocks Agreement).

[179] The Commission subsequently adopted draft Articles on Prevention of Transboundary Damage (2001).   [180] Para 140.

[181] Only France, China and Turkey opposed adoption of the Convention, on which see S. McCaffrey, *The Law of International Watercourses* (Oxford, 2001) 301–22; P. Wouters, 'The Legal Response to International Water Conflicts: The UN Water Convention and Beyond', 42 *GYBIL* (1999) 293; C. Bourne, 'The Primacy of the Principle of Equitable Utilization in the 1997 Watercourses Convention', 35 *CYBIL* (1997) 222.

it wishes with the portion of an international watercourse within its territory'.[182] Given the ILC's inclusion of prior notification in the Watercourses Convention and in the draft Articles on Prevention of Transboundary Harm there can be little doubt that this too is customary law.[183] Thus the Commission's work has a potential double impact: on the one hand it provides good evidence of the existing law, on the other its work helps constitute new law, sometimes quite quickly. We return to this very important point in our consideration of the law-making effect of treaties in the next chapter.

The ICJ has not always been quite so generous in its application of ILC conventions. The 1969 *North Sea Continental Shelf* cases[184] represent an earlier, less successful, attempt to rely on ILC law-making. The case advanced by Denmark and the Netherlands rested principally on the contention that the 1958 Geneva Convention on the Continental Shelf reflected or had crystallised into customary international law, and that Germany, a non-party, was therefore bound by the same rules as parties. The Continental Shelf Convention had been drafted initially by the ILC, and was adopted in modified form by a diplomatic conference attended by all three states. It was accepted on all sides that Articles 1–3 of the 1958 Convention were based on state practice, including the 1945 Truman Proclamation on the Continental Shelf, and reflected customary law which had developed with remarkable rapdity.[185]

The disagreement concerned Article 6, the Convention's provision on boundary delimitation. Germany did not accept that this article represented or had become customary law. The Court considered the ILC's deliberations on the subject in some detail. It noted that the Commission had discussed various possible rules and that Article 6 had only been adopted following a report by hydrographical experts 'actuated by considerations not of legal theory but of practical convenience and cartography'.[186] The conclusion was thus that Article 6 was proposed by the Commission 'with considerable hesitation, somewhat on an experimental basis, at most *de lege ferenda*, and not at all *de lege lata* or as an emerging rule of customary international law'.[187] Given this record it would of course be difficult to hold that Article 6 reflected pre-existing law. Nor had the equidistance/special circumstances element become law: it did not possess the character of a rule of law, first, because the principal duty was to negotiate and second, because it was open to reservation. Finally, there was no subsequent record of widespread and consistent state practice applying an equidistance/special circumstances rule; even among parties to the Convention several had made reservations excluding Article 6.

Nevertheless, the Court's dicta show some appreciation of the ILC's special role in the international law-making process. It was not persuaded by the argument that

---

[182] 92 *AJIL* (1998) 103. Only Ethiopia, Rwanda and Turkey, all upstream states, opposed the inclusion of articles on transboundary notification and consultation.

[183] See also 1992 Rio Declaration on Environment and Development, Principle 19, and *Lac Lanoux Arbitration* (1957) 101 ILR 101.   [184] (1969) ICJ Reports 4.

[185] W. Friedmann, 'The North Sea Continental Shelf Cases—A Critique', 64 *AJIL* (1970) 229, 232.

[186] (1969) ICJ Reports 4, para 53.   [187] Ibid, para 62.

'the process of definition and consolidation of emerging customary law took place through the work of the International Law Commission, the reaction of governments to that work and the proceedings of the Geneva Conference' had crystallised a new rule of customary law when states adopted the 1958 Convention.[188] But the Court did not deny the possibility; it merely rejected it with regard to Article 6. Judge Sorensen put the point more positively: 'it should be considered as a relevant element that a convention has been adopted in the process of codification and development of international law under the UN Charter'.[189] In his view, 'The adoption of the Geneva Convention on the Continental Shelf was a very significant element in the process of creating new rules of international law in a field which urgently required legal regulation'.[190] Sorensen's approach of giving special weight to ILC conventions appears very close to that taken by the Court in the *Gabčíkovo* case. Ironically, although states continued to disagree on the applicable rule for continental shelf delimitation during UNCLOS III negotiations, the Court's later jurisprudence on Article 6 has departed from its earlier conclusion and now assimilates it to the customary rule of delimitation based on equitable principles.[191]

While the *North Sea* case shows that a distinction between codification of existing law and progressive development of new law can be important, the *Gabčíkovo* case nevertheless suggests that the International Court is willing to give considerable weight to the ILC's work regardless of its genesis. If the Commission's proposals are cogent, even if novel, considerable potential for law-making may in practice result, more especially where, as Sorensen observed in 1969, the outcome of diplomatic conferences or UN reaction is favourable.[192] Where these factors are absent, as in the earlier stages of 'International Liability for Injurious Consequences', then of course no such effect will ensue.[193]

6. Codification by Other Bodies

6.1 The International Committee of the Red Cross

In Chapter 2 we noted briefly the participation of the International Committee of the Red Cross (ICRC) in promoting and negotiating treaties on international humanitarian law. Part of the ICRC's role in this respect is to keep the treaties up-to-date, based on its experience in the field and its understanding of developments in modern warfare. Although formally an NGO, the Statutes of the ICRC are adopted by conferences in which states participate, and the ICRC functions in many respects as the competent organisation for the 1949 Geneva Conventions

---

[188] (1969) ICJ Reports 4, para 61.   [189] Ibid 246.   [190] Ibid.
[191] *Jan Mayen Case* (1993) ICJ Reports 38, para 56.
[192] See R. Y. Jennings, 'Recent Developments in the International Law Commission: Its Relation to Sources of International Law', 13 *ICLQ* (1964) 390; Sinclair, *The ILC*, 121–7.
[193] See below. For other cautionary examples see Sinclair, *The ILC*, 125.

and their later Protocols, under which it has important powers and responsibilities.[194] It has its own legal advisers and secretariat, and as we saw earlier, it also enjoys observer status at the UN, enabling it to participate actively in UN law-making. Although the Geneva Conventions have attained near universal participation, later protocols and other humanitarian treaties have not. Accordingly, the 26th Annual Conference of the Red Cross and Red Crescent in 1995 invited the ICRC to prepare a report on customary international law related to armed conflicts in consultation with experts from governments and international organisations. In effect this was a project to codify international law on the subject.

The result was a large work published in 2005 and setting out what the rules are believed to be, with a commentary and explanatory text. It is described by the ICRC as an attempt to 'capture the clearest possible "photograph" of customary international humanitarian law as it stands today'.[195] At the same time, as the foreword also notes, 'the study's conclusion will serve as a valuable basis for identifying areas in the law that should be clarified or developed and for engaging in whatever dialogue or negotiation is necessary . . . '.[196] It might be said that taking snapshots of existing law and identifying problems and uncertainties is more in the nature of a scholarly text than an exercise in codification and progressive development. In reality, however, whatever the intention, the result is more than a mere snapshot, precisely because the authors cannot avoid filling in the gaps, taking a position on uncertainties, or trying to state the law on matters where neither treaties nor state practice cover the field. The law relating to internal armed conflict is an example. The state practice is sparse, and it is often possible only to draw analogies from the international law of armed conflict, where the treaty law is extensive.

Whether all of this can accurately be described as customary law may be open to debate, which is the main problem with such an exercise. The study is the work of a group of academic rapporteurs whose experience and background are not unlike that of many members of the ILC. In deciding what is customary law they have followed the methodology of the ILA Committee on the Formation of General Customary International Law.[197] The ICRC also deployed a research team, and governmental experts were consulted. Nevertheless, unlike the ILC, the ICRC exercise has not had the benefit of an ongoing dialogue with the UN 6th Committee, so the input from states is less obvious, although it is known that some have provided comments and do have views on the matter which are not necessarily consistent with the study. Writers of textbooks face the same problem; however good, they cannot command the authority of articles developed by the ILC, commented on by states, and adopted after negotiations by the UNGA. Another subtle but important difference is that the ILC rarely indicates what is

---

[194] J.-P. Lavoyer and L. Maresca, 'The Role of the ICRC in the Development of International Humanitarian Law', 4 *International Negotiation* (1999) 508.

[195] J.-M. Henckaerts and L. Doswald-Beck, *Customary International Humanitarian Law* (Cambridge, 2005), vol I, xi.   [196] Ibid xvii.

[197] See n. 5 above.

and what is not customary law, and as we saw in the previous section, that is one of the reasons why it can sometimes succeed in developing the law. The ILC's methods are thus quite different from those of the ICRC study. Whatever the process and methodology employed, however, like any other codification the ultimate test of this study will be its influence, particularly on governments and courts.

6.2   UNIDROIT

The International Institute for the Unification of Private Law (UNIDROIT) is not part of the UN system but an independent IGO. Its mandate is to modernise, harmonise and coordinate national commercial law—in effect a form of international codification and progressive development of national laws.[198] Like the ILC, it has been the preparatory body for a number of conventions adopted at diplomatic conferences. In Chapter 2 we discussed the input of non-state actors in the negotiation of the 2001 UNIDROIT Convention on International Interests in Mobile Equipment and its Protocol on Matters Specific to Aircraft Equipment. Here we look more generally at the UNIDROIT law-making processes. UNIDROIT's focus on harmonisation or unification of commercial law requires in many instances attention to technical detail to facilitate the changes to municipal law that will be required in many cases. It has accordingly adopted working methods appropriate to this context.

Preliminary work is undertaken by the Secretariat to determine the desirability and feasibility of a particular project, which may include an examination of the comparative law on the issue in question. The Secretariat's report is considered by the UNIDROIT Governing Council, which advises on the most appropriate course of action. Normally this will mean convening a study group of independent experts in the particular field where the Council judges the preparation of an international instrument to be both feasible and useful. The Secretariat is responsible for determining the membership of these study groups and for ensuring that different areas of expertise are covered (for example a particular convention may require legal, technical, commercial and industry-specific knowledge), as well as a balanced representation of different geographical regions and legal systems. The study group prepares a preliminary draft which is then brought before the Governing Council for further consideration. If the Council approves the project, it will normally authorise the transmission of the preliminary draft to governments with a view to convening a committee of experts made up of the representatives of member governments, appropriate IGOs and professional associations; non-member governments may also be invited. This committee seeks to prepare the text for a diplomatic conference,

---

[198] UNIDROIT was established in 1926 as a League of Nations auxiliary organ and re-established in 1940 by international agreement; see http://www.unidroit.org, from which much of this account is drawn. Another comparable organisation is the Hague Conference on Private International Law, which despite its name is a permanent intergovernmental organisation for promoting the adoption of harmonisation conventions.

the establishment of which must be approved by the Governing Council. Diplomatic conferences are invariably open to all states, not just member states.

In addition to its contribution to 'hard' law-making UNIDROIT has been responsible for a number of soft law instruments such as model laws, legislative guidelines and statements of general principles. There is a particular reason for this: UNIDROIT Conventions by their very nature often require detailed and technical amendments to domestic law which can be time consuming within parliamentary timetables and burdensome for states. The need for domestic law reform tends to delay the ratification process with the risk of conventions becoming out-dated before their entry into force. Model laws offer a non-binding set of legal precedents that can be adopted, modified or rejected by states when considering domestic law reform. Adoption of model laws by a sufficient number of states can achieve the required legal consistency without the formalities of treaty acceptance.[199] Statements of general principles are directed at users (contracting parties) and decision-makers (arbitrators and judges) rather than at governments. Their status thus depends upon their acceptability to those whose work is directly affected rather than the form in which they are adopted.

7. Conclusions

It is self-evident that a comprehensive codification of the whole of international law is no longer a realistic or even desirable objective, if it ever was. It is equally apparent that many of the fundamental elements of international law have been progressively codified, perhaps not in the systematic fashion envisaged in 1947, but a great deal has nevertheless been done to clarify, modernise and develop the law. It is not particularly useful to assess the impact of post-1945 codification by reference to treaties adopted and in force. As earlier sections have shown, the real importance of codification to an international lawyer lies in its influence on state practice and judicial decisions—on customary law rather than on the corpus of treaty law binding on states. In that sense codification is an important element of the process for identifying and developing general international law, particularly when supported by the collegiate authority and commentary which the ILC can bring to the task. Except for topics where the main objective is to harmonise national laws (such as state immunity), or to establish institutions (such as the ICC) or to provide for dispute settlement, it is of secondary importance whether codification takes the form of a treaty or a non-binding declaration or guidelines. There are advantages and disadvantages to both forms, a point that we develop further in the next chapter, but they need to be assessed in their particular context and not in general or dogmatic terms.

---

[199] Another organisation that has been responsible for influential model laws is UNCITRAL. The 1985 UNCITRAL Model Law on International Commercial Arbitration has become the basis of modern arbitration law in many states including the UK.

It is also apparent both that the UN Charter gives the ILC no monopoly over codification and progressive development and that for a steadily increasing range of topics other less independent and more political processes are preferred, as we saw in Chapter 3. This is an inevitable trend as the focus of international law-making shifts away from codification of existing law towards the negotiation of new law. Nevertheless, with better guidance from the 6th Committee, and a much closer relationship with states, the ILC can assist this process, as we saw in relation to the ICC, but it cannot lead it. It could to that extent play a greater and potentially more creative role in international law-making. In that event, as Hafner has observed, 'the Commission has to perform a totally different role: it no longer only formulates rules reflecting the general practice of states; it acts as a mediator between states and becomes part of a real negotiation process'.[200] Giving the Commission a role of this kind would pose other questions. Should its membership be selected entirely by states? Is there a role for NGOs, whether in nominating members, or simply in having more of an opportunity to influence the Commission's deliberations? Not all members of the Commission, or all states, share this vision of a potentially wider role for the Commission. Pellet, for example, argues that the Commission can only codify norms that are '*déjà dans l'air*'; it cannot simply invent new ones.[201] Fundamentally, like many other members, he views the making of new law as an essentially political process for which the ILC is unsuited, and would remain unsuited even if reformed. From this perspective increasing the independence and capacity of the ILC is likely to make it less attractive to governments, not more. We can see that doctrinal debates about the nature of codification have lost none of the vitality on display in the early days of the League of Nations.

Failing to enlarge its role need not spell obsolescence for the ILC, or for the concept of codification and progressive development. Existing law will continue to require periodic restatement, revision and modernisation, a task still best undertaken by the Commission in most cases. Equally importantly, both the proliferation of international law-making bodies and courts and the increasing complexity and diversity of international law require some body capable of giving coherence to the system as a whole. Courts can contribute to this process, as we observe in Chapter 6, but they cannot direct it. It remains true that only the ILC can stand back and give the necessary overview. In the next chapter we address some of the problems posed by the decentralised nature of international law-making and the abundance of law-making instruments. Ensuring coherence is the greatest challenge posed by modern international law: this is certainly a task to which the ILC could and should rise.

---

[200] UN, *The ILC Fifty Years After*, 140.
[201] Ibid 22.

Further Reading

M. Anderson, A. E. Boyle, A. V. Lowe and C. Wickremasinghe (eds), *The International Law Commission and the Future of International Law* (London, 1998).

J. Crawford, 'The ILC's Articles on State Responsibility for Internationally Wrongful Acts: A Retrospect', 96 *AJIL* (2002) 874.

—— and S. Olleson, 'The Continuing Debate on a UN Convention on State Responsibility', 54 *ICLQ* (2005) 959.

R. Dhokalia, *The Codification of Public International Law* (Manchester, 1970).

W. Friedmann, 'The North Sea Continental Shelf Cases—A Critique', 64 *AJIL* (1970) 229.

M. Koskenniemi, 'International Legislation Today: Limits and Possibilities', 23 *Wis ILJ* (2002) 60.

S. McCaffrey, 'Is Codification in Decline?', 20 *Hastings ICLR* (1997) 639.

C. Redgwell, 'Universality or Integrity? Some Reflections on Reservations to General Multilateral Treaties', 64 *BYBIL* (1993) 245.

I. Sinclair, *The International Law Commission* (Cambridge, 1987).

Y. Tyagi, 'The Conflict of Law and Policy on Reservations to Human Rights Treaties', 71 *BYBIL* (2000) 181.

5

Law-Making Instruments

1. Introduction

Our task in this chapter is twofold. First, to explain how the instruments employed by international law-making processes evolve into international law. We develop the conclusion reached in Chapter 3 that multilateral processes promote law-making insofar as the instruments they adopt become generally binding, are translated into customary international law, or evidence general principles of law. The instruments which typically constitute the products of these multilateral processes include resolutions, conference declarations, and multilateral treaties and agreements. Some are formally binding on states, but others are not; while the distinction between 'hard' and 'soft' law instruments is clearly important, as we shall see it is not necessarily decisive in law-making terms. Moreover, contemporary international law is often the product of a complex and evolving interplay of instruments, both binding and non-binding, and of custom and general principles. Only in this broader context can the significance of so-called 'soft law' and multilateral treaties be fully appreciated.

Second, we consider how these instruments interact, both with each other and with the rest of international law, and whether they do so in a coherent or merely fragmentary fashion. When governments make law they also make policy choices about how to balance competing political, social, economic or cultural objectives. These choices may be reflected in the agreements they negotiate or in the state practice that contributes to general international law. The relationship between competing policy concerns—such as international trade and environmental protection, or human rights and international criminal law, for example—is at its most transparent when agreed explicitly by states acting through the UN system, the WTO and other international organisations. However, no government can foresee in detail all the consequences of the commitments they make; even when they do foresee them, it is not always possible to secure the agreement of other governments on how to address whatever tensions may arise out of the interaction of the commitments into which they have entered. This is where the role of courts and of the International Law Commission may assume special importance.

How courts resolve the potential for conflict between competing norms in these situations is essentially a matter of judicial technique, but the case law of the

International Court of Justice suggests that where possible it prefers an integrated conception of international law to a fragmented one.[1] Interpretation of one rule or treaty in the light of other rules or treaties, or the characterisation of one body of rules as a *lex specialis* governing the decision of the case, are the doctrines most often relied on to avoid a conflict of norms. The ICJ has shown no inclination whatever to resort to rules on the priority or validity of treaties when determining the applicable law in international disputes, nor has any other international tribunal approached the decision of any case from such a hierarchical perspective. Apart from highlighting the formative role of international courts in determining the applicable law, a point to which we return in Chapter 6, this conclusion points to the danger of viewing any part of international law in isolation from the whole. Not only are the rules dynamic, but potentially so is their interaction.

It is not the purpose of this chapter to describe or assess the sources of international law as such, whether those articulated in Article 38 (1) of the Statute of the ICJ or in some broader sense. Nor do we consider the impact of unilateral action by individual states on the development of customary international law, or the process by which the accumulation of state practice over time, when supported by *opinio juris*, can amount to customary international law. There is no doubt that custom in its oldest and most classical sense manifested itself in those forms. As we saw in earlier chapters, however, it is rarely possible in the modern world to make new law without recourse to the multilateral processes considered there, even if the initial impetus may come from one or more states acting individually. Sir Robert Jennings long ago pointed out that contemporary international law-making is far removed from the classical conception of custom. He preferred to use the term 'general international law'.[2] A further question we have to confront in this chapter, therefore, is whether it is possible to explain the product of contemporary international law-making processes within the dated and increasingly misleading terms of Article 38 (1).

2. Soft Law

2.1 The Significance of Soft Law

'Soft law' is a frequently misunderstood phenomenon, although evidence of its importance as an element in modern international law-making is abundant, most notably in the declarations or resolutions adopted by states in international conferences or in the United Nations General Assembly. While the relationship

---

[1] See *Gabčíkovo-Nagymaros Case* (1997) ICJ Reports 7, at paras 112 and 140; *Advisory Opinion on the Legality of the Use or Threat of Nuclear Weapons (UNGA)* (1996) ICJ Reports 226; *Oil Platforms Case* (2003) ICJ Reports 161. See R. Higgins, 'A Babel of Judicial Voices? Ruminations from the Bench', 55 *ICLQ* (2006) 791, and Section 4 below.

[2] R. Y. Jennings, 'What is International Law and How Do We Tell It When We See It? 37 *Swiss YBIL* (1981) 59.

between treaty and custom is well understood, the interplay between soft law and treaties, custom, or general principles of law is less often appreciated, but it is no less important, and has great practical relevance to the law-making and regulatory work of international organisations.

Perhaps the most important point to make at the outset is that some of the forms of 'soft law' under consideration here are potentially law-making in much the same way that multilateral treaties are potentially law-making. The proposition is not that non-binding declarations or resolutions of the General Assembly or any other soft law instrument are invariably law *per se*, but that they may be evidence of existing law, or formative of the *opinio juris* or state practice that generates new law. Brownlie, for example, refers to the 'decisive catalytic effect' of certain UNGA resolutions.[3] Moreover, widespread acceptance of soft law instruments will tend to legitimise conduct and make it harder to sustain the legality of opposing positions.[4] They may additionally acquire binding legal character as elements of a treaty-based regulatory regime,[5] or constitute a 'subsequent agreement between the parties regarding the interpretation of the treaty or the application of its provisions',[6] or otherwise assist in the development and application of general international law.[7]

It is certainly a fallacy to dismiss soft law, properly understood, as not law: it can and does contribute to the corpus of international law, as the examples considered below will show. Nor is reliance on soft law to be confused with the application of *lex ferenda* or 'evolving law'.[8] If it is true that some soft law instruments are—like some treaties—part of the process by which law evolves, then it is equally true that in the evolutionary stage they have not yet generated actual law, and we should not pretend otherwise. Identifying when law in the making has become law is of course precisely the point on which states and international lawyers will often disagree, but it is precisely at that point that 'soft law' is in reality no longer soft. Our focus in this book is on the law-making process precisely because in our view it leads to law, not to something less than law.

2.2   What is Soft Law?

'Soft law' has a range of possible meanings.[9] From a law-making perspective the term is simply a convenient description for a variety of non-legally binding instruments used in contemporary international relations. It encompasses *inter alia*

---

[3] I. Brownlie, 'The Legal Status of Natural Resources', 162 *Recueil des Cours* (1979) 261.

[4] See C. M. Chinkin, 'The Challenge of Soft Law: Development and Change in International Law', 38 *ICLQ* (1989) 850, 866.

[5] eg under the 1982 UN Convention on the Law of the Sea, Articles 210–11, or the 1994 Nuclear Safety Convention, on which see below.

[6] Article 31 (3) (a), 1969 Vienna Convention on the Law of Treaties.

[7] *Gabčíkovo-Nagymaros Case* (1997) ICJ Reports 7, para 140.

[8] *Gabčíkovo-Nagymaros Case* (1997) ICJ Reports 7, para 140; *OSPAR Arbitration* (2003) PCA, paras 101–4. On the applicability of evolving law see the very sensible comments of T. McDorman, 'Access to Information under Article 9 of the OSPAR Convention', 98 *AJIL* (2004) 330.

[9] The literature is extensive. See especially R. R. Baxter, 'International Law in "Her Infinite Variety" ', 29 *ICLQ* (1980) 549–66; Chinkin, 38 *ICLQ* (1989) 850–66; P. -M. Dupuy, 'Soft Law and

inter-state conference declarations such as the 1992 Rio Declaration on Environment and Development; UN General Assembly instruments such as the 1948 Universal Declaration of Human Rights, the 1970 Declaration on the Principles of Friendly Relations Among States, and resolutions dealing with disarmament, outer space, the deep seabed, decolonisation, or natural resources; interpretative guidance adopted by human rights treaty bodies and other autonomous intergovernmental institutions; codes of conduct, guidelines and recommendations of international organisations, such as UNEP's 1987 Guidelines on Environmental Impact Assessment, FAO's Code of Conduct on Responsible Fisheries or many others adopted by IMO, IAEA, FAO and so on. Also potentially included within the category of soft law are the common international standards adopted by transnational networks of national regulatory bodies, NGOs, and professional and industry associations.[10] Finally, the term 'soft law' can also be applied to non-treaty agreements between states or between states and other entities that lack capacity to conclude treaties.[11]

Soft law in this sense can be contrasted with hard law, which is always binding. Seen from this angle, the legal form is decisive: treaties that have entered into force are by definition hard law, at least for the parties. So are mandatory UN Security Council Resolutions adopted under Chapter VII of the UN Charter, because all UN member states have agreed to accept and carry out these decisions.[12] If the form is that of a non-binding agreement, such as the Helsinki Accords,[13] or the 1998 Belfast Agreement on the future of Northern Ireland,[14] or a UN General Assembly resolution or declaration, it will not be a treaty for precisely that reason and we will have what is in effect a 'soft' agreement. Of course, it is not necessarily easy to determine whether an agreement is a binding treaty, as we can observe in the *Qatar-Bahrain Maritime Delimitation* case.[15] The question is one of substance and intent; the label attached to the instrument is not decisive. Moreover, an agreement involving a state and another entity may be binding, even if it is not a treaty,[16] so the distinction between hard and soft agreements is not simply synonymous with the distinction between treaties and other instruments. Furthermore, once soft law begins to interact with binding instruments its non-binding character may be lost or altered.

---

the International Law of the Environment', 12 *Mich JIL* (1991) 420–35; J. Sztucki, 'Reflections on International "Soft Law"', in J. Ramberg et al (eds), *Festskrift till Lars Hjerner: Studies in International Law* (Stockholm, 1990) 549–75. For more sceptical views see P. Weil, 'Towards Relative Normativity in International Law?', 77 *AJIL* (1983) 413; J. Klabbers, 'The Undesirability of Soft Law', 67 *Nordic JIL* (1998) 381–91.

[10] See Chapter 2.   [11] H. Hillgenberg, 'A Fresh Look at Soft Law', 10 *EJIL* (1999) 499–15.
[12] UN Charter, Article 25.
[13] See O. Schachter, 'The Twilight Existence of Non-Binding International Agreements', 71 *AJIL* (1977) 296–304.   [14] Hillgenberg, 10 *EJIL* (1999) 501.
[15] *Maritime Delimitation and Territorial Questions between Qatar and Bahrain* (1994) ICJ Reports 112. See C. Chinkin, 'A Mirage in the Sand? Distinguishing Binding and Non-Binding Relations between States', 10 *LJIL* (1997) 223.
[16] See *Anglo-Iranian Oil Case* (1952) ICJ Reports 93; *Texaco v. Libya* (1977) 53 *ILR* 389.

As we have seen, reliance on soft law as part of the law-making process takes a number of different forms. While the legal effect of declarations, resolutions, guidelines and other soft law instruments is not necessarily the same in all cases,[17] it is characteristic of nearly all of them that they are carefully negotiated, often carefully drafted statements. Not infrequently states express reservations. Evidently, some soft law instruments are expected to have normative significance despite their non-binding, non-treaty form. There is at least an element of good faith commitment,[18] evidencing in some cases a desire to influence state practice or expressing some measure of law-making intention and progressive development. In this sense non-binding soft law instruments are in some cases not fundamentally different from those multilateral treaties which serve much the same law-making purposes. They may also be both an alternative to and part of the process of multilateral treaty-making. In the following sections we will explore the uses of soft law and consider what legal effect it may have.

2.3   Treaties or Soft Law?

There are several reasons why soft law instruments may represent an attractive alternative to law-making by treaty.[19] First, it may be easier to reach agreement when the form is non-binding. Use of soft law instruments enables states to agree to more detailed and precise provisions because their legal commitment, and the consequences of any non-compliance, are more limited. Second, it may be easier for some states to adhere to non-binding instruments because they can avoid the domestic treaty ratification process, and perhaps escape democratic accountability for the policy to which they have agreed. Of course this may also make it comparably harder to implement such policies if funding, legislation or public support are necessary. Third, soft law instruments are more flexible. They will normally be easier to supplement, amend or replace than treaties, particularly when all that is required is the adoption of a new resolution by an international institution. Two good examples are the nuclear safety standards adopted by the International Atomic Energy Agency, which amplify and interpret the basic obligations contained in the Nuclear Safety Convention, and the non-binding 'Plans of Action' adopted by FAO for the purpose of implementing fisheries agreements.[20] Lastly, soft law instruments may provide more immediate evidence of international support and consensus than a treaty whose impact is heavily qualified by reservations and the need to wait for ratification and entry into force. As we saw in Chapter 4,

---

[17]   In UN practice a 'declaration' is used in preference to a 'resolution' when 'principles of great and lasting importance are being enunciated'. See UN Doc E/CN4/L610 (1962), cited in B. Cheng (ed), *International Law Teaching and Practice* (London, 1982) 237.

[18]   In the *OSPAR Arbitration* (2003) PCA, para 90, it was accepted that a soft law declaration *may* in appropriate cases result in binding unilateral obligations based on good faith: see generally *Nuclear Tests Cases* (1974) ICJ Reports 253 and 457.

[19]   For a detailed examination see K. Abbott and D. Snidal, 'Hard and Soft Law in International Governance', *54 Int. Org* (2000) 421–56; Hillgenberg, 10 *EJIL* (1999) 499–515.

[20]   See next section.

codification of the law of state responsibility in the form of a General Assembly resolution reflects the advantages of a soft law form which in this context is viewed by many states and the ILC as sufficient for the purpose.

The argument for using a treaty rather than a soft law instrument is stronger in the case of new law-making or the revision of existing treaty-based law, such as the re-negotiation of the law of the sea or the elaboration of human rights law, although in many of these cases institutions with extensive powers were also established at the same time and a treaty was thus desirable in any event. NGOs often prefer treaties over soft law, especially on human rights issues, but like states they may be willing to settle for what can best be achieved. Even for new law, non-binding instruments may still be useful if they can help generate widespread and consistent state practice and/or provide evidence of *opinio juris* in support of a customary rule. There are good examples of UN General Assembly resolutions and intergovernmental declarations having this effect in the *Nicaragua case*,[21] the *Nuclear Weapons* Advisory Opinion[22] and the *Western Sahara* Advisory Opinion.[23] It is noteworthy, however, that despite some academic opinion to the contrary, no international tribunal has ever suggested that the mere act of voting for such resolutions of itself constitutes the state practice necessary to create a customary rule. We return to this question below.

What all of this suggests is that the non-binding form of an instrument is of relatively limited relevance in the context of customary international law-making. Treaties do not generate or codify customary law because of their binding form but because they either influence state practice and provide evidence of *opinio juris* for new or emerging rules, or because they are good evidence of what the existing law is. In many cases the potential effect of non-binding soft law instruments is no different. Both treaties and soft law instruments can be vehicles for focusing consensus on rules and principles, and for mobilising a consistent, general response on the part of states. Depending upon what is involved, treaties may be more effective than soft law instruments for this purpose insofar as they become part of national law on ratification, or because they indicate a stronger commitment to the principles in question. To that extent they may carry greater weight than a soft law instrument, but the assumption that they are necessarily more authoritative is misplaced. To take only one example, the 1992 Rio Declaration on Environment and Development both codifies existing international law and tries to develop new law. It is not obvious that a treaty with the same provisions would carry greater weight or achieve its objectives any more successfully. On the contrary, it is quite possible that such a treaty would, several years later, still have far from universal participation, whereas the 1992 Declaration secured immediate consensus support, with such authority as that implies. At the same time, it seems clear that agreements such as those on climate change and biological diversity could only be in treaty form, because of the combination of their status as new law, their more detailed terms and their institutional and dispute

---

[21] (1986) ICJ Reports 14.   [22] (1996) ICJ Reports 226.   [23] (1975) ICJ Reports 12.

settlement provisions. Similarly, as we saw in Chapter 4, the ILC articles on state immunity were adopted as a treaty in order to effect the necessary changes in national law. These are good examples of cases where because of the content of an agreement, incorporation in a treaty is the right option for pragmatic reasons and does carry a greater sense of commitment than a soft law instrument.

2.4   Soft Law as Part of the Multilateral Treaty-Making Process

Some non-binding soft law instruments are significant mainly because they are the first step in a process of negotiation eventually leading to the conclusion of a multilateral treaty. Thus the non-binding Universal Declaration of Human Rights was adopted long before agreement on the 1966 UN Covenants became possible, but it was always intended by the Commission on Human Rights that further binding agreements would follow. Apart from facilitating early agreement on principles, a declaration would not be overloaded with details, nor would it contain the institutional provisions found in the Covenants.[24] Other examples include General Assembly resolutions on outer space, the deep seabed and climate change[25] all of which acted as precursors for later agreements; the IAEA Guidelines,[26] which formed the basis for the rapid adoption of the 1986 Convention on Early Notification of a Nuclear Accident following the Chernobyl accident; UNEP Guidelines on Environmental Impact Assessment,[27] which were subsequently substantially incorporated in the 1991 UN Economic Commission for Europe Convention on Environmental Impact Assessment in a Transboundary Context; and UNEP's Guidelines on Land-based Sources of Marine Pollution,[28] which provided a model for regional treaties.

Soft law instruments are also used as mechanisms for authoritative interpretation or amplification of the terms of a treaty, and to that extent must be taken into account. The ILC commentary to what is now Article 31 (3) (a) of the Vienna Convention on the Law of Treaties notes simply that '. . . an agreement as to the interpretation of a provision reached after the conclusion of the treaty represents an authentic interpretation by the parties which must be read into the treaty for purposes of its interpretation'.[29] There are well-known instances of General

---

[24] See G. Alfredson and A. Eide (eds), *The Universal Declaration of Human Rights* (The Hague, 1999) 10.

[25] UNGA Res 1962 XVIII, 13 December 1963, Declaration of Legal Principles Governing the Activities of States in the Exploration and Use of Outer Space; UNGA Res 2749 XXV, 17 December 1970, Declaration of Principles Governing the Sea Bed and Ocean Floor and Subsoil Thereof Beyond the Limits of National Jurisdiction; UNGA Res 43/53, 6 December 1988, Protection of Global Climate for Present and Future Generations of Mankind.

[26] IAEA/INFCIRC/321 (1985).   [27] UNEP/GC14/25 (1987).

[28] UNEP/WG120/3 (1985).

[29] ILC, 'The Law of Treaties', commentary to Article 27, at para (14), in A. D. Watts (ed), *The ILC 1949–1998* (Oxford, 1999), vol II, 689. On the level of participation required in such agreements see Section 4.4.2 below.

Assembly resolutions interpreting and applying the UN Charter, including the Universal Declaration of Human Rights, the Declaration of Principles of International Law Concerning Friendly Relations, and others dealing with decolonisation, terrorism or the use of force.[30]

In contrast to soft law interpretations agreed by the General Assembly, in the case of UN human rights treaties this function is performed by committees of independent experts that we considered in Chapter 3. Since 1971, when the Committee on the Elimination of Racial Discrimination adopted its first General Recommendation,[31] the UN human rights committees have regularly adopted General Comments or Recommendations. These are often drafted with NGO input. They explain the Committee's understanding of particular articles of the relevant Convention, or proffer the Committee's opinion on general issues, or on associated rights not spelled out. As we noted in Chapter 3, General Recommendation No. 19 of the Committee on the Elimination of Discrimination against Women[32] explains how gender-specific violence against women contravenes the Convention despite the absence of any such article in the Convention. The Committee on Economic and Social Rights has interpreted the CESCR to provide a right to clean water, again going beyond the Convention's terms.[33] States play no part in the adoption of General Comments and this may cause some friction where they consider the Committee has gone beyond the treaty obligations. For example France, the United Kingdom and the United States reacted adversely to the Human Rights Committee's General Comment on Reservations.[34] On the one hand a state is bound only by the terms of a treaty to which it has become party. On the other hand, states have accepted the role of the human rights treaty bodies in supervising and monitoring the treaties. In some instances the Committee is explicitly mandated to make general recommendations,[35] and in all cases the Committee is supervised through annual reporting to the GA. General Comments might be understood as a form of delegated soft law. They supplement the limited jurisprudence under UN human rights treaties[36] and contribute to their status as 'living instruments'.

---

[30] UNGA Res 1514 XV, 14 December 1960, Declaration on the Granting of Independence to Colonial Countries and Peoples; UNGA Res 2625 XXV, 24 October 1970, Declaration on Principles of International law Concerning Friendly Relations and Co-operation Among States in Accordance with the Charter of the United Nations; UNGA Res 49/60, 9 December 1994, Declaration on Measures to Eliminate International Terrorism. See *Western Sahara Advisory Opinion* (1975) ICJ Reports 12; *Military and Paramilitary Activities in and against Nicaragua* (1986) ICJ Reports 14, and A. V. Lowe and C. Warbrick (eds), *The UN and the Principles of International Law* (London, 1994).

[31] CERD, General Recommendation No. 1, States parties' obligations (Article 4), 25 February 1972.

[32] CEDAW, General Recommendation, No. 19, Violence against women, 29 January 1992.

[33] CESCR, General Comment 15, The right to water, 20 January 2003.

[34] Observations by Governments of the United States and United Kingdom on General Comment No. 24 (52) relating to reservations, reprinted in 16 *Human Rights Law Journal* (1995) 433. See for comment R. Higgins, 'Introduction', in J.P. Gardner (ed), *Human Rights as General Norms and a State's Right to Opt Out* (London, 1997) xvii.

[35] CERD, Article 9 (2); CEDAW, Article 18 (1); CROC, Article 45 (d).

[36] The right of individual complaint is limited to the ICCPR, Optional Protocol; the Convention on the Elimination of All Forms of Racial Discrimination, Article 14; the Convention against

The same task of giving guidance on or amplifying the terms of a treaty is performed more frequently by resolutions, recommendations and decisions of other international organisations, and by the conferences of parties to treaties. Environmental soft law is quite often important for this reason, setting detailed rules or more general standards of best practice or due diligence to be achieved by the parties in implementing their obligations. These 'ecostandards' are essential in giving hard content to the open-textured terms of framework environmental treaties.[37] Thus UNEP's Cairo Guidelines on the Transport of Hazardous Wastes[38] can be regarded as an amplification of the obligation of 'environmentally sound management' provided for in Article 4 of the 1989 Basel Convention on the Control of Transboundary Movements of Hazardous Wastes. The advantages of regulating environmental risks in this way are that the detailed rules and standards can easily be changed or strengthened as scientific understanding develops or as political priorities change. They could of course be adopted in treaty form, using easily amended annexes to provide flexibility, but the parties may prefer a more cautious option. It was a resolution of the parties to the Montreal Protocol to the Ozone Convention which first set out the terms of the non-compliance procedure provided for in the Protocol.[39] The procedure was subsequently revised and once states had become comfortable with the idea it was then incorporated by amendment as an annex in the Protocol, showing again how non-binding soft law can be transformed into binding form.

The IAEA has made particular use of formally non-binding standards, through its nuclear safety codes and principles. These generally represent an authoritative technical and political consensus, approved by the Board of Governors or General Conference of the Agency. The preamble to the 1994 Nuclear Safety Convention recognises that internationally formulated safety guidelines 'can provide guidance on contemporary means of achieving a high level of safety', and they would be the obvious starting point for determining what constitute the 'appropriate steps' required by the Convention and by the customary obligation of due diligence in the regulation and control of nuclear activities. However, in order to further strengthen the nuclear safety regime, the 1994 Convention and the 1997 Joint Convention on the Safety of Spent Fuel and Radioactive Waste Management now incorporate in binding treaty articles the main elements of IAEA's safety standards for nuclear installations, radioactive waste management and radiation protection, including most of its former Code of Practice on the Transboundary Movement of Radioactive Waste. These various agreements have significantly strengthened the

Torture, Article 22; the Convention on the Elimination of All Forms of Discrimination against Women, Optional Protocol; Convention on Migrant Workers, Article 77. In all cases states parties must 'opt in' to the right of individual complaint.

[37] See P. Contini and P. Sand, 'Methods to Expedite Environment Protection: International Ecostandards', 66 *AJIL* (1972) 37; D. Bodansky, 'Rules vs Standards in International Environmental Law', 98 *ASIL Proceedings* (2004) 275.   [38] UNEP/WG122/3 (1985).

[39] Decision II/5, UNEP/OzLPro/WG3/2/2, Annex III (1990).

legal force of IAEA standards and, in conjunction with the remaining soft law standards, have created a more convincing legal framework for the international regulation of nuclear risks. They exemplify how soft law and treaties can interact in a complex regulatory framework.

Nor is IAEA unique in this respect. FAO uses a mixture of hard and soft law instruments to promote implementation of the fisheries provisions of the 1982 UNCLOS. The 1993 Agreement to Promote Compliance with Conservation Measures on the High Seas is a binding treaty, but it forms an integral part of the non-binding 1995 Code of Conduct on Responsible Fishing, which is itself further implemented by other soft law measures including the 2001 Plan of Action on Illegal, Unreported and Unregulated Fishing. The choice of soft law instruments can partly be explained by the opposition of some states to binding agreements. Another reason, however, is that they are aimed at regional fisheries organisations and the fishing industry as well as states, and contain some elements which are unlikely to find their way into treaty form. They are also easier to amend or replace than treaties, requiring simply the adoption of another instrument. Negotiated in the same manner as treaties, and adopted by consensus in FAO,[40] these non-binding 'voluntary instruments' also complement the 1995 UN Fish Stocks Agreement and seek to promote implementation of elements of that agreement by non-parties. Reviewing the effect of all these inter-related measures, a former FAO Legal Adviser concludes that 'There can be little doubt that the sum total of the changes introduced has substantially strengthened the regime of the 1982 UN Convention, leaving aside the question whether there has been a *de facto* amendment of it in some respect.'[41]

Sometimes binding force is conferred on soft law instruments by incorporating them into the terms of a treaty by implied reference. The 1982 UN Convention on the Law of the Sea makes use of this technique, impliedly incorporating recommendations and resolutions of IMO, as well as regulatory annexes to treaties such as the 1973/78 MARPOL Convention, under provisions variously requiring or permitting states to apply 'generally accepted rules and standards established through the competent international organisation or general diplomatic conference'.[42] Thus although IMO has no general power under its constitution to adopt binding resolutions, UNCLOS may indirectly render some of these resolutions obligatory.

In a few cases soft law declarations have been used to codify and restate principles already adopted in treaty form. An example in the practice of the International

---

[40] See W. Edeson, 'The International Plan of Action on Illegal, Unreported and Unregulated Fishing: The Legal Context of a Non-Legally Binding Instrument', 16 *IJMCL* (2001) 603. However some states expressed significant reservations when adopting the Plan of Action: see FAO, *Report of the Committee on Fisheries*, 24th Session (2001).

[41] W. Edeson, in A. E. Boyle and D. Freestone (eds), *International Law and Sustainable Development* (Oxford, 1999) 165. See also Edeson, 'Soft and Hard Law Aspects of Fisheries Issues', in M. Nordquist, J. N. Moore and S. Mahmoudi (eds), *The Stockholm Declaration and Law of the Marine Environment* (The Hague, 2003) 165.   [42] See Section 4.4.3 below.

Labour Organisation is the 1998 Declaration on Fundamental Principles and Rights at Work, which distils the core principles of the ILO's numerous conventions.

Lastly, as we saw earlier, soft law instruments may operate in conjunction with a treaty to provide evidence of *opinio juris* for the possible emergence of a rule of customary international law. ICJ case law, including the *Nicaragua* case,[43] shows how the interplay between the UN Charter and resolutions of the General Assembly can have this effect.

These examples all point to the conclusion that the non-binding force of soft law can be overstated. In many of the above examples states are not free to disregard applicable soft law: even when not incorporated directly into a treaty, it may represent an agreed understanding of the terms of the treaty. Thus, although of themselves these instruments may not be legally binding, their interaction with related treaties may transform their legal status into something more.

2.5   Treaties as Soft Law

An alternative view of soft law focuses on the contrast between 'rules', involving clear and reasonably specific commitments which are in this sense hard law (for example, 'No State may validly purport to subject any part of the high seas to its sovereignty'), and 'norms' or 'principles', which, being more open-textured or general in their content and wording, can thus be seen as soft.

The point was made many years ago by the late Judge Baxter that some treaty provisions are soft in the sense that they impose no real obligations on the parties.[44] Though formally binding, their vagueness, indeterminacy or generality may deprive them of the character of 'hard law' in any meaningful sense. The 1992 Framework Convention on Climate Change provides another example. Adopted by consensus at the Rio Conference, this treaty imposes some commitments on the parties, but its core articles, dealing with policies and measures to tackle greenhouse gas emissions, are so cautiously and obscurely worded and so weak that it is uncertain whether any real obligations are created. The United States' interpretation of Articles 4 (1) and (2) was that 'there is nothing in any of the language which constitutes a commitment to any specific level of emissions at any time . . . '. Moreover, Article 4 (7) makes whatever commitments have been undertaken by developing states conditional on provision of funding and transfer of technology by developed states parties.

Such treaty provisions are almost impossible to breach and in that limited sense Judge Baxter is justified in calling them soft law. More of a political bargain than a legal one, these are 'soft' undertakings of a fragile kind. They are not normative and cannot be described as creating 'rules' in any meaningful sense. This is probably true of many treaties, a point recognised by the International Court in the

---

[43] (1986) ICJ Reports 14. See also *Western Sahara Advisory Opinion* (1975) ICJ Reports 12.
[44] 29 *ICLQ* (1980) 549–66.

North Sea Continental Shelf case when it specified that one of the conditions to be met before a treaty could be regarded as law-making is that it should be so drafted as to be 'potentially normative' in character.[45]

There is, however, a second and more significant sense in which a treaty, like a non-binding resolution or declaration, may be potentially normative, but still 'soft' in character, because it articulates 'principles' rather than 'rules'. Here it is the *formulation* of the provision which is decisive in determining whether it is hard or soft, not its form as a treaty or binding instrument. An example of a soft formulation, which nevertheless has binding form, is Article 87 (2) of the 1982 UNCLOS, providing that high seas freedoms 'shall be exercised by all States with due regard for the interests of other states in their exercise of the freedoms of the high seas . . . '. What is meant by 'due regard' for the interests of other states will necessarily depend on the particular circumstances of each case and in that sense the provision is more of a 'principle' than a rule.[46] The rule of customary law providing for equitable delimitation of maritime boundaries is another example of a comparably 'soft' formulation.[47]

The Convention on Climate Change once again provides other good examples of such principles explicitly included in a major treaty. Indeed, given how weak the rest of the treaty is, the principles found in Article 3 are arguably the most important 'law' in the whole agreement because they prescribe how the regime for regulating climate change is to be developed by the parties. It is worth quoting the main elements of this provision:

Article 3: Principles
In their actions to achieve the objective of the Convention and to implement its provisions, the parties shall be guided, *inter alia*, by the following:

1. The Parties should protect the climate system for the benefit of present and future generations of humankind, on the basis of equity and in accordance with their common but differentiated responsibilities . . .
3. The Parties should take precautionary measures to anticipate, prevent, or minimise the causes of climate change and mitigate its adverse effects . . .
4. The Parties have a right to, and should, promote sustainable development . . .

These elements of Article 3 are all drawn directly from the non-binding Rio Declaration on Environment and Development; they reflect norms which are not simply part of the Climate Change Convention, but which are also emerging at the level of general international law, even if it is premature or inappropriate to accord them the status of custom. They are not expressed in obligatory terms: the use of 'should' qualifies their application, despite the obligatory wording of

---

[45] *North Sea Continental Shelf Cases* (1969) ICJ Reports 3, para 72.
[46] See *Fisheries Jurisdiction Cases* (1974) ICJ Reports 3 and 175; *Nuclear Tests Cases* (1974) ICJ Reports 253 and 457.
[47] 1982 UNCLOS, Articles 74 and 83; *North Sea Continental Shelf Cases* (1969) ICJ Reports 3; *Gulf of Maine Case* (1984) ICJ Reports 246; *Jan Mayen Case* (1993) ICJ Reports 38.

the *chapeau* sentence. All of these principles are open-textured in the sense that there is considerable uncertainty concerning their specific content and they leave much room for interpretation and elaboration. They are not at all like rules requiring states to conduct an environmental impact assessment, or to prevent harm to other states.

Given their explicit role as guidance and their softer formulation, the 'principles' in Article 3 are not necessarily binding rules which must be complied with or which entail responsibility for breach if not complied with; yet, despite all these limitations, they are not legally irrelevant. At the very least Article 3 is relevant to interpretation and implementation of the Convention as well as creating expectations concerning matters which must be taken into account in good faith in the negotiation of further instruments.

Article 3 takes a novel approach to environmental protection, but in the context of a dynamic and evolutionary regulatory regime such as the Climate Change Convention it has the important merit of providing some predictability regarding the parameters within which the parties are required to work towards the objective of the Convention. In particular, they are not faced with a completely blank sheet of paper when entering subsequent protocol negotiations or when the Conference of the Parties takes decisions under the various articles empowering it to do so. Thus it is significant that the relevance of Article 3 was reiterated in the mandate for negotiation of the Kyoto Protocol[48] and is referred to in the preamble to the Protocol. It is a nice question whether the parties collectively are entitled to disregard the principles contained in Article 3, or what the legal effect of decisions that do so may be, but however weak it may seem, parties whose interests are affected do have a right to insist on having the principles of Article 3 taken into account. As we shall see in the following section, sustainable development, intergenerational equity or the precautionary principle are all more convincingly seen in this sense: not as binding obligations which must be complied with, but as principles, considerations or objectives to be taken account of—they may be soft, but they still have legal effects.

2.6   Soft Law General Principles

The idea that general norms or principles can affect the way courts decide cases or the exercise of discretionary powers by an international organisation is not confined to treaty regimes. Indeed in modern international relations such general norms or principles are more often found in the form of non-binding declarations or resolutions of international organisations than in the provisions of multilateral treaties. The Universal Declaration of Human Rights remains one of the most influential examples of soft law of this kind.[49] International courts have of course

---

[48] The so-called 'Berlin mandate': Decision 1/CP1, in, *Report of the Conference of the Parties on its 1st Session*, UN Doc FCCC/CP/1995/7/Add 1.
[49] See Alfredson and Eide, *The UDHR*, xviii–xxii.

always had the power under Article 38 (1) (c) of the ICJ Statute to refer to general principles of law. In most cases this entails borrowing by analogy from common elements of national law, such as non-discrimination or the right to a fair hearing.[50]

However, it is also possible for states to adopt general principles not derived from national law, with the intention that courts and states should apply them when relevant. Such general principles do not have to create rules of customary law to have legal effect, nor do they need to be incorporated in treaties. They cannot over-ride or amend the express terms of a treaty,[51] so their importance derives principally from the influence they may exert on the interpretation, application and development of other rules of law. Article 31 (3) of the 1969 Vienna Convention on the Law of Treaties appears to include reference to general principles as an aid to treaty interpretation.[52] Thus in *Golder* the ECHR referred to access to a court as a 'general principle of law' when interpreting Article 6 of the European Convention on Human Rights.[53] The point is not applicable only to treaty interpretation, however. A general principle of this kind may also influence the interpretation and application of customary law.

The precautionary principle or approach, endorsed by consensus in Principle 15 of the 1992 Rio Declaration on Environment and Development, is a case in point. The precautionary approach is a common feature of almost all the Rio and post-Rio global environmental agreements. Principle 15 provides as follows:

> In order to protect the environment, the precautionary approach shall be widely applied by states according to their capabilities. Where there are threats of serious or irreversible damage, lack of full scientific certainty shall not be used as a reason for postponing cost-effective measures to prevent environmental degradation.

Its purpose is thus to make greater allowance for uncertainty in the regulation of environmental risks and the sustainable use of natural resources.

Some writers and governments have argued that the precautionary principle or approach is a rule of customary international law, but international courts and many governments have been noticeably hesitant to accept this characterisation.[54] If, however, it is viewed as a general principle of law, on which decision-makers and courts may rely when deciding cases and interpreting treaties, then its subsequent use by national and international courts, and by international organisations, is easier to explain. As the *Southern Bluefin Tuna* cases show, the interpretation and

---

[50] *S W Africa Cases* (1966) ICJ Reports 294–301 (Judge Tanaka); *Golder v. UK* (1975) 1 EHRR 524, paras 10–36, but compare dissenting opinion of Judge Fitzmaurice, paras 18–46 and 48. See generally A. Cassese, *International Law in a Divided World* (Oxford, 1986) 170–4; B. Cheng, *General Principles of International Law* (London, 1953); W. Friedmann, 'The Uses of General Principles in the Development of International Law', 57 *AJIL* (1963) 279; O. Elias and C. Lim, ' "General Principles of Law", "Soft" Law and the Identification of International Law', 28 *NYBIL* (1997) 3.

[51] *Beef Hormones Case* (1998) WTO Appellate Body, paras 124–5.

[52] See *Report of the ILC*, GAOR A/60/10 (2005), para 477.

[53] *Golder v. UK* (1975) 1 EHRR 524, paras 10–36.

[54] See eg *Beef Hormones Case*, paras 120–5; *Southern Bluefin Tuna Cases* Provisional Measures (1999) ITLOS Nos. 3 and 4, paras 77–9.

application of treaties may be affected.[55] Moreover, as Brownlie observes, 'The point which stands out is that some applications of the principle, which is based on the concept of foreseeable risk to other states, are encompassed within existing concepts of state responsibility'.[56] The ILC special rapporteur on transboundary harm has taken the same view, concluding that the precautionary principle is already a component of existing customary rules on prevention of harm and environmental impact assessment, 'and could not be divorced therefrom'.[57]

Much the same could be said of sustainable development. Lowe makes the essential point with great clarity:

Sustainable development can properly claim a normative status as an element of the process of judicial reasoning. It is a meta-principle, acting upon other rules and principles— a legal concept exercising a kind of interstitial normativity, pushing and pulling the boundaries of true primary norms when they threaten to overlap or conflict with each other.[58]

Sustainable development thus becomes a mediating principle between the right to development and the duty to control sources of environmental harm. Mediating norms or principles need not impose obligations or regulate conduct, they do not depend on state practice and they do not need the same clarity or precision as rules.

What gives general principles of this kind their authority and legitimacy is simply the endorsement of states—*opinio juris* in other words.[59] Such principles have legal significance in much the same way that Dworkin uses the idea of constitutional principles.[60] They lay down parameters which affect the way courts decide cases or how an international institution exercises its discretionary powers. They can set limits, or provide guidance, or determine how conflicts between other rules or principles will be resolved. They may lack the supposedly harder edge of a 'rule' or 'obligation', but they should not be confused with 'non-binding' or emerging law. That is perhaps the most important lesson to be drawn from the ICJ's references to sustainable development in the *Case Concerning the Gabčíkovo-Nagymaros Dam.*[61] Even if sustainable development is not in the nature of a legal obligation, it does represent a policy goal or principle that can influence the outcome of litigation and the practice of states and international organisations, and it may lead to significant changes and developments in the existing

---

[55] Ibid, paras 77–9, and Judges Laing, paras 16–19, Treves, para 9, and Shearer.

[56] *Principles of Public International Law* (6th edn, Oxford, 2003), 276.

[57] *Report of the ILC* (2000) GAOR A/55/10, para 716.

[58] A. V. Lowe, in Boyle and Freestone, *International Law and Sustainable Development*, 31.

[59] Lowe, ibid, 33, dispenses even with *opinio juris*, but unless such norms emerge from thin air at the whim of judges the endorsement of states must be a necessary element. All the norms Lowe relies on do in fact have such endorsement.

[60] R. Dworkin, *Taking Rights Seriously* (London, 1977). This argument is developed by P. Sands in W. Lang (ed), *Sustainable Development and International Law* (London, 1995), chapter 5.

[61] (1997) ICJ Reports 7, para 140.

law.[62] In that important sense, international law appears to require states and international bodies to take account of the objective of sustainable development, and to establish appropriate processes for doing so.

What these examples show is that subtle changes in the existing law and in existing treaties may come about through the application of such general principles. In Chapter 6 we will see how courts have made use of soft law principles in developing international law. In any system of law the ability to make changes on a systemic basis is important. How else could this be done in international law? New *rules* of customary law are not necessarily appropriate to the elaboration of such general principles and could not be created quickly enough; moreover, to take an obvious example, a treaty endorsing the precautionary principle would only bind the parties. A binding resolution of the UNSC may be a possible option, but only where questions of international peace and security are at stake. Thus, the consensus endorsement by states of a general principle enshrined in a soft law declaration is an entirely sensible solution to such law-making challenges.

Use of soft law techniques does not diminish the need for consensus among states, however. On the contrary, while amendments to treaties or implementing agreements may limp into force with only partial participation, adopting soft law principles without consensus support has little if any impact on the law-making process. The main advantage of adopting principles in soft law form is simply that the need to go through the process in treaty form is avoided. Once adopted, no ratification is necessary. This does not mean that soft law principles are an alternative to treaty amendment or implementation agreements in every case: far from it. Much will depend on what is proposed. But if the issue can be formulated in terms of interpretation or application of the existing terms of a treaty or other rule of law—as it could be in the case of the precautionary principle or sustainable development—there is no necessity to go further than soft law.

2.7   Soft Law and Customary Law

Resolutions of international organisations and multilateral declarations by states may also have effects on customary international law.[63] Whether they provide evidence of existing law, or of the *opinio juris* necessary for new law, or of the practice of states, will depend on various factors which must be assessed in each case. A law-making resolution or declaration need not necessarily proclaim rights or principles as law, but as with treaties, the wording must be 'of a fundamentally norm-creating character such as could be regarded as forming the basis of a general rule of law'.[64]

---

[62] See for example the inclusion of provisions on sustainable use or sustainable development in the 1994 WTO Agreement, the 1995 UN Fish Stocks Agreement and the 1997 UN Convention on International Watercourses.

[63] See eg G. Abi-Saab, 'Cours Général de Droit International Public', 207 *Recueil des Cours* (1987) 33, 160–1.   [64] *North Sea Continental Shelf Cases* (1969) ICJ Reports 3, para 72.

It is also obvious that declarations or resolutions setting out agreed norms or general principles 'will usually have greater influence than recommendations'.[65] The context within which soft law instruments are negotiated and the accompanying statements of delegations will also be relevant if assessing the *opinio juris* of states. Lastly, the degree of support is significant. A resolution adopted by consensus or by unanimous vote will necessarily carry more weight than one supported only by a two-thirds majority of states. Resolutions opposed by even a small number of states may have little effect if those states are among the ones most immediately affected.[66] The attempt by the General Assembly in the 1970s to change the law on expropriation of foreign investments is a well-known example of the inability of majorities of states to legislate for minorities in this fashion.[67] The General Assembly's ban on deep seabed mining outside the framework of UNCLOS is another. In this case, the minority of objecting states maintained their own parallel regime, until eventually an agreement was reached.[68]

In an international system where the consent or acquiescence of states is still an essential precondition for the development of new law or changes to existing law, these examples show that opposing votes matter. Even if such resolutions can change the law for states which vote in favour, it is clear that they do not do so for the dissenting minority.[69] Moreover, even consensus adoption will not be as significant as it may at first appear if accompanied by statements which seriously qualify what has been agreed, or if it simply papers over an agreement to disagree without pressing matters to a vote. For all these reasons, the adoption of resolutions by international organisations or of declarations by states should not be confused with law-making *per se*.

Some scholars have argued that General Assembly resolutions and declarations could create 'instant' customary law.[70] Cheng concludes that the clearly articulated expression of *opinio juris* through the medium of a non-binding resolution or declaration may be enough, without further state practice, to afford evidence of

---

[65] H. Schermers and N. Blokker, *International Institutional Law* (The Hague, 1995) 777.

[66] See the cautionary dissent of Schwebel in the *Nuclear Weapons Advisory Opinion* (1996) ICJ Reports 226, 318–9. On the question which states are 'specially affected' see Chapter 1.

[67] See Charter of Economic Rights and Duties of States, UNGA Res 3281 XXX, 12 December 1974 and *Texaco v. Libya* (1977) 53 ILR 422, paras 80–91. A hundred and twenty states voted for the resolution, six voted against, ten abstained.

[68] The Declaration of Principles Governing the Seabed and Ocean Floor, UNGA Res 2749 XXV, 17 December 1970 was adopted by 108 votes in favour with 14 abstentions. For an account of the subsequent disagreements over the legal status of the deep seabed and the reciprocating states regime established by Western states see R. R. Churchill and A. V. Lowe, *The Law of the Sea* (Manchester, 1999) 224–35.

[69] *Texaco v. Libya* (1977) 53 ILR 422. But for a different view compare J. Charney, 'The Persistent Objector Rule and the Development of Customary International Law', 58 *BYBIL* (1987) 1, and see Section 4.2 below.

[70] B. Cheng, 'United Nations Resolutions on Outer Space: "Instant" Customary Law?', 5 *Indian JIL* (1965) 23–48, reprinted in B. Cheng (ed), *International Law Teaching and Practice* (London, 1982) 237. See also A. Roberts, 'Traditional and Modern Approaches to Customary International Law: A Reconciliation', 95 *AJIL* (2001) 757, who makes a rather similar argument.

a new rule of customary or general international law. For anyone seeking to use the UN General Assembly as a law-making instrument this is an attractive but generally unsustainable argument. Cheng himself rightly cautions against the facile assumption that UNGA resolutions make law, and his view of instant law-making is limited to very specific circumstances. First, it depends on a strong consensus in favour of such a resolution.[71] Second, it requires appropriate wording. The principal UNGA resolutions on outer space fail this test, because they merely articulate principles by which states 'should be guided',[72] rather than normative rules. Cheng was also writing before any of the leading modern ICJ cases on the creation of customary law were decided, and even his cautious formulation may now be too generous. The jurisprudence is not favourable, it must be said, to notions of instant law-making, but stresses instead the need for confirmatory practice, or at least the absence of contrary practice.[73] Moreover, although certain more appropriately worded UNGA declarations (for example the Universal Declaration of Human Rights and the Declaration on the Granting of Independence to Colonial Territories and Peoples) have undeniably had law-making effect, neither of these resolutions was adopted by consensus and it is doubtful that their impact was ever instantaneous.

If the resolutions on outer space did not make instant law, and were meant to be replaced by treaties,[74] why adopt them at all? Apart from practical considerations of simplicity and speed of adoption compared to treaties, the importance of resort to the UNGA lies in the collective affirmation thereby provided for general rules of space law otherwise only impliedly asserted by the space states. The resolutions provided both a record of what all states believed the relevant rules should be, and evidence of *opinio juris* demonstrating the law-making significance of their earlier practice. As Brownlie observes, 'In the face of a relatively novel situation the General Assembly provides an efficient index to the quickly growing practice of States.'[75] Elsewhere he refers to the 'decisive catalytic effect' which such resolutions may have on state practice.[76]

In those circumstances it would be safe for space states to proceed on the assumption that there would be no opposition to activities conducted in conformity with the principles endorsed by the resolutions. That these principles were

---

[71] Resolutions 1721 (XVI) (1961) and 1962 (XVIII) (1963) were agreed first by the USA and USSR (the only space states at that time), then adopted unanimously by the Outer Space Committee, the 1st Committee and the UNGA.

[72] UNGA Res 1962 XVIII, 13 December 1963. The wording of UNGA Res 1721 XVI, 20 December 1961 is even weaker: 'The General Assembly . . . commends to States for their guidance . . . the following principles.'

[73] See *Nicaragua Case* (1986) ICJ Reports 14, para 184, and Section 4.2 below.

[74] See now the 1967 Outer Space Treaty and the 1979 Moon Treaty. The USSR had from the start argued in favour of a treaty; Cheng, 5 *Indian JIL* (1965) 28, 31, surmises that it agreed to the adoption of a resolution out of concern that any treaty might be vetoed by the US Senate.

[75] I. Brownlie, *Basic Documents on International Law* (3rd edn, Oxford, 1991) 204.

[76] I. Brownlie, 'The Legal Status of Natural Resources', 162 *Recueil des Cours* (1979) 261.

subsequently reaffirmed in treaty form shows both the value of soft law precedents as a prelude to later agreement on a more detailed international regime, and the preference for treaties as a means of stabilising the law within an appropriate institutional framework once the views and practice of states are settled. This may suggest a perception that soft law is too fragile an instrument to sustain the long-term regulation of common areas such as space or the deep seabed, but it is certainly an effective starting point when states need reassurance before commencing novel and previously unregulated activities.

The adoption of non-binding resolutions or declarations can also lead to changes in the existing law, in some cases quite quickly. The termination of driftnet fishing on the high seas is a good example of the successful use of UNGA resolutions in this way.[77] Although the resolutions themselves have no legal force, and do not make 'instant' law, the widespread opposition to such fishing has been effective in pressuring many of the states involved to comply with the resolutions and phase out the use of driftnets. Today it seems unlikely that any state would wish to assert the right to use driftnets, although the practice has not yet been universally banned. Such changes in the law can of course only come about as a result of changes in practice by those states most closely involved. Moreover, even states initially voting against such resolutions may eventually conform to the general will. The initial opposition of colonial powers to UN resolutions on self-determination soon faded, and as the *Western Sahara* and *East Timor* cases show,[78] former colonial states became the principal advocates of self-determination for their former colonies.

Why use non-binding resolutions for such purposes? Negotiating a global treaty on driftnets would have taken as long or longer; it would not have entered into force until there were enough ratifications, and if the relevant states failed to become parties they would not be bound anyway. In the latter case the law would not change unless these states changed their practice, which is no less true of the non-binding resolutions adopted by UNGA. In such cases, if the consensus for a change in practice is strong enough, a treaty is not necessary. If it is not strong enough a treaty will not necessarily strengthen it.

Banning a specific form of fishing is a relatively simple change in the law. Soft law instruments may not be as useful when more complex changes are needed. When it became apparent that the provisions of the 1982 UNCLOS relating to the high seas would not be sufficient to ensure sustainable fishing, an additional treaty was negotiated. Between the parties the 1995 UN Fish Stocks Agreement in effect elaborates and amends the 1982 UNCLOS. It is an important and far-reaching instrument that makes notable changes in the law on high seas fishing. *Inter alia*, freedom of fishing is confined to states which operate within the rules of

---

[77] UNGA Res 44/225, 22 December 1989 and UNGA Res 46/215, 20 December 1991 on Large Scale Pelagic Driftnet Fishing, and other instruments collected in FAO, *Legislative Study 47: The Regulation of Driftnet Fishing on the High Seas* (Rome, 1991).
[78] *Western Sahara Advisory Opinion* (1975) ICJ Reports 12; *East Timor Case* (1995) ICJ Reports 2.

regional fisheries organisations; fisheries law is given a newly environmental focus, emphasising sustainability and conservation of biological diversity and ecosystems; the enforcement powers of other states are extended, and regional agreements are brought within the UNCLOS dispute settlement system. However strong the consensus in favour of these changes, given their far-reaching nature and impact on other treaties, a treaty was clearly the only possible instrument in this situation. In reality, some of these measures have been controversial, and many fishing states remain non-parties to the 1995 Agreement, but resort to soft law would not have been any more effective in such circumstances. But if the weakness of soft law is that states are not obliged to comply, the same is no less true of an unratified or poorly ratified treaty. Whether the 1995 Agreement changes the law will still depend on how far it influences the practice of states, rather than on its binding force.

2.8   Conclusions

Soft law is manifestly a multi-faceted concept, whose relationship to treaties, custom and general principles is both subtle and diverse. At its simplest soft law facilitates progressive evolution of international law. It presents alternatives to law-making by treaty in certain circumstances, at other times it complements treaties, while also providing different ways of understanding the legal effect of different kinds of treaty. Those who maintain that soft law is simply not law have perhaps missed some of the points made here; moreover those who see a treaty as necessarily having greater legal effect than soft law have perhaps not looked hard enough at the 'infinite variety' of treaties, to quote Baxter once more. Soft law in its various forms can of course be abused, but so can most legal forms, and it has generally been more helpful to the process of international law-making than it has been objectionable.

3.   UN Security Council Resolutions

3.1   The Power to Take Binding Decisions

We saw in Chapter 3 how the UNSC has begun to use its considerable power, and noted how some resolutions have a distinctly legislative character and purpose, despite obvious concerns about the Council's legitimacy in this role. While General Assembly resolutions are at best only soft law, the legal effect of UNSC resolutions is more complicated. The Security Council has power to adopt decisions binding on all UN member states by virtue of Article 25 of the UN Charter. Not all provisions of UNSC resolutions are binding, however, including those which merely 'recommend', 'call upon' or 'urge' states to do or refrain from doing something. The wording, context and intent are all relevant, as is the UN Charter provision relied upon.[79] 'Decisions' taken under Chapter VII of the Charter to maintain or restore international peace and security are the most important category of binding resolutions. A binding resolution may have legal significance in various ways, as we shall see below.

Are there any limits on the power of the UNSC to take binding decisions? Herein lies a profound debate on the constitutional limits of an admittedly powerful institution. It is not necessary to explore this debate in depth here,[80] but some understanding of the issues is necessary because they impact directly on the law-making potential of the Council. The Council does not have absolute power; two obvious limitations are suggested by the wording of the Charter itself. First, Article 24 provides expressly that in carrying out its duties the Security Council 'shall act in accordance with the Purposes and Principles of the United Nations',[81] while Article 25 refers to the obligation of member states to 'accept and carry out the decisions of the Security Council in accordance with the present Charter'. Delbrück gives this phrase a narrow reading limited to procedural compliance with the Charter,[82] but as Martenczuk argues, the ICJ's treatment of the *Lockerbie* cases suggests that it has 'resisted all attempts to remove Chapter VII of the Charter from the ambit of legal interpretation'.[83] It might thus be argued that the Council's assumption of a more general law-making authority under Chapter VII falls outside the substantive scope of its powers as intended by the negotiators of the Charter.[84] More probably, however, the purposive reading of the Charter adopted by the ICJ in the *Certain Expenses* case[85] would lend support to the Council's law-making activities so long as they can reasonably be related to the maintenance or restoration of international peace and security under Article 39.[86] In Chapter 3 we saw how the Council has made generous use of Chapter VII, asserting the right to act even in respect of internal humanitarian crises, civil war, governmental breakdown or racist oppression. In some of these cases the threat to 'international peace and security' is tenuous. Given the breadth of the discretion afforded to the Council, however, it is not surprising that judicial decisions have shown considerable deference to its political judgments and treated its decisions as presumptively

---

[79] *Namibia Advisory Opinion* (1971) ICJ Reports 16, 52–3; R. Higgins, 'The Advisory Opinion on Namibia: Which Resolutions are Binding under Article 25 of the Charter?', 21 *ICLQ* (1972) 270, 283; B. Simma (ed), *The Charter of the UN: A Commentary* (2nd edn, Oxford, 2002) 454–64.

[80] The literature is extensive. See T. Franck, 'Who is the Ultimate Guardian of UN Legality?', 86 *AJIL* (1992) 519; V. Gowlland-Debbas, 'The Relationship between the ICJ and the Security Council', 88 *AJIL* (1994) 643; J. Alvarez, 'Judging the Security Council', 90 *AJIL* (1996) 1; D. Akande, 'The ICJ and the Security Council', 46 *ICLQ* (1997) 309.

[81] See *Prosecutor v. Tadic* (1996) 35 *ILM* 32, paras 28–9.

[82] In Simma, *The Charter of the United Nations*, 455.

[83] B. Martenczuk, 'The Security Council, the International Court and Judicial Review', 10 *EJIL* (1999) 517.

[84] See M. Happold, 'SC Resolution 1373 and the Constitution of the UN', *13 LJIL* (2003) 593.

[85] (1962) ICJ Reports 151.

[86] UN Charter, Article 39. See F. Kirgis, 'The Security Council's First 50 Years', 89 *AJIL* (1995) 506, 520–8.

valid.[87] Nevertheless, it is possible that the legality of a resolution could be challenged on the ground that it is far removed from peace and security.

A second limitation may flow from the concept of *jus cogens*. Some of the Council's resolutions relating to the war in Bosnia have been challenged on this basis because, it was argued, they facilitated genocide by denying Bosnia the right to defend itself.[88] This argument would at least support the conclusion that Council resolutions cannot legitimise torture, genocide, war crimes or any other activity falling within the narrow category of *jus cogens* presently supported by judicial decisions. In the context of possible Security Council action against international terrorism these may prove to be significant limitations.

More questionably, it might be argued that in using its powers the Council must respect general international law. A possible example is the *Tadic* case, considered in Chapter 3, which addresses human rights limitations on the Council's power to establish criminal tribunals. However, interpreting and applying UNSC resolutions in accordance with human rights law, or with other relevant rules of international law, does not tell us that the Council cannot lawfully pass resolutions inconsistent with general international law; it merely compels it to do so in appropriate terms. More pertinently, it has been suggested that the Council cannot force states to agree to third party settlement of disputes, or impose territorial boundaries, or compel states to extradite suspected terrorists, because to do so would be inconsistent with existing law, procedural due process or treaty commitments.[89] If that were correct, then the Council's power to legislate generally about such matters would be similarly constrained. It is doubtful that this is a good argument, however. In UNSC 687 the Council carefully refrained from imposing a boundary on Iraq, but it is not clear that its reasons for doing so were constitutional rather than political.[90] In *Lockerbie* incompatibility with an existing treaty did not persuade the ICJ to restrain implementation of a UNSC resolution regarded by the court as *prima-facie* valid.[91] Moreover, if the Council is bound to act within existing international law then its power to act at all will be severely compromised and open to challenge in most, if not all, cases. Why, for example, should a state which claims to be acting lawfully in self-defence pay any attention to a resolution imposing a ceasefire? Why should it evacuate territory it believes to be lawfully its own, however implausibly? Why should it do anything that general international law does not already require or empower it to do? On that basis the Council would find itself constantly embroiled in endless argument about the legality of its decisions, with serious consequences for its effectiveness. This outcome is a

---

[87] *Namibia Advisory Opinion* (1971) ICJ Reports 16, para 20; *Prosecutor v. Tadic* (1996) 35 *ILM* 32, para 29.

[88] See *Prevention and Punishment of the Crime of Genocide case* (1993) ICJ Reports 3, especially the judgment of Judge Lauterpacht.

[89] I. Brownlie, 'The Decisions of Political Organs of the United Nations and the Rule of Law', in R. Macdonald (ed), *Essays in Honour of Wang Tieya* (Dordrecht, 1993) 91.

[90] M. Mendelson and S. Hulton, 'The Iraq-Kuwait Boundary', 64 *BYBIL* (1993) 135, 144–50.

[91] Provisional Measures (1992) ICJ Reports 114.

recipe for emasculation, and as we shall see in Section 3.2 below it is inconsistent with Article 103 of the UN Charter as interpreted by the ICJ, and unlikely to appeal to any international tribunal. In his classic work on the United Nations, Kelsen concluded that 'The Charter does not provide that decisions . . . in order to be enforceable must be in conformity with the law which exists at the time they are adopted.'[92]

While the precise limits on the Council's power of decision remain uncertain, and the procedures for challenging the constitutionality of its decisions are unsatisfactory,[93] it is nevertheless clear that at a minimum there must be some threat to international peace and security before the Council can take binding decisions under Chapter VII. This might justify action to restore the environment, or ensure democratic elections,[94] but it is less likely that it would cover measures designed to save the whale, or to secure education rights for indigenous peoples, for example. The next section shows that the Council's resolutions have greater legal effects than the General Assembly's but it is already clear that it can only exercise its powers within narrower limits.

3.2   UNSC Resolutions and their Relationship to International Law

Valid and binding decisions of the UNSC not only affect all states, the jurisprudence suggests that they also over-ride inconsistent international law. Customary law will necessarily yield to binding UNSC decisions, if that is the intention and if the resolution is so worded, on the straightforward basis that parties to a treaty are free to contract out of custom and will in this case have done so under Article 25 of the Charter. Furthermore, under Article 103 of the Charter a valid and binding UNSC decision will also prevail over inconsistent international agreements. This was the clear view of the ICJ in the *Lockerbie* case.[95] The Court refused an application by Libya for provisional measures on the ground that, *prima facie*, resolution 748 requiring Libya to surrender terrorist suspects for trial was binding and thus prevailed over the inconsistent provisions of the 1972 Montreal Convention for the Suppression of Unlawful Acts against the Safety of Civil Aviation. The Court left the matter open for reconsideration on the merits only in respect of the question whether resolution 748 was indeed binding. Moreover, reviewing UNSC resolutions which expressly or by implication assert priority over other treaties, Bernhardt concludes that 'the principle that binding SC decisions taken under Chapter VII supersede other treaty commitments seems to be generally recognised . . . '.[96]

[92] H. Kelsen, *The Law of the United Nations* (New York, 1950) 294–5.

[93] See the *Lockerbie Cases* Preliminary Objections (1998) ICJ Reports 9 and 115; *Namibia Advisory Opinion* (1971) ICJ Reports 16, 45, and Alvarez, 90 *AJIL* (1996) 1, 24 ff.

[94] See SC Res 687, 3 April 1991 on environmental damage in Kuwait and SC Res 940, 31 July 1994 on elections in Haiti.

[95] Provisional Measures (1992) ICJ Reports 114, paras 39 and 42. See commentary on Article 103 in Simma, *The Charter of the UN*.

[96] In Simma, ibid. See also T. Sato, in J.-M. Coicaud and V. Heiskanen, *The Legitimacy of International Organisations* (Tokyo, 2001) 309, 321–3. Article 16 of the Statute of the International

The significance of this conclusion cannot be over-estimated. Unlike any other international organisation, it gives the UNSC the power to rewrite or dispense with existing international law in particular situations, and possibly in more general terms.[97] Potentially, Security Council resolutions may thus have as great or greater significance than the concept of *jus cogens*. In effect the capacity to override other treaties and general international law amounts to a claim to formal legislative capacity. While challenges to their validity may be a tenable response, it is neither possible for states to opt out of binding UNSC resolutions, nor to formulate reservations. Nor, since they are not treaties, is it clear on what basis UNSC resolutions should be interpreted.[98] Used vigorously, and on the basis of the liberal interpretation it has given to 'peace and security', the Council could make immediate, mandatory, and enforceable changes to international law. In this respect its resolutions are very different from the soft law adopted by the General Assembly. This is not in itself an objectionable outcome and it is one which promotes coherence in international law-making; what matters more, as we saw in Chapters 1 and 3, is the legitimacy of the process, not the capacity to over-ride existing law.

4. Treaties as Law-Making Instruments

4.1 The Variety of Treaties

Treaties are necessarily the product of negotiation, and their legal force *as treaties* depends entirely on the consent of the parties, variously expressed by signature, ratification, accession or in any other agreed way. A party to a treaty is bound to comply with its terms and entitled to act in accordance with them; a non-party is not, unless the parties to the treaty intend to create rights or obligations for third states.[99] Viewed simply from the perspective of the law of treaties, therefore, treaties are a source of rights and obligations for the parties; most were never intended to be law for all states. Whether they are contracts, conveyances or constitutions, the vast majority are thus of no further significance for a work on international law-making.[100]

Paradoxically, however, much of the most important international law-making in the modern world is undertaken in treaty form. There are several good reasons for this development. As we saw in Chapters 3 and 4, both the process of negotiation and the binding character of treaties have made them the closest analogy to an international legislative instrument so far devised, even if the analogy is inexact.

Criminal Court specifically empowers the Council to over-ride the operation of the Statute for 12 months by barring investigations and prosecutions, on which see discussion of SC 1497 in Chapter 3.

[97] For examples see discussion of SC 1373 and 1540 in Chapter 3.
[98] M. Wood, 'The Interpretation of Security Council Resolutions', 2 *Max Plank UNYB* (1998) 73.
[99] See below, Section 4.3.
[100] The same can be said of nearly all memoranda of understanding whether or not they are binding treaties.

The potential for treaties to become sources of international law was acknowledged as early as 1920 in Article 38 (1) (a) of the Statute of the Permanent Court of International Justice, insofar as they establish 'rules expressly recognised by the contesting States'. The UN Charter, the 1949 Geneva Conventions on humanitarian law, the 1969 Vienna Convention on the Law of Treaties, the 1982 UN Convention on the Law of the Sea, and the 1994 WTO Agreement all illustrate such rules. Thus the idea that some treaties are 'law-making', or '*traités-lois*', is neither new nor controversial, but it poses some distinct and difficult questions that we try to address in the following sections.

It needs to be appreciated, moreover, that a treaty may be 'law-making' in several different senses. At its simplest, a treaty such as the UN Charter is effectively law for all states because it sets out important general rules, powers and principles and nearly every state is a party. Such universal participation is unusual, and the Charter is a rare example. However, as we saw in Chapter 3, there are many other multilateral treaties which, even if they do not enjoy universal participation, nevertheless create regimes which are in force and effectively law for a large number of states parties. These regimes need to evolve in response to new policies and problems, and as we shall see below there are various mechanisms for achieving this.

Even where participation is much less than universal, a multilateral treaty may nevertheless affect other states because certain provisions either confer rights on 'all states' or through practice or intent have become accepted by parties and non-parties alike as the basis of new customary law. On the other hand there are also a significant number of multilateral treaties with few parties, sometimes many years after adoption. These agreements remain 'limping' for various reasons:[101] some simply do not meet real needs; others may encounter domestic opposition; a few are merely symbolic. This does not mean that poorly supported treaties cannot influence the emergence of customary law—a point excellently illustrated by the Vienna Convention on Treaties itself—but the reasons for poor ratification may also limit their wider impact. Finally, a treaty may afford evidence of existing law, as we saw in our discussion of codification in Chapter 4.

4.2   Treaties and Customary Law

A treaty does not 'make' customary law, but like soft law it may both codify existing law and contribute to the process by which new customary law is created and develops. The process has been fully explored by the ICJ in two cases, the *North Sea Continental Shelf* case and the *Nicaragua* case. The approach taken by the court is subtly different in both cases. As we saw in Chapter 4, in the *North Sea* case the Court accepted that a normatively worded provision of a multilateral

---

[101] See generally UN, *Review of the Multilateral Treaty-Making Process*, UN Doc ST/LEG/SERB/21 (1985), and A. Aust, 'Limping Treaties: Lessons from Multilateral Treaty-Making', 50 *NILR* (2003) 243.

treaty could contribute to the formation of a new rule of customary law if the subsequent practice of a sufficiently widespread and representative selection of non-parties conformed to the treaty and there was additionally evidence of *opinio juris*.[102] In the *Nicaragua* case, the ICJ reiterated that 'the shared view of the parties as to the content of what they regard as the rule is not enough. The Court must satisfy itself that the existence of the rule in the *opinio juris* of states is con-firmed by practice.'[103] However, that practice need not be perfectly consistent nor conform rigorously in order to establish its customary status, provided inconsist-ent conduct is treated by the states concerned as a breach of the rule, not as an indication of a new rule. Attempts to justify inconsistent conduct serve, on this view, merely to confirm the rule in question. In this context only conduct amounting to an outright rejection of the alleged rule will constitute genuinely inconsistent practice. The *Nicaragua* case also recognised that the embodiment of a rule in a treaty provision (in this case the UN Charter) does not displace an exist-ing rule of customary international law or prevent its continued development.[104]

The Court's findings of law in *Nicaragua* do not rest only on the normative impact of the UN Charter. The point has already been made that the *opinio juris* of states was also evidenced by consensus adoption of comparable resolutions in the UN General Assembly. Although the Court is careful to avoid any suggestion that custom can be established simply by states declaring the law in treaties and soft law resolutions, it comes close to doing so. The only significant caveat is that there must be no *inconsistent* state practice. This reverses the approach taken in the *North Sea* case, where the Court emphasised the need for *consistent* state practice. The circumstances of the two cases are different, however. In *North Sea*, the sup-posed equidistance rule was not acceptable to a number of states, and certainly not to Germany, nor was the practice of non-parties to the treaty consistent. By con-trast, both parties in the *Nicaragua* case consistently expressed support for the same rule on the use of force, even in the face of flagrant violations. Moreover, it should not be forgotten that the United States is a party to the UN Charter, even if in the circumstances of the *Nicaragua* case the Court was precluded from applying the Charter to the dispute. Finally, the use of force in violation of international law contravenes a norm of *jus cogens*. By definition, such rules are recognised by the international community as whole. The delimitation of seabed boundaries on the basis of equidistance is not in the same category.

In the *Malta/Libya Continental Shelf* case[105] the International Court had the opportunity to consider once again the effect of a law-making treaty on the evolu-tion of customary law relating to seabed boundaries. The 1982 UNCLOS was not at that time in force, nor were Malta or Libya parties, but both had participated in its negotiation and were signatories. Both states accepted for the purposes of the litigation that 'some of its provisions constitute, to a certain extent, the expression

---

[102] (1969) ICJ Reports 3.   [103] (1986) ICJ Reports 14, para 184.
[104] Ibid, paras 174–9.   [105] (1985) ICJ Reports 13.

of customary international law in the matter'.[106] The Convention had introduced the new concept of the 200-mile exclusive economic zone (EEZ), conferring on coastal states sovereign rights over seabed minerals and living resources within that area, independently of the geographical continental shelf. The question before the Court was: what legal principles now applied to delimitation of the parties' shared continental shelf in customary law? The Court saw no difficulty in holding that the Convention had changed the law. Although neither Libya nor Malta claimed an EEZ, the practice of other states based on the Convention demonstrated that the EEZ had become part of customary law;[107] the Convention showed how the EEZ and continental shelf are inter-linked in modern international law, and the development in the customary law of the continental shelf is reflected in Articles 76 and 83.[108]

Here we can see how novel provisions of a convention negotiated using the consensus/package deal procedure discussed in Chapter 3 and adopted by 'an overwhelming majority of states'[109] are rapidly translated into law on the basis of state practice—and something more. Because of course there was no state practice on the relationship between the 200-mile EEZ and the delimitation of the continental shelf: that relationship could only be inferred from the provisions of the Convention itself. In effect, once state practice based on the Convention had endorsed the EEZ regime, the Court had to accept that consequential changes in the customary law of the continental shelf law resulted. The only basis for doing so was the Convention itself. Hence the attitude of both states to the treaty, and the general acceptability of the negotiated text, were important elements, as in the *Nicaragua* case.

What conclusions about the normative force of law-making treaties can we draw from these three cases? First, the Court had no difficulty accepting that treaties 'may have an important role in recording and defining rules deriving from custom, or indeed in developing them'.[110] Second, the cases accept that there is a law-making intention behind the negotiation of certain multilateral treaties. This can constitute evidence of *opinio juris* in favour of new general rules of international law, especially if the treaty was negotiated by consensus or has the consistent support of a large majority of states. Third, we can see that support for a treaty rule, however universal, cannot by itself create 'instant' law. Such treaties will only create new law if supported by consistent and representative state practice over a period of time. That practice can in appropriate cases consist mainly of acquiescence, or the absence of inconsistent practice. How long a time is required will depend on the circumstances. It may be very short indeed if the subsequent practice is widespread and consistent, as in the case of the exclusive economic zone, or if the treaty is a codification treaty, as we saw when considering

[106] (1985) ICJ Reports 13, para 26.
[107] See *Tunisia/Libya Continental Shelf Case* (1982) ICJ Reports, paras 47 and 100.
[108] Ibid, paras 33, 34, 77.   [109] Ibid, para 27.   [110] Ibid.

the *Gabčíkovo* case.[111] Fourth, it evidently matters little whether the treaty is in force, or widely ratified. What is most important is simply that the more widely supported the treaty text is shown to be, the easier it will be to establish its law-making effect. The longer it takes to establish consistent *opinio juris* or consistent state practice the harder it will be to establish a new rule of customary law.

This leads on to a final question: is the Court right in these cases to place so much emphasis on state practice? Could it be that the adoption of a consensus text is itself enough, or should be? Let us take another example from the 1982 UNCLOS. Article 218 gives port states express power to investigate and prosecute discharge violations wherever they have taken place. This power covers both high seas offences, and violations within the coastal zones of another state, although in the latter case the port state may only act in response to a request from the state concerned. In effect Article 218 has created a form of universal jurisdiction based on the presence of the vessel within the port.

It is, however, a novel development in the law of the sea to confer jurisdiction on port states in this way. Although the *Lotus* case did permit Turkey to prosecute a foreign vessel present in a Turkish port for an offence which had occurred on the high seas, that decision owed much to the erroneous equation of ships with floating territory, and the Court's specific conclusion regarding collisions has since been reversed by treaty.[112] Thus it cannot convincingly be asserted that the exercise of port state jurisdiction over high seas pollution offences contemplated by Article 218 (1) is based on pre-UNCLOS customary law. Only a few states are known to have implemented Article 218 (1); port state practice otherwise appears to remain within the more limited regime provided by jurisdiction over offences committed within internal waters. However, given the extensive and largely unopposed way in which port state control and jurisdiction in general have developed since 1982, and the consensus surrounding the relevant UNCLOS provisions, it may be that no state would now deny that Article 218 has become customary law.[113] The point is a simple one: once there is international consensus on the basic rule, it is highly unlikely that any state will object if it is then implemented, however rarely, in state practice. From this perspective, the practice of two states and the acquiescence of many may be enough to satisfy even the ICJ that a new form of universal jurisdiction now exists in 'customary' law. If so, then we can see why it is worthwhile to negotiate a law-making treaty by consensus, but this does not as such show that consensus alone is sufficient to create new customary rules. Some measure of

---

[111] See Chapter 4.

[112] (1927) PCIJ Series A, No. 10, 169 and cf 1952 Brussels Convention for the Unification of Certain Rules Relating to Penal Jurisdiction; 1958 High Seas Convention, Article II; 1982 UNCLOS, Article 97.

[113] Compare Judge Anderson, in Boyle and Freestone (eds), *International Law and Sustainable Development*, 343 with the more cautious views of B. Kwiatkowska, *The 200 Mile EEZ* (Dordrecht, 1989) 184 and Churchill and Lowe, *Law of the Sea*, 352–3. See generally T. McDorman, 'Port State Enforcement: A Comment on Article 218 of the 1982 Law of the Sea Convention', 28 *JMLC* (1997) 305.

implementation and acquiescence appears essential, if only to test the reality of what has been agreed. Given the sometimes ambiguous nature of consensus described in Chapter 3, any other conclusion would be problematic for states which subsequently decide not to ratify the treaty, for reasons considered in the next paragraph.

While it is clear that multilateral treaties can initiate the development of new customary international law, and in that sense some of them can be described as 'law-making', it does not follow that law which develops in this fashion will necessarily bind all states. Apart from the obvious proviso that customary law may be regional or local rather than global, certain states may also object to attempts to change the law. They may do so in the form of reservations,[114] or they may remain outside and oppose the treaty, even if they participated in its consensus negotiation— a position in which the United States frequently finds itself. Either way, if they maintain their persistent objection to new rules that emerge from a treaty, these rules will be unopposable against those states.[115] Charney argues that persistent objectors can at best maintain this position only while the status of a new rule is in doubt; they will be bound once the rule is firmly established.[116] As a matter of diplomatic reality this will be true in many cases, including those on which Charney relies, but much depends on the circumstances and the states involved. Moreover, if customary law can be local or regional in scope, there can be no inherent reason why persistent objectors cannot successfully remain bound by different rules, unless one accepts the possibility that majorities make law for minorities.[117] We return to these arguments at the end of this chapter but, as our earlier discussion shows, there is little explicit support for such a view in the case law of the ICJ.

4.3   Treaties and Third States

As the above discussion makes clear there is a synergy between treaties and customary international law whereby the former can declare, crystallise or generate new rules of custom. In Article 34 of the Vienna Convention on the Law of Treaties this situation is cast as an exception to the classic rule that treaties only bind parties and do not create rights or obligations for third parties: *pacta tertiis nec nocent nec prosunt*. This rule epitomises the requirement of consent, equates treaties to contracts under municipal law (*traité-contrat*) and denies them any autonomous law-making effect. But there are other exceptions within the Vienna Convention itself. The Convention distinguishes between rights and obligations for third parties and spells out when each may be incurred. Obligations can only be imposed if the parties so intend and the third party accepts the obligation in

---

[114] See eg *Anglo-French Continental Shelf Arbitration* (1977) 54 ILR 6.
[115] See *Fisheries Jurisdiction Case* (1974) ICJ Reports 3, 6–7, 22–35.
[116] J. Charney, 'The Persistent Objector Rule and the Development of Customary International Law', 58 *BYBIL* (1987) 1.   [117] See Charney's discussion of the literature.

writing, a requirement that in effect creates a side agreement.[118] Rights can be conferred on a third party where the parties so intend and the third party assents, not necessarily in writing. Third party assent is assumed unless there is evidence to the contrary.[119] For example, Article 38 of the 1982 UNCLOS establishes the right of transit passage for the ships and aircraft of 'all states', not merely those that are parties to the Convention. The assent of such non-parties to this right is assumed and supported by practice. This last example indicates that the classic exposition does not provide the full story today. Further analysis reveals other situations where treaties do indeed have legal consequences for non-parties:[120] various techniques have been devised and concepts evolved to avoid the adverse and restrictive consequences of the classic rule.

First, the rule that a treaty is void if it conflicts with a peremptory norm of *jus cogens*[121] makes it clear that a non-party to, for example, the Genocide Convention is nevertheless bound by its confirmation that genocide is a crime under international law. In the *Reservations* case the ICJ both affirmed the rule that a state cannot be bound by a treaty without its consent and, without using the language of *jus cogens*, considered that the 'special characteristics' of the Genocide Convention must be taken into account. The Convention represents the 'will of the General Assembly' to condemn and punish genocide and consequently the 'principles underlying the Convention are principles which are recognized by civilised nations as binding on States, even without any conventional obligation'.[122]

Second, dispositive treaties, such as those establishing a boundary or an international legal regime, create obligations *erga omnes* binding on all other states. Express words may extend rights to 'all states' (as in the transit passage cited above) or through necessary implication.[123] Article 1 of the 1959 Antarctic Treaty asserts that 'Antarctica shall be used for peaceful purposes', not that the states parties agree that they will so act. Twelve states established a regime beyond national jurisdiction in which the territorial claims of some of those states were put aside by Article 4, but not relinquished.[124] The Antarctic Treaty has been supplemented by other treaties that in turn incorporate and sustain Article 4. Although it is not the intent of the treaty to establish an objective regime of rights and obligations *erga omnes*, one commentator has concluded that 'through state practice and recognition of and acquiescence in the regime, . . . turning back to the traditional concepts of state sovereignty will become unacceptable both to the parties and to the international community'.[125]

---

[118] VCLT, Article 35.   [119] VCLT, Article 36.

[120] This section considers only third party states. For a full discussion of the effects of treaties on other third party actors see C. Chinkin, *Third Parties in International Law* (Oxford, 1993) 89–133.

[121] VCLT, Article 53.

[122] *Reservations to the Convention on the Prevention and Punishment of the Crime of Genocide* (1951) ICJ Reports 15.   [123] eg UN Charter, Article 2(6).

[124] Antarctic Treaty, Article 4.

[125] G. Triggs, *International Law: Contemporary Principles and Practices* (Chatswood, 2006), 259–60.

Closely related to dispositive treaties are those establishing communication rights, for example through international waterways. In the *SS Wimbledon*, the first case brought before it, the PCIJ noted that the Kiel Canal:

> . . . has ceased to be an internal and national navigable waterway, the use of which by the vessels of other states other than the riparian state is left entirely to the discretion of that state, and that it has become an international waterway intended to provide under treaty guarantee [Treaty of Versailles, article 380] easier access to the Baltic for the benefit of all nations of the world.[126]

Various rationales have been offered for the binding effect on third parties of treaties establishing communication routes: that they create an international servitude, third party beneficiary rights, the concept of dispositive treaties, or a theory of dependence or reliance.[127] At the core of such reasoning is a functional argument—that international waterways and similar transit routes must be maintained open for the smooth operation of international commerce and security. This contrasts with the moral-based arguments of international community values for norms of *jus cogens*, although perhaps the two are not so distinct. Where treaty parties have dedicated a particular route as 'international' and open to all states, those third party rights are not readily lost,[128] although there remains controversy over the lawfulness of, for example, the closing of the Suez Canal by Egypt in 1956 and 1967. The correct approach may be that third party rights may be lawfully suspended when necessary as part of lawful self-defence but that such closure must be judged against the criteria of necessity and proportionality and must not be discriminatory.[129]

Third, the constitutive instruments of international organisations create objective international legal personality.[130] This may be made explicit, as in Article 2 (6) of the UN Charter. This is one of the concerns of the US about the International Criminal Court (ICC): Article 12 (2) (a) of the Rome Statute provides jurisdiction when the territorial state (where the alleged offences are committed) is a party to the Statute even if the state of nationality of the accused is not. This provision would accord the ICC jurisdiction over a US national accused of war crimes, crimes against humanity or genocide in a territorial state party to the Rome Statute despite the US refusal to become a party. If one of the main concerns of the US is to ensure that American service personnel are not subject to prosecution before the ICC, remaining outside the Statute does not achieve that result. As discussed in Chapter 3, it is precisely to redress this potential situation that the US has sought bilateral agreements under Article 98 (2) of the Statute and various SC resolutions.[131]

---

[126] *SS Wimbledon (UK, France, Italy and Japan v. Germany)* (1923) PCIJ Series A, No. 1, 22.
[127] R. Baxter, *The Law of International Waterways* (Cambridge, Mass, 1964) 177–84.
[128] VCLT, Article 37 (2) states that a third party right may not be revoked by the parties if it is established that the right was intended not to be revocable without the third party's consent.
[129] Chinkin, *Third Parties in International Law*, 86.
[130] *Reparation for Injuries Suffered in the Service of the United Nations* (1949) ICJ Reports 174.
[131] SC Res 1422, 12 July 2002; SC Res 1487, 12 June 2003 and SC Res 1497, 1 August 2003.

However by undertaking these steps the US has in effect conceded the constitutive effect of the Rome Statute.

In order to promote universal acceptance and participation in such treaties, formal adherence is generally facilitated, for example by clauses that leave the way open to participation even by states that have earlier repudiated the treaty. But where a state refuses to adhere there is an obvious tension between the desire for universality and the freedom of all states to remain aloof from a treaty to which they have not consented.[132] As we discussed in Chapter 1, this tension can generate broad claims of customary international law that are divorced from empirical evidence of state practice and *opinio juris*. It is to ameliorate such tensions and to avoid the formalities of the third party rule and the traditional approach to the creation of customary international law that Jonathan Charney advocated a universal international law 'binding on all subjects regardless of the attitude of any particular state'.[133] Such general international law would be generated through international institutions 'established on less formal indications of consent or acquiescence'.[134] Although there is considerable flexibility in treaty-making and interpretation, such visionary approaches to law-making remain as yet unaccepted. We return to this point in the conclusions to this chapter.

4.4 Treaties as Evolving Regimes

Despite their importance as modern instruments of international law-making, treaties have the obvious disadvantage that, like all written law, they will become obsolete unless some mechanisms exist to ensure the possibility of subsequent modification and evolution. Some treaties, frequently described as framework or 'umbrella' treaties, are specifically designed to facilitate further development through the addition of protocols, annexes or additional agreements.[135] We saw in Chapter 3 how international organisations and conferences of the parties to many multilateral treaties can act as law-making bodies for this purpose. These bodies can determine how such treaties are to be interpreted, they can adopt amendments or additional protocols, or they may add further treaties, creating an increasingly complex regime that does not necessarily apply in full between all the parties to the original treaty. In this section we therefore consider some of the problems that can arise when these techniques are employed. Moreover, treaties do not exist in isolation. The larger question which must also be considered in the subsequent sections is how different law-making treaties interact. This is one of

---

[132] See Chapter 1.   [133] J. Charney, 'Universal International Law', 87 *AJIL* (1993) 529.
[134] Ibid 551.
[135] For example the 1973/78 MARPOL Convention, the 1985 Ozone Convention and the 1992 Climate Change Convention all provide for the adoption of annexes and protocols containing more detailed rules. The 1982 UNCLOS is not a framework agreement in this sense, but it does envisage further elaboration in other ways: see A. E. Boyle, 'Further Development of the 1982 Law of the Sea Convention: Mechanisms for Change', 54 *ICLQ* (2005) 563–84.

the most difficult and frequently debated issues in contemporary international law-making and one we return to in Chapter 6.

4.4.1   Amendment

The most obvious way of keeping a treaty up to date is through formal amendment. Most multilateral treaties make some provision for amendment, usually exercisable by qualified majority vote, or sometimes by unanimity or consensus, subject to subsequent ratification by states parties. Amendments to annexes often take effect for all states save those which specifically object within a specified time.[136] Article 40 of the Vienna Convention provides a residual procedure to be followed.[137] The most important point is that all parties have the right to participate in the process and to become parties to the amendment. For example the Convention on the Elimination of Discrimination against Women allows any state party to make a request for revision of the Convention to the UN Secretary-General.[138] The General Assembly then decides upon the steps to be taken. It has in this way amended Article 20 (1) by providing for longer meeting sessions than originally stipulated. Another process for amendment is through a Conference of States Parties, usually on the initiative of a state party. The form in which this is done varies. In some cases existing articles of a treaty are simply amended by decision of the parties; in others a protocol of amendment may be adopted, while in a few cases a new treaty is adopted by protocol, completely replacing the earlier text on entry into force.[139]

Formal amendments are in practice easier to adopt when treaties are administered by international organisations or when there is a conference of the parties that meets regularly. Otherwise it becomes necessary to convene a special conference. Two problems can then arise. The first is political: once one state proposes an amendment, others may follow, and the outcome of any negotiating conference becomes inherently unpredictable. One of the principal reasons why amendments to the UN Charter are much discussed but rarely proposed is the risk that the existing *modus vivendi* would unravel in the bargaining between states that would be necessary to secure adoption and ratification by two-thirds of the General Assembly and all of the permanent members of the Security Council. In its first 60 years the only successful amendments of the Charter merely increased the size of the Security Council and ECOSOC.

Amendment of the 1982 UNCLOS has proved even less attractive to states parties. Amendments proposed at a negotiating conference can be adopted by vote when all efforts to reach consensus have failed,[140] but once such a conference is

---

[136] See eg the 1972 London Dumping Convention, Article 14. The Convention was extensively amended in 1993 and a new convention adopted in 1996.

[137] For ILC commentary see Watts, *The ILC*, vol II, 708–15.   [138] Article 26.

[139] Compare for example the 1978 Protocol amending the 1973 Convention for the Prevention of Marine Pollution from Ships prior to the latter's entry into force; the 1996 Protocol amending and replacing the 1972 London Dumping Convention; the 1997 Protocol replacing the 1963 Vienna Convention on Civil Liability for Nuclear Damage.   [140] Article 312.

convened there is again no means of controlling what other amendments are put forward. A simplified procedure provided for in Article 313 eliminates this risk by dispensing with the need for a negotiating conference. Non-objection will secure adoption of an amendment, but it only takes one objection for the procedure to fail. A further drawback is that only the treaty parties can initiate amendment procedures. The non-parties, including the United States, would have no vote in such procedures, yet their participation in UN discussions on law of the sea shows their continuing interest in further development of the Convention and related agreements. In practice, therefore, the main amendments and additions to the corpus of UNCLOS law have come through 'implementing' agreements, notably the 1994 Agreement Relating to Part XI,[141] and the 1995 UN Fish Stocks Agreement,[142] deliberately negotiated in this form in order to permit non-party participation and avoid resort to 'amendment' of the Convention. Nevertheless, the 1994 Agreement on Part XI disapplies certain provisions of Part XI and revises others. It also prevails over inconsistent provisions of the Convention. Non-parties are assumed to have acquiesced in the changes made to the Convention. While the UNCLOS amendment procedures thus remain unused, it seems clear that UNCLOS has in fact been amended by the 1994 Agreement and quite possibly by other agreements.

The second problem is constitutional. Although adopted by the parties or a majority of them, amendments typically enter into force only for ratifying states. In the absence of contrary intention, this is the residual rule in Article 40 of the Vienna Convention. Inertia will inevitably result in some states failing to ratify amendments, even if they are not otherwise opposed. The treaty will then be amended for some states, but not for others, and the result will be an awkward and overlapping network of old and new obligations between different sets of parties. One of the better examples of the confusion which can ensue is the 1929 Warsaw Convention Relating to International Carriage by Air.[143] Problems may also arise in determining the relationship between the main treaty and the Protocol. For example the US has ratified both Optional Protocols to the Convention on the Rights of the Child without becoming a party to the original Convention. Does this entail any of the rights or obligations of the main Convention? The US must report to the Committee on the Rights of the Child on its steps to implement each Protocol.[144] Might this mean that the US could claim to nominate a member to

---

[141] See D. H. Anderson, 'Further Efforts to Ensure Universal Participation in the UNCLOS', 43 *ICLQ* (1994) 886; J. Charney, 'Entry into Force of the 1982 UNCLOS', 35 *VJIL* (1995) 381.

[142] See D. H. Anderson, 'The Straddling Fish Stocks Agreement of 1995—An Initial Assessment', 45 *ICLQ* (1996) 463; D. Balton, 'Strengthening the Law of the Sea: The New Agreement on Straddling Fish Stocks and Highly Migratory Fish Stocks', 27 *ODIL* (1996) 125.

[143] See R. Gardiner, 'Revising the Law of Carriage by Air: Mechanisms in Treaties and Contract', 47 *ICLQ* (1998) 278.

[144] Optional Protocol to the Convention on the Rights of the Child on the Involvement of Children in Armed Conflicts, Article 8; Optional Protocol to the Convention on the Rights of the Child on the Sale of Children 2000, Child Prostitution and Child Pornography 2000, Article 12.

the Committee on the Rights of the Child and to participate in the elections in accordance with Article 43 of the Convention (which is not referred to in the Protocols), or could the Committee require the US to include wider information than that required by the Protocols? The better view would seem that the US is not bound by any articles of the Convention, although this seems artificial in light of the expressed relationship between the two.

Exceptionally, some treaties, of which the UN Charter is the leading example,[145] can be amended for all member states if the amendment is adopted and ratified by the necessary majority. This at least avoids the difficulty of asymmetric participation. One method of eliminating the need for ratification of amendments altogether is for the parties to adopt the necessary text by consensus in the form of a resolution interpreting the treaty. As we saw earlier in our discussion of soft law, a treaty must be interpreted in accordance with such agreements.[146] Whether this will be sufficient to ensure *de facto* amendment will depend on what is proposed; moreover, it may be impermissible to use a resolution of the parties for this purpose if the amendment provisions of the treaty are thereby undermined.[147] A few treaties make specific provision for such resolutions to be adopted by majority vote.[148] The 'Elements of Crimes' adopted by states parties under Article 9 of the Statute of the International Criminal Court (ICC) can be amended by a two-thirds majority vote of the parties without requiring either an amendment of the Statute or ratification by the parties. Once adopted, however, the elements, or any amendment of them, become immediately applicable *as law* by the Court.[149]

4.4.2 Evolutionary Interpretation

One of the most important approaches to the integration of different bodies of law is based on techniques of interpretation, taking account of one treaty or legal norm in order to assist in the interpretation or application of another treaty or norm. Interpretative techniques may help to avoid conflicts between agreed norms, and save negotiated agreements from premature obsolescence, or the need for constant amendment. Changing social values can be reflected in the jurisprudence, a point particularly well observed in international human rights law. The European Court of Human Rights has consistently held that 'the Convention is a living instrument which . . . must be interpreted in the light of present-day conditions'.[150] Changes in international law can also be accommodated where appropriate. Article 31 (3) (c) of the Vienna Convention accordingly provides that in interpreting a treaty account shall be taken of 'any relevant rules of international law applicable in the relations between the parties'.[151] This notably Delphic formulation conceals more

---

[145] UN Charter, Articles 108–9.   [146] VCLT, Article 30 (3) (a). See above, Section 2.
[147] See eg 1994 WTO Agreement, Article IX (2), last sentence.
[148] eg 1994 WTO Agreement, Article IX (2).   [149] ICC Statute, Article 21 (1) (a).
[150] See eg *Soering v. UK* (1989) 11 EHRR 439, para 102, and Chapter 6.
[151] See eg *Loizidou v. Turkey* (Merits) (1996) ECHR Reports VI, paras 43–5 (invalidity of acts of unrecognised states); C. McLachlan, 'The Principle of Systemic Integration and Article 31(3)(c) of

than it reveals, and it is currently the subject of further study by the ILC. How far, if at all, might reinterpretation of a law-making treaty be possible under this provision?

The terms within which 'evolutionary interpretation' is permissible under Article 31 (3) (c) have been narrowly circumscribed in the jurisprudence, and over-ambitious attempts to reinterpret or 'cross-fertilise' treaties by reference to later treaties or other rules of international law have had only limited success.[152] Nevertheless, while accepting 'the primary necessity of interpreting an instrument in accordance with the intentions of the parties *at the time of its conclusion*' (emphasis added), the ICJ has acknowledged that treaties are to be 'interpreted and applied within the framework of the entire legal system prevailing at the time of the interpretation'.[153] Thus, its approach in cases such as the *Namibia Advisory Opinion* and the *Aegean Sea* is based on the view that the concepts and terms in question 'were by definition evolutionary',[154] not on some broader conception applicable to all treaties. The WTO Appellate Body has given a similarly evolutionary interpretation to certain terms in the 1947 GATT Agreement. In the *Shrimp-Turtle* decision, for example, it referred *inter alia* to the 1992 Rio Declaration on Environment and Development, the 1982 UNCLOS, the 1973 CITES Convention, the 1979 Convention on Conservation of Migratory Species and the 1992 Convention on Biological Diversity in order to determine the present meaning of 'exhaustible natural resources'.[155]

In all of these cases the question at issue was not general revision or reinterpretation of the treaty. Rather, each case was concerned with the interpretation of particular provisions or phrases, such as 'natural resources', or 'jurisdiction', which necessarily import—or at least suggest—a reference to current general international law. Ambulatory incorporation of the existing law, whatever it may be, enables treaty provisions to change and develop as the general law itself changes, without the need for any amendment. As the ICJ points out in the *Oil Platforms* case, such treaty provisions are not intended to operate independently of general international law.[156]

---

the Vienna Convention', 54 *ICLQ* (2005) 279; D. French, 'Treaty Interpretation and the Incorporation of Extraneous Legal Rules', 55 *ICLQ* (2006) 281.

[152] eg Ireland's unsuccessful attempt to rewrite UNCLOS in the *Mox Plant Arbitration* (PCA, 2002). For a contrary view see Sands, in Boyle and Freestone, *International Law and Sustainable Development*, 39.

[153] *Namibia Advisory Opinion* (1971) ICJ Reports 16, 31; *Aegean Sea Continental Shelf Case* (1978) ICJ Reports 3, 32–3. See also *Bankovic v. Belgium* (2002) 41 ILM 517, paras 55–66; *Al-Adsani v. UK* (2001) 123 ILR 24; *Fogarty v. UK* (2001) 123 ILR 54; *Mc Elhinney v. Ireland* (2001) 123 ILR 73. The ICJ's approach, combining both an evolutionary and an intertemporal element, reflects the ILC's commentary to what became Article 31 (3) (c). See ILC, 'The Law of Treaties', commentary to draft Article 27, para (16), in A. D. Watts (ed), *The ILC 1949–1998* (Oxford, 1999), vol II, 690.

[154] See also *Oil Platforms Case* (2003) ICJ Reports 161, paras 40–1; *La Bretagne Arbitration* (Canada/France) (1986) 82 ILR 591, paras 37–51.

[155] *Import Prohibition of Certain Shrimp and Shrimp Products*, WTO Appellate Body (1998) WT/DS58/AB/R, paras 130–1.

[156] (2003) ICJ Reports 161, paras 40–1. See also *Gabčíkovo-Nagymaros Case* (1997) ICJ Reports 7, paras 140–1.

Evolutionary interpretation is thus a relatively limited task, usually justified by reference to the intention of the parties. It does not entitle a court or tribunal to engage in a process of constant revision or updating every time a newer treaty is concluded that relates to similar matters.[157] On this view, interpretation is interpretation, not amendment or rewriting of treaties. The result must remain faithful to the ordinary meaning and context of the treaty, 'in the light of its object and purpose'.[158]

Whether another treaty is regarded as an agreement on interpretation, or as a guide to the interpretation of inherently evolutionary provisions, or simply as evidence of a common understanding of comparable provisions, the level of participation cannot be ignored. Some authors read Article 31 (3) (c) as referring only to rules applicable between all the parties to a treaty *dispute*, rather than all the parties to a treaty. Apart from being inconsistent with the ILC commentary to Article 31 (3), this interpretation leaves unanswered the question how the article should be applied in other contexts, for example by treaty COPs, the UN, or foreign ministries, and risks a serious Balkanisation of global treaties implemented by regional agreements. It is true that under many treaties individual states are free to agree alternative interpretations *inter se*, within the terms of VCLT Article 41.[159] However, where there is a clear need for uniform interpretation, given the express terms of Article 31 (3) and the ILC commentary thereto the stronger argument is that a treaty cannot realistically be regarded as an agreement on interpretation or as a 'relevant rule applicable in relations between the parties' unless it has the consensus support of all the parties, or there is no objection.[160] This does not mean that all the parties to one treaty would have to be party to the other treaty. The 1994 Agreement on the Implementation of UNCLOS is assumed to be effective on the basis that non-parties have tacitly consented to or acquiesced in the revision of UNCLOS. Alternatively, a treaty rule may also be binding in customary international law, and become applicable on that basis. Thus in *Shrimp-Turtle* the WTO Appellate Body noted that although not a party to UNCLOS, the US did accept the relevant provisions as customary law. These are significant qualifications to the ILC's general principle regarding universality.

An agreement lacking general support will no longer fall strictly within the obligatory terms of Article 31 (3) (a) or (c), and its persuasive force as a basis for evolutionary interpretation will necessarily be weaker the fewer parties there are. In the

---

[157] *Gabčíkovo-Nagymaros Case*, Judge Bedjaoui sep op, para 12. See also *SW Africa Case* (1966) ICJ Reports 3, 48.

[158] VCLT, Article 31 (1). See also *OSPAR Arbitration* (PCA, 2003) paras 101–5.

[159] See eg L. Bartels, 'Article XX of GATT and the Problem of Extraterritorial Jurisdiction', 36 *JWT* (2002) 353, 361, and see the next section.

[160] ILC commentary in Watts, *The ILC*, vol II, 688–9. The arguments are reviewed extensively by J. Pauwelyn, 'The Role of Public International Law in the WTO: How Far Can We Go?', 95 *AJIL* (2001) 535, 575–6; McLachlan, 54 *ICLQ* (2005) 279, 315, para 16 (but note his qualifications at para 17); French, 55 *ICLQ* (2006) 300–7.

OSPAR Arbitration the arbitrators declined even to take into account a convention which was not in force, and which Ireland had not ratified, although the better view is probably that of Griffith, who notes that such an agreement may nevertheless provide some guidance.[161] In practice much will depend on whether other non-parties acquiesce or not, and on the issue in dispute. In *Shrimp-Turtle* the United States did not object to the Appellate Body taking the Biological Diversity Convention into account. It is difficult to see how any tribunal could do otherwise, given the almost universal participation by other states in this treaty.

4.4.3 Incorporation by Reference

Some treaties avoid the need for frequent amendment or reinterpretation by referring in general terms to standards set by other treaties or soft law instruments. As these standards change, so in effect does the principal treaty. We saw above how the Nuclear Safety Convention makes use of this technique to incorporate IAEA soft law standards.[162] The 1982 UNCLOS similarly makes reference to 'generally accepted international rules and standards' established by international organisations such as IMO and IAEA. The essential point in these cases is that states must give effect to or apply rules and standards no less onerous than 'generally recognised international rules and standards'. Although not all writers are agreed on the correct interpretation, the importance of Articles 208, 210 and 211 of the 1982 Convention seems to be that they have the effect of incorporating into the terms of UNCLOS the current pollution control requirements agreed and adopted by a preponderance of maritime states under the 1973/78 MARPOL Convention, the 1974 SOLAS Convention, and in IMO and IAEA codes and guidelines, *inter alia*.[163] States parties to the 1982 UNCLOS may thus be compelled to adopt the standards set by the above treaties, as they evolve and even if they are not parties to them.[164] Moreover, the same standards will also define the content of customary international law based on the relevant provisions of UNCLOS, such as jurisdiction to regulate pollution in the exclusive economic zone.[165] The 1994 Nuclear Safety Convention and the 1982 UNCLOS can thus promote universal application of current rules and standards agreed in the relevant international organisations without the need for amendment. This has proved to be a highly effective regulatory technique.

---

[161] *OSPAR Arbitration* (PCA, 2003), paras 101–5.   [162] Section 2 (4).

[163] A. E. Boyle, 'Marine Pollution under the Law of the Sea Convention', 79 *AJIL* (1985) 347. On the variety of meanings attributed to the phrase 'generally accepted', see B. Vukas, in A. H. Soons (ed), *Implementation of the Law of the Sea Convention through International Institutions* (Honolulu, 1990) 405; E. Molenaar, *Coastal State Jurisdiction over Vessel-Source Pollution* (The Hague, 1998), chapter 5; P. Birnie, in H. Ringbom (ed), *Competing Norms in the Law of Marine Environmental Protection* (The Hague, 1997), 31.   [164] G. Handl, in Ringbom, *Competing Norms*, 217–40.

[165] 1982 UNCLOS, Article 211. See P. Birnie and A. E. Boyle, *International Law and the Environment*, chapter 7.

4.5   Treaty Relations in Theory: Successive Treaties and *Lex Specialis*

In our discussion of regulatory and framework treaties, we have seen that the adoption of successive treaties, protocols and related instruments on the same subject is an increasingly common phenomenon. Moreover, even treaties not directly related in this sense may nevertheless overlap or affect the same issue. As we shall see in the next section, it is not possible, for example, to discuss the law relating to the marine environment without taking into account both the 1982 UNCLOS and the 1992 Convention on Biological Diversity. Whenever states adopt successive or related agreements the question necessarily arises how these inter-relate, especially if they contain no express provision on the matter, or if their parties differ, as will often be the case. Interpretation can only take the systematic integration of such treaties so far, and it cannot readily deal with genuine conflicts. It then becomes necessary to consider what other rules may govern the inter-relationship of treaties. How treaties inter-relate cannot be determined in any *a priori* sense. In general international law the relationship between successive treaties is partly governed by the intention of the parties, partly determined by the nature of the treaty, partly regulated by the relationship between special and general rules, partly determined by residual rules based on the time of conclusion of incompatible treaties, and partly dictated by operation of law.[166] A regime of such complexity is not well suited to ensuring a coherent integration.

Moreover, given the diversity of law-making institutions, and the varying participation by states in all such treaties, a measure of incoherence and uncertainty in the relationship between specific treaties may be inevitable. The relationship between any two agreements may not be policy-driven or reflect any particular appreciation of priorities on the part of the negotiators. Two treaties which are the result of a different 'legislature'—to use Pauwelyn's description—will also be 'the reflection of a different balance of interests and one state may well have been able to push through its interests more under one treaty than under another'.[167] It is therefore necessary to consider how international law presently caters for such situations.

4.5.1   Replacing an Earlier Treaty

It is always open to the parties to an earlier treaty to replace it by a new one.[168] This may be done expressly, as for instance when one treaty 'supersedes', 'replaces' or is 'successor to' another. Under Article 59 of the Vienna Convention an earlier treaty

---

[166] 1969 VCLT, Articles 30, 41, 53. See J. Pauwelyn, *Conflict of Norms in Public International Law* (Cambridge, 2003), chapters 6 and 7; A. Aust, *Modern Treaty Law and Practice* (Cambridge, 2000), chapter 12; W. Czaplinski and G. Danilenko, 'Conflict of Norms in International Law', 21 *NYBIL* (1990) 3; C. W. Jenks, 'The Conflict of Law-Making Treaties', 30 *BYBIL* (1953) 401.

[167] *Conflict of Norms*, 369. For an example see the discussion of FAO in Chapter 3.

[168] 1969 VCLT, Article 59. See Watts, *The ILC*, vol II, 751–2; I. Sinclair, *The Vienna Convention on the Law of Treaties* (2nd edn, Manchester, 1984), 181–5.

will also terminate if its terms are so far incompatible 'that the two treaties are not capable of being applied at the same time', or if the intention to terminate can be otherwise implied.[169] Even a clause in the earlier treaty specifically prohibiting later inconsistent treaties will normally be ineffective to prevent termination because the parties 'are fully competent to abrogate or modify the earlier treaty which they themselves drew up'.[170] The earlier treaty will normally terminate on entry into force of the new agreement, as between the states which at that point are parties to the later one. Non-participation in the later agreement by some states can, however, leave the older treaty with a 'limping' existence. The 1954 Convention for the Prevention of Pollution of the Sea by Oil retains a ghostly existence for a small number of parties with little or no shipping industry and no incentive to become parties to the successor agreement concluded in 1973 by IMO. Some treaties require parties to denounce the older treaty once enough states have become bound by its replacement.[171]

4.5.2   *Preserving an Earlier Treaty*

The parties may wish to leave earlier agreements unaffected in whole or in part, and it is open to them to do so.[172] Thus where the later treaty is 'subject to', or 'without prejudice to', or 'does not derogate from', or 'does not impair', or is 'not incompatible with' an earlier agreement, that agreement will prevail should any apparent conflict arise. This is essentially a matter of interpretation, and to avoid doubt it is better regulated expressly. In some cases it may be enough to indicate that the later agreement 'supplements' earlier treaties.[173] Other treaties are more explicit. Article 4 of the 1991 Antarctic Protocol on Environmental Protection provides:

1. This protocol shall supplement the Antarctic Treaty and shall neither modify nor amend that treaty.
2. Nothing in this protocol shall derogate from the rights and obligations of the Parties under other international instruments in force within the Antarctic Treaty system.

Clearly, the effect of Article 4 is that this protocol does not directly modify any earlier agreement. The next article nevertheless recognises that there may be some inconsistency with earlier agreements, but the parties agree to regulate this through further consultation and cooperation. Similarly, the 1997 UN Convention on International Watercourses does not alter existing agreements, such as those governing the Nile or the Amazon, nor does it require that future watercourse agreements be

---

[169] In the *Free Zones Case* (1932) PCIJ Series A/B, No. 46 the contention that the 1919 Treaty of Versailles had impliedly terminated relevant provisions of earlier treaties was considered but rejected.
[170] ILC Commentary, in Watts, *The ILC*, 677, para 7. But see discussion of VCLT, Article 41 below.
[171] See eg the 1992 Protocol to the 1971 Convention on the Establishment of an International Fund for Compensation for Oil Pollution Damage, Article 31.
[172] 1969 VCLT, Article 30 (2).   [173] eg 1977 Protocol I to the 1949 Geneva Conventions.

consistent with its basic principles. Instead Article 3 allows parties to later agreements to 'apply and adjust' the provisions of the Convention to the characteristics and uses of specific watercourses. The 1997 Convention is thus an optional framework code or 'guideline' whose provisions are not only subject to reservation, but may be departed from *ad hoc*. This approach does no more than recognise the normal freedom of states when negotiating specific bilateral or regional agreements to depart *inter se* from the general rules of international law on the subject. The point of such a codification treaty is not to over-ride that freedom, but simply to provide some certainty about the law applicable in situations where the parties have been unable to reach an *inter se* agreement.

4.5.3   Priority in Time

Priority in time is potentially relevant to the relationship between treaties, but it is simplistic and fallacious to assume that in the absence of contrary wording a later treaty will necessarily prevail over an earlier one. True, Article 30 (3) of the 1969 Vienna Convention provides that, when not terminated under Article 59, 'the earlier treaty applies only to the extent that its provisions are compatible with those of the later treaty'. However, it would be unwise to take this wording at face value. In reality, the matter is more complex and open to various approaches, for several reasons. First, it not always clear when one treaty pre-dates another. Does the date of adoption, or entry into force, or entry into force for the relevant parties determine the timing of a treaty for the purposes of Article 30?[174] States become parties to multilateral treaties at different times: is it possible that the same treaty may be an earlier treaty for one state and a later one for another? For example, for a state party to the 1982 UNCLOS at the date of its entry into force (November 1994), the 1994 WTO Agreement is a later treaty whether the date of adoption or entry into force is decisive.[175] But for a state becoming a party to UNCLOS after ratification and entry into force of the WTO Agreement, UNCLOS could arguably be the later treaty since only on becoming a party does a potential conflict arise *for that state*. Moreover, what is the effect of frequent amendments, or the addition of new protocols or implementing agreements, to evolving treaties such as UNCLOS or various multilateral environmental agreements? As several commentators have pointed out, 'in certain circumstances, given the character of modern treaty-making, it will often be difficult to define two conflicting treaties as "successive in time" '.[176] In many of these situations it is difficult to identify any principled reason why the date of adoption of one instrument should be decisive in determining the applicable treaty provision. The intent of the parties is probably not a plausible justification, even assuming they had the same intentions.[177] These

---

[174] See E. Vierdag, 'The Time of Conclusion of a Multilateral Treaty: Article 30 of the VCLT and Related Provisions', 59 *BYBIL* (1988) 75; Pauwelyn, *Conflict of Norms*, 367–84.

[175] Adopted 15 April 1994; in force 1 January 1995.

[176] Pauwelyn, *Conflict of Norms*, 378–80. See also Sinclair, *The Vienna Convention*, 98, and Vierdag, 59 *BYBIL* (1988) 75.   [177] Pauwelyn, *Conflict of Norms*, 368–70.

problems illustrate the unsatisfactory nature of Article 30. Fortunately, Article 30 is a residual rule, easily avoided by express or implied terms, and further limited in its operation by other provisions, including Articles 41 and 58, considered below.

Moreover, on its own terms Article 30 applies only to successive treaties 'relating to the same subject matter'. What this means has never been authoritatively addressed, except by scholars. It does *not* mean that Article 30 only applies between treaties dealing with law of the sea, for example, but not to the relationship between, say, the 1982 UNCLOS and the 1994 GATT Agreement. As we note below, it is possible for such different agreements to conflict and to that extent they necessarily relate to the same subject matter.[178] The most widely expressed view is that cases of genuine conflict to which Article 30 applies must be distinguished from the relationship between treaty provisions of a general character and more specific ones. A *lex specialis* will normally apply in preference to a *lex generalis*, unless the negotiating history or context suggest otherwise.[179] Reuter thus notes that: 'The rule of article 30 would therefore only apply to treaties with subject matters of a comparable degree of "generality".'[180] On this view priority in time ceases to be relevant when dealing with the relationship between a *lex specialis* and a more general rule. The point can be illustrated hypothetically by contrasting an earlier treaty providing that territorial sea boundaries shall be delimited by equidistance with a later treaty providing for maritime boundaries to be delimited by agreement in accordance with international law. In the absence of any contrary wording the later treaty would not prevail despite Article 30 because its general terms are not intended by the parties to over-ride the more specific rule of the earlier treaty. Here, the two provisions do not address the same issue. Article 30 never comes into play.

This is an important conclusion. If correct, it means, for example, that Article 30 will not operate to give general WTO trade rules adopted in 1994 priority as treaty law over earlier more specific trade restrictions in the 1973 Convention on International Trade in Endangered Species or the 1989 Basel Convention on the Control of Transboundary Movement of Hazardous Wastes. If that had been the intention of the WTO negotiators in 1994 they should have said so expressly. The issue is thus primarily one of interpretation rather than precedence.[181] As Pauwelyn points out, this approach has implicit support from the ICJ's *Advisory Opinion on the Legality of the Threat or Use of Nuclear Weapons Case*, where the Court found that environmental treaties and customary rules of a later but more general character did not displace specific treaty rules on the use of force and

---

[178] Ibid 364 and references there cited.

[179] *Mavrommatis Palestine Concessions, Jurisdiction* (1924) PCIJ Series A No. 2, 30–1; *Iran-US Case A/2* (1981) I *Iran-US CTR* 101, 104. See below.

[180] P. Reuter, *Introduction to the Law of Treaties* (London, 1995) 132, para 201. See also Aust, *Modern Treaty Law and Practice*, 183; Sinclair, *The Vienna Convention*, 96–8; P. Daillier and A. Pellet, *Droit International Public* (7th edn, Paris, 2002) 271. A few writers disagree and would continue to apply the *lex specialis* only where it is later in time or where Article 30 is otherwise inapplicable: Pauwelyn, *Conflict of Norms*, 364–6 and 406–9.   [181] Sinclair, *Vienna Convention*, 96.

international humanitarian law.[182] It did not refer to Article 30 or to rules on the precedence of later treaties. Given all the problems with a priority in time rule, it seems unlikely that any international tribunal would choose to base its decision in a contentious case solely on that element of Article 30. There will almost always be better ways of deciding cases on a basis that more closely accords with the intention of the parties and the interpretation of treaties in good faith.

4.5.4   Lex Specialis

Lex specialis is one of the concepts more frequently employed by international courts to explain the relationship between one body of law and another, or one rule and another. As we saw above it avoids the appearance of conflict or hierarchy by focusing on the more specific rule as the governing or decisive norm.[183] A rule may be 'special' in various ways, either because it is more specific in its wording, or because it applies between a limited group of states.[184] This does not necessarily mean that other more general rules are excluded or trumped, although that may be the result, as for example between parties to a bilateral or regional trade treaty, or where a treaty creates its own self-contained regime of remedies.[185] More often it enables a court to locate a specific rule or body of law within a broader set of rules whose content will influence the interpretation and application of the *lex specialis*.[186] As the ILC report notes, 'preference was often given to a special standard because it not only best reflects the requirements of the context, but because it best reflected the intent of those who were to be bound by it'.[187] From this perspective the *lex specialis* doctrine is essentially a technique for interpreting and applying treaties, although the determination that one rule rather than another has a more specific character is not necessarily free from doubt, and the resulting choice may indeed have the appearance of giving priority to one body of law over another on policy grounds. To that extent it can also be seen as a conflict-resolving device.

These points can all be observed in the *Advisory Opinion on the Legality of the Threat or Use of Nuclear Weapons*.[188] Here the ICJ was faced with a case in which treaties and customary law relating to the use of force, international humanitarian law, human rights law and international environmental law were relied on by

---

[182]   Pauwelyn, *Conflict of Norms*, 408. See below.
[183]   *Mavrommatis Palestine Concessions* (1924) PCIJ Series A, No. 2, 31.
[184]   ILC, *Report of the Study Group on Fragmentation of International Law*, A/CN4/L663/Rev 1 (2004), para 9.
[185]   See eg *Tehran Hostages Case* (1980) ICJ Reports 3, para 86, where the Vienna Convention on Diplomatic Relations excluded certain remedies available under general international law.
[186]   *Gabčíkovo-Nagymaros* (1997) ICJ Reports 7, para 132; *Amoco International Finance Corp. v. Iran* (1987) US-Iran CTR 189, para 112; *Ambatielos, Preliminary Objections* (1952) ICJ Reports 28, 44; *Southern Bluefin Tuna Arbitration* (2000) 39 ILM 1359, para 52. See generally Pauwelyn, *Conflict of Norms*, 385–416.   [187]   *Report of the Study Group* (2004), para 12.
[188]   (1996) ICJ Reports 226.

various parties to the proceedings. The court did not try to decide the case on the basis that any of these bodies of law were inapplicable or took priority over any other; it accepted that in the appropriate context the use of nuclear weapons might engage some or all of the rules in question. Thus human rights law continued to apply in wartime, but 'the test of what is an arbitrary deprivation of life . . . falls to be determined by the applicable *lex specialis*, namely the law applicable in armed conflict which is designed to regulate the conduct of hostilities'.[189] Similarly, environmental obligations continued to apply during an armed conflict and were relevant to assessing whether a particular use of force was necessary and proportionate but, in the Court's view, environmental treaties 'could not have been intended to deprive a State of the exercise of its right of self-defence'.[190] On the general question of the legality of nuclear weapons the Court concluded that 'the most directly relevant applicable law governing the question of which it was seised, is that relating to the use of force enshrined in the United Nations Charter and the law applicable in armed conflict which regulates the conduct of hostilities, together with any specific treaties on nuclear weapons . . . '.[191] Given the generality of the question the Court was asked, this looks like the only plausible answer, but it also shows that what constitutes the relevant *lex specialis* may depend on the focus of the question.

4.5.5 *Third Party Rights*

There is no general rule invalidating a treaty simply because it is inconsistent with an earlier treaty commitment to third states. The ILC had considered the desirability of such a rule, but cautiously concluded against it, mainly on the ground that many law-making treaties are revised by later agreements but only rarely are the parties the same in both cases.[192] Article 30 (4) (b) of the Vienna Convention on the Law of Treaties thus provides that 'as between a State Party to both treaties and a State Party to only one of the treaties, the treaty to which both States are parties governs their mutual rights and obligations'. What this means in practice is that states may conclude later agreements with other parties, but they cannot thereby relieve themselves of their earlier treaty commitments to states which have not become parties to the later treaty. Third party rights cannot be abrogated in this way, as we saw earlier. If the state which has concluded two incompatible agreements cannot then comply with or implement both of them, it may become necessary to choose which one to breach, with whatever consequences flow from such a wrongful act.[193] Some treaties for this reason have a savings clause for existing treaty obligations to third parties. Others seek to ameliorate the problem by

---

[189] Ibid, para 25.   [190] Ibid, para 30.   [191] Ibid, para 34.

[192] *Report of the ILC* (1964) II YBILC, 189–92, paras 14–17.

[193] Article 30 (5) leaves open the possibility of termination for breach and responsibility for breach of treaty. See ILC, Commentary, in Watts, *The ILC*, vol II, 676, para 6.

providing that earlier agreements must be implemented in a manner consistent with the later agreement.[194] This formulation may in some cases enable a state party to fulfil its obligations under both agreements.

A few treaties go further, however, by expressly seeking to regulate the conclusion of future agreements on the same subject matter. Given the general rule in Article 30 of priority for later treaties, and the ability of all the parties to terminate or modify an earlier treaty, the question arises whether such attempts at regulation are effective. The important point is that unless all parties to the first treaty also participate in the second, concluding a later treaty in breach of an earlier prohibition will be an illegal act *vis-à-vis* those states which remain parties only to the earlier agreement. Although the later treaty will not normally be invalid, it can be applied and enforced only between its own parties.[195]

But what if the later treaty also affects enjoyment of the rights and obligations of other parties to the earlier treaty, or defeats the object and purpose of that treaty? In this case a stronger argument can be made for refusing to allow the later treaty to be applied or enforced at all. Article 41 of the Vienna Convention provides in part that *inter se* modification of an earlier multilateral treaty is permissible provided the modification neither affects third party rights or obligations, nor 'relates to a provision derogation from which is incompatible with the effective execution of the object and purpose of the treaty as a whole'. The point here is that some treaties seek to create integral regimes for the common benefit of all states, often reinforced by a prohibition on reservations. It would be counterproductive to allow some states parties in effect to contract out by concluding later incompatible agreements *inter se*. This argument leads on to the conclusion that in the event of a conflict, for example, between WTO treaties and earlier multilateral environmental agreements, the latter will prevail by virtue of Article 41. The necessary assumption here is of course that the MEA provisions in question are 'integral' agreements for the common benefit of all states, from which derogation *inter se* must be controlled, and that WTO agreements create a network of principally bilateral relations, from which derogation *inter se* will usually be permissible.[196]

A clearer example is the 1982 UNCLOS. Negotiated by consensus and as a package deal, not only are reservations prohibited,[197] but the terms of Article 311 also confer express priority over existing treaties and limit the right of parties to derogate from the Convention in later agreements. Article 311 (3) is modelled on

---

[194] eg UNCLOS, Article 237 (2).

[195] See *Austro-German Customs Case* (1931) PCIJ Series A/B, No. 41; Pauwelyn, *Conflict of Norms*, 300.

[196] Pauwelyn, *Conflict of Norms*, 315–24; id, 'A Typology of Multilateral Treaty Obligations: Are WTO Obligations Bilateral or Collective in Nature?', 14 *EJIL* (2003) 907, 925–41. Pauwelyn acknowledges the possibility that some WTO treaty obligations may be collective in character. Equally, some MEA provisions may not be.   [197] Article 309.

Articles 41 and 58 of the Vienna Convention,[198] with the addition of a reference to treaties affecting the application of the 'basic principles' of UNCLOS. The drafters' concern for the integrity of UNCLOS thus reflects general treaty law. The assumption is that, in the event of the kind of conflict envisaged in Article 311 arising, UNCLOS will prevail over a later treaty dealing with the same subject matter, notwithstanding the *lex posteriori* rule enshrined in Article 30 of the Vienna Convention.[199] When considering such clauses, the ILC commentary concludes:

> The chief legal relevance of a clause asserting the priority of a treaty over subsequent treaties which conflict with it therefore appears to be in making explicit the intention of the parties to create a single 'integral' or 'interdependent' treaty regime not open to any contracting out; in short, by expressly forbidding contracting out, the clause predicates in unambiguous terms the incompatibility with the treaty of any subsequent agreement concluded by a party which derogates from the provisions of the treaty.[200]

It has accordingly been suggested by Pauwelyn that in such cases later inconsistent agreements of this kind are unenforceable, even between the parties, not simply illegal as a breach of treaty. He concludes that ' . . . although the *inter se* agreement is not invalid or void under the law of treaties, as a result of its illegality grounded in Art. 41 or Art. 58 and the law of state responsibility, the *inter se* agreement must be ended and cannot, therefore, be enforced, *not even as between the parties to it* . . . This explains why Arts. 41 and 58 provide for an exception to the contractual freedom of states.'[201] On this view Article 311(3) of UNCLOS would produce the same result. In all such cases it would be unsafe to assume that later *inter se* treaties are either applicable or enforceable in any form or forum.

The conclusions are obvious. First, that techniques of interpretation, including the *lex specialis* doctrine, will in general better serve the interests of integration than resort to rules on priority, which are less likely to promote a nuanced and coherent approach to international law-making. Second, there is sufficient uncertainty about the impact of Vienna Convention to make it unwise to rely solely on these rules to resolve difficulties predictably and with certainty. Third, the only way to ensure predictable and coherent integration of law-making treaties is to make express provision for the relationship between the relevant treaties at the negotiating stage. We can now consider these points further in the context of three agreements: the 1982 UNCLOS, the 1992 Convention on Biological Diversity and the 1994 WTO Agreements.

---

[198] M. Nordquist (ed), *UN Convention an the Law of the Sea: A Commentary* (Dordrecht, 1985), vol V, 238–40.

[199] In such cases the residual rules of priority found in Article 30 of the Vienna Convention are displaced in favour of Article 41: 1969 VCLT, Article 30 (5). This includes the *lex posteriori* rule. See generally Pauwelyn, *Conflict of Norms*, 302–15.

[200] ILC, Commentary to draft article 26, para 7, in Watts, *The ILC*, vol II, 678.

[201] Pauwelyn, *Conflict of Norms*, 311–13. He relies in part on S. Rosenne, *Breach of Treaty* (Cambridge, 1985) 89, who argues that such agreements *may* be invalid.

4.6 Treaty Relations in Practice: UNCLOS, Biological Diversity and WTO Law

The relationship between the 1982 UNCLOS and the 1992 Convention on Biological Diversity (CBD) shows how successive treaties on rather different topics can nevertheless contribute to the development of an integrated legal regime.[202] As we noted earlier, the 1982 Convention makes no reference to biological diversity. A decade later the 1992 Rio Conference on Environment and Development adopted the CBD, whose provisions apply both to terrestrial and marine biodiversity. Clearly, each agreement is relevant for the purpose of interpreting the other. Equally clearly, the increasingly devastating effect of unsustainable fishing practices on marine biodiversity and ecosytems is a matter that directly affects implementation of the CBD. There is undoubtedly a possibility that implementing the later treaty could affect rights and obligations under UNCLOS.

The CBD does not prevail over UNCLOS, nor does it give blanket priority to UNCLOS. On marine environmental matters Article 22 specifically requires parties to implement the CBD 'consistently with the rights and obligations of States under the law of the sea'. This suggests that they could not, for example, ignore the rights of ships to freedom of navigation in the EEZ and high seas, whether under UNCLOS or under customary law. To that extent Article 22 of the CBD reinforces the terms of Article 311 (3) of UNCLOS. Within these limits UNCLOS will prevail in any conflict. On the other hand, under Article 237 of UNCLOS, agreements relating to the marine environment do not have to conform to Part XII of the Convention, but need only be carried out in a manner consistent with the 'general principles and objectives' of the Convention. This would allow CBD parties much greater latitude to depart from the terms of Part XII than from other parts of the Convention, since as a *lex specialis* Article 237 over-rides Article 311 (3).[203] Save in an extreme case, the CBD regime will therefore prevail over Part XII of UNCLOS.

More importantly, however, while Article 22 also provides that existing treaty rights and obligations are not affected by the CBD, this exclusion does not apply where 'the exercise of those rights and obligations would cause serious damage or threat to biological diversity'. While in general terms the effect of Article 22 is to ensure that UNCLOS will normally prevail, states parties to the CBD cannot rely on UNCLOS to justify—or to tolerate—fishing which causes or threatens serious damage to biodiversity. To that extent the CBD may have modified UNCLOS. Is this permissible within the terms of Article 311 (3) of UNCLOS? Here the answer is probably yes. Since conservation of marine living resources and protection and

[202] See UN/CBD, *Study of the Relationship between the CBD and UNCLOS with Regard to the Deep Seabed* (2004) UNEP/CBD/SBSTTA/8/INF/3/Rev. 1.
[203] Nordquist, *UNCLOS Commentary*, vol IV, 423–6.

preservation of 'rare or fragile ecosystems' and the habitat of 'depleted, threatened or endangered species and other forms of marine life' are already envisaged by UNCLOS,[204] the Convention's objects and purposes can readily be interpreted to include measures aimed at protection of marine biodiversity. Thus, for example, the adoption under the CBD of protected zones intended to reduce serious damage to biodiversity on the high seas would not be incompatible with UNCLOS, and would be consistent with Article 22 of the CBD. However, such zones would not be opposable to non-parties to the CBD, whose UNCLOS rights Article 311 expressly protects. Any meaningful attempt to regulate marine biodiversity thus in practice depends principally on the parties to UNCLOS, not on the parties to the CBD.

The relationship between UNCLOS and the CBD is relatively complex, and operates at several different levels. It should be obvious that this relationship could not be reproduced simply on the basis of Vienna Convention rules, nor indeed on the basis that either one is necessarily a *lex specialis* in relation to the other. It clearly had to be negotiated and carefully considered in advance.[205] We can also see how a major law-making treaty such as UNCLOS has an ongoing impact on the structuring of later law-making agreements that affect matters regulated by UNCLOS. This effect is not limited to biodiversity or fisheries, but can also be observed in relation to security,[206] narcotics control,[207] trade in hazardous cargoes[208] or the protection of cultural heritage,[209] *inter alia*. Moreover, it also has implications at an institutional level. Much the most important contribution so far made by international law to the protection of marine biodiversity is the 1995 UN Fish Stocks Agreement. For the first time this agreement brings an environmental and biodiversity perspective to international fisheries regulation. Notice however that it is an agreement implementing UNCLOS, not an agreement implementing the CBD. At one level the reason is simply that this was how the UN General Assembly chose to proceed. But at another level, it makes sense, given the priority which UNCLOS enjoys both as a matter of law and of UN policy.[210] The range of matters covered by the 1995 Agreement simply could not have been addressed with the same freedom or priority as an addendum to the CBD.

If the relationship between UNCLOS and other treaties has been carefully considered and reflects a strong international consensus in favour of UNCLOS, the same cannot be said about the WTO Agreement of 1994, and its principal

---

[204] Articles 61, 64–7, 117–20, 194 (5).

[205] Article 22 (2) of the CBD originated in a US proposal aimed at protecting freedom of navigation. It was introduced very late in the negotiations.

[206] 2003 Proliferation Security Initiative.

[207] 1988 Convention against Illicit Traffic in Narcotic Drugs, Articles 4 and 17.

[208] 1989 Basel, Convention on Transboundary Movement of Hazardous Waste, Article 4 (12).

[209] 2001 Convention on the Protection of Underwater Cultural Heritage, Article 3.

[210] See Agenda 21, Chapter 17, in UN, *Report of the UN Conference on Environment and Development* (1992) UNDoc A/Conf151/26/Rev1, vol I; UNGA Res 54/33, 12 November 1999.

component, the 1947/94 GATT. Neither agreement contains any provision governing its relationship with non-WTO treaties. Whether through arrogance, oversight, disagreement or a misplaced belief in the self-contained character of WTO law, the omission is a major source of controversy. Theses have been written on the relationship between WTO law and the rest of international law;[211] whole forests have disappeared addressing the question whether WTO treaties or multilateral environmental agreements have priority over each other. As we shall see this is not really the right question.

WTO law is not a closed system. Article 3 (2) of the WTO Dispute Settlement Understanding, and the decision of the WTO Appellate Body in the *Shrimp-Turtle* case,[212] make it clear that WTO agreements must, like any other treaty, be interpreted and applied in accordance with general rules of international law. In effect this means the Vienna Convention on the Law of Treaties, including the provisions we have already considered earlier. Without a priority clause, or any provision comparable to Article 311 of UNCLOS, the relationship between WTO agreements and other treaties can only be determined in accordance with general rules of international law, or with the relevant provisions of other treaties. Articles 30, 41 and 58 of the Vienna Convention are no easier to apply in this context than in any other, nor are they any more likely to be relied upon by courts. As we saw in the previous section, however, a *lex specialis* will not be displaced by the more general rules of the GATT, and on that basis an environmental agreement making specific provision for trade restrictions will usually provide the applicable norm.[213] So will integral treaties, such as UNCLOS, in preference to the mainly bilateral relationships which arise under GATT.

This may be exactly what WTO members intended. States have on several occasions shown that they are perfectly capable of including in other instruments a specific savings clause in respect of WTO agreements if they wish to,[214] although the practice is more remarkable by its rarity. As the comparison with UNCLOS shows only too clearly, it is easy to confer entrenched priority on a treaty where the parties are in agreement. The effect of doing nothing, however, is that the relationship between WTO law and other treaties is determined elsewhere. But this will only work as between parties to those other treaties. Simply by staying out of UNCLOS, the CBD and the Biosafety Protocol, the United States or any other

---

[211] See especially Pauwelyn, *Conflict of Norms*.

[212] *Import Prohibition of Certain Shrimp and Shrimp Products*, WTO Appellate Body (1998) WT/DS58/AB/R. See R. Howse, in J. Weiler (ed), *The EU, the WTO and the NAFTA* (Oxford, 2000) 54.

[213] eg 1973 Convention on International Trade in Endangered Species; 1987 Ozone Protocol; 1989 Basel Convention on the Control of Transboundary Movements of Hazardous Wastes. On *lex specialis* see previous section.

[214] 1994 Agreement Relating to the Implementation of Part XI, Annex, section 6 (1) (b); 2001 FAO Plan of Action to Prevent Illegal, Unreported and Unregulated Fishing, paras 65–8. Compare the somewhat ambiguous terms in which the preamble to the 2000 Biosafety Protocol refers to trade agreements. See A. Qureshi, 'The Cartagena Protocol on Biodiversity and the WTO—Co-existence

WTO member can ensure that it retains its trade rights under WTO law regardless of the provisions of these agreements. At worst, WTO trade rights may be interpreted in the light of other agreements, as in *Shrimp-Turtle*, but they cannot be abrogated or amended *vis-à-vis* non-parties who are members of WTO. How significant a limitation this may prove to be will depend on the circumstances.

At the time of writing, the 1982 UNCLOS remains the only environmental agreement whose inter-relationship with WTO law has been explored by an international tribunal. The case law suggests that GATT need not interfere with implementation of UNCLOS, and that recourse to residual rules on priorities is unlikely to be necessary. In *Shrimp-Turtle* the Appellate Body held that unilateral restrictions on trade in marine living resources are more likely to be regarded as arbitrary or discriminatory under GATT if the state concerned has not first sought a cooperative solution through negotiation with other affected states.[215] Moreover, the unwillingness of the US to negotiate a possible solution made it harder to rely convincingly on the exceptions provided for in Article XX, however broadly interpreted. Together, these findings effectively reinforce rather than threaten the duty under UNCLOS Articles 116–19 and in customary international law to cooperate in the conservation and management of high seas marine living resources. Although the WTO ruling did not specifically require further negotiations between the parties, in practice the US found that the easiest way to achieve its objectives was by returning to the negotiating table to conclude a regional conservation agreement for marine turtles. Unilateral trade sanctions remained a legitimate option had other parties refused to negotiate in good faith.

Once again we can see the value of interpretation in this case. This does not mean that conflicts between WTO law and international environmental law cannot arise, but it is noteworthy that the trade and environment case law has involved unilateral action by individual states, and the decisions have focused on issues of arbitrariness, lack of justification or discriminatory treatment, rather than posing a straight challenge to the applicability of environmental agreements.[216] On the contrary, guided by the Preamble to the WTO Agreement and Principle 12 of the 1992 Rio Declaration on Environment and Development, the Appellate Body has been rather sensitive to environmental obligations and concerns. This may not satisfy some WTO lawyers, but so far it has posed no discernible threat to the viability of international trade law, and has strengthened the coherent application of international law as a whole.

---

or Incoherence?', 49 *ICLQ* (2000) 835; T. Schoenbaum, 'International Trade in Living Modified Organisms: The New Regimes', 49 *ICLQ* (2000) 856.

[215] (1998) WT/DS58/AB/R, paras 166–72. But not the failure to reach a negotiated solution: see *Shrimp-Turtle Art 21.5 Report* WT/DS58/AB/RW (2001) 37.

[216] *Standards for Reformulated Gasoline*, WT/DS2/AB/R (1996); *EC Measures Concerning Meat and Meat Products* (*Beef Hormones*) WT/DS26/AB/R (1998), paras 120–5; *EC—Measures Affecting Asbestos*, WT/DS135/AB/R (2001).

5. Conclusions

In this chapter we can see clearly that much of modern international law is the product of multilateral agreements, Security Council and General Assembly resolutions, intergovernmental declarations and various forms of soft law adopted by international organisations and other bodies. The relationship between different instruments is not always coherent or predictable, and this is a matter which undoubtedly merits further study and reform by the ILC. Nevertheless, there is no doubt that in many instances the process of negotiating and adopting these instruments, whether they are binding or not, helps to promote the coordination of state practice and *opinio juris*, and thereby to clarify, create and change international law on a more or less global basis. As Charney explains:

> Those solutions that are positively received by the international community through state practice or other indications of support will rapidly be absorbed into international law, notwithstanding the technical legal form in which they emerged from the multilateral forum.[217]

Many of the examples referred to here and in Chapter 3 show that consensus support combined with widespread implementation of or acquiescence in that practice, can have a particularly powerful impact on customary international law. This is not far removed from traditional custom. It largely exemplifies a different, more proactive method of generating custom, rather than a radical change in the nature of customary law. On this view, state practice and *opinio juris* are still necessary, but they are far more likely to develop quickly, consistently and widely when the rules are negotiated and agreed multilaterally.

Can we go further, however, to argue convincingly that this 'evolution in the law-making process' no longer requires us to have recourse to customary law and the evidence of state practice? We have considered various examples supporting such a view. The articulation of general principles by states constitutes one development which does not depend on implementation in state practice, and which is very different from traditional general principles borrowed from national law. Cheng's conception of instant custom is another example, questionable perhaps in the context of UNGA resolutions, but rather more persuasive when applied to the consensus adoption of treaties such as UNCLOS. Here we can observe a marked tendency to legitimise implementation in practice without waiting for widespread ratification or entry into force. Examples of this kind may suggest that the notion of custom emerging through practice over time diminishes to vanishing point when new norms are clearly articulated and unambiguously supported by a strong consensus.[218]

Roberts makes perhaps the most radical argument. For her, 'modern custom' need not reflect actual practice at all, but instead takes the form of ideal standards

---

[217] Charney, 87 *AJIL* (1993) 529, 545.   [218] Ibid 546.

prescribed by states. For that reason it may be 'descriptively inaccurate',[219] like the law relating to torture, but morally right. However, the example of torture highlights an obvious weakness in this argument: it focuses on widespread breach of the rule as evidence of practice when it should focus instead on national laws, which almost universally outlaw torture.[220] The same could be said of genocide and war crimes. There is no doubt that much contemporary international law-making responds to moral perceptions about right and wrong, but it does not follow that a new theory of customary international law is necessary to accommodate these developments.

Nevertheless, there is no reason in principle why the UN General Assembly or other international bodies could not assume the power to make law *ipso facto*; the important questions are whether the international community accepts that such an evolution in the *grundnorm* of international law has occurred, and whether the instruments adopted by such bodies are treated as law by international courts. These are essentially empirical questions. Both Charney and Jennings stop short of suggesting that multilateral fora have acquired authority to declare new law, but they were writing several decades ago and the world has moved on. At present only the Security Council appears to have taken upon itself the power to make law *ipso facto*, and it remains to be seen how far this will be accepted. As we argued in Chapter 3 it is still premature to conclude that other intergovernmental bodies or international conferences have crossed the boundary between promoting law-making and making law, although they have come closer to doing so in fora such as UNCLOS III.

Questions of legitimacy, participation, and transparency considered in earlier chapters are also relevant here. We saw in Chapter 3 that it is impossible to separate the process of law-making from the authority of law itself; from that perspective modern law-making represents a marked advance over classical customary international law.[221] It is more inclusive and more authoritative. It relies less on the uncertain practices of relatively few states and more on texts negotiated and agreed multilaterally. The agreement of states to the rules and principles is more obvious, and at an earlier stage. What this and earlier chapters show is that in modern international society both the processes and the legal instruments which *could* constitute a legislative system already exist.

Nevertheless, the one remaining but vital feature which continues to differentiate contemporary international law-making from a genuine legislative system is that in most cases the capacity to impose new rules on dissenting states, or to change the law for those states, is absent. With the sole exception of the UNSC, it is not, as we saw earlier, a system of majoritarian law-making. Only when the 'persistent objector' has been driven from the scene can we truly say that normative instruments adopted by multilateral fora are *ipso facto* law. Charney concludes that 'state practice and other evidence do not support the existence of the persistent objector rule'.[222] That is a matter of debate, and the present authors conclude

---

[219] Roberts, 95 *AJIL* (2001) 769.   [220] See earlier discussion of the *Nicaragua* case.
[221] Charney, 87 *AJIL* (1993) 538–47.   [222] Ibid 540.

that, on the contrary, the evidence generally points in the opposite direction. Moreover, even when states join in the consensus adoption of negotiated texts, many of our examples show that consensus may mask opposition, or be subject to reservation, or become the object of subsequent objection or non-participation. What happens after adoption and how states subsequently react plainly remain important when assessing legal effects.

We are left therefore with the conclusion that only the Security Council can as such adopt immediately binding law in non-derogable form, albeit episodically, in restricted fields, and contingently on an appropriate majority and the non-exercise of the veto. The political and legal implications of the Council's extended law-making power have not yet been fully comprehended. Everything else contributes to international law-making through custom or general principles, but does not *per se* make law. Whether one should call the product of this process general international law, or retain the terminology of custom and general principles, is largely a matter of choice rather than doctrine. It has to be admitted, however, that Jennings' preference for 'general international law' more accurately reflects the reality of what has become a subtle and complex interaction of form and process.

Further Reading

R. R. Baxter, 'International Law in "Her Infinite Variety"', 29 *ICLQ* (1980) 549.

A. E. Boyle and D. Freestone (eds), *International Law and Sustainable Development* (Oxford, 1999), chapter 2.

J. Charney, 'The Persistent Objector Rule and the Development of Customary International Law', 58 *BYBIL* (1987) 1.

B. Cheng, 'United Nations Resolutions on Outer Space: "Instant" Customary Law?' 5 *Indian JIL* (1965) 23, reprinted in B. Cheng (ed), *International Law Teaching and Practice* (London, 1982) 237.

C. M. Chinkin, 'The Challenge of Soft Law: Development and Change in International Law', 38 *ICLQ* (1989) 850.

T. Franck, 'Who is the Ultimate Guardian of UN Legality?', 86 *AJIL* (1992) 519.

M. Happold, 'SC Resolution 1373 and the Constitution of the UN', *13 LJIL* (2003) 593.

R. Higgins, 'A Babel of Judicial Voices? Ruminations from the Bench', 55 *ICLQ* (2006) 791.

W. Jenks, 'The Conflict of Law-Making Treaties', 30 *BYBIL* (1953) 401.

R. Y. Jennings, What is International Law and How Do We Tell It When We See It?', 37 *Swiss YBIL* (1981) 59.

C. McLachlan, 'The Principle of Systemic Integration and Article 31(3)(c) of the Vienna Convention', 54 *ICLQ* (2005) 279.

J. Pauwelyn, 'The Role of Public International Law in the WTO: How Far Can We Go?', 95 *AJIL* (2001) 535.

—— *Conflict of Norms in Public International Law* (Cambridge, 2003).

A. Roberts, 'Traditional and Modern Approaches to Customary International Law: A Reconciliation', 95 *AJIL* (2001) 757.

P. Weil, 'Towards Relative Normativity in International Law?', 77 *AJIL* (1983) 413.

6

Law-Making by International Courts and Tribunals

1. Introduction

The proliferation of international courts and tribunals is one aspect of the development of specialist international regimes and the apparent fragmentation of the international legal system discussed in earlier chapters. Although the International Court of Justice (ICJ) is the 'principal judicial organ' of the United Nations, and all UN members are *ipso facto* parties to the Statute of the Court,[1] the ICJ does not have automatic compulsory jurisdiction over all international legal disputes, it is not a court of appeal from other international tribunals, nor do its judgments enjoy a superior status. It has no power to ensure systematic coherence between the judgments of different international courts and tribunals. Constitutionally it is simply one court among many.

There are differing views as to the effects of the proliferation of judicial bodies on the international legal system as a whole and whether it is beneficial or otherwise.[2] Some see this as a judicialisation of international relations with a corresponding enhancement of international law through the maturing of the legal system. Others fear that such fragmentation will undermine the coherence of international law in that specialist regimes in, for example human rights and international trade, will diverge from their international law roots and expound specialist rules of limited application.[3] The existence of specialist sectoral courts delivering judgments on a regular basis can have systemic impact.[4] Judge Oda, for example, has argued that the ITLOS is a futile and unnecessary institution that

---

[1] UN Charter, Articles 92–3.

[2] See the articles in 'Symposium: The Proliferation of International Tribunals: Piecing Together the Puzzle', 31 *NYU JILP* (1999); T. Buergenthal, 'The Proliferation of International Courts and Tribunals: Is It Good or Bad?', 14 *LJIL* (2001) 267; R. Higgins, 'The ICJ, the ECJ and the Integrity of International Law', 52 *ICLQ* (2003) 1.

[3] The concept of a *lex specialis* has been accepted by the ICJ; *Legality of the Use or Threat of Nuclear Weapons* (1996) ICJ Reports (Adv Op) para 25.

[4] S. Charnovitz, 'Judicial Independence in the World Trade Organization', in L. Boisson de Chazournes, C. Romano and R. MacKenzie, *International Organizations and International Dispute Settlement: Trends and Prospects* (Ardsley, 2002) 219, 227.

will result in an unwise separation of law of the sea from the rest of international law, of which it is an integral part. It has, he suggests, the potential to diminish the ICJ's authority and centrality as the principal judicial organ of the UN and fragment the jurisprudence on the law of the sea, instead of promoting the desirable uniformity that Judge Oda considers more likely to result from leaving the general development of the law in the hands of the ICJ.[5] In reality these fears appear overblown.[6] There is little evidence to suggest that the creation of the ITLOS has undermined the ICJ, if only because it has decided so few cases. Nevertheless, the awards of arbitral tribunals under the 1982 UNCLOS do highlight special problems arising out of the fragmentation of compulsory jurisdiction, and we return to these below.

The creation of the Permanent Court of International Justice (PCIJ) in 1920 heralded a new era in international law through the establishment of a permanent forum for the exercise of international adjudication. Until the latter part of the 20th century consideration of international law-making through judicial bodies would have required consideration only of this Court, its successor the ICJ, mixed arbitral commissions, *ad hoc* international arbitrations and some attempts at regional judicial decision-making.[7] The picture has now changed significantly and many other international adjudicatory bodies operate alongside the ICJ. The Project on International Courts and Tribunals has determined that there were in 2004 some 125 international judicial bodies and mechanisms that are staggering in their diversity.[8] There is a now a body of persons of a kind that did not exist a hundred years ago—international judges.[9] International, regional and sub-regional courts have been established in particular areas of international law, notably human rights,[10] the law of the sea,[11] economic integration,[12] international trade,[13]

---

[5] Judge S. Oda, 'The ICJ viewed from the Bench', 244 *Recueil des Cours* II (1993) 127–55. See also Judge G. Guillaume, 'The Future of International Judicial Institutions', 44 *ICLQ* (1995) 848.

[6] See A. E. Boyle, 'Dispute Settlement and the Law of the Sea Convention: Problems of Fragmentation and Jurisdiction', 46 *ICLQ* (1997) 37.

[7] eg the Central American Court of Justice was founded in 1907 to maintain peace and resolve disagreements among Central American states. It decided approximately ten cases, including *El Salvador v. Nicaragua*, judgment 9 March 1917 which was instrumental to the *Land, Island and Maritime Frontier Dispute (El Salvador/Honduras)* Nicaragua Intervening (1992) ICJ Reports 4, 351.

[8] Project on International Courts and Tribunals, Synoptic Chart, available <http://www.pict-pcti.org/publications/synoptic_chart.html>. See P. Sands, R. Mackenzie and Y. Shany (eds), *Manual on International Courts & Tribunals* (London, 1999).

[9] J. Alvarez, 'The New Dispute Settlers: (Half) Truths and Consequences', 38 *Texas ILJ* (2003) 405, 406.

[10] European Court of Human Rights (ECHR); American Court of Human Rights (IACHR); African Court of Human and Peoples' Rights (AfCHPR).

[11] International Tribunal for the Law of the Sea (ITLOS), UN Convention on the Law of the Sea, 1982, Annex VI.

[12] European Court of Justice (ECJ); Court of Justice of the Common Market for Eastern and Southern Africa; Court of Justice of the Andean Community. The African Court of Justice has not yet been established and the African Union Assembly has determined that it should be merged with the AfCHPR.

[13] Dispute Settlement System of the World Trade Organization (WTO); North American Free Trade Area (NAFTA) Dispute Settlement Procedures.

international criminal law[14] and international administrative and employment law.[15] Many of these have been established since the 1990s and more are envisaged. In addition to international courts there are institutional arbitral bodies[16] and a number of quasi-judicial bodies such as the UN human rights treaty bodies[17] that issue non-binding decisions on whether state behaviour complies with the relevant treaty on the basis of an individual complaint. Other bodies include dispute resolution or inspection processes leading to the issuing of recommendations or guidelines, the UN Claims Commission,[18] and compliance mechanisms primarily under international environmental law treaties.

A plethora of international courts raises the spectre of competing jurisdictions and legal orders[19] resulting in conflicting decisions that will undermine the authority of the law (and in particular that of the ICJ), encourage forum shopping and create uncertainty. However Charney considered such concerns to be overstated. Based on a study of the jurisprudence of some leading bodies, he found that in core areas of international law different tribunals share relatively coherent views. Despite differences of detail they all use a familiar language. Charney concluded that '[o]n the basis of the available evidence, no substantial breakdown in the unity of central norms of general international law has developed'.[20] Indeed commonality may develop whereby principles gain in authority and expectation through their repetition in a number of different arenas. However Charney's study was published in 1999 and it may be that as the case-load of different bodies increases this conclusion carries less weight. Certainly the issue of conflicting jurisdictions has gained in significance, as discussed below.

One effect is however evident: there is a larger number of judicial bodies and a greater number of international judges whose pronouncements may contribute to the corpus of international law. There was always a danger of simplification in describing the attitude of the ICJ towards the judicial function in international law. The requirements of judicial diversity in Article 9 of the Statute of the Court have ensured a judiciary drawn from diverse legal and political backgrounds who

---

[14] International Criminal Tribunal for the Former Yugoslavia (ICTY); International Criminal Tribunal for Rwanda (ICTR); International Criminal Court (ICC); Special Court for Sierra Leone.

[15] The UN Administrative Tribunal established by the GA has been followed by administrative tribunals within other specialised agencies and international organisations. Until 1995 the decisions of the UNAT could be reviewed by the ICJ but the GA stopped this (Res 50/54, 29 January 1996) because the procedure had not been a 'constructive or useful element in adjudication of staff disputes'. The jurisprudence of these tribunals contributes to the development of international employment and administrative law.

[16] eg the Permanent Court of Arbitration established by the Convention for the Pacific Settlement of International Disputes, The Hague, 1899 and Convention for the Pacific Settlement of International Disputes, The Hague, 1907; International Centre for the Settlement of Investment Disputes (ICSID), Convention on the Settlement of Investment Disputes between States and Nationals of other States, 1965.   [17] See Chapter 3.

[18] Established in accordance with SC Res 687, 3 April 1991, paras 16–19. See Chapter 3.

[19] Y. Shany, *The Competing Jurisdictions of International Courts and Tribunals* (Oxford, 2003).

[20] J. Charney, 'Is International Law Threatened by Multiple International Tribunals?', 271 *Recueil des Cours* (1998) 373.

do not necessarily share the same perspective on international judicial law-making in general or on specific issues as they arise. The proliferation of international courts has multiplied the number of judges who may perceive their tasks from a variety of viewpoints. The different institutional frameworks also mean that the tasks of the various courts cannot unquestioningly be equated. It is difficult to generalise about judicial decision-making without regard, *inter alia* to the particular tribunal, its institutional setting, the context of the dispute, the identity of the parties and the makeup of the decision-making body. Whatever view is taken of this development, any consideration of international law-making must take account of this proliferation and consider the contribution of courts and tribunals in very different sectors of international law.

This chapter provides an overview of some of the law-making attributes of contemporary international courts and tribunals.[21] Despite the increase in the number of international courts and tribunals its emphasis is upon the position of the ICJ and its predecessor. Not only has the jurisprudence of the World Court been subject to greater analysis, it remains the single international court of general jurisdiction.[22] Reference will be made to the law-making attributes of other international adjudicative bodies where appropriate.

## 2.	Do International Courts Make Law?

There is an initial question which is whether international judicial bodies can be called law-making at all. The extent to which courts should appropriately make law and do so act is contested within all jurisdictions. This is especially the case in the international legal order where state consent remains paramount and is the basis for the exercise of jurisdiction.[23]

The primary function of the ICJ is not law-making but the application of law in the settlement of disputes. The PCIJ was 'competent to hear and determine any dispute of an international character' submitted to it[24] and the ICJ's role in the peaceful settlement of disputes was made integral to the UN Charter's overall schema for the maintenance of international peace and security. Other international courts have been established explicitly to this end. For example the ICTY and ICTR were both created by the Security Council under its UN Charter, Chapter VII powers.[25] The Preamble of the Rome Statute recognises that crimes

---

[21]	The chapter does not discuss the impact of national courts on the development of international law. For a brief discussion see Chapter 2.

[22]	The Statute of the ICJ, Article 36 (1) provides that 'The jurisdiction of the Court comprises all cases which the parties refer to it and all matters specially provided for in the Charter of the United Nations or in treaties or conventions in force'.

[23]	E. Lauterpacht, *Aspects of the Administration of International Justice* (Cambridge, 1991) 23–6.

[24]	Treaty of Versailles, 1919, Article 14.

[25]	SC Res 827, 25 May 1993 (ICTY); SC Res 955, 8 November 1994 (ICTR). See Chapter 3.

within its jurisdiction 'threaten the peace, security and well-being of the world' and reaffirms the Purposes and Principles of the Charter.

The records of the debate of the Advisory Committee of Jurists in 1920 reveal that the members were clear that judicial settlement of disputes does not necessarily entail law-making and that the decisions of the proposed PCIJ would not make law.[26] Baron Descamps unequivocally described the international judicial function:

Doctrine and jurisprudence no doubt do not create law; but they assist in determining rules which exist. A judge should make use of both jurisprudence and doctrine, but they should serve only as elucidation.[27]

In conformity with this view the Statute of the PCIJ (and subsequently ICJ), Article 59, limited the effect of decisions in contentious cases[28] by asserting that 'The decision of the Court has no binding force except between the parties and in respect of that particular case.'[29] This proviso 'was primarily intended to underline the opinion that the Court should not be considered a law-making or law-creating institution'.[30] This is repeated for other international courts,[31] although exceptionally the ICC is mandated that it 'may apply principles and rules of law as interpreted in its previous decisions'.[32] Consistently with Article 59, Article 38 (1) (d) assigns to judicial decisions only a subsidiary status as a source of law.[33] 'Decisions binding on the parties in the particular case could be overruled the next day by the same court in a new case.'[34]

States have been ready to increase the number and scope of international tribunals but less willing to acknowledge the possibility of judicial law-making. Some states remain anxious to ensure that even the ICJ (let alone 'lesser' courts) remains within what they consider its proper limits. For example, in their submissions in the *Legality of the Use or Threat of Nuclear Weapons* some states expressed their concern that the Court should not go beyond 'delivering opinions in legal

---

[26] G. Van Hoof, *Rethinking the Sources of International Law* (Deventer and London, 1983) 169–70.

[27] PCIJ, Advisory Committee of Jurists, *Procès-Verbaux* of the Proceedings of the Committee, 16 June–24 July (The Hague, 1920) 336.

[28] The advisory jurisdiction of the ICJ is by its terms non-binding, UN Charter, Article 96; Statute of the ICJ, Article 65.

[29] On the grey area between precedent (the effect of a decision on third parties) and *res judicata* (determinative of the rights and obligations of the parties *inter se*), see R. Jennings, 'The Judiciary, International and National and the Development of International Law', 45 *ICLQ* (1996) 1, 6–12.

[30] A. Zimmermann, C. Tomuschat and K. Oellers-Frahm, *The Statute of the International Court of Justice: A Commentary* (Oxford, 2006) 1233 (per R. Bernhardt).

[31] eg Statute of the International Tribunal for the Law of the Sea, Article 33 (2); NAFTA, articles 1136; WTO Agreement, Annex 2, Understanding on Rules and Procedures Governing the Settlement of Disputes, 1994, Article 3 (2) states that 'the recommendations and rulings of the DSB cannot add to or diminish the rights and obligations provided in the covered agreements'.

[32] Rome Statute of the ICC, Article 21 (2).

[33] The Statute of the PCIJ, Article 38(1) (d) differed only from the text of the Statute of the ICJ in that the 'the power of the Court to decide a case *ex aequo et bono*' is contained in a separate numbered paragraph (Article 38 (2)) in the latter.

[34] Zimmermann et al, *The Statute of the International Court of Justice*, 1244.

matters' and slip into an improper 'law-making' capacity. The Court responded by asserting the orthodoxy that:

It is clear that the Court cannot legislate . . . Rather its task is to engage in its normal judicial function of ascertaining the existence or otherwise of legal principles and rules . . . The contention that the giving of an answer to the question posed would require the Court to legislate is based on a supposition that the present *corpus juris* is devoid of relevant rules in this matter. The Court could not accede to this argument; it states the existing law and does not legislate. This is so even if, in stating and applying the law, the Court necessarily has to specify its scope and sometimes note its general trend.[35]

However theoretical assertions that deny law-making power to international judicial bodies ignore the reality that, as we have seen in earlier chapters, international courts—in particular the ICJ—do play a major law-making role.

As a subsidiary, or indirect consequence of its role in the settlement of disputes,[36] 'the Court [ICJ] has made a tangible contribution to the development and clarification of the rules and principles of international law'.[37] President of the ICJ Judge Higgins concurs: the 'very determination of specific disputes, and the provision of specific advice, does develop international law'.[38] To this end:

Making orders and delivering opinions in legal matters is the proper function and judicial responsibility of the Court and when the Court properly discharges its obligations in this regard the Court's determination will naturally have its repercussions in many spheres including the political.

Included among the 'many spheres' is the increasingly sophisticated legal order occupied by the many international adjudicative bodies listed above. In a decentralised system without a legislative body or authoritative law-making process and where unwritten law is developed through the amorphous processes of state practice and *opinio juris*, judicial decision-making carries great weight through exposition of the law. International courts, in particular the ICJ, play a significant role both in crafting and ensuring consistency in contemporary international law. They also develop our understanding of how it is made through the processes described in earlier chapters of this book. We have seen for example that the ICJ has drawn upon soft law instruments and given impetus to the process of transformation

---

[35] *Legality of the Use or Threat of Nuclear Weapons*, para 18.

[36] Indeed an ICJ decision may have little impact on the outcome of a dispute but nevertheless develop the law. Eg judgment in the *Oil Platforms Case* was given 15 years after the negotiated settlement in the Iran–Iraq war which was the setting for the claims, *Oil Platforms (Iran v. US)* Merits (2003) ICJ Reports (Judgment of 6 November 2003). Similarly the *Application of the Convention on the Prevention and Punishment of the Crime of Genocide (Bosnia and Herzegovina v. Serbia and Montenegro)* is to be decided in 2006, 11 years after the Dayton Peace Agreement, 1995.

[37] H. Lauterpacht, *The Development of International Law by the International Court* (London, reprinted 1982) 5. See also G. Schwarzenberger, *International Law as Applied by International Courts and Tribunals* (4 vols, London, 1957–86); W. Jenks, *The Prospects of International Adjudication* (London, 1964).

[38] R. Higgins, *Problems and Process: International Law and How We Use It* (Oxford, 1993) 202.

from soft to hard law (Chapter 5); has expounded on the relationship between treaty and customary international law, specifically in the context of 'law-making' treaties (Chapter 5); and has given authoritative weight to the process of ILC codification, even before finalisation of the Commission's work (Chapter 4). In a decentralised legal system the ICJ offers an authoritative voice on the meaning of international instruments and unwritten principles. Its position as the primary judicial organ of the UN ensures it a constitutional role, determining the competencies of the other principal organs and specialised agencies of the UN and their inter-relationship.[39] Other courts have played a similar role within sectoral[40] and regional[41] regimes. More broadly international courts are a significant vehicle for the integration of international law into international affairs.

The impact of international courts and tribunals on the evolution of international law largely depends upon how many cases are brought before them and the significance of those cases in terms of raising new and contested legal issues. The logical corollary of the greater number of international courts is that there is a greater—and ever-growing—body of primarily judge-made law that supplements and complements the jurisprudence of the ICJ.

3. Judicial Process

A brief description of the ways in which judges come to articulate their opinions is useful. The process varies according to different courts. In the ICJ the accepted practice is for judges to seek to reach collectively a single majority opinion through a drafting committee. The process through which the judges reach their majority opinion was first adopted as a resolution of the PCIJ in 1931. In the current Rules of Court a resolution concerning the Internal Judicial Practice of the Court was adopted on 12 April 1976 and is footnoted to Article 19.[42] The resolution makes it clear that judicial decision-making is a deliberative process giving rise to collegiate responsibility[43] for the outcome. It provides for the judges to exchange their views both before and after the commencement of oral proceedings. The judges have an initial joint deliberation after the end of oral proceedings and then exchange written notes expressing each individual judge's views on the

---

[39] eg *Case Concerning Certain Expenses of the United Nations* (1962) ICJ Reports 151 (Adv Op 20 July); *Legal Consequences for States of the Continued Presence of South Africa in Namibia (South West Africa) notwithstanding Security Council Resolution 276* (1970) (1971) ICJ Reports (Adv Op 21 June).

[40] D. Cass, *The Constitutionalization of the World Trade Organization: Legitimacy, Democracy, and Community in the International Trading System* (Oxford, 2005). See Chapter 3.

[41] E. Stein, 'Lawyers, Judges and the Making of a Transnational Constitution', 75 *AJIL* (1981) 1.

[42] ICJ, Rules of Court, 1978 as amended 5 December 2000.

[43] R. Jennings, 'The Collegiate Responsibility and Authority of the International Court of Justice', in Y. Dinstein (ed), *International Law at a Time of Perplexity: Essays in Honour of Shabtai Rosenne* (Dordrecht, 1989) 343, 344.

case. After a further joint deliberation a drafting committee is elected by secret ballot. A first draft is circulated among the judges and amendments suggested for revision. After a formal first reading (that is paragraph by paragraph) of the draft, further amendments are made for a second reading, after which a final vote is taken. Thus 'even Judges intending a thoroughly dissenting opinion are expected to work with the Court on the draft judgment . . . up to and including the final stages of its drafting'.[44] Judge Higgins has described the current process as ensuring 'that every single judge is engaged in the deliberation processes' and that the preliminary note system provides a guarantee that points are not overlooked or ignored. The disadvantage is that it is time consuming.[45] In response to concerns about the lengthy nature of the Court's processes some changes have been introduced, for example dispensing with the note in some cases.

Other international courts follow different processes. Not all such courts sit as plenary bodies. The ICTY and ICTR operate through trial chambers of three judges, with the possibility of appeal to a common five-judge appeal chamber. The ECHR sits in chambers of seven judges with the possibility of a Grand Chamber of 17 judges.[46] Sitting as chambers facilitates the hearing of a greater number of cases but may prevent the development of collegiality that prevails where the norm is that all judges participate in all cases.[47] The Working Procedures of the Appellate Body of the WTO (where three members out of seven sit on each case) have explicitly addressed collegiality. Rule 4 (1) provides that '[t]o ensure consistency and coherence in decision-making, and to draw on the individual and collective expertise of the Members, the Members shall convene on a regular basis to discuss matters of policy, practice and procedure'.[48]

The process of reaching judgment may also not be as coordinated as in the ICJ. For example in the ICTY each Trial Chamber has a senior legal officer (SLO), each judge has an Assistant Legal Officer and there are usually one or two 'floating' Legal Officers who are assigned to the Chamber, not to a particular judge. In many cases law clerks do the initial drafting with guidance from the judges. Each case has a presiding judge, and generally one judge is assigned as the primary author. Typically, the Chamber's SLO assigns each law clerk a particular section for preliminary drafting, such as the facts, elements of crimes, the application of law or relevant principles for sentencing. The SLO coordinates the drafting

---

[44] Ibid 345.

[45] R. Higgins, 'Remedies and the International Court of Justice: An Introduction', in M. Evans (ed), *Remedies in International Law: The Institutional Dilemma* (Oxford, 1998) 1, 2–5. Hersch Lauterpacht compared this process favourably with that of the US Supreme Court, noting that it avoids the imprint of the 'intellectual effort of a single individual' and seeks to reconcile 'legitimate diversities of judicial outlook'; Lauterpacht, *The Development of International Law by the International Court*, 65.

[46] European Convention on Human Rights, as amended by Protocol 11, Article 27.

[47] The Statute of the ICJ, Article 26 provides for the Court to sit in chambers of three or more judges but only a few cases have been so decided.

[48] Working Procedures for Appellate Review, WT/AB/WP/5, 4 January 2005.

efforts. Where there are several accused persons, a different person might work on aspects specific to each accused. One Chamber however, tends to have a person responsible for the drafting, and gives assignments to the various Associate Legal Officers to do research on specific issues. The Appeal Chamber works in essentially the same way, with one judge and his/her legal advisor taking the lead, and the SLO acting as coordinator to the other legal officers. The ICTY and ICTR common appellate chamber protects against conflicting judgments and, as in other courts, the authority of an appellate body (or Grand Chamber as in the ECHR) gives greater weight to their decisions.

Like the UK House of Lords and US Supreme Court, the decisions of the ICJ (and all other international courts) are made by majority vote with scope for dissenting and separate opinions. The need for space to put forward individual views is especially potent in an international order characterised by diverse cultures, traditions and concepts of reason and justice.[49] Furthermore the 'negotiation' process, whereby majority decisions are constructed, allows for the inclusion of dicta on peripheral issues. Dicta may expressly reaffirm important legal principles.[50] All these contribute to clarification and elaboration of the law[51] despite the legal formality that not even the decision and core reasoning of the majority judgment are binding except for the parties. There are numerous examples of influential dicta and individual opinions. One need only refer to the frequently cited dicta of the majority in *Barcelona Traction* relating to obligations owed *erga omnes*,[52] the separate opinion of Judge Ammoun in the *Namibia* case on the status of the Universal Declaration of Human Rights as customary law, in particular provisions relating to racial discrimination,[53] or that of Vice President Weeramantry on the right to development (including sustainable development) in *Gabčíkovo*[54] to realise that careful expositions of legal positions that do not form part of the decision can develop a life of their own, often forming the basis of subsequent legal argument by a range of international actors. While dissenting and separate opinions provide a platform for individual judges to develop their own theories of international adjudication, it has also been suggested that regular dissent limits

---

[49] M. Koskenniemi, 'The Pull of the Mainstream', 88 *Mich LR* (1989–90) 1946, 1947.

[50] eg In the *Oil Platforms* case Judge Simma asserted that the Court should have taken the opportunity to use 'strong unequivocal obiter dicta' to reassert the Charter principles on the use of force; *Oil Platforms (Iran v. US)* Merits (2003) ICJ Reports (Judgment of 6 November 2003) sep op Judge Simma, para 6.

[51] R. Jennings, 'The United Nations at Fifty: The International Court of Justice after Fifty Years', 89 *AJIL* (1995) 493, 498 (about separate opinions).

[52] *Barcelona Traction, Light and Power Co. Ltd.* (*Belgium v. Spain*) (second phase) (1970) ICJ Reports, 3, para 33 (judgment of 5 February). See M. Ragazzi, The Concept of International Obligations Erga Omnes (Oxford, 2000) for an analysis of the evolution of the concept from this starting point.

[53] Judge Ammoun, *Legal Consequences for States of the Continued Presence of South Africa in Namibia (South West Africa)* (1970) ICJ Reports 78–81. See also Judge Tanaka, *South West Africa* Cases (second phase) (1966) ICJ Reports 298 (judgment of 18 July).

[54] *Gabčíkovo-Nagymaros Project (Hungary/Slovakia)* (1997) ICJ Reports sep op V-P Weeramantry (judgment of 25 September).

the opportunities for a judge to influence the majority in its crafting of the court's opinion.[55]

The ICJ has remained largely impervious to the receipt of information or argument from any source other than the parties in contentious cases[56] and even in its advisory jurisdictions accepts arguments or information only from an international organisation considered 'likely to be able to furnish information on the question'.[57] As discussed in Chapter 2 other international courts are more receptive to submissions from non-parties, including from NGOs in the form of *amicus* briefs. Unless explicitly referred to in the judgment, the extent to which such information is influential in the process of decision-making remains unclear.

4. International Courts: Interpretation and Application of Law

The greater number of multilateral instruments containing compulsory or optional dispute resolution clauses has ensured that judicial tribunals have had greater opportunity both to amplify (and sometimes confuse) the understanding of how international law derives from the sources listed in Article 38 (1) of the ICJ Statute and have developed substantive rules and principles. Clauses in multilateral treaties providing for the jurisdiction of the ICJ invariably do so in cases of disputes over the interpretation or application of the particular convention. Other clauses may spell out the law to be applied by the ICJ in making its determination. All three of these interlocking tasks—determining the applicable law, application and interpretation of the convention—assume existing law to be applied but in fact contribute to the processes of law-making. Determination of the applicable law may frame an issue as falling within the parameters of general international law or a regional or subject-specific *lex specialis*. This initial categorisation then shapes the development of law in that area. Judicial reliance upon, and interpretation of, some principle or instrument (whether in hard or soft law form) bestows it with meaning and authoritative weight.[58] It is not only the ICJ that carries out these functions. Other courts, including national courts, may look to the ICJ's interpretation of international law and to its methodology when determining the existence and content of a rule of conventional or customary international law.[59] This

---

[55] J. Crawford, 'Public International Law in Twentieth Century England', in J. Beatson and R. Zimmermann (eds), *Jurists Uprooted: German-Speaking Emigré Lawyers in Twentieth Century Britain* (Oxford, 2004) 681, 684 n. 17.

[56] It has taken a generally restrictive approach to requests to intervene from third party states; Zimmermann et al, *The Statute of the International Court of Justice*, 1331–68 (per Chinkin).

[57] Statute of the ICJ, Article 66 (2).

[58] The Statute of the ICJ, Article 63 (declaration of intervention) assumes that interpretation of a treaty will have law-making effect.

[59] eg the UK House of Lords referred to the ICJ's methodology in the *North Sea Continental Shelf* cases with respect to the formation of customary international law in the entirely different context of the treatment of asylum claimants. *R v. Immigration Officer at Prague Airport and another ex parte European Roma Rights Centre and others* [2004] UKHL 55, [2005] 2 WLR 1, para 23 per Lord Bingham.

section looks at some aspects of adjudication in the development and clarification of international law through determination of applicable law, application and interpretation.

4.1 Applicable Law

It should not be assumed that in deciding cases brought before them international courts and tribunals always apply the whole of international law. They have jurisdiction to decide cases only insofar as the parties have conferred jurisdiction on them to do so. No court exercises universal compulsory jurisdiction over legal disputes, although some specialised tribunals, such as the WTO Dispute Settlement Body, or a tribunal established under the 1982 UNCLOS, have compulsory jurisdiction within their particular field. The political processes involved in the creation of international courts and the negotiation of dispute settlement clauses in treaties significantly affect the discretion left to adjudicators in determining the substantive law they are to apply. The widest discretion is accorded by Article 38 (2) of the Statute of the ICJ which envisages that with agreement of the parties the Court may decide a case *ex aequo et bono*—in effect a decision not necessarily based on legal rules.[60] Although this choice has never been exercised, states have sometimes agreed that a dispute will be adjudicated on the basis of rules that are not yet law. Thus in the *Tunisia–Libya Continental Shelf* case the *compromis* provided that the Court would apply international law including 'the recent trends admitted at the Third Conference on the Law of the Sea'.[61]

There are many other formulae for determining the applicable law. The simplest is where judges are directed to decide cases in accordance with the 'applicable rules of international law'.[62] In other instances the general rules of international law are incorporated as a yardstick against which claims or defences are to be measured, thereby bringing into a convention legal principles of international law external to it. For example, in the *Oil Platforms* case, the ICJ interpreted the provisions of a treaty of friendship in such a way that international law on the use of force became applicable for the purpose of applying the treaty.[63] Similarly, the European Convention on Human Rights, Protocol 1, Article 1 provides that no one shall be deprived of property 'except . . . by the general principles of international law'. The applicable law may also include related treaties or soft law instruments which set standards with which the parties to the principal treaty are required to conform. As we saw in Chapter 5, the 1982 UNCLOS makes reference for this purpose to 'generally accepted international rules and standards established through the competent international organisation or general diplomatic conference'.[64]

---

[60] See also 1982 UNCLOS, Article 293.   [61] (1982) ICJ Reports 18.
[62] NAFTA, Article 1131.   [63] (2003) ICJ Reports, paras 40–1. See Chapter 5.
[64] Article 211 (2). See also Articles 207, 208, 210. Other articles also make express reference to international law at various points: see Articles 19, 21, 23, 31, 32, 34, 39, 58, 74, 83 87, 221 and 235.

Many treaties do not incorporate other rules of international law quite so liberally or at all. Some impose explicit limits on the application of other rules. One result of limiting the applicable law in this way is that some disputes cannot easily be decided in accordance with all the relevant international law potentially applicable between the parties.[65] This is particularly a phenomenon of treaty disputes arising under compulsory jurisdiction clauses. For example, in accordance with Article 293 of the 1982 UNCLOS a court or tribunal must apply the 'Convention and other rules of international law not incompatible' with it. It has been argued that Article 293 allows a court to adjudicate an UNCLOS dispute on the basis of customary law or other treaties binding on the parties to the dispute, and that the only limit on doing so is compatibility with the Convention. On that basis in the *Mox Plant Arbitration* Ireland sought to persuade a tribunal that it could decide the case in accordance with the more detailed rules on environmental impact assessment and the precautionary principle found in European law and European regional treaties.[66] The problem with this view is that it would turn a dispute settlement system that confers only limited compulsory jurisdiction for the purposes of a particular treaty into a general jurisdiction clause over non-UNCLOS aspects of a dispute. Using an applicable law provision for this purpose is not an argument that any international tribunal has so far found persuasive.[67] The alternative view is that UNCLOS tribunals may adjudicate on questions of general international law only insofar as it is within their jurisdiction and not inconsistent with UNCLOS to do so: that is, only where other rules of law are expressly incorporated by specific articles of the Convention, or where it is necessary to apply other rules in order to decide the UNCLOS dispute.[68] For example, if the question is whether freedom of fishing on the high seas can be suspended in order to carry out nuclear tests, the legality of such tests under general international law would have to be decided in order to apply the Convention's rule on use of the high seas with 'due regard' for the rights and interests of other states.[69] On that basis, Article 293 does not extend the jurisdiction of tribunals under the Convention and its reference to applicable law should be read accordingly.

The problem of ensuring coherent application of international law in such situations can partially be addressed through interpretation. Article 31 (1) of the Vienna Convention on the Law of Treaties provides for a treaty to be interpreted in its context. Article 31 (2) gives a broad meaning to a treaty's context by including any instrument made 'in connection with the conclusion of the treaty'. The WTO adjudicating bodies have brought in under this rubric[70] the Harmonised

---

[65] See *Military and Paramilitary Activities in and against Nicaragua* (*Nicaragua v. United States*) (*Nicaragua* case) (1984) ICJ Reports 392; *Oil Platforms Case* (2003) ICJ Reports.

[66] *Mox Plant Arbitration* (PCA, 2003).

[67] Ibid. See also *OSPAR Arbitration* (PCA, 2003), paras 101–5.

[68] *MOX Plant Arbitration* (PCA, 2003), para 19.

[69] 1982 UNCLOS, Article 87. See *Nuclear Tests Cases* (*Australia v. France; New Zealand v. France*) (1974) ICJ Reports 253 and 457.

[70] The Agreement Establishing the WTO, Annex 2, Understanding on Rules and Procedures Governing the Settlement of Disputes, Article 3 (2) envisages this approach by authorising the

System—a treaty negotiated under the auspices of the World Customs Organisation—recognising it as relevant context for the interpretation of obligations under the WTO.[71] Moreover, as we saw in Chapter 5, Article 31 (3) also allows other rules of international law to be taken into account when interpreting a treaty. In all these ways the applicable law of a particular convention can be extended beyond its own terms, allowing up to a point for consistent judicial application across connected subject matters. They maintain the fiction that the law is there simply to be identified and applied by the judges. But in reality, by extending the scope of applicable law, adjudicators may in effect incorporate principles outside those specifically agreed by the parties to the dispute and thereby develop the law beyond the framework of the convention upon which jurisdiction is founded.

In other instances, however, states may be concerned that they will not view such judicial determinations favourably and thus seek in advance to pre-empt any law-making effect. For example the NAFTA Agreement provides that the parties may collectively issue interpretations of their specific agreements under NAFTA and that any such interpretative statement is binding on the Tribunal.[72] Similarly, Article 3 (2) of the WTO Dispute Settlement Understanding provides that 'Recommendations and rulings of the DSB [Dispute Settlement Body] cannot add to or diminish the rights and obligations provided in the covered agreements'. In this way the parties have asserted their own competence to interpret these agreements, thereby prioritising their own political determinations over potential judicial decisions. There is an interesting contrast between the Statutes of the ICTY and ICTR on the one hand and the ICC on the other in this regard. The former provide virtually no guidance to the judges in formulating the applicable rules of international criminal law and procedure. The Report of the Secretary-General that was preparatory to the establishment of the ICTY stated that the Tribunal would apply international humanitarian law that exists in conventional and customary law.[73] The Secretary-General emphasised that the Tribunal should 'apply rules of international humanitarian law which are beyond any doubt part of customary law'. However no definitions of offences were provided (other than genocide) and there had been no international war crimes trials since the adoption of the 1949 Geneva Conventions for the Tribunal to draw upon. The Nuremberg and Tokyo Tribunals did provide a body of case law but these Tribunals were established over 50 years ago, with different jurisdiction and before the evolution of much contemporary international law, for example international human rights law. It was evident that the ICTY (and subsequently the ICTR) would have to

dispute settlement bodies to interpret the agreements 'in accordance with customary rules of interpretation of public international law'.

[71] ILA, *Report of the Committee on International Trade Law* (Toronto, 2006), para 20.
[72] NAFTA, Articles 1131, 1132. See also WTO Agreement, Article 9 (2).
[73] Report of the S-G pursuant to paragraph 2 of SC Resolution 808 (1993), 3 May 1993, UN Doc S/25704, paras 33–4.

determine its own definitions, processes and rules. Indeed the judges were entrusted with drawing up the Rules of Procedure and Evidence,[74] again without any directional guidance.

In contrast, in the highly politicised negotiations for the Rome Statute of the ICC, states sought to minimise the Court's future law-making capacity by determining that the Elements of Crimes and the Rules of Procedure and Evidence would be set out through negotiation by states at the Assembly of States Parties. These important matters were thus not left to the judges to determine through judicial decision-making or adoption of an instrument.

Nevertheless, despite the conclusion of the Elements of Crimes and the Rules of Procedure and Evidence, the ICC judges will have the detailed and comparatively prolific jurisprudence of the *ad hoc* Tribunals before them as well as that of other courts such as the ICJ. In some instances this jurisprudence was incorporated into the ICC definitions adopted by states parties, in others it was not. But legal history cannot be turned back and it is certain that lawyers arguing before the ICC will draw upon these cases. Assuming the ICC develops a reasonable caseload, it may have to choose whether to seek consistency with the jurisprudence of the *ad hoc* Tribunals, in effect recognising an applicable international criminal law, and regarding itself as justified by this drafting history in deviating from that law by applying the law of the Statute. If it favours the former approach it will assist in the evolution of a coherent body of international criminal law emanating from a mix of SC resolutions, treaty negotiation and the case law of the *ad hoc* Tribunals. If it relies heavily on its own Statute to the exclusion of these other sources it could marginalise the work of the *ad hoc* (and time limited) Tribunals and may retrospectively undermine their authority.

4.2   'Living Instruments' and Judicial Interpretation

We saw in Chapter 5 how some treaties evolve through interpretation, a point of particular resonance in the field of human rights. For example the European Convention on Human Rights was adopted in 1950. Its provisions are short and claims are made for rights that do not fall within their precise terms. The ECHR has to strike a balance between interpreting the Convention in such a way that it continues to have validity in changing social, economic and political conditions and not asserting new rights that have not been accepted by the parties. New rights can be introduced by adoption of a Protocol and it is not the Court's role to usurp the 'legislative power' of states parties.

The concept of a 'living instrument' has been the Court's answer, that is using existing treaty articles to reach innovative outcomes that reflect society's changing

---

[74] ICTY Statute, Article 15. The ICJ has drawn up its own Rules of Procedure, Statute of the ICJ, Article 30. The UN Convention on the Law of the Sea, Annex VI, Article 16 authorises the ITLOS judges to draw up its Rules of Procedure.

attitudes. The ECHR has said that the Convention is 'a living instrument which . . . must be interpreted in the light of present day conditions'[75] enabling decisions that would not have been anticipated at the time of its adoption. A frank admission of the consequences of the judicial role was made by Judge Garlicki in *Öcalan v. Turkey*:

This may result (and, in fact, has on numerous occasions resulted) in judicial modifications of the original meaning of the Convention . . . The Strasbourg Court has demonstrated such a creative approach to the text of the Convention many times, holding that the Convention rights and freedoms are applicable to situations which were not envisaged by the original drafters.[76]

Thus in *Soering v. UK*[77] the Court stated that it 'cannot but be influenced by the developments and commonly accepted standards in the penal policy in the member states of the Council of Europe'.[78] In this case the Court noted the 'virtual consensus' within such states that the death penalty should not be imposed for crimes committed in times of peace as it is no longer 'consistent with regional standards of justice'. This was not the case in 1950. Accordingly the Court found it to be a violation of Article 3 (prohibition of torture, cruel, inhuman treatment) to extradite a person to a state (outside the Council of Europe) where he might face the death penalty and thus be subjected to the agonies of detention on death row. In *Öcalan* itself, after taking account of the current attitude towards the death penalty in the member states of the Council of Europe, the Court went further, holding that 'capital punishment in peacetime has come to be regarded as an unacceptable, if not inhuman, form of punishment which is no longer acceptable under Article 2'.[79] Similarly there are no articles specifically protecting the human rights of lesbians, gay men, transexuals and bisexuals. However, the Court has interpreted the Convention to bring such rights within Article 8 (the right to privacy). Although there is neither a right to health nor to a clean environment within the Convention the ECHR has also relied on Article 8 to develop environmental rights. For example it has found a violation of the right to respect for private and family life through a government's failure to regulate environmental nuisances, or to enforce the law in such cases, or to warn of the associated dangers and health risks.[80] It considered that serious harm to the environment may affect the welfare of persons and deprive them of the enjoyment of their homes in such a way as to damage their private and family life.

The law-making effect of such decisions is especially powerful because of the direct effect of the European Convention in the domestic law of many member

---

[75] eg *Tyrer v. UK* (Appl. No. 5856/72), ECHR (Series A) No. 26 (25 April 1978) 15–16.
[76] *Öcalan v. Turkey* (Appl. No. 46221/99), GC (2005) partly concurring, partly dissenting opinion of Judge Garlicki, para 4.
[77] *Soering v. UK* (Appl. No. 14038/88), ECHR (Series A) No. 161 (1989).
[78] Ibid, para 102. [79] *Öcalan v. Turkey* (2003) 37 EHRR 10, para 196.
[80] See *Lopez Ostra v. Spain* (1994) 20 EHRR 277; *LCB v. UK* (1999) 27 EHRR 212; *Guerra v. Italy* (1998) 26 EHRR 357.

states. In the UK (where incorporation of a treaty into national law is required) the Human Rights Act 1998, section 2 requires any court or tribunal making a determination relating to a Convention right to take into account any 'judgment, decision, declaration or advisory opinion' of the ECHR. ECHR decisions are argued before UK courts as authoritative precedents and analysed by judges as such. Decisions of national courts are formative of state practice and *opinio juris* for the formation of at least a regional customary international law of human rights. The cross-fertilisation of human rights principles between the human rights bodies of the Inter-American and African systems and the UN treaty bodies strengthens arguments of customary international law standards emergent from the terms of the conventions and contributes to the development of general principles of law.

4.3   Application of Customary International Law

The Statute of the ICJ, Article 38 (1) sets out where the ICJ should look for existing law where there is no relevant treaty.[81] Other courts deciding issues on the basis of international law look to the same sources. The first listed is 'international custom, as evidence of a general practice accepted as law'. Judicial decision-making does not of course constitute customary international law, which long pre-dates the establishment of the PCIJ.[82] But judicial reasoning may clarify its mysteries. In particular the ICJ has had many occasions to consider the processes by which customary international law is formed and identified. Thus although the 'existence and content of custom is usually determined by states and academics . . . the Court remains the ultimate arbiter in some cases'.[83] The choices a court (and individual judges) makes in determining its recourse to, and application of, customary international law (and the other listed sources) are political, value choices. The Court's approach and structure of legal argument with respect to custom have been subject to significant analysis and critique, most notably in recent years from critical legal scholars.[84]

It is commonplace that the ICJ has set out what it regards as the appropriate criteria for determination of customary international law: the actual practice of states and *opinio juris*.[85] As we saw in Chapter 5, it has asserted in a number of cases

---

[81] For a brief overview see R. Kearney, 'Sources of Law and the International Court of Justice', in L. Gross (ed), *The Future of the International Court of Justice* (New York, 1976), vol II, 610.

[82] B. Chigara, *Legitimacy Deficit in Custom: Towards a Deconstructionist Theory* (Dartmouth, 2001) 2–7.

[83] A. Roberts, 'Traditional and Modern Approaches to Customary International Law: A Reconciliation', 95 *AJIL* (2001) 757, 772.

[84] The issue continues to generate literature; see J. Beckett, 'Countering Uncertainty and Ending Up/Down Arguments: *Prolegomena* to a Response to NAIL', 16 *EJIL* (2005) 213.

[85] *Lotus* Case (*France v. Turkey*) (1927) PCIJ (Series A) No. 10, 28; *Continental Shelf (Libyan Arab Jamahiriya/Malta)* (1985) *ICJ Reports*, 13, para 27. This classic approach to customary international law has been termed the 'pedagogical approach', that is what international lawyers impart to their

whether there is, or is not, a rule of customary international law, and the content of particular rules. It has refined understandings of custom (for example the existence of regional customary law)[86] and procedural requirements for pleading custom (for example that the state relying on custom must prove it). These have in turn become part of the body of customary international law. The Court has recognised its constraints and has refrained from blatant law-making, for example by speculating what future law might be.[87] However, applying the criteria for establishing custom is not a scientific process, the accuracy of which can be measured. Rather it requires an evaluation of the facts and arguments selected for presentation to the Court by advocates appearing before it. Indeed it has been observed that 'custom, if considered from a technical point of view, is not so much the rule; it is the procedure of creating the rule',[88] that is a methodology.

The Court has considered customary international law in a great many cases, only a few of which can be referred to here.[89] However even a brief examination of the way the Court has addressed the making of customary international law shows both the law-making potential in this process and how the Court has not been consistent in applying its own criteria for the determination of customary international law.

In a number of early cases the PCIJ developed its approach to determining when a rule of customary international law exists, the content of the rule, to whom it is applicable and the limits of its application.[90] Despite these pronouncements it has been inconsistent in its examination of state practice and *opinio juris* and in the respective weight it has given to these distinct elements. For example in the 1951 *Anglo-Norwegian Fisheries* case[91] it referred to no practice with respect to the drawing of straight baselines around the *skjaregaard* from any state other than Norway and indeed noted that the Second Sub-Committee of the Second Committee of the 1930 Conference for the Codification of International Law had formulated the low water mark rule 'somewhat' strictly.

In the 1974 *Fisheries Jurisdiction* case the Court found two concepts to have crystallised as customary international law: the concept of a 12-mile exclusive fishing zone and that of preferential rights for coastal states beyond 12 miles. These concepts were said to have arisen out of the general consensus revealed at the 1960

students; D. Fidler, 'Challenging the Classical Concept of Custom: Perspectives on the Future of Customary International Law', 39 *GYBIL* (1996) 198.

[86] *Asylum Case (Colombia/Peru)* (1950) ICJ Reports 266.

[87] *Fisheries Jurisdiction Case (UK v. Iceland)* (1974) ICJ Reports 3, para 40; this does not mean that the Court should declare the law between the parties as it might be at the date of expiration of the interim agreement, a task beyond the powers of any tribunal.

[88] A. Cassese and J. Weiler, *Change and Stability in International Law-Making* (Berlin, 1988) 10 (per Georges Abi-Saab).

[89] See also Chapter 5 for discussion of the ICJ's analysis of the interplay between treaty and custom.

[90] eg *Lotus* Case.

[91] *Fisheries (UK v. Norway)* (1951) ICJ Reports (judgment of 18 December 1951) 116, 129.

Geneva Conference on the Law of the Sea—which had failed to reach agreement on the extent of fishery rights. Furthermore, UNCLOS III (which had commenced in 1973)[92] had not yet reached any conclusions—as it would not for another eight years. Without citing any concrete instances of state practice the Court noted that it was 'aware that a number of States has asserted an extension of fishery limits'.[93] It left unspoken such questions as: how was it aware of this? By arguments presented before it? If so why not acknowledge the fact? How many states? How great an extension of fishery limits? Have they been widely accepted? By whom? The Court was also 'aware' of the manifest desire of states to codify the law through UNCLOS III. While asserting that it could not usurp the legislator by anticipating the law, the Court did precisely that. In the same case at its jurisdiction stage the Court noted that the Vienna Convention on the Law of Treaties, 1969, Article 62 'may in many respects be considered as a codification of existing customary law'.[94] Again this leaves open many questions: in what respects? On what basis? It did not refer to its own methodology expounded in the *North Sea Continental Shelf* cases on when a treaty provision may be regarded as customary international law.[95] No state practice was offered as evidence. There was no reference to the ILC commentaries on Article 62, nor to the debates at the Vienna Conference. Unlike the Law of the Sea Convention, at least in this instance the treaty had been completed, although it was not yet in force. Such failure to act consistently with its own asserted methodology[96] undermines the legitimacy of judicial decision-making, and the content of the espoused customary laws. Indeed the 'practice of the ICJ to vary at will, and without acknowledging standard rules is not legitimacy enhancing for both the new norms of law created and for law creating mechanism involved'.[97]

As discussed in Chapter 5, in the 1986 *Nicaragua* case the Court apparently reversed its traditional approach of seeking state practice supported by *opinio juris* by finding first *opinio juris* in the form of UNGA resolutions and then looking for state practice.[98] The Court discounted the inconvenient fact that much state practice was inconsistent with the ideals expressed in those resolutions as constituting evidence weighing against the *opinio juris* but instead viewed such practice as breaches of those rules.[99] Nor did it inquire whether there was any state practice or *opinio juris* to support its opinion that Articles 1 and 3 of the Geneva Conventions on the Laws of War had become customary international law.[100]

---

[92] See Chapter 3.

[93] *Fisheries Jurisdiction* Case (*UK v. Iceland*) Merits (1974) ICJ Reports 3, para 53 (judgment of 25 July 1974).

[94] *Fisheries Jurisdiction* Case (*UK v. Iceland*) Jurisdiction (1973) ICJ Reports 3, para 36 (judgment of 2 February 1973). See Chapter 4.

[95] *North Sea Continental Shelf* Cases (*Federal Republic of Germany/Denmark; Federal Republic of Germany/Netherlands*) (1969) ICJ Reports 3, para 71 (judgment of 20 February 1969). See Chapter 5.

[96] In contrast in its discussion of preferential rights the Court did refer to state practice; *Fisheries Jurisdiction* Case (*UK v. Iceland*) Merits, para 58.   [97] Chigara, *Legitimacy Deficit in Custom*, 209.

[98] *Nicaragua* Case Merits (1986) ICJ Reports 14, para 184 (judgment of 27 June).

[99] Ibid, para 186.

[100] T. Meron, *Human Rights and Humanitarian Norms as Customary Law* (Oxford, 1989) 36.

The Court's inconsistency with respect to the weight to be accorded to state practice and *opinio juris* has elicited different responses. Schachter has argued that there are different types of customary rules.[101] The first type is 'the great body of customary rules' such as those on jurisdiction, immunity and state responsibility where consistent state practice must still be sought. The second type comprises those rules that prohibit state conduct that offends against core values and sustain the international order: the prohibition of aggression, genocide, torture, slavery and systematic racial discrimination. These norms are 'brittle' in their susceptibility to violation and must therefore be reaffirmed even in the face of such violations.[102] Kirgis has similarly argued for different processes according to the substantive nature of the proposed rule. Greater consistency in state practice is required where there is little evidence of *opinio juris* but contradictory practice is tolerated where there is expressed consensus about illegality, for example through UNGA resolutions.[103]

These analyses fuse the making of customary international law with its content. The use of ethical and human rights values in this way adds to the inherent uncertainties that surround customary international law and dispel any pretence at an objective methodology. They assume that international law is imbued with the core values of an international community which debates about universalism make uncertain.[104] But in any case such analyses are further confused by subsequent decisions of the Court. For example, in the 2002 *Arrest Warrant* case the ICJ had to determine whether a foreign minister has immunity from the criminal jurisdiction of foreign states asserted under principles of universal jurisdiction. The case therefore involved one of Schachter's 'great body of customary rules'— immunity. There was at that time no international treaty on sovereign immunity[105] and there remains much disagreement about the substantive content of any customary rule on criminal immunities. Further this was the first opportunity for the ICJ to consider immunity of state officials after the ruling of the UK House of Lords in the *Pinochet* case[106] which had held there to be no immunity (for a former Head of State) in the case of alleged torture. According to Schachter's analysis above, evidence of consistent state practice would be required for the pronouncement of a rule of customary international law. In these circumstances it might

---

[101] O. Schachter, 'New Custom: Power, *Opinio Juris* and Contrary Practice', in J. Makarczyk (ed), *Theory of International Law at the Threshold of the 21st Century: Essays in Honour of Krzysztof Skubiszewski* (The Hague, 1996) 531, 538.

[102] Henkin has been more dismissive, saying that customary human rights law is not derived from state practice or consent; L. Henkin, 'Human Rights and State "Sovereignty"', 25 *Georgia JICL* (1995) 31.

[103] R. Kirgis, 'Custom on a Sliding Scale', 81 *AJIL* (1987) 146. See also C. Tomuschat, 'Obligations Arising for States without or against their Will', 241 *Recueil des Cours* (1993), vol IV, 195.

[104] See Chapter 1.

[105] This was before the adoption of the United Nations Convention on the Jurisdictional Immunities of States and their Property, 2004. GA Res 59/38, 16 December 2004. See Chapter 4.

[106] *R v. Bow Street Metropolitan Stipendiary Magistrate, ex parte Pinochet Ugarte (No. 3)* [1999] 2 WLR 827.

have been anticipated that the Court would be especially conscientious in this regard. However the Court made no reference to any methodology for reaching its conclusion on the immunity of a foreign minister. It cited no state practice (although it claimed to have examined some)[107] nor any evidence of *opinio juris* and decided on the basis of its conclusions about the functions of a foreign minister. Similarly with respect to Belgium's claim that under customary international law immunity is displaced in the case of war crimes and crimes against humanity, the Court stated that it had examined state practice, but did not provide any information about what state practice, from which states and in what context. Nor was there any reference to the need for, or existence of, *opinio juris*. In this instance its decision upheld state sovereignty and implicitly rejected the moves to develop the law along the lines commenced by the House of Lords.[108]

Judge *ad hoc* Van Den Wyngaert regretted the lack of a 'principled perspective'[109] in the majority's approach and stressed that there is no support for the proposition that foreign ministers enjoy immunity under customary international law. In criticising the majority's methodology and structure of its argument, the disregard of its own case law, the failure to undertake a 'rigorous approach', the flaws in drawing an analogy between Heads of State and Foreign Ministers, and the brevity of the judgment, Judge Van Den Wyngaert provides grounds for questioning the legitimacy of the decision and the rule of customary law pronounced therein.

In contrast in the 1996 advisory opinion on the *Legality of the Threat or Use of Nuclear Weapons* the Court had considered both the consistency of state practice and the normative effect of UNGA resolutions. On this occasion there was consistent state practice but it was of omission not commission—no state had used a nuclear weapon since the end of World War II. The Court concluded that it could not be sure if states had refrained from the use of such weapons out of a conviction of their illegality or because they favoured the political policy of deterrence. In these circumstances there was no evidence of *opinio juris* to be derived from state practice. The Court then looked to whether UNGA resolutions could be used as evidence of *opinio juris*. The relevant factors for making this determination are the 'content and the conditions' of the adoption of the resolution and 'whether an *opinio juris* exists as to its normative character'. It also accepted that while a single resolution is not determinative 'a series of resolutions may show the gradual evolution of the *opinio juris* required for the establishment of a new rule'.[110] In light of the fact that several relevant resolutions were adopted with negative votes and abstentions they fell 'short of establishing the existence of an *opinio juris* on the

---

[107] *Arrest Warrant* Case (*Democratic Republic of the Congo v. Belgium*) (2002) ICJ Reports 3, para 58 (judgment of 14 February).

[108] In *Jones v. Ministry of the Interior* the House of Lords distinguished *Pinochet* in finding there is no exception to immunity in civil claims for torture; [2006] UKHL 26.

[109] *Arrest Warrant* Case, 137 diss op *ad hoc* Judge Van Den Wyngaert.

[110] *Legality of the Threat or Use of Nuclear Weapons*, para 70.

illegality of the use of such weapons'.[111] The Court accepted that the series of resolutions indicated the concern of the international community about the issue, and even that there was an evolving principle of customary international law, but that the conflicting evidence as to *opinio juris* denied the existence of an existing law.

In *Nicaragua* the Court had given effect to UNGA resolutions as constituting *opinio juris* while in the *Legality of Nuclear Weapons* it did not. It is evident that it is not the 'soft law' nature of UNGA resolutions that determines the issue. In the *Legal Consequences of the Construction of a Wall in the Occupied Palestinian Territory* case the Court drew broadly on soft law. It accepted the opinions of a 'soft' tribunal, the Human Rights Committee, given through a soft adjudicative process (individual complaints procedure) and a non-binding General Comment[112] to find the International Covenant on Civil and Political Rights to be applicable in the Occupied Territories.[113] The suggestion has been made that greater recourse to adjudication through the proliferation of international courts might lessen the importance of soft law because of a judicial preference for hard law sources, made less vague through their interpretation and application and given effect through hard remedies. This 'half-truth' has been exposed by José Alvarez[114] and is well illustrated by this case.

The Court may adopt one of three procedures: declaring existing law; crystallising a rule of customary international law, that is by articulating an emergent rule and transforming it into an existent rule; and generating or constituting a rule whereby the Court's pronouncement becomes the 'focal point of a subsequent practice of states which, in due course, hardens into a rule of customary international law'.[115] An oft-cited example is the *Anglo-Norwegian Fisheries* case where Norway's novel assertion of the legality of the use of straight baselines and long usage was accepted by the ICJ, despite strong legal argument from the UK that this was against general international law and lack of supporting practice. The judgment has been described as serving one purpose: sanctioning the Norwegian government's breach of international law on the acquisition of maritime territory.[116] Nevertheless it generated practice both from the UK itself and from other states. Only seven years later the substance of the ruling was incorporated into the Geneva Convention on the Territorial Sea and Contiguous Zone, 1958, Article 4 and in almost identical language into the 1982 Convention on the Law of the Sea, Article 7.

Where there is no previous practice or other sources (hard or soft) the Court must use other techniques to support its reasoning. In *Anglo-Norwegian Fisheries*

---

[111] Ibid, para 71.   [112] See Chapter 3.

[113] *Legal Consequences of the Construction of a Wall in the Occupied Palestinian Territory* (2004) ICJ Reports (Adv Op) paras 102–12, 127–9, 134–6 where the Court makes reference to these instruments.

[114] Alvarez, 38 *Texas ILJ* (2003) 405, 421–8.

[115] This typology was set out by former Judge Jiménez de Aréchaga in the context of codification conferences. It seems more broadly applicable to the Court's role in the development of customary international law; Cassese and Weiler, *Change and Stability*, 3.

[116] Chigara, *Legitimacy Deficit in Custom*, 209 (discussing in particular Norway's claim of historic title).

the Court paid attention to what it termed 'the realities' of the situation: that the coast of the mainland is exceptional in that it 'does not constitute, as it does in almost all other countries, a clear dividing line between land and sea'; that along the coast are shallow banks that are veritable fishing grounds, known to the Norwegian fishing people since time immemorial; and that in these barren regions the inhabitants derive their livelihoods essentially from fishing.[117] The Court also stressed 'certain basic considerations' that determine the relevant criteria for the drawing of straight baselines, for example the 'close dependence of the territorial sea upon the land domain', and the 'more or less close relationship existing between certain sea areas and the land formations which divide or surround them' and the economic factors peculiar to the region, 'the reality and importance of which are clearly evidenced by a long usage'.[118] Finally the Court also found that the 'general toleration of foreign states with regard to the Norwegian practice is an unchallenged fact'.[119] In contrast, Norway's rejection of the ten-mile rule meant that it was not bound. David Kennedy has concluded that:

It seems that doctrines about the creation of custom seem to be about the conditions of justice or the nature of the system of international law, while doctrines about the limits of custom seem to be about the failure of consent by the state to be bound.[120]

In selecting one of the three procedures (declaring existing law, crystallising a rule of customary international law or constituting a rule) the Court has fluctuated in the respective weight it has given to the components of state practice and *opinio juris* and the amount of evidence it has required for either. At times it has placed greater emphasis on state practice (termed the classic or traditional approach[121]), although varying its requirements as to time, number of states, identity of states and consistency of practice. In other decisions it has favoured expressions of *opinio juris* over inconsistent state practice (termed the modern approach). Koskenniemi has famously termed this the dilemma of apology and utopia: law that is reliant on state practice defers too much to the realities of power while that which rests on principles unrelated to actual behaviour is Utopian and destined never to be achieved.[122] In other instances it has given little attention to the need to ascertain either. While the ICJ has identified a methodology for identifying rules of customary international law it follows it neither consistently nor rigorously. Nor has it clarified the 'mysteries' of customary international law expounded by academics[123]

---

[117] *Anglo-Norwegian Fisheries*, 128.   [118] Ibid 133.   [119] Ibid 138.

[120] D. Kennedy, 'The Sources of International Law', 2 *AM UJILP* (1987) 1, 71.

[121] Roberts, 95 *AJIL* (2001) 757, 758.

[122] M. Koskenniemi, *From Apology to Utopia: The Structure of International Legal Argument* (Helsinki, 1989, 2nd edn with epilogue, 2006).

[123] eg M. Byers, 'Custom, Power and the Power of Rules: Customary International Law from an Interdisciplinary Perspective', 17 *Mich JIL* (1995) 109; N. Dunbar, 'The Myth of Customary International Law', 8 *Australian YBIL* (1983) 1; J. Tasioulas, 'In Defence of Relative Normativity: Communitarian Values and the *Nicaragua* Case', 16 *Oxford JLS* (1996) 85.

relating to its theoretical incoherence and empirical inadequacy, or attempted to reconcile its own inconsistencies. It is hard to reach any conclusion except that where the Court's own requirements present an obstacle it will discount them in order to find custom—or not—where it wishes to do so and to find supporting evidence in either case as it seems fit. Indeed it appears to treat 'all non-written norms—whatever their basis, character or significance—. . . as customary'.[124]

In light of the failure of the ICJ to provide theoretical or analytical consistency it is unsurprising that other courts have also not been rigorous in determining the existence of rules of customary international law. For example the ICTY has made a number of assertions of customary international law without seeking evidence of state practice or *opinio juris*. It has also found sufficient evidence in the provisions of the Rome Statute before its entry into force, noting in *Tadic* that although the Rome Statute was not legally binding 'it already possesse[d] significant legal value'.[125] This legal value derived from its adoption by an overwhelming majority of states and its substantial endorsement by the 6th Committee of the GA, showing the text to be supported by a 'great number of States and may be taken to express the legal position i.e. *opinio iuris* of those States'.[126]

When courts ignore the traditional requirements for customary international law or fail to subject them to any strict scrutiny they risk giving tacit weight to what has been called the 'rush to champion new rules of law'.[127] Particularly in areas such as human rights or environmental law there is a tendency to assert new norms of customary law at will in order to advance political and social agendas— an activity pursued especially by NGOs. Scant regard is given to the niceties of state consent or the likelihood of compliance with such easily pronounced norms.[128]

4.4 Application of General Principles of Law

If an international court concludes that there is no applicable rule of customary international law what should be its response? Members of the 1920 Advisory Committee of Jurists responsible for the drafting of the Statute of the PCIJ were concerned about the prospect of lacunae in the law. In the words of De Lapradelle: 'It is not possible to admit a declaration of a *non-liquet* by an international court; denial of justice must be excluded from the international court.'[129] Since the Advisory Committee was also agreed that judges should not have legislative

---

[124] Koskenniemi, 88 *Mich LR* (1989–90) 1946, 1948.

[125] *Prosecutor v. Dusko Tadic*, IT-94-1 (judgment of 15 July 1999), para 223 (AC). The Appeal Chamber referred to an earlier decision of the Trial Chamber showing how reiteration of a principle can create its own authority.   [126] Ibid.

[127] Fidler, 39 *GYBIL* (1996) 198, 224.

[128] Alston describes this phenomenon in P. Alston, 'Making Space for New Human Rights: The Case of the Right to Development', 1 (3) *Harv HRYB* (1988) 3.

[129] PCIJ, Advisory Committee of Jurists, *Procès-Verbaux* of the Proceedings of the Committee, 16 June–24 July (The Hague, 1920) 312.

power,[130] other techniques or 'useful devices'[131] were needed to serve the Court when the usual sources are inadequate. Courts derive such devices from their constitutive instruments and from external factors.

The ICJ Statute, Article 38 (1) (c) provides one such device: recourse to general principles of law. Article 38 (1) (c) was drafted as a compromise by the Advisory Committee of Jurists between those who considered that general principles derive from natural law and those who considered their origin to be national legal systems. It is now considered that they apply to principles of both national and international law.

It has been suggested that as the inadequacies of custom and treaty law are exposed by the increased interdependence associated with globalisation, greater weight should be given to general principles of law to fill the gaps.[132] But since the Statute offers no guidance as to how general principles are to be ascertained, exactly how they are to be extracted from the specific rules and the 'underlying principles of national legal systems' is a matter of discretion for individual judges. Like any actions that cannot be achieved through purely technical and mechanical means they may be subject to legal evaluation by a court and thereby bestowed with subjective weight and meaning.[133]

In this process other international courts have been rather more proactive than the ICJ,[134] perhaps because of their greater need to respond to contemporary demands. An international criminal court cannot abdicate its responsibility for determining guilt or innocence because there is no definition of the offences with which an accused is charged. But this has been exactly the case with a number of the offences within the jurisdiction of the *ad hoc* international criminal tribunals. For instance, since neither the Geneva nor the Hague Conventions define the crime of rape, the ICTY and ICTR have had to reach their own definitions. The ICTY has sought assistance 'by reference to the general principles of law common to the major national legal systems of the world'. In *Kunarac* the Trial Chamber explained this judicial process:

The value of these sources is that they may disclose 'general concepts and legal institutions' which, if common to a broad spectrum of national legal systems, disclose an international approach to a legal question which may be considered as an appropriate indicator of the international law on the subject. In considering these national legal systems the Trial

---

[130] For discussion of these two incompatible viewpoints see Van Hoof, *Rethinking the Sources of International Law*, 136–9; 169–70.

[131] T. Elias, *The International Court of Justice and Some Contemporary Problems* (The Hague, 1983) 14.

[132] M. Bassiouni, 'A Functional Approach to "General Principles of International Law" ', 11 *Mich JIL* (1990) 768, 769.

[133] U. Fastenrath, 'Relative Normativity in International Law', 4 *EJIL* (1993) 305, 321.

[134] The exception is Judge Simma who in the *Oil Platforms* case concluded from a comparative survey of national tort laws that 'the principle of joint-and-several responsibility . . . can properly be regarded as a "general principle of law" under article 38 (1) (c) of the Statute of the ICJ'. (*Oil Platforms* (*Islamic Republic of Iran v. United States of America*) Merits (2003) ICJ Reports, sep op Judge Simma, para 74.)

Chamber does not conduct a survey of the major legal systems of the world in order to identify a specific legal provision which is adopted by a majority of legal systems but to consider, from an examination of national systems generally, whether it is possible to identify certain basic principles, or in the words of the *Furundžija* judgement, 'common denominators', in those legal systems which embody the *principles* which must be adopted in the international context.[135]

The Chamber proceeded to examine the criminal laws in a large number of countries (civil law and common law, including states from Africa and Asia) in order to derive the basic principle underlying the crime of rape in national jurisdictions. It has been noted that there are dangers of drawing general principles primarily from Anglo-American jurisprudence[136] in moulding international law. In *Kunarac* the ICTY showed that this need not be the case and included the criminal laws of such countries as South Korea, Japan, India, South Africa, Bangladesh and Zambia in reaching its decision.[137] The Appeal Chamber noted that the Trial Chamber had drawn on 'domestic laws from multiple jurisdictions' and concurred with the definition of rape it had derived in this way.[138] The Appeal Chamber's statement diminishes the Trial Chamber's methodology: the latter did not look simply at the substance of the rape laws of a number of states but sought the underlying principles they revealed.

In *MC v. Bulgaria* the ECHR recognised that the ICTY's jurisprudence on the definition of rape 'reflects a universal trend'[139] with which it agreed. It too examined the rape laws of a number of states, evidence of which had been submitted to it in the form of an NGO *amicus* brief. It did not identify its methodology as clearly as the ICTY but rather deduced a trend 'towards effective equality and respect for each individual's sexual autonomy'[140] from the domestic statutes and case law presented to it. It is however noticeable that unlike the ICJ's terse references to national legislation as state practice in the *Arrest Warrant* case, large portions of such legislation are reproduced and general principles deduced therefrom.

The Rome Statute makes detailed provision for the applicable law. Article 21 limits judicial discretion by setting out in order what judges should make reference to in deciding cases. Article 21 enumerates the Statute, the Elements of Crimes and Rules of Procedure and Evidence; other treaties and the principles and

---

[135] *Prosecutor v. Dragoljub Kunarac, Radomir Kovac and Zoran Vukovic*, IT-96–23 and IT-96–23/1, judgment of 22 February 2001 (TC), para 439 (footnotes omitted). The earlier case referred to is *Prosecutor v. Anto Furundžija*, IT-95–17, judgment of 10 December 1998 (TC).

[136] Koskenniemi, 88 *Mich LR* (1989–90) 1946, 1950.

[137] The ICTY appellate chamber has also drawn on African case law, *Pius Nwaoga v. The State*, 52 ILR 494, at 496–7 (Nig S Ct 1972) where the Supreme Court of Nigeria held that rebels must not feign civilian status while engaging in military operations; *Prosecutor v. Tadic*, Decision on the Defence Motion for Interlocutory Appeal on Jurisdiction, 2 October 1995, para 125.

[138] *Prosecutor v. Dragoljub Kunarac, Radomir Kovac and Zoran Vukovic*, IT-96–23 and IT-96–23/1, judgment of 12 June 2002 (AC), para 127.

[139] *MC v. Bulgaria* (Application no. 39272/98) 15 *Butterworths Human Rights Cases* 627, para 163.

[140] Ibid, para 165.

rules of international law, including the international law of armed conflict. Where these sources are inadequate the Court must look to 'general principles of law derived by the Court from national laws of legal systems of the world including, as appropriate, the national laws of States that would normally exercise jurisdiction over the crime, provided that those principles are not inconsistent with this Statute and with international law and internationally recognized norms and standards'. Finally, the 'application and interpretation of law' by the Court 'must be consistent with internationally recognized human rights' and non-discriminatory.

Unusually the Rome Statute sets out specific standards against which the Court's decisions must be assessed rather than making reference to vague criteria such as justice or fairness. The judges who will use these various sources in development of principles of international criminal law have different legal expertise, not only in criminal law and criminal procedure within the civil and common law traditions but also in military law, in different religious legal traditions, in different areas of international law and in accordance with Article 36 (8) (b) in 'specific issues, including, but not limited to, violence against women or children'. In addition the ICC is the first international court that is required to ensure a 'fair representation of female and male judges'.[141] It is not known what impact (if any) the presence of a 'critical mass' of women will have on the judicial process.[142]

Another judicial device is equity. The ICJ has indicated that when selecting between a range of plausible interpretations of the positive international law before it 'the Court may choose among several possible interpretations of the law the one which appears, in the light of the circumstances of the case, to be closest to the requirements of justice'.[143] Recourse to equity is a way of delivering justice. Unlike other constitutive instruments that explicitly require decision-makers to take account of equity or to reach an equitable solution,[144] the ICJ Statute makes no reference to equity. It may however be understood as coming within the notion of general principles of law.[145] The Court has had recourse to equity in a number of ways, including applying equitable procedures, effecting an equitable division, reaching an equitable result and ensuring an equitable solution.[146] It has adopted equitable principles, equitable procedures and equitable methods through its application of treaties, custom and judicial decisions.[147] Use of equity by the ICJ

---

[141] Rome Statute of the ICC, Article 36 (8) (a) (iii).

[142] H. Charlesworth and C. Chinkin, *The Boundaries of International Law: A Feminist Analysis* (Manchester, 2000) 80–3.

[143] *Case Concerning the Continental Shelf (Tunisia/Libya)* (1982) ICJ Reports 18, 60; *Case Concerning the Continental Shelf (Libya/Malta)* (1985) ICJ Reports 13, 39.

[144] eg 1982 UNCLOS, Article 83 (continental shelf delimitation between opposite or adjacent states to be agreed 'on the basis of international law . . . in order to achieve an equitable solution'); NAFTA, Article 1105 (foreign investors to be treated 'in accordance with international law, including fair and equitable treatment').

[145] 'The legal concept of equity is a general principle directly applicable as law.' *Case Concerning the Continental Shelf (Tunisia/Libya)* (1982) ICJ Reports 18, para 71.

[146] *Maritime Boundary in the Area between Greenland and Jan Mayen (Denmark v. Norway)* (1993) ICJ Reports (judgment of 14 June) sep op Judge Weeramantry, para 7 (describing the majority decision).   [147] Ibid, para 10.

has been criticised for its subjectivity, vagueness, for being a principle of morality not of law and as going beyond its powers—in effect law-making.[148] In the words of Judge Tanaka, 'Reference to the equitable principle is nothing else but begging the question'.[149] But resort to equity—in the many ways described by Judge Weeramantry—has undoubtedly become part of the international judicial armoury, most significantly in the context of boundary delimitation.[150]

In addition to equity and the general principles of law imported from national systems, or derived from the international plane,[151] Judges have looked to values that they can use as a 'judicial lodestar'[152] in determining cases, that is what they consider as the 'values that international law seeks to promote and protect'.[153] As far back as the *Corfu Channel* case the Court referred to 'elementary considerations of humanity'[154] while in the *Legality of the Threat or Use of Nuclear Weapons* Judge Higgins refers to the 'physical survival of peoples' as such a value. Such approaches are reminiscent of the Yale School's theory of international law with its central placing of the promotion of human dignity but are also open to the assertion of selective evaluation and subjective law-making.[155]

4.5 Gaps in the Law

Despite these various devices to ensure a legal basis for decision-making it may be that a court is unable to find any applicable legal doctrine. In the *Nuclear Weapons* advisory opinion, no doubt aware of the suspicions that had been expressed about it over-stepping its proper role, the ICJ eschewed any law-making function. In the absence of any relevant treaty and having found insufficient evidence to establish a rule of customary international law, it declined to 'conclude definitively whether the threat or use of nuclear weapons would be lawful or unlawful in an extreme circumstance of self-defence in which the very survival of a State would be at stake'.[156]

The Court's failure to reach a definitive conclusion in the *Nuclear Weapons* advisory opinion, in effect a *non liquet*,[157] was greatly regretted by Judge Higgins[158] who saw it as a failure of judicial function, which was asserted by her to be 'to take principles of general application, to elaborate their meaning and to

---

[148] M. Janis, 'Equity in International Law', 7 *Encyclopedia of Public International Law* (Oxford, 1984) 76–7.

[149] *North Sea Continental Shelf* Cases (1969) ICJ Reports, 172, 196 diss op Judge Tanaka.

[150] See A. V. Lowe, 'The Role of Equity in International Law', 12 *Australian YBIL* (1992) 54; T. Franck', *Fairness in International Law and Institutions* (Oxford, 1995), chapter 3 'Equity as Fairness'.

[151] On soft law declarations as sources of general principles, see Chapter 5. See also P. Alston and B. Simma, 'The Sources of Human Rights Law: Custom, Jus Cogens and General Principles', 12 *Australian YBIL* (1992) 82.

[152] The expression of Judge Higgins, *Legality of the Threat or Use of Nuclear Weapons* (1996) ICJ Reports (Adv Op) diss op Judge Higgins, para 41.   [153] Ibid, diss op Judge Higgins, para 41.

[154] *Corfu Channel* Case (*UK v. Albania*), (1949) ICJ Reports 4, 22.   [155] See Chapter 1.

[156] *Legality of the Threat or Use of Nuclear Weapons*, para 105.

[157] P. Weil, ' "The Court Cannot Conclude Definitively . . ." *Non Liquet* Revisited', 36 *Col JTL* (1998) 109; M. Aznar-Gomez, 'The 1996 Nuclear Weapons Advisory Opinion and *Non-Liquet*', 48 *ICLQ* (1998) 3.   [158] Ibid, diss op Judge Higgins, para 7.

apply them to specific situations'.[159] Many years earlier as a scholar, Judge Higgins had argued that unless international law was to remain in a rudimentary state the judicial function must include 'developing and applying international law to hitherto untested situations'.[160] Consistent with this position Judge Higgins, from the Court, provides a vigorous description of the judicial role:

It is the role of the judge to resolve, in context, and on grounds that should be articulated, why the application of one norm rather than another is to be preferred in the particular case. As these norms indubitably exist, and the difficulties that face the Court relate to their application, there can be no question of judicial legislation.[161]

The Court may have been reluctant to reach a clear conclusion, apprehending that any pronouncement would undermine its credibility: with nuclear states for determining the existence of a rule of customary international law in the light of weak evidence and with non-nuclear states for failing to take a stand for the illegality of such weapons.

However the Court did stress the importance of the obligation in the Nuclear Non-Proliferation Treaty, Article VI, to negotiate in good faith on disarmament.[162] It described this obligation not as simply one of conduct but rather as an obligation of result.[163] It also emphasised the Security Council's affirmation of this obligation that 'remains without any doubt an objective of vital importance to the whole of the international community today'. In so doing the Court reminded states of the primary method of law-making—transactional negotiation[164] and of the different functions of the Court and states, whether acting through the UN organs or other multilateral treaty processes. It is for the latter to make and change the law, not the former.

5.   Role of Lawyers

The role of other actors in the judicial process should also be noted. In an adversarial process the judiciary are dependent on the legal arguments made and the evidence adduced by advocates in support of their claims. Judge Simma has also pointed to the importance of counsel's argument in clarifying the legal situation

---

[159] Ibid, diss op Judge Higgins, para 32.
[160] R. Higgins, 'Aspects of the Case Concerning the Barcelona Traction, Light and Power Company, Ltd' 11 *VJIL* (1971) 327, 341.
[161] *Legality of the Threat or Use of Nuclear Weapons*, Judge Higgins, para 40.
[162] *Legality of the Threat or Use of Nuclear Weapons*, para 99.
[163] The Court has long encouraged friendly settlement and negotiation, no doubt mindful of its potential to generate state practice and acquiescence. In the *Free Zones* case the PCIJ recognised that 'the judicial settlement of international disputes . . . is simply an alternative to the direct and friendly settlement of such disputes between the Parties; as consequently it is for the Court to facilitate, so far as is compatible with its Statute, such direct and friendly settlement'. *Case of the Free Zones of Upper Savoy and the District of Gex* (1929) PCIJ, Series A, No. 22, 13.
[164] *Legality of the Threat or Use of Nuclear Weapons*, para 103.

for the Court, for example that individuals are not deprived of legal protection through gaps in the application of international humanitarian and human rights law.[165] What might be called an epistemic community of the comparatively small body of lawyers appearing before international courts has emerged. This ensures a common set of perspectives about the appropriate way to present an international case and has a tangible impact upon the way international courts function, and thus on their law-making potential. A novel argument that is based on sound reasoning and well supported can in turn lead to an innovative judgment and thus to changes in the substance of international law.

In the context of international criminal law the prosecutorial framing of the indictment determines the course of the hearing and the contents of the judgment. The importance of this process to the formation of international criminal law is shown by the initial omission from the indictment of charges of rape and sexual violence in the *Akayesu* case in the ICTR. It was amended to include such charges after evidence of the commission of such offences was spontaneously offered during the trial.[166] This opened the way for the important rulings on the definition of rape under international law and the meaning of genocidal rape.

It is self-evident that lawyers want to win their cases. The texts of previous cases are pored over by international lawyers in search of the strongest authorities in support of their arguments and intent on making indeterminate language serve their cause in subsequent litigation through creative lawyering. International lawyers have their own political and moral preferences that may affect their advocacy, even where they assert the neutrality of lawyering[167] and their obligations to their clients.

Another aspect of lawyering is selection of international forum. As discussed above, the proliferation of international courts means that an international dispute may be susceptible to proceedings in more than one tribunal, creating choice as to forum. Cases may be framed differently to fit within one forum rather than another. For example the *Mox Plant* case could be variously described as an environmental pollution law case, a law of the sea case, a case concerning general international law with respect to sovereignty, use of territory and the rights of neighbouring states, or a case concerning European Community law. The decision as to forum may be restricted, as where there is no jurisdictional basis before certain tribunals or where there is exclusive jurisdiction in one tribunal. Where there are apparently jurisdictional options, an important task for the applicant state's legal team is to weigh those choices and select the most favourable forum. Different factors influence this strategic decision; whether particular procedures

---

[165] *Armed Activities on the Territory of the Congo* (*Democratic Republic of the Congo v. Uganda*) (2005) ICJ Reports (judgment of 19 December), sep op Judge Simma, para 19.

[166] *Prosecutor v. Jean-Paul Akayesu*, ICTR-96–4, judgment of 2 September 1998, para 23 and amended indictment, charges 12A and 12B.

[167] See the different views expressed as to whether international lawyers can be ideologically neutral: Cassese and Weiler, *Change and Stability*, 136–63, 178–82.

are available, the remedy sought, the need for a speedy decision, how the lawyers 'feel' about the different tribunals available to them are all potential considerations. The *Southern Bluefin Tuna* and *Mox Plant* cases also show that lawyers' choices may be wrong. The lawyers' initial choice will impact upon the way the case is framed (whether in general or specialist terms), the way it is argued and the tribunal's decision and thus on the evolution of the law.

An example involves the repeated failure of the US to accord consular access to detained persons, especially those facing capital charges, as required by the Vienna Convention on Consular Relations, 1963, Article 36. This situation has been the subject of separate litigation before the ICJ[168] and hearings before the American Commission on Human Rights.[169] Before the American Commission the Vienna Convention provisions were categorised as 'concerning the protection of human rights' in the Americas and the failure to accord consular protection was determined to constitute a denial of due process. Before the ICJ the case was not adjudicated from a human rights perspective but rather as a violation of treaty obligations. By reformulating cases to fit the jurisdictional requirements of a particular tribunal, restrictive provisions such as those prohibiting the same matter from being examined 'under another procedure of international investigation or settlement'[170] may be avoided, although there is little jurisprudence on this point. From the point of view of law-making, it allows for authoritative interpretation of concepts from differing perspectives. This may be viewed as inculcating troubling incoherence or as enabling a richer consideration of the many facets of international law.

The fact that forum choices are available may have other legal consequences. Courts and tribunals seek to improve their own processes and to encourage litigants before them. Bodies may assess their own procedures in light of the potential benefits of procedures available in other fora. For example the 1982 UNCLOS, Article 290 (6) spells out that parties 'shall comply promptly with any provisional measures prescribed'. There is no similar wording in the Statute of the ICJ, Article 41. In *LaGrand* the ICJ was called upon to determine the legal effect of interim measures under Article 41, a point not previously decided by either the ICJ or the PCIJ. In determining Article 41 to give rise to binding interim measures the Court made no reference to the explicit power of the ITLOS,[171] but it is possible that it was a factor in their decision. Whatever the motivation of the ICJ in this case, the decision has had law-making effect.[172]

---

[168] *Vienna Convention on Consular Relations (Paraguay v. United States)* Request for the Indication of Provisional Measures (1998) ICJ Reports 248 (Order of 9 April); *LaGrand (Germany v. United States)* Merits (2001) ICJ Reports 466 (judgment of 27 June 2001); *Avena and other Mexican Nationals (Mexico v. US)* (2004) ICJ Reports (judgment of 31 March).

[169] *The Right to Information on Consular Assistance in the Framework of the Guarantees of the Due Process of Law*, Adv Op OC-16/99, 1 October 1999, IACHR (Series A), No. 16 (1999).

[170] International Covenant on Civil and Political Rights, First Optional Protocol, 1966, Article 5 (2) (a). There are similar provisions in other human rights treaties including the American Convention on Human Rights, 1969, Article 46 (1) (c).   [171] *LaGrand*, Merits, para 109.

[172] In *Mamatkulov v. Turkey* the ECHR Grand Chamber reconsidered an earlier decision that found there to be no obligation under the European Convention on states to comply with interim

6.   Precedential Weight of Judicial Decisions

As stated above the formal position is that there is no doctrine of precedent in international law and that international judicial decisions are binding only on the parties to the particular case. The reality is of course quite different and in many ways judicial decisions have law-making effect. Within the international legal system decisions of the ICJ are especially authoritative for a number of reasons. First is the ICJ's status as the principal judicial organ of the UN.[173] Second, the Court behaves as though its decisions have precedential value and thus consciously contributes to substantive law-making. It assumes the role of authoritative interpretation of procedural and substantive international law and its pronouncements are widely accepted as such by states, other international courts and tribunals, academic writers, expert bodies such as the ILC and NGOs.

From the outset, many of the judgments of the PCIJ and subsequently the ICJ have contained extensive references to, and extracts from, its previous decisions, relating to both procedural and substantive issues.[174] As Shabtai Rosenne has noted, there is 'a general desire for consistency and stability in the Court's case-law when the Court is dealing with legal issues which have been before it in previous cases'.[175] In the *Avena* case the ICJ was explicit, spelling out that:

To avoid any ambiguity, it should be made clear that, while what the Court has stated concerns the Mexican nationals whose cases have been brought before it by Mexico, the Court has been addressing the issues of principle . . . from the viewpoint of the general application of the Vienna Convention, and there can be no question of making an *a contrario* argument in respect of any of the Court's findings in the present Judgment. In other words, the fact that in this case the Court's ruling has concerned only Mexican nationals cannot be taken to imply that the conclusions reached by it in the present Judgment do not apply to other foreign nationals finding themselves in similar situations in the United States.[176]

In expectation of conformity with previous case law, lawyers arguing before the Court use the language of precedent and urge for the following, or distinguishing, of an earlier case. Members of Court engage similar language.[177] The meaning of a

---

measures and found there to be such an obligation. In reaching this decision the GC considered the provisions and case law of a number of international courts and tribunals including the *LaGrand* case; 41 EHRR (2005).

[173]   UN Charter, Articles 7 (1) and 92.

[174]   '[T]he practice of referring to its previous decisions has become one of the most conspicuous features of the Judgments and Opinions of the Court'; Lauterpacht, *The Development of International Law by the International Court*, 9.

[175]   S. Rosenne, *The Law and Practice of the International Court 1920–1996*, vol III, Procedure (The Hague, 1997) 1610; *Armed Activities on the Territory of the Congo (DRC v. Uganda)* sep op Judge Elaraby, para 19.   [176]   *Avena and other Mexican Nationals*, para 151.

[177]   In *Legal Consequences of the Construction of a Wall in the Palestinian Occupied Territory* Judge Higgins (admittedly from a common law jurisdiction) refers to the '*ratio decidendi*' of the *Eastern Carelia* case—an opinion which is theoretically advisory only; sep op Judge Higgins, paras 8–9.

case is never closed in the dynamic process of adjudication and decided cases generate further litigation. In the words of President of the Court Judge Higgins:

States which have no dispute before the Court follow the judgments of the Court with the greatest interest, because they know that every judgment is at once an authoritative pronouncement on the law, and also that, should they become involved in a dispute in which the same legal issues arise, the Court, which will always seek to act consistently and build on its own jurisprudence, will reach the same conclusions.[178]

The ICJ regularly makes statements such as 'according to its settled jurisprudence'.[179] Cases decided under its contentious jurisdiction and advisory opinions are replete with references to, and dicta from, previously decided cases. The jurisprudence on third party intervention offers many examples: the assertion made in *Haya de la Torre* that 'Every intervention is incidental to the proceedings in a case'[180] is reiterated in every subsequent case on third party intervention; the assumption of consistency in determinations of a request to intervene under ICJ Statute, Article 62 is made clear by the Chamber in the *Case Concerning the Land, Island and Maritime Frontier Dispute*, where it commenced its consideration of Nicaragua's application to intervene with the words: 'As the Court has made clear in previous cases';[181] in the *Case concerning the Land and Maritime Boundary between Cameroon and Nigeria* the Court simply cited extracts from the earlier *Case Concerning the Land, Island and Maritime Frontier Dispute* in acceding to Equatorial Guinea's request.[182]

Alongside the need for judicial consistency, international courts must also retain the flexibility to depart from earlier decisions where for example they have become obsolete through evolving state practice or treaty law. It is for instance inconceivable that the decisions in the *Lotus* case or the *Icelandic Fisheries* cases would be followed today given subsequent developments in the law of the sea in the 1958 and 1982 Conventions. Where the Court determines not to follow one of its previous decisions it normally explains why the earlier case is not applicable in the later case—that is it adopts the language of distinguishing. For example in *Monetary Gold* the Court formulated the principle that it will not determine a case where the interests of a third state that is not before the Court form the very subject matter of

---

[178] Higgins, *Problems and Process*, 202–3.
[179] *Arrest Warrant* Case, para 26 (that jurisdiction must be established at the time the case is filed).
[180] *Haya de la Torre (Colombia v. Peru)* (1951) ICJ Reports 71, 82 (judgment of 13 June 1951).
[181] *Case Concerning the Land, Island and Maritime Frontier Dispute* (El Salvador/Honduras) Application by Nicaragua for Permission to Intervene (1990) ICJ Reports 92, para 52 (judgment of 13 September).
[182] However, in upholding Nicaragua's request to intervene, the Chamber barely referred to earlier decisions where requests had failed. It is difficult to determine why Nicaragua's application succeeded where Italy's had failed in the *Continental Shelf* Case (Libyan Arab Jamahiriya/Malta) Application by Italy to Intervene (1984) ICJ Reports 3 (judgment of 21 March 1984). In Equatorial Guinea's request to intervene the Court did not refer to the apparent conflict between the Chamber in the *Land, Island and Maritime Frontier* Case and the Court in the *Italy* Case.

the case. This principle was applied in the *East Timor* case and distinguished in *Nicaragua*,[183] *Nauru*[184] and *Armed Activities on the Territory of the Congo*.[185]

Third, as discussed above, a decision may generate the requisite state practice and *opinio juris* to establish customary international law. Principles the Court enunciates are also likely to be influential in inter-state negotiations in similar situations,[186] again contributing to the body of applicable state practice. Fourth, the Court makes decisions with dispositive effect. The particular need for certainty in boundary delimitation and consequential resource allocation has led to an especially high number of land and maritime boundary disputes being submitted to the ICJ. A boundary determination 'achieves a permanence which the treaty itself does not necessarily enjoy'[187] and effectively determines the territorial disposition for the two states concerned and for all other states. The *Libya/Chad* case illustrates the law-making nature of a boundary determination which was reinforced by the parties' subsequent agreement on execution of the judgment that provided for the complete withdrawal of Libyan troops from the disputed territory to be observed by a United Nations observer group.[188]

It is precisely because of the definitive nature of such territorial disputes that the incidental procedure of intervention has been most used in the context of boundary delimitation. In a number of instances a third state has viewed with concern a bilateral boundary dispute, apprehending that the disposition might impinge upon an area to which it lays claim. Intervention is available when a state considers that it has 'an interest of a legal nature' which may be affected by a decision in a case to which it is not a party.[189] Theoretically Article 59 renders unnecessary any requirement for a third party intervention procedure since the decision is binding only on the parties to the case. But intervention has been allowed and some judges have made explicit that they do not consider Article 59 to afford adequate third party protection. In effect they accept the law-making effects of judicial determination. Judge Jennings, for example, has stated that Article 59 is solely to prevent legal principles accepted by the Court in a particular case from being binding also

---

[183] 'None of the States referred to can be regarded as in the same position as Albania in that case, [*Monetary Gold*] so as to be truly indispensable to the pursuance of the proceedings.' *Nicaragua Case*, Jurisdiction and Admissibility (1984) ICJ Reports 431, para 88.

[184] The Court found that the interests of New Zealand and the UK 'do not constitute the very subject matter of the judgment . . . and the situation is in that respect different from that . . . in *Monetary Gold*' *Certain Phosphate Lands in Nauru (Nauru v. Australia)* (1992) ICJ Reports, 240, para 55.

[185] *Armed Activities on the Territory of the Congo (DRC v. Uganda)* (2005) ICJ Reports, paras 203–4.

[186] M. Shaw, 'A Practical Look at the International Court of Justice', in M. Evans (ed), *Remedies in International Law: The Institutional Dilemma* (Oxford, 1998) 11, 13.

[187] *Territorial Dispute* (Libyan Arab Jamahiriya/Chad) (1994) ICJ Reports 6, para 73 (judgment of 13 February).

[188] On May 30 1994, representatives of the two parties jointly declared that the withdrawal had been completed.

[189] Statute of the ICJ, Article 62. C. Chinkin, *Third Parties in International Law* (Oxford, 1993) 147–85.

upon other states or in other disputes.[190] He considered that Article 59 cannot alter the persuasive effect of Court decisions, and that in a dispositive judgment such as one allocating rights and duties, it provides a purely technical protection. Similarly, Judge Oda has stated that Article 59 may not be accepted as guaranteeing that a decision of the Court in a case regarding title *erga omnes* would not affect a claim by a third state to the same title.[191]

Fifth, assertions by the Court of obligations owed *erga omnes* are applicable to all members of the international community,[192] for example the right to self-determination.[193] Sixth, the Court makes determinations with objective and constitutive legal effect, in particular through its advisory jurisdiction where the Court furnishes the requesting international organisation[s] with 'the elements of law necessary for them in their action'.[194] Such pronouncements effectively make law for all member (and non-member states) as for example in the determination of the legal personality of the United Nations,[195] the implied powers of the UNGA,[196] or through a declaration of illegality from which certain legal consequences flow, whether or not they are spelled out by the Court. As is well known, the Court determined South Africa's obligations under the continued Mandate in South West Africa through a chain of advisory opinions and in *Namibia* it affirmed that '[a] binding determination made by a competent organ of the United Nations to the effect that a situation is illegal cannot remain without consequence'.[197] The required consequence for member states was the recognition of the illegality of South Africa's continued presence in Namibia, in which obligation it was 'incumbent' on non-member states to give assistance. Similarly all states are under an obligation not to recognise the illegal situation resulting from the construction of the Israeli security wall.[198] In some instances the Court has openly gone beyond, and changed, existing law as for example in the *Reservations* case[199]

---

[190] *Libya/Malta Continental Shelf Case*, Application for Permission to Intervene (1984) ICJ Reports 3, diss op Judge Jennings, para 27. Judge Jennings was referring to the objective of Article 59 as defined by the PCIJ in *Certain German Interests in Polish Upper Silesia* PCIJ, Series A, No. 7, 3, 19 (judgment of 25 March 1926).   [191] Ibid, diss op Judge Oda, para 28.
[192] The development of the concept from the dicta in *Barcelona Traction* is another example of the law-making impact of decisions of the ICJ; *Barcelona Traction Light and Power Company, Limited* (New Application: 1962) (*Belgium v. Spain*) (1970) ICJ Reports 3, para 33.
[193] *East Timor* Case (*Portugal v. Australia*) (1995) ICJ Reports 90, para 29 (judgment of 30 June).
[194] *Legal Consequences of the Construction of a Wall in the Occupied Palestinian Territory* (2004) ICJ Reports (Adv Op 9 July 2004) para 60.
[195] *Reparation for Injuries Suffered in the Service of the United Nations* (1949) ICJ Reports (Adv Op 11 April 1949) 185–7.
[196] eg *Certain Expenses of the United Nations* (1962) ICJ Reports 151 (Adv Op 20 July).
[197] *Legal Consequences for States of the Continued Presence of South Africa in Namibia (South West Africa) notwithstanding Security Council Resolution 276 (1970)* (1971) ICJ Reports 3, para 117 (Adv Op 21 June). The most evident consequence is to put an end to an illegal situation; *Haya de la Torre*, 82.
[198] *Legal Consequences of the Construction of a Wall in the Palestinian Occupied Territory*, para 163. Judge Higgins considered the assimilation with the *Namibia* opinion to be incorrect; sep op Judge Higgins, para 2.
[199] *Reservations to the Convention on the Prevention and Punishment of the Crime of Genocide* (1951) ICJ Reports 15 (Adv Op 28 May).

where its disregard of the unanimity rule has become largely accepted.[200] The strongly worded dissent asserted that the majority view was contrary to existing law and 'current practice' and that change should be achieved through express treaty provision, carrying the implication that judicial law-making of this sort was not appropriate.[201]

The ICJ gives precedential effect to its own decisions but rarely makes any reference to the decisions of other international courts and tribunals as offering it persuasive authority or analogous reasoning,[202] although individual judges may do so.[203] There is little similar reluctance to look to the jurisprudence of other courts among other international judges who use ICJ jurisprudence and that of other judicial bodies to support their decisions.[204] There are many examples of the ICTY and ICTR citing ICJ cases, especially with respect to issues of competence and procedure. For example, the Appellate Chamber in *Tadic* drew upon *Nottebohm*, the *Namibia* opinion, and the *Effect of Awards* case in determining that it had jurisdiction to determine the validity of its establishment by the Security Council;[205] the *Expenses* case in determining that it was not barred from making a decision because the case involved a political question;[206] the *Nicaragua* case for the proposition that Article 1 of the four Geneva Conventions, has become a 'general principle . . . of humanitarian law to which the Conventions merely give specific expression'.[207] In developing substantive international criminal law the ICTY has regularly analysed the jurisprudence of the European and American Courts of Human Rights—which in turn have drawn upon that of international criminal courts—and case law and legislation from national legal systems. Illustrating again from *Tadic*, the Appellate Chamber drew upon the *Eichmann* case from the Supreme Court of Israel and the *Barbie* case from the French *Cour de Cassation*.[208]

We can speculate on the reasons for such mutual borrowing. First, may be the desire to support what might be novel legal conclusions with persuasive authority from other international tribunals and thus to enhance the legitimacy of the decision. The unique authority of the ICJ may be especially important in this respect.

---

[200] The Court's opinion is largely replicated in the Vienna Convention on the Law of Treaties, 1969, Articles 19–23. The law on reservations is currently under reconsideration by the International Law Commission; see Chapter 4.

[201] *Reservations to the Convention on the Prevention and Punishment of the Crime of Genocide*, 31, diss op Judges Guerrero, Sir Arnold McNair, Read and Hsu Mo.

[202] The majority opinion unusually referred to the case law of the Human Rights Committee in the *Legal Consequences of the Construction of a Wall in the Palestinian Occupied Territory*, para 109.

[203] eg in *Armed Activities on the Territory of the Congo* (*DRC v. Uganda*) Judge Simma drew on the jurisprudence of the ICTY; paras 23, 29, sep op Judge Simma. Judge Simma also referred to the opinion of the Venice Commission, an expert body established by the Council of Europe; ibid, para 27.

[204] For ECJ citation of ICJ jurisprudence see A. Rosas, 'With a Little Help from my Friends: International Case Law as a Source of Reference for the EU Courts', 5 *The Global Community Yearbook of International Law and Jurisprudence* 2005 (2006) 203.

[205] *Prosecutor v. Tadic*, Decision on the Defence Motion for Interlocutory Appeal on Jurisdiction, 2 October 1995, paras 14–22.   [206] Ibid, paras 23–5.

[207] Ibid, para 93.   [208] Ibid, paras 57–9.

Second, may be the desire for transnational judicial consistency. Third, is the comparatively small group of international lawyers who appear before these various tribunals and these are the tools with which they are most familiar and rely upon in argument. Fourth, may be the perceived audience of such courts and tribunals—other international lawyers and legal institutions. Judges may wish to impress this audience with their knowledge of and respect for international law, even while they are progressively developing it.[209] Fifth, judges may be conscious of gaps or uncertainties in the law applicable in the case before them and look to other international law institutions to assist in reaching a decision. This law-making through institutional dialogue is part of what Anne-Marie Slaughter has described as 'Courts . . . talking to each other all over the world'.[210] This too supports the argument that proliferation of international courts has not in fact led to fragmentation and inconsistency in the development of international law but rather to commonality whereby principles are repeated and gain in authority and expectation.

But international courts of limited jurisdiction have not just routinely applied earlier rulings of the ICJ without considering their appropriateness in the particular context and have upon occasion departed from them. In *Tadic* the ICTY Appeal Chamber rejected what the ICJ had 'authoritatively' suggested in the *Nicaragua* case to be the legal test for the degree of control required for individuals to be considered as acting on behalf of a state.[211] It considered factors that made the *Nicaragua* test unpersuasive, including what it saw as inconsistency with judicial and state practice, and concluded by setting out its own test. The Appellate Chamber's lengthy analysis showed that it did not depart lightly from ICJ authority and its sense of responsibility for judicial reasoning in development of the law. In another example, the ICTY affirmed the definition of torture in the Convention against Torture and Other Cruel, Inhuman or Degrading Treatment, 1984 as constituting customary international law.[212] However it subsequently distinguished its criminal law jurisdiction from the human rights framework of the Torture Convention holding that 'the public official requirement is not a requirement under customary international law in relation to the criminal responsibility of an individual for torture outside of the framework of the Torture Convention'.[213] This differentiation is adopted in the Rome Statute,[214] thereby demonstrating law-making though a blend of judicial decision and treaty negotiation.

The last examples illustrate how many of the newer international courts have played a leading role in developing international law within their areas of specialist

---

[209] These reasons reflect those put forward by McCrudden in explaining why judges in domestic courts use foreign law; C. McCrudden, 'Human Rights and Judicial Use of Comparative Law', in E. Orucu, *Judicial Comparativism in Human Rights Cases* (London, 2003) 1, 9 ff.

[210] A. -M. Slaughter, 'A Typology of Transjudicial Communication', 29 *University of Richmond LR* (1994) 99, cited McCrudden, 'Human Rights and Judicial Use of Comparative Law', 5. See Chapter 2.

[211] *Prosecutor v. Dusko Tadic*, IT-94-1, judgment of 15 July 1999 (AC), para 99.

[212] *Prosecutor v. Anto Furundžija*, IT-95-17 (judgment of 21 July 2000), para 111 (AC).

[213] *Prosecutor v. Dragoljub Kunarac, Radomir Kovac and Zoran Vukovic*, IT-96-23 and IT-96-23/1 (judgment of 12 June 2002) (AC), para 148.   [214] Rome Statute of the ICC, Article 7 (2) (e).

jurisdiction. Many of the judges elected to specialist courts such as the ITLOS, international criminal courts, human rights courts, WTO dispute settlement procedures have expertise within the relevant areas of law and particular qualifications may be required. ICJ judges are required to have qualifications for election to high judicial positions in their own country or to be 'jurisconsults of recognized competence in international law'.[215] In contrast the ITLOS Statute, Article 2 specifies that judges shall have 'recognised competence in the field of the law of the sea'; the Rome Statute of the ICC, Article 36 (3) that judges have competence in criminal law and procedure and relevant experience in criminal proceedings, or competence in international humanitarian law or human rights law and relevant professional legal experience;[216] and the WTO Annex on Dispute Settlement, Article 8 that Panels include people with experience under GATT, whether by teaching or publishing on international trade law or policy, or through service as a senior trade policy official.

Nevertheless while focusing on their particular area of law they have in many instances reaffirmed the authority of general international law and have contributed to its development. For example, the ECHR and ACHR have built up significant bodies of jurisprudence that flesh out the requirements of the relevant treaties. Both Courts routinely apply and develop general international law,[217] with respect to such principles as treaty interpretation, the exhaustion of domestic remedies,[218] state responsibility, jurisdiction and legal consequences of non-recognition. Where their assertions of legal principle have been fed back into other law-making processes, legal coherence and consistency are promoted. For example, as discussed in Chapter 2, state responsibility for the internationally wrongful acts of non-state actors through the duty of due diligence was articulated by the ACHR in *Velasquez Rodriguez v. Honduras*.[219] The Court did not cite any judicial authority and articulated the principle from its interpretation of Article 1 of the American Convention. Nevertheless reports and instruments of various UN bodies have picked up the standard of due diligence and applied it in other contexts. It is included in soft law instruments such as the General Assembly Declaration on the Elimination of Violence Against Women, 1993,[220] the UN Office of the High Commissioner for Human Rights Model Principles and Guidelines on Trafficking,[221] reports of the special rapporteurs of the UN Commission on Human Rights (for example those on torture, on extrajudicial, summary and arbitrary executions, and on the use of

[215] Statute of the ICJ, Article 2.

[216] Rome Statute of the ICC, Article 36 (8) (b) requires states also to take into account the need for judges with specific legal expertise including on violence against women.

[217] eg the ECHR has interpreted European Convention on Human Rights, Article 1, 'within their jurisdiction' from the 'standpoint of public international law'; *Bankovic v. Belgium and 16 Other States* (Appl. No. 52207/99), para 59 (judgment of 12 December 2001).

[218] eg European Convention on Human Rights, Article 35 and American Convention on Human Rights, Article 46 both require domestic remedies to be 'exhausted in accordance with generally recognized rules ["principles" in the American Convention] of international law'.

[219] IACHR (Series C), No. 4 (1988) para 172 (judgment of 29 July 1988).

[220] UNGA Res 48/104, December 1993.

[221] *Report of the Office of the United Nations High Commissioner for Human Rights to the Economic and Social Council*, UN Doc E/2002/68/Add 1, 20 May 2002.

mercenaries), reports by representatives of the Secretary-General, (for example the S-G SR on internally displaced persons); by human rights treaty bodies (for example the Committee on the Elimination of All Forms of Discrimination against Women, General Comment No. 19 and the Committee on the Elimination of All Forms of Racial Discrimination); by expert group meetings (for example the meeting on children and juveniles in detention).[222] The standard is not applied only in human rights cases: ICSID arbitrations have determined that a host country must treat a foreign investor with 'due diligence'.[223] It is difficult to argue that this has not become the required customary international law standard of conduct with respect to state responsibility for the internationally wrongful acts of non-state actors.

It is not only judicial bodies that have law-making effect. Despite the centrality of party autonomy in international arbitration, some arbitral awards have also been influential in developing principles of international law. The reporting of arbitral awards—despite their 'private' character—enhances their law-making potential. The contribution of regular reporting of the decisions of international courts and tribunals and the greatly increased availability of jurisprudence through the internet, to law-making should also not be underestimated.[224] Successive adjudicative bodies have contributed to the rules and principles of international law on diplomatic protection. As well as the PCIJ and ICJ, decisions of the General Claims Commission,[225] the Special Claims Commission (in the particular context of revolutionary events), the US/Iran Claims Tribunal, ICSID and NAFTA arbitral awards (foreign investment) have been widely drawn upon. The case law of the earlier General Claims Commission and Special Claims Commission was extensively used by the Harvard Research Programme and subsequently by successive ILC rapporteurs in their respective work on state responsibility, and are still widely cited.

7.   Legitimacy of Law-Making by International Courts

The significance of international tribunals in the international law-making process depends upon the weight that is given to their decisions. Ultimately '[t]he authoritativeness of the decision will essentially be founded upon the constitutional function, perceived role and reputation of the Court'.[226] This applies to whichever court has made the decision. If states (and other international actors) accept the

---

[222] These are listed in the Report of the Special Rapporteur on violence against women, its causes and consequences, Ms Radhika Coomaraswamy, on trafficking in women, women's migration and violence against women, submitted in accordance with Commission on Human Rights Res 1997/44, E/CN 4/2000/68, 29 February 2000, para 52.

[223] *Asian Agricultural Products Ltd v. Republic of Sri Lanka* ICSID Case No. ARB/87/3 (award of 27 June 1990) 30 ILM (1991) 577.

[224] R. Jennings, 'The Judiciary, International and National, and the Development of International Law', 45 *ICLQ* (1996) 1.

[225] Established by the General Claims Convention, 8 September 1923 (USA and Mexico).

[226] Shaw, 'A Practical Look at the International Court of Justice', 11, 27.

decisions of international courts and build practice around them then their law-making impact is substantial, as was seen in the aftermath of the *Anglo-Norwegian Fisheries* and *Reservations* cases.[227] If they do not, the decision may become marginalised, seen as exceptional and have minimal law-making effect. The short-lived concept of preferential fishing zones endorsed by the ICJ in the *Icelandic Fisheries* case but quickly abandoned at the UNCLOS III negotiations, or the PCIJ's extension of port state jurisdiction to collisions between ships on the high seas,[228] but repudiated by the Convention on the High Seas, 1958, Article 11 are two well-known examples.

The adoption by states of practice deriving from judicial decision-making will depend *inter alia* on the degree of legitimacy accorded to the relevant body. Any court's role in the law-making process is likely to be accepted if it is perceived by the international community as a credible, impartial and legitimate institution which reaches reasoned decisions in accordance with accepted legal principles. Legitimacy is likely to be improved if the decision is also perceived as fair in procedure and outcome. The introduction of an appellate chamber (as at the ICTY and ICTR) or of a Grand Chamber (as at the European Court of Human Rights) enhances legitimacy through the availability of appeal and the greater number of judges participating in these decisions.

The WTO Appellate Body is especially important in this respect. The WTO Dispute Settlement Panels, which hear cases at first instance, are not staffed by lawyers, but by trade officials and diplomats. The Appellate Body, however, is composed of international lawyers with expertise not only in trade law but also in general international law. As we noted in Chapter 5, WTO appellate decisions have shown considerable sensitivity to international law techniques of treaty interpretation, and to the integration of WTO law and general international law.[229] They have also ensured that WTO agreements are interpreted and applied consistently, and have generally raised the standard of reasoning expected of panels.

Although legitimacy is crucial for all international courts this section focuses on the ICJ as the court at the heart of international adjudication. In Franck's words:

The ICJ represents such a major advance in the twentieth century progress towards the institutionalizing of a community of states that its methods and procedures for manifesting the fairness of its decisions require careful examination, evaluation and recognition.[230]

---

[227] The more flexible and law-making approach of the majority in the *Reservations* case has been revisited. In the *Democratic Republic of the Congo v. Rwanda* Judges Higgins, Kooijmans, Elaraby, Owada and Simma stated that the *Reservations* case did not 'foreclose legal developments' which are taking place in other fora (for example the ILC) and through the practice of the regional and international human rights insitutions. The 1951 Opinion was not a barrier to 'developing the law to meet contemporary realities' and should not be viewed as such. (*Democratic Republic of the Congo v. Rwanda* (2006) ICJ Reports (Joint separate opinion Judges Higgins, Kooijmans, Elaraby, Owada and Simma.) [228] *Lotus* case (1927) PCIJ Series A, No. 10, 31.

[229] See in particular *Import Prohibition of Certain Shrimp and Shrimp Products*, WTO Appellate Body (1998) WT/DS58/AB/R, at paras 130–1.

[230] Franck, *Fairness in International Law and Institutions*, 316. Franck asserts that fairness comprises two ingredients: legitimacy and distributive justice.

Among the many factors that enhance or decrease the legitimacy of decisions is the public nature of all written and oral pleadings and of the judgment allowing for analysis of all aspects of the process, including the judicial reasoning. The availability of these documents on the ICJ website (and those of other international courts) is an enormous boon to demystifying its processes and increasing its legitimacy.[231] It is also 'an essential requirement of the judicial process that a court should show the steps by which it reaches its conclusions'.[232] The collegiate working methods of the ICJ described above are an important component of this. Judge Jennings has explained how separate and dissenting judgments also contribute to the overall legitimacy of the process for 'unless one fully understands what the choices were, one cannot fully understand the choice that was made; whether for example the chosen view was a median view, or nearer to one extreme of the spectrum of views from which choice was made'.[233] The presence of dissenting and separate opinions palpably demonstrates that the decision of the Court was based on juridical argument, not political bias.[234]

Another factor that enhances a court's credibility is its reliance on previous jurisprudence and the reputation of judicial consistency. Unpredictable decisions which do not rest upon previous jurisprudence may be intolerable to governments.[235] Where a decision is novel the Court engages a slew of techniques to support its decision. For example in the *LaGrand* case the ICJ bolstered its novel ruling (that provisional measures are binding on the parties) through the following means: comparison of the French and English texts; interpretation of the Statute of the ICJ, Article 41 in accordance with the object and purpose of the Statute; the long-standing principle of international law that 'parties to a case must abstain from any measure capable of exercising a prejudicial effect in regard to the execution of the decision to be given, and, in general, not allow any step of any kind to be taken which might aggravate or extend the dispute';[236] and analogous measures indicated by the Court to avoid aggravation of a dispute. The Court considered that these were sufficient to obviate any necessity to look at the *travaux préparatoires* of Article 41 of its Statute and then proceeded, at some length to do so. Finally it determined that the UN Charter, Article 94 did not preclude any such decision. The Court evidently sought to provide the strongest possible basis for its unprecedented decision.

Another concern is where the language of the Court is open-ended and insufficiently precise to make clear the legal obligations that flow. Indeterminate language

---

[231] However as of 2006 NGO submissions made in accordance with ICJ Practice Direction XII, 2004 (discussed in Chapter 2) are not available on the web and there is no easy means of identifying whether such submissions have been made, their source, content or whether the judges have had reference to them.

[232] *Legality of the Threat or Use of Nuclear Weapons*, diss op Judge Higgins, paras 7, 9.

[233] R. Jennings, 'The Collegiate Responsibility and Authority of the International Court of Justice', in Y. Dinstein (ed), *International Law at a Time of Perplexity: Essays in Honour of Shabtai Rosenne* (Dordrecht, 1989) 343, 352.   [234] Ibid 353.

[235] R. Jennings, 'The Identification of International Law', in B. Cheng, *International Law: Teaching and Practice* (London, 1982) 3.   [236] *LaGrand*, para 103.

is one of Tom Franck's criteria for denying legitimacy.[237] Judge Higgins critiqued the Court's *dispositif* in the *Legality of the Threat or Use of Nuclear Weapons* for its lack of specificity:

I do not consider it juridically meaningful to say that the use of nuclear weapons is 'generally contrary to the rules of international law applicable in armed conflict, and in particular the principles and rules of humanitarian law'. What does the term 'generally' mean? Is it a numerical allusion, or is it a reference to different types of nuclear weapons, or is it a suggestion that the rules of humanitarian law cannot be met save for exceptions? If so, where is the Court's analysis of these rules, properly understood, and their application to nuclear weapons? And what are any exceptions to be read into the term 'generally'?[238]

Another factor that can undermine the legitimacy, and therefore the compliance 'pull', of an opinion is where it is considered that a court 'did not have before it the requisite factual bases for its sweeping findings'.[239] The ICJ has specified that it must have 'sufficient information and evidence to enable it to arrive at a judicial conclusion on any disputed questions of fact the determination of which is necessary for it to give an opinion'.[240] However the ICJ is not a sophisticated finder of facts. Only rarely have witnesses of fact appeared before it[241] and evidentiary matters have not received much attention. Yet understanding of law as expressed by any court depends upon the facts that it has found. Disputed versions of the facts have contributed to repudiation of the judgment. For example, in *Nicaragua* the US withdrawal from the merits of the case meant that it did not present evidence before the Court. The Court's determinations of fact were based primarily upon Nicaragua's written and oral submissions and witnesses called by Nicaragua.[242] The Statute of the Court, Article 53 requires the Court to satisfy itself that the case of the appearing party is 'well-founded in fact and law', which reinforces their interdependence as the basis for the judgment. Findings of fact and law that are not based upon properly presented evidence cannot be sustained. In the words of Judge Buergenthal in the *Security Wall* case: 'the critical question in determining whether or not [the Court should] exercise its discretion in acting on an advisory opinion request is "whether the Court has before it sufficient information and evidence to enable it to arrive at a judicial conclusion upon any disputed questions of fact the determination of which is necessary for it to give an opinion in conditions compatible with its judicial character".'[243] Judge Buergenthal continued to

---

[237] T. Franck, 'Legitimacy in the International System', 82 *AJIL* (1988) 705, 712.

[238] *Legality of the Threat or Use of Nuclear Weapons*, diss op Judge Higgins, para 25.

[239] *Legal Consequences of the Construction of a Wall in the Occupied Palestinian Territory*, Declaration, Judge Buergenthal, para 1.

[240] *Western Sahara* (1975) ICJ Reports 12, para 46 (Adv Op 16 October); *Legal Consequences of the Construction of a Wall in the Occupied Palestinian Territory*, para 56.

[241] Witnesses gave factual evidence before the ICJ in the oral proceedings in the *Application of the Convention on the Prevention and Punishment of the Crime of Genocide (Bosnia and Herzegovina v. Serbia and Montenegro)*, 2006.

[242] *Nicaragua* Case, Merits (1986) ICJ Reports 14, para 13.

[243] *Legal Consequences of the Construction of a Wall in the Occupied Palestinian Territory*, Declaration Judge Buergenthal, para 1 (citing *Western Sahara*, para 46).

explain just what issues had not been properly brought before the Court and considered by it:

> The nature of these cross-Green Line attacks and their impact on Israel and its population are never really seriously examined by the Court, and the dossier provided the Court by the United Nations on which the Court to a large extent bases its findings barely touches on that subject. I am not suggesting that such an examination would relieve Israel of the charge that the wall it is building violates international law, either in whole or in part, only that without this examination the findings made are not legally well founded. In my view, the humanitarian needs of the Palestinian people would have been better served had the Court taken these considerations into account, for that would have given the Opinion the credibility I believe it lacks.[244]

The logic of this view is that the Court's opinion on important issues of international law is weakened by insufficient factual grounding and consequently its contribution to the law-making process is undermined.

Following the appropriate procedures is also important, although it may be hard to disentangle procedural flaws and those which go to the heart of the judicial process. This point is also well illustrated by the Request for Provisional Measures in the *LaGrand* case. Germany filed its application on 2 March 1999 and since Walter LaGrand was due to be executed the following day the Court heard the request without any exchange of pleadings or oral hearing, the next day. The US disputed this procedure, arguing that the Court should not make an order without first hearing both parties. Further, there had been lengthy criminal proceedings in the US and Germany had made its request very late, indeed at the last minute.[245] The Court made an Order for provisional measures.

It has been suggested that the rushed and one-sided proceedings before the ICJ undermined the weight of the Order. Judge Schwebel in a separate opinion expressed his profound reservations about this unprecedented departure 'in critical measure from a basic rule of the judicial process'.[246] Before the US Supreme Court the US Solicitor-General took the position that 'an order of the International Court of Justice indicating provisional measures is not binding and does not furnish a basis for judicial relief'. One reason for his position was 'the extraordinarily short time' (four hours[247]) between the issuance of the Order and the scheduled execution. This merges into considerations of inappropriate use of the international judicial process.

In the judgment on the merits Judge Buergenthal thought the question of the binding nature of provisional measures to be inadmissible because of Germany's 'lack of diligence' in pursuing the *LaGrand* case, which was the reason for the first rushed proceedings. He thought that Germany's negligence in this regard should have been scrutinised by the Court at the merits hearing. He further considered

---

[244] *Legal Consequences of the Construction of a Wall in the Occupied Palestinian Territory*, Declaration, Judge Buergenthal, para 3.
[245] *LaGrand*, Request for Provisional Measures (1999) ICJ Reports 9, para 12.
[246] Ibid 21, sep op Judge Schwebel.
[247] *LaGrand*, Merits, 548, para 7, diss op Judge Buergenthal.

that Germany had acted unfairly through a 'litigation strategy prejudicial to the United States' in that it knew of the Solicitor-General's rejection of the binding nature of provisional measures consequent upon the earlier *Breard* case.[248] Judge Buergenthal concluded that Germany's behaviour:

amounted to procedural misconduct prejudicial to the interests of the United States as a party to the instant proceedings. Such misconduct provides the requisite justification—it compels it, in my opinion—for declaring Germany's third submission inadmissible.

In Judge Buergenthal's view the ruling on the binding nature of provisional measures should never have been given—a position that undermines the legitimacy of the holding.

Another, related, concern is that adjudication is being used for political ends,[249] or that judicial and political functions are becoming blurred. For example concerns have been expressed about the respective functions of the WTO Dispute Settlement Panels and the appellate body on the one hand and political organs on the other. Roessler has argued that 'the now independent judicial organs should . . . refrain from using their interpretative power to confer decision-making authority upon themselves that the Members of the WTO have explicitly assigned to bodies composed of the Members'.[250] If they do so their actions are likely to be considered illegitimate. An example is the controversy over the acceptance of *amicus* briefs from non-state actors. The constitutive rules of the Dispute Settlement Understanding are silent on this issue but the appellate body has allowed both itself and the Panels to receive such submissions. In the *Asbestos* case in 2000 the Appellate Body set out guidelines for applications to admit such briefs and received 17 applications to do so. At a special meeting of the WTO General Council member states reacted strongly against this process asserting that the Appellate Body had exceeded its judicial function by in effect legislating. The Appellate Body in fact rejected all seventeen applications but on the grounds that they were not within their guidelines, not that it was acting inappropriately to consider acceptance of such briefs. However the juxtaposition of the meeting of the General Council and the rejection of the applications also raised concerns about political interference in the judicial process.[251] In either case there are concerns about legitimacy.

Some have perceived the ICTY to be politically biased because of its failure to indict NATO leaders with respect to the bombing of Serbia in 1999 while former Serbian leader Milosevic was brought to trial. Decisions and opinions of the ICJ

---

[248] *Vienna Convention on Consular Relations (Paraguay v. United States)* Request for the Indication of Provisional Measures (1998) ICJ Reports 266 (Order of 9 April).

[249] Reisman has called this a 'factititous' concern 'for all courts are political institutions'. M. Reisman, 'International Politics and International Law—Reflections on the So-Called "Politicization" of the International Court', in W. Heere (ed), *International Law and its Sources: Liber Amicorum Maarten Bos* (Deventer, 1989) 77.

[250] Cited Charnovitz, 'Judicial Independence in the World Trade Organization', 219, 232.

[251] Charnovitz, 'Judicial Independence in the World Trade Organization', 235.

have also been denounced because of their alleged political bias.[252] An advisory opinion may be undermined because the nature of the question it was required to address risked politicising the Court.[253] Since a request for an advisory opinion must be made by an international organisation it is likely to have been the subject of political debate within the relevant body. The concern has been expressed that if the Court is perceived as politicised it will be unable to contribute to global security and will undermine respect for the rule of law.[254] In response to such claims the Court has stressed that the presence of political issues does not deprive a question of its legal character. For example, in the *Legal Consequences of the Construction of a Wall in the Occupied Palestinian Territory* the Court opined that:

Whatever its political aspects, the Court cannot refuse to admit the legal character of a question which invites it to discharge an essentially judicial task, namely, an assessment of the legality of the possible conduct of States with regard to the obligations imposed upon them by international law.[255]

Indeed, the Court reiterated its earlier statement that 'in situations in which political considerations are prominent it may be particularly necessary for an international organization to obtain an advisory opinion from the Court as to the legal principles applicable with respect to the matter under debate'.[256] Nevertheless the Court's position on this may not satisfy all participants, especially those who had voted against the resolution requesting the opinion or had argued before it for the impropriety of complying with the request.[257]

External factors which relate to the ICJ's position as the 'principal judicial organ of the United Nations' may also lead to it being perceived as lacking legitimacy. These include the alleged non-democratic nature of the Court, its representative deficiency and that giving weight to judicial decision-making offends domestic commitment to the separation of powers and lack of judicial independence. Criticisms have rarely been so vociferously expressed as by Harvard Law Professor Alan Dershowitz in his editorial on the Court in respect of its 2004 advisory opinion in the *Wall* case. Dershowitz attacked the 'questionable status' of the ICJ in that:

No Israeli judge may serve on that court as a permanent member, while sworn enemies of Israel serve among its judges, several of whom represent countries that do not abide by the rule of law. Virtually every democracy voted against that court's taking jurisdiction over the

---

[252] E. McWhinney, 'Historical Dilemmas and Contradictions in U.S. Attitudes to the World Court: The Aftermath of the Nicaragua Judgments', in Y. Dinstein (ed), *International Law at a Time of Perplexity* (Dordrecht, 1989) 423 provides an overview of political condemnation of the *Nicaragua* decision.

[253] eg written statement, United States of America, para 1.4; this is not just a concern in advisory opinions; see *Legality of the Use of Force (Serbia and Montenegro v. Belgium)* Request for the Indication of Provisional Measures (1999) ICJ Reports, diss op V-P Weeramantry (Order of 2 June).

[254] *Legal Consequences of the Construction of a Wall in the Occupied Palestinian Territory*, sep op Judge Koojimans, para 20.

[255] *Legal Consequences of the Construction of a Wall in the Occupied Palestinian Territory*, para 41.

[256] Ibid.

[257] In Chapter 1 we discuss the different opinions about whether the influence of non-state actors in seeking the advisory opinion *Legality of the Threat or Use of Nuclear Weapons* undermined its legitimacy.

fence case, while nearly every country that voted to take jurisdiction was a tyranny. Israel owes the International Court absolutely no deference. It is under neither a moral nor a legal obligation to give any weight to its predetermined decision.[258]

Arguing that a 'judicial decision can have no legitimacy when rendered against a nation that is wilfully excluded from the court's membership by bigotry', Dershowitz likened the ICJ to 'a Mississippi court in the 1930s'.

Dershowitz's complaints show little understanding of the composition and structure of the ICJ. No state has a legal right to a permanent judge on the Court and indeed the Statute of the ICJ, Article 2 states that judges are to be 'elected regardless of their nationality'. Article 9 requires representation of forms of civilisation and legal systems, not of states. Indeed representation of all states would be impossible in a court of 15 judges. Admittedly there has been a long practice of ensuring the presence of a judge from each of the Permanent Members of the SC, but this is not a legal entitlement under the Statute.

The composition of the ICJ has been a cause of concern to different states at different periods throughout its history.[259] Inadequate representation from Africa and Asia in its early years made it appear inimical to the interests of such states—a perception that was enhanced by the 1966 *SW Africa* cases.[260] However after the 1971 *Namibia* opinion with its resounding defeat for apartheid South Africa, this perception was gradually reversed and since the 1980s a growing number of cases involving such states have been brought before the Court. These include both cases that involve a less-developed state (not necessarily from Africa or Asia) against a developed state and disputes between two or more developing states from within the same region. In the contemporary world it is the US that is less willing to accept the legitimacy of international adjudication. After the high spot (from its point of view) of the *Tehran Hostages* case[261] it has become hostile to the ICJ as exemplified by its withdrawal of its Article 36 (2) Declaration accepting the compulsory jurisdiction of the Court in 1984.[262] In the aftermath of the *Nicaragua* case American international lawyers saw the Court as in crisis. While this was averted through the many cases on the Court's docket in the 1990s,[263]

---

[258] Alan Dershowitz, 'Israel follows its own law, not bigoted Hague decision', *Jerusalem Post*, 11 July 2004, repeated *Jewish World Review*, 12 July 2004 at <http://www.jewishworldreview.com/0704/dershowitz_hague_ruling.php3>. The editorial was written before the publication of the Court's opinion.

[259] Another cause of concern (but not normally to states) is the inadequate representation of women across all international courts and tribunals. J. Linehan, 'Women and Public International Litigation' (2001, Project on International Courts and Tribunals), available at <http://www.pict-pcti.org/publications/PICT_articles/Women1.pdf>.

[260] *SW Africa* (*Ethiopia v. South Africa; Liberia v. South Africa*, Second phase (1996) ICJ Reports (judgment of 18 July).

[261] *United States Diplomatic and Consular Staff in Tehran* (*United States of America v. Iran*) Merits (1980) 3 ICJ Reports (judgment of 24 May).   [262] 1354 UNTS (1984) 452.

[263] In 1979 McWhinney spoke of 'dwindling—almost to the vanishing point—of the Court's business in recent years'; E. McWhinney, *The World Court and the Contemporary International Lawmaking Process* (Alphen aan den Rijn, 1979) 164. For the change in attitude just over ten years later see K. Highet, 'The Peace Palace Heats Up: The World Court in Business Again', *85 AJIL* (1991) 646.

US experiences have remained largely negative through the cases brought against it by Libya, Iran, Serbia, Paraguay, Germany and Mexico. As discussed in Chapters 1 and 2 it has also campaigned against the ICC. One of its reasons for doing so is that there is no 'effective mechanism to prevent politicized prosecutions of American service members and officials',[264] that is concern about the political bias of the prosecutor. There is no way to escape the obvious fact that 'Those who see themselves as excluded from these fora [or unjustly brought before them] are likely to resist and resent the expansion of law that these processes represent and entail'.[265]

Another aspect of the legitimacy of a tribunal is confidence in the independence of the judiciary. Although the requirement for election to an international judicial post is typically that the person must be of 'high moral character, impartiality and integrity'[266] international judges are nominated by governments and elections are highly politicised. Further, candidates are frequently drawn from within government departments including those handling foreign affairs. It is not surprising that occasions arise where judges are asked to sit on cases involving issues with which they have had some dealings. But as Judge Buergenthal emphasised '[j]udicial ethics . . . are matters of perception and of sensibility to appearances that courts must continuously keep in mind to preserve their legitimacy'.[267] A Study Group of the International Law Association and the Project on International Courts and Tribunals has pointed out that there are no international codes of ethics or standards with respect to judicial independence. The Study Group has drafted such a Code and hopes that adoption of its proposed principles will allay concerns about conflict of interest or lack of judicial independence.[268] This example of a soft law code of conduct negotiated by academic and legal practitioner experts (with participation by international judges) has the potential to change international judicial behaviour and offers an answer to those who challenge the legitimacy of international adjudication.

The institution of *ad hoc* judges before the ICJ gives rise to a related concern, that counsel in a case may appear to have some influence on the ICJ because he or she has previously acted as an *ad hoc* judge and thus has personal knowledge of the permanent judges and the decision-making processes. In Practice Directions the ICJ has stated that 'it is not in the interest of the sound administration of

---

[264] Secretary Rumsfeld Statement on the ICC Treaty, Defense Link, US Department of Defense, 6 May 2002.

[265] Alvarez, 38 *Texas ILJ* (2003) 405, 417.

[266] Rome Statute of the ICC, Article 36 (3) (a); see also Statute of the ICJ, Article 2; UN Convention on the Law of the Sea, Annex VI, Statute of the International Tribunal for the Law of the Sea, Article 2 (1) ('highest reputation for fairness and integrity'); International Covenant Civil and Political Rights, 1966, Article 28 (2) (Human Rights Committee).

[267] *Legal Consequences of the Construction of a Wall in the Occupied Palestinian Territory*, Composition of Court (2004) ICJ Reports 3, para 10, diss op Judge Buergenthal (Order of 30 January 2004).

[268] Burgh House Principles on the Independence of the International Judiciary, available at <http://www.ucl.ac.uk/laws/cict/docs/burgh_final_21204.pdf>.

justice that a person sit as judge *ad hoc* in one case who is also acting or has recently acted as agent, counsel or advocate in another case' and that persons who are acting as agent, counsel or advocate in a case before the Court or have acted in that capacity in the previous three years should not be nominated. Similarly those who have acted as an *ad hoc* judge should not be designated as agent, counsel or advocate within the same time period.[269]

The impartiality of the individual judges hearing a case is also an important aspect of legitimacy. In the *Security Wall* case Israel had argued that Judge Elaraby should not sit on the advisory opinion as he had played an 'active, official and public role' in advocating for the issues raised by the case. Judge Elaraby had at various times acted as legal adviser to the Egyptian government. The Court considered that Judge Elaraby should not be regarded as having taken part in the case in any capacity.[270] He had acted in a diplomatic capacity many years before the construction of the wall and had not expressed any opinion on this issue. Judge Buergenthal dissented in far more reasoned language than that of Professor Dershowitz. He considered that an interview given by Judge Elaraby in his personal capacity shortly before his election to the Court in which the latter addressed issues relating to the occupation of Palestine created an appearance of bias that should preclude his sitting on the case.[271] The ICTY too has had to consider claims of bias. In *Furundžija* the appellant argued that Judge Mumba should have been disqualified from hearing the case because of her personal interest in the UN Commission on the Status of Women, which had a legal and political agenda relevant to the issues in the case—international criminal charges of rape and sexual violence. The Appellate Chamber rejected the appeal on the grounds that there was no actual bias, nor any basis for a reasonable and informed person to apprehend bias. It stated that even if Judge Mumba's opinions with respect to the promotion and protection of the human rights of women were established, these would be general views that are 'distinguishable from an inclination to implement those goals and objectives as a Judge in a particular case. It follows that she could still sit on a case and impartially decide upon issues affecting women.'[272]

Decisions of the ICJ—and other international courts—are generally accorded a high degree of legitimacy. Franck concluded that

In terms of fairness, most of the criticisms brought against it are remarkably toothless. Its judges' intellectual autonomy compares favorably with that of most national judiciaries, let alone that of delegates to the political organs of the international system.[273]

---

[269] Practice Direction VII. Practice Direction VIII imposes similar restraints upon those who have been a Member of the Court, judge *ad hoc*, Registrar, Deputy-Registrar or higher official of the Court (principal legal secretary, first secretary or secretary) appearing as agent, counsel or advocate; available at <http://www.icj-cij.org/icjwww/ibasicdocuments/ibasictext/ibasic_practice_directions_20040730_I-XII.htm>.

[270] *Legal Consequences of the Construction of a Wall in the Occupied Palestinian Territory*, Composition of Court (2004) ICJ Reports. [271] Ibid 7, para 13, diss op Judge Buergenthal.

[272] *Prosecutor v. Anto Furundžija*, IT-95–17/1, 21 July 2000, para 200 (AC).

[273] Franck, *Fairness in International Law and Institutions*, 346.

Since 1995 when Franck reached this conclusion the ICJ has been asked to adjudicate in some highly controversial areas including the legality of nuclear weapons; the legality of the Security Wall; issues arising out of conflict in Bosnia-Herzegovina and the Democratic Republic of the Congo; the legality of the NATO action in Serbia in 1999. There have been those who have criticised particular judgments and opinions but the Court's popularity is evidenced by the continuing submission of cases to it. New courts have been established since 1995 (the ICC, African Court of Human Rights) and others have become operational (ITLOS, the ICTY and ICTR, WTO Dispute Settlement Panels and Appellate Body). There appears little evidence that international adjudication is rejected as illegitimate.

Adjudicative processes allow states to seek to counter-balance weaker political power with legal argument (and in many cases achieve success). In addition to some contentious cases where this was done (for example *Nauru*, *Nicaragua*, *Oil Platforms*) advisory opinions have been sought to clarify the law despite the unwillngness of powerful states. Forty-two states submitted written pleadings in the *Legality of the Threat or Use of Nuclear Weapons* where the opinion was given over the strenuous objections of the nuclear states. Similarly states from Europe and the US voted against the UNGA resolution seeking an advisory opinion on the *Legal Consequences of the Construction of a Wall in the Occupied Palestinian Territory*. Commentators have supported the law-making advantages of seeking such opinions:

> The contribution of the judge to the development of international law, especially if it emanates from advisory opinions, has certain advantages, notably that it may reduce the undue influence of the most politically powerful States. This contributes towards a levelling of the playing field, as well as allowing all States to express their views.[274]

The democratic deficit by the multilateral political organs makes international judicial determination 'legitimized by . . . principled process[es] of decision-making',[275] an important feature of contemporary international law-making. The vast amount of international legal regulation and the law-making activities of regulatory bodies make their oversight by judicial and quasi-judicial bodies of increasing significance with their corresponding enhancement of law-making powers.

8.　Conclusions

International courts and tribunals do more than apply the law. As we have seen in this chapter, they are also part of the process for making it. In some cases this involves affirming the law-making effect of multilateral agreements, UN resolutions, ILC codification or other products of the international law-making processes we

---

[274] L. Boisson de Chazournes, 'Advisory Opinions and the Furtherance of the Common Interest of Humankind', in Boisson de Chazournes et al, *International Organizations and International Dispute Settlement*, 105, 115.　　　[275] Franck, *Fairness in International Law and Institutions*, 347.

have considered in this book. In other cases, judges have drawn upon a rather broader legal basis for their decisions, and articulated rules and principles of law that can only be described as novel and are not necessarily supported by evidence of general state practice or *opinio juris*. How states in general and other actors respond to such decisions may deprive them of lasting impact, as we observed in regard to the *Fisheries Jurisdiction* cases, or may alternatively help establish a new rule or principle of international law for all states, not just those party to the case. To that extent the law-making effect of all judicial decisions, like all multilateral treaties, is contingent on the response of a broader international community and cannot be presumed in advance.

But international courts also make law in another, perhaps more important sense, for it may fall to them to address the problems of coherence and fragmentation we have highlighted throughout this book. Courts, as we pointed out in Chapter 5, tend to prefer an integrated conception of international law to a fragmented one. An understanding of the mechanisms by which different bodies of law can be integrated is an important contribution to that process. We have seen in this chapter that it may not always be possible to achieve such a goal within a system of limited compulsory jurisdiction and constraints on the law that may be applied in particular disputes. What also seems clear is that conflicts between rules and the values they represent are an inevitable feature of a legal system, which states, courts and other actors can only resolve *ad hoc*, as best they can. Rules of interpretation, priority of treaties or a balancing of competing interests, have generally provided an ample range of techniques for promoting coherence in the application of international law. This does not mean there are no problems. On the contrary, there will always be uncertainty about how different legal regimes or different bodies of law interact. An examination of the inter-relationship of trade, environment and human rights law, to take three topics frequently referred to in this book, shows that difficult judgments have to be made, and that there remains much for lawyers to argue over. Do they interact at all? Has the right balance between environmental regulation and individual rights been maintained? Are the terms of a treaty fixed in time or inherently evolutionary? Are environmental trade restrictions a *lex specialis* or a *lex generalis*, or do they form part of an integral, non-derogable, regime that will prevail over subsequent agreements? What law is applicable in any dispute? How is the content of any relevant rules of customary law or general principles of law to be established? What role should broader values play in the decision? The answers to such questions will rarely be obvious and the outcomes are unlikely to be predictable. For those reasons, these are in practice some of the most challenging questions about international law-making that any international lawyer will have to deal with.

Further Reading

'Symposium: The Proliferation of International Tribunals: Piecing Together the Puzzle', 31 *NYU JILP* (1999).

D. Cass, *The Constitutionalization of the World Trade Organization: Legitimacy, Democracy, and Community in the International Trading System* (Oxford, 2005).

J. Charney, 'Is International Law Threatened by Multiple International Tribunals?', 271 *Recueil des Cours* (1998).

L. Gross (ed), *The Future of the International Court of Justice* (New York, 1976).

A. Zimmermann, C. Tomuschat and K. Oellers-Frahm, *The Statute of the International Court of Justice: A Commentary* (Oxford, 2006).

Bibliography

Abbott, K., and Snidal, D., 'Hard and Soft Law in International Governance', *54 Int Org* (2000) 421.

Abi-Saab, G., 'Cours Général de Droit International Public', 207 *Recueil des Cours* (1987) 33.

Ago, R., 'Nouvelles réflexions sur la codification du droit international', 92 *Revue Générale de Droit International Public* (1988) 532.

Akande, D., 'The ICJ and the Security Council', 46 *ICLQ* (1997) 309.

Akehurst, M., 'Custom as a Source of International Law', 47 *BYBIL* (1974–5) 1.

_____ 'International Liability for Injurious Consequences Arising out of Acts Not Prohibited by International Law', 16 *NYBIL* (1985) 8.

Aldrich, G., and Chinkin, C., 'The Hague Peace Conferences: A Century of Achievement and Unfinished Work', 94 *AJIL* (2000) 90.

Alfredson, G., and Eide, A. (eds), *The Universal Declaration of Human Rights* (The Hague, 1999).

Allott, P., 'Power Sharing in the Law of the Sea', 77 *AJIL* (1983) 1.

Alston, P., 'Making Space for New Human Rights: The Case of the Right to Development', 1 *Harv HRYB* (1988) 3.

_____ (ed), *The United Nations and Human Rights* (Oxford, 1992).

_____ 'The Myopia of the Handmaidens: International Lawyers and Globalization', 8 *EJIL* (1997) 435.

_____ 'Ships Passing in the Night: The Current State of the Human Rights and Development Debate seen through the Lens of the Millennium Development Goals', 27 *HRQ* (2005) 755.

_____ 'Reconceiving the UN Human Rights Regime: Challenges Confronting the New Human Rights Council', 7 *Melbourne Journal of International Law* (2006) 185.

_____ and Simma, B., 'The Sources of Human Rights Law: Custom, Jus Cogens and General Principles', 12 *Australian YBIL* (1992) 82.

Alvarez, J., 'Judging the Security Council', 90 *AJIL* (1996) 1.

_____ 'The New Dispute Settlers: (Half) Truths and Consequences', 38 *Texas ILJ* (2003) 405.

_____ '*International Organizations as Law-Makers* (Oxford, 2005).

Anaya, J., *Indigenous Peoples in International Law* (Oxford, 1996; 2nd edn 2000).

Anderson, D., 'Further Efforts to Ensure Universal Participation in the UNCLOS', 43 *ICLQ* (1994) 886.

_____ 'The Straddling Fish Stocks Agreement of 1995—An Initial Assessment', 45 *ICLQ* (1996) 463.

Anderson, K., 'The Ottawa Convention Banning Landmines, the Role of International Non-Governmental Organizations and the Idea of International Civil Society', 11 *EJIL* (2000) 91.

_____ and Rieff, D., ' "Global Civil Society": A Sceptical View', in H. Anheier, M. Glasius and M. Kaldor (eds), *Global Civil Society 2004/5* (London, 2005) 26.

Anderson, M., Boyle, A. E., Lowe, A. V., and Wickremasinghe, C. (eds), *The International Law Commission and the Future of International Law* (London, 1998).

Anghie, A., *Imperialism, Sovereignty and the Making of International Law* (Cambridge, 2004).

Anheier, H., Glasius, M., and Kaldor, M. (eds), *Global Civil Society 2001* (Oxford, 2001).

Arsanjani, M., 'The Rome Statute of the International Criminal Court', 93 *AJIL* (1999) 22.

Aust, A., *Modern Treaty Law and Practice* (Cambridge, 2000).

_____ 'Counter-Terrorism—A New Approach', 5 *Max Planck UNYB* (2001) 1.

_____ 'Limping Treaties: Lessons from Multilateral Treaty-Making', 50 *NILR* (2003) 243.

Axworthy, L., *Human Security: Safety for People in a Changing World* (Ottawa, 1999).

Aznar-Gomez, M., 'The 1996 Nuclear Weapons Advisory Opinion and *Non-Liquet*', 48 *ICLQ* (1998) 3.

Baldwin, S., 'The International Congresses and Conferences of the Last Century as Forces Working towards the Solidarity of the World', 1 *AJIL* (1907) 565.

Balton, D., 'Strengthening the Law of the Sea: The New Agreement on Straddling Fish Stocks and Highly Migratory Fish Stocks', 27 *ODIL* (1996) 125.

Bantekas, I., and Nash, S., *International Criminal Law* (2nd edn, London, 2003).

Baratta, R., 'Should Invalid Reservations to Human Rights Treaties be Disregarded?', 11 *EJIL* (2000) 413.

Barnes, R., 'Refugee Law at Sea', 53 *ICLQ* (2004) 47.

Bartels, L., 'Article XX of GATT and the Problem of Extraterritorial Jurisdiction', 36 *JWT* (2002) 353.

_____ 'The Separation of Powers in the WTO: How to Avoid Judicial Activism', 53 *ICLQ* (2004) 861.

Bassiouni, M., 'A Functional Approach to "General Principles of International Law"', 11 *Mich JIL* (1990) 768.

Baxter, R., *The Law of International Waterways* (Cambridge, Mass, 1964).

_____ 'International Law in "Her Infinite Variety"', 29 *ICLQ* (1980) 549.

Beckett, J., 'Countering Uncertainty and Ending Up/Down Arguments: *Prolegomena* to a Response to NAIL', 16 *EJIL* (2005) 213.

Benedick, R., *Ozone Diplomacy* (London, 1998).

Bianchi, A., 'Ad-hocism and the Rule of Law', 13 *EJIL* (2002) 263.

Birnie, P., 'International Legal Issues in the Management and Protection of the Whale: A Review of Four Decades of Experience', 29 *NRJ* (1989) 913.

_____ 'Are 20th Century Marine Conservation Agreements Adaptable to 21st Century Goals and Principles?', 12 *IJMCL* (1997) 488.

_____ and Boyle, A. E., *International Law and the Environment* (2nd edn, Oxford, 2002).

Bleicher, M., 'The Ottawa Process: Nine Day Wonder or a New Model for Disarmament Negotiations?' 2 *Open Forum* (2000) 69.

Bloom, E., 'Protecting Peacekeepers', 89 *AJIL* (1995) 621.

Blum, Y. Z., 'Proposals for UN Security Council Reform', 99 *AJIL* (2005) 632.

Boczar, B., 'Avenues for Direct Participation of Transnational Corporations in International Environmental Negotiations', 3 *NYU Environmental LJ* (1994–5) 1.

Bodansky, D., 'The UN Framework Convention on Climate Change', *Yale JIL* (1993) 451.

_____ 'The Legitimacy of International Governance', 93 *AJIL* (1999) 596.

_____ 'Rules vs Standards in International Environmental Law', 98 *Proceedings ASIL* (2004) 275.

_____ and Crook, J. R., 'Symposium: The ILC's State Responsibility Articles', 96 *AJIL* (2002) 773.

Boisson de Chazournes, L., Romano, C., and MacKenzie, R., *International Organizations and International Dispute Settlement: Trends and Prospects* (Ardsley, 2002).

_____ and Sands, P. (eds), *International Law, the International Court of Justice and Nuclear Weapons* (Cambridge, 1999).

Bos, M., *A Methodology of International Law* (North Holland, 1984).

Bourne, C., 'The Primacy of the Principle of Equitable Utilization in the 1997 Watercourses Convention', 35 *CYBIL* (1997) 215.

Bowett, D., 'Reservations to Non-restricted Multilateral Treaties', 48 *BYBIL* (1976–7) 67.

Boyle, A. E., 'Marine Pollution under the Law of the Sea Convention', 79 *AJIL* (1985) 347.

_____ 'State Responsibility and International Liability for Injurious Consequences of Acts Not Prohibited by International Law: A Necessary Distinction?', 39 *ICLQ* (1990) 1.

_____ 'Dispute Settlement and the Law of the Sea Convention: Problems of Fragmentation and Jurisdiction', 46 *ICLQ* (1997) 37.

_____ 'Further Development of the 1982 Law of the Sea Convention: Mechanisms for Change', 54 *ICLQ* (2005) 563.

_____ 'EU Unilateralism and the Law of the Sea', 21 *IJMCL* (2006) 15.

_____ and Freestone, D. (eds), *International Law and Sustainable Development* (Oxford, 1999).

Breen, C., 'The Role of NGOs in the Formulation of and Compliance with the Optional Protocol to the Convention on the Rights of the Child on Involvement of Children in Armed Conflict', 25 *HRQ* (2003) 453.

Briggs, H. W., *The International Law Commission* (Cornell, 1965).

Brown Weiss, E., *Environmental Change and International Law* (Tokyo, 1992).

Brownlie, I., 'The Legal Status of Natural Resources', 162 *Recueil des Cours* (1979) 261.

_____ *System of the Law of Nations: State Responsibility Part I* (Oxford, 1983).

_____ *Basic Documents on International Law* (3rd edn, Oxford, 1991).

_____ 'The Decisions of Political Organs of the United Nations and the Rule of Law', in R. Macdonald (ed), *Essays in Honour of Wang Tieya* (Dordrecht, 1993).

_____ *Principles of Public International Law* (6th edn, Oxford, 2003).

_____ and Apperley, C., 'Kosovo Crisis Inquiry: Memorandum on the International Law Aspects', 49 *ICLQ* (2000) 878.

_____ Chinkin, C., Greenwood, C., and Lowe, V., 'Kosovo: House of Commons, Foreign Affairs Committee, 4th Report, June 2000, Memoranda', 49 *ICLQ* (2000) 878.

Brunnée, J., 'COPing with Consent: Law-Making under Multilateral Environmental Agreements', 15 *LJIL* (2002) 1.

_____ and Toope, S., 'International Law and Constructivism: Elements of an Interactional Theory of International Law', 39 *Col JTL* (2000) 19.

Buchanan, R., 'Perpetual Peace or Perpetual Process: Global Civil Society and Cosmopolitan Legality at the World Trade Organisation', 16 *LJIL* (2003) 673.

Buergenthal, T., 'The Proliferation of International Courts and Tribunals: Is It Good or Bad?', 14 *LJIL* (2001) 267.

Burci, G. L., and Vignes, C.-H., *WHO* (The Hague, 2004).

Buzan, B., 'United We Stand: Informal Negotiating Groups at UNCLOS III', 4 *Marine Policy* (1980) 183.

Buzan, B., 'Negotiating by Consensus: Developments in Technique at the UN Conference on the Law of the Sea', 75 *AJIL* (1981) 324.

Byers, M., 'Custom, Power and the Power of Rules: Customary International Law from an Interdisciplinary Perspective', 17 *Mich JIL* (1995) 109.

____ *Custom, Power and the Power of Rules: International Relations and Customary International Law* (Cambridge, 1999).

____ (ed), *The Role of Law in International Politics* (Oxford, 2000).

____ and Nolte, G. (eds), *United States Hegemony and the Foundations of International Law* (Cambridge, 2003).

Byrnes, A., and Connors, J., 'Enforcing the Human Rights of Women: A Complaints Procedure for the Women's Convention?', 21 *Brooklyn JIL* (1996) 679.

Cameron, M., Lawson, M., and Tomlin, B. (eds), *To Walk Without Fear: The Global Movement to Ban Landmines* (Canada, 1998).

Caminos, H., and Molitor, M., 'Progressive Development of International Law and the Package Deal', 79 *AJIL* (1985) 871.

Cardinale, H., *The Holy See and the International Order* (Toronto, 1976).

Caron, D., 'The Legitimacy of the Security Council', 87 *AJIL* (1993) 552.

Carty, A., 'Critical International Law: Recent Trends in the Theory of International Law', 2 *EJIL* (1991) 66.

Cass, D., *The Constitutionalization of the World Trade Organization: Legitimacy, Democracy, and Community in the International Trading System* (Oxford, 2005).

Cassese, A., *International Law in a Divided World* (Oxford, 1990).

____ Gaeta, P,. and Jones, J. (eds), *The Rome Statute of the International Criminal Court: A Commentary* (Oxford, 2002).

____ and Weiler, J., *Change and Stability in International Law-Making* (Berlin, 1988).

Chambers, B., 'Emerging International Rules on the Commercialisation of Genetic Resources', 6 *J World Intellectual Property* (2003) 311.

Charlesworth, H., 'Women as Sherpas: Are Global Summits Useful for Women?', 22 *Feminist Studies* (1996) 537.

____ 'International Law: A Discipline of Crisis', 65 *MLR* (2002) 377.

____ and Chinkin, C., 'The Gender of *Jus Cogens*', 15 *HRQ* (1993) 63.

____ and ____ *The Boundaries of International Law: A Feminist Analysis* (Manchester, 2000).

Charney, J., 'The Persistent Objector Rule and the Development of Customary International Law', 58 *BYBIL* (1987) 1.

____ 'Universal International Law', 87 *AJIL* (1993) 529.

____ 'Entry into Force of the 1982 UNCLOS', 35 *VJIL* (1995) 381.

____ 'Is International Law Threatened by Multiple International Tribunals?', 271 *Recueil des Cours* (1998) 101.

Charnovitz, S., 'Two Centuries of Participation: NGOs and International Governance', 18 *Mich JIL* (1997) 183.

____ 'Judicial Independence in the World Trade Organization', in L. Boisson de Chazournes, C. Romano and R. Mackenzie, *International Organizations and International Dispute Settlements: Trends and Prospects* (Ardsley, 2002) 219.

____ 'Non-Governmental Organizations and International Law', 100 *AJIL* (2006) 348.

Chayes, A., and Chayes, A., *The New Sovereignty: Compliance with International Regulatory Agreements* (Cambridge, Mass, 1998).

Cheng, B., *General Principles of International Law* (London, 1953).

_____ 'United Nations Resolutions on Outer Space: "Instant" Customary Law?', 5 *Indian JIL* (1965) 23.

_____ (ed), *International Law Teaching and Practice* (London, 1982).

Chigara, B., *Legitimacy Deficit in Custom: Towards a Deconstructionist Theory* (Dartmouth, 2001).

Chinkin, C., 'The Challenge of Soft Law: Development and Change in International Law', 38 *ICLQ* (1989) 850.

_____ *Third Parties in International Law* (Oxford, 1993).

_____ 'A Mirage in the Sand? Distinguishing Binding and Non-Binding Relations between States', 10 *LJIL* (1997) 223.

_____ 'The Role of Non-Governmental Organisations in Standard Setting, Monitoring and Implementation of Human Rights', in J. Norton, M. Andenas and M. Footer (eds), *The Changing World of International Law in the Twenty First Century: A Tribute to the Late Kenneth R. Simmonds* (The Hague, 1998) 45.

_____ 'International Environmental Law in Evolution', in T. Jewell and J. Steele (eds), *Law in Environmental Decision-Making* (Oxford, 1998) 229.

_____ 'The Legality of NATO's Action in Yugoslavia', 49 *ICLQ* (2000) 910.

Churchill, R., and Ulfstein, G., 'Autonomous Institutional Arrangements in Multilateral Environmental Agreements', 94 *AJIL* (2000) 623.

_____ and Lowe, A. V., *The Law of the Sea* (Manchester, 1999).

Cohen, C., 'The Role of Non-governmental Organizations in the Drafting of the Convention on the Rights of the Child', 12 *HRQ* (1990) 137.

Cohen, R., and Rai, S., *Global Social Movements* (London, 2000).

Coicaud, J.-M., and Heiskanen, V. (eds), *The Legitimacy of International Organisations* (Tokyo, 2001).

Connors, J., 'NGOs and the Human Rights of Women at the United Nations', in P. Willetts (ed), '*The Conscience of the World*': *The Influence of Non-Governmental Organisations in the UN System* (Washington, 1996) 147.

Contini, P., and Sand, P., 'Methods to Expedite Environment Protection: International Ecostandards', 66 *AJIL* (1972) 37.

Coomaraswamy, R., 'The Varied Contours of Violence against Women in South Asia', Paper Presented to Fifth South Asia Regional Ministerial Conference, Celebrating Beijing + 10, Pakistan, May 2005, 2.

Crawford, J., 'Democracy and International Law', 64 *BYBIL* (1993) 113.

_____ 'The ILC's Draft Statute for an International Criminal Tribunal', 88 *AJIL* (1994) 140.

_____ (ed), *The International Law Commission's Articles on State Responsibility: Introduction, Text and Commentaries* (Cambridge, 2002).

_____ 'The ILC's Articles on State Responsibility for Internationally Wrongful Acts: A Retrospect', 96 *AJIL* (2002) 874.

_____ 'Public International Law in Twentieth Century England', in J. Beatson and R. Zimmermann (eds), *Jurists Uprooted: German-Speaking Emigré Lawyers in Twentieth Century Britain* (Oxford, 2004) 681.

_____ and Olleson, S., 'The Continuing Debate on a UN Convention on State Responsibility', 54 *ICLQ* (2005) 959.

Cromwell White, L., and Ragonatti Zocca, M., *International Non-Governmental Organizations: Their Purposes, Methods and Accomplishments* (New Brunswick, NJ, 1951).

Cryer, R., 'Déjà vu in International Law', 65 *MLR* (2002) 931.

Czaplinski, W., and Danilenko, G., 'Conflict of Norms in International Law', 21 *NYBIL* (1990) 3.

Daillier, P., and Pellet, A., *Droit International Public* (7th edn, Paris, 2002).

D'Amato, A., *The Concept of Custom in International Law* (Ithaca, NY, 1971).

Danilenko, G., 'International *Jus Cogens*: Issues of Law-Making', 2 *EJIL* (1991) 42.

_____ *Law-Making in the International Community* (Dordrecht, 1993).

Davies, I., 'The New *Lex Mercatoria*: International Interests in Mobile Equipment', 52 *ICLQ* (2003) 151.

Davies, P., 'EC-Canada Fisheries Dispute', 44 *ICLQ* (1995) 927.

de Búrca, G., and Scott, J. (eds), *The EU and the WTO: Legal and Constitutional Issues* (Oxford, 2001).

de La Fayette, L., 'The MEPC: The Conjunction of the Law of the Sea and International Environmental Law', 16 *IJMCL* (2001) 155.

De Visscher, C., *Theory and Reality in Public International Law* (2nd edn, P. Corbett trans, Princeton, 1968).

de Wet, E., 'The International Constitutional Order', 55 *ICLQ* (2006) 51.

de Yturriaga, J., *The International Regime of Fisheries* (Leiden, 1997).

Dhokalia, R., *The Codification of Public International Law* (Manchester, 1970).

Dickinson, A., 'Status of Forces under the UN Convention on State Immunity', 55 *ICLQ* (2006) 427.

Duffy, H., *The 'War on Terror' and the Framework of International Law* (Cambridge, 2005).

Dunant, H./ICRC, *A Memory of Solferino* (Geneva, 1986).

Dunbar, N., 'The Myth of Customary International Law', 8 *Australian YBIL* (1983) 1.

Dupuy, P. -M., 'Soft Law and the International Law of the Environment', 12 *Mich JIL* (1991) 420.

Dworkin, R., *Taking Rights Seriously* (London, 1977).

Edeson, W., 'The Code of Conduct for Responsible Fisheries: An Introduction', 11 *IJMCL* (1996) 97.

_____ 'The International Plan of Action on Illegal, Unreported and Unregulated Fishing: The Legal Context of a Non-Legally Binding Instrument', 16 *IJMCL* (2001) 603.

El Baradei, M., Franck, T. and Trachtenberg, F., *The ILC: The Need for a New Direction* (UNITAR, 1981).

Elias, O., and Lim, C., ' "General Principles of Law," "Soft" Law and the Identification of International Law', 28 *NYBIL* (1997) 3.

Elias, T., *The International Court of Justice and Some Contemporary Problems* (The Hague, 1983).

Esty, D., 'NGOs and the WTO', 1 *JIEL* (1998) 123.

Evans, M. D., and Haenni-Dale, C., 'Preventing Torture: The Development of the Optional Protocol to the UNCAT', 4 *HRLR* (2004) 19.

Evensen, J., 'Working Methods and Procedures in the 3rd UNCLOS', 199 *Recueil des Cours* (1986-IV) 425.

Falk, R., 'The Nuclear Weapons Advisory Opinion and the New Jurisprudence of Global Civil Society', 7 *Transnational Law and Contemporary Problems* (1997) 333.

_____ and Strauss, A., 'On the Creation of a Global Peoples Assembly: Legitimacy and the Power of Popular Sovereignty', 36 *Stan JIL* (2000) 191.

Fassbender, B., 'The United Nations Charter as Constitution of the International Community', 36 *Col JTL* (1998) 529.

Fastenrath, U., 'Relative Normativity in International Law', 4 *EJIL* (1993) 305.

Fidler, D., 'Challenging the Classical Concept of Custom: Perspectives on the Future of Customary International Law', 39 *GYBIL* (1996) 198.

_____ 'The Future of the WHO: What Role for International Law?', 32 *Vand JTL* (1998) 1079.

Fitzmaurice M., 'International Environmental Law as a Special Field', 25 *NYBIL* (1994) 181.

Fox, H., *The Law of State Immunity* (Oxford, 2002).

Francioni, F., and Scovazzi, T. (eds), *International Law for Antarctica* (2nd edn, The Hague, 1996).

Franck, 'Legitimacy in the International System', 82 *AJIL* (1988) 705.

_____ *The Power of Legitimacy Among Nations* (New York, 1990).

—— 'The Emerging Right to Democratic Governance', 86 *AJIL* (1992) 46.

_____ 'Who is the Ultimate Guardian of UN Legality?', 86 *AJIL* (1992) 519.

_____ *Fairness in International Law and Institutions* (Oxford, 1995).

_____ 'The Power of Legitimacy and the Legitimacy of Power: International Law in an Age of Power Disequilibrium', 100 *AJIL* (2006) 88.

_____ and El-Baradei, M., 'The Codification and Progressive Development of International Law: A UNITAR Study', 76 *AJIL* (1982) 630.

_____ and Lockwood, B., 'Preliminary Thoughts Towards an International Convention on Terrorism', 68 *AJIL* (1974) 69.

Freestone, D., 'The Road from Rio: International Environmental Law After the Earth Summit' (1994) 6 *JEL* 193.

French, D., 'Treaty Interpretation and the Incorporation of Extraneous Legal Rules', 55 *ICLQ* (2006) 281.

Friedmann, W., *Law in a Changing Society* (London, 1959).

_____ 'The Uses of General Principles in the Development of International Law', 57 *AJIL* (1963) 279.

_____ *The Changing Structure of International Law* (2nd edn, New York, 1966).

_____ 'The North Sea Continental Shelf Cases—A Critique', 64 *AJIL* (1970) 229.

Gamble, J., and Ku, C., 'International Law—New Actors and New Technologies: Center Stage for NGOs?', 31 *Law and Policy in International Business* (2000) 221.

Gardiner, R., 'Revising the Law of Carriage by Air: Mechanisms in Treaties and Contract', 47 *ICLQ* (1998) 278.

Gardner, J. P. (ed), *Human Rights as General Norms and a State's Right to Opt Out* (London, 1997).

Garibaldi, O., 'The Legal Status of General Assembly Resolutions: Some Conceptual Observations', 73 *ASIL Proceedings* (1979) 324.

Gaskell, N., 'Decision Making and the Legal Committee of the IMO', 18 *IJMCL* (2003) 155.

Gattini, A., 'The UNCC: Old Rules, New Procedures on War Reparations', 13 *EJIL* (2002) 161.

Glasius, M., 'Expertise in the Cause of Justice: Global Civil Society Influence on the Statute for an International Criminal Court', in M. Glasius, M. Kaldor and H. Anheier (eds), *Global Civil Society 2002* (London, 2003).

Glendon, M. A., *A World Made New: Eleanor Roosevelt and the Universal Declaration of Human Rights* (New York, 2001).

Goldsmith, J., and Posner, E., *The Limits of International Law* (Oxford, 2005).

Goode, R., *Convention on International Interests in Mobile Equipment and Protocol Thereto on Matters Specific to Aircraft Equipment Official Commentary* (Rome, 2002).

Goodman, R., 'Human Rights Treaties, Invalid Reservations and State Consent', 96 *AJIL* (2002) 531.

Gowlland-Debbas, V., 'The Relationship between the ICJ and the Security Council', 88 *AJIL* (1994) 643.

_____ (ed), *Multilateral Treaty-Making* (The Hague, 2000).

Graefrath, B., 'The ILC Tomorrow: Improving its Organization and Methods of Work', 85 *AJIL* (1991) 595.

Gray, C., 'Iraq, the Security Council and the Use of Force', 65 *BYBIL* (1994) 135.

Greenwood, C., 'International Law and the NATO Intervention in Kosovo', 49 *ICLQ* (2000) 926.

Gross, L. (ed), *The Future of the International Court of Justice* (New York, 1976).

Guillaume, G., 'The Future of International Judicial Institutions', 44 *ICLQ* (1995) 848.

Gunning, I., 'Modernizing Customary International Law: The Challenge of Human Rights', 31 *VJIL* (1991) 211.

Gurowitz, A., 'International Law, Politics and Migrant Rights', in C. Reus-Smit (ed), *The Politics of International Law* (Cambridge, 2004) 131.

Guzman, A., 'Global Governance and the WTO', 45 *Harv ILJ* (2004) 303.

Haas, P., 'Do Regimes Matter? Epistemic Communities and Mediterranean Pollution Control', 43 *Int Org* (1989) 377.

Hall, C., 'The First Two Sessions of the UN Preparatory Committee on the Establishment of an ICC', 91 *AJIL* (1997) 177.

_____ 'The Third and Fourth Sessions of the UN Preparatory Committee on the Establishment of an ICC', 92 *AJIL* (1998) 124.

_____ 'The Fifth Session of the UN Preparatory Committee on the Establishment of an ICC', 92 *AJIL* (1998) 331.

_____ 'The Sixth Session of the UN Preparatory Committee on the Establishment of an ICC', 92 *AJIL* (1998) 548.

_____ 'UN Convention on State Immunity: The Need for a Human Rights Protocol', 55 *ICLQ* (2006) 411.

Happold, M., 'SC Resolution 1373 and the Constitution of the UN', 13 *LJIL* (2003) 593.

Harding, C., and Lim, C., 'The Significance of Westphalia: An Archaeology of the International Legal Order', in C. Harding and C. Lim, *Renegotiating Westphalia: Essays and Commentary on the European and Conceptual Foundations of Modern International Law* (The Hague, 1999) 1.

Harlow, C., *Accountability in the European Union* (Oxford, 2002).

Haslam, E., 'Non-Governmental War Crimes Tribunals: A Forgotten Arena of International Criminal Justice', in C. Harding and C. Lim, *Renegotiating Westphalia: Essays and Commentary on the European and Conceptual Foundations of Modern International Law* (The Hague, 1999) 153.

Hathaway, J., 'America, Defender of Democratic Legitimacy?', 11 *EJIL* (2000) 121.

Hayashi, M., 'Toward Elimination of Sub-standard Shipping: The Report of the International Commission on Shipping', 16 *IJMCL* (2001) 501.

Heere, W. P. (ed), *International Law and its Sources: Liber Amicorum Maarten Bos* (Deventer, 1989).

Held, D., *Democracy and the Global Order: From the Modern State to Cosmopolitan Governance* (Cambridge, 1995).

Henckaerts J.-M., and Doswald-Beck, L., *Customary International Humanitarian Law* (Cambridge, 2005).

Henkin, L., 'Human Rights and State "Sovereignty" ', 25 *Georgia JICL* (1995) 31.

Hey, E. (ed), *Developments in International Fisheries Law* (The Hague, 1999).

Higgins, R., *The Development of International Law through the Political Organs of the United Nations* (Oxford, 1963).

_____ 'Aspects of the Case Concerning the Barcelona Traction, Light and Power Company, Ltd.', 11 *VJIL* (1971) 327.

_____ 'The Advisory Opinion on Namibia: Which Resolutions are Binding under Article 25 of Charter?', 21 *ICLQ* (1972) 270.

_____ *Problems and Process: International Law and How We Use It* (Oxford, 1993).

_____ 'The Reformation of International Law', in R. Rawlings (ed), *Law, Society and Economy: Centenary Essays for the London School of Economics and Political Science 1895–1995* (Oxford, 1997) 208.

_____ 'Remedies and the International Court of Justice: An Introduction', in M. Evans (ed), *Remedies in International Law: The Institutional Dilemma* (Oxford, 1998) 1.

_____ 'The ICJ, the ECJ and the Integrity of International Law', 52 *ICLQ* (2003) 1.

_____ 'A Babel of Judicial Voices? Ruminations from the Bench', 55 *ICLQ* (2006) 791.

Highet, K., 'The Peace Palace Heats Up: The World Court in Business Again', *85 AJIL* (1991) 646.

Hill, N., *The Public International Conference* (Stanford, Calif, 1929).

Hillgenberg, H., 'A Fresh Look at Soft Law', 10 *EJIL* (1999) 499.

Hollick, A., *US Foreign Policy and the Law of the Sea* (Princeton, 1981).

Humphrey, J., *Human Rights and the United Nations: A Great Adventure* (Dobbs Ferry, 1984).

Hurd, I., 'Legitimacy and Authority in International Politics', 53 *Int Org* (1999) 379.

International Alert, 'Women Building Peace from the Village Council to the Negotiating Table', No. 4, October–December 2000, 3.

Jain, N., 'A Separate Law for Peacekeepers: The Clash between the SC and the ICC', 16 *EJIL* (2005) 239.

Janis, M., 'Equity in International Law', 7 *Encyclopedia of Public International Law* (Oxford, 1984) 76–7.

_____ 'Protestants, Progress and Peace: Enthusiasm for an International Court in Early Nineteenth Century America', in M. Janis (ed), *The Influence of Religion on the Development of International Law* (Dordrecht, 1991).

Jenks, C. W., 'Some Constitutional Problems of International Organisations', (1945) 22 *BYBIL* 34.

_____ 'The Conflict of Law-Making Treaties', 30 *BYBIL* (1953) 401.

_____ *The Common Law of Mankind* (New York, 1958).

_____ *The Prospects of International Adjudication* (London, 1964).

Jennings, R. Y., 'The Progressive Development of International Law and its Codification', 24 *BYBIL* (1947) 301.

_____ 'Recent Developments in the International Law Commission: Its Relation to Sources of International Law', 13 *ICLQ* (1964) 390.

_____ 'What is International Law and How Do We Tell It When We See It?', 37 *Swiss YBIL* (1981) 59.

Jennings, R. Y., 'The Identification of International Law', in B. Cheng (ed), *International Law: Teaching and Practice* (London, 1982) 3.

____ 'The Collegiate Responsibility and Authority of the International Court of Justice', in Y. Dinstein (ed), *International Law at a Time of Perplexity: Essays in Honour of Shabtai Rosenne* (Dordrecht, 1989) 343.

____ 'The United Nations at Fifty: The International Court of Justice after Fifty Years', 89 *AJIL* (1995) 493.

____ 'The Judiciary, International and National and the Development of International Law', 45 *ICLQ* (1996) 1.

____ and Watts, A. D., *Oppenheim's International Law* (London, 1996).

Jessup, P., *Transnational Law* (New Haven, 1956).

Joyner, C. (ed), *The UN and International Law* (Cambridge, 1997).

Kammerhofer, J., 'Uncertainty in the Formal Sources of International Law: Customary International Law and Some of its Problems', 15 *EJIL* (2004) 523.

Kaufmann, J., *Conference Diplomacy* (3rd edn, Basingstoke, 1996).

Kearney, R., 'Sources of Law and the International Court of Justice', in L. Gross (ed), *The Future of the International Court of Justice* (New York, 1976) vol II, 610.

Keck, P., and Sikkink, K., *Activists beyond Borders: Advocacy Networks in International Politics* (Ithaca, NY, 1998).

Kelly, P., 'The Twilight of Customary International Law', 40 *VJIL* (2000) 449.

Kelsen, H., *The Law of the United Nations* (New York, 1950).

Kennedy, D., 'The Sources of International Law', 2 *Am UJILP* (1987) 1.

____ 'The International Human Rights Movement: Part of the Problem?' 15 *Harvard Human Rights Journal* (2002) 101.

Kimball, L., *Treaty Implementation: Scientific and Technical Advice Enters a New Stage* (Washington, 1996).

Kingsbury, B., 'The Concept of Compliance as a Function of Competing Conceptions of International Law', 19 *Mich JIL* (1998) 345.

____ 'Operational Processes of International Institutions as Part of the Law-Making Process: The World Bank and Indigenous Peoples', in G. Goodwin-Gill and S. Talmon (eds), *The Reality of International Law* (Oxford, 1999).

____ 'The International Legal Order', in P. Cane and M. Tushnet, *The Oxford Handbook of Legal Studies* (Oxford, 2003) 272.

____ Krisch, N., Stewart, R., and Wiener, J. (eds), 'The Emergence of Global Administrative Law', 68 *Law and Contemporary Problems* (2005).

Kirgis, F., 'Custom on a Sliding Scale', 81 *AJIL* (1987) 146.

____ 'The Security Council's First Fifty Years', 89 *AJIL* (1995) 506.

Kirsch, P., and Holmes, J., 'The Rome Conference on an International Criminal Court: The Negotiating Process', 93 *AJIL* (1999) 2.

Klabbers, J., 'The Undesirability of Soft Law', 67 *Nordic JIL* (1998) 381.

Knop, K., 'Re/statements: Feminism and State Sovereignty in International Law', 3 *Transnational Law and Contemporary Problems* (1993) 293.

____ and Chinkin, C., 'Remembering Chrystal Macmillan: Women's Equality and Nationality in International Law', 22 *Mich JIL* (2001) 523.

Koh, H., 'Why Do Nations Obey International Law?', 106 *Yale LJ* (1996–7) 2599.

Kolb, R., 'The Jurisprudence of the Yugoslav and Rwandan Criminal Tribunals on their Jurisdiction and on International Crimes', 71 *BYBIL* (2000) 259.

Kopelman, E., 'Ideology and International Law: The Dissent of the Indian Justice at the Tokyo War Crimes Trial', 23 *NYU JILP* (1990–1) 373.

Korelia, K., 'New Challenges to the Regime of Reservations under the ICCPR', 13 *EJIL* (2002) 437.

Korey, W., *NGOs and the Universal Declaration of Human Rights: A Curious Grapevine* (New York, 1998).

Koskenniemi, M. *From Apology to Utopia: The Structure of International Legal Argument* (Helsinki, 1989, 2nd edn with epilogue, 2006).

—— 'The Pull of the Mainstream', 88 *Mich LR* (1989–90) 1946.

—— 'Solidarity Measures: State Responsibility as a New International Order', 72 *BYBIL* (2001) 337.

—— *The Gentle Civilizer of Nations: The Rise and Fall of International Law 1870–1960* (Cambridge, 2001).

—— ' "The Lady Doth Protest Too Much": Kosovo and the Turn to Ethics in International Law', 65 *MLR* (2002) 159.

—— 'International Legislation Today: Limits and Possibilities', 23 *Wis ILJ* (2002) 61.

Krueger, R. B., and Riesenfeld, S. (eds), *The Developing Order of the Oceans* (Honolulu, 1984).

Krut, R., *Globalization and Civil Society: NGO Influence in International Decision-Making* (Geneva, 1997).

Kwiatkowska, B., *The 200 Mile EEZ* (Dordrecht, 1989).

Lang, W. (ed), *Sustainable Development and International Law* (London, 1995).

Lasswell H., and McDougal M., *Jurisprudence for a Free Society: Studies in Law, Science and Policy* (New Haven, 1992).

Lauren, P., *The Evolution of International Human Rights: Visions Seen* (Philadelphia, 1998).

Lauterpacht, E., 'The Legal Effect of Illegal Organisations', in *Cambridge Essays in International Law: Essays in Honour of Lord McNair* (London, 1965) 88.

—— *Aspects of the Administration of International Justice* (Cambridge, 1991).

Lauterpacht, H., 'Westlake and Present Day International Law', 15 *Economica* (1925) 307.

—— *The Development of International Law by the International Court* (London, reprinted 1982).

Lavoyer, J.-P., and Maresca L., 'The Role of the ICRC in the Development of International Humanitarian Law', 4 *International Negotiation* (1999) 508.

Lee, R. (ed), *The International Criminal Court: The Making of the Rome Statute: Issues, Negotiations, Results* (The Hague, 1999).

Llewellyn, H., 'The Optional Protocol to the 1994 Convention', 55 *ICLQ* (2006) 718.

Lorimer, J., *Institutes of the Law of Nations* (Edinburgh, 1884).

Lowe, A. V., 'The Role of Equity in International Law', 12 *Australian YBIL* (1992) 54.

—— 'Sustainable Development and Unsustainable Arguments', in A. E. Boyle and D. Freestone (eds), *International Law and Sustainable Development* (Oxford, 1999).

—— 'The Politics of Law-Making: Are the Method and Character of Norm Creation Changing?', in M. Byers (ed), *The Role of Law in International Politics* (Oxford, 2000).

—— 'International Legal Issues Arising in the Kosovo Crisis', 49 *ICLQ* (2000) 934.

—— and Warbrick, C. (eds), *The UN and the Principles of International Law* (London, 1994).

Lowenfeld, A., *International Economic Law* (Oxford, 2002).

McCaffrey, S., 'Is Codification in Decline?', 20 *Hastings ICLR* (1997) 639.

McCaffrey, S., *The Law of International Watercourses* (Oxford, 2001).

McCrudden, C., 'Human Rights and Judicial Use of Comparative Law', in E. Orucu, *Judicial Comparativism in Human Rights Cases* (London, 2003) 1.

Macdonald, R., and Johnston, D. M. (eds), *The Structure and Process of International Law: Essays in Legal Philosophy, Doctrine and Theory* (Dordrecht, 1986).

_____ _____ (eds), *Towards World Constitutionalism* (Leiden, 2005).

McDorman, T., 'Port State Enforcement: A Comment on Article 218 of the 1982 Law of the Sea Convention', 28 *JMLC* (1997) 305.

McLachlan, C., 'The Principle of Systemic Integration and Article 31(3)(c) of the Vienna Convention', 54 *ICLQ* (2005) 279.

McWhinney, E., *The World Court and the Contemporary International Law-Making Process* (Alphen aan den Rijn, 1979).

_____ 'Historical Dilemmas and Contradictions in U.S. Attitudes to the World Court: The Aftermath of the Nicaragua Judgments', in Y. Dinstein (ed), *International Law at a Time of Perplexity* (Dordrecht, 1989) 423.

Marceau, G., and Pedersen, P., 'Is the WTO Open and Transparent?', 33 *JWT* (1999) 5.

Marks, S., 'Reservations Unhinged: The Belilos Case before the ECHR', 39 *ICLQ* (1990) 300.

Martenczuk, B., 'The Security Council, the International Court and Judicial Review', 10 *EJIL* (1999) 517.

Maslen, S., *Commentaries on Arms Control Treaties, Volume I, The Convention on the Prohibition of the Use, Stockpiling, Production and Transfer of Anti-Personnel Mines and on their Destruction* (Oxford, 2004).

Matthews, J., 'Powershift', 76 *Foreign Affairs* (1997) 50.

Mayer, F., 'Europe and the Internet: The Old World and the New Medium', 11 *EJIL* (2000) 149.

Mendelson, M., and Hulton, S., 'The Iraq-Kuwait Boundary' 64 *BYBIL* (1993) 135.

Meron, T., *Human Rights and Humanitarian Norms as Customary Law* (Oxford, 1989).

Mertus, J., 'Considering Non-state Actors in the New Millennium: Toward Expanded Participation in Norm Generation and Norm Application', 32 *NYU JILP* (2000) 537.

M'Gonigle, R. and Zacher, M. W., *Pollution, Politics and International Law* (London, 1979).

Milano, E., *Unlawful Territorial Situations in International Law: Reconciling Effectiveness, Legality and Legitimacy* (Leiden, 2006).

Mintzer, I., and Leonard, J. (eds), *Negotiating Climate Change* (Cambridge, 1994).

Molenaar, E., *Coastal State Jurisdiction over Vessel-Source Pollution* (The Hague, 1998).

Morgenthau, H., *Politics Among Nations: The Struggle for Power and Peace* (5th edn, New York, 1978).

Mosler, H., 'The International Society as a Legal Community', 140 *Recueil des Cours* (1974) 17.

Murphy, S., *Humanitarian Intervention: The United Nations in an Evolving World Order* (Philadelphia, 1996).

Nelson, D.M., 'Declarations, Statements and Disguised Reservations with Respect to the Convention on the Law of the Sea', 50 *ICLQ* (2001) 767.

Nolke, A., 'Introduction to the Special Issue: The Globalization of Accounting Standards', 7 (3) *Business and Politics* (2005) 1.

Nordquist, M. (ed), *UN Convention on the Law of the Sea: A Commentary* (Dordrecht, 1985).

——— and Moore, J. (eds), *Current Maritime Issues and the IMO* (The Hague, 1999).

——— ——— and Mahmoudi, S. (eds), *The Stockholm Declaration and Law of the Marine Environment* (The Hague, 2003).

Nurser, J., 'The "Ecumenical Movement", Churches, "Global Order" and Human Rights', 25 *HRQ* (2003) 841.

O'Connell, M. E., 'New International Legal Process', 93 *AJIL* (1999) 334.

Oberthür, S., and Ott, H. (eds), *The Kyoto Protocol* (Berlin, 1999).

Obokata, T., 'Trafficking Human Beings as a Crime Against Humanity', 54 *ICLQ* (2005) 445.

Oda, S., 'The ICJ viewed from the Bench', 244 *Recueil des Cours* II (1993) 127–55.

Orford, A., 'The Politics of Collective Security', 17 *Mich JIL* (1996) 373.

Otto, D., 'Non-Governmental Organisations in the United Nations System: The Emerging Role of International Civil Society', 18 *HRQ* (1996) 107.

Our Global Neighbourhood: Report of the Commission on Global Governance (Oxford, 1995).

Pace, W., and Schense, J., 'The Role of Non-Governmental Organisations', in A. Cassese, P. Gaeta, and J. Jones, *The Rome Statute of the International Criminal Court: A Commentary* (Oxford, 2002).

Palmer, G., 'New Ways to Make International Environmental Law', 86 *AJIL* (1992) 259.

Parlett, K., 'Immunity in Civil Proceedings for Torture: The Emerging Exception', 1 *EHRLR* (2006) 49.

Pauwelyn, J., 'The Role of Public International Law in the WTO: How Far Can We Go?', 95 *AJIL* (2001) 535.

——— 'A Typology of Multilateral Treaty Obligations: Are WTO Obligations Bilateral or Collective in Nature?', 14 *EJIL* (2003) 907.

——— *Conflict of Norms in Public International Law* (Cambridge, 2003).

——— 'The Sutherland Report', 8 *JIEL* (2005) 329.

Petersmann E. -U. (ed), *Reforming the World Trade System* (Oxford, 2005).

Peterson, M. J., *The General Assembly in World Politics* (Boston, 1986).

Petit, M., et al, *Why Governments Can't Make Policy: The Case of Plant Genetic Resources* (Lima, 2001).

Pictet, J., (ed), *The Geneva Conventions of 12 August 1949: Commentary* (Geneva, 1952–60).

Posner, M., and Whittome, C., 'The Status of Human Rights NGOs', 25 *Col HRLR* (1994) 283.

Princeton Project on Universal Jurisdiction, *Princeton Principles on Universal Jurisdiction* (Princeton University, 2001).

Qureshi, A., 'The Cartagena Protocol on Biodiversity and the WTO—Co-existence or Incoherence?', 49 *ICLQ* (2000) 835.

Ragazzi, M., *The Concept of International Obligations Erga Omnes* (Oxford, 2000).

Rajagopal, B., *International Law from Below: Development, Social Movements and Third World Resistance* (Cambridge, 2003).

Ratner, S., 'Does International Law Matter in Preventing Ethnic Conflict?', 32 *NYU JILP* (2000) 591.

Raustiala, K., and Victor, D. G., 'The Regime Complex for Plant Genetic Resources', 58 *Int Org* (2004) 277.

Redgwell, C., 'Universality or Integrity? Some Reflections on Reservations to General Multilateral Treaties', 64 *BYBIL* (1993) 245.

Reisman, M., 'International Lawmaking: A Process of Communication', *Proceedings of the 75th Anniversary Convocation of the American Society of International Law* (1981) 101.

——— 'International Politics and International Law—Reflections on the So-called "Politicization" of the International Court', in W. Heere (ed), *International Law and its Sources: Liber Amicorum Maarten Bos* (Deventer, 1989) 77.

——— 'The View from the New Haven School of International Law', 86 *ASIL Proceedings* (1992) 118.

——— 'Unilateral Action and the Transformation of the World Constitutive Process: The Special Problem of Humanitarian Intervention', 11 *EJIL* (2000) 3.

——— 'Assessing Claims to Revise the Laws of War', 97 *AJIL* (2003) 82.

——— and Willard, A. (eds), *International Incidents: The Law that Counts in World Politics* (Princeton, 1988).

Report of the International Commission on Intervention and State Sovereignty, *The Responsibility to Protect* (Ottawa, 2001).

Reus-Smit, C. (ed), *The Politics of International Law* (Cambridge, 2004) 35.

Reuter, P., *Introduction to the Law of Treaties* (London, 1995).

Ringbom, H. (ed), *Competing Norms in the Law of Marine Environmental Protection* (The Hague, 1997).

Roberts, A., 'Traditional and Modern Approaches to Customary International Law: A Reconciliation', 95 *AJIL* (2001) 757.

——— and Kingsbury, B. (eds), *United Nations, Divided World* (2nd edn, Oxford, 1993).

Rosas, A., 'With a Little Help from my Friends: International Case Law as a Source of Reference for the EU Courts', 5 *The Global Community Yearbook of International Law and Jurisprudence* 2005 (2006) 203.

Rosenne, S. (ed), *League of Nations Conference for the Codification of International Law* (New York, 1975).

——— *Breach of Treaty* (Cambridge, 1985).

——— *The Law and Practice of the International Court 1920–1996* (The Hague, 1997) vol III, 'Procedure'.

Roth, B., 98 *AJIL* (2004) 798.

Sabel, R., *Procedure at International Conferences* (Cambridge, 1997).

Sand, P., 'UNCED and the Development of International Environmental Law', 3 *YBIEL* (1992) 3.

——— 'Whither CITES? The Evolution of a Treaty Regime on the Borderland of Trade and Environment', 8 *EJIL* (1997) 29.

Sands, P., Mackenzie, R., and Shany, Y. (eds), *Manual on International Courts & Tribunals* (London, 1999).

Schabas, W., *An Introduction to the International Criminal Court* (Cambridge, 2001).

Schachter, O., 'The Invisible College of International Lawyers', 72 *Northwestern ULR* (1977) 217.

——— 'The Twilight Existence of Non-Binding International Agreements', 71 *AJIL* (1977) 296.

——— 'Entangled Treaty and Custom', in Y. Dinstein (ed), *International Law at a Time of Perplexity* (Dordrecht, 1989).

_____ 'Recent Trends in International Law-Making', 12 *Australian YBIL* (1989) 1.

_____ 'New Custom: Power, *Opinio Juris* and Contrary Practice', in J. Makarczyk, *Theory of International Law at the Threshold of the 21st Century: Essays in Honour of Krzysztof Skubiszewski* (The Hague, 1996) 531.

_____ and Joyner, C. (eds), *United Nations Legal Order* (ASIL, 1995).

Schermers, H., and Blokker, N., *International Institutional Law* (The Hague, 1995).

Schoenbaum, T., 'International Trade in Living Modified Organisms: The New Regimes', 49 *ICLQ* (2000) 856.

Scholte, J. A., O'Brien, R., and Williams, M., *The WTO and Civil Society*, Centre for the Study of Globalisation and Regionalisation, University of Warwick, Working Paper No. 14 (1998) 17.

Schwarzenberger, G., *International Law as Applied by International Courts and Tribunals* (4 vols, London, 1957–86).

Serdy, A., 'Bringing Taiwan into the International Fisheries Fold: The Legal Personality of a Fishing Entity', 75 *BYBIL* (2005) 185.

Shany, Y., *The Competing Jurisdictions of International Courts and Tribunals* (Oxford, 2003).

Shaw, M., 'A Practical Look at the International Court of Justice', in M. Evans (ed), *Remedies in International Law: The Institutional Dilemma* (Oxford, 1998) 11.

_____ *International Law* (5th edn, Cambridge, 2003).

Shelton, D. (ed), *Commitment and Compliance: The Role of Non-binding Norms in the International Legal System* (Oxford, 2000).

Simma, B., 'From Bilateralism to Community Interest in International Law', 250 *Recueil des Cours* (1994) 217.

_____ (ed), *The Charter of the United Nations: A Commentary* (2nd edn, Oxford, 2002).

_____ and Paulus, A., ' "The International Community": Facing the Challenge of Globalization', 9 *EJIL* (1998) 266.

_____ _____ 'The Responsibility of Individuals for Human Rights Abuses in Internal Conflicts: A Positivist View', 93 *AJIL* (1999) 302.

Simpson, G., *Great Powers and Outlaw States: Unequal Sovereigns in the International Legal Order* (Cambridge, 2004).

Sinclair, I., *The Vienna Convention on the Law of Treaties* (Manchester, 1982).

_____ *The International Law Commission* (Cambridge, 1987).

Slaughter, A.-M., 'A Typology of Transjudicial Communication', 29 *University of Richmond LR* (1994) 99.

_____ 'The Real New World Order', 76 *Foreign Affairs* (1997) 183.

_____ 'Governing the Global Economy through Government Networks', in M. Byers (ed), *The Role of Law in International Politics* (Oxford, 2000) 177.

_____ *A New World Order* (Princeton, 2004).

_____ 'Sovereignty and Power in a Networked World Order', 40 *Stan JIL* (2004) 283.

_____ 'Security, Solidarity and Sovereignty: The Grand Themes of UN Reform', 99 *AJIL* (2005) 619.

Sloan, B., 'General Assembly Resolutions Revisited (Forty Years After)', 58 *BYBIL* (1987) 39, 93.

Sohn, L., 'Voting Procedures in United Nations Conferences for the Codification of International Law', 69 *AJIL* (1975) 310.

Soons, A. H. (ed), *Implementation of the Law of the Sea Convention through International Institutions* (Honolulu, 1990) 405.

South Centre, *Environment and Development: Towards a Common Strategy of the South in the UNCED Negotiations and Beyond* (Geneva, 1991).

——— *For a Strong and Democratic United Nations* (London, 1997).

Spinedi, M., and Simma, B. (eds), *UN Codification of State Responsibility* (New York, 1987).

Spiro, P., 'New Global Potentates: Nongovernmental Organizations and the "Unregulated" Marketplace', 18 *Cardozo LR* (1996) 957.

Steains, C., 'Gender Issues', in R. Lee (ed), *The International Criminal Court: The Making of the Rome Statute—Issues, Negotiations, Results* (The Hague, 1999) 357, 368.

Stein, E., 'Lawyers, Judges and the Making of a Transnational Constitution', 75 *AJIL* (1981) 1.

——— 'International Integration and Democracy', 95 *AJIL* (2001) 489.

Steinberg, R. H., 'Judicial Law-Making at the WTO', 98 *AJIL* (2005) 247.

Steyn, J., 'Guantánamo Bay: The Legal Black Hole', 53 *ICLQ* (2004) 1.

Stokke, O., and Vidas, D. (eds), *Governing the Antarctic: The Effectiveness and Legitimacy of the Antarctic Treaty System* (Cambridge, 1996).

'Symposium: Assessing the Work of the International Law Commission on State Responsibility', 13 *EJIL* (2002) 1037.

'Symposium: Method in International Law', 93 *AJIL* (1999) 291.

'Symposium: The Boundaries of WTO', 96 *AJIL* (2002) 1.

'Symposium: The Proliferation of International Tribunals: Piecing Together the Puzzle', 31 *NYU JILP* (1999).

'Symposium: UNCED', 4 *Col JIELP* (1993) 1.

Szasz, P., 'The Security Council Starts Legislating', 96 *AJIL* (2002) 901.

Sztucki, J., 'Reflections on International "Soft Law"', in J. Ramberg, O. Bring and S. Mahmoudi (eds), *Festskrift till Lars Hjerner: Studies in International Law* (Stockholm, 1990).

Tasioulas, J., 'In Defence of Relative Normativity: Communitarian Values and the *Nicaragua* case', 16 *Oxford JLS* (1996) 85.

Teson, F., 'Realism and Kantianism in International Law', 86 *ASIL Proceedings* (1992) 113.

Teubner, G. (ed), *Global Law without a State* (Aldershot, 1997).

Tieleman, K., 'The Failure of the Multilateral Agreement on Investment (MAI) and the Absence of a Global Public Policy Network', UN Vision Project on Global Public Policy Networks, available at, <http://www.globalpublicpolicy.net/>.

Tolbert, D., in R. Churchill and D. Freestone (eds), *International Law and Global Climate Change: International Legal Issues and Implications* (London, 1991) 95.

Tomuschat, C., 'Obligations Arising for States without or against their Will', 241 *Recueil des Cours* (1993), vol IV, 195.

——— 'The Concluding Documents of World Conferences', in J. Makarczyk, *Theory of International Law at the Threshold of the 21st Century: Essays in Honour of Krzysztof Skubiszewski* (The Hague, 1996) 563.

Toope, S., 'Powerful but Unpersuasive? The Role of the United States in the Evolution of Customary International Law', in M. Byers and G. Nolte, *United States Hegemony and the Foundations of International Law* (Cambridge, 2003).

Trachtman, J., 'The Domain of WTO Dispute Resolution', 40 *Harv ILJ* (1999) 333.

Triggs, G., *International Law: Contemporary Principles and Practices* (Chatswood, 2006).

Tyagi, Y., 'The Conflict of Law and Policy on Reservations to Human Rights Treaties', 71 *BYBIL* (2000) 181.

UN, *Survey of International Law in Relation to the Work of the International Law Commission* (1949) UN Doc A/CN 4/Rev 1.

—— *Review of the Multilateral Treaty-Making Process*, UN Doc ST/LEG/SER.B/21 (1985).

—— *The Work of the ILC* (5th edn, New York, 1996).

—— *The ILC Fifty Years After: An Evaluation* (New York, 2000).

—— *We the Peoples of the United Nations in the 21st Century*, Millennium Report of the Secretary-General (New York, 2000).

—— *A More Secure World: Our Shared Responsibility*, Report of the High Level Panel on Threats, Challenges and Change, UN Doc A/59/565, 2 December 2004.

Van Hoof, G., *Rethinking the Sources of International Law* (Deventer and London, 1983).

Vierdag, E., 'The Time of Conclusion of a Multilateral Treaty: Article 30 of the VCLT and Related Provisions', 59 *BYBIL* (1988) 75.

Vignes, D., 'Will the Third Conference on the Law of the Sea Work According to the Consensus Rule?', 69 *AJIL* (1975) 119.

Vohrah, Lai Chand, 'Pre-trial Procedures and Practices', in G. K. McDonald and O. Swaak-Goldman (eds), *Substantive and Procedural Aspects of International Criminal Law*, vol 1 (The Hague, 2000) 481.

Waltz, S., 'Universal Human Rights: The Contribution of Muslim States', 26 *HRQ* (2004) 799.

Watts, A. D., *The International Law Commission 1949–1998* (Oxford, 1999).

Weil, P., 'Towards Relative Normativity in International Law?', 77 *AJIL* (1983), 413.

—— ' "The Court Cannot Conclude Definitively . . ." *Non Liquet* Revisited', 36 *Col JTL* (1998) 109.

Weiler, J. (ed), *The EU, the WTO and the NAFTA* (Oxford, 2000).

—— and Paulus, A., 'The Structure of Change in International Law or Is There a Hierarchy of Norms in International Law?' 8 *EJIL* (1997) 545.

Wickremasinghe, C. (ed), *The International Lawyer as Practitioner* (London, 2000).

Wolfke, K., *Custom in Present International Law* (2nd rev edn, Dordrecht, 1993).

Wood, M., 'The Interpretation of Security Council Resolutions', 2 *Max Planck UNYBL* (1998) 73.

Wouters, P., 'The Legal Response to International Water Conflicts: The UN Water Convention and Beyond', 42 *GYBIL* (1999) 293.

Wright, Q., 'Activities of the Institute of International Law', *ASIL Proceedings* (1960) 195.

WTO, *The Legal Texts: The Results of the Uruguay Round of Multilateral Trade Negotiations* (Cambridge, 1999).

Zimmermann, A. (ed), *International Criminal Law and the Current Development of Public International Law* (Berlin, 2003).

—— and Hoffmann, R., *Unity and Diversity in International Law* (Berlin, 2005).

—— Tomuschat, C., and Oellers-Frahm, K., *The Statute of the International Court of Justice: A Commentary* (Oxford, 2006).

Index